Gerard Brennan's Articles and Speeches

Maintaining the Law's Skeleton of Principle

VOLUME 1

Justice According to Law

Father Frank Brennan SJ

EDITOR

Connor Court Publishing Pty Ltd

Published in 2025 by Connor Court Publishing Pty Lrd

Connor Court Publishing Pty Ltd
PO Box 7257
Redland Bay QLD 4165
sales@connorcourt.com
www.connorcourt.com

NATIONAL LIBRARY OF AUSTRALIA

A catalogue record for this book is available from the National Library of Australia

ISBN: 9781923224698 (vol 1)
ISBN: 9781923224704 (vol 2)

Cover Design by Maria Giordano
Cover image: (Francis) Gerard Brennan by Robert Lyall Hannaford, 1996. Oil on canvas, 122 x 91.4 cm. Historic Memorials Collection, High Court of Australia.

Printed in Australia.

Contents

Dedication

On the day of Gerard Brennan's swearing of the oath as a Justice of the High Court of Australia 'to do right to all manner of people according to law without fear or favour, affection or ill-will', his cousin Father Grove Johnson inscribed a bible: '*Salus animorum suprema lex* (The salvation of the soul is the supreme law) – when the lawyer perceives this truth with perfect clarity, embraces it with total surrender and applies it with impeccable professional skill, holiness and genius have met. I can wish you no greater success.'

Dedicated

to

the future generations of lawyers committed to justice according to law

Foreword

Gerard Carney

This rich collection of articles and speeches by Sir Gerard Brennan, spanning over half a century, reveals his humanity, his morality, his perspicacity, but above all else, his commitment to the practical implementation of the rule of law within a democratic state. His essential message was that the rule of law must recognize the individual dignity of every person. Yet in delivering justice according to law, the judicial role required disciplined restraint to avoid breaching the appropriate division of powers. Sir Gerard's extra-judicial writings demonstrate his sophisticated antennae for this delicate balance. Like an engineer attending complex machinery or a surgeon operating, he delivered justice without fracturing the skeleton of our legal system.

I was very privileged to join Sir Gerard's chambers in 1995 as he assumed the heavy burden of Chief Justice of the High Court of Australia. A key aspect of my role as his Executive Associate was to assist in the preparation of his speeches. My first task was to undertake research for the inaugural Deakin Oration in Melbourne, which he entitled: "Courts for the People – not people's courts" (3.7 below). As his first address as Chief Justice, Sir Gerard emphasized its importance to me. Neither of us was prepared, however, for *The Canberra Times* headlining his very short comment about the ongoing difficulty of attracting talented lawyers to the bench!

Sir Gerard readily embraced his new role as Chief Justice, conscious of the great responsibility he bore as the chief representative of the Australian judiciary. While it provided him with a broader platform from which to advance and explain the rule of law, he remained extremely careful to avoid treading on political or controversial issues. As a judge, he was acutely concerned to ensure that his extra-judicial statements and activities could not be perceived in any way to undermine public confidence in his judicial independence. Nor would he elaborate on his judgments or those of his fellow judges. He always maintained that his written reasons for judgment 'must speak for themselves'. (see 6.2).

Consequently, Sir Gerard's favourite topics for his articles and speeches were those which explained the judicial role as part of the rule of law, emphasising the importance of judicial independence, encouraging and guiding the ethical role of lawyers. Another favourite topic was the important role of the Administrative Appeals Tribunal, of which he was its first President in 1976. The chapters of Volume One reflect these topics. I think no other judge in the common law world has focused in such a disciplined way on the institutional importance of the legal profession and the judiciary. In pursuing that focus, Sir Gerard's extrapolation of legal principle is the closest he gets to the political or controversial rockface of public opinion.

Volume Two reflects in part his other great passion: exploring the relationship between law, Christianity and morality. His devout spirituality clearly influenced his legal philosophy, in particular the protection of human dignity. After retirement, Sir Gerard felt a little less retrained to embrace controversial political issues, such as asylum seekers and the republic.

Father Frank's adroit arrangement of his father's articles and speeches in these two volumes highlights the major themes of Sir Gerard's extra-judicial writings. Many were previously published. Some previously unpublished materials such as Sir Gerard's letter to Michael Kirby of 2 September 1979 (4.1) in which he explains his reasons for resigning from the Administrative Appeals Tribunal and the Administrative Review Council make a notable contribution to the public record.

Most chapters encompass papers written during Sir Gerard's legal career as a barrister, a judge, Chief Justice, and thereafter. How much his views evolved over that 50 years can now be assessed. While the many papers he was invited to deliver during his three years as Chief Justice added considerably to his workload, he always relished the opportunity to remind and to encourage the legal profession of the importance of their role, and to share this with a wider audience. Retirement from the High Court at the statutory age of 70 afforded Sir Gerard much more time to write papers and to accept numerous invitations to speak at conferences, both nationally and overseas. These two volumes attest to the prodigious range of articles and speeches he wrote over the next 25 years following his "retirement".

Sir Gerard's articles and speeches contain many literary turns of phrase, such as this pithy comment in his inaugural *Deakin Oration*: 'Want of impartiality poisons the stream of justice at its source; an appearance of partiality dries it up.' (3.7 below). While in his inaugural *Gerard Brennan Lecture* at Bond University, he observed how government bureaucracies sometimes regarded the Administrative Appeals Tribunal as 'an irksome trespasser on their territory - a cuckoo in the administrative nest' (6.3 below).

I am sure that those who delve into Sir Gerard's articles and speeches will readily perceive his admirable qualities, celebrated in the tributes included at the end of Volume Two. An added delight for the reader is a sprinkling of humorous legal anecdotes, a legacy of his love for the Irish. But most significantly for future generations are the principles he espoused by which the rule of law needs to be protected and nourished by an independent judiciary and a competent legal profession.

Those of us who had the extraordinary privilege of knowing him can testify that he was a man who, with humility and good humour, truly practised what he preached.

Gerard Carney

Gold Coast

February 2025

Introduction

Frank Brennan

My father, Francis Gerard Brennan, was introduced to the law by his father, Frank Tenison Brennan who had been a member of the Queensland Parliament before becoming a Judge of the Supreme Court of Queensland. As a boy, Gerard would visit his father's chambers, first in Rockhampton and later in Brisbane. Each year, the High Court would come on circuit to Brisbane for a week or two of sittings. For 89 years, the High Court when on circuit in Brisbane had sat in the Supreme Court building. At the 1993 Brisbane sittings, Sir Gerard Brennan presided over the final sitting of the High Court in the Supreme Court of Queensland. Thanking the Queensland court for its hospitality and preparing for the High Court's move to the new Commonwealth Courts Building in Brisbane, Brennan observed: 'We are conscious of the personal courtesies which we have received from the judges of the Supreme Court who have given us their chambers during the Brisbane sittings of the High Court. In earlier and easier days – now almost half a century away – the High Court sittings might require the judges of the Supreme Court to take a vacation for weeks on end! I remember that in those days Sir George Rich was a welcome visitor to my father's chambers.'[1] Brennan had been introduced to the law and to the High Court at a very young age.

There was a ceremonial welcome in Brisbane for Brennan when he became Chief Justice of the High Court in 1995. Brennan expressed his great pleasure at being welcomed by the Queensland profession. He said, 'The Queensland Bar is my professional home and I enjoyed a long and satisfying relationship with the solicitors of this state. This occasion affords me the opportunity to acknowledge my indebtedness to colleagues in both branches of the Queensland legal profession who, by their high standards and personal dispositions, made life at the Bar in this State a source of great personal satisfaction and of happy and oftentimes amusing memories.'[2]

Brennan was admitted to the Bar in 1951 having already been associate to Justice Kenneth Townley on the Supreme Court of Queensland. His time as an associate was life-changing. Townley had been appointed to conduct war crimes trials of Japanese soldiers on Manus Island in Papua New Guinea. Brennan observed the death penalty being imposed. He became a lifetime opponent of capital punishment.

On his return to Brisbane, Brennan commenced practice at the Bar and he married Patricia O'Hara in 1953. They had seven children over the next nine years. Over those years, Patricia gave up her practice as a doctor and took on primary responsibility for the rearing of the children. In his early years at the Bar, Brennan was mentored by the legendary Dan Casey, especially in criminal and defamation cases. Brennan said, 'Casey's pre-eminence and strength were derived from his utter independence.... He feared no judge, nor did he seek confrontation with the bench. His respect for the judicial office and the institutions of the law ensured that any passage at arms was on a point of principle to which not the slightest exception could be taken, though he bridled under the observations of some judges whose approach to the administration of criminal justice was more severe than his own.'[3] Being a successful junior barrister practising in criminal and civil matters, Brennan took silk in 1965 at the early age of 37. As a QC, he took a strong interest in the Bar's community obligations. By 1971, he was Vice-President of the Queensland Bar. He played a prominent role in the biennial Australian Legal Conventions in 1971, 1973 and 1975.

At the opening of the 16th Australian Legal Convention in 1971, Lord Diplock was the guest of honour. At the opening ceremony, he joined issue with John Bray, Chief Justice of South Australia, who was to speak at the forthcoming plenary session on 'law, liberty and morality'. Having read Bray's paper on the plane from London, Diplock objected to Bray's assertion: 'It is not a question of what the law is, with which Judges are alone normally concerned, but with what it ought to be.' Diplock expressed his 'utter, profound and complete disagreement with what is implicit in that sentence'. Diplock noted: 'The common law ... works empirically and works mainly by nudges. It is not often that one gets the epoch-making case, it is not often that the opportunity occurs of saying, as Lord Mansfield could, "the air of England is too pure for any slave to breathe, let the black go free." There are great opportunities from time to time ... But in so many more there is the opportunity of giving a little nudge which sends the law along the direction that it ought to go, the opportunity of saying what the law ought to be.'[4]

The first respondent to Bray at the plenary session was the young silk from Brisbane, Gerard Brennan. He observed: 'It is now two centuries since Lord Mansfield was able to say "Let the black go free," and the problem which we have today is of the same nature as his Lordship faced then. On the one hand, there is the risk that if law goes too far there is rebellion in the name of freedom; if law stops short of its proper role, then freedom itself is at risk.'[5]

Brennan concluded his remarks presciently half a century ago with the observation about the contested relationship between law, liberty and morality: 'It is not so much about the present content of the law, it is about the way in which we ascertain new views as to what the law should be. We may find out if we create these structures that the new morality will have relatively little concern about changes in sexual morality and may exhibit a very great concern about problems relating to poverty and privilege and race.'[6]

At the end of the legal convention, he returned home to Brisbane where the premier Sir Joh Bjelke-Petersen was proclaiming a State of Emergency to facilitate police control of protesters during the last all-white Springbok rugby tour. Brennan published a letter to the editor objecting to the tactics being adopted both by government and protesters. He made a plea for maintenance of the rule of law. He wrote: 'When legitimate protest degenerates into unlawful disruption, governments are invited to assume powers of doubtful legality, and to condone unlawful actions by police. When governments do not exercise their powers honestly and fairly and with statesmanship, they invite disruptive expressions of protest. In either case both the rulers and the ruled attack the concept of law and order. Is it not time for both to examine their consciences?'[7]

That night he came home and told his wife Patricia and me that he had been confronted at lunch in the Bar common room by Peter Connolly, one of the doyens of the Queensland Bar, who told him: 'That's it, Brennan. Now you'll never be a judge.' He matter of factly said to us: 'Well so be it.' But that wasn't it at all. Within a decade he was a Justice of the High Court of Australia.

At the 17th Australian Legal Convention in 1973, he came to national prominence when he was a panellist on the ABC's *Monday Conference* program focusing on the legal profession's community responsibilities. Chief Justice Barwick had been overseas when the program went to air but he told Brennan that he had heard that he had 'saved the legal profession'. On 14 September 1973, Barwick wrote to Prime Minister Whitlam suggesting names for prospective High Court appointments. Barwick wrote: 'As a starter, I attach on a separate slip a few names that might be kept in mind. The performances of the persons named might be watched over the next year or so. The list will need to be revised from time to time both by addition and deletion.' He specified that the 9 names were 'not in any order of preference and all, indeed the majority, not ready yet.' It's still worth noting that Brennan was second on the list, after John McIntosh Young who became Chief Justice of Victoria the following year. The list included only two future High Court appointments: Ronald Wilson in 1979 and Brennan in 1981, each appointed by the Fraser government long after the dismissal of the Whitlam government.

In 1975 at the 18th legal convention, Brennan delivered the closing address 'Where Now?!' reflecting on 'how the profession sees itself at present, and how it is geared to handle the problems that will occur within the next decade'.[8] Answering the question 'Where Now?', he responded:

> I would suggest that in the world outside Australia we might be generous with our judicial talents, in our region we might cooperate to devise methods by which our courts can be made more efficient, and in our profession, I suggest that we might devote ourselves to fashioning the structures of unity.

He then quoted his mentor and friend Sir Maurice Byers, Commonwealth Solicitor-General, who had spoken at the opening church service for the convention: 'that the just exercise of our calling requires us to remember, that each of our decisions is about our fellow man, and that our procedures must recognise and admit his equal and constant presence.' Brennan concluded, 'In answering the question of where we as a profession, as a united profession, go from here, I would answer it by the answer given in that Service: "Go forth into the world in peace!"'[9]

As a QC at the Brisbane Bar, Brennan appeared annually as senior counsel for the Queensland sugar cane growers before the Central Sugar Cane Prices Board which determined any disputes with the millers about the price payable for sugar cane. The main mill operator was the Colonial Sugar Refinery (CSR). In 1969, Brennan was briefed by the Fijian Alliance Party to come to Fiji and appear before Lord Denning in an arbitration to determine sugar cane prices payable to growers and landholders by the South Pacific Sugar Mills (SPSM), a subsidiary of CSR. The mill owners were perceived to be foreigners with a colonial mindset. The landowners were mostly Fijian. And many of the growers were Indian. This was Brennan's introduction to land rights, race relations and the rule of law.

In 1972, Brennan was briefed by the Commonwealth to prosecute a politically charged murder trial in Papua New Guinea. Disaffected Tolai landholders had killed Jack Emanuel, an Australian who worked for the government as a District Commissioner in the Gazelle Peninsula. Five Tolai were convicted and eight acquitted. Chief Justice John Minogue presided at the trial and paid tribute to Brennan for his sensitive handling of the prosecution. This was Brennan's second introduction to land rights and the rule of law.

In 1973, at the 17th Australian Legal Convention in Perth, Sir Edward Woodward asked Brennan if he would be open to accepting the brief as counsel for the Northern Land Council in the royal commission on land rights he was conducting for the newly elected Whitlam Government. Despite the protracted absences from home this would cause, Brennan's wife Patricia told him that he should take the brief. This led to Brennan's third schooling in land rights, and over a protracted period.

Brennan maintained a varied practice as a silk, including regular appearances before the High Court. He became president of the Queensland Bar and then President of the Australian Bar Association. He was appointed to the Australian Law Reform Commission in 1975 under the dynamic youthful leadership of Michael Kirby where he often locked horns robustly and happily with Gareth Evans.

Horizons kept opening, taking him beyond the Queensland Bar and beyond the strict parameters of the law. Conducting a long running Commonwealth inquiry into the failed Barton companies, he was often in Sydney, and from time to time he saw Robert Ellicott who was Attorney-General in the Fraser government after the dismissal of the Whitlam Government. Ellicott invited Brennan to spearhead the Commonwealth administrative law reforms and then to become a founding judge of the Federal Court of Australia. The Administrative Appeals Tribunal (AAT) and the Administrative Review Council (ARC) were established on 1 July 1976.

As President of the AAT, Brennan set the contours for judicial review of administrative decisions made by Commonwealth ministers and public servants exercising statutory functions. Asking whether the minister's decision in a deportation case affecting the applicant was the correct or preferable decision, the Tribunal needed to consider what weight to give to policy. In *Re Drake and Minister for Immigration and Ethnic Affairs (No 2)*, Brennan J said:

> It is one thing for the Minister to apply his own policy in deciding cases; it is another thing for the Tribunal to apply it. In point of law, the Tribunal is as free as the Minister to apply or not to apply that policy. The Tribunal's duty is to make the correct or preferable decision in each case on the material before it, and the Tribunal is at liberty to adopt whatever policy it chooses, or no policy at all, in fulfilling its statutory function.[10]

Urging caution, he went on to say:

> When the Tribunal is reviewing the exercise of a discretionary power reposed in a Minister, and the Minister has adopted a general policy to guide him in the exercise of the power, the Tribunal will ordinarily apply that policy in reviewing the decision, unless the policy is unlawful or unless its application tends to produce an

> unjust decision in the circumstances of the particular case. Where the policy would ordinarily be applied, an argument against the policy itself or against its application in the particular case will be considered, but cogent reasons will have to be shown against its application, especially if the policy is shown to have been exposed to Parliamentary scrutiny.[11]

Brennan was sworn in as a founding judge of the new Federal Court on 7 February 1977. Initially the court was composed of 16 existing federal judges. In time, other judges were added. The Chief Justice Nigel Bowen often rostered Brennan with judges like William Deane and John Toohey to sit on appeals. This added workload together with tension between judicial office and the lobbying of public servants and ministers to grant jurisdiction to the AAT over a vast range of administrative decisions proved too much to bear. After three years of labour establishing the AAT and the ARC, Brennan resigned from the AAT and the ARC so as to devote his energies to the development of the Federal Court and its jurisprudence, including judicial review of AAT decisions.

On 12 February 1981, Brennan became the first of a succession of Federal Court judges promoted to the High Court. At his ceremonial welcome, Attorney-General Peter Durack who had known Brennan since university days when they both served on the National Union of Australian University Students (Brennan being President), observed: 'The effectiveness of the administrative reforms which have been introduced over the last few years were due in no small way to the fact that you identified the major theoretical problems and contributed substantially to their solution.'[12]

During his early years on the High Court, the Northern Territory government appealed a string of decisions under the *Aboriginal Land Rights (Northern Territory) Act 1976* (Cth). By the time the first *Mabo* hearing occurred in March 1988, all members of the High Court were familiar with the issue of land rights. John Toohey having been the first Aboriginal Land Commissioner in the Northern Territory brought a wealth of grounded experience as did Brennan having been counsel in the Woodward Royal Commission.

Brennan's passion for justice, quest for legal principle, unfailing courtesy, honest intellectual inquiry and judicious contribution to what he often described as 'a free and confident nation' was highlighted in the exchange between him and Geoff Davies, Solicitor-General of Queensland, on the third day of argument in the *Mabo* proceedings:

> Brennan J: If your argument be right, Mr Solicitor, it seems that the common law as applied in England, and perhaps the law as applied

> in Canada and the United States, was no more than a device to ensure that the indigenous people had nothing.
>
> Mr Davies: Your Honour, historically unpalatable as that may appear to be today to us looking back at that in retrospect, historically it seems to have been correct, but it was no rights against the government.
>
> Brennan J: No rights against those who exercise the power of control?
>
> Mr Davies: Yes, that seems to be the case.
>
> Brennan J: It is scarcely an enabling doctrine for a common law.[13]

In the wake of the *Mabo* decision in 1992, Hugh Morgan, CEO of Western Mining, and his speech writer Ray Evans agitated about what they perceived as the Catholic thinking behind the High Court's *Mabo* decision.[14] They suggested that the majority of judges who had been educated at Catholic schools must have allowed their Catholic perspective or values to influence their decision as it was inconceivable to these good Protestant gentlemen how else the court could have reached such a decision. They were particularly concerned that the lead judgments were written by Justice Brennan 'regarded as a conservative Catholic' and by Justice Deane, 'a Catholic of some standing'.[15] Their anxiety was heightened by my relationship to Justice Brennan. Hugh Morgan offered public advice that I should have been particularly conscious of my father's standing, 'and sensitive to the implications of remarks which could quite incorrectly, give rise to suggestions of influence'.[16] At the commencement of the *Mabo* proceedings back in March 1988, my father had made this declaration from the bench:

> I have informed counsel appearing in this case that my son Fr Frank Brennan SJ is an adviser to the Australian Catholic bishops on matters relating to the land rights of Aboriginal and Islander peoples and that he is actively engaged in a ministry to these peoples. As this matter raises for consideration the question whether Islander people enjoy traditional rights with respect to land, not being rights arising under a statute, it is appropriate that the information I have given counsel should appear on the public record.[17]

Counsel offered no comment and neither did the likes of Evans and Morgan until four years later when the litigation was well complete. I regarded my father's statement as an excess of judicial scrupulosity. Morgan was convinced that 'in *Mabo*, and all that followed from it, we are engaged in a struggle for the political and territorial future of Australia'.[18] Evans discerned a 'Gnostic heresy which seized the collective minds of the High Court'.[19] By 1999, Evans was publicly lamenting that 'Justice Brennan not only sat on the case but wrote the lead judgment, despite the fact that, in

Australia, his son was, and has been for a decade, one of the most active and influential advocates for the revolutionary policies which were embodied in the *Mabo* judgment.'[20]

In *Mabo*, Brennan wrote: 'In discharging its duty to declare the common law of Australia, this Court is not free to adopt rules that accord with contemporary notions of justice and human rights if their adoption would fracture the skeleton of principle which gives the body of our law its shape and internal consistency.'[21] He went on to say:

> It is not possible, *a priori,* to distinguish between cases that express a skeletal principle and those which do not, but no case can command unquestioning adherence if the rule it expresses seriously offends the values of justice and human rights (especially equality before the law) which are aspirations of the contemporary Australian legal system. If a postulated rule of the common law expressed in earlier cases seriously offends those contemporary values, the question arises whether the rule should be maintained and applied. Whenever such a question arises, it is necessary to assess whether the particular rule is an essential doctrine of our legal system and whether, if the rule were to be overturned, the disturbance to be apprehended would be disproportionate to the benefit flowing from the overturning.[22]

Thereafter, Brennan often returned to consider how contemporary or enduring values of society could inform the development of principles from which particular rules could be incorporated into the common law.

Four years after *Mabo*, Brennan, then Chief Justice, dissented in the *Wik Case* which considered whether native title could co-exist on a pastoral lease. The court decided 4 to 3 that native title could co-exist. In *Mabo*, Brennan had written the lead judgment for the majority in a 6-1 decision. In *Wik*, he wrote the lead judgment for the minority in a 4-3 decision. As a barrister appearing for the Northern Land Council before the Woodward Commission, Brennan had argued forcefully for the recognition of Aboriginal rights on pastoral leases. Then he was the advocate, now he was the judge on the final court of appeal. He was constrained as a judge. There were limits to how far the courts could go. In *Wik*, the plaintiffs, proposing the co-existence of native title rights on a pastoral lease, argued that any limitation on pre-existing native title rights would be contingent on the pastoralist taking legally authorised action on the pastoral lease such as the fencing of the land. They argued that prior to the taking of any such action, native title could continue to exist. In dissent, Brennan rejected this submission:

> The law can attribute priority to one right over another, but it cannot recognise the co-existence in different hands of two rights that cannot both be exercised at the same time. To postulate a test of inconsistency not between the rights but between the manner of their exercise would be to deny the law's capacity to determine the priority of rights over or in respect of the same parcel of land. The law would be incapable of settling a dispute between the holders of the inconsistent rights prior to their exercise, to the prejudice of that peaceful resolution of disputes which reduces any tendency to self-help. To postulate extinguishment of native title as dependent on the exercise of the private right of the lessee (rather than on the creation or existence of the private right) would produce situations of uncertainty, perhaps of conflict. The question of extinguishment of native title by a grant of inconsistent rights is – and must be – resolved as a matter of law, not of fact. If the rights conferred on the lessee of a pastoral lease are, at the moment when those rights are conferred, inconsistent with a continued right to enjoy native title, native title is extinguished. [23]

Brennan the judge willingly conceded that this reasoning could produce an injustice. But he was constrained by his understanding of the judicial function and the need for the common law to maintain certainty. He concluded:

> The Wik and Thayorre Peoples' claims fail because native title was extinguished on the issue of the leases under s 6 of the 1910 Act. … The principles of the law may thus be thought to reveal 'a significant moral shortcoming' which can be rectified only by legislation or by the acquisition of an estate which would allow the traditions and customs of the Wik and Thayorre Peoples to be preserved and observed. Those avenues of satisfaction draw on the certainty of proprietary rights created by the sovereign power. Such rights, unlike the rights of the holders of native title, are not liable to extinguishment by subsequent executive action. [24]

Brennan's decisions in *Mabo* and *Wik* nicely highlight the creative tension he lived and thought as a judge committed to the rule of law and to justice for all.

Having already served on the High Court for 14 years, Brennan was the court's most senior judge when Chief Justice Mason retired in 1995. Having been first appointed to the court by Malcolm Fraser, Brennan was appointed Chief Justice by Paul Keating. When introducing his Native Title Bill to Parliament in 1993, Keating had commenced his second reading speech with these words: 'Today is a milestone. A response to another milestone: the High Court's decision in the *Mabo Case*. The High Court has determined that Australian law should not, as Justice Brennan said, be "frozen in an era of racial discrimination". Its decision in the *Mabo* case ended the pernicious legal deceit of *terra nullius* for all of Australia – and for all time.'[25] Brennan served as Chief Justice for just over three years. After Brennan's death, Paul Keating explained why as Prime Minister he had appointed Brennan for such a brief period:

> Some asked me at the time, 'Why appoint Gerry as chief justice when he would have only a little over three years to run?' The answer was clear. Moral clarity and incisiveness. If you appoint someone to the top job, even for a short time, with moral clarity and incisiveness, they can help shape the country for the better.

Mr Keating added: 'In public life, there is a confusion between insight and progress with the idea that it is time in the job that matters. The creative spark is the source of all progress and sparks do not linger. Gerry possessed a vast panoply of legal understandings and experience – and from that cumulus he could manage the odd lightning strike.'[26]

Having retired from the High Court at the constitutional retirement age of 70, Brennan was still at the peak of his intellectual powers. He served briefly on the Supreme Court of Fiji and then spent twelve years sitting periodically on the Hong Kong Final Court of Appeal. At the end of his judicial career, Brennan delivered the 2012 Hal Wootten Lecture. He was introduced by Wootten who had been the foundation dean of the University of New South Wales Law School and then a judge and royal commissioner investigating Aboriginal deaths in custody. Like Brennan, Wootten had attended the 1971 Australian Legal Convention where Lord Diplock had spoken of Lord Mansfield and the little nudgers who shape the common law.

Lord Mansfield would not have come to decide *Somerset's Case* in 1772 but for the actions of a public servant Granville Sharp who was outraged by the treatment of a slave on the streets of London. It then took generations of campaigning by people like Lord Wilberforce and little people of whom we have never heard to agitate for change. Ultimately the House of Commons passed the *Slavery Abolition Act* in 1833.

Each of us wonders what contribution we can make to a better world. How can we make a difference? Each of us can be a little nudger like Granville Sharp. We can nudge things in the right direction – within our profession, within our discipline, in our relationships and within our world. If each of us keeps nudging, every now and again, there will be a Lord Mansfield moment. And every now and again there will be a Lord Mansfield.

Wootten suggested that Australia had its own Lord Mansfield moment when the High Court of Australia recognised the rights of Aboriginals and Torres Strait Islanders to their traditional lands in the 1992 *Mabo* decision. In his introduction to Brennan's lecture, Wootten said: 'In the end we little nudgers need the Lord Mansfields. We depend on there being people in high places who have the wisdom, the vision and the courage to seize the opportunity and bring the work of the little nudgers to fruition in a form that will command authority and survive.'[27]

Wootten declared that while all six judges in the majority in *Mabo* joined in the Mansfield role, 'one had to write what would become the leading judgment, find the words and the arguments that could command a majority—the reasons that would survive the scrutiny of future generations of judges and ultimately win the support of the community . . . and that role fell to Justice Brennan'.

Twenty years after *Mabo,* Brennan concluded his Wootten lecture entitled 'Lessons from a Life in the Law' with a parting joyful attestation: 'It has been a great adventure to have been in the company of those whom I have respected for their devotion to justice according to law, not least when we have not been unanimous in our definitions of the law.'

In this book of my father's extra-judicial writings and speeches, I set out some of the key landmarks, some of the many quandaries, and many of the little nudges made by him in his contribution to the law and to what he was fond of calling a free and confident nation. Hopefully this collection, letting him speak for himself, can complement existing publications reflecting on his judicial method and achievements. His contributions to administrative law and the jurisprudence of judicial review have been set out in *The Brennan Legacy: Blowing the winds of legal orthodoxy* edited by Professors Robin Creyke and Patrick Keyzer in 2002.[28] Jeff Fitzgerald published a detailed biography *Sir Gerard Brennan: The Law's Good Servant* in 2024.[29]

Brennan had the good fortune to be a founder of many aspects of our contemporary legal system. As counsel for the Aboriginal people in the Woodward Commission in 1974 and as judge in the 1992 High Court *Mabo* decision, he founded so many of the principles of Aboriginal land rights. He was a founding judge of the Federal Court of Australia. He was the founding president of the Administrative Appeals Tribunal and the Administrative Review Council and a founding member of the Australian Law Reform Commission. He was a Justice of the High Court when the *Australia Act 1986* (Cth) was passed establishing the High Court as the ultimate court of appeal in all matters and the Commonwealth Parliament as the sovereign parliament in all matters for the nation. In all these roles, he was committed to maintaining the skeleton of principle while developing the law to the contemporary needs of justice for all.

On his retirement as Chief Justice of Australia, Brennan said, '[T]he law is not an ever-expanding cosmos containing rules for the solution of the problems of every generation and awaiting only a judicial telescope to capture their text. As each generation faces new problems, the rules must be crafted by the judges of the time.' Brennan became one of the finest craftsmen of his generation. Brennan's predecessor as chief justice, Sir Anthony Mason, described him as 'above all else a principled common lawyer'[30]. Speaking of 'The Legacy of Sir Gerard Brennan to Australian Public Law', the present chief Justice Stephen Gageler has said, 'To the question of what he added to Australian public law, the answer can be given with a precision that would have pleased him. He added its essential unity, its guiding principle, and its moral compass.'[31] This book of Brennan's extra-judicial writings traces his development of the craft as he confronted problems, old and new. It offers insights into his life and work as an Australian, a Christian, a Catholic, a barrister and a judge who wrestled constantly with the tensions of his promise to 'do right to all manner of people according to law without fear or favour, affection or ill-will'. When taking his oath as Chief Justice of the High Court, he attested publicly that he was 'responsible not only to this Court and this country but also to his Creator'.

Brennan held together the highest legal method, absolute judicial integrity and commitment to his Catholic faith. He demonstrated this in the four points he made in 1992 when speaking at the ecumenical service for the opening of the legal year at the Lutheran church in Canberra. While judgment was reserved in *Mabo*, he told his fellow believers and fellow lawyers: (1) 'Declarations of solidarity with or sympathy for a neighbour who suffers an injustice are no substitute for, or solvent of, the duty to do whatever lies within our power to see that justice is done according to law.' (2) 'We have no divine mandate to administer justice in disregard of human law. To the contrary, the professional duty of the Christian lawyer is to administer the law created by the competent organs of society's government.' (3) 'If the law itself is an obstacle to justice, the duty of a Christian lawyer extends to seeking its reform.' (4) 'To aspire to perform our duties, we need wisdom and knowledge, humility and compassion, courage and strength. These are gifts for which we pray and which we commit ourselves to employ.'[32]

I've been privileged to have such a father. It is with love and pride that I share and honour his legacy.

I record my thanks both to Catherine Fitzgerald for her generous and professional assistance with the preparation of this publication and to Michael Gilchrist who responded to the editors' many typesetting needs.

I also acknowledge Robyn Martine who did so much to place Dad's papers in order. I thank my sister Madeline KC and Dad's former associates who advised on appropriate papers for inclusion in this collection. I thank Gerard Carney for his splendid Foreword. Having been my father's Executive Associate when Dad was Chief Justice, Gerard knew well the judicial mind and humane temperament at work in these pages. I thank Chief Justices Kiefel and Gageler and Justice Keane for their insights into their much admired judicial forebear. I thank Dad's friend and colleague Sir William Deane for his eulogy and Patrick Dodson for his First Nations tribute. I thank Connor Court and Anthony Cappello for committing to a two-volume work, allowing the publication of my father's religious and philosophical musings as well as his legal deliberations. I thank my colleagues at the P M Glynn Institute and the Thomas More Law School at Australian Catholic University. This year, I mark 40 years as a priest and 50 years as a Jesuit. I thank my brother Jesuits for their ongoing encouragement as well as for their pastoral support for my parents in years past. Hopefully this work will allow future generations of lawyers and interested citizens to understand more of the moral formation and legal discipline of Australia's Lord Mansfield who in *Mabo* would 'find the words and the arguments that could command a majority—the reasons that would survive the scrutiny of future generations of judges and ultimately win the support of the community.'[33]

---

1. High Court of Australia, Transcript of Proceedings, 2 July 1993.
2. High Court of Australia, Transcript of Proceedings, 19 June 1995.
3. F G Brennan, Toast to Dan Casey, Bar Association of Queensland, Annual Bar Dinner, 26 June 1984.
4. (1971) 45 *Australian Law Journal* 449, 451.
5. (1971) 45 *Australian Law Journal* 463.
6. Ibid, 464.
7. See *The Australian*, 2 August 1971
8. (1975) 49 *Australian Law Journal* 672.
9. Ibid, 677.
10. See *Re Drake and Minister for Immigration and Ethnic Affairs (No 2),* (1979) 2 ALD 634, 642.
11. Ibid, 645.
12. High Court of Australia, Transcript, 12 February 1981.
13. Transcript of Proceedings, *Mabo* v *The State of Queensland*, 30 May 1991,305-6.

14. See R Evans, 'Gnosticism and the High Court', *Quadrant*, June 1999, 20-26 (See also my response 'Justice Brennan and Mabo', *Quadrant*, September 1999, Letters, 5-6)
15. Ibid. 24,25.
16. H Morgan, 'The Dangers of Aboriginal Sovereignty', *News Weekly*, 29 August 1992 11, 12.
17. The statement appears in the court transcript of 15 March 1988.
18. Letter to author, 19 September 1994.
19. R Evans, 'Gnosticism and the High Court' (n 14) 2.
20. Ibid, 24.
21. See *Mabo & Others v The State of Queensland (No. 2)* (1992) 175 CLR 1, 29.
22. Ibid, 30.
23. See *The Wik Peoples* v *The State of Queensland* (1996) 187 CLR 1, 87.
24. Ibid, 97-8.
25. Commonwealth, House of Representatives, 16 November 1993, 2877 (Paul Keating, Prime Minister).
26. Justice James Elliott, endorsed by his colleague Justice Tony Cavanough (former Associates of Sir Gerard Brennan and judges of the Supreme Court of Victoria), *Tribute to Sir Gerard Brennan*, (2022) 172 *Victorian Bar News* 64. Their Honours note: 'On 18 August 2022, a commemorative sitting of the High Court was held in memory of Sir Gerard, which was attended by many, including the Hon Paul Keating, Prime Minister of Australia from 1991 to 1996. Mr Keating has authorised the inclusion of this account in this publication.'
27. Hal Wootten, Response to Sir Gerard Brennan's 2012 Wootten Lecture, University of New South Wales at <http://www.law.unsw.edu.au/sites/law.unsw.edu.au/files/images/2012_hwl_response_final_1.pdf>.
28. Robin Creyke and Patrick Keyzer, *The Brennan Legacy: Blowing the winds of legal orthodoxy*(The Federation Press, 2002).
29. Jeff Fitzgerald, *Sir Gerard Brennan: The Law's Good Servant* (The Federation Press, 2024).
30. Sir Anthony Mason, 'Judicial Review: The Contribution of Sir Gerard Brennan', in Robin Creyke and Patrick Keyzer (eds), *The Brennan Legacy*(The Federation Press, 2002)38.
31. Stephen Gageler, 'The Legacy of Sir Gerard Brennan to Australian Public Law' (2023) 33 *Public Law Review* 303, 307.
32. Sir Gerard Brennan, 'The Christian Lawyer', Address at Ecumenical Church Service, Reid, ACT, 28 January 1992, (1992) 66 *Australian Law Journal* 259, 260-261.
33. Hal Wootten, Response to Sir Gerard Brennan's 2012 Wootten Lecture, University of New South Wales (n 27).

First Nations Tribute

Senator Patrick Dodson

Editor's Note

Patrick Dodson had known Gerard Brennan since 1976 when they both spoke on land rights at the annual conference of the Queensland Aboriginal and Islander Catholic Council. At that time, Brennan was a barrister, having concluded his appearance for the Northern Land Council in the Woodward Royal Commission on land rights, and Dodson was a Catholic priest. At the time of Brennan's death, Senator Dodson was the Australian Government's Special envoy for Reconciliation and the Implementation of the Uluru Statement from the Heart. At Brennan's funeral in St Mary's Church, North Sydney, on 17 June 2022, Dodson delivered this tribute together with an acknowledgment of country. Other tributes delivered at the funeral appear in Volume 2, Chapter 15.

I am a Yaruwu man from the Kimberley. This is not my traditional land. I acknowledge and pay our respects to the Eora nation and their contemporary leaders and assure them that we come in peace.I thank them for allowing us to return this great Australian to the soil of this ancient land where he will be welcomed as a man of courage, truth and a listening heart – a man we Yaruwu people call *ngarli birragah* – a true boss of the Gadiya law.

I placed upon his coffin some leaves from the gum tree.They are often used for smoking and healing. Today in this church which represents the importance of his own spiritual beliefs, the leaves symbolise the emissaries that will introduce his spirit to those of the ancient peoples who come from this Eora country.

Someone said of the former Chief Justice whose life and achievements we are celebrating today that he grappled or wrestled with the tension between the law and justice. But I remember one Sunday afternoon in Melbourne at the home of the late Ron Castan and Nelly. Amongst us there was Sir Ronald Wilson, a former High Court judge himself. We were discussing the long tortuous path of *Mabo* in the courts. Sir Ronald summed it up after an afternoon of legalistic discussion with the opinion that ultimately in their judgment of *Mabo*, the chief and his colleagues had listened with their hearts to the truth of the law, and justice was the outcome. By confronting the myth of *terra nullius* and to name it a legal fiction that made unjust deeds by the crown legal in the taking of First Nations lands, waters and way of life, the court had bequeathed both a gift and a challenge to the nation. Against the tide of an unrecognised flawed legal system, truth and justice prevailed. He and his fellow justices held in *Mabo* the seeds of our liberation. They held a light to the lie of *terra nullius* when many would have preferred continuing in the dark and the comfort of the legal fiction that had for centuries justified the legal dispossession of First Nations of this country with all its disastrous effects.

Today's invitation by First Nations 'to walk with us' in the Uluru Statement from the Heart holds up to all Australians the need for Voice, Treaty and Truth as the way to redress the tyranny of our indigenous dispossession. Injustice and illegality as the foundational pillars of our nationhood can perhaps be discarded to the wastebasket of history.

Others today will speak of his stature amongst jurists, his achievements as a father and a husband. Sir William Deane will speak of these and many other contributions that he has made to his family, our nation, and the significance of his life as a celebrated Australian. These and all his other achievements will be acknowledged and recognised as it's only right that we do so. For you must celebrate the lives of good people. But when we have completed our eulogies, it will be worth remembering that perhaps this Old Man's greatest achievement was that he had the courage and listening heart to seek the truth of our history and to use the law to which he was dedicated to confront the truth so long denied. Peace be with you, Old Man. Travel well, and take with you the thanks of a people seeking reconciliation in this country to which you have given so much. *Kulia.*

Timeline

1928 Born 22 May.

1946 Enrols at University of Queensland, BA/LLB.

1949 National President of National Union of Australian University Students (NUAUS).

1950 Associate to Townley J (Manus Island war crimes trials).

1951 Admitted to Queensland Bar.

1953 Marries Patricia O'Hara.

1959 First appearance in High Court.

1965 Takes silk (QC).

1969 Fiji Sugar Inquiry before Lord Denning.

1971 16th Australian Legal Convention – Response to Chief Justice Bray.

1971 Letter to *The Australian* re Springbok Rugby Tour and Queens land State of Emergency.

1972 Jack Emanuel Murder trial (PNG).

1973 17th Australian Legal Convention – Appearance on ABC *Monday Conference*.

1973-4 Counsel for the Northern Land Council, Aboriginal Land Rights Royal Commission.

1974-6 President of Queensland Bar Association.

1975 Appointed to the Australian Law Reform Commission.

1975 18th Australian Legal Convention – Closing Address: 'Where now?'

1975-6 President of Australian Bar Association.

1976 Founding President of Administrative Appeals Tribunal.
Founding Chair of the Administrative Review Council.
Judge of the Industrial Court, the Supreme Courts of the Northern Territory and the Australian Capital Territory.

1977 Founding judge of the Federal Court.

1979 Resigns from Administrative Appeals Tribunal and Administrative Review Council.

1981 Appointed to High Court.

1992 *Mabo* Decision.

1995 Appointed Chief Justice.

1996 *Wik* Decision.

1998 Retires from the High Court.
Appointed Chancellor, University of Technology, Sydney (UTS).

1999 Appointed to Supreme Court of Fiji.

2000 Resigns from Supreme Court of Fiji.

2000 Appointed to Hong Kong Final Court of Appeal.

2004 Retires as Chancellor of UTS.

2012 Retires from Hong Kong Final Court of Appeal.

2022 Died 1 June.

Table of Cases

ACKNOWLEDGMENTS

Some of the articles in this publication have appeared in journals including: *Australian Bar Review, Australian Journal of Public Administration, Australian Law Journal, Australian Law Librarian, Australian Quarterly, Bar News: Journal of the NSW Bar Association, Compass: A Review of Topical Theology, Constitutional Law and Policy Review, Deakin Law Review, James Cook University Law Review, Journal of Contemporary Health Law and Policy, Judicial Review, Medical Journal of Australia, Australian Journal of Forensic Sciences, Melbourne University Law Review, Monash University Law Review, University of New South Wales Law Journal, Irish Jurist, Public Law Review*, and *Utopia: The Journal of the St Thomas More Society.*

Others have appeared in books published by The Federation Press, LexisNexis Butterworths and Oxford University Press.

All permissions have been sought and, where necessary, obtained.

About the Editor

Fr Frank Brennan SJ AO, a son of Sir Gerard, is Adjunct Professor at the Thomas More Law School at ACU and Adjunct Research Professor at the Australian Centre for Christianity and Culture. He chaired the Media Entertainment and Arts Alliance's Review of the Australian Journalists' Code of Ethics. He chaired the National Human Rights Consultation for the Rudd Government and was a member of the Turnbull Government's expert panel which conducted the Religious Freedom Review. The Morrison Government appointed him to the Voice Co-Design Senior Advisory Group to help guide the Co-Design process to develop options for an Indigenous voice to parliament. His Order of Australia was for services to Aboriginal Australians, particularly as an advocate in the areas of law, social justice and reconciliation. He is the author of 16 books.

Chapter 1

The Common Law, Liberty and Justice

1.1 Law, Liberty and Morality

Editor's note

At the 16th Australian Legal Convention held in Melbourne in 1971, John Bray, Chief Justice of South Australia presented a paper 'Law, Liberty and Morality' in which he expressed his views on the Hart-Devlin debate in the United Kingdom. Professor HLA Hart had published 'Law, Liberty and Morality' in 1963.[1] Lord Devlin had published 'The Enforcement of Morals' in 1965.[2] The two chief respondents to Bray were Brennan, then Vice-President of the Queensland Bar, and Professor Enid Campbell, Dean of the Faculty of Law, Monash University. Lord Diplock was guest of honour at the convention. In his opening remarks, he observed that the common law 'works empirically and works mainly by nudges. It is not often that one gets the epoch-making case, it is not often that the opportunity occurs of saying, as Lord Mansfield could, the air of England is too pure for any slave to breathe, let the black go free.'[3] Another overseas guest was Judge Minor Wisdom from the United States Court of Appeal Fifth Circuit. Wisdom's many opinions helped end segregation in the south of the United States. Wisdom told his Australian audience that he had a bone to pick with Mansfield: 'Lord Mansfield was one of the greatest judges the English-speaking world has ever had and he took a very expansive view with regard to the judicial functions in commercial matters and other matters. I am sorry to say that when it came to the slave, Somerset, he ruled that he had to decide only the question before him – the liberty of that particular slave who happened to be in England at the time. Now, if Judge Mansfield had just indulged in a little obiter dictum, if he had just said "the law of England and the Colonies is too pure an air for a slave to breathe" he might have saved us a war and a lot of trouble today.'[4] This was Brennan's response to Bray's paper.[5]

Mr F G Brennan QC (Queensland): Mr Chairman, My Lord, Your Honours, Ladies and Gentlemen: It should not be thought that the debate which we are taking further today lay dormant between the time when Mill wrote his thesis and the publication of the *Wolfenden Report*. In the case of *R v Haddock,* the matter was once more agitated and you will remember that when Albert took his appeal to the Court of Appeal one of his grounds was that England was a free country and a man could do as he likes if he did nobody any harm. The response that he got on that occasion was one which might cause us to pause today. 'It is like the thirteenth stroke of a crazy clock,' said Lord Light, which not only is itself discredited but casts a shade of doubt over all previous assertions. It cannot be too clearly understood that this is not a free country and it will be an evil day for the legal profession when it is.

Now, the paper on which we are engaged today is one which is not confined to philosophic debate, but it is one which has tremendous practical implications, as Lord Light saw. It is now two centuries since Lord Mansfield was able to say, 'Let the black go free,' and the problem which we have today is of the same nature as his Lordship faced then. On the one hand, there is the risk that if law goes too far there is rebellion in the name of freedom; if law stops short of its proper role, then freedom itself is at risk. As Lord Denning pointed out, 'The freedom of the just man is not worthwhile to him if he can be preyed upon by the murderer or thief.' There would be many who would say that our laws are oppressive and who claim a moral right of non-compliance with the law. There are others who say that there should be more extensive legal control, for example, in fields such as the marketing of securities in order that the freedom of investment will not be impaired by those who would otherwise be free to manipulate the market.

Now, in determining the proper role of law and adjusting the niceness of this balance, the criteria which the Chief Justice's paper discusses seem to me to be utterly inadequate. It is no real answer to say that we are concerned with questions of private or sexual morality. There must be some wider test which can be applied to say how far the law might go. Morality, I should not think, is something which is intrinsically bad with which the law can never have any concern. Morality is not something which stands outside the fabric of our social life. Morality is part and parcel of our ways of life, just as financial adjustments may be and just as physical integrity is, and I would not have thought that any criterion is one which can be adequate for the task if it simply says, 'We will stop short of the enforcement of morality,' or on the other hand, 'We will enforce more morality.' After all, it is a moral judgment to say that murder is wrong, and yet we have no compunction in enforcing a law against murder.

Now, the criteria which have been discussed seem to me to be inadequate because if we take Mill's proposal that each may go to the devil in his own way, that really overlooks the fundamental proposition that the community has a very real interest in the individual. If the heroin addict collapses on the footpath and the harm which he has undergone, though of his own making, is affecting him in this way, does the community act the Levite and let him lie, or does it act the Good Samaritan and take him to the inn? And in the latter case, who pays the innkeeper's charges? Can the law say nothing to the addict before he starts, and can it not restrain him before he goes too far? Professor Hart would say that the law might protect him from his weaknesses. The Chief Justice would say that the harm in this case is physical. Let me vary the example. The family finances are damaged by the sickness of the breadwinner, and the alternatives are repossessions under the hire-purchase contracts or borrowing from the moneylender. Has the community no interest in curtailing the liberty of contract of either the hire-purchase company or of the moneylender? Consent to harm, to adopt Mill's proposition, can be no criterion for the limit of the law, because the individual cannot be empowered to give or to barter away the real interest which the community has in him. Physical harm can be no criterion, because the community interest in the individual is in the whole social person, and not simply in the bodily frame. Paternalism is no criterion at all, but rather an umbrella under which all manner of legal prohibitions may be gathered.

The difficulty, I would suggest, in determining the proper role of law arises from the difficulty in appreciating what law does in fashioning the fabric of life. As lawyers, we are accustomed to the analytical process and we, therefore, tend to examine law as though it were an isolated phenomenon, defined in terms of the source of its creation, the listed contents of its rules, the sanctions imposed for enforcement, and the mode and agency of their imposition. These tell us what law is. They tell us nothing about what law does. I suggest if we can turn from what law is to what law does, we can see more clearly the positive role which law plays in fashioning our social environment. Lord Lloyd has observed that 'for all the philosophic doubts, experience has shown that law is one of the great civilising forces in human society.' I rather thought this is what his Lordship was referring to yesterday when he told us of the seedlings of the law planted in foreign and new climes and when they grew the plants of civilisation reflected the values of the community from which they were drawn. The community was fashioned in this way by the law. The ultimate role of law is not the solution of individual cases–that is but the long stop after the law has failed. The law is fulfilled when murder is not committed, rather than when the murderer is punished; when contracts are performed, rather than when damages are awarded for their breach. I would suggest, for example, that regulations relating to aircraft maintenance may be judged good, not because they were made within power, or because provision is made for their summary enforcement, but rather because they help to engender a climate of skill and care in the engineering workshops. The objective of the law is education in attitudes. Law thus helps to form the conscience of the community. I would suggest the community's moral sense is as much a function of the enforcement of its laws as its laws are a function of the community's moral sense.

Viscount Simonds in the noted *Ladies Directory Case* (*Shaw v Director of Public Prosecutions* [1962] AC 200) said that the fundamental purpose of the law was the conservation of 'not only the safety and order but also the moral welfare of the state.'[6] It seems to me, with respect, that that has a great deal of reality as well as sense to commend it. The Chief Justice, of course, would say: Men cannot be made virtuous by legislation. And that is quite true. But legislation might help us who are of indifferent moral calibre for the most part to practise virtue more easily. Professor Hart, I think, might even accept that proposition if it were not for his fear that the law might freeze the State's moral standards into immobility. The Chief Justice adverts not to immobility but to the possible additions to the tensions of society by the existence of a set of laws relating to sexual morality in an age when there is general disagreement on moral issues. Well, what is the answer? Surely not the withdrawal of the law from all areas of supposed disagreement, because that would amount to a repeal by an uncertain vote and a repeal of standards which have served us well and which have formed the conscience of our community. We have had the advantage of a system which has fused the morality of Christianity with the pragmatism of the Anglo-Saxon character, and the most cursory reading of the views expressed in *Bowman v Secular Society Ltd*[7] will illustrate the point which I wish to make. Do we want the community standards to be changed now under the influence of the law? Do we want to withdraw laws from areas of supposed disagreement? What is the pragmatic solution to a problem when the community is supposed to have varying standards of personal morality? We cannot, as it were, think that law is simply the manifestation of these standards. The law itself affects the standards and the consciences which are adopted.

The Chief Justice expresses the opinion that 'there are indications that belief in the wickedness of fornication, adultery, abortion, and homosexuality may be following belief in the account of creation given in the book of Genesis into the shadow of minority opinion.' Passing over this singularly fundamentalist interpretation of Genesis, one can only ask whether society may not have been better and healthier in the past for its having adopted the Christian view. However, let it be said that there is the prospect of tension; let it be said that there is the prospect of immobility unless there are changes in the law. Does this not argue the necessity for creating some method for ascertaining a new and reasoned consensus as to what the law should be? I suggest this is really the problem which we face today. If there is to be a consensus upon a new morality, then a method of ascertaining it must be found. It is not to be ascertained by the cry of vocal minorities, nor by academic debate which proceeds with logical inevitability from fundamental ethical premises which are unacceptable to our society. So many today feel themselves ineffectual to influence any change in the fabric of society. The frustrations of impotence spill over into breaches of the law, not because the law is thought to be bad, but because breaking the law becomes the only effective method of protest. The Establishment as represented by government and the other institutions which the law upholds can be made to listen only by breaking the law. How sad a commentary on us all – on those who have power because they cannot make others believe they understand their protests; on those who protest because they attack the law which protects their right to protest; on those of us who do nothing because they care nothing for the problems of a quickly changing society. The rule of law is the victim in all this, and I would suggest that we appreciate the price of insisting on the rule of law is the creation of efficient machinery for its change.

I would suggest this, which is a tremendous topic in itself, is the real problem with which this paper is ultimately concerned. It is not so much about the present content of the law, it is about the way in which we ascertain new views as to what the law should be. We may find out if we create these structures that the new morality will have relatively little concern about changes in sexual morality and may exhibit a very great concern about problems relating to poverty and privilege and race.

---

1. HLA Hart, *Law Liberty and Morality* (Stanford University Press, 1963).
2. Patrick Devlin, *The Enforcement of Morals* (Oxford University Press, 1965).
3. 'Opening Ceremony', The Sixteenth Legal Convention of the Law Council of Australia, Melbourne (1971) 45 *Australian Law Journal* 449, 451.
4. J J Bray, 'Law, Liberty and Morality' (1971) 45 *Australian Law Journal* 452, 468.
5. J J Bray, 'Law, Liberty and Morality' (n 4) 463 – 4.
6. See *Shaw* v *Director of Public Prosecutions* [1962] AC 200, 267.
7. [1917] AC 406.

1.2 Letter to *The Australian* during the 1971 State of Emergency

Editor's note

In July 1971, there were widespread protests against the all-white Springbok Rugby team touring Australia. On 14 July 1971, the day after the conclusion of the 16th Australian Legal Convention in Melbourne, Sir Joh Bjelke Petersen had the Governor of Queensland declare a 'state of emergency' under the *State Transport Act 1960 (Qld)*. The Springboks arrived in Queensland on 22 July 1971. On 2 August 1971, *The Australian* published this letter from Brennan, the Vice President of the Queensland Bar. Though the Springboks were still within the jurisdiction, the 'state of emergency' was prematurely terminated.

The contemporary discussion of law and order has been overlaid with other issues: apartheid and football (as to which there is little disagreement), politics and protest (as to which there will always be disagreement).

The fact remains that law and order are essential to a civilised community. Law binds both the ruler and the ruled. The ruler who contemns the law can scarcely insist upon its observance by the ruled.

Each must obey the law in the appropriate way – the ruler, by exercising no more power than the law gives him, and by exercising that power honestly and fairly and with statesmanship; the ruled, by refraining from deliberate infringements of the laws properly enforced by the rulers.

Law and order are bilateral – if either side rejects law and order the other side is encouraged to do the same. The moral obligation of obedience is diminished.

When legitimate protest degenerates into unlawful disruption, governments are invited to assume powers of doubtful legality, and to condone unlawful actions by police. When governments do not exercise their powers honestly and fairly and with statesmanship, they invite disruptive expressions of protest.

In either case both the rulers and the ruled attack the concept of law and order. Is it not time for both to examine their consciences?

F G BRENNAN, QC

North Quay, Qld

1.3 The Naming of Magna Carta Place

Editor's note

In preparation for the centenary of federation, the ACT Branch of the Australia-Britain Society oversaw the design and construction of Magna Carta Place on Langton Crescent adjacent to the Old Parliament House Senate Garden. As Chief Justice, Brennan dedicated Magna Carta Place on 12 October 1997, the 700th anniversary of the sealing by King Edward I of the 1297 issue of Magna Carta.

Magna Carta was not an Act of Parliament. There was no Parliament. Magna Carta was not a constitution born of a revolution. Henry II's structures of government stayed in place. It was a bargain struck between King John and the Barons who thought themselves oppressed by his demands. Its terms were hammered out between them on the banks of the Thames at Runnymede between 15 June and 19 June 1215. Then the Great Seal was affixed to Magna Carta. It was not granted because of a desire for reform but merely as concessions wrung from a King whose position had been weakened by his disastrous campaigns in Flanders and France the year before. Historically, Magna Carta can be understood only by reference to the turbulent history of the times in the context of a feudal system. John repudiated Magna Carta and the repudiation was confirmed by Pope Innocent III. Both men died in the following year. But that is not the history that matters.

There are three factors which make today's occasion significant. The first is that the Barons' particular grievances against the King were extended to include provisions of potential benefit to a wider segment of the people. These ameliorating and beneficial provisions were largely the work of the Archbishop of Canterbury, Stephen Langton, whose election John had refused to confirm and whom he kept out of the Kingdom for years until 1213. It was Langton who brought the precedent of a Royal Charter to the notice of the Barons;[1] it was Langton who looked beyond the interests of the Barons to the protection of the people.[2] How appropriate it is that Magna Carta Place should be dedicated in a site bounded by Langton Crescent.

After John's death in 1216, Magna Carta was reissued by the Regents of the infant, Henry III in 1216 and again in 1217. In 1225, with Henry having come of age, he made the final and definitive reissue of the text under his seal. The original 63 Chapters were reduced to 37. But the enduring influence of Magna Carta depended on events that were to occur more than 70 years later.

On this day 12 October in 1297, the Royal Seal of Edward I was affixed to inscribed and attested copies of Magna Carta. They were distributed throughout the land to implement Edward's confirmation of the Charter. By letters patent, he directed his justices to administer the Charter as common law. No judgments were to be given henceforth that were contrary to the Charter – else they would be 'undone and holden for naught'.[3] Magna Carta, whether as common law or statute, entered the law of the land and, as part of the law of England from that time forward, became part of the law of all those Imperial colonies and possessions to which English law was carried. It is Edward's confirmation of the Charter – of the 1225 re-issue, not of the 1215 original – which is of greatest significance in the history of our institutions. It is this event that we commemorate today, the 700th Anniversary of its occurrence. In the Parliament building, close by, there is one of Edward's sealed copies of the Charter intended for the County of Surrey. That copy and this Place will be tangible reminders of the origin and centuries of growth of the constitutional principles which inform our national life.

The third significant factor is not the text itself but the beneficial misinterpretations – indeed, the myth – with which, from age to age, the text has been invested. Four centuries after the Charter was granted, Sir Edward Coke called it 'the Charter of Liberty, because it maketh freemen.'[4] This is not the occasion to rehearse the textual or historical support for all that has been said about the Charter. Today it is regarded as providing a traditional mandate for trial by jury, equal and incorrupt justice for all, no arbitrary imprisonment and no taxes without Parliament's approval. It does not matter that the text is seldom invoked in today's courts. At base, the importance of Magna Carta is that it contains the principle that the King, like all his subjects, is subject to the rule of law. On the doctrine that government, as well as the governed, is subject to the rule of law, depends on every step in our constitutional progress.

Above all, Magna Carta has lived in the hearts and minds of our people. It is an incantation of the spirit of liberty. Whatever its text or meaning, it has become the talisman of a society in which tolerance and democracy reside, a society in which each man and woman has and is accorded his or her unique dignity, a society in which power and privilege do not produce tyranny and oppression. It matters not that this is the myth of Magna Carta, for the myth is the reality that continues to infuse the deepest aspirations of the Australian people. Those aspirations are our surest guarantee of a free and confident society.

Today, in commemorating the launching of this enduring myth into our lives and our law, we gather to name this Place. We do so with a sense of gratitude for those who brought the law with them to these shores, a law that enures for the benefit of those who were here before and those who have come after to make Australia their home. We name this Place in our National Capital with gratitude for our forebears who have kept alive the spirit of Magna Carta. I am therefore honoured to unveil this plaque which names Magna Carta Place.

---

1. Sir William Holdsworth, *History of English Law*, vol 2, 210.
2. Ibid 304.
3. Allan, 'Magna Carta – An English Masterpiece' (1987) 21 *Law Society Gazette* 120, 123.
4. Geoffrey Hindley, *The Book of Magna Carta* (Constable, 1990), 189.

1.4 Institutions of Government in Australian Democracy

Editor's note

Brennan retired as Chief Justice on 22 May 1998. On 4 August 1998, the University of Technology, Sydney conferred him with an honorary LLD. Shortly thereafter, he became Chancellor of the university until 2004. This was his graduation address.

Mr Chancellor,

Retirement is an occasion for reflection. Retirement from practice of law and service in the judicial branch of government brings many reflections – of human drama, of humour, of friendships made, of insights into the human condition, of venality and arrogance, of generosity and compassion. The overwhelming reflection, however, is that we in Australia enjoy the priceless benefit of freedom under the law. Freedom under the law is a high-sounding phrase, suitable for inclusion in a piece of rhetoric, but full of meaning to a judge before whose court issues of great public moment are debated. When he or she picks up the tablets of the law in order to fashion a judgment, the tradition and culture of freedom are clearly inscribed and the law – not each integer but the entirety of the law – is found to command respect for the dignity of each person, for the institutions of a democratic government and for as much liberty as is consistent with the security of person and property and the good order of society needed for human development and social intercourse.

At base, freedom under the law is not obtained by the power of the State; to the contrary, the power of the State is confined by the law that secures the freedom. Freedom under the law is secured by the will of the Australian people and will be maintained so long as it remains the will of the people. We shall have freedom under the law so long as we retain that confidence in the institutions of government which is needed to sustain the rule of law. The rule of law depends on a voluntary acceptance of the authority of those institutions. In a democracy, the authority of an institution flows from a consensus that it is performing its allotted function.

Our two basic institutions, modelled on the government of England, are Parliament and the courts, the Executive Government being politically responsible to the Parliament and subject to judicial review by the courts. Lord Bridge of Harwich has observed: 'The maintenance of the rule of law is in every way as important in a free society as the democratic franchise. In our society the rule of law rests upon twin foundations: the sovereignty of the Queen in Parliament in making the law and the sovereignty of the Queen's courts in interpreting and applying the law.'[1]

His Lordship's observation echoes the declaration of Chief Justice Marshall in *Marbury v Madison*: 'It is, emphatically, the province and duty of the judicial department to say what the law is'.[2]

The mechanisms which regulate the functions of our several institutions are not the same, but they are calculated to create and maintain public confidence in the manner in which the different classes of governmental power are exercised. Public respect for and confidence in judicial institutions is safeguarded by the requirements of judicial method. Public respect for and confidence in the political institutions of government must be secured in a different manner, for the functions of the political institutions are separate from the functions of the judicial institutions.

Of course, confidence in any institution has to be earned and maintained by the members' performance of their proper duties. If politicians were merely self-seeking or the puppets of interest groups, if bureaucrats were indolent or incompetent, if judges were ignorant or corrupt, there would be no confidence in the legislature, the executive or the judiciary. The public needs to be satisfied that politicians, bureaucrats and judges are capable of performing and are duly performing their allotted functions. But human institutions are never perfect and there will always be grounds for criticism of the work of particular individuals. Reasonable freedom to expose the alleged or actual shortcomings of public officials and to comment fairly on them and their activities is the right of every citizen in a free society and a stimulus to the due performance of public duty. These are considerations that underpin the modern law of defamation in the common law countries. The High Court of Australia in *Lange* v *Australian Broadcasting Corporation*, declared: '... that each member of the Australian community has an interest in disseminating and receiving information, opinions and arguments concerning government and political matters that affect the people of Australia. ... The common convenience and welfare of Australian society are advanced by – discussion – the giving and receiving of information – about government and political matters.'[3]

In New Zealand, the Court of Appeal referred to similar considerations in *Lange* v *Atkinson and Australian Consolidated Press NZ Ltd*.[4] And the English Court of Appeal in *Reynolds* v *Times Newspapers Ltd*, said:

> We do not for an instant doubt that the common convenience and welfare of a modern plural democracy such as ours are best served by an ample flow of information to the public concerning, and

> by vigorous public discussion of, matters of public interest to the community.
>
> Recognition that the common convenience and welfare of society are best served in this way is a modern democratic imperative which the law must accept. In differing ways and to somewhat differing extents the law has recognised this imperative, in the United States, Australia, New Zealand and elsewhere, as also in the jurisprudence of the European Court of Human Rights.[5]

But freedom to criticize is insubstantial if the matter for criticism is unknown. Hence the modern insistence on transparency in government. Here, the judicial method provides a safeguard of public confidence in the courts. The judicial method requires that, subject to narrow exceptions, every word that is uttered from the opening sentence of a case to the closing words of an appellate judgment be open to scrutiny. Nothing must be hidden.[6] In *Russell* v *Russell*,[7] Gibbs J[8] wrote that the rule requiring proceedings to be conducted 'publicly and in open view'[9] has

> … the virtue that the proceedings of every court are fully exposed to public and professional scrutiny and criticism, without which abuses may flourish undetected. Further, the public administration of justice tends to maintain confidence in the integrity and independence of the courts. The fact that courts of law are held openly and not in secret ... distinguishes their activities from those of administrative officials, for 'publicity is the authentic hallmark of judicial as distinct from administrative procedure'.[10]

The process of the judge's reasoning, as well as the proceedings in the trial, must be exposed to public examination. Sir Frank Kitto's classic paper on 'Why Write Judgments?' asserted that full publicity for the judge's process of reasoning: '… must be exposed to the light of day so that all concerned may understand what principles and practice of law and logic are guiding the courts, and so that full publicity may be achieved which provides, on the one hand, a powerful protection against any tendency to judicial autocracy and against any erroneous suspicion of judicial wrongdoing and, on the other hand, an effective stimulant to judicial high performance.'[11]

Judicial decisions are made on material the whole of which is on the public record and for reasons which are publicly stated. But the judicial method cannot be transposed to govern political institutions. In the first place, political decisions, often relating to issues more diffuse and less particular than the issues before a court, do not always admit of proof of facts already in existence. Such decisions must be made on the best information available. Some years ago, a Lord Chancellor told me that, if he were sitting judicially, he had to study the Appeal Book minutely in order to apprehend precisely the facts of the case but, if he were acting politically, he had to do the best he could with such facts as were given to or known by him. Hence the importance of the work of the departments of State charged with the responsibility of assembling and evaluating material relevant to political decisions and tendering honest advice fearlessly to Ministers or others who must make those decisions.

Secondly, while confidential communications have no place in the work of the judicial branch of government, many communications with the political branches of government are necessarily con-fidential. The national interest could sometimes be prejudiced and the workings of government could be inefficiently delayed if the procedures governing legislation and administration required all material to be received, tested and evaluated in public. However, Parliamentary procedures elicit much information from the Executive and the enactment of Freedom of Information legislation in many jurisdictions has permitted some *ex post facto* examination of administration. Useful as these procedures are, the public does not and cannot always have the same level of access to the material on which political and bureaucratic decisions are made as it has to the material on which judicial decisions are made.

Hence, it is not always possible for the public to know whether political decisions are soundly based or whether the reasons advanced in support of a political decision are truly stated. Moreover, political decisions are not necessarily made according to their correspondence with existing fact or conformity with *a priori* rules; they may be made because they are calculated to produce a future effect that cannot be tested in advance. Confidence in the institutions empowered to make political decisions must be supported by mechanisms different from those which are capable of supporting confidence in judicial institutions.

Although the Parliament is, in a sense, the people's forum and although political figures and their activities are subjected to considerable, sometimes unduly intrusive, scrutiny by the media, the public are conscious that many political decisions of great importance are hammered out behind closed doors and that Parliamentary debates may be set pieces which put a particular complexion on decisions already made. Confidence in Parliament rests not so much on the procedures of Parliament but on the calibre and personality of politicians and the public's power at the ballot box. Confidence in politicians depends on their relationship with and sensitivity to the aspirations, needs and values of their constituents. When political decisions answer those aspirations, satisfy those needs and correspond with those values, confidence in the political institutions of government is high. In other words, a tolerable harmony between the policies implemented by a government and the aspirations, needs and values of the people bolsters confidence in our democratic political institutions. When the harmony is interrupted, it is the ballot box which secures confidence in the political institutions. So long as the people are confident that they can have a say in their political future in the reasonably foreseeable future, the habit of obedience to the law will secure the stability of our democratic political institutions. But if protest at the ballot box were practically ineffectual and if the policies of government continued to be substantially at odds with the aspirations, needs and values of the people, a free and democratic society would be at risk. Confidence in political institutions therefore depends on two factors: a fair and transparent electoral system which is likely to produce a Parliament that is broadly representative of the constituents and reflective of their opinions and, consequentially, government policies that are tolerably harmonious with public aspirations, needs and values. By what method are those policies to be resolved upon?

Here a divergence appears between the judicial method and the process which leads to the exercise of political power. The judicial method requires the ascertainment, sometimes the development, and always the articulation, of the principle or rule which determines the judgment or order to be made. (I leave aside those cases where the judgment or order is discretionary.)

Where the law is settled, the judge simply applies it. But even when the existing law does not contain a rule appropriate to the case in hand, the judge is not at liberty simply to enunciate a rule of his or her own choosing. Scholarship and experience must be employed. If an existing rule is to be modified or a new rule declared, analogy derived from existing principles is the primary source. Moreover, the modified or new rule must be articulated as an integer of the existing body of law, interlocking with related rules. This is no idiosyncratic exercise.

Minds may legitimately differ in the identification of the principles and purpose of the law and, infrequently, in the identification of enduring community values. But legal development does not depend on the law's pragmatic acceptability to the majority. Judges do not approach their function in that way.

The judicial method is rigorous and, when cases require the courts to make new law, I venture to suggest that it has become more patently rigorous. The reasons for judgment in the higher appellate courts increasingly look behind the legal rule to discover the informing legal principle and behind the informing legal principle to discover the basic value. Legal development then proceeds in the reverse order: provided the basic value is consistent with the enduring values of the community, the informing legal principle is stated in contemporary terms consistent with other legal principles and the new legal rule is stated in terms interlocking with related legal rules. The judge's legislative power is hedged about with restrictions. Judge Cardozo said, in a well-known description of the judicial method, that the judge is 'to exercise a discretion informed by tradition, methodised by analogy, disciplined by system, and subordinated to 'the primordial necessity of order in the social life". Wide enough in all conscience is the field of discretion that remains.'[12] Courts are tribunals of law – law that is settled or law that is developed within the confines of the judicial method. The judge is not free to innovate at pleasure although it is possible to conceive of some problems, notably in the fields of bio-ethics, where no analogy with existing principles can offer guidance.

Political and, to a great extent, bureaucratic decision-making cannot adopt the judicial method. To the extent that decision-making in these fields is not idiosyncratic, it is governed by policy rather than law. And policy may be chameleon-like, taking its colour from the decision-maker's assessment of the political, social or economic exigencies of the moment. Policy is the well-spring of new rights and obligations; law generally defines existing rights and obligations on which people can rely in charting their conduct and their relationships. Policy is the proper domain of the political branches of government, just as interpretation of statute law or the definition of the common law are the proper domain of the judicial branch.

In the resolution of policy, pragmatism has an important role to play. But public confidence will not be maintained in the political process if decisions are based on nothing but pragmatic considerations. Polls and personalities are no substitute for principle. Pragamatism without principle turns political power into a force of oppression and, whatever level of approval can be temporarily procured for a particular pragmatic decision, in time the people will perceive the absence of principle. Then, even if the government of the day, retains power, confidence in the political institutions of government is eroded. The judicial method of developing and articulating a principle is inapplicable to political decision-making but it does not follow that principle is foreign to politics. Public confidence in political institutions is enhanced if those who are entrusted by the people with political power exercise that power according to principles publicly espoused and publicly endorsed.

As a people, we have not developed a taste for the mature consideration of political principles, much less have we adopted an hierarchy of principles prescribing which principle prevails over another. We seek the instant answer to any political problem. The media, who live in a symbiotic relationship with the political branches of government, sense that we have a limited span of attention. Indeed, the media have entrenched the habit.

So, if the discussion of principle in political debate is superficial and fragmentary, we, the people, must assume much of the responsibility. At all events, we share that responsibility with the media and with the political professionals.

Our unwillingness to examine at length and in depth the nature of political problems and to debate political policies with tolerance and mutual respect is a serious flaw in our democracy. In today's world, political policies that answer the aspirations of the people, that satisfy their needs and that correspond with their values are not easily developed, much less implemented. That calls for leadership.

Political leadership today demands two capacities. First, a leader must have the capacity to understand a rapidly changing world in which technology and economics have leapt national boundaries, in which international relations preclude the quarantining of national policies from international scrutiny and in which the values of one generation are modified by the values of the next.

Secondly, a leader must have the capacity to carry the people with him or her in a mature debate in which the aspirations, needs and values of the people are re-assessed by them in the hard light of contemporary reality. Unless political leaders can stimulate our reflection on the real world in which we live and articulate the principles which will inform our policies, the political institutions will fail our people. Alienation will follow.

Alienation from the political process means a loss of confidence in political institutions. And that is a threat to the peace, order and freedom of our society.

There is little inherently wrong with the constitutional provisions governing our institutions, whether judicial or political. The greatest weakness lies in the level of political debate which seems to be marked increasingly by ignorance, prejudice and stridency. The peace, order and freedom that we have experienced and take for granted is arguably unequalled in any other country. We must not forfeit those blessings by failing to take an informed, open and tolerant part in the political debates that contemporary reality demands.

In this, Mr Chancellor, Universities have an important role to play, not only in contemporary policy formulation but in the excitement of curiosity in young intellects and in fostering a passion for the institutions that will keep Australia a free and confident nation. I thank you and the University for the honour you have bestowed on me. It is an honour which asserts the respectful support of the University for the judicial and quasi-judicial institutions on which I have served and which fulfil their purpose by service of the Australian people.

---

1. See *X Ltd v Morgan-Grampian (Publishers) Ltd* [1991] 1 AC 1, 48.
2. (1803) 1 Cranch 137, 177; 5 U.S. 87, 111.
3. (1997) 189 CLR 520, 571.
4. (unreported), 25 May 1998, CA 52/97; [1998] NZCA 252.
5. [1998] 3 All ER 961, 1004.
6. See Lord Devlin, *The Judge* (Oxford University Press, 1979) 26 – 27.
7. (1976) 134 CLR 495, 520.
8. And see *Dickason* v *Dickason* (1913) 17 CLR 50, 51. *H (falsely called C)* v *C* (1859) 29 LJ (P&M) 29, 30.
9. *Scott* v *Scott* [1913] AC 417, 441. See *Skope Enterprises Ltd* v *Consumer Council* [1973] 2 NZLR 399.
10. See *McPherson* v *McPherson* [1936] AC 177, 200.
11. (1973), see Sir Frank Kitto, 'Why write Judgments' (1992) 66 *Australian Law Journal* 787, 790.
12. Benjamin N Cardozo, *The Nature of the Judicial Process* (Yale University Press, 1921), 141.

1.5 Principle and Independence: The Guardians of Freedom

Editor's note

On 24 March 2000, Brennan delivered the Sir Ninian Stephen Lecture at the University of Newcastle.[1]

I begin this lecture by paying my respects to the jurist in whose honour this series of lectures has been established. My acknowledgment of Sir Ninian Stephen is more than the ritual courtesy of a lecturer in the series, for I had the honour of sitting with Sir Ninian in his last year and my first year as a member of the High Court bench. I witnessed the working of an incisive and cultivated mind responding with seeming ease to an unrelenting caseload. There were moments of apprehension when, immediately before walking through the court door to take his seat on the bench, Sir Ninian would tuck a fuming pipe into the pocket of his bar jacket. A sense of relief grew only with the passing minutes, although there was never a sign of conflagration.

Collegiality in a numerically small court can be a fragile thing, especially when issues of great moment fall for decision. Sir Ninian's scholarship and experience, his urbanity and especially his openness of mind made professional association as easy and agreeable as personal friendship. We missed Sir Ninian and Lady Stephen greatly when a wise Government cast upon him the duties of Governor-General. Our consolation was the appointment of his successor in both judicial and vice-regal offices, Sir William Deane. Both jurists and their wives have contributed to the building of a free and confident nation, and it is no diminution of their personal contributions to examine this evening the foundations of our freedom.

A satisfactory definition of freedom, or of its synonym liberty, is as elusive as the means of securing it. Abraham Lincoln told the American people that –

> The world has never had a good definition of the word liberty, … We all declare for liberty; but in using the same word we do not all mean the same thing. With some the word liberty may mean for each man to do as he pleases with himself, and the product of his labor; while with others the same word may mean for some men to do as they please with other men, and the product of other men's labor.[2]

The term may connote both liberty of the individual and liberty in the exercise of power, yet these meanings are not only different – they are opposed. There is and will always be a tension between these two types of liberty. The ambiguity of the term appears in modern debates. In a free market, the exercise of market power by some persons, some corporations or some nations can result in a widespread restriction or destruction of freedom. The free exercise of majoritarian power in a democracy may trample on the freedom of minorities. And, at the individual level, the exercise of our own freedom can sometimes impair a neighbour's freedom to act as he or she would otherwise choose to act.

If the essence of freedom is the absence of control, freedom can never be absolute. In the long years of controversy over the meaning of 'absolutely free' in s 92 of the *Constitution*, there was never any dissent from Sir Samuel Griffith's dictum that 'We boast of being an absolutely free people, but that does not mean that we are not subject to law.'[3] A P Herbert's fictitious litigant, Albert Haddock, learned that freedom can never be absolute when he lost his appeal.[4] He had jumped into the Thames in front of a regatta and was convicted of sundry offences, including endangering the lives of mariners. He had good grounds of appeal against each conviction but he foolishly added the tendentious ground that England 'is a free country and a man can do what he likes if he does nobody any harm.' This led Lord Chief Justice Light to dismiss all grounds of appeal, observing that that ground was 'like the thirteenth stroke of a crazy clock which not only is itself discredited but casts a shade of doubt over all previous assertions.'

Freedom cannot be absolute, but no limitations need to be imposed on the freedom of thought or action that has neither impact on society nor threat to our own safety; it is the freedom to exercise power which must be amenable to control. In an insightful article, RWM Dias pointed out: 'It is the exercise of power that matters. Therefore, one aspect of the problem is that behind every form of power lies the freedom of power-holders to exercise it or not, which makes the abusive exercise of this freedom the crux of the matter, not simply possession of power.'[5]

Once we acknowledge that freedom to exercise power can never be absolute and that controls of one sort or another are essential to social peace and order, the problem of guarding my freedom focuses on the nature and extent of the controls which limit the freedom of those who have power to affect me or my interests. To the extent that their power is controlled, I am free to think and to act as I choose. The guarantors of freedom are to be found in the mechanisms by which the possessors of power are controlled in its exercise. Before we look at those mechanisms, we should be clear about the reasons why we value freedom.

The value of freedom can be appreciated most vividly if we contemplate its absence. We are distressed by the memory of Hitler youth conditioned to think and act as the Nazi propaganda machine decreed, or of the children sent to work in the pits in 19th Century England, or of the Aboriginal mothers whose children were taken from them, or of the political dissenters in the hands of Pinochet's torturers – men, women and children who were denied their humanity, their capacity to be themselves, to develop and to reach their true potential. Or, to take examples more familiar to ourselves: the drug addict dependent on the supplier; the young prisoner enslaved to the hardened criminal in the gaol; the untrained and unemployed without prospect of employment. These are but some of the instances we can call to mind of those whose dignity is suppressed by their loss of freedom. The freedom we seek is not absolute. If it were, it would degenerate into licentiousness or even tyranny. It would destroy our own dignity. Freedom is needed to allow us to be ourselves – to allow us to develop and to express ourselves truly; to live in the dignity which comes from autonomy of thought and action.

As our autonomy can be enjoyed only in the society in which we live, it must be limited to allow a due measure of autonomy to others. We are social beings, so we cannot seek a freedom which poses a substantial risk of destroying the freedom of others and, if we are truly egalitarian, we would not want the freedom of others to be reduced below the freedom which we enjoy. So, we can define the freedom we seek as the maximum degree of autonomy of thought and action consistent with the enjoyment of a corresponding degree of autonomy by others. The implications of this definition are stated by Joseph Raz:[6]

> Three main features characterize the autonomy-based doctrine of freedom. First, its primary concern is the promotion and protection of … the capacity for autonomy, consisting of the availability of an adequate range of options, and of the mental abilities necessary for an autonomous life. Second, the state has the duty not merely to prevent denial of freedom, but also to promote it by creating the conditions of autonomy. Third, one may not pursue any goal by means which infringe people's autonomy unless such action is justified by the need to protect or promote the autonomy of those people or of others.

How is freedom in that sense to be secured? What controls on power are needed? A preliminary question is whether we always need mechanisms of control to protect our freedom. In a pluralist, multi-cultural society, tolerance is essential to allow others to think and act in ways with which we disagree. Albert Einstein said:'Laws alone cannot secure freedom of expression; in order that every man may present his views without penalty there must be a spirit of tolerance in the entire population.'[7]

Tolerance is a virtue for it respects the dignity of others without requiring an adoption of others' thoughts or actions or an abandonment of one's own. It facilitates that social intercourse, peace and order in which individual personalities can develop and express themselves. It can diminish the need for the introduction of controls designed to protect personal freedom. It is only when there is some risk to social peace and order, or some risk of offence to personal dignity that we need to think in terms of mechanisms to control the exercise of power.

Mechanisms to Control Power

It is tempting for a lawyer to propose that the law be regarded as the chief mechanism for the control of power, but a moment's reflection will show us that that is the solution of last resort. If all conduct were regulated by law, our society would be anything but free; equally, of course, if there were no laws to regulate conduct, untrammelled force and power would destroy our freedom. The fabric of the law is essential to freedom, but it cannot be the sole or ordinary guarantor. Indeed, the ultimate sanction of the law is required only when other mechanisms of control fail. The real assurance of a free society comes from the people's spirit of freedom, informing their customs and their institutions.

Power comes in various forms. A submissive wife may be cowed by a dominant husband; a powerful intellect may tower over those around him; a campaign by the media may change the opinions of a community. The control of one kind of power may not be suited to the control of another and there are some powers, of a socially private or familial kind, which are properly exercised only by self-control. In the relationships of a family or a group of friends, affection or the lack of it or good manners or the want of them have the greatest effect on the autonomy of a member of the family or group. In the ordinary, day to day intercourse of the family or group, no external intervention is needed and none would be appropriate to control any power possessed by one member over another. Generally speaking, it is unacceptable that an external control should intrude into the relationship of parent and child, in the relationship of siblings, in the social discourse of a group of friends. It is only when those relationships become dysfunctional and when individuals need external authority to protect their interests against those who have neglected or oppressed them that it is legitimate for any external mechanism to intervene.

Just as there are various forms of power, so there are various mechanisms for its control. Some can be exercised by the possessor of the power, others only by an external authority exercising a countervailing power. The paradigm instance of an external authority exercising a power to control the exercise of another's power is the court in its enforcement of the law. The principles found in the law are applied to the particular facts and the exercise of the court's power follows in the judgment pronounced. That is the way in which freedom under the law is secured in judicial proceedings. Therein lies the key to the control of all forms of power, whether the control is exercised by the possessor of the power or by an external authority exercising its supervening and countervailing power. Power should be exercised according to principle. Principles encapsulate values and can govern the way in which power is exercised by its possessor. Principles do govern the way power is exercised if the possessor is independent of influences which would induce the possessor not to act in accordance with the principles he or she espouses. Principles are susceptible of rational evaluation and, whether or not articulated, they develop in the religious, social and economic environment in which we live. So, in a free society, it is reasonable to expect that principles which govern the exercise of public power will themselves reflect the spirit of freedom and that the people in general assent to principles which reflect that spirit. Provided those principles are faithfully implemented – a function of independence – the maximum autonomy of thought and action for all members of the society should be assured.

In considering the various mechanisms of power control, it must be remembered that the law has a significant limitation: it cannot directly abridge freedom of thought. That is because, as Oliver Wendell Holmes correctly observed, '[a]ll law is directed to conditions of things manifest to the senses'[8] Thoughts can be translated into action and the law can constrain action, but it cannot control thought. This was the point which Thomas More made at his trial when he repelled the charge of treason based on his non-acceptance of the King's ecclesiastical supremacy. 'I answer that', he said, 'for this my taciturnity and silence, neither your law nor any law in the world is able justly and rightly to punish me unless you may besides lay to my charge either some words or some fact in deed.'[9]

Freedom of thought depends on our education (in the broadest sense), our social and financial situation and the environment in which we live. These are variables. If we leave aside the effects of mind-altering drugs, of torture, of some psychiatric therapies and of brainwashing by cults or like groups – all of which receive some attention from the law – the peril to freedom of thought comes chiefly from deception which distorts the individual's understanding of reality. The protection of freedom of thought therefore depends in part on the control of conduct and substances which might overpower the mind and in part on the control of conduct which is likely to deceive.

The most basic and important mechanism for the control of power is the moral sense of the possessor of the power. I will not exercise the power that I possess over another if I do not think I ought to exercise it. Oftentimes it is said that law is the force which governs and secures acceptable conduct. It is not. The law can always be disobeyed, even if the offender must suffer some penalty in consequence. The law provides an incentive to socially acceptable conduct and it can have a valuable educative effect, but the most immediate and coercive force affecting the conduct of men and women is the force of conscience. Conscience is the voice which sums up the values which we embrace and the influences we have experienced in life.

If the Biblical injunction to 'love one another as I have loved you' were fully appreciated and fully implemented, power would be exercised not for the benefit of the possessor of the power but for the benefit of others. But that counsel of moral perfection is seldom seen, much less emulated. However, although religious belief as the mainspring of a moral system has diminished in our society, Judaeo-Christian moral values which respect the dignity of others have become part of the secular culture. They are esteemed as humanitarian values and inform many of the judgments that we make.

Each of us lives by a moral code. It may be good, bad or indifferent, but we act out of the principles which we accept.[10] The principles of morality by which most people govern their thoughts and actions are not necessarily articulated; it is often times a matter of 'what one does' rather than the reason why one does it. Those principles, whether articulated or not, determine whether and in what circumstances and in what manner any power we possess will be exercised. We describe a person of fine moral calibre as 'highly principled' by which we mean that his or her thoughts and acts are informed by moral standards which are not abandoned for expediency or under pressure.

In a stable community, the moral principles of individuals govern the exercise of private power, and the entirety of their individual principles produces a moral consensus to govern the exercise of public power. In a stable community, the moral consensus may support the exercise of public power to serve the common good.[11] The common good, as it is understood in a free society, seeks to achieve a maximum and equal degree of autonomy for its members. But how it is achieved is, in large measure, a matter for political opinion, judgment and action. Some find in the economics of laissez-faire the greatest stimulus to the general population's initiative, independence and wealth; some think it essential to provide a welfare state with a tightly controlled economy to prevent the less fortunate from a loss of human dignity; some again find the political and economic solution somewhere between these two extremes. Generally speaking, it is impossible to determine for every society, at all times and in all circumstances, the precise form of government and economic control which yield the optimum benefits. That is why we repose political and other public powers in a Parliament and a Government that is democratically elected. Provided the political will of the majority of the people is reflected at the polls, we obtain as best we can, a political assurance of the maximum autonomy of thought and action – for at least that majority.

The system has some weaknesses. Those who possess or seek political or other public power engage the media to disseminate their particular policies and viewpoints and provide the media with selected material for that purpose. That is an inevitable phenomenon in an elective democracy. And, as the acquisition and retention of political power requires only majority support, the power may be exercised to advantage the majority at the expense of a minority.

Mechanics needed to safeguard democracy

An effective democracy depends on an informed electorate. Demo-cracy is a charade if the electorate is ignorant of or deceived about the matters that are relevant to the exercise of power purportedly to achieve the common good. The chief sources of political education are political parties and the media. The freedom of each group is important – the political parties so that they may devise and advocate for popular consideration the course which they invite the people to endorse; the media so that they can convey the information and make the comments that can assist the public in evaluating the options before them.

We expect political groups to lay out their policies – the practical steps to implement the principles they espouse. Those principles determine the frames of political reference, the options open to the people to endorse. Those principles must be open to public debate, otherwise the public lack the understanding which would allow them to pass judgment on a proposed or past exercise of political power. Nor, without public debate, can a political party obtain a true picture of political sentiment.

The necessity of publicity and free discussion in a democracy is obvious. In recent times it has been affirmed repeatedly in the High Court.[12] Public discussion is the mechanism by which public morality emerges to define the principles which should govern the exercise of power. Dennis F Thompson, an American academic reminds us that –

> It was Kant who first emphasized the deep connection between morality and publicity. He presented the criterion of publicity as

> a fundamental test of morality … 'All actions which relate to the right of other men are contrary to right and law [if their] maxim… does not permit publicity.' That a principle can be made public is not sufficient to make the principle moral, but it is necessary. If a principle must be kept secret, it is because the principle cannot be generally and freely accepted on its merits … . A legislator could not legitimately act on the principle that he will tell the truth except when it could jeopardize his re-election. Making that principle public would defeat its purpose.[13]

But how are principles made public? By the media. The vitality, even the continuing legitimacy, of our constitutional institutions depends in no small measure on the media. It has long been so. Thomas Carlyle tells us that Edmund Burke said: '… there were Three Estates in Parliament; but, in the Reporters' Gallery yonder, there sat a Fourth Estate more important far than they all. It is not a figure of speech or a witty saying, it is a literal fact – very momentous to us in these times…. Whoever can speak, speaking now to the whole nation, becomes a power, a branch of government, with inalienable weight in law-making, in all acts of authority.'[14]

Now if the media enjoy that power, they too must be under an obligation to declare the principles which govern their exercise of it. The media assert a right to publish freely in service to the community and that is a right which can be readily acknowledged – indeed, which provides the raison d'être of a free press. But there is no freedom that is absolute and the freedom to publish is no exception. I am not speaking here of the limitations imposed by the law relating to defamation and contempt of court; I am speaking of the obligation of the media to apply the principle that matter be published to serve the community. It is not sufficient for the media in a free society to publish material merely to entertain or to titillate a passing interest; their function in disseminating information accurately, explaining it adequately and commenting on it fairly is critical to a free, democratic society

The need for accurate, informed reporting and incisive comment has perhaps never been greater. Governments, political parties and other organizations equip themselves with public relations consultants, speech writers and others whose function it is to obtain the best possible media coverage for their employers. The spin doctors may feed the media with selected information and slanted comment and it becomes the function of the media to evaluate what they are given, to correct or amend it as needed, or to reject it. To publish media handouts without evaluation or without identifying them as handouts from the originating source impedes the flow of information to the public or falsifies its significance.

It is inevitable that media comment will be influenced by media ownership, and that influence can be patently acknowledged without departure from the principle of community service. What is unacceptable, and a real danger to freedom, is undisclosed bias which affects the matter published. If reporters, news editors, producers or publishers cede their independence, whether to a proprietor, to a political party, to a commercial interest or even to a friend, the principle of community service which ought to be a guardian of the people's freedom becomes an instrument of deception and a danger to their autonomy.

Deception attacks autonomy of thought by denying the individual the material to be thought about. Our laws insist, and rightly, that trading and financial corporations and some other categories of persons should refrain from deceptive and misleading conduct in trade or commerce but, in elections, our law imposes no sanction on the politician who engages in deceptive or misleading conduct designed to induce the voters to favour that politician with their vote. In *Evans* v *Crichton-Brown*, the High Court acknowledged that: 'In a campaign ranging over a wide variety of matters, many of the issues canvassed are likely to be unsuited to resolution in legal proceedings; and a court should not attribute to the Parliament an intention to expose election issues to the potential requirement of legal proof in the absence of clear words.'[15]

No doubt the disparity in our law between deception in trade or commerce on the one hand and deception in elections on the other simply acknowledges the hyperbole and suppression which are characteristic of democratic elections. We console ourselves with the notion that the good sense of the people will ultimately arrive at the principle best suited to serve the common good as they see it. At all events, subject to an important qualification relating to human rights, there are no better principles by which a legislature and a government should act than the principles openly stated by a party seeking government and endorsed by the majority of the people. That is sometimes called "the mandate" and it is not to be departed from by a government after the compact is made with the people unless there be unexpected, supervening circumstances which warrant the departure. The bleak cry of broken promises alienates the people from the political process.

Provided the people are adequately informed about the prin-ciples by which political power is to be, and is being, exercised and provided the majority approve of those principles, their implementation will not trespass upon the freedoms of the majority unless it is to secure the common good as the majority understand it. Of course, in a perfect society which rejoices in a culture of freedom, the common good would be seen to include the good of minorities as well as the good of the majority and political power would be so confined as not to trespass on the freedom of minorities. But no society is perfect and, as the Founding Fathers were confident of the liberal spirit of the Australian people and declined to follow the American precedent of a constitutional Bill of Rights,[16] the protection of minority rights is a responsibility of the parliamentary process.

Democracy by itself does not assure the freedom of all members of the community. The tyranny of a majority may need to be controlled.[17] It is the risk of that tyranny and perhaps a growing mistrust of the political process that has stimulated interest in an Australian Bill of Rights. The warrant for such a measure is the potential of democratic power to be used tyrannically over a minority. The common good, if it were represented to be in the interests or will of the majority, would oftentimes be secured only by the oppression of a minority. Majoritarian benefit is likely to be the result of an exercise of legislative or executive power in a democracy: benefits are conferred on some, while others either go without or are made to bear corresponding burdens. But the burden which a majority might impose on a minority is exceeded when the human rights of the minority are infringed. This is, or ought to be, the boundary beyond which State power must not trespass. Human rights prescribe the minimum conditions in which an individual can live in society with his or her dignity respected. The infringement of human rights is a refusal to recognize the dignity of the person. And with the loss of that dignity is the loss of freedom. That was the truth proclaimed by the United Nations in its 'Universal Declaration of Human Rights' in 1948, the first recital of which declared that: 'recognition of the inherent dignity and of the equal and inalienable rights of all members of the human family is the foundation of freedom, justice and peace in the world'.

Two factors have combined to expose human rights and fundamental freedoms to danger from an exercise of power by the political branches of Government. First, our society has become more diverse in its ethnic, cultural, religious, and economic composition. Or, to put it another way, there are more minority groups whose particular interests are liable to be overreached by the exercise of legislative or executive power. The control of the political process by political parties favours the creation of poll-driven policies which will appeal to the majority of the electorate whether or not they unjustifiably discriminate against minority groups or against the weak. There is a consequent risk that factors which justify special consideration of the position of a minority or special support of the weak will be disregarded.

A Bill of Rights is seen by many as a necessary protection of minorities and the weak. Lord Scarman advances this as the chief political argument for a Bill of Rights in the United Kingdom:

> ... if you are going to protect people who will never have political power, at any rate in the foreseeable future (not only individuals but minority groups with their own treasured and properly treasured social customs, religion and ways of life), if they are going to be protected it won't be done in Parliament – they will never muster a majority. It's got to be done by the courts and the courts can only do it if they've got the proper guide-lines.[18]

A further danger to human rights and fundamental freedoms is posed by the dominance of the executive Government, supported by its bureaucracy, over the Parliament. This dominance has undermined the theory that the Westminster model of responsible Government effectively guarantees democratic control of executive power. Indeed, the influence of a Cabinet, itself substantially under the influence of the Prime Minister of the day, over the Parliament substantially justifies Lord Hailsham's comment[19] that '[w]e live under an elective dictatorship, absolute in theory if hitherto thought tolerable in practice'.[20] A Bill of Rights is seen as a protection against the oppressive exercise of this enormous mass of power. As Sir Anthony Mason put it: 'Human rights are seen as a countervailing force to the exercise of totalitarian, bureaucratic and institutional power – widely identified as the greatest threats to the liberty of the individual and democratic freedom in this century. One result has been the wide-spread entrenchment of fundamental rights in Constitutions throughout the world.'[21]

The various international instruments which declare human rights and which have been ratified by Australia can provide us with a set of principles observance of which would be effective to safeguard the freedom of minorities. For example, in *Minister for Immigration and Ethnic Affairs* v *Teoh*[22] the High Court affirmed the setting aside of a deportation order on the ground that the maker of the order had not taken account of the obligation to protect the interests of an alien's child under the *International Convention on the Rights of the Child.*

We can apply these principles to the controversy over mandatory sentencing. It is, so far as we know, valid law in Western Australia and the Northern Territory. What were the principles which led their respective Parliaments to enact such legislation? Clearly, that the law should provide a deterrent to the commission of particular kinds of offences, even minor property offences. And it is asserted that a majority of the respective electorates support these laws. So, the problem for the legislatures and governments of Western Australia and the Northern Territory was whether the laws trespass on human rights. If so, the laws were inappropriate in a free society. The better view seems to be that those laws do trespass on human rights. Moreover, they deny the courts the ability to do justice and thereby strike at one of the foundations of a civilised society.

Then there arises the question whether Commonwealth legislative power should be exercised to protect human rights. A question of principle arises: is it right for the Commonwealth Parliament to override the laws of a State or self-governing Territory? If so, in what circumstances? Minds may differ on this issue. In my respectful opinion, the autonomy of States and self-governing Territories in matters of domestic concern should generally be maintained. Yet, when human rights of life and liberty are trampled on, albeit with the consent of an electoral majority, I would contend that no Parliament and no Government ought to stay its hand. Freedom at so basic a level is not to be forfeited to satisfy the demands of any group, whether a majority in an electorate or not. Political expediency offers no reason for refraining from ensuring basic human rights, for the power to rectify is conferred in order to maintain fundamental freedoms and the basic institutions of a society.

Of course, there is an argument for the constitutional entrenching of the Bill of Rights and thereby remitting to the courts the protection of the human rights which the Bill would declare. That would certainly bring the courts into play as an element in the political process but, in entering the process, there would be a risk to the courts themselves of becoming politicized. This is not the occasion to debate the desirability of a constitutionally entrenched Bill of Rights but it is instructive to consider why there should be any movement to transfer into the hands of an unelected judiciary a highly political power. Of all the institutions of government, the courts retain – and need to retain – the greatest public confidence. It is a commonplace that the freedom of a society depends on a free and competent judiciary, so we can examine the judicial method in order to discover what are the features on which that reputation is built.

Principle and independence in the judicial method

The judiciary resolves the controversies of litigants by finding the facts, applying the law, sometimes exercising discretions within narrow and definable limits and then and thereby pronouncing judgment.[23] The courts act according to established principles: the principles of the law. Generally speaking, those principles are in existence before they are to be applied in a particular case. The rule of law has at its core the 'principled faithful application of the law'.[24] As Lord Bridge of Harwich has observed: 'The maintenance of the rule of law is in every way as important in a free society as the democratic franchise. In our society the rule of law rests upon twin foundations: the sovereignty of the Queen in Parliament in making the law and the sovereignty of the Queen's courts in interpreting and applying the law.'[25]

The common law is the basis of our legal system and it encapsulates the values of a free society. These values include the dignity and integrity of every person, substantive equality before the law, the absence of unjustified discrimination, the peaceful possession of one's property, the benefit of natural justice, and immunity from retrospective and unreasonable operation of laws. In applying the law, there are occasions when the circumstances of a particular case show that the literal application of some rule or precedent would be productive of injustice. The court must then re-examine the rule or precedent and, if the court is not constrained by the authority of a superior court or by a statutory text, the court may think it right and timely to reformulate the rule or precedent to accord with the enduring values of the contemporary community.[26]

As the basic principles of the common law are protective of freedom,[27] those principles govern the approach of the courts to the construction of statutes. The High Court has said that the courts do 'not impute to the legislature an intention to interfere with fundamental rights. Such an intention must be clearly manifested by unmistakable and unambiguous language.'[28] In the *Cambridge Law Journal*, Dr TRS Allan lauded this approach of the courts, proclaiming that:

> Properly articulated and developed, the basic constitutional principle of the rule of law provides a powerful breakwater, if not an impenetrable dam, against encroachment on important rights and liberties by means of statutory authority. Nor can the scope of the principle be limited to those liberties and interests – chiefly liberty of the person and property interests – which have received the most assiduous judicial attention in the past. The traditional political liberties, especially freedoms of speech and assembly, which constitute important features of modern bills of rights, fall equally naturally within its compass.[29]

It would read too much into this comment to assume that the courts can or would defy statutory law, but the approach is right and the endeavour to preserve freedom by application of the rule of law is a continuous element in curial decisions. In developing the law, the courts are not set loose on the acquisition of discretionary powers by leaving new principles so open textured as to allow judges to decide cases according to their idiosyncratic notions of justice. The law should state principles capable of application to the case in hand and to future cases arising the same issue. The point was made dramatically by Geoffrey Robertson in criticism of an aspect of the genius of Lord Denning who, I might add, was one of his, and one of my, legal icons of the past century. Robertson wrote that his generation had been:

> ... taken in by a most charismatic and controversial judge, Lord Denning, whose slogan was 'I must do justice, whatever the law may be'. His invitation to tear up the rule book in order to reach popular results suited the iconoclasm of the time. That it was dangerously simplistic only became evident years later, as I sat in courtrooms in Singapore and Kenya and South Africa, listening to his idiosyncratic judgments being quoted by State prosecutors as warrant for locking up dissidents without trial, as threats to national security; Denning played Prospero to lawyers of his generation, creating the result his own opinionated mind believed 'just' through the alchemy of obscure precedents he found in the common law: his prejudices were his principles. 'Trust the judges' became his motto, and although my cases show that judges usually favour liberty more than governments do, they need advocates to push them and principles to protect them.[30]

The judicial method reduces any antinomy between justice and law to a minimum. This is the method which gives effect to the rule of law.

Dias comments that:[31]

> ... it is commonplace that in this task [the judges] are guided by their sense of values according to which they balance the interests in dispute.
>
> This explanation, brief as it is, makes it possible to relate judicial independence to the 'rule by law'/'rule of law' dichotomy. Where 'rule by law' obtains, the judiciary is a tool of government, which, along with others, reflects and implements official policies and interests. Where 'rule of law' obtains, judges are free to decide on values of their own, and the check on power derives from their being able to hold governmental interests in balance against others. In this way the British judiciary has built up its tradition of independence over the centuries. By and large judges have contrived to preserve as much balance of power in society as they could by siding with the weaker side whenever the balance tilted against it.

In exercising their power according to principle, the courts must, of course, be independent. The purpose of independence is the maintenance of the rule of law. Without independence the rule of law would be destructive of the interests which the law must protect. Chief Justice Gleeson has pointed out that the law is not the instrument of the popular but the protector of the unpopular: 'Those for whose rights we need to be zealous are the unpopular, those against whom campaigns of public vilification may be waged, those whose activities, even though lawful, are sought to be made the object of public disapproval.'[32]

To ensure that effect is given to the values of the common law when they stand in the way of an exercise of power, especially the power of governments, a judiciary of unquestioned independence is essential. The judge stands in the lonely no-man's-land between the government and the governed, between the wealthy and the poor, the strong and the weak. She or he can identify with neither, for partisanship robs the judge of the authority essential to discharge the judicial office. Independence has been the characteristic of the judiciary for 300 years since the *Act of Settlement 1701*. And it assures the impartial application of the principles of law in every case. It is the ultimate guarantee of a free society.

The freedom of society generally and the autonomy of each of its members require the legislature, the executive, the judiciary and the media – the great repositories of public power – to exercise their respective powers according to principle and to be independent of the influences that tend to divert them from that duty. Whether an entrenchment of human rights with its consequent transference of power to the judiciary is expedient to protect the human rights of minorities is a question that should receive more public examination and debate. But as the ultimate guarantor of freedom is our sensitivity to the dignity and autonomy of others as well as ourselves and our vigilance in insisting on the patent adherence to principle by the great repositories of public power, the future of a free society is in our hands.[33]

---

1. This lecture was published in (2000) 74 *Australian Law Journal* 749.
2. At Baltimore in 1864, printed in R Basler (ed), *The Collected Works of Abraham Lincoln* (Rutgers University Press, 1953), 301.
3. See *Duncan v State of Queensland* (1916) 22 CLR 556, 573.
4. Herbert A P, *Uncommon Law* (Methuen & Co, 3rd ed, 1937) 24-29.
5. Dias RWM, 'Götterdammerung – gods of the law in decline' (1981) 1(1) *Legal Studies* 3, 5.
6. Joseph Raz, *The Morality of Freedom* (Clarendon Press, 1986), 425.
7. Albert Einstein, *Out of My Later Years* (Greenwood Press, 1950) 12,13.
8. O W Holmes, *The Common Law* (MacMillan & Co, 1881), 49.
9. Peter Ackroyd, *The Life of Thomas More* (Chatto & Windus, 1998), 383.
10. Milton Rokeach, *Beliefs Attitudes and Values* (Jossey-Bass, 1980), 161.
11. David Beetham, *The Legitimation of Power* (Atlantic Highlands: Humanities Press, 1991) 22, 46-47, 59.
12. See *Australian Capital Television Pty Ltd v Commonwealth* (1992) 186 CLR 168; *Theophanous v Herald & Weekly Times Ltd* (1994) 185 CLR 243; *Nationwide News Pty Ltd v Wills* (1992) 186 CLR 168; *Lange v Australian Broadcasting Corporation* (1997) 189 CLR 596.

13. D F Thompson, *Political Ethics and Public Office* (Harvard University Press, 1987) 116 -117.
14. 'The Hero as man of Letters' published in Thomas Carlyle, *On Heroes, Hero-Worship and the Heroic in History* (Oxford University Press, 1904), 219. This book was first published in 1840.
15. (1981) 147 CLR 169 at 208. The High Court was sitting as the Court of Disputed Returns under the *Electoral Act* s 19.
16. Sir Owen Dixon, *Jesting Pilate* (Law Book Co, 1965), 102; Sir Robert Men-zies, *Central Power in the Australian Commonwealth* (Cassell & Company Ltd, 1967), 54.
17. See J S Mill in D Tannenbaum D & D Schultz (eds), *Inventors of Ideas* (St Martin's Press, 1998), 232.
18. Lord Scarman, 'Britain and the Protection of Human Rights' [1948] *New Zealand Law Journal* 175, 177.
19. Though some media commentators deny the proposition.
20. Lord Hailsham, *Elective Dictatorship* (British Broadcasting Corporation, 1976) 5. The Richard Dimbleby Lecture 1976.
21. Sir Anthony Mason, 'A Bill of Rights for Australia' (1989) 5 *Australian Bar Review* 79.
22. (1995) 183 CLR 273.
23. See *R v Trade Practices Tribunal; Ex parte Tasmanian Breweries Pty Ltd* (1970) 123 CLR 361, 374-375 (Kitto J).
24. J Raz, *Ethics in the Public Domain* (Clarendon Press, 1994), 357.
25. See *X Ltd v Morgan-Grampian Ltd* [1991] 1 AC 1, 48.
26. See *Mabo v Queensland (No2)* (1992) 175 CLR 1.
27. K Zweigert & H Kötz , *An Introduction to Comparative Law* (Clarendon Press, 2nd ed, 1992), 202.
28. See *Coco v The Queen* (1994) 179 CLR 427, 437 (Mason CJ, Brennan, Gaudron, McHugh JJ).
29. TRS Allan 'Legislative Supremacy and the Rule of Law' (1985) 44(1) *Cambridge Law Journal* 111, 133.
30. Geoffrey Robertson, 'Obituary – Lord Denning' *The Guardian (6 March 1999)* 21.
31. RWM Dias, 'Götterdammerung – gods of the law in decline' (1981) 1(1) *Legal Studies* 3, 71.
32. Chief Justice Murray Gleeson, 'The Rule of Law and the Independence of the Judiciary' (1989) 1 *Judicial Officers' Bulletin* 2.
33. I acknowledge with thanks the research and assistance of Ms Heidrun Blackwood of the Faculty of Law, University of New South Wales, in the preparation of this Lecture.

1.6 The Common Law: Law for a Time, Law for a Place

Editor's note

This was an address to the Judicial Conference of Australia on 3 September 2005. Brennan drew on his experience as a judge on the final courts of appeal in Australia, Fiji and Hong Kong.

Mr David Coltart, the shadow Minister of Justice in Zimbabwe, visited Australia a few weeks ago. He spoke about the tragic situation in that country, where the poorest of the poor are oppressed by the Mugabe regime and obscene riches flow to those in government favour. Human rights are without protection and the economy is in free fall. The rule of law is moribund. Of course, the breaking down of the rule of law is a commonplace in every society in which tyrants impose their will. It is achieved either by denying the judiciary any effective jurisdiction or by making the judiciary the servile instrument of the executive government.

When we hear a powerful speaker describing the breakdown of law in his own country, we realize that we have hardly any appreciation of the destructive and corrosive force of a judicial power wielded in sympathy with political power, nor the depressing hopelessness of a people who have no effective remedy for injustice. In a society where the rule of law has no sway, remedies must be bought by corruption of the powerful. Liberty, which may stand in the way of power, is obtained only by subservience. Natural justice has no meaning; its place is taken by the adventitious will of the tyrant. Although we in Australia boast that we live under the rule of law, we seldom reflect on the laws, the traditions, the institutions and their personnel which make the rule of law the basic underpinning of our society. Nevertheless, Donald Horne says that the first of the civic values which most Australians would share is maintenance of the rule of law.

The rule *of* law is not the same as rule *by* law. There is a distinction to be drawn between them. Rule by law requires the courts to be the unreflective instruments of the political branches of government, or even to be a mere integer in the implementing of a political policy. It may be that Nazi Germany was ruled by law, many of Hitler's heinous policies being implemented by courts which applied laws framed in accordance with the prevailing ideology. The rule of law, on the other hand, seeks to do justice within the law; it operates when the courts are empowered to take account of the demands of justice in interpreting and applying the law and in exercising the discretions which they possess. The Cambridge academic, RWM Dias speaking of the application of legal rules, commented:

> Rules do not of themselves decide disputes. Their structure, the fluidity of the meaning of words at their fringes and the possibility of making different statements to describe the same fact-situation combine to allow leeways to judges as to how they state, interpret and apply rules to facts. Likewise, it is commonplace that in this task they are guided by their sense of values according to which they balance the interests in dispute.
>
> This explanation … makes it possible to relate judicial independence to the 'rule by law'/'rule of law' dichotomy. Where 'rule by law' obtains, the judiciary is a tool of government, which, along with others, reflects and implements official policies and interests. Where 'rule of law' obtains, judges are free to decide on values of their own, and the check on power derives from their being able to hold governmental interests in balance against others. In this way the British judiciary has built up its tradition of independence over the centuries.[1]

There are many aspects to the rule of law and many conditions that must be satisfied before a system can be said to be entirely congruent with the rule of law. At base, there must be a separation of judicial power from the legislative and executive powers of government. Then the judges must be wholly independent – independent of government, independent of the rich and powerful, independent of pressure groups and ideologies. And the judges, whose task it must be to interpret and apply the law, must be given a sufficient leeway by the law to allow its application so as not to work injustice in particular cases or in cases of a particular kind.[2] If the judges do not have that leeway, issues which ought properly be decided by courts are effectively determined by the will of government expressed in a law created by government. Injustice is the inevitable result, and injustice leads to an erosion of the rule of law.

That is the evil to be seen in laws which deprive the courts of their ordinary jurisdiction – such as the restriction on the Federal Court's and Federal Magistrates Court's jurisdiction in judicial review under the *Migration Act 1958* (Cth).[3] When courts are stripped of their jurisdiction over a particular subject matter, to that extent the subject matter is without legal control – an area of unbridled power. It is fortunate that s 75(v) of our *Constitution* reposes in the High Court a jurisdiction over the exercise of federal power that cannot be diminished by the political branches of government, though the burdening of that Court with cases that ought properly be decided elsewhere is unacceptable. The decision of the High Court in *Ex parte Aala*[4] and in *Plaintiff S157*[5] establish the limitation on legislative power to preclude curial challenges for jurisdictional error. There is evil to be seen also in legislation which prescribes mandatory or minimum sentencing regimes – regimes which remove a judge's ability to do justice in particular cases. Such legislation imposes a legislative judgment on a set of facts that, by tradition and by common sense, demand judicial evaluation.

These thoughts lead me to say something about three topics: first, the importance of the values which a judge brings to bear in decision-making and how that makes the role of the judge basic to the rule of law; second, the significance of values in the evolution of the common law; and, third, the critical importance of courts, constituted and working in accordance with the common law, to the peace and order of societies, especially if there is any concern about social stability.

The common law allows judges a leeway in rendering a judgment. But Mr Dias over-eggs the omelet in suggesting that judges 'are free to decide on values of their own', although the context shows that he was speaking of those elements or stages in making a decision where more than one view is open. In a majority of cases, the value which affects a judge's decision is an ordinary community value – was the defendant negligent? What is a fair and reasonable price? Was the conduct dishonest? What is in the best interests of a child? Or, more controversially, what sentence would be just? In answering these questions, the judge reaches a decision in much the same way as a jury would reach its decision if the issue were to be determined by a jury. The judge draws on the same set of community values subject, however, to a qualification. Especially in sentencing, but in determining other issues as well, the value that the contemporary community would favour might be affected by prejudice or passion or might fail to take into account factors which the law declares to be relevant, for example, the prospect of reformation of an offender. The value which the judge applies is shorn of prejudice or passion and takes account of all factors that are legally relevant.

When we appreciate the way in which the common law underpins our society and depends on the judgment of the judge in the circumstances of individual cases, we can see how pivotal is the role of the judge in maintaining the rule of law. The judge is not a juridical robot. He or she has an active role to perform in every case. It may be in the evaluation of evidence, in determining the application of a rule of law (including a determination whether to distinguish a precedent), in exercising a discretion, in the granting or refusal of relief or in the imposition of punishment. The judge's active participation in the process is an integral element in the rule of law; it is an essential characteristic of the rule of law.

The work-a-day aspect of the rule of law may not be very glamorous, yet it is the role of the judge in the run of the mill cases in the trial courts which commends the rule of law to most of the people involved in litigation. These cases call for the judicial qualities of knowledge of the relevant legal principles, familiarity with the current community standards, a sound sense of justice, common sense and, of course, a robust independence and unquestioned integrity.

Sometimes I wonder if judges realize the pivotal role they play in creating and preserving the way of life that makes us proud to be Australian. Perhaps judges are depressed by captious criticism in some of the media, or the apparent indifference of the political branches of government towards the judicial branch, or the want of popular acclaim. It is easy for a judge to see himself or herself to be doing no more than shifting, Sisyphus-like, an ever extending case list, or repeating the same process day by day without public adulation or even public awareness. Yet a moment's reflection on what our society would be without a competent, dutiful, independent judiciary should be sufficient to convince the dispirited and the cynical of the importance of judicial work.

So, I am privileged to join this Judicial Conference, to see again many old friends and colleagues and to say something about the primary trade tool of the Australian judge – the common law. The common law is not only the basis of the legal system; it is the champion of what we regard as civilized values and its principles. The rules of law are an articulation of the way in which the members of a society customarily act towards one another and structure their relationships. Judge Cardozo in his definitive work on the judicial process said, 'Law is indeed an historical growth for it is an expression of customary morality which develops silently and unconsciously from one age to another.'[6]

Of course, if we seek the ultimate foundation for our way of life, it must be found in the moral fibre of our people. But the moral fibre of a people and the system of law by which they are governed live in a symbiotic relationship. The moral fibre of a society is supported by the law and the underlying power of the State. If there were major disparities between the moral values of a society and its laws, there would be chaos or tyranny. Notions of equality before the law, the obligation not to use your property so as to damage another, the desirability of fulfilling a promise, the non-culpability for conduct that is affected by ignorance, mistake or insanity, the duty to hear a party before making an adverse finding – these are all concepts drawn from the community's sense of values. Yet those values inform principles of the common law.

Judicial values have, as we know, accounted for the development of the common law and today are the cause of, and justification for, the continuing development of common law. The occasions for modifying the common law are much less frequent than other occasions for the judicial application of values but it should not be thought that modification of the common law is dramatic and is to be found only in decisions of the higher appellate courts. It is a slow and incremental process, drawing on the experience of judges in contemporary cases. Cardozo saw this saying 'This work of modification is gradual. It goes on inch by inch. Its effects must be measured by decades and even centuries. Thus measured, they are seen to have behind them the power and the pressure of the moving glacier'.[7]

Thus, the fortunes of plaintiffs in negligence cases has waxed and more recently waned; judicial attitudes to the admissibility of 'voluntary' confessions has become more sophisticated, forcing changes in police methods. Rarely, but only rarely, an appellate court may work a more substantial change in the common law. When a court, having authority to do so, is contemplating such a change in the common law, the values to which the court gives effect in making the change are not an idiosyncratic set of values but the historical values of the common law system and the enduring values of the contemporary community. That must be so, for the law cannot change merely to accommodate ephemeral changes in contemporary opinion.

But am I overstating the significance of values in judging? Are not the rules of the law sufficient by themselves for the disposition of cases without troubling about values? Oliver Wendell Holmes might have said so and 'strict and complete legalism' might deny the existence of any leeway in the application of legal rules. After all, when, 50 years ago, Sir Owen Dixon spoke of the judicial method applied in our courts he said:

> Such courts do in fact proceed upon the assumption that the law provides a body of doctrine which governs the decision of a given case. It is taken for granted that the decision ... conforms with ascertained legal principles and applies them according to a standard of reasoning which is not personal to the judges themselves. It is a tacit assumption. But it is basal. The court would feel that the function it performed had lost its meaning and purpose, if there were no external standard of legal correctness.[8]

Today we should have to qualify this statement to allow for the exercise of some novel jurisdictions. The troublesome bioethical cases dealing with the beginning and ending of human life or surgical or medical intervention in the care of those incompetent to give consent raise issues which do not fall within settled legal doctrine. Judges have to decide such cases and they cast around for the values that can provide an external and expressible criterion for decision-making. Sir Owen's own judgments show that values played an unexpressed but important role in his decision-making. Else why, when appeal still lay to the Privy Council, would Sir Owen have chosen in *Parker* v *R* [9] to refuse to follow *Director of Public Prosecutions* v *Smith*? [10] Whence did he derive his definition of duty of care owed to a trespasser in *Commissioner for Railways (NSW)* v *Cardy*? [11] And why did he attribute a particular operation to s 90 of the *Constitution* in *Parton* v *Milk Board (Victoria)*? [12]

It is clear that the common law has developed to its present sophisticated condition by artisan judges who, with knowledge of existing rules, have moulded, added, rejected or resected them, to achieve a measure of justice in particular cases. And that is a technique which is essential to maintaining the law in a state that is serviceable for the community. It is a technique which distinguishes a society living under the rule of law from a society that is ruled by law.

Axiomatically, the common law judge must be familiar with the relevant law, not only to apply it precisely but also to be conscious of the measure of leeway which the judge has in reaching a decision that is just according to law. And the judge will have to attribute a meaning and operation to the relevant law by reference to the values inherent in the common law. That requires some familiarity with authoritative expositions of legal rules, and with their history and application. Usually this familiarity is acquired by reference to precedent but the mere words of a passage extracted from an earlier case may not fully express the value. Indeed, particular cases may need analysis to ascertain the underlying principle and the principle may need analysis to discover the informing value.

Occasionally, but only occasionally, changes in the enduring values of a society may evoke changes in the common law. Perhaps *Mabo [No 2]*[13] is the most dramatic modern example. The recognition of native title flowed from the change in the values of a society which, in earlier times (to adopt the language of Lord Sumner) had perceived Aborigines as 'so low in the scale of social organization that their usages and conceptions of rights and duties are not to be reconciled with the institutions or the legal ideas of civilized society. Such a gulf cannot be bridged. It would be idle to impute to such people some shadow of the rights known to our law and then to transmute it into the substance of transferable rights of property as we know them.'[14]

But now we are in a society which regards all people as equal before the law. Thus, the enduring value which led to the decision in *Mabo* was the value of equality.

Such judicial leeway as is allowed in applying a legal principle may seem to be in tension with legislative supremacy. Trevor Allen argues that the two are reconciled by the adoption of principles of interpretation which serve to protect fundamental rights.[15] And fundamental rights are to be found in the values of the common law. They may be broadly expressed but their influence on the development and application of the common law is profound. Sir Anthony Mason recently identified several of the values of the common law. He said: 'The common law stands for a set of concepts, interests and values which it has protected during the course of its long history. They include the rule of law, the independence of the judiciary, access to the courts, the separation of the powers of government, liberty of the individual, freedom of expression, freedom of association, no detention or imprisonment without lawful authority and natural justice, to mention but a few of them. These values have both generated and informed legal principles, including the rules of statutory interpretation.'[16]

The values of the common law are, to use a computer metaphor, a program running in the back of the judicial mind when a case is being heard and determined. But we should not overstate the legal relevance of values nor try to expand the areas of choice in decision making. Certainty in the law is itself a value of the common law that cannot be diminished by excesses of judicial enthusiasm.

The common law is noted for both its antiquity and its adaptability. The one contributes to its wisdom and certainty; the other to its relevance and utility in the modern world. As to its antiquity Holdsworth says that it was in the reign of Henry II when the courts were expanded in jurisdiction that we see 'the beginnings of a centralised judicial system which administered a law common to the whole country'.[17] Blackstone notes that the judges drew on English custom,[18] though the content was affected by the practices of the judges and lawyers of the time assisted by scholars familiar with Roman Law.[19] So, the gestation period of the modern common law extends back for centuries. It is not surprising that the vast judicial experience during so lengthy a period has fashioned a sophisticated legal system the justice and the practicality of which is attested by generations of litigants and their lawyers.

But the common law is not immutable and we should not be reticent about the manner of change. Lord Goff of Chieveley has written: 'It is universally recognized that judicial development of the common law is inevitable. If it had never taken place, the common law would be the same now as it was in the reign of King Henry II; it is because of it that the common law is a living system of law, reacting to new events and new ideas, and so capable of providing citizens of this country with a system of practical justice relevant to the times in which they live.'[20]

Precisely because of its daily application from generation to generation and from place to place, it changes in response to the needs and aspirations of particular communities. The daily and ubiquitous application of the common law's values explains the practicality and the vitality of the common law. As the High Court said in the *Native Title Case*, 'The content of the common law will, in the ordinary course of events, change from time to time according to the changing perception of the courts'.[21] The pace of change may be slow but when a legal rule is varied and followed so that the variation becomes settled law, there is an assurance that it has been found to be just and practical in actual situations. Conversely, if experience shows that a proposed development of the common law is impractical or unjust, it is dismissed, even if the proposal emanates from a superior court. That is what happened to the Beaudesert Shire[22] tort of unlawful activity causing damage which was discarded in *Northern Territory v Mengel*.[23]

The technique of development has itself been developed by common law judges. They eschewed the implementation of idiosyncratic ideas, but they have taken account of the exigencies of their societies. Benjamin Cardozo summed it up when he said that judicial development of the law is ' … informed by tradition, methodised by analogy, disciplined by system, and subordinated to the primordial necessity of order in the social life.'[24] Sir Owen Dixon's adoption of Maitland's description of the common law's development as 'strict logic and high technique'[25] does not really bring out the diverse influences of which Cardozo spoke, though the term 'high technique' might be intended to comprehend those influences. Cardozo expressed what underlies, albeit unacknowledged, the development of law when the mantra of strict and complete legalism is recited.

There was a time prior to the abolition of appeals from the High Court to the Privy Council when Australian law was constrained by the decisions of English judges, since, as Sir Anthony Mason noted, 'the colonial common law inheritance was the English common law. The notion that the inheritance might ripen into an Australian, Canadian, New Zealand or Hong Kong common law took some time to develop'.[26] Once the constraints of Privy Council appeals were removed, the High Court was able to assume responsibility for declaring the common law of Australia.[27] That Court necessarily possesses a wide power to mould the law, conformably with constitutional and statutory law and in accordance with judicial method, to serve the contemporary needs of Australian society and to reflect contemporary society's enduring values.[28] Thus, the High Court has been free to develop new principles of Australian law. That can be seen in cases such as *Commercial Bank of Australia Ltd* v *Amadio,*[29] *David Securities Pty Ltd* v *Commonwealth Bank of Australia*[30] and *Trident General Insurance Co Ltd* v *McNiece Bros Pty Ltd*[31] to name a few. The Australian common law is free to develop differently from the common law of England, a recent example being *D'Orta Ekenaike* v *Victoria Legal Aid*[32] which maintained immunity for negligence in the conduct of court proceedings when the House of Lords had abandoned that principle in *Arthur JS Hall & Co* v *Simons.*[33]

None of this is novel to an Australian Judicial Conference. We were all instructed that the common law has grown over the centuries and that its development has been a judicial creation. We have all known of Oliver Wendell Holmes' observation: 'The life of the law has not been logic: it has been experience. The felt necessities of the time, the prevalent moral and political theories, intuitions of public policy, avowed or unconscious, even the prejudices which judges share with their fellow-men, have had a good deal more to do than the syllogism in determining the rules by which men should be governed. The law embodies the story of a nation's development through many centuries'.[34]

Now I should like to say something about the influence of the courts on social stability. Since retirement, I have had the privilege of sitting in two overseas jurisdictions where the common law system is in force. I know that some of you have already had that experience. There may be peculiarities of address or etiquette in each place – Australian judges find it a heady experience to be addressed as 'My Lord' – but the ways of thought are the same. As the values derived from the history of the common law are shared in all common law courts constituted by independent and competent judges, there is a core of values which inform decision-making in each jurisdiction. The experience shows that the constitutional and statutory law of the overseas jurisdiction may be quite different from constitutional and statutory law of one's home jurisdiction but, because of the common principles and values of the common law, it is possible for Australian judges to take a full and equal part with their overseas colleagues in the administration of justice. Perhaps the great change that has taken place since the abolition of appeals to the Privy Council from virtually all of the erstwhile British dominions and colonies is the recourse to precedent from other common law countries.

Common law courts in every jurisdiction, I believe, look to the decisions of other common law courts as persuasive precedents, the weight of any precedent being dependent on the authority of the court and the cogency of its reasoning.

Prior to the last coup in Fiji, Chief Justice Tuivaga, Sir Anthony Mason, Justice John Toohey, Lord Cooke of Thorndon and I sat together in the Supreme Court of the Republic of Fiji. For the Australians, of course, the sittings were very much a reunion of former colleagues and, having been declared constitutionally senile in this country, we enjoyed the opportunity of serving in another jurisdiction where we were deemed to be compos mentis and where the judicial techniques were the same as those in Australia. The coup put an end to our sitting on the Court. We had each sworn to uphold the Constitution of Fiji but, with the advent of the coup and the dismissal by the President of the Prime Minister, for my part I felt it was no longer possible to continue to discharge the obligations of that oath. I know that Sir Anthony was of the same view and that may have been the view of the other erstwhile members of that Court. All of us have ceased to be members now but I am pleased to see that Chief Justice Fatiaki has succeeded in having the Supreme Court reconstituted and it includes noted Australian jurists. In the interim, the Fiji Court of Appeal decided a case of political significance. I recount the decision because it shows that, when the peace and order of society are in question, the community must place its trust in a court which displays the independence and integrity demanded by the common law.

For a time after the military had wrested control from George Speight, the Court of Appeal was the final Court of Fiji. Its members included Mr Justice Handley. In *Republic of Fiji v Prasad*[35] the Court heard an appeal against a decision by Mr Justice Gates in the High Court that the 1997 *Constitution of Fiji* had not been abrogated and was still the governing Constitution of the Republic. The de facto administration, headed by Interim Prime Minister Laisenia Qarase appealed against that decision. Professor George Williams, who was one of the counsel briefed to appear on behalf of the respondent Prasad describes the scenario:

> There was little to suggest that the decision of Justice Gates would affect political developments in Fiji. Given that the Military had already sought to abrogate the 1997 Constitution, why would it or its Interim Civilian Government obey a decision of a court of law? Indeed, no steps were taken to recall Parliament. Nevertheless, the proceedings took a decisive turn after the High Court decision when, instead of ignoring the orders of Justice Gates, the Interim Civilian Government decided to appeal to the Court of Appeal of

> Fiji and to submit to the jurisdiction of that Court. It was one thing to abrogate the Constitution, but it proved to be another thing entirely to deny the force of a decision of a respected judge, particularly when it was strongly and unequivocally backed by the international community. Even after the coup, respect for the rule of law and the judiciary prevailed as a fundamental principle of Fijian political culture. Certainly, a decision in favour of the Interim Civilian Government by the Court of Appeal would also have greatly assisted its aim of being seen domestically and internationally as the legitimate government of Fiji.[36]

The appeal was, in a sense, a constitutional curiosity. It raised the question whether 'a court created by a constitution lacks jurisdiction to determine the legality of that constitution or to do otherwise than to assume its ongoing effect.'.[37] A negative answer to this question had been given by Fieldsend AJA in the High Court of Southern Rhodesia in *Madzimbamuto* v *Lardner-Burke*[38] who said, 'It is my firm conviction that a court created in terms of a written constitution has no jurisdiction to recognize either as a de jure or de facto government any government other than that constitutionally appointed under that Constitution.'[39]

However, when an appeal against that Court's decision was taken to the Privy Council, it was accepted by the majority that a court sitting in a territory has to determine the status of a new regime which has usurped power and acquired control of the territory.[40] The members of the Fiji Court of Appeal adopted this view, holding that it was their duty 'as Judges of Fiji' to consider whether, in accordance with the Kelsen doctrine of effectiveness the new regime had effectively supplanted the old.[41] The Court held that the Interim Government had failed to prove the elements necessary to establish that the new regime was constitutionally effective. But would the decision be accepted? In a note in the *Law Quarterly Review*, N W Barber observed 'The effectiveness of any Supreme Court forced to decide on the legality of an attempted usurpation will depend on the respect it commands within the society and the willingness of the revolutionaries to submit to judgment. In Fiji the Court rejected outright the claims of the usurper; the effectiveness of this decision will depend on the political strength of the court, a strength that can only be assessed in the reception of the judgment.'[42]

The reception of the judgment is described by Professor Williams:

> The decisions of the High Court and Court of Appeal of Fiji demonstrate that the judiciary can play an important role in maintaining the rule of law even in the immediate period after a coup. The decisions of these Courts are unique in that they represent

> the only time that a domestic court has pronounced a coup illegal and the abrogation of a nation's constitution legally ineffective. Perhaps even more remarkable was that, immediately after this decision, the Prime Minister of the Interim Civilian Government, Qarase, announced that the nation would be returned to democratic rule under the 1997 *Constitution*. His government then resigned.[43]

However, Parliament was not recalled. Instead, it was dissolved by the President who called a general election under the 1997 Constitution and re-appointed the Interim Civilian Government as a caretaker administration. The general election held from 25 August to 5 September 2001 returned a coalition government led by Qarase.

So, the decision in *Prasad* paved the way for a return to constitutional normalcy. *Prasad's* case shows that the rule of law depends ultimately on the authority of the court in the community and, where democracy is practised, the people will favour the rule of law if they have confidence in the judiciary.

Next, I turn to Hong Kong. To an Australian judge sitting in Hong Kong, the public confidence in – indeed, enthusiasm for – the judiciary comes as an unusual and welcome surprise. To explain this, I must contrast the legal systems of two parts of the People's Republic of China: the Mainland and the Special Administrative Region of Hong Kong. One country, two systems.

First, the mainland system – the system of Chinese socialist legalism, as described by Mr Lay-Hong Tan in his recent article in the *Australian Law Journal*.[44] The foundation of this system is the Marxist theory that law rests on class struggle, but it has been modified in the People's Republic and the system is now described by the author as 'legal pragmatism'. He identifies the following characteristics:

1. It over emphasises the instrumental facets of law.
2. It regards law as an outcome of "actuality"
3. It treats law as a servant of policy.
4. It does not treat individual rights seriously.

According to this approach, the law is an instrument of the Chinese Communist Party (CCP). What this means is that after establishing 'actuality', the CCP uses the law as an instrument to legislate appropriate policy.

Clearly enough, the values which underlie this system are different from the values which underlie the common law system of Hong Kong. I do not venture to criticize the system in the People's Republic or its suitability for the Chinese people. I mention it to contrast the role which falls to the judiciary in the Hong Kong Special Administrative Region of the People's Republic. Hong Kong, as you know, is governed under the Basic Law as agreed by the PRC and the British Government. The Basic Law is a statute of the National People's Congress. However, as Sir Anthony Mason has pointed out,[45] 'the Basic Law maintains the principles of the common law and basic elements of a common law judicial system in the Region. The conjunction of such a common law system under a national law within the larger framework of Chinese constitutional law is itself a fundamental aspect of the principle 'one country, two systems' recited in the Preamble to the Basic Law.' In 1997, when Hong Kong reverted to China, the Court of Final Appeal was created to take the place of the Judicial Committee of the Privy Council in the Hong Kong hierarchy. Among others, judges or former judges from Australia, New Zealand and Britain were invited to sit with the Permanent Judges of Hong Kong to constitute the Court. At present, Sir Anthony Mason and I are honoured to sit on that Court.

Recently, the Court gave judgment in a case in which convictions had been recorded against participants in an unauthorized procession protesting against the earlier conviction of an 'activist' for assault and obstruction of a public officer. The protesters relied on a provision[46] of the *Bill of Rights Ordinance* which recognizes the 'right of peaceful assembly'.[47] This provision evoked from the majority judgment this opening passage:

> The freedom of peaceful assembly is a fundamental right. It is closely associated with the fundamental right of the freedom of speech. The freedom of speech and the freedom of peaceful assembly are precious and lie at the foundation of a democratic society.
>
> These freedoms are of cardinal importance for the stability and progress of society for a number of inter-related reasons. The resolution of conflicts, tensions and problems through open dialogue and debate is of the essence of a democratic society. These freedoms enable such dialogue and debate to take place and ensure their vigour. A democratic society is one where the market place of ideas must thrive.[48]

This declaration of the importance of values at the heart of a democracy, made by a Court whose competence, incorruptibility and independence is unquestioned, is characteristic of the approach taken by common law courts. The *Bill of Rights Ordinance* conferred an individual right which could not be overridden by an ordinary law regulating the conduct of processions but the values are said to be 'fundamental' precisely because they are values at the heart of the common law system. The response of the public to such a judgment can be gathered from a comment which appeared in an article in the *South China Morning Post.*[49] The article was critical of some interpretations of the Basic Law which had been earlier issued by the Beijing Standing Committee of the National People's Congress pursuant to Article 158 of the Basic Law. These interpretations, it was said, 'have caused considerable damage to Hong Kong's confidence in the rule of law.' But, the article continued 'In contrast, confidence in the judiciary remains strong, especially in the aftermath of the decision last Thursday by the Court of Final Appeal exonerating Falun Gong practitioners who were arrested in 2002 while protesting outside the central government's liaison office in Hong Kong.'

In another article dealing with the same case, Professor Yash Ghai wrote:

> Judges now accept unequivocally their responsibility to review legislation as well as the policies and conduct of public agendas. They are the ultimate custodians of rights and freedoms, entrusted with the task of determining when rights may be legitimately restricted. There is no compelling reason for subservient deference to legislative and executive authorities, because the Basic law has put the duty of applying the law squarely on the courts.
>
> .....it is no surprise that the Court of Final Appeal is well on its way to establishing a reputation as a court of great distinction and learning, whose judgments are read, and cited, with respect in other jurisdictions.[50]

The authority of a court depends to no small degree on public confidence in its capacity to apply the law in a way which preserves and protects the social conditions under which the public lives. If the courts are independent, competent and incorruptible and if the legal system vests in the courts an effective authority to do justice, the courts command public confidence and society is stable. Indeed, those characteristics measure the state of a society under the rule of law for they assure protection of individual freedom, respect for human rights irrespective of race or religion, peaceful order, the just settlement of disputes and the just distribution of benefits – all the attributes of a society which treasures human dignity. And popular esteem of the judiciary follows.

In Australia, it is taken for granted that the courts are independent, competent and incorrupt and that they protect the rights of individuals according to law. Hence there is little public comment about the functions of the judiciary. There are occasional criticisms of particular decisions – usually in relation to a sentence pronounced in a case that has stirred the public's passions – but the criticisms proceed only on the footing that a particular decision is said not to accord with the standard of decision-making that is taken as the norm. The norm itself is assumed to be set at a high level of independence, competence and incorruptibility and a sensitivity to community values qualified by law. Institutionally, the courts are secure because the public insists that they be so.

Judges may feel that there is insufficient acknowledgement of the anxiety and effort that go into keeping up the high standard which the public expects but the rewards of judicial office are neither in public adulation nor in financial returns. The rewards are in the profound conviction that they are the guardians and ministers of the common law and, as such, they are effective in preserving Australia as a free, peaceful, ordered and confident nation.

---

1. RWM Dias, 'Gotterdammerung – gods of the law in Decline' (1981) 1 *Legal Studies* 3, 13.
2. See *Marbury* v *Madison* 5 US 137; 1 Cranch 137; 2 Law Ed. 60 (1803).
3. See *Migration Act 1958* (Cth), ss 475, 476
4. See *Re Refugee Review Tribunal; Ex parte Aala* (2000) 204 CLR 82.
5. See *Plaintiff S157/2002* v *Commonwealth* (2003) 211 CLR 476.
6. Benjamin N Cardozo, *The Nature of the Judicial Process* (1921 Yale University Press, 21st Printing, 1963) 104-105.
7. Ibid 25.
8. Sir Owen Dixon, 'Concerning Judicial Method' (1955) published in Sir Owen Dixon, *Jesting Pilate* (Law Book Co, 1965) 152, 155.
9. (1963) 111 CLR 610.
10. [1961] AC 260.
11. (1960) 104 CLR 274.
12. (1949) 80 CLR 229.
13. (1992) 175 CLR 1.
14. See *In re Southern Rhodesia* [1919] AC 211, 233-234.
15. TRS Allen, 'The Common Law as Constitution' in Cheryl Saunders (ed) *Courts of Final Jurisdiction* (Federation Press, 1996) 146, 156.
16. Sir Anthony Mason, 'The Role of the Common Law in Hong Kong', (15 March 2005) par 3.
17. Sir William Holdsworth, *History of English Law,* (Methuen, 1924) Vol I, 47-53.
18. See *Blackstone's Commentaries on the Laws of England* Vol 1 (Clarendon Press, 1769) 17, 68. The content was affected by the practices of the judges and lawyers of the time (AWB Simpson, *History of the Common Law* (Clarendon Press, 1987) 376) assisted by scholars familiar with Roman Law. Sir William Holdsworth, *History of English Law,* (Methuen, 1924) Vol I, 175 – 176 pays tribute to the beneficial influence of the works of Glanvil and Bracton on the laying of the foundations of the common law.
19. AWB Simpson, *A History of the Common Law of Contract* (Clarendon Press, 2nd ed, 1987) 376.
20. See *Kleinwort Benson Ltd* v *Lincoln City Council* [1999] 2 AC 349, 377.

21. (1995) 183 CLR 373, 486; see McHugh J in *Re Colina, Ex parte Torney* (1999) 200 CLR 386, 400-401.
22. See *Beaudesert Shire Council* v *Smith* (1966) 120 CLR 145.
23. (1995) 185 CLR 307.
24. Benjamin Cardozo, *The Nature of the Judicial Process* (Yale University Press, 1921) 113-114.
25. Sir Owen Dixon, 'Concerning Judicial Method' in *Jesting Pilate* (Law Book Co, 1965) 152, 153.
26. Sir Anthony Mason, 'The Break with the Privy Council and the Inter-nationalisation of the Common Law' in Peter Cane (ed) *Centenary Essays for the High Court of Australia* (Lexis Nexis, 2004) 66, 68-69.
27. See *Mutual Life and Citizens' Assurance Co Ltd* v *Evatt* (1968) 122 CLR 556 (Barwick CJ); Mabo *[No. 2]* (1992) 175 CLR 1, 29 (Brennan J).
28. See *McKinney* v *The Queen* (1991) 171 CLR 468, 485) (Brennan J).
29. (1983) 151 CLR 447.
30. (1992) 175 CLR 353.
31. (1988) 165 CLR 107.
32. (2005) 79 ALJR 755.
33. [2002] 1 AC 615.
34. Oliver Wendell Holmes, *The Common Law* (Houghton Mifflin Company, 43rd printing, 1949).
35. [2001] 2 LRC 743.
36. George Williams, 'The Case that stopped a Coup? The rule of law in Fiji', 2003 Quentin-Baxter Memorial Trust Lecture, Victoria University of Wellington. 27 November 2003.
37. Ibid 13.
38. [1968] (2) SA 284, 431 quoted by Lord Reid at [1969] 1 AC 645, 724.
39. [1969] 1 AC 645, 724.
40. Lord Pearce's position on this issue seems to be closer to the view of Fieldsend AJA though Lord Pearce's comment relates to a situation where there is a 'true Sovereign' asserting sovereignty: see [1969] 1 AC 645, 732.
41. Hans Kelsen writes: 'According to international law, the constitution of a state is valid only if the legal order established on the basis of this constitution is, by and large, effective. It is this general principle of effectiveness, a positive norm of international law, which, applied to an individual national legal order, provides the basic norm of this national legal order.' *Principles of International Law* (Rinehart & Company, 1952), 414-5.
42. (2001) 117 *Law Quarterly Review* 408, 411.
43. George Williams, 'The Case that stopped a Coup? The rule of law in Fiji', 2003 Quentin-Baxter Memorial Trust Lecture, Victoria University of Wellington. 27 November 2003, 16.
44. Unravelling the complexities of the Chinese legal system: A primer for foreign investors' (2005) 79 *Australian Law Journal* 97, 98. Lay-Hong Tan, 'Unravelling the complexities of the Chinese Legal System' (2005) 79 *Australian Law Journal* 97.
45. Sir Anthony Mason, 'The Role of the Common Law in Hong Kong', University of Hong Kong, 15 March 2005, par 12.
46. The Basic Law provides that the provisions of the International Convention on Civil and Political Rights should be implemented through the domestic laws of Hong Kong. The Bill of Rights Ordinance (cap 383) was enacted pursuant to the Basic Law.
47. Article 17.

48. See *Leung Kwok Hung and Others v Hong Kong Special Administrative Region* [2005] HKCFA 41.
49. 12 May 2005.
50. Professor Yash Ghai, 'Great Guardian of Human Rights', *South China Morning Post*, (10 May 2005).

1.7 Law and Liberty in the War on Terror

Editor's note

This address was delivered at the Symposium Dinner in NSW Parliament House convened by the Gilbert and Tobin Centre for Public Law's Terrorism and Law Project on 4 July 2007.

The speakers at this Symposium have canvassed or will canvass a number of issues about law and liberty in the war on terror, whatever that term may connote. How do we strike the right balance between preventing and detecting terror and infringing human rights and fundamental freedoms? Of course, we know that human rights and fundamental freedoms are not inviolable. That was Albert Haddock's mistake. You remember Albert, AP Herbert's legendary litigant in *Misleading cases in the Common Law*. He had been convicted on a number of charges because he leapt off Hammersmith Bridge during a regatta. The Court of Criminal Appeal upheld his grounds of appeal and would have quashed all his convictions. But then they reached the last of his stated grounds. Albert had submitted that 'this is a free country and a man can do what he likes if he does nobody any harm'. Lord Light, LCJ dismissed the appeal, observing that this ground 'is like the thirteenth stroke of a crazy clock, which not only is itself discredited but casts a shade of doubt over all previous assertions'.[1] Albert had overstated his case. It was immaterial that he had done no harm to anybody. He should have submitted that he could do what he liked subject only to the provisions of the law. A unanimous High Court said so in *Lange v Australian Broadcasting Commission.*[2]

In a Conference to discuss terrorism and the law, the focus of attention must be on the extent to which human rights and fundamental freedoms have been, or should be, pared back in order to avoid some greater harm. I would not offer comment on the constitutional validity of any of the provisions relating to terrorism and, when I was first invited to speak to you this evening, my first reaction was that I should not offer any other comment on the legislation. It is undesirable, in my view, for judges to comment publicly on issues which may have political significance or which question the wisdom of legislative or executive policy, for such comments are likely to cast doubt on their courts' impartiality and thus weaken the courts' authority. That inhibition can affect, but it does not exclude, comment on these topics by retired judges. So I thought it permissible at least to note the impact of statute or executive action on the values of the common law. It is not in controversy – indeed, it is the very reason for this Symposium – that the terrorism legislation and the actions to be taken under it do impair the freedoms and immunities which the common law protects. I confess that the impact of the legislation on common law immunities troubled me when I discovered its extent.

The legislation is voluminous and detailed. Its principal provisions will no doubt be canvassed in the papers that have been delivered or are awaiting delivery. I have selected a couple of issues which attracted my attention, for reasons that will appear. The starting point of any discussion about the terrorism legislation is the canon of construction which applies to any provision affecting freedoms and immunities. It is assumed that it is: 'in the last degree improbable that the legislature would overthrow fundamental principles, infringe rights, or depart from the general system of law, without expressing its intention with irresistible clearness'.[3]

That assumption is weakened by the purposely draconian provisions of the legislation but it indicates nevertheless that the courts, conscious of their role as the branch of government invariably concerned with individual rights and liabilities, strive to preserve the values of the common law so far as is consistent with their duty to apply the law as laid down by the Parliament.

Sir Anthony Mason has spoken of the values of the common law: '… personal liberty, freedom of expression, no imprisonment without trial, procedural fairness are commonly identified by judges as values which inform legal principle and require an unambiguous expression of statutory intention to override them. This emphasis on values protected by the common law is in one sense an instance of institutional values or morality.'[4]

I respectfully agree.

A lawyer's focus is on the freedom of the individual. Some years ago, I expressed[5] what I regard as the law's approach in striking the balance: 'It is of the essence of a free society that a balance is struck between the security that is desirable to protect society as a whole and the safeguards that are necessary to ensure individual liberty. But in the long run the safety of a democracy rests upon the common commitment of its citizens to the safeguarding of each man's liberty, and the balance must tilt that way.'[6]

That approach accords with the policy statement made by Sir Robert Menzies as Prime Minister immediately after the outbreak of the Second World War: 'Whatever may be the extent of the power that may be taken to govern, to direct and to control by regulation' he said, 'there must be as little interference with individual rights as is consistent with concerted national effort … the greatest tragedy that could overcome a country would be for it to fight a successful war in defence of liberty and to lose its own liberty in the process.'[7]

Now these are voices of the past. They belong to a mindset which can be described as 'pre-9/11'. No doubt the events since 9/11 – the bombs in Bali, the London Tube and Madrid Station, the explosive vehicles in London and Glasgow, and the daily bombs in Iraq – reveal attacks that are less expected and more precisely targeted on civilians than the bombing raids of World War II, albeit the number of casualties and the amount of damage have been much less than in a real war. In substance, terrorists have committed or been party to the commission of crimes of a familiar kind – murder, the infliction of bodily harm, wilful destruction of property and going armed so as to cause terror. The ordinary criminal law already proscribes such acts. But as the crimes are both organized and secretive, it is thought that more police power is needed than is allowed under the general law. Both wisdom and sensitivity are needed to strike the right balance between freedom and police power.

Hanging over us today is the threat of terrorism by Islamic extremists. This threat is facilitating intolerance towards and suspicion of peace-loving Muslim citizens and some of the rhetoric surrounding the anti-terrorism legislation is fanning that intolerance and suspicion. Intolerance and suspicion preclude any minority from entry into the mainstream community. Intolerance and suspicion produce division, isolation and alienation to the prejudice of peace and the rule of law.

It was surprising to read last Friday of the reported remarks of that prolific writer-judge Richard Posner. He is said to have advocated the use of surveillance technology to answer the questions: 'Are there terrorist plots that are at a formative stage among the large US Muslim community of two to three million people? In the 600,000 Canadian Muslim population, are there people planning attacks on the US?'[8]

To expose an entire community, marked out by their religious belief, to special surveillance is a proposition from which I recoil. Perhaps Posner has been quoted out of context, for such discriminatory treatment would be offensive to that freedom of conscience which is central to human dignity and which is essential in a free society.

Discrimination is counter-productive. It is the unified resolve of the people that gives criminal law its true force and provides both a disincentive to crime and public support for the enforcement of the criminal law. It is a unified society which, sharing a common aspiration for peace and freedom, is the best guarantee of the maintenance of the rule of law. Crime cannot flourish in a community which rejects crime and such a community is the most successful in preventing crime and detecting criminals. But if laws are seen as directed against, or as discriminating against, a group of citizens, that group can be alienated from society. They become less willing to co-operate in the enforcement of those laws and may even be induced to make common cause with those who are thinking of committing the proscribed acts. Laws which drive a wedge between elements of our society are destructive of the social fabric and may be a danger to our national security. For this reason, I have some concerns about the key definition of a 'terrorist act' in s100.1 of the *Criminal Code Act 1995* (Cth).

It contains a curious element: a specific intention which is really a motive. An act is not a terrorist act unless it is engaged in 'with the intention of advancing a political, religious or ideological cause'. Leaving aside the distinction between intention and motive, one may wonder why the advancing of political, religious and ideological causes should be an element in the definition of a criminal offence or in the provisions which depend on the definition of 'terrorist act'. If the terrible crimes proscribed by reference to that definition – killing or seriously injuring a person or causing serious damage to property or to an electronic system – were engaged in to advance the interests of, say, organized crime, or industrial espionage or – like the bombing of the 'Rainbow Warrior' – to stifle dissent, would the crime be any the less reprehensible? The motive adds nothing to the criminality of the acts constituting terrorism. Inclusion of the motivational element in the definition may easily be misunderstood as targeting the entire group who wish to advance the religious cause of Islam. A law which leaves itself open to such an interpretation fosters dissent. Indeed, it brands the advancing of a religious cause as an element in a heinous crime. A law which strikes at terrorist acts should not divide, but unite. It should not foster dissent which festers into an ambition to destroy the values which the law is intended to defend.

Another question is the desirability of conferring on the Australian Security Intelligence Organisation (ASIO) the extensive powers of detention and questioning for which Division 3 of the *Australian Security Intelligence Organistion Act* 1979 (Cth) provides. These powers allow a person to be detained, kept in detention for up to a week and subjected to questioning for periods of eight hours or more at a time. There is an obligation to answer the questions. The answers are not admissible in the person's prosecution for an offence but evidence acquired from the information extracted can be used. The questioning may be designed to obtain information that might be quite remote from any terrorism offence. It suffices that the information should 'substantially assist' in the collection of other information. It is the other information that is required to have an 'important' relationship with a terrorism offence. ASIO can secure the detention and questioning of a person in the hope of obtaining that kind of assistance, whether or not the information sought itself helps to prevent a terrorist act or the detection of the terrorist. This is a remarkable infringement on a person's common law rights, especially when the person is not a suspect and may not be even a sympathizer of terror. Fifty years ago, Fullagar J spoke of an interference with a person's person and liberty as 'prima facie a grave infringement of the most elementary and important of all common law rights'.[9] How is that infringement to be authorized? Apart from the ASIO and police personnel who would initiate or carry out the procedures, the persons authorized to issue the necessary warrants are selected serving judges or magistrates or other persons in a class specified by regulation and the persons authorized to supervise the detention and questioning are selected retired or serving judges or presidential members of the Administrative Appeals Tribunal (AAT). These *personae designatae* are not <u>all</u> the members of a court or <u>all</u> the previous members of a court or <u>all</u> the Presidential members of the AAT who might consent to appointment – they are only those selected for appointment by the Attorney General or persons selected by executive regulation. Why some and not others?

The use of judicial officers as *personae designatae* in tribunals such as the AAT is acceptable when their authority is to be exercised in a judicial manner and the power to be exercised is only the ordinary power to confer or cancel rights or privileges that are within the authority of the executive government. The ASIO powers are not ordinary powers and some of them cannot be exercised in a judicial manner. Warrants to detain a person for questioning are made without notice to the potential detainee who may have no knowledge or means of knowledge of the grounds on which the warrant has been sought or issued and has no means of questioning the sufficiency of those grounds. Again, a detainee may not be informed even of an application to extend the time for questioning, much less the grounds of the application.[10] Does it make any difference that these extraordinary powers are being exercised by *personae designatae* who are nominees of the executive government?

Compare these powers with the values of the common law. Remember the centuries old wisdom of Blackstone who warned that: 'if once it were left in the power of any, the highest, magistrate to imprison arbitrarily whomever he or his officers thought proper there would soon be an end of all other rights and immunities.'[11]

It must be acknowledged, however, that many Australians, believing that there must be sacrifices made in the so-called war on terror and that they will not be affected personally, are willing to accept incursions on the personal freedom of others and even some restriction on legal remedies which protect freedom.

Yet experience has shown that the due exercise of any form of executive power, particularly a power of detention, demands transparency of operation and accountability, both legally and politically. It is not a sufficient safeguard – indeed, it is not any kind of safeguard – to have assurances given by ASIO agents or police officers or Ministers who are advised by them, that the powers were justifiably exercised or that their exercise was justified in the result. Nor is it sufficient that judicial or quasi-judicial officers are involved in the procedure, their authority being circumscribed by the information which is given them and by the statute under which they are acting.

A minimum safeguard should be an effective pathway to a court exercising *habeas corpus* jurisdiction, casting on the Commonwealth authorities the burden of justifying the warrant and action taken under it. The first step would be free and automatic contact with the detainee's lawyer of choice or lawyers on a panel provided by a Law Society or Bar Association. A judge – not a judge selected by government, but one selected by the internal process of the court – can provide whatever confidentiality is reasonably required by national security in the course of a hearing, if the jurisdiction of the court is invoked.

We must never allow fear – that most malleable of political emotions – to transfer the protection of individual liberty from the judicial to the executive branch of government. Nor should our laws isolate and alienate peaceful citizens, robbing us of that solidarity and communal courage that has preserved us in past perils.

I do not doubt that it is difficult to strike the right balance, but I would place my trust in a united nation which accepts and welcomes all peaceful minorities, and which sees the courts as the proper guardians of the rule of law and the faithful protector of individual rights and immunities. That is the way to a free and confident nation: it is the way to keep the Australia I have known and loved.

---

1. A P Herbert, *Uncommon Law* (Methuen & Co, 3rd ed, 1937), 24, 28.
2. See *Lange v Australian Broadcasting Commission* (1997) 189 CLR 520, 564.
3. See *Bropho v Western Australia* (1990) 171 CLR 1, 18; *Potter v Minahan* (1908) 7 CLR 277, 304 and see also *Ex parte Walsh and Johnson; In re Yates* (1925) 37 CLR 36, 93.
4. Sir Anthony Mason,'Reshaping Australian Institutions', ANU Public Lecture, 13 August

1996, edited version published: Sir Anthony Mason, 'Rights, Values and Legal Institutions: Reshaping Australian Institutions' (1997) *Australian International Law Journal* 1.

5. See *Alister v R* (1984) 154 CLR 404, 456.
6. Compare *Sankey v Whitlam* (1978) 142 CLR 1, 42, 61- 62 referred to in *Alister v R* (1984) 154 CLR 404, 456.
7. Commonwealth, *Parliamentary Debates,* House of Representatives, 7 September 1939, 164,165 (Robert Menzies, Prime Minister).
8. Richard Posner, *The Australian,* (29 June 2007) 8.
9. See *Trobridge v Hardy* (1955) 94 CLR 147, 152.
10. See *Australian Security Intelligence Organisation Act 1979* (Cth), s 34R.a
11. William Blackstone, *Commentaries on the Laws of England* (Clarendon Press,1765), Bk1, 120-121,130-131 cited in *Williams v R* (1986) 161 CLR 278, 292.

1.8 Law for All; Justice for Each

Editor's note

This address was delivered at the Law and Justice Foundation Justice Awards Dinner at the NSW Parliament House on 31 October 2007.

Tonight, we gather, as you have gathered over the years, to pay tribute to those who have contributed to the fairness of the justice system – fairness which includes accessibility to justice especially by those who are socially or economically disadvantaged. The very existence and title of the Foundation, as well as the purpose of our gathering, invites us to consider the relationship between law and justice.

We know, of course, that law and justice are not synonymous. Law is a social regulator, justice is a moral value. In the second century AD, Ulpian defined justice as 'the constant and perpetual will to allot to every man his due.' When justice is compared with law, we can see that law affects a community; justice and injustice are experienced by individuals. What brings us together tonight is not so much a devotion to law as an abstract conception, but to law as an instrument of achieving justice – a means by which society facilitates the allotment 'to every man his due'. It is only when the law works no injustice to individuals that we can proclaim our adherence to the rule of law. It was the lawyer's thirst for justice that led Justice Cardozo to tell the lawyers of New York County that: 'The tradition, the ennobling tradition, though it be myth as well as verity, that surrounds as with an aura the profession of the law, is the bond between its members and one of the great concerns of man, the cause of justice upon earth.'

In a diverse and pluralist democracy, however, laws may be promoted which attract majority support though they bear harshly on a minority. Then the will of the majority can be an instrument of tyranny for the minority. Individual interests may, on occasions, be a source of frustration for a majority of the people, but laws which cause injustice to individuals are hard to justify. We, as a community, cannot justify seeking our own advantage if that advantage is to be underwritten by the visiting of injustice on an individual, or on a few, or on a minority. This is the reason why lawyers are essential to a free society. By 'lawyers' I mean all those who have an active role in the operation of the law. Their focus is on the individual and the justice of the individual's position.

Justice is the fundamental value which monitors the scope and content of the law. No law, however beneficial it may be to the majority, should be supported if it works injustice to some. However, we should be clear about what we mean by injustice. In a free society we start with the notion that law's restrictions on freedom should be kept to a minimum and there has to be some good reason for imposing any limitation. Freedom allows the fullest expression of the human person and the fullest opportunity to achieve the human potential – physical freedom as well as freedom of conscience, freedom of expression, freedom of association, freedom of movement, freedom from the arbitrary exercise of power. That is not to say that freedom is unlimited. To allow uncontrolled freedom to the powerful and the rich is to prejudice the freedom of the weak and the poor. A law which imposes duties or liabilities restrictive of freedom must be justified by the need to protect or advance the common good. Those duties or liabilities must be precisely targeted to protect the common good, they must be proportionate to the damage that would be reasonably apprehended if there were no such law and they must refrain from inflicting individual injustice. It is not unjust to limit an individual's freedom in order to protect the common good but only if, by reason of some attribute of, or conduct by, an individual, his freedom poses a threat to or has been used to offend the common good. That is why a law which imposes a duty or liability should be precisely drawn, defining objectively the attribute of, or the conduct by, an individual which justifiably attracts the law's operation. Thus is the rule of law maintained. Unjust laws undermine the rule of law, for injustice even to the few ultimately foments resentment in the many and erosion of the law's authority. These elementary considerations have significance for both the content of the law and for the role of lawyers.

In recent times, there has been much debate about the content of particular laws. We are in the midst of an election campaign when the parties are locked in dispute about the Industrial Relations laws. Are the Work Choices provisions protective of the economy in the interests of the common good? Do they impose unjust burdens on vulnerable workers to the benefit of the rest of the community? These are issues for others to debate, but they are the relevant issues for determining the justice of those laws. Consider the laws providing for intervention in the Aboriginal communities of the Northern Territory. All are agreed that sexual abuse of children must be prohibited, but the question is whether the intervention is targeted on that evil and whether the new laws unnecessarily impose discriminatory disadvantages on Northern Territory Aboriginal families. Again, these are questions material to the determination of the justice of the laws.

Perhaps the most tendentious laws in force at present – though they are not the subject of political campaigns – are the anti-terrorism laws for they trespass upon the basic notion of natural justice. That is a notion that is dear to the heart of all those concerned with justice, so it is worthwhile trying to determine whether these important laws give us both security and justice. Nobody doubts the need for laws conferring special powers enabling authorities to identify terrorists and potential terrorists and to neutralize any terrorist activity. But do they work injustice to individuals? Legislation empowering the Australian Securities and Investment Organisation (ASIO) or the Federal Police to carry out surveillance, or to search and to seize property can be justified when there are reasonable grounds shown, provided such powers are precisely targeted on the detection and prevention of terror and the apprehension of terrorists. But what of the power to compel submission to interrogation or the power to detain and interrogate without charge, or the power to charge, detain and submit to interrogation or the power of preventative detention?

Clearly, an exercise of these powers constitutes a remarkable invasion of common law rights, especially if the person is not a suspect and may not be even a sympathizer of terror. Fifty years ago, Fullagar J spoke of an interference with an individual's person and liberty as 'prima facie a grave infringement of the most elementary and important of all common law rights'.[1] There should be an effective mechanism to safeguard personal liberty, but the anti-terrorism laws vest the power to interfere with a person's liberty in the Executive branch of Government which controls the procedure and those laws deny natural justice to the person who is the subject of the power.

A warrant to compel a person to submit to interrogation or a warrant to detain and question a person is issued on the application of the Director-General of ASIO who has the Minister's consent to apply. The warrant may be issued once the issuing authority is satisfied 'that there are reasonable grounds for believing that the warrant will substantially assist the collection of intelligence that is important in relation to a terrorism offence'.[2] A semblance of legality is provided by limiting the issuing authorities to Federal Magistrates and Judges who consent to being appointed by the Minister. They do not act in a judicial capacity but as *personae designatae* exercising executive authority. The procedure for obtaining a warrant does not resemble standard judicial procedure. The ASIO application is made *ex parte* and the subject is not informed of the grounds advanced for the warrant. If the subject should want to challenge the sufficiency of the grounds on which the warrant is issued, his or her legal adviser is not entitled to see any document other than the warrant itself.[3] In any event, contact with that legal adviser, if permitted at all, is monitored by a person exercising authority under the warrant.[4] Unless the warrant allows a person who is being detained, either by the warrant or by a "prescribed authority"[5] to contact somebody, he or she can be prevented from contacting anyone.[6] In summary, a person may be detained in custody, virtually incommunicado, without even being accused of involvement in terrorist activity, on grounds which are kept secret and without effective opportunity to challenge the basis of his or her detention. When statute exempts a repository of power from the obligation to observe natural justice, an exercise of the power is attended with the risk of injustice – injustice which is not curable by judicial intervention and which may not even be revealed if the repository of the power does not have to disclose the material on which he or she acted. It was John Locke who pithily observed: 'Where-ever law ends, tyranny begins'.[7]

A similar problem arises in relation to preventative detention orders under Division 105 of the *Criminal Code Act 1995* (Cth). These orders are issued on application by a member of the Australian Federal Police to a judicial or quasi-judicial or former judicial officer who has consented to being appointed by the Minister as an issuing authority.[8] The order may be issued if the issuing authority is satisfied that it is necessary to detain the subject *either* to assist in preventing the occurrence of an imminent terrorist act in which the subject is suspected on reasonable grounds of being involved *or* to preserve evidence of a terrorist act occurring within the previous 28 days.[9] The detainee may also be subject to a prohibited contact order, including contact with specified lawyers, similar to the situation of detainees under the ASIO Act. Effective judicial review is impossible. So long as the detention order is in force, resort to any Court is denied[10] although, presumably, the jurisdiction of the High Court under s 75 (v) of the *Constitution* cannot be excluded. After the detention order has expired, the detainee can apply for review, but only to the Security Appeals Division of the Administrative Appeals Tribunal which can award compensation if it would have held the order to be void.[11] If a detention order has been made under a state law as well as under the *Criminal Code*, state courts can review both after the warrants have expired, but the Australian Federal Police are not required to disclose any information that 'is likely to prejudice national security'.[12] The meaning of that term is extremely wide – it covers, inter alia, not only prejudice to physical security, but also prejudice to Australian political, military and economic relations with foreign governments and international organisations and our interest in avoiding disruption to national and international efforts relating to law enforcement or criminal intelligence and in protecting informants.[13] In other words, effective judicial review is excluded.

Granted the desirability of confidentiality in dealing with many issues of security, can it be just to repose these powers in agencies of the Executive without judicial supervision exercised in accordance with natural justice? Courts certainly value publicity as a safeguard against the adventitious use of power, but they are not antipathetic to national security, nor are they incapable of preserving confidentiality of information when confidentiality is essential for national security. If effective access to the courts were available to those against whom warrants are issued, there would be an assurance that the powers conferred on ASIO and on the Federal Police are exercised reasonably and for the purpose for which they were conferred. The sad experience of the *Haneef* case has eroded public confidence in the agencies entrusted to safeguard public security. The misinformed attack on Stephen Keim SC for releasing a transcript of the interview with Haneef after extracts prejudicial to Haneef had been leaked suggested a fear that an incompetent or arrogant misuse of power would be exposed.

To exclude access to the courts and to restrict a court's access to the material on which to determine the validity of an exercise of power is to deny the rule of law. Experience has shown that, whenever unexaminable power is conferred, there is a tendency – no, more, a likelihood – that the power will be abused. As United States Justice Stevens said in *Rumsfeld v Padilla*: 'Unconstrained executive detention for the purpose of investigating and preventing subversive activity is the hallmark of the Star Chamber. Access to counsel for the purpose of protecting citizens from official mistakes and mistreatment is the hallmark of due process.'[14]

The courts and their processes are the only sure protection of individuals – and ultimately the only sure protection of a community – against illegal injustice. In the struggle against terror, we must be careful not to expose ourselves to the risk of oppression by those with unaccountable power. Some may be prepared to accept the risk of injustice to others, believing themselves to be immune from the risk of suffering injustice at the hands of executive agencies. Perhaps they might reflect on Pastor Niemoller's lament in Hitler's Germany: '... they came first for the Communists, and I didn't speak up because I wasn't a Communist. Then they came for the Jews, and I didn't speak up because I wasn't a Jew. Then they came for the trade unionists, and I didn't speak up because I wasn't a trade unionist. Then they came for the Catholics, and I didn't speak up because I was a Protestant. Then they came for me, and by that time no one was left to speak up.'

Democracy is our prized possession, but we must not be blind to the reality that democracy by itself does not assure justice to all members of the community. Passivity by a majority in the face of injustice may be destructive of freedom. Five years passed before David Hicks was brought home – and even then, under a bargain which does not bear comparison with the situation of the British detainees who were released to freedom years before. In the absence of effective judicial remedies or timely popular protest, it was the passion for justice of Michael Mori, Stephen Kenny and others, including Lex Lasry, which ultimately secured for Hicks some relief from the injustices of Guantanamo Bay.

Experience of the anti-terrorism laws and their operation, like the experience of Mamdouh Habib and David Hicks in Guantanamo Bay, starkly illustrate the injustices that can occur when power is exercised without effective judicial review. Judicial review is not designed to frustrate the reasonable exercise of legitimate powers – it is but the means by which the rule of law is maintained. You who have given so much of your time and energy to justice and the law know only too well that the absence of law walks hand in hand with injustice to the detriment of individual liberty, individual rights and, importantly, public confidence in the rule of law. Yet, in Australia in recent times, we have witnessed a series of erosions of the jurisdiction of the courts to apply the rule of law.

It was a denial of access to the courts and of effective judicial review that allowed injustices to be visited on many asylum seekers held in detention. Port Headland and Baxter, Tampa and the Pacific solution were designed to preclude effective access to the courts. And the full scope of judicial review has been denied by Part 8 of the *Migration Act 1958* (Cth).[15] When courts are stripped of their jurisdiction over a particular subject matter, to that extent the subject matter is without legal control – an area of unbridled power. Then it is foolish to place complete trust in the integrity of executive agencies to act justly in all circumstances. Of course, we must place trust in those agencies – we trust them to fulfil the very purpose of their existence, whether it be to protect us against terrorism or to administer the *Migration Act 1958* (Cth) or to perform some other function which, in a modern complex state, must be performed by a skilled and committed bureaucracy. But it is the very devotion to their allotted task that carries the risk of individual injustice – injustice that may follow sometimes from an excess of enthusiasm to achieve their purpose, sometimes from incompetence or human error. The Council of Europe, in a preface to its Guidelines on Human Rights and the Fight Against Terrorism, said this: 'The temptation for governments and parliaments in countries suffering from terrorist action is to fight fire with fire, setting aside the legal safeguards that exist in a democratic state. But let us be clear about this: while the State has the right to employ to the full its arsenal of legal weapons to repress and prevent terrorist activities, it may not use indiscriminate measures which would only undermine the fundamental values they seek to protect. For a State to react in such a way would be to fall into the trap set by terrorism for democracy and the rule of law.'[16]

Sometimes injustice consists in the infliction of punishment for crime that is either disproportionate to the circumstances of the offence or does not accord with what we accept as reasonable. Thus we provide for appeals against sentences imposed by Australian courts. But we have no juridical means of reviewing sentences imposed by foreign courts. In recent years, we have become acutely conscious of the imposition of the death penalty by courts in our region. Many of you are too young to remember the last execution in Australia. It was 8 o'clock on the morning of 3 February 1967 when Ronald Ryan was hanged from the gallows in the Melbourne gaol. Most Australians shuddered at that moment. Just as most of us were distressed by the hanging of Barlow and Chambers in Pudu Prison in Malaysia in July 1986 and by the hanging of Van Nguyen in Changi Gaol in December 2005. These events were each described as 'barbaric' by leading political figures of the day: Bob Hawke in relation to the hanging of 1986,[17] Philip Ruddock in 2005.[18] Coming from Queensland, where the death penalty was abolished in 1922, I was largely shielded from involvement in the terrible process of pronouncing the death penalty but I was present as a minor court officer at the last of the Japanese War Crimes trials in Manus Island in 1950 when I heard that dread sentence pronounced. I sensed the horror of the sentence but not as much as did the members of the Court Martial who imposed it – tough men, good men who had lived through some of the terrors of the war; they exhibited distress and mental anguish in the days that followed. Such a reaction is the inevitable and widespread accompaniment of taking any part in a judicial killing, however awful the crime. Capital punishment brutalises the society that tolerates it and may destroy not only the person killed but also those involved or associated with the gruesome event.

Australia long ago decided that capital punishment is not to be practised. We joined 132 other nations in that resolve.[19] In 1991, we acceded to the Second Optional Protocol to the *International Convention on Civil and Political Rights* which not only binds Australia not to execute anyone within the jurisdiction[20] but also recites that the Parties to the Protocol are: 'Convinced that all measures of abolition of the death penalty should be considered as progress in the enjoyment of the right to life,' and the Parties are: 'Desirous to undertake … an international commitment to abolish the death penalty'.

One of the latest nations to endorse the policy was Rwanda. In July this year, Louise Arbour, the United Nations Commissioner for Human Rights lauded the Rwandan decision, saying: 'A country that has suffered the ultimate crime and whose people's thirst for justice is still far from quenched has decided to forego a sanction that should have no place in any society that claims to value human rights and the inviolability of the person'.[21]

Nevertheless, on 16 February 2003 the Australian Prime Minister said that the Bali bombers 'should be dealt with in accordance with Indonesian law. ... and if [the death penalty] is what the law of Indonesia provides, well, that is how things should proceed.' But Ronald Ryan and Barlow and Chambers and Van Nguyen were hanged as the law provided. When Mr McClelland pointed out that death sentences were pronounced on Van Nguyen and Amrozi, one of the Bali bombers, at the same time, and proposed that Australia would join Asian countries to persuade others in the region to abolish capital punishment, his statement was repudiated by both the main political parties. It was repudiated not merely on the ground that it was made insensitively in the week of the anniversary of the Bali bombings but on the ground that Australia's interventions on behalf of those sentenced to death should be limited to Australian prisoners. This elicited a comment from Mr Malcolm Fraser: 'It is sad to see principle being thrown overboard and an expedient argument, which politicians believe will be the popular argument, pursued. So often matters of principle need to be explained and supported by those in positions of authority – and then, more often than not, those principles will find general support.'[22]

If the Bali 9 should be spared the firing squad, why do we repudiate a proposal to persuade those South East Asian nations who still carry out executions to change? The effectiveness of intervention on behalf of Australians under the death sentence is surely problematic. We decline extradition unless the country seeking extradition undertakes that the prisoner will not be executed, yet our policy for co-operation with Indonesian police allowed, perhaps required, that the Australian Federal Police facilitate the arrest and possible execution in Indonesia of Australians who were employed to bring drugs to Australia. When the Bali 9 were arrested, the then political leaders of both major parties supported the policy. Scott Rush's parents had asked that he be warned off becoming a drug mule but he was allowed to go lest the police operation be compromised. Mr Keelty, the Commissioner, said: 'We'd do the same thing again and we're doing it each and every day.'[23] We can only hope that Australia can effectively intervene to save the lives of those condemned, including 21 year old Scott Rush after exposing him to the very risk of execution.

The political responses to the capital sentences imposed by Indonesian courts on some of the Bali 9 and on some of those involved in the Bali bombing raise acutely the distinction between law and justice. All of us would support laws which are effective to suppress the trade in destructive drugs and to punish those involved in the horrible murder of the bombing. But if we espouse the equal application of law as the essential characteristic of the rule of law, how can nationality be the ground of distinction? We cannot declare the execution of Australians to be barbaric and the execution of Indonesians to be acceptable. Yet that now seems to be bipartisan policy. Principle is sacrificed for political advantage. A country which speaks about such an important issue with a forked tongue can hardly lay claim to the rule of law and forfeits its credibility in the international forum.

It is, I suppose, inevitable that an election campaign should be pitched at the majority, and that the protection of the few against injustices would not be an election issue. We have not been moved by the case of David Hicks to press for the restoration of the rule of law by the United States in its treatment of so-called 'enemy combatants'; nor has the case of Mohamed Haneef elicited a call to revisit the provisions of the anti-terrorism laws to provide detainees with effective access to justice. The injustices that have marked both the provisions and the administration of the *Migration Act 1958* (Cth) have stimulated only partial reforms and apparently have no resonance today in the political sphere. And even our international commitments to the ideals of the Second Optional Protocol are sacrificed on the altar of political expediency.

But, on nights like this, when men and women devoted to the cause of justice gather to celebrate their commitment and to validate the rights of the outcast and the underprivileged, there are grounds for optimism. It is their work which employs the law in its most important role – the equal application of the law to all, irrespective of class, creed, ethnic origin, popularity or lack of it, status or wealth. Ultimately, political rhetoric about the rule of law may be exposed to be as genuine as the electoral kissing of babies, but there is a brave core of Australians, including many in the legal profession, who are truly devoted to the rule of law and the securing of justice for all. They are the ones who see the law as a way to justice, who give real meaning to the notion of a fair go. They represent the values of a free and confident nation. We greet you, we thank you and we wish you well in your noble endeavours.

---

1. See *Trobridge v Hardy* (1955) 94 CLR 147, 152.
2. See *Australian Securities and Investigation Organisation Act 1979* (Cth), ss 34E(1)(b), 34G(1)(b).
3. Ibid s 34ZQ(4)(b).
4. Ibid s 34ZQ(1).
5. Ibid s 34K(1)(d).
6. Ibid s 34K(10).

7. John Locke, *Second Treatise of Government* (1690), Chap XVII, s 202 (Cambridge University Press, 1988), quoted by Lord Bingham in *The Rule of Law,* the Sixth Sir David Williams Lecture, Cambridge, 16 November 2006.
8. Ibid *Criminal Code Act 1995* (Cth), s 105.2.
9. Ibid s 105.4.
10. Ibid s 105.51, 105.52(5)(b).
11. Ibid s 105.51.
12. Ibid s 105.52(4).
13. Ibid s 105.53(4) and (6), *National Security Information (Criminal and Civil Proceedings) Act 2004* (Cth) ss 8, 10, 11, 17.
14. 542 US (2004).
15. See *Migration Act 1958* (Cth) ss 475, 476.
16. Adopted by the Committee of Ministers, 11 July 2002, at the 804th Meeting of the Ministers' Deputies, 5, cited by Hon Arthur Chaskalson, sometime Chief Justice of South Africa and President of the Constitutional Court in his Seventh Sir David Williamson Lecture: *The Widening Gyre: Counter-terrorism, human rights and the rule of law*.
17. Damien Murphy, *The Sydney Morning Herald* (Sydney, 30 November 2005).
18. ABC News, 28 November 2005.
19. See the Amnesty report of October 2007: http://web.amnesty.org/pages/deathpenalty-facts-eng.
20. Article 1.
21. Office of the High Commission for Human Rights, 'High Commissioner for Human Rights Hails Abolition of Capital Punishment in Rwanda', 27 July 2007, https://www.ohchr.org/en/statements/2009/10/high-commissioner-human-rights-hails-abolition-capital-punishment-rwanda'
22. Malcolm Fraser, 'The Death Penalty: Where is the moral leadership' originally published on the *Australians All* website.
23. See *The Sydney Morning Herald* (Sydney, 15 February 2006).

1.9 The Constitution, Good Government and Human Rights

Editor's note

This address was delivered at the Human Rights Law Resource Centre, Melbourne, on 12 March 2008.[1]

Our *Constitution*, the powers of Government and the human rights recognised by the law identify the basic politico/legal structures affecting the well-being of our people. We need to consider these structures from time to time to ensure that they facilitate the realisation of our social aspirations.

What are these social aspirations? At base, personal freedom – freedom of conscience including freedom of religious belief and practice, physical freedom, freedom to use and dispose of property, freedom to choose a partner and found a family, freedom of association, freedom of speech, freedom from the exercise of arbitrary power. Then, so far as the resources of the community allow, each person should have reasonable access to education and an opportunity for employment, together with access to the social services required to maintain health and personal dignity and to allow for personal development. The marshalling of those resources and their application is a function of good government – a government of laws and not of men.

In a democracy, laws find acceptance when the power to make them is subject as far as practicable to popular control and when the enforcement of the law is left to competent, fair and impartial tribunals. So, we should assess our constitutional laws, the way in which those laws and governmental practices operate and the extent to which each individual's human rights and fundamental freedoms are respected.

In recent times there has been a welcome interest in human rights and their legal recognition. But it would be a mistake to think that our well-being and the protection of individual interests depend entirely, or even chiefly, on the enactment of a Bill of Rights. Human rights and fundamental freedoms find their chief protection in the twin pillars of the constitutional legal system the rule of law and the jurisdiction of the courts to enforce the law.

The underlying principle of our constitutional law – the principle that gives essential protection to individual freedom and dignity – is the principle of the rule of law. That is because, as John Locke pithily observed, 'Where-ever law ends, tyranny begins'.[2] The rule of law is not to be found in a statutory text; it is simply the axiomatic basis of the politico/legal system.

In the *Communist Party Case,*[3] Dixon J observed that among the traditional conceptions in accordance with which our *Constitution* is framed 'it may fairly be said that the rule of law forms an assumption'.[4] What does the rule of law mean? A V Dicey gave this as the primary meaning: '– … the absolute supremacy or predominance of regular law as opposed to the influence of arbitrary power ... It means ... equality before the law or the equal subjection of all classes to the ordinary law of the land administered by the ordinary law courts; the "rule of law" in this sense excludes the idea of any exemption of officials or others from the duty of obedience to the law which governs other citizens or from the jurisdiction of the ordinary tribunals.'[5]

As the law is applied equally to all – the government and the governed, the powerful and the weak, the rich and poor alike – it has been held that the criminal law allows no exemption to those who breach the law under the purported authority of the executive government.[6]

The 'regular law … administered by the ordinary law courts' is that 'everybody is free to do anything, subject only to the provisions of the Law'.[7] That was the approach of the *Declaration of the Rights of Man*, Article 4 which reads: 'Liberty consists in the freedom to do everything which injures no one else; hence the exercise of the natural rights of each man has no limits except those which assure to the other members of the society the enjoyment of the same rights. These limits can only be determined by law'.

Individual freedom is protected by the common law – personal physical freedom is protected by the law of assault, battery and false imprisonment; reputation by the law of libel and slander; a variety of interests by the torts of negligence and trespass; possessions by detinue and conversion; the quiet enjoyment of where we live is protected by the torts of trespass and nuisance.[8]

The common law also gives a measure of freedom to the artisan and trader and strengthens the economy by invalidating unreasonable restraints of trade. The common law of real property secures title (including native title) to interests in land, and the principles of equity go far to ensuring that the courts are able to enforce obligations the neglect of which would be unconscionable. The common law as it has developed is calculated to protect human rights and fundamental freedoms and it has done so with tolerable success without a Bill of Rights. Of course, the established common law principles have been modified or built on by statute but the significant point for present purposes is the importance of the ordinary, but general, jurisdiction of the courts to administer and enforce the general law.

The law that rules is the law that is interpreted and applied by the courts.

In the familiar words of Chief Justice Marshall in *Marbury* v *Madison*: 'It is emphatically the province and duty of the judicial department to say what the law is'.[9] To maintain the integrity of the law, we invoke the constitutional principle that the courts should be separate from and independent of influence by the political branches of government. The judges must be kept impartial, free not only from bias but also from any reasonable apprehension of bias.[10] As Lord Bingham has pointed out: '... the function of independent judges charged to interpret and apply the law is universally recognised as a cardinal feature of the modern democratic state, a cornerstone of the rule of law itself.'[11]

Professor Winterton, commenting on the *Communist Party Case*[12] said that it: '... demonstrated that our freedom depends upon impartial enforcement of the rule of law, of which courts are the ultimate guardians. Although, of course, not infallible, impartial and fearless courts determined to exercise their proper powers are our final defence against tyranny'.[13]

There are a number of other rules and practices which underpin our legal system and which are protective of individual rights: the public promulgation of the law and the public sittings of the courts administering the law, the presumption against retrospectivity and the presumption that laws are not intended to trespass on rights and fundamental freedoms. In *Wentworth* v *NSW Bar Association*,[14] the High Court said that: 'There are certain matters in relation to which legislative provisions will be construed as effecting no more than is strictly required by clear words or as a matter of necessary implication.[15] They include important common law rights,[16] procedural[17] and other[18] safeguards of individual rights and freedoms and the jurisdiction of superior courts.'[19]

The law assumes good government.

If the rule of law is to apply universally, however, the jurisdiction of the courts to judicially review an exercise of governmental power is essential.

If the courts are denied jurisdiction to enforce the law governing the exercise of power, the repository of the power can refuse to obey the law with impunity, individual interests are at risk and the rule of law is negated. Although State Parliaments have power to deny jurisdiction to the courts, that power has been sparingly exercised.[20] By force of s 75(v) of the Commonwealth *Constitution*, decisions taken in exercise of federal power cannot be totally exempt from judicial review. The High Court has pointed out[21] that the jurisdiction conferred on the High Court by that provision: '... is a means of assuring to all people affected that officers of the Commonwealth obey the law and neither exceed nor neglect any jurisdiction which the law confers on them.'

The law, and the courts which administer the law, are the primary protectors against tyranny and any abuse of power. Respect for our human rights and fundamental freedoms in this country stems from, and still largely depends on, the constitutional authority of the courts to vindicate those rights and protect those freedoms by application of the general law.

The responsibility does not rest with the courts alone. Respect for fundamental freedoms and human rights is a function of good government in the ordinary exercise of legislative and executive powers. Each of us individually and Australians collectively have an interest in the distribution and control of these powers – their distribution between the Commonwealth and the States and between the legislature and the executive. Consider first the distribution of powers between the Commonwealth and the States. In a federation, good government requires legislative power to be distributed between the central and local governments according to the need for national laws and efficiency in their implementation and in the provision of governmental services. Between 1986 and 1988, a Constitutional Commission inquired into the working of the *Constitution*. The Commission and its Committees were constituted by members possessing formidable political, practical and legal expertise. The Commission recommended changes. Yet its Report, pre-empted by a Bill[22] hastily cobbled together and submitted to referendum, was buried in the rubble of the Referendum's failure. It would be desirable to revisit, in a cooler climate, the recommendations of the Commission. Those recommendations covered, inter alia, minimum 3 year and maximum four year terms for the House of Representatives,[23] the Senate's power over money bills,[24] disagreement between the two Houses of Parliament,[25] an extension of Commonwealth power to make laws with respect to intra State trade and commerce,[26] and nuclear material, nuclear energy and ionising radiation.[27] The rapid growth of technology in fields that affect human existence (the cloning of humans and animal genome engineering, for example), the ecosystem (genetic modification of plants and animals, control of rivers and waterways) and privacy now call for a power to intervene, if necessary, by enacting uniform or coordinated national laws. The new issues should not produce political division. Some of these subjects may fall within the Commonwealth's external affairs power if there be international conventions to which Australia is a party but it is preferable to confer the power to make laws with respect to specified areas of technology in order to facilitate laws appropriate to Australian conditions. The Commission also recommended that the High Court be invested with jurisdiction to give advisory opinions,[28] a proposition that would not command universal support, but it may need some consideration if it were desired to invest the Court with a declaratory jurisdiction under a statutory Bill of Rights – a topic to which we must return.

The *Uniform Tax* cases in 1942[29] and 1957[30] sanctioned the Commonwealth's acquisition of the most important categories of taxation. In *Ha v New South Wales*[31] in 1997, the High Court's interpretation of the excise power excluded the States from some of the residual sources of taxation that they had hitherto enjoyed. However, although there is an undoubted fiscal imbalance as between the central and state governments, the concentration of financial power in the central government has been conducive to effective control of the national economy. Nevertheless, there may be a need to consider whether this financial power should be used to purchase control over specific areas of activity, egg universities that do not fall within the legislative powers of the Commonwealth and are not covered by grants to the States under s 96.

Next, consider the relationship between the Executive and the Legislature. Parliamentary control of the Executive is, of course, the characteristic of responsible government. A century ago, Lord Haldane thought that that institution permeated the Constitution.[32] But it has been eroded by the growth of executive power and the dominance of the Executive over the Parliament. In Australia, as in England, Lord Hailsham's more modern statement[33] is substantially true: '[we live under an elective dictatorship, absolute in theory if hitherto thought tolerable in practice.[34]'

When an executive government is able to escape the scrutiny of the parliament and may even control the parliament so that scrutiny is impotent against executive maladministration, responsible government can become a misnomer and good government can fall captive to undisciplined authority.

Recently a problem has surfaced in relation to parliamentary supervision of expenditure by the central government. This is a problem with a long history. It lay at the heart of the great constitutional struggles of the late 17th century. At least from the time of the *Appropriation Act* in the reign of Charles II, executive powers have been substantially constrained by the 'undisputed principle' that 'supplies granted by Parliament are only to be expended for particular objects specified by itself.'[35] Holdsworth adopted the opinion that the principle was 'established for the better securing the rights, liberties, and privileges of the people' and he noted that :'[t] he very act of appropriating specific sums to this or that need of the government involved a decision upon the question which need was more, and which was less pressing and the right to make these decisions gave a power, not only to criticize but also, in some measure, to control the conduct of the government.'[36]

In conformity with this principle, the *Constitution* provides that money cannot be 'drawn from the Treasury except under appropriation made by law',[37] that a proposed law cannot be passed unless the purpose of the appropriation has been recommended by message of the Governor

General,[38] and that money can be appropriated only for a purpose of the Commonwealth.[39] To the extent that Parliament prescribes the objects of expenditure by the Executive, the Executive is made responsible to the Parliament. The drafting of recent Appropriation Bills for the 'ordinary annual services of government' has circumvented parliamentary control of particular objects of expenditure by appropriating funds as a 'departmental item', listing them under the heading 'Departmental Outputs', which can be expended as the departmental minister chooses. A challenge to the efficacy of this practice failed in *Combet* v *The Commonwealth*[40] (the Work Choices advertising case). A majority of the High Court[41] observed: '… at least since the mid-1980s the chief means of limiting expenditures made by departments of State that has been adopted in annual appropriation Acts has been to specify the **amount** that may be spent rather than further define the purposes or activities for which it may be spent.'[42]

Arguably, the appropriation provisions of the *Constitution* need tightening, or the drafting practices amended.[43] The diminution of parliamentary supervision over executive expenditure weakens the practical observance of the system of responsible government.

It is not surprising that the *Constitution* shows some strain after more than a century during which it has proved to be obdurately resistant to change. It is time to overhaul its provisions to ensure that it meets the needs of the present and foreseeable future times. Take, for example, the corporations power. As it has been interpreted by the High Court,[44] it denies the Commonwealth power to make laws with respect to the formation of trading and financial corporations though it has power to legislate for those corporations after their formation. The bifurcation of the power precludes the enactment of a comprehensive national code for the incorporation and control of trading and financial corporations, although the qualified reference of power in a *State Corporations (Commonwealth Powers) Act* goes some way towards resolving the problem. It is not the constitutionally preferable solution.

Again, s 80 has proved to be an inadequate protection of the right to trial by jury for serious crimes. Its provisions are engaged only when the crime charged is triable on indictment.[45] Let the crime be defined as triable summarily, and the right to jury trial disappears. Section 80 has been described as 'a mere procedural provision',[46] the effect of which can be avoided merely by a device of drafting.[47] If s 80 is to be an effective guarantee of trial by jury for serious Commonwealth offences, it should be amended.

A problem that may seem at first glance to be merely technical, but which raises jurisdictional difficulties productive of cost and frustration, is the constitutional inability of federal courts to be invested with State jurisdiction.[48] There is no obstacle to the vest-ing of federal jurisdiction in State courts – the 'autochthonous expedient' was one of the masterstrokes of the founding fathers. Nor is there any objection to the vesting in federal courts of jurisdiction to determine 'matters' which arise in part under State law where the matter arises also under federal law.[49] It may not be possible to create a single judicial system in a federation such as ours, but it is unacceptable to maintain a system that places jurisdictional difficulties in the way of enforcement of rights, whether those rights be derived from State or Federal laws. The Constitutional Commission recommended changes to remedy all of these anomalies.[50]

Then there are the transitional and obsolete provisions of the *Constitution* which are littered throughout the text, cloud the true nature of the Constitutional framework and impair its readability.[51] The Commission recommended repeal of the race power (s 51 (xxvi)) to be replaced with a power to make laws with respect to Aborigines and Torres Strait Islanders.[52] Section 25, which authorises disqualification from the franchise on grounds of race, should be repealed. It is high time to be rid of s 74, the dead letter which still purports to provide for appeals to the Privy Council, and the provisions of ss 58, 59 and 60 which permit the reservation of a law for the Queen's pleasure and reserve the Queen's power to disallow a law even after it has been assented to by the Governor-General. The provisions, which confer powers on the Queen, with one exception, have become anachronistic. The removal of these provisions should not be seen as dependent upon the adoption of a republican form of government. It is an anachronism that the *Constitution* should repose in the Queen powers that are obsolete; but the power to appoint the Governor-General must remain unless and until an alternative provision is inserted for the appointment of an Australian Head of State. The Commission observed that the obsolete provisions could be repealed with no practical effect on the operation of the *Constitution*.[53] Dr Helen Irving makes the same plea: '[R]emove the detritus … Send them to a constitutional elephants' graveyard for historians like myself to lament.'[54]

The *Constitution* is not easily changed by referendum, but a clean-up of the *Constitution* is long overdue. It is time to dust off the recommendations of the Constitutional Commission and to make amendments that would eliminate known inefficiencies, strengthen our democratic controls and bring our *Constitution* into shape to cope with the scientific and technological problems of the 21st century. Agreement on the principal issues should not be too difficult to attain, but it would require statesmanship and commitment from the leaders on both sides of the political divide to commend the desirable amendments to the Australian people. With adequate explanation, the people can be trusted to repair defects in our *Constitution* at least to the point where the document can operate effectively in 21st century conditions.

Of course, the *Constitution* does not determine the way in which the powers it confers will be exercised. That depends chiefly on the values, ability and political acumen of the members of the Executive and Legislature. If we accept that, in a democracy, the powers of government should be exercised for the common good, the definition of what is the common good must in turn depend on the values and aspirations of the people. If the people aspire to a society that is free and in which all citizens are equal before the law, the common good must include respect for individual freedom and dignity. That leaves no room for drawing distinctions based on race or colour, class or creed, physical or mental perfection or defect. Governmental power must be exercised to ensure that at least the basic social benefits are available to all, especially to the marginalised and disadvantaged. Those benefits cannot be exhaustively listed for the infinite variety of personal circumstances and social phenomena evoke different needs at different times.

To achieve the common good, political leaders have a variety of courses that they might follow and opinions will differ about the way in which they should be achieved. In an ideal, but unreal, world the concept of the common good would guide all exercise of governmental power but in a democratic, materialist society which places a premium on individual benefits, the interests of a majority may be preferred at the expense of a minority. Policies which benefit or appeal to a majority may prevail to the prejudice of the common good. A brake on majoritarian tyranny is provided by raising public consciousness of the importance of human rights. Our common humanity can inspire us to seek a community in which, by respecting human rights, all may live in freedom and dignity. That has long been realised and it has played its part in the development of some legal rules.

John Locke, in the 17th century, had asserted that, as the natural law, discoverable by reason, holds all persons to be 'equal and independent, no one ought to harm another in his life, health, liberty or possessions'.[55] In France, Rousseau's theory of popular sovereignty led to a democratic espousal of human rights and to their expression as a basis for political action.[56] In 1786, the American Declaration of Independence asserted that 'all men are created equal ... endowed by their Creator with certain inalienable rights … amongst them … Life, Liberty and the pursuit of Happiness'. Holdsworth believed that American independence was 'the first great victory of the democratic ideas preached by Rousseau' but it was the success of the French Revolution that gave those ideas 'their great importance in the succeeding century.'[57] Those ideas informed the Declaration of the Rights of Man which, on 26 August 1789, the National Assembly of France 'recognize[d] and proclaime[d], in the presence and under the auspices of the Supreme Being'. It proclaimed, inter alia, that 'men are born and remain free and equal in rights' and that 'the aim of all political association is the preservation of the natural and imprescriptible rights of man. These rights are liberty, property, security, and resistance to oppression.'

Popular democracy as proposed by Rousseau, however, led to no constitutional revolution in England. Absolute monarchy had departed with the Stuarts; the Bill of Rights had ended the monarch's power to suspend the laws. The British Constitution was defended by Edmund Burke, who revolted 'against the individualism which magnified the rights of each separate man'. Holdsworth agreed, although he accepted that the extension of the franchise in England owed something to the 'loose theories of the equality of men and their natural right to share in the government of the country' despite 'the intellectual differences between human beings, and the intellectual and physical differences between men and women'.[58] Objections to the magnification of individual rights had been consolidated in England by the horrors of the French Revolution, which delayed the reform of British law.[59]

In the 20th century, however, the world was faced with the inhuman laws of Nazi Germany, inspiring the General Assembly of the United Nations in 1948 to proclaim the Universal Declaration of Human Rights 'as a common standard of achievement for all peoples and all nations'. It began by declaring that 'All human beings are born free and equal in dignity and rights' and that 'Everyone is entitled to all the rights and freedoms set forth in this Declaration'. The Universal Declaration can be seen as the launch of the modern movement for the protection of human rights. Of course, the Universal Declaration was not directly effective in domestic law, but the movement for human rights was effective – at least in western societies – to elevate public consciousness of the need to protect the human rights and fundamental freedoms of individuals. The need for recognition of human rights was expressed by Sir Anthony Mason: 'Human rights are seen as a countervailing force to the exercise of totalitarian, bureaucratic and institutional power – widely identified as the greatest threats to the liberty of the individual and democratic freedom in this century.'[60]

In 1950 the European Convention on Human Rights was agreed by the member States of the Council of Europe. The rights were intended to be at least prima facie barriers against infringing legislative or executive action.

They were enforceable by judgment binding on the States Parties given by the Court in Strasbourg.[61] The Convention allowed some limited restrictions on the rights declared[62] and the Court has allowed governments a 'margin of appreciation' in those cases.[63]

The common law does not attribute to individuals any right which gives immunity from legislative or executive power. For a time, the notorious provisions of s 92 of our *Constitution* were thought to have the effect of conferring an individual right to destroy legislative or executive action but that heresy has now been extirpated.[64] Laws operate in accordance with their terms, although the terms are interpreted so far as possible to respect human rights and fundamental freedoms. Once human rights are enacted as domestic law, however, it is necessary to determine whether and to what extent such rights affect the exercise of the constitutional powers of the legislature and the executive. That question did not arise for the framers of the Commonwealth *Constitution*, because, as Mason CJ explained: '... the prevailing sentiment of the framers [was] that there was no need to incorporate a comprehensive Bill of Rights in order to protect the rights and freedoms of citizens. That sentiment was one of the unexpressed assumptions on which the *Constitution* was drafted.'[65]

Thus, our constitutional history was against the creation of human rights that might limit or be incompatible with the exercise of legislative or executive power. The balancing of individual interests with the interests of the community has been seen as a purely political issue, in which the courts have no role to play.

Nevertheless, the exigencies of modern politics have sometimes led Governments to ignore human rights in order to achieve objectives that are said to be for the common good. Commonwealth laws relating to national security and immigration and executive action under those laws provide the most obvious recent examples. Recent international history and domestic concerns about the untrammelled authority of the political branches of government to infringe upon the rights and freedoms of individuals has led to the translation of some international instruments into domestic statute. In Victoria, many of the provisions of the *International Covenant on Civil and Political Rights* have been incorporated in the *Charter of Human Rights and Responsibilities Act 2006*, similarly, in the *Human Rights Act 2004* in the ACT. When domestic human rights laws are enacted, it is necessary to include some modifying provision to allow a balance between the rights enacted and other rights and interests, including the interests of the wider community.[66] Some overseas laws provide that prescribed human rights are not to be taken to be incompatible with other laws which infringe those rights only to an extent demonstrably justified in a free and democratic society.[67] That test which is in substance reproduced by the Victorian Act[68] is, by our constitutional standards, political.

In Canada as in the United States, the courts are required to make that political decision in order to apply constitutionally entrenched rights in determining the legal validity of statutes and executive action. That has resulted in a relocation of political power from the legislature and the executive to the judiciary. In the United Kingdom, the European Convention on Human Rights has been substantially incorporated into domestic law[69] and the courts have been directed to interpret statutes so as to vindicate the Convention rights even though the statute would be incompatible with Convention rights if it were interpreted by the ordinary legal rules.[70] To repose these kinds of political power in an Australian court would run counter to our constitutional history. The American experience shows that the reposing of ultimate responsibility in the judiciary for invalidating legislative and executive action to give effect to human rights raises a popular expectation that many controversial political issues are to be solved by judges, not by the democratically elected branches of government. Thus the judiciary is itself politicised.

The legislatures of Victoria and the Australian Capital Territory[71] have taken a more conservative approach, respectful of the separation of judicial power, which is characteristic of our Constitutional system. The courts have been directed to interpret statutes compatibly with statutorily defined human rights but only so far as it is possible to do so *consistently with the statutory purpose.*[72] The court's function is to give effect to the legislature's purpose in accordance with the legislature's directions, including the direction to give the statutory language, if possible, a meaning consistent with prescribed human rights. Under these statutes, the validity of a law is not affected by any incompatibility with human rights. If there is incompatibility, the court's jurisdiction is limited to the making of a declaration of inconsistency, leaving remedial action, if any, to be taken by the legislature. The courts will from time to time have to decide the political question whether a law infringes a human right 'only to such reasonable limit as can be demonstrably justified in a free and democratic society' but they will not be empowered to strike down a law if the law is found to exceed that limit. That will be for the legislature to consider.

Of course, if the court, construing a provision in accordance with the legislature's directions, concludes that an executive action is in disconformity with statutory power construed as the Charter directs, the court will review the executive action and grant the appropriate remedy.

But jurisdiction to review executive action for disconformity with statutory power is a commonplace in our constitutional arrangements, applying the rule of law to government as well as to the governed.[73]

In Victoria and the ACT, the legislative code of human rights awaits judicial interpretation, but the innovative mechanism for giving effect to the listed human rights is most significant. The primary responsibility for giving human rights their intended operation rests not with the courts but with the Parliament. The Victorian Act requires that, before any second reading speech on a Bill introduced into the Parliament, a statement of compatibility must be laid before the House, showing either the Bill's compatibility or incompatibility with the defined human rights.[74] A Parliamentary Committee must report on compatibility,[75] and the Parliament may include a declaration of override in an Act, declaring that the Act or a provision of the Act is effective despite any incompatibility.[76] Although the courts are directed to interpret a statute compatibly with human rights so far as it is possible to do so consistently with the purpose of the statute,[77] the purpose is the Parliament's purpose ascertained in accordance with the ordinary rules of interpretation.[78] Public authorities are directed to act compatibly with the Charter rights, subject to certain exceptions.[79] The significance of a wide definition of 'public authority' is pointed out in a valuable paper by the Solicitor General, Ms Pamela Tate.[80] The term extends to statutory bodies, local councils, Victoria police and '[i]mportantly, [it] extends to those bodies that discharge functions of a public nature' thus sweeping in private corporations to which government might contract out public functions such as the control and management of prisons.

Although many of the rights listed in the Charter are already familiar to, and would in any event have found a measure of protection in, the common law, their enactment might affect the interpretation of ambiguous terms[81] and, one might surmise, will heighten judicial sensitivity to circumstances in which human rights are possibly at risk. But, having interpreted a statute or statutory instrument as the Charter directs, a court which finds the provision to be incompatible with a Charter right has no jurisdiction to affect the operation of the provision. The court is limited to the making of a declaration of inconsistency which, in turn, enlivens a statutory obligation on the part of the responsible Minister to prepare and lay before the Parliament a written response.[82] The political branches of government may repeal, amend or leave standing the incompatible provision. Political responsibility remains with the political branches. The traditional separation of powers is unaffected.

The courts have an important role in the interpretation of the Charter rights.

The construction which a Victorian court places on a statutory provision affecting the rights or duties in issue, whether affected by a Charter right or not, is open to review in the course of an appeal to the Court of Appeal. There may be a question whether a further appeal would lie to the High Court under s 73 of the *Constitution* against a mere declaration of inconsistency if the declaration does not affect the interests involved in the litigation. The Solicitor General gives an affirmative answer to this question, noting that such a declaration is made only in litigation which determines the issues between parties. Ms Tate relies inter alia on the judgment of the High Court in *Mellifont* v *Attorney General (Queensland).*[83] In that case, the High Court entertained an appeal from a Court of Criminal Appeal deciding a point of law on an Attorney General's reference after acquittal.

There will be a degree of forensic fascination with the jurisprudence, which emerges under the Charter. But it may not be premature to make two suggestions. First, as the Victorian model does no violence to the traditional separation of political and judicial powers, adoption of the model by the Commonwealth would work no change to the current distribution of federal powers. The genius of the Charter is the solution of the problem which beset earlier models, namely, the risks of transferring political powers to the judiciary. The Charter has brought the judiciary into constructive dialogue with the Parliament, but that is no more than utilising the interpretative skills of the courts to promote good government in the interests of the community. However, if a judicial declaration of incompatibility had no effect on a litigant's rights or liabilities, there would be a question whether such a declaration can be made in the exercise of federal jurisdiction.[84] An appeal to the High Court from Victoria or the ACT under s 73 may indicate an answer to this question.

Second, a statutory enactment of human rights in the Victorian model would surely inhibit legislative or executive infringement of those rights – and thus enhance the quality of good government; it would also heighten judicial sensitivity to possible infringements and sharpen judicial ability to construe provisions so as to avoid infringements. If, for example, a Commonwealth statute in terms similar to the Victorian Charter had been in force in 2004 when *Al-Kateb*[85] came before the High Court, the Court may not have held that a stateless migrant who could not be deported in the foreseeable future was liable to be held in executive detention for an indefinite and unlimited period. The relevant provision[86] prescribed detention of the migrant until deportation or the grant of a visa; it did not contemplate the situation of refusal of a visa and practical impossibility of deportation. Had the Court been directed to give effect, if possible, to the right to liberty and freedom from arbitrary detention,[87] a majority[88] may have construed 'detention' as meaning detention limited to the time needed and taken for the processing of Mr Al-Kateb's visa application and ascertaining the prospects of deportation.[89]

By mandating legislative machinery to ensure that individual human rights are not improvidently overridden in the course of legislating for the community at large, and by requiring the courts to understand that the Parliament has no such intention unless the contrary is expressed, the Charter of Human Rights and Responsibilities Act is a valuable instrument of good government. It leaves the constitutional distribution of powers intact, allowing the political branches of government to do what is needed to secure the common good while protecting human rights and fundamental freedoms except to the extent that 'can be demonstrably justified in a free and democratic society based on human dignity, equality and freedom'. These are lofty ideals. It will be the satisfying privilege of both the political and the judicial branches of government to implement the Act's provisions and to make those ideals a reality.

---

1. This address was first published in the *Australian Law Librarian*, see Sir Gerard Brennan, 'The *Constitution*, good government and human rights' (2008) 16 (2) *Australian Law Librarian* 83.
2. John Locke, Second Treatise of Government (1690), Chap XVIII 'Of Tyranny', sec. 202, Cambridge University Press, 1988, quoted by Lord Bingham.
3. See *Australian Communist Party* v *The Commonwealth* (1951) 83 CLR 1, 193.
4. Ibid 193.
5. Albert Venn Dicey, *Introduction to the study of the law of the Constitution* (Macmillan, 10th ed, 1959), 202 – 203.
6. See *A* v *Hayden* (1984) 156 CLR 532; *Ridgeway* v *The Queen* (1995) 184 CLR 19.
7. See *Attorney-General* v *Guardian Newspapers [No 2]* [1990] 1 AC 109, 283, cited by the High Court in *Lange v Australian Broadcasting Commission* (1997) 189 CLR 520, 564.
8. Thus, in *Entick v Carrington (*1765) 19 St Tr 1029, 1066, Lord Campbell LCJ declared that – 'By the laws of England, every invasion of private property, be it ever so minute, is a trespass. No man can set his foot upon my ground without my licence, but he is liable to an action, though the damage be nothing ... If he admits the fact, he is bound to shew by way of justification, that some positive law has empowered or excused him.' and see *Plenty* v *Dillon* (1991) 171 CLR 635.
9. 5 US (1 Cranch) 137, 177 (1803).
10. See *Ebner* v *Official Trustee in Bankruptcy* (2000) 205 CLR 337, 344-345.
11. See *A* v *Secretary of State for the Home Department* [2005] 2 AC 68, [2004] UKHL 56, para 42.
12. See *Australian Communist Party* v *The Commonwealth* (1951) 83 CLR 1.
13. George Winterton, 'The Significance of the Communist Party Case' (1992) 18 (3) *Melbourne University Law Review* 630, 658.
14. (1992) 176 CLR 239, 252 (Deane, Dawson, Toohey & Gaudron JJ).

15. See *Bropho* v *Western Australia* (1990) 171 CLR 1, 17- 18 for a general statement of the rule.
16. Ibid 17,18; See also *Corporate Affairs Commission (NSW)* v *Yuill* (1991) 172 CLR 319, 322, 338 and cases there cited, 346-347. As to property rights see *American Dairy Queen (Q) Pty Ltd* v *Blue Rio Pty Ltd* (1981) 147 CLR 677, 682-683. As to the right to carry on business, see the *Commonwealth* v *Progress Advertising & Press Agency Co Pty Ltd* (1910) 10 CLR 457, 464.
17. As to procedural fairness, see *Annetts v McCann* (1990) 170 CLR 596, 598 and cases there cited; *Ainsworth v Criminal Justice Commission* (1992) 175 CLR 564, 575-576.
18. As to the privilege against self-incrimination, see *Hammond* v *The Commonwealth* (1982) 152 CLR 188, 197-198, 200; *Sorby* v *Commonwealth* (1983) 152 CLR 281, 289-290, 294-295, 309, 311; *Hamilton* v *Oades* (1989) 166 CLR 486, 495, 500-501. As to the right to trial by jury see *Tassell* v *Hayes* (1987) 163 CLR 34, 41, 50. As to the right to personal liberty see *Re Bolton; Ex parte Beane* (1987) 162 CLR 514, 523. As to legal professional privilege see *Baker* v *Campbell* (1983) 153 CLR 52, 96-97, 104, 116-117, 123; *Corporate Affairs Commission (NSW)* v *Yuill* (1991) 172 CLR 319, 322, 331, 338, 348-349.
19. See *Clancy* v *Butchers' Shop Employees Union* (1904) 1 CLR 181, 196-197, 204; *Hockey* v *Yelland* (1984) 157 CLR 124, 130, 142; *Bropho* v *Western Australia* (1990) 171 CLR 1, 17; *Public Service Association (SA)* v *Federated Clerks' Union of Australia (SA) Branch* (1991) 173 CLR 132, 160.
20. See s 85 of the *Constitution Act 1975* (Vic) which confers general jurisdiction on the Supreme Court of the State, but some exceptions have been legislated, eg, *Australian Crime Commission (State Provisions) Act 2003* (Vic), ss 36, 49, 56, 64.
21. See *Plaintiff S157/2002* v *Commonwealth of Australia* (2003) 211 CLR 476, 513-514; [2003] HCA 2 and see *Re Minister for Immigration and Multicultural Affairs; Ex parte Applicant S20/2002* [2003] HCA 30; 77 ALJR 1165.
22. See *Constitution Alteration (Rights and Freedoms) Bill* 1988 (Cth).
23. See *Final Report of the Constitutional Commission, Summary Volume*, (Australian Government Publishing Service, 1988).
24. Ibid 9.
25. Ibid 10-11.
26. Ibid 64-66.
27. Ibid 47-48.
28. Ibid 29.
29. See *South Australia* v *The Commonwealth* (1942) 65 CLR 373.
30. See *Victoria* v *The Commonwealth* (1957) 99 CLR 575.
31. (1997) 189 CLR 465.
32. Cited in *Amalgamated Society of Engineers v Adelaide Steamship Co Ltd (Engineers' Case)* (1920) 28 CLR 129, 147.
33. Lord Hailsham, *Elective Dictatorship*, The Richard Dimbleby Lecture (British Broadcasting Corporation, 1976) 5.
34. Ibid.
35. See Thomas Pitt Taswell-Langmead, *English Constitutional History* (Stevens and Haines, 4th ed, 1890), 645. The 4th edition was revised by CHE Carmichael.
36. Sir William Holdsworth, *History of English Law*, Volume VI (Methuen, 1924), 253-254.
37. Section 83.

38. Section 56.
39. Section 81.
40. (2005) 224 CLR 494.
41. Gummow, Hayne, Callinan and Heydon JJ.
42. (2005) 224 CLR 494, 577.
43. See Geoffrey Lindell, 'The Combet Case and the Appropriation of Tax-payers' Funds for Political Advertising - An Erosion of Fundamental Principles?' (2007) 55(3) *The Australian Journal of Public Administration* 307.
44. In *New South Wales* v *The Commonwealth; The Incorporation Case* (1990) 169 CLR 482.
45. See *Li Chia Hsing* v *Rankin* (1978) 141 CLR 182.
46. See *Spratt* v *Hermes* (1965) 114 CLR 126, 244 (Barwick CJ); and see the *Final Report of the Constitutional Commission, Summary Volume*, (Australian Government Printing Service, (1988) AGPS 35 hereinafter referred to as *Constitutional Commission Summary*.
47. See *Kingswell* v *The Queen* (1985) 159 CLR 264.
48. See *Re Wakim, Ex P McNally* (1999) 198 CLR 511.
49. See *Fencott* v *Muller* (1983) 152 CLR 570.
50. See *Constitutional Commission Summary*, 66 (corporations), 34-35 (trial by jury), 25 (cross-vesting).
51. The Commission's list of repealable provisions 'include ss 26, 41, 52(ii.), 69, 84, 85, 86, 87, 89, 93, 95, 97 and the second paragraph of s 83, the second paragraph of s 90, the second paragraph of s 92 and the introductory words of s 96. Expended words should also be removed from other sections including ss 3, 15, and 66'.
52. See *Constitutional Commission Summary*, 54-56.
53. See *Constitutional Commission Summary,* 78.
54. Helen Irving, 'Australia's Constitutional Identity: a Conundrum for the 21st century?' (2001) Barton Lecture, ABC Radio National, 15 April 2001, Transcript, 5.
55. See *Two Treatises of Government,* 1690 (Second Essay II, 6). Writing shortly after the Glorious Revolution of 1688, he rejected absolute monarchy as 'inconsistent with civil society' and insisted that the authority of civil society is derived from the agreement of all members to submit to society's laws to which even the monarch is subject (*Second Essay II*, 90, 94). So we might conclude that the need for both the constitution and the general law to respect fundamental human rights was part of British political thinking by the beginning of the 18th century.
56. Jean-Jacques Rousseau, *The Social Contract*, (1762).
57. Sir William Holdsworth, *History of English Law*, Volume VI (Methuen, 1924), 14.
58. Ibid 19, 22, 23.
59. Theodore Plucknett, *A Concise History of the Common Law* (Stevens, 3rd ed, 1940), 71.
60. Sir Anthony Mason, 'A Bill of Rights for Australia' (1989) 5 *Australian Bar Review* 79, 79-80.
61. Articles 33, 34, 46.
62. See, inter alia, Articles 15, 18.
63. For example, *Hatton and Others* v. *United Kingdom* [Grand Chamber], Application no. 36022/97, 8 July 2003; *Aksoy* v *Turkey,* Application no. 21987/93,18 December 1996.
64. See *Cole* v *Whitfield* (1988) 165 CLR 365.

65. See *Australian Capital Television Pty Ltd* v *Commonwealth* (1992) 177 CLR 106, 135-136; see also Dawson J, 182.
66. David Kretzmer, 'Basic Laws as a surrogate Bill of Rights' in Philip Alston (ed) *Promoting Human Rights through Bill of Rights* (Oxford University Press, 1999), 75,82.
67. See, for example, *Canadian Charter of Rights and Freedoms*, s. l, *Bill of Rights Act 1990 (*NZ), s 5 and *Moonen* v *Film and Literature Board of Review* [2000] 2 NZLR 9, [1999] NZCA 329, [18].
68. See *Charter of Human Rights and Responsibilities Act 2006 (*Vic) s 7(2).
69. [7]By the *Human Rights Act 1998* (UK).
70. See *Ghaidan* v *Godin-Mendoza* [2004] 2 AC 557; [2004] UKHL 30.
71. See *Human Rights Act 2004* (ACT).
72. See *Charter of Human Rights and Responsibilities Act 2006* (Vic), s 32(1); *Human Rights Act 2004* (ACT), s 30.
73. See *Church of Scientology* v *Woodward* (1982) 154 CLR 25; *Attorney General (NSW)* v *Quin* (1990) 170 CLR 1, 35-36.
74. Section 28.
75. Section 30.
76. Section 31
77. Section 32.
78. See *Interpretation of Legislation Act 1984* (Vic) s 35 (b).
79. Section 38.
80. Pamela Tate, 'Protecting Human Rights in a Federation' (2007), 33(2) *Monash University Law Review* 220..
81. As the Solicitor-General illustrated by reference to *Hopkinson* v *Police* [2004] 3 NZLR 704.
82. See *The Charter of Human Rights and Responsibilities Act 2006* (Vic) s 37.
83. (1991) 173 CLR 289.
84. See *In re Judiciary and Navigation Acts* (1921) 29 CLR 257.
85. (2004) 219 CLR 562.
86. See *Migration Act 1958* (Cth), s 196.
87. See *Charter of Human Rights and Responsibilities Act 2006* (Vic).
88. See the reference by Justice McHugh to the absence of a Bill of Rights in his reference to *Al Kateb* in 'The Need for Agitators – the Risk of Stagnation' in a speech at Sydney University Law Society Public Forum, Sydney, 12 October 2005 reported at <http://www.hcourt.gov.au/speeches/mchughj/ mchughj12octO5.pdf>, viewed 29 July 2008.
89. Cf *Minister for Immigration and Multicultural and Indigenous Affairs* v *Al Masri* (2003) 126 FCR 54.

Chapter 2

The Legal Profession

2.1 Ministers of the Third Branch of Government

Editor's note

Brennan was appointed a Justice of the High Court of Australia in February 1981. This was his address to a luncheon organized by the Young Lawyers' Section of the Law Society of New South Wales on 29 March 1982.

I thank you for your invitation to join you for lunch today, and to speak to you for a short time before you return to your practices. No doubt those practices comprehend a variety of legal work – criminal and civil, litigious and non-litigious corporate and non-corporate, large cases and small. But through all kinds of professional legal work there is a common thread – a thread which distinguishes legal tapestries from those of other professions and occupations. It is the thread which connects what is done with the orders which a court might make if the work should be put to the test of litigation. A lawyer's work is always done with his eye cocked over his shoulder, so to speak, to see how the Court would respond to what he is doing. I should make it clear that I am not speaking about those other kinds of work in which practitioners may engage, however time-consuming or interesting or lucrative those other kinds of work may be, which do not take the court's response as the touchstone of efficacy and which is not professional work in the sense in which I have used that term.

In their professional work, lawyers – both judges and practitioners – are ministers of the third branch of government: the judicial branch. We are all of us committed to the work of the only non-political branch of government, professionally unconcerned with the ebb and flow of political fortune, or with the policies which a government elects to pursue. That is not to decry the importance of the political arts, nor to deny the distinct and essential functions of the legislative and executive branches of government. Nor is it to deprecate the frequent and useful contributions which have been made by lawyers to politics or the broadening of their own experience thereby.

It is simply to observe that professional activity is unaffected by political controversy, and that the principles and practices with which we are professionally familiar are not amenable to variation or suspension according to political will until the will finds expression in a positive law. You may think I paint a fairly drab picture of a lawyer, with never a challenge to take up, and with only the most stylised battles to fight. Nothing could be further from the truth; but it is as well to ensure that we do not take up challenges or try to fight battles that are not our affair. We are the ministers of what has been called 'the weakest branch of the three departments of power'. In 1788 Alexander Hamilton so described the judicial branch. He was writing in 'The Federalist' (No78), contributing to the debate among the erstwhile colonists of America with respect to a draft constitution. He also held the judiciary to be the least dangerous branch:

> Whoever attentively considers the different departments of power must perceive, that, in a government in which they are separated from each other, the judiciary, from the nature of its functions, will always be the least dangerous to the political rights of the Constitution; because it will be least in a capacity to annoy or injure them. The Executive not only dispenses the honors, but holds the sword of the community. The legislature not only commands the purse, but prescribes the rules by which the duties and rights of every citizen are to be regulated. The judiciary, on the contrary, has no influence over either sword or the purse; no direction either of the strength or of the wealth of the society; and can take no active resolution whatever. It may truly be said to have neither FORCE nor WILL, but merely judgment; and must ultimately depend upon the aid of the executive arm even for the efficacy of its judgments.

The division of powers might be too absolutely stated, but the thrust of Hamilton's observation is right. The judicial branch is concerned with the legal principles and concepts which govern the relationships of people and institutions. The judicial branch gives expression to and moulds its judgments according to principles and concepts which are powerful to inform our relationships one with another and to govern our institutions; but those notions are powerful precisely because they are enforced by little other than their intrinsic validity and utility.

It is a rarity for a judgment not to be accepted as binding by its own force; seldom is acceptance imposed upon the unwilling (as distinct from the unable) by force of execution. And when the reasons for judgment contain a new element – and the profusion of law reports suggests that the softwood forests may be hard put to keep up with judicial innovation – the practitioners, cocking their eyes to perceive the curial response, put the principle into practice.

As a profession, we are concerned with ideas and the words in which they are expressed. We are concerned with ideas, not with force; with principles, not with the exercise of political will. And a reference to history will show that the most powerful of influences are organized ideas. So in the long run, I should not hold the judicial branch of government to be the weakest; it furnishes the bonds of an ordered society, marking the boundaries between freedom and control, limiting the power which might be exercised by individuals or groups, defining the modes of acquisition use and disposition of property and defining the conduct which is not acceptable to society at large or to particular members of it. All this is obvious. But its implication is worth stating. The judicial branch of government – and I include all of its professional ministers – performs two main functions.

First, it gives effect to, and sometimes expresses, the basic norms of society. For the most part, these basic norms do not find expression in positive law. They are drawn from the values which a society commonly respects – perhaps intuitively respects. Notions of justice, dignity, fair dealing, respect for others, mercy – these are notions which are not often found in the statute books, though they affect statutory interpretation. They affect the finding of facts, and often they are translated into principles of law.

What underlies the rules of natural justice, or negligence, nuisance or breach of trust or contract but values which are drawn from the ethos of society? And when we construe statutes to avoid absurdity, what gives us an understanding of the absurd?

The greatest efforts of the codifiers, of the positive lawyers, require to be supplemented by – perhaps mellowed by – the values of the society which the law is to serve. It is the function of the judicial branch of government to give effect, subject to the overriding will of the legislature, to the values of our civilization.

Recently Lord Hailsham, the Lord Chancellor, wrote a stimulating article which he called 'Reflections on a Remark by Cicero'.[1] He happened upon Cicero's remark: 'We have a natural propensity to love our fellow men, and that after all is the foundation of all law.'

And the Lord Chancellor asks whether the remark sheds a new light on the nature of law. Perhaps it does. At least it emphasizes the role of law as a civilizing discipline. And it is the function of the weakest branch of government to give effect to civilized values when conflict breaks out.

The second main function that the judicial branch of government performs is to remove the sense of injustice, which strikes at every man from time to time, and which might destroy him if he could find no avenue of relief.

To prevent the sense of injustice arising, the day-to-day work of advising, drafting, settling – the machinery of our system of social organization – takes place. When the sense of injustice reasonably arises and it is of grave proportions, some avenue of relief must be provided. Litigation is not, of course, the only method of dispute settlement; indeed, sometimes it may promote a conflict which is amenable to settlement in a less dramatic way.

But litigation is one of the essential weapons in the armoury of an ordered society. The search for adequate and efficient machinery to remove a reasonable sense of injustice when it is of grave proportions demands a continuing professional commitment to appropriate law reform programmes and legal aid schemes.

To perform these functions of the judicial branch, its ministers require three qualities: independence, competence and a sense of humour.

Independence is the quality most expected by the community of the legal profession. It is essential to impartiality which Lord Devlin has called the supreme judicial virtue. As his Lordship said, 'The Judge who does not appear impartial is as useless to the process as an umpire who allows the trial by battle to be fouled or an augurer who tampers with the entrails.'[2]

Last year Lord Denning, delivering the BBC Dimbleby Lecture, spoke on 'The Misuse of Power' and observed that the judges 'must be free from any influence by those who wield power. Otherwise, they cannot be trusted to decide whether or not the power is being abused or misused.'[3]

Judicial independence was the great battle of Chief Justice Coke. It was buttressed by the *Act of Settlement* (UK) in 1700. The battle for judicial independence has been won, though the prize must be jealously watched.

Professional independence is under continuous siege and is often beset by subtle and undermining influences. Yet the community's expectation of the profession, and the condition upon which it is respected, is that it shall be entirely and fiercely independent. The paradigm of independence in the professional sphere is counsel for the accused in a criminal case. Standing against the power of the State, accepting instructions only within defined limits from the accused, occupying a pivotal role in the trial, he discharges heavy responsibilities in consultation with those instructing him. In the community's mind, the Rumpoles of this world are the principal justification for an independent legal profession. Absent the role of the profession as those who hold the ground of legal rights between the various concentrations of power and those who lack it, and the *raison d'etre* of an independent legal profession disappears.

Independence in the day-to-day work of the profession is sometimes difficult to achieve. A client may expect that the payment of the fee entitles him to use of the lawyer's skills according to the client's demands without regard to the duty which the lawyer owes to the court and the opponent; or a show of independence – giving advice which the client does not wish to hear – may alienate the client. But any substantial experience in the profession shows that the advantages of too zealous a commitment to the client or cause are outweighed by the disadvantages of lost independence. I need not pause to dwell on that.

The second quality which a minister of the judicial branch requires is sheer professional competence. The consequences of incompetence are all too clear in the memories of most of us, and they are particularly vivid if the remembered incompetence was our own.

By professional competence I do not mean merely a knowledge of legal rubrics. I mean a knowledge of why the law is as it is, and what object it serves. An opinion, soundly formed, that a rule does not really fit the exigencies of a particular case is the trigger for developing the law, moulding it according to the needs of contemporary society, expanding or resecting its growth so that the law reflects the current consensus of the community.

I do not mean that the judicial branch should legislate to achieve some radical departure from established principle. Lord Devlin has warned that judges should not be unbridled legislators, especially in a time of change. 'For change, in the measure of its beneficence to the many, causes hardship and displacement to the few. It is essential to the stability of society that those whom change hurts should be able to count on even handed justice calmly dispensed, not driven forward by the agents of change.'[4]

Yet this is no plea for legal atrophy. The values which underlie legal principle may need restatement, and the organic growth of legal principle inevitably follows from the task of doing justice according to law in the myriad permutations of human relationships.

To strike the balance between stability and organic development, professional competence is needed in courts and in the extra curial work of counsel and solicitors.

Finally, we need a sense of humour. It helps us to serve the community and our clients; and it reminds us that, however grave and important be the work in hand, it is part of the human experience which we share with others. And thus, our work is put in perspective, and we are likely to do better in performing the two main functions of the judicial branch.

---

1. Lord Hailsham, 'Reflections on a remark by Cicero' (1981) 56 *Encounter*, Congress for Cultural Freedom, February 1981, 42-49.
2. Lord Devlin, 'Judges and Lawmakers' (1976) 39 (1) *Modern Law Review* 1, 4.
3. Lord Denning, *Misuse of Power: The 1980 Richard Dimbleby Lecture,* British Broadcasting Corporation reprinted as ' Misuse of Power ' (1981) 55 *Australian Law Journal* 720, 720.
4. Lord Devlin, 'Judges and Lawmakers' (n 2) 9.

2.2 The Bar as Ministers of Justice

Editor's note

This was the closing lecture delivered at the Victorian Bar Practice Course on 1 November 1984.

This is the closing lecture of a course in which you have given consideration to the rules of ethics and etiquette of the Bar, the techniques of advocacy and the traditional relationships of a barrister with lay and solicitor clients and with the judiciary. These rules, techniques and relationships govern the members of the Bar in order that they may work effectively, compete fairly and conduct their professional activities in a civilised manner. They have a wider purpose. They enhance the administration of justice according to law, which is the work of the judicial branch of government to which you and I belong. Holdsworth states one of its chief functions: 'The judges hold an office to which is annexed the function of guarding the supremacy of the law. It is because they are the holders of an office to which the guardianship of this fundamental constitutional principle is entrusted, that the judiciary forms one of the three great divisions into which the power of the State is divided.'[1]

Tonight, I should like to speak to you about the judicial branch of government, and your function as ministers of that branch. We work in the only non-political branch, professionally unconcerned with the ebb and flow of political fortune, or with the policies which a government elects to pursue. That is not to claim a remote dignity above the legislature and the executive, nor is it to deprecate the frequent and useful contributions which lawyers make to politics or the broadening which political experience gives them. It is simply to observe that professional activity in the judicial branch is unaffected by political controversy, and that there are many issues of great importance that are not our affair.

What is our affair is the supremacy of the law. Law, with all its complexities and minutiae, with all its nice distinctions and categories, is what displaces the tyranny of untrammelled power. Sometimes we hear the observation that there are too many laws, and that may be true. But much worse would it be if there were too few laws – too few to prevent excesses of power and the subjection of one man to discretionary treatment at the hands of another. The supremacy of the law is the means by which we protect individual rights against infringements by the political branches of government or by the more powerful persons, corporate or natural, in society.

Sometimes the symbolic figure of Justice is shown brandishing a sword. I prefer the symbol of the shield. As you enter through the doors of No 1 Court in the High Court, you will see that Sir Garfield Barwick had that symbol emblazoned upon them. It is the symbol of law as a defence – a defence alike to the weak and the powerful, to the poor and the rich, to minorities and majorities, to the subject and the government. As the powerful, the rich, the majorities and the government might do tolerably well without the law's protection and as they sometimes find the law an impediment to action, the law is often seen to be standing between them and the weak, the poor, the minorities, or the individual. And so the law does stand as a defence of their interests, but it is effective in doing so only because the third branch of government asserts even-handedly the supremacy of the law over both. If the third branch of government were to be identified either with the powers that be or those who struggle against them, partisanship would rob it of its power.

At base, that is the reason why a barrister cannot decline a brief that offers a fair fee in a jurisdiction in which he/she ordinarily practises. Professionally it is immaterial that the barrister has no sympathy with the cause to be advocated. If access to the court and the even-handed application of the law were impeded by the political or social predilections of counsel, the judicial branch of government would be politicised and powerless. The rule is fundamental to the adversary system, and the qualifications on its operation – fair fee and jurisdiction – must be invoked with awareness of the cardinal importance of access to the courts.

The judicial branch, being singularly non-political must be and be seen to be independent of the other branches of government. There are, of course, many points of contact between them – the executive provides the facilities for the administration of justice, it appoints the judges and court staff, it enforces judgments in the criminal jurisdiction and is under the ultimate duty of enforcing judgments in the civil jurisdiction; the Parliament enacts law affecting the administration of justice, votes supply for the provision of court facilities, judicial and staff salaries and is empowered to remove judges in certain circumstances. Without a robust tradition of independence, sustained by professional sentiment and public insistence, you may think that the judicial branch might yield to the pressures of the political branches. How is the independence of the judicial branch sustained without which the supremacy of the law would be eroded?

To guard the supremacy of the law against powerful interests, you might think that the judicial branch needed to be vested with great power. Yet Alexander Hamilton in 1788 described the judicial branch as 'the least dangerous branch' of the three departments. He wrote in The Federalist for circulation among the erstwhile colonists of America:

> Whoever attentively considers the different departments of power must perceive, that, in a government in which they are separated from each other, the judiciary, from the nature of its functions, will always be the least dangerous to the political rights of the Constitution; because it will be least in a capacity to annoy or injure them. The Executive not only dispenses the honors, but holds the sword of the community. The legislature not only commands the purse, but prescribes the rules by which the duties and rights of every citizen are to be regulated. The judiciary, on the contrary, has no influence over either sword or the purse; no direction either of the strength or of the wealth of the society; and can take no active resolution whatever. It may truly be said to have neither FORCE nor WILL, but merely judgment; and must ultimately depend upon the aid of the executive arm even for the efficacy of its judgments. [2]

The division of powers might be too absolutely stated, but the thrust of Hamilton's observation is right.

Lacking force or will, on what does the power of the judicial branch depend? It is a paradox that its very strength lies in the fact that it has no influence over either the sword or the purse. Its strength lies chiefly in the power of public, independent, impartial and reasoned judgment to command the continuing confidence of the community. That confidence is a necessary foundation for the authority of the courts. As the supremacy of the law over both the legislative and the executive branches is entrusted to the judicial branch, it is manifest that an authority greater than the power of the purse, more irresistible than the power of the sword, is essential to a society which relies on the law to protect the interests of each group or individual. That authority, and the consequential supremacy of law, is conferred and sustained by public confidence. Given public confidence, the supremacy of the law can be guarded, the independence of the judicial branch can be insisted on, the separation of powers can be maintained and the freedom and order of society is secured. Absent public confidence, the separation of powers and the supremacy of the law would be eroded, and some excesses of power would go unchecked. Though the retention of public confidence in the judicial branch of government is imperative, the giving of that confidence is not a civic virtue which the community, or even the coordinate branches of government, are bound to practise without regard to the way in which the courts and the legal profession perform their function. Nor is public confidence obtained by proclamations by the courts and the legal profession of their own satisfaction with the way in which justice is being administered. Public confidence is painfully built by the day-to-day work of the courts, according to the standards which the community expects. I might adopt what Chief Justice Stone wrote in 1941: 'The Court ... has of late suffered from overmuch publicity. After all, its only claim to public confidence is the thoroughness and fidelity with which it does its daily task.'[3]

What is the daily task in which we are engaged? And what do we have to do to perform it with thoroughness and fidelity? Mr Justice Kitto stressed the essentially syllogistic nature of the judicial process when he said: '... the process to be followed must generally be an inquiry concerning the law as it is and the facts as they are, followed by an application of the law as determined to the facts as determined.'[4]

The applicable principles – 'the law as it is' – provide the major premise; 'the facts as they are' provide the minor premise; and judgment follows inexorably by applying 'the law as determined to the facts as determined'. In each step of this process, the rules, whether of law or practice, are calculated to ensure that public confidence is maintained. In the first two steps – the inquiry concerning the law as it is and the facts as they are – the barrister has a critical role to perform.

The first step – An inquiry concerning the law as it is

The search for a rule to be applied in resolving a particular case is not, as you have found, always a clear and simple task. Yet it is a search for the law not for a political or social policy, and for the law as it is, not the law as it ought to be. Though the syllogistic approach has been criticised as unsuited to meeting the need for practical rules to govern the resolution of diverse conflicts,[5] the real question is not whether a legal rule should be applied in the instant case but whether a rule stated in an earlier case is the relevant legal rule for the case in hand.[6]

The distinction between the law on the one hand and social and political policies on the other is fundamental. The administration of justice according to law cannot be deflected by considerations of policy, however desirable. This obvious point was reaffirmed recently by the majority judgment of the High Court in *Clunies-Ross v The Commonwealth* in these terms:

> It would be an abdication of the duty of this Court under the *Constitution* if we were to determine the important and general question of law which the demurrer has raised according to whether we personally agreed or disagreed with the political and social objectives which the Minister sought to achieve ... As a matter of constitutional duty, [the] question must be considered objectively

> and answered in this Court as a question of law and not as a matter to be determined by reference to the political or social merits of the particular case. We have so considered and determined it. [7]

Sir Ninian Stephen defined an independent judiciary by reference to its disregard of policies:

> My definition of an independent judiciary is a judiciary which dispenses justice according to law without regard to the policies and inclinations of the government of the day; such a judiciary will ... unhesitatingly accept and give full effect to whatever valid legislation may be enacted ... it is only when a government's wishes have been ... translated into valid law, and not before, that those wishes, now expressed in legal form, become of relevance to an independent judiciary; until then those wishes will be no part of the body of law which alone is the judiciary's task to administer. [8]

Of course, where the exercise of a discretionary power is challenged, it is sometimes necessary to decide whether an exercise of the power in pursuit of a particular policy is valid. That is not a decision on the merits of the policy, but on the scope of the power. The widening of the sources to which regard may be had in construing a statute[9] and the purposive approach to statutory construction[10] should not be understood, or rather misunderstood, as authorising decisions which, to adapt a phrase from the late Mr Justice Philip, tip their hat to the law and go off arm in arm with policy. The barrister whose argument is based on political or social policy has missed the point in the case: he has missed the governing legal principle, or he has mistaken the nature of a judicial discretion (if it be a case of discretion). The disregard of political and social policies which do not represent the common values of the community – an important qualification – ensures that the courts do not, and are not seen to be, the instruments of sectional interests.

The search is for law as it is, not for the law as it ought to be. Judges are not legislators. The legal rights of litigants are not to be denied because the judge thinks the law is not as it ought to be. It is not the function of the court to ignore the legal rights of litigants in order to propound what might be thought to be a better principle of law. Viscount Simonds made the point in *Midland Silicones Ltd v Scruttons Ltd*:

> For to me heterodoxy, or, as some might say, heresy, is not the more attractive because it is dignified by the name of reform. Nor will I easily be led by an undiscerning zeal for some abstract kind of justice to ignore our first duty, which is to administer justice according to law, the law which is established for us by Act of Parliament or

> the binding authority of precedent. The law is developed by the application of old principles to new circumstances. Therein lies its genius. Its reform by the abrogation of those principles is the task not of the courts of law but of Parliament.[11]

There is a difference between the development of the law to meet new circumstances and an abrogation of applicable principle. Where the line is to be drawn is often a matter of contention, but development cannot be effected in a case where an applicable and binding rule is at hand. Lord Devlin cautioned against the impermissible exercise of judicial power to achieve social change: 'For change, in the measure of its beneficence to the many, causes hardship and displacement to the few. It is essential to the stability of society that those whom change hurts should be able to count on evenhanded justice calmly dispensed, not driven forward by the agents of change.'[12]

These warnings, from judges of high authority, do not mean that the law is ossified and that there are no legitimate judicial techniques for its development; but these observations are powerful reminders that the primary function of the courts is to declare and enforce the legal rights and obligations of litigants. Public confidence in the judicial branch would not be maintained if that function were subordinated to the function of developing the law.

But, equally, public confidence would not be maintained if antique rules, intended for application in a context that has passed, were applied uncritically to any case that comes within their literal scope. Nobody nowadays would deny that the law changes and develops under the influence of judicial decisions, particularly the decisions of appellate courts. But the techniques by which old rules are refashioned and new rules emerge are well known. Distinguishing an earlier authority, reasoning by analogy, expanding an established and useful principle, confining another to the facts of the earlier case: these are well known means for judicially developing the law. None of them permits judicial legislation according to the judge's idiosyncratic notions of justice, though values – reflecting what the judge regards as the values generally held in the community or what he believes to be inherent in the legal system – often affect the choices that are made. In my respectful opinion, Lord Scarman's observations in *McLoughlin* v *O'Brian* are very nearly right if his reference to policy is a reference to common contemporary community values and not to political or social policy:

> The function of the court is to decide the case before it, even though the decision may require the extension or adaptation of a principle or in some cases the creation of new law to meet the justice of the case. But, whatever the court decides to do, it starts from a baseline of

> existing principle and seeks a solution consistent with or analogous to a principle or principles already recognised.
>
> The distinguishing feature of the common law is this judicial development and formation of principle. Policy considerations will have to be weighed: but the objective of the judges is the formulation of principle. And, if principle inexorably requires a decision which entails a degree of policy risk, the court's function is to adjudicate according to principle, leaving policy curtailment to the judgment of Parliament. Here lies the true role of the two law-making institutions in our constitution. By concentrating on principle the judges can keep the common law alive, flexible and consistent, and can keep the legal system clear of policy problems which neither they, nor the forensic process which it is their duty to operate, are equipped to resolve. If principle leads to results which are thought to be socially unacceptable, Parliament can legislate to draw a line or map out a new path.[13]

Legal research and advocacy by the Bar of the future is likely to be more sophisticated than it was in earlier times when society was more settled, when change was less rapid. This is not because the courts wish to assume a pace-setting role in effecting social change. The reason is that society is changing with such rapidity that earlier decisions reached in the context of a simpler society oftentimes do not provide the coercive guidance of precedent for contemporary cases, and the relationships and conflicts of interest and power that are the subjects of contemporary litigation oftentimes call for refashioned rules to govern them. If legal reasoning were merely deductive and the major premise of the judicial syllogism were at hand in every case, the system could serve only a static society in which no new rights, interests or relationships ever emerged. Such a society would be lifeless. Such a system is useless to our society. Under our system, practitioners must be capable of ascertaining what is meant by the law 'as it is' in a dynamic society.

The tension between literal application of old rules and the judicial development of rules is healthy but the balance is a delicate one. If the balance is rightly struck, the judicial branch will not encroach on the function of the legislature but the principles which grew out of the common values of earlier times will be refashioned to reflect the common values of today. It should not be surprising that minds differ on the striking of the balance in many cases, and the function of the barrister in finely balanced cases is of particular importance. Barristers' research cannot be limited to discovery of a formula with words that can be made to cover the case in hand; they are engaged in a search for principle that can be tested by contemporary experience. Ideas, not words, are at the heart of the judicial process, though the accuracy and elegance with which ideas are expressed affect their power and operation.[14] For this reason – that is, our concern with ideas rather than the words used to express them – it would be a mistake to think that the uncreative memories of the computer age will suffice to keep the law in good repair or the judicial branch in high regards.

In renewing the law and keeping the balance right, the barrister has an important role to play. The barrister has, as you know, a duty to bring to the court's attention statutory provisions and antecedent authority which bear upon the case in hand whether or not they favour the client's cause. If this rule were abrogated, the judicial process would be impaired. The risk that cases would be decided in disconformity with law would be enhanced. If the application of law were adventitious or slipshod, confidence in the administration of justice would be impaired. Lord Birkenhead LC, speaking for the House of Lords said: '... the withholding from their Lordships of any authority which might throw light upon the matters under debate was really to obtain a decision from their Lordships in the absence of the material and information which a properly informed decision required; it was, in effect, to convert this House into a debating assembly upon legal matters, and to obtain a decision founded upon imperfect knowledge. The extreme impropriety of such a course could not be made too plain.'[15]

Counsel cannot be satisfied in every case with arguments that proceed no further than the established authorities. If the literal application of a precedent would yield an unjust decision, it may be that the precedent is no longer applicable or no longer applicable without qualification. It is for counsel to propose the qualification. One cannot give an *a priori* definition of what is or is not unjust – notions of justice cannot be expressed exhaustively – yet the appearance of injustice is the instigator of legal development. It is the warning light that some new factor has entered and may require either the distinction of existing precedents or their development to do justice to the case in hand. In appropriate cases, it is necessary for counsel to consider the judicial techniques of distinguishing precedents or fashioning new rules. This is no narrow function. Mr Justice Cardozo pointed to the wide variety of factors which, when the occasion for judicial development of the law is at hand, may influence the judges: 'My analysis of the judicial process comes then to this, and little more: logic, and history, and custom, and utility, and the accepted standards of right conduct, are the forces which singly or in combination shape the progress of the law. Which of these forces shall dominate in any case, must depend largely upon the comparative importance or value of the social interests that will be thereby promoted or impaired.'[16]

However, the judicial development of the law is not free wheeling. Its starting point is existing principle and the organic development of new rules requires that they be fashioned consistently with other rules of the legal system. The technique of development is important, for orderly development of legal principle is essential to the preservation of public confidence. Sir Owen Dixon has noted that in the 'classical' period of English law:

> Principles were not only used, they were developed. There was a steady, if intuitive, attempt to develop the law as a science. But this was done not by an abandonment of the high technique and strict logic of the law. It was done by an apt and felicitous use of that very technique and, under the name of reasoning, of that strict logic which it seems fashionable now to expel from the system.[17]

A leap of principle which rests only upon judicial assertion would give grounds for suspecting an encroachment by the judiciary upon the territory of the legislature. Moreover, it would undermine the ability of the judge to perform his function: 'His authority and his immunity depend upon the assumption that he speaks with the mouth of others: the momentum of his utterances must be greater than any which his personal reputation and character can command, if it is to do the work assigned to it – if it is to stand against the passionate resentments arising out of the interests he must frustrate.'[18]

I suspect that counsel have not yet appreciated their creative and difficult role in the ascertainment of the law as it is in the present day, yet recent decisions have manifested the need for structured and sophisticated research and provide examples of judicial developments in the law. Omitting reference to cases in fields of public law, cases such as *O'Dea v Allstates Leasing (WA) Pty Ltd*;[19] *Legione v Hateley*[20] and *Commercial Bank of Australia v Amadio*[21] come to mind. Without the assistance of counsel, the judges will be less adequately equipped than they ought to be in keeping the balance right in developing the law.

The second step – The facts as they are

The curial method of dispute resolution is the adversary process. Other methods, adopted by tribunals, boards and commissions are less formal, more inquisitorial, often cheaper. Why do we retain the adversary system? A powerful reason for doing so is that it is the system which best commands public confidence in the finding of disputed facts. The role of the judge is essentially passive. He decides between the parties on the evidence that they place before him. He can and must be impartial. He does not undertake independent inquiries or pursue his own hypotheses: either of those courses would predispose, or appear to predispose, the court to find the facts consistently with its own discoveries of hypotheses. The judge sits above the arena lest his vision be clouded by the dust of conflict[22] and leaves the parties to produce the evidence on which the facts are to be found.[23] Not only is the judge kept out of the arena of conflict to give him the appearance of an impartial arbiter, he must be impartial in fact; and there can be no reasonable apprehension to the contrary: 'The view that a judge shall not sit to hear a case if in all the circumstances the parties or the public might reasonably suspect that he was not unprejudiced and impartial, and that if a judge does sit in those circumstances, prohibition will lie, is not only supported by the balance of authority as it now stands but is correct in principle.'[24]

So rigid is the view of the judicial branch on this subject that decisions made in the course of earlier cases may disqualify a judge from sitting. If a judge has already expressed 'clear views either about a question of fact which constitutes a live and significant issue in the subsequent case or about the credit of a witness whose evidence is of significance on such a question of fact' he ought to refrain from sitting unless it is necessary for him to sit to constitute a court, or the parties consent to his sitting or some extraordinary circumstances intervene: *Livesey v The NSW Bar Association.*[25]

The provision of an impartial arbiter is one function of the judicial branch; the adducing of evidence and the presentation of argument by the legal representatives is another. The assembling and presenting of evidence is a responsibility of the parties and their legal representatives, the importance of which is hard to overstate: it is important to the case of a particular client and to the general regard of the litigating public. It is a sad truth that notorious miscarriages of justice have been caused by a failure to appreciate the significance of available evidence or a failure to exercise due diligence in producing it. The legal representatives furnish the raw materials on which the judicial branch of government works so that public confidence in the trial process is largely in their hands.

The diligence of legal adversaries is essential to the adjudicative function, but they have no adjudicative role to play. Nevertheless, partisan advocacy must be fair. Some aspects of that rule are easy of application: it is clear that a judgment which is obtained by deception in a material matter will be set aside[26] and that counsel must not knowingly adduce evidence to deceive the court.[27] Other aspects of the rule require anxious consideration: for example, in a criminal case if counsel's hands are bound by his knowledge of the truth, it remains, as the High Court said in *Tuckiar* v *The King* where murder was charged, the duty of counsel: '… both to his client and to the court, to press such rational considerations as the evidence fairly gave rise to in favour of complete acquittal or conviction of manslaughter only.'[28]

In adducing evidence, the rules of evidence, sometimes ridiculed as archaic and unnecessary, must be observed. It is well to remember that fairness is the reason for their existence. As Evatt J said: 'After all, they represent the attempt made, through many generations, to evolve a method of inquiry best calculated to prevent error and elicit truth. No tribunal can, without grave danger of injustice, set them on one side and resort to methods of inquiry which necessarily advantage one party and necessarily disadvantage the opposing party.'[29]

Even the niceties of address – 'my learned friend', 'may it please the Court' – may seem archaic, but they provide powerful constraints upon the excesses of language which might turn a trial from a civilised process into disorderly abuse.

In an adversary system, independence is essential to the performance of counsel's role. Owing no allegiance to government, corporation or partner, the barrister is free to give advice objectively or to devote his talents to the interests of his client for the day. Independence is promoted by two factors. The first is sheer professional competence. The barrister who does not know what to do or why he is doing it has no confidence in himself and does not understand the part that he is playing in the judicial branch of government. He is likely, albeit without malice, to falter in the performance of his duty and to exercise the privileges that he is given to impede rather than facilitate the administration of justice. The second factor which promotes rugged independence at the Bar is common professional sentiment – peer group pressure, if you like. The Bar is one of the few boastfully independent professions. It is a fortunate fact that those who fail to respect their own independence lose the respect of colleagues and of the court. The progress of a barrister of real ability will be slowed, halted or reversed if, for the sake of a fashionable brief or a well-paid retainer or an impermissible victory, he sacrifices the independence which his colleagues or the courts expect of him. The expectation is not of a professional group alone; it is an expectation which the community insists should be fulfilled. In the public mind the Rumpoles of the Bar, who stand robustly independent between the forces of government and the liberty of the individual, earn the Bar much of its reputation and foster the sentiment that a thoroughly independent Bar is essential to a free society.

Independence is essential to candour and by candour the confidence of other barristers and of the court is won. As Sir Owen Dixon reminded the law students at Melbourne University: 'The obligation of candour rests on simple moral grounds. But at the same time it is a paradoxical if cynical truth which needs no elaboration that in advocacy candour is a weapon.'[30]

Candour in argument, diligence in adducing evidence, courtesy in demeanour, fairness in presentation are the contributions by counsel to public confidence in the trial process. Impartiality, both real and apparent, are the reciprocal contributions on the part of the judge.

The third step – Judgment

When the trial is over, the lonely work of the judge begins. The judgment he delivers, whether delivered orally or in writing, must not only show to the unsuccessful party why he has lost; it must show the public why the case was decided in that way. The delivery of reasons for judgment is a salutary safeguard against unconscious prejudice and a corrective to judicial impetuosity that might tend to overlook or unduly to diminish the rights of a party or the strength of his case. The judge must reason his way to judgment by steps that he knows are subject to public and critical scrutiny. The publication of judgments and the mere existence of appellate courts sharpens judicial sensitivity to the need for thoughtful solutions. Mr Justice Kitto in his paper, 'Why Write Judgments' said:

> The process or reasoning which has decided the case must itself be exposed to the light of day, so that all concerned may understand what principles and practice of law and logic are guiding the Courts, and so that full publicity may be achieved which provides on the one hand a powerful protection against any tendency to judicial autocracy and against any erroneous suspicion of judicial wrongdoing and on the other hand an effective stimulant to judicial high performance. Jeremy Bentham put the matter in a nutshell … when he wrote, in a passage which Lord Shaw quoted in *Scott v Scott* … 'Publicity is the very soul of justice. It is the keenest spur to exertion and the surest of all guards against improbity. It keeps the judge himself while trying on trial.'[31]

Let me continue the quotation from Lord Shaw:

> The security of securities is publicity'. But amongst historians the grave and enlightened verdict of Hallam, in which he ranks the publicity of judicial proceedings even higher than the rights of Parliament as a guarantee of public security, is not likely to be forgotten: 'Civil liberty in this kingdom has two direct guarantees; the open administration of justice according to known laws truly interpreted, and fair constructions of evidence; and the right of

> Parliament, without let or interruption, to inquire into, and obtain redress of, public grievances. Of these, the first is by far the most indispensable.[32]

Now all this is known to you. I have told you nothing that is not the common understanding of the Bar. But I wanted to put it in a context, to show that the rules of law and the practices of bench and bar are calculated to foster and maintain public confidence in the administration of justice by the courts – the confidence on which the supremacy of the law depends. The public dispassionate examination of facts in contest between litigants by an impartial arbiter who has no interest in the matter and of whom the litigants can entertain no reasonable suspicion of bias, the presentation of facts by skilled advocates according to rules designed to see that no party is treated unfairly, the hearing of argument and reply, the application of established principles that are subject to orderly modification to ensure that they are consonant with common contemporary community values, and the giving of reasons for judgment which are subject to public scrutiny and to review on appeal are the features of the working of the judicial branch of government. Though slow and expensive, it is a system which commands public confidence, The part that each of us plays in the administration of justice tends to enhance or diminish public confidence in the work of the judicial branch, to strengthen or erode the supremacy of the law. Though these considerations are proper stimuli to the discharge of our respective functions, public confidence is built upon the rules which govern the work of the judicial branch as well as upon the ministers of that branch. The confidence which is essential is confidence in the performance by the judicial branch of its constitutional function of administering justice even-handedly according to law. That kind of confidence is not often expressed yet it is fundamental to the supremacy of the law and to the freedom that our society enjoys under it. Our responsibility is the maintenance of that confidence; our challenge is to preserve the supremacy of the law. I wish you well as you accept that responsibility and that challenge.

---

1. The citation is taken from Justice Sydney Robins, 'The role of the independent judiciary' in Law Society of Upper Canada (ed), *The Abuse of power and the role of an independent judicial system in its regulation and control* (R DeBoo, 1979) 24.
2. No 78.
3. Alpheus Thomas Mason, 'Extra-Judicial Work for Judges: The Views of Chief Justice Stone (1953) 67 (2) *Harvard Law Review* 193, 200.
4. See *R* v *Trade Practices Tribunal; Ex parte Tasmanian Breweries Pty Ltd* (1970) 123 CLR 361.

5. See, for example, Dennis Lloyd, 'Reason and Logic in the Common Law' (1948) 64 *Law Quarterly Review* 468.
6. Cf Anthony Gordon Guest, 'Logic in the Law' in Anthony Gordon Guest (ed), *Oxford Essays in Jurisprudence* (Oxford University Press, 1961), 176.
7. (1984) 155 CLR 193.
8. Sir Ninian Stephen, 'Southey Memorial Lecture 1981: Judicial independence – a fragile bastion', (1982) 13 (3) *Melbourne University Law Review* 334; and see Nutley JA in *Corporate Affairs Commission* v *Bradley* [1974] 1 NSWLR 391, 403.
9. See for example, s 15AB of the *Acts Interpretation Act 1901* (Cth).
10. See, for example, *Cooper Brookes (Wollongong) Pty Ltd* v *Commissioner of Taxation (Cth)* (1981) 147 CLR 297; 55 ALJR 434.
11. [1962] AC 446, 467-468.
12. Lord Devlin, 'Judges and Lawmakers' (1976) 39 (1) *Modern Law Review* 1, 8.
13. [1983] 1 AC 410, 430.
14. See the interesting discussion by Frank Maher: Frank Maher, 'Words, Words, Words' (1984) 14 (3) *Melbourne University Law Review* 468.
15. See In *Glebe Sugar Refining Company Ltd* v *Trustees of the Port and Harbours of Greenock* [1921] WN 85.
16. Margaret Esther Hall (ed), *Selected Writings of Benjamin Nathan Cardozo* 1879-1938 (Fallon Law Book Co, 1947), 153. (.
17. 'Concerning Judicial Method' in Sir Owen Dixon, *Jesting Pilate* (Law Book Co, 1965), 157; and see *Myers* v *Director of Public Prosecutions* [1965] AC 1001, 1021 (Lord Reid).
18. Judge Learned Hand, 'Mr Justice Cardozo' (1939) 52 *Harvard Law Review* 361.
19. (1983) 152 CLR 359.
20. (1983) 152 CLR 406.
21. (1983) 151 CLR 447.
22. See *Yuill* v *Yuill* [1945] P 15, 20.
23. Save in the most exceptional circumstances in a criminal trial: *R.* v *Apostilides* (1984) 154 CLR 563 — though this case was not decided under the *Criminal Code Act 1899* (Qld).
24. See *R* v *Watson; Ex parte Armstrong* (1976) 136 CLR 248, 262.
25. (1983) 151 CLR 288, 300.
26. See *Meek* v *Fleming* [1961] 2 QB 366, 379.
27. See *Re Gruzman; Ex parte Prothonotary* (1968) 70 SR (NSW) 316, 323.
28. (1934) 52 CLR 335, 346.
29. See *R* v *War Pensions Entitlement Appeal Tribunal; Ex parte Bott* (1933) 50 CLR 228, 256.
30. In 1953: see Sir Owen Dixon, 'Professional Conduct' in Sir Owen Dixon, *Jesting Pilate* (Law Book Co, 1965) 134.
31. Sir Frank Kitto, 'Why write judgments' in Blackburn (ed) *Judicial Essays* (Law Foundation of New South Wales and Victorian Law Foundation, 1975), 9: an article that should be on the reading list of legal practice courses. This article was later republished in (1992) 66 *Australian Law Journal* 787.
32. [1913] AC 417,473.

2.3 The Irish and Law in Australia

Editor's note

This paper was delivered at a conference held at the Australian National University in Canberra in August 1985 on Ireland and Irish-Australia 1750-1950. The conference was convened by Professors Oliver MacDonagh and William Mandle.[1]

Let me start with an Irish statement: the subject is too big for me to talk on. I am not an expert on the Irish people, and I do not know all the law in Australia. Well, you may ask, if the subject is too big, why did you agree to speak on it? The primary answer is simple: a request by Oliver MacDonagh is not easy to refuse. The secondary answer is more complex. I and many other lawyers in Australia are indebted to the Irish, not only for our biological heritage, but for such gifts of compassion, generosity, humour and irreverence as we have ourselves inherited or have enjoyed in our colleagues. I and other lawyers in this nation are indebted to the law in Australia. It is the emanation of our people's culture, a reference point of principle in an increasingly turbulent sea of pragmatism, a system which we help to mould and by which we in turn are moulded. It is our hearth and our home. And so, I undertake this task as a kind of penitential work – perhaps an expiation for sins of ingratitude to those who, in myriad ways, have given to my generation a legal system which, if kept in good repair, can serve the needs of a free and confident nation.

The Irish contribution to this system is at once significant and indefinable. Its significance can be charted in part by reference to some of the great lawyers who came from Ireland to this country, and who were distinguished practitioners, judges and legislators in the infant colonies. Their contribution, though of the highest importance, does not exhaust the Irish influence on law in this country. For my part, I think more of some of the counsel of Irish origin with whom I practised at the Bar in Queensland and whose facility with language and whose refusal to regard life too seriously made them powerful advocates before the jury. They belonged, so it was said – and not always in laudatory tones - to the Irish school of advocacy. When they would address themselves, usually after a dramatic pause, to the gentlemen of the jury – for30 years ago sex discrimination was the norm in jury panels – the turning point in the case was reached and the cognoscenti would wander in to listen to the flowing oratory. The Old Munster Circuit had no better stories to tell, no more pungent witticisms to recall. There was, of course, an earnestness of purpose to it all. Justice was not an abstract virtue; it was something to strive for day by day. And if, at the end of the day, a sense of failure or injustice lingered, you might find counsel being consoled and refreshed by listening to Emmet's Speech from the Dock or Padraig Pearse's Oration at the grave of O'Donovan Rossa. (A record of the same was frequently played to the faithful in a set of Chambers renowned for good conversation, unshakeable views and some humour.)

I must not get lost in reminiscence. I must go back to the beginning and recall some of the eminent few and the contributions which they made to the establishment of a legal system in this country. Of course, legislators and administrators played critical parts in the establishment of Australia's legal system, but I have put most of them aside to focus on the professional lawyer. To try to keep these remarks within tolerable limits, I have largely passed by the mass of Australian lawyers born of Irish parents, although they were the chief means by which Irish traditions and values influenced Australian legal institutions. I shall mention those of Irish birth who played a significant role in establishing the Australian legal system, though I must caution that the list is not exhaustive and emphases may be misplaced.

The British settlements which were established in various parts of what is now Australia were governed by and under English law. Colonial modification of, or abrogation of, English laws that were applicable to the colonies were valid only to the extent authorised by English law. Until recent times, that has been the underlying theory and the practical reality of legal development in this country. The laws of the Aboriginal peoples were largely unknown by the colonial governments and have received little recognition by the Anglo-Australian legal system,[2] although the practices of some Aboriginal peoples have sometimes been taken into account in imposing criminal punishment. The application of English law – imperial legislation, common law and equity – was administered by courts from which appeals lay to the Privy Council. The Privy Council, whose remaining jurisdiction has become anachronistic and a source of inconsistency in Australian legal principle,[3] was in earlier times the tribunal which kept Australian law uniform and in conformity with the law of England.

It follows, of course, that Irish lawyers in the Australian colonies had but a limited opportunity to contribute to the development of a peculiarly Australian legal system. They were necessarily priests of an established oracle, and it was an oracle with which they were familiar.

Prior to the Federation of the Australian colonies on 1 January 1901, each colony had its own legal system connected with the other colonial systems by their common stock of English law, including English legislation, and by their common subjection to Privy Council appeals. The history of Irish participation in these systems must therefore be approached colony by colony.

New South Wales

Roger Therry was a Dublin man, whose father was one of the early Catholic barristers admitted to that profession when the penal laws were relaxed at the end of the eighteenth century. Roger was born in 1800 and though he went to Trinity College, Dublin (TCD) he did not take a degree. He was called to the English and Irish Bars and, having been private secretary to Canning, the United Kingdom Prime Minister, he was appointed Commissioner of the Court of Requests in New South Wales. With his wife, Anne, he arrived in Sydney[4] on 4 November 1829, a town in which he found a 'variety of strange sounds and divers tongues that met the ear ... a City of Babel on a small scale'.[5] His was the tenth name on the roll of New South Wales barristers and he conducted a successful practice while discharging his duties in the humble jurisdiction of the Court of Requests.

Therry was joined in Sydney by a fellow student whom he had met at TCD, John Hubert Plunkett, born in 1802, who had been a successful barrister on the Connaught Circuit. Daniel O'Connell gave him the credit for the success of his candidates in Connaught in 1830. Plunkett was appointed Solicitor-General of New South Wales. He arrived in Sydney in 1832. In 1836 he became Attorney-General.

Plunkett and Therry were men of ability and integrity. In 1838, they prosecuted to conviction the perpetrators of the infamous Myall Creek massacre in which a large number of Aboriginals – men, women and children – were slaughtered. The rigorous enforcement of the law in protection of the Aboriginal people excited a great deal of comment, but the Attorney-General and his junior counsel earned public respect for their impartial enforcement of the law.

In 1839, Plunkett and Therry each declined appointment as an acting Judge of the Supreme Court of New South Wales. At that time, they were regarded by Governor Gipps as 'the two most distinguished barristers of New South Wales'.[6]

Plunkett's contribution to the law in New South Wales was made chiefly in the political forum. He secured the passage of the *Church Act* in 1836 which established legal equality between Anglicans, Catholics and Presbyterians, and was later extended to Methodists. He became President of the Legislative Council and he was elected to the Legislative Assembly for a term. He was a noted leader of Catholic opinion, a firm supporter of Caroline Chisholm, a force in the establishment of St Vincent's Hospital and a protector of the hospital against ecclesiastical administrators. He sat on the Wentworth Committee for the establishment of the University of Sydney and became its Vice-Chancellor. He was a founding fellow of St. John's College within the University. He died in East Melbourne just short of his 67th birthday and was buried in Sydney near Archpriest John Joseph Therry.

Therry's career followed a different course. For a time, he was Attorney-General during Plunkett's absence in England, then he applied to be, and was, appointed as Resident Judge at Port Phillip. That appointment was not well received by the Port Phillip community at first, but during the year he spent in Melbourne (1845) he earned their respect. From 1846 to 1859 he was a judge of the Supreme Court in New South Wales. During most of that time he was the Primary Judge in Equity. In May 1850 he held the first Circuit Court for the district of Moreton Bay. He pleased the Circuit dinner held in his honour in Brisbane when he told them: 'I feel that I am in the presence of a scene that cannot be exceeded in the loveliness of its landscape'.[7] After Therry retired, he lived in Paris and London before returning to his native Dublin. He wrote his Reminiscences which received a more enthusiastic reception in London than in the Antipodes. In 1869 he was knighted and five years later he died.

Both Plunkett and Therry were champions of the Irish community in Sydney and proud defenders of the interests of their Catholic coreligionists. They were not the only Irish lawyers in the early days of the colony. Thomas Callaghan, another Dublin man, came to New South Wales as an immigrant in 1839 shortly after graduating from TCD. He earned an income as a barrister, supplemented by legal reporting for the *Sydney Herald*. In 1844 he published in two volumes the imperial and colonial legislation in force in the colony – Callaghan's Acts (*Acts and Ordinances of the Governor and Council of New Wales*). He became Chairman of Quarter Sessions and one of the first three District Court Judges. In 1863, he died in a riding accident at Braidwood where, in St Bede's Church, an obelisk was erected in memory of his impartiality and ability.

Sir James Martin and Sir Frederick Darley were Chief Justices of New South Wales in virtual succession. Both were born in Ireland. Martin arrived in Sydney in 1821 as a child aged 18 months. His parents were poor but they made great sacrifices to secure an education for their brilliant son. He became a solicitor and a passionate if conservative patriot. He became a barrister and Attorney-General. On two occasions, he was Premier of the State. Sir Henry Parkes thought him to be an imperious man who 'loved power for power's sake', but when he became Chief

Justice in 1873, he discharged the duties of his office to the satisfaction of profession and public alike. He died in 1886 and was succeeded, after a brief interregnum, by Darley.

Darley was ten years younger, educated in Ireland, a graduate of TCD and a member of the Munster Circuit. He came to Sydney to practise as a barrister in 1862 and became Queen's Counsel in 1878. He was prevailed upon to accept appointment as Chief Justice in the public interest and at considerable financial sacrifice. He was a sound judge, especially in equity and company law. He was jealous of judicial independence. He sought no public recognition though he was laden with honours. Desiring to be remembered only as 'an old Irish gentleman' he died while in London in 1910 and was buried in the family vault at Dublin.

In turn, he was succeeded by a noted Irish-Australian, Sir William Portus Cullen, born near Kiama in New South Wales in 1855. He graduated with first class honours in classics from Sydney University and later took a degree in law. He favoured Federation, was a member of the Legislative Council, and – almost alone among the conservative lawyers of his time – he favoured the abolition of Privy Council appeals.[8] He became Chief Justice of New South Wales in 1910, an office which he held until 1925. He continued for some years as Lieutenant Governor and Chancellor of Sydney University. He died in 1935.

Another Australian-born lawyer of Irish parentage who should be mentioned was Daniel Deniehy, the son of two transportees from Ireland, whom William Bede Dalley described as 'the most gifted Irish-Australian of our history'. Born in 1828, he was taken on a visit to Europe, England and Ireland before he was16, returning to study law in Sydney. Admitted as a solicitor in 1851, and elected to the Legislative Assembly in 1856, he was a man of letters and a gifted orator. But his capacities for liquor and satire lost him the influence which his genius would otherwise have commanded. He left a touching indication of his spirit in a letter he wrote to his wife a few hours before his death in 1865: 'Brave things have been written on the love, and truth, and goodness, and heroism, and courage, and suffering, and faith of women, but one year's history of your life would be sufficient for all that has entitled them to the honour and veneration and gratitude of mankind.'[9]

Victoria

The first barrister to arrive in Victoria was Edward Jones Brewster, a nephew of the Lord Chancellor of Ireland. The second was James Croke, the third was Redmond Barry. All three were graduates of TCD and members of the Irish

Bar. Brewster left the Bar to engage in land dealing and, later, to become a clergyman in the Church of England. Croke became Crown Prosecutor, renowned for his ability and independence. Barry became not only a distinguished judge but a leading figure in the colony.

In 1841, a resident judge was appointed for the Port Phillip district, but the appointee had to be replaced after a short time. William Jeffcott of Tralee took his place briefly, followed by Judge Therry from Sydney for eighteen months. After separation from New South Wales in 1851, a'Beckett was Chief Justice until 1857 when the long reign of Irish Chief Justices began. Stawell, Higinbotham, Madden and Irvine successively filled the office until 1935. All were Irish-born; all save Madden a graduate of TCD. They were joined on the Supreme Court by other Irish lawyers of great distinction, notably Sir Redmond Barry and Sir Robert Molesworth. They too were TCD graduates. Barry was a leading barrister at the time of separation and was the first Victorian Solicitor-General. He was appointed to the Supreme Court in 1852 but, despite his application to be appointed Chief Justice when a'Beckett retired, he was never appointed to that office. He was active in the foundation of the Philosophical Institute, the Philharmonic Society, the Horticultural Society, the Melbourne Hospital, the Melbourne Library, the Victorian National Gallery, the Melbourne Club[10] and Melbourne University of which he was the first Chancellor, an office which he held until his death in 1880. He presided over the trial of the now legendary bushranger Ned Kelly whose response to the sentence of death was: 'I will see you there where I go'. Sir Arthur Dean comments: 'Much has been made by the superstitious of the fact that Barry died unexpectedly twelve days after Kelly was hanged'.[11]

Molesworth served as a Supreme Court Judge for 30 years (1856-1886) with great distinction. He was appointed also to be Chairman of the Court of Mines over which he presided during years of feverish mining activity and in which he developed the basic principles of mining law that were adopted in other Australian colonies.[12]

Charles Gavan Duffy declared himself to be the first emancipated Catholic in Ireland, but his conflict with ecclesiastical power as much as his conflict with the power of government decided him to leave Ireland. 'An Ireland where Mr Keogh typified patriotism and Dr Cullen the Church was an Ireland in which I could not live'.[13] He arrived in Melbourne with his wife Susan and three of their children including Frank in January 1856. There he was greeted by a welcoming committee. He hung up his barrister's shingle but he was soon constrained to enter Parliament and in time became Premier of

Victoria. After Susan, who was his second wife, died in 1878, he returned to Europe. In France, he married Louise who bore him four children including George. Frank became Chief Justice of the High Court of Australia. George became the President of the High Court of Ireland.

Of the Victorian Chief Justices, George Higinbotham should be especially mentioned. He arrived in Melbourne in 1854 as one of the 300,000 immigrants who swept into Victoria in the nine years up to 1860.[14] He became editor of the *Argus* newspaper in the columns of which he espoused radical views that he later carried into politics as Attorney-General. Professor Manning Clark says that he:

> … was a man with Christ-like qualities who spent much of his time with lawyers and accountants, a gentle spirit who found himself with the measurers, an enlarger surrounded by straiteners. He had a face of such delicacy, mildness and sweetness that those in his company felt they were in the presence of a cherub, an angel who had been vouchsafed a vision of God's throne. He was kind to drunks, whom he sheltered from the abuse of the self-righteous, tender with women and very gentle with little children.[15]

He was elected on a platform of 'manhood suffrage, total separation of Church from state, state aid to denominational education, reform of land tenures and an abhorrence of faction and cabal'.[16] Whether as politician or, later, as judge, he held strongly, indeed idiosyncratically, to the view that the Victorian Constitution conferred on the colonial government 'very large and, in my opinion, almost plenary powers of internal self government'.[17] As Chief Justice in 1887, he made it clear that, if he were appointed Acting Governor, or Lieutenant Governor while the Governor was on leave he would refuse to communicate with the Colonial Office.[18] He refused the customary knighthood. During the maritime strike of 1891, he publicly sent £50 and a further £10 per week towards the relief of the strikers' families. Alfred Deakin held him to be a man of magnetic influence, radical thought and dominating will. 'Such a man,' wrote Deakin, 'rare in the world, seemed rarer still in Australia where his inflexible purity of life and aim, his irresistible charm and grace, and his transcendent power of convincing and being convinced, left an indelible impression upon so many minds and characters'.[19]

Tasmania

Sir Valentine Fleming was born in England though his family hailed from Tuam. He graduated from TCD, became Solicitor-General in Hobart in 1844 and Chief Justice in 1854. He held that office until 1869 and again he acted as

Chief Justice from 1872 to 1874. The Bar presented him with a testimonial which spoke of his ability, care, courtesy and constant impartiality.

Queensland

The second barrister to sign the roll in Queensland was Charles William Blakeney. Born in County Roscommon in 1802 he was a grandson of Archbishop Newcome, Primate of Ireland. He entered but did not graduate from Trinity College, was called to the Bar in England and Ireland, gambled away an inheritance and settled in Brisbane in 1859 and became the Member for Brisbane in the first Legislative Assembly in the following year. In 1865 he became the first judge of the Western District Court. He stimulated a controversy over the competence of the juries in Roma, prompting a juror to write to the press complaining of Blakeney's severity. He resigned in 1875 and died in the following year.

Patrick Real was from Limerick. He arrived in Brisbane as a child with his recently widowed mother in 1851. He left school at twelve and worked as a carpenter and in railway workshops. In those days, entry to the Bar was reserved to those who could be supported or who could support themselves for the three-year period before a student at law submitted himself to his examinations. During this period, a student at law could not be engaged in any trade, business or employment other than that of judge's associate or principal secretary to a minister of the Crown. Real was therefore obliged to save enough from his trade to support himself and his mother for the three years during which he completed his legal studies. He did so. In 1874, he was admitted to the Bar. He soon entered the front rank of the profession.[20] He was appointed a judge of the Supreme Court in 1890, retired in 1922 and died in 1928. Real was a member of the Commission for the establishment of the University of Queensland. One of Real's pupils was a young and brilliant barrister of Irish parentage, Thomas Joseph Byrnes, whom Sir Samuel Griffith was to appoint Solicitor-General and who became Premier of the State and one of its legendary heroes.

Virgil Power, though born in Queensland, received his secondary education in Ireland and graduated with a Bachelor of Arts from Dublin University. He returned to the Queensland Bar where he was an outstanding advocate. He was a Crown Prosecutor and was appointed a judge of the Supreme Court when the first appointment was made to Rockhampton.

Although the Irish Bar did not staff the Queensland profession, the Irish influence in Queensland has been extensive and enduring. Among the Chief Justices of the State there have been several of Irish lineage: Hugh Macrossan,

Neil Macrossan, Thomas McCawley and Sir William Webb, later a Justice of the High Court.

South Australia

Irish immigration to South Australia was limited, but an Irishman, Sir Robert Torrens, Premier of the State for a time, made a lasting contribution to the Australian legal system and, indeed, to legal systems in other parts of the common law world. He graduated with a Master of Arts from TCD but he was not a lawyer. In South Australia he became Treasurer and Registrar-General in 1852 and five years later he introduced a *Real Property Act* which created a workable system of land title by registration. The Torrens System which radically altered conveyancing procedures, was quickly adopted throughout the Australian colonies.

The first Chief Justice was Sir John Jeffcott, whose brother William served for a time as the second resident judge at Port Phillip. Born in Tralee in 1796 and a graduate of TCD, John had been Chief Justice of Sierra Leone, a post not coveted by many. During a visit to England, when he was knighted, he engaged in a duel. His opponent was wounded but lingered for a time. The judge left for Africa but returned to England to face a charge of murder after his opponent died. In the meantime, his seconds had been indicted and tried. Despite a strong Crown case against them and an adverse summing-up by the trial judge, the jury acquitted.[21] When the judge was ultimately brought to trial, the prosecution offered no evidence and he was acquitted. Then he was unemployed for a time, but successfully pressed his application for appointment as Chief Justice of South Australia. He arrived in Adelaide via Van Diemen's Land in April 1837, but his term of office was brief. He drowned in a boating accident at the mouth of the Murray River in December of that year.

A more conventional figure was Mr Justice Crawford born in County Longford, son of the Vicar-General of the diocese of Armagh. A barrister and a Trinity College man, he served as the puisne judge of the Supreme Court between 1850 and his death in 1852 at the age of 40. In his short career, he had a powerful influence in establishing the authority of the court and setting higher professional standards.

Western Australia

Sir Walter Dwyer, born 1875, was a Tipperary man who, like Patrick Real, came to Australia at a young age. He was admitted as a legal practitioner in Western Australia in 1907, was a noted advocate and the founder of the firm

Dwyer, Durack and Dunphy. In 1926 he became the first President of the Western Australia Court of Arbitration. He was one of the first trustees of the Public Library, Museum and Art Gallery of Western Australia. He retired from office in 1945 and died in 1950.

Federation and the High Court

The creation of the Commonwealth of Australia was achieved after much debate both in the Colonies and in London. This is not the occasion to note the parts played by Irishmen in the federal movement. One of them was Cardinal Moran, the Archbishop of Sydney, whose candidature for election to a Federal Convention was both unsuccessful and the occasion of a resurgence of sectarian bitterness.[22] When the High Court was established in 1903, three justices were appointed. Sir Samuel Griffith, Chief Justice of Queensland, was appointed Chief Justice of the High Court. Barton, the first Prime Minister, was the second Justice. Richard O'Connor, Sydney-born of Irish parents, was the third. O'Connor had been a protagonist of Federation with Barton and a member of Barton's federal ministry. The three foundation justices were judges of great ability. They established the authority of this Court in the Australian judicial hierarchy and confirmed it in its role as the keystone of the federal arch.

They were joined by two other justices when the membership of the Court was expanded to five in 1906 – Isaac Isaacs and Henry Bourne Higgins. Higgins, one of the greatest jurists that this Court has known and one of the greatest patriots and reformers that this nation has known, was born on 30 June 1851 in County Down, the second of the nine children of John and Anne Higgins. John was a Wesleyan preacher who decided to emigrate, sending his family ahead of him to Melbourne in 1870. Henry went to work and later, aided by a university exhibition, he completed degrees in Arts and Law at Melbourne University. One of the professors who influenced him was W E Hearn, a Trinity College man and a constitutional lawyer of distinction. In 1876 Higgins was called to the Bar, where his practice brought him financial security that he had not earlier known. He was an ardent federalist, a champion of religious tolerance and devoted to the interests of working men and women. He secured the insertion of the industrial conciliation and arbitration clause in the *Constitution* and became, in succession to O'Connor, the President of the Arbitration Court. He proclaimed the new jurisdiction to be 'A New Province for Law and Order'.[23] In the *Harvester* (*Ex parte H V McKay*) judgment,[24] he propounded a test for fixing a basic wage sufficient to provide food and water, shelter and rest for employees and their families 'and a condition of frugal comfort estimated by current human standards'. A recent biographer says that Higgins adopted the phrase 'reasonable and frugal comfort' from Pope Leo XIII's encyclical letter, *Rerum Novarum.*[25] He was instrumental in effecting the High Court's reversal of its original approach to constitutional interpretation. In the *Engineers Case*[26] when principles favourable to the growth of the Commonwealth's power were espoused, he wrote a separate and perhaps a more closely reasoned judgment than the majority. Higgins was an industrious and successful equity lawyer who became a champion of the labor movement; a non-Labor man who accepted appointment as Attorney-General in the first federal Labor Government under Prime Minister Watson in 1904; a man of great personal reserve and dignity who engaged in public controversy with Prime Minister Hughes in defence of the Arbitration Court. He was a rebel for causes which were identified with the aspirations of the young Commonwealth. He was held in universal esteem and when he died in early 1929 he was described by Sir Frank Gavan Duffy as 'a man of the most sterling integrity and kindliest nature'. His name can be seen inscribed in the High Court without the title of the customary knighthood which has hitherto been accepted by most Justices of the Court.

Sir Frank Gavan Duffy, son of Sir Charles Gavan Duffy, was educated at Stonyhurst and the University of Melbourne. In 1874 he was admitted to the Bar. He was a powerful advocate, 'quick-witted and of sparkling vitality'.[27] He founded the *Australian Law Times*. One of the leaders of the Victorian Bar, he was appointed a Justice of the High Court in 1913 to succeed Sir Richard O'Connor and Chief Justice in 1931. He retired in 1935.

Of course, this selection of Australian lawyers who were born in Ireland does not give us a full or balanced picture of the contribution which the Irish have made to the Australian legal system. But some themes emerge. It is clear that Trinity College and the King's Inn in Dublin imparted much of the learning which was essential to establish a working legal system in Australia – learning which colonial training might not have imparted adequately in the early days. It is clear also that many of the eminent Irish lawyers who made such a significant contribution to the colonial courts were drawn from the ranks of the Protestant Ascendancy. It is not surprising that few of the emigrant Irish lawyers were Catholics, for it was only in 1791 that the penal laws prohibiting Catholics from the practice of the law in Ireland were withdrawn.[28] Though nineteenth-century Australia was the scene of several bitter sectarian conflicts, the Irish lawyers – both Protestant and Catholic – were generally and genuinely tolerant and open men.

Two Irishmen of the Protestant tradition were among Australia's greatest judges: Higinbotham and Higgins. Dr. H V Evatt, when a Justice of this Court, writing in the *Harvard Law Review,*[29] nominated four great Australian judges: Griffith, Isaacs, Higinbotham and Higgins. He summarised their contributions thus:'whereas Griffith emphasized State rights as against those of the Commonwealth, and Isaacs emphasized Commonwealth rights as against those of the States, and Higinbotham emphasized the rights of colonial self-government as against the claims of British imperialism, Higgins' principal concern was that, wherever possible, the law should lay its protecting shield over the poor, the weak and the oppressed.'

It is no accident that independence and compassion were the qualities that shone through the judicial work of these Irish-Australians.

A theme which emerges from the lives of Martin, Higgins and Real is the opportunity which legal practice offered for the children of poor Irish immigrants to achieve eminence and financial security in one generation. The Irish love of language and sense of independence were natural endowments which carried many Irish-Australians to success in the profession. It needed the addition of great intellect and industry to produce such jurists as Sir Richard O'Connor and Sir Leo Cussen, of the Victorian Supreme Court, but there have been many other distinguished Irish-Australian lawyers. And that consideration raises two questions which would prove fascinating to pursue. To what extent has the legal profession been the means of securing the social and intellectual advancement of the children of immigrants, and particularly Irish immigrants, to Australia? And in what respects have Australian laws and legal institutions been formed by the ideas and values which are characteristic of immigrant families? I must leave to others the pursuit of these questions, but I hazard two opinions. The first is that a legal profession which is easy of entry but demanding in its standards is essential to a free and confident nation and conducive to social mobility within it. The second is that the ideals and values which the Irish contributed to Australian life – sometimes vital, sometimes diluted – have been reflected in those laws and institutions which were established before the Second World War.

If these opinions be valid, the true Irish influence on Australian laws and institutions is no less than, and no different from, the Irish influence on Australia as a whole. And that has been enormous.

---

1. See Oliver MacDonagh and William Frederick Mandle (eds), *Ireland and Irish Australia: Studies in Cultural and Political History* (Croom Helm, 1986). This book was republished in 2024 as part of the Routledge Revivals series. This paper was also published in the *Irish Jurist*, see Gerard Brennan, 'The Irish and Law in Australia' (1986) 21(1) *Irish Jurist* 95.
2. Other than in some land rights legislation, for example s 71(1) of the *Aboriginal Land Rights (Northern Territory) Act 1976* (NT), which provides: ' Subject to this section,

an Aboriginal or a group of Aboriginals is entitled to enter upon Aboriginal land and use or occupy that land to the extent that that entry, occupation or use is in accordance with Aboriginal tradition governing the rights of that Aboriginal or group of Aboriginals with respect to that land, whether or not those rights are qualified as to place, time, circumstances, purpose, permission or any other factor.'

3. Appeals to the Privy Council were terminated in 1986: see s 11, *Australia Act 1986* (Cth).
4. Roger Therry, *Reminiscences of Thirty Years Residence in New South Wales* (facsimile ed, Sydney University Press [for] Royal Australian Historical Society, 1974), 13.
5. Ibid 40.
6. Ibid 19.; Frederick Watson (ed), *Historical Records of Australia, Series 1, Volume 20, 1914-1925* (Library Committee of the Commonwealth Parliament, 1924), 59.
7. Roger Therry, *Reminiscences of Thirty Years Residence in New South Wales* (facsimile ed, Sydney University Press [for] Royal Australian Historical Society, 1974), 29.
8. John Michael Bennett, 'Sir William Portus Cullen' (1977) *Canberra Historical Journal* 83.
9. Cited in Bernard Thomas Dowd, 'Daniel Henry Deniehy' (1947) 33(2) *Journal of Royal Australian Historical Society* 57, 91.
10. Peter Ryan, *Redmond Barry* (Oxford University Press, 1972), 20.
11. Arthur Dean, *A Multitude of Counsellors: a History of the Bar of Victoria* (Cheshire for the Bar Council of Victoria, 1968) 71.
12. Ibid 66.
13. Cyril Pearl, *The Three Lives of Gavan Duffy* (New South Wales University Press, 1979), 155.
14. N Stephen, 'George Higinbotham', (1983 Daniel Mannix Memorial Lecture, Newman College, University of Melbourne, 17 September 1983), unpublished, 11.
15. Manning Clark, *A History of Australia* (Melbourne University Press, 1978), vol. 4, 109.
16. N Stephen, 'George Higinbotham', (1983 Daniel Mannix Memorial Lecture, Newman College, University of Melbourne, 17 September 1983), unpublished, 16-17.
17. See *Toy* v *Musgrove* (1888) 14 VLR 349 – see Zelman Cowen, 'Sir John Latham and Other Papers' (Oxford University Press, 1965), referred to in N Stephen, 'George Higinbotham', (1983 Daniel Mannix Memorial Lecture, Newman College, University of Melbourne, 17 September 1983), unpublished, 27.
18. Arthur Dean, *A Multitude of Counsellors: a History of the Bar in Victoria* (Cheshire for the Bar Council of Victoria, 1968) 77.
19. Alfred Deakin, *The Federal story: the inner history of the Federal cause 1880 – 1900* (Melbourne University Press, 2nd ed, 1963) 8.
20. Sir Harry Gibbs, 'Some Aspects of the History of the Queensland Bar' (1982) 53 *Australian Law Journal* 63, 66.
21. R M Hague, *Sir John Jeffcott*: portrait of a colonial judge (Melbourne University Press, 1963), 46-47.
22. Richard Ely, *Unto God and Caesar: religious issues in the emerging Commonwealth 1891-1906* (Melbourne University Press, 1976) Ch 3.
23. The title of the book, which was published by Constable, London in 1922, following a series of earlier articles in the *Harvard Law Review*.
24. (1907) 2 CAR 1
25. John Rickard, *HB Higgins, the Rebel as Judge* (Allen and Unwin, 1984), 173-4.

26. See *Amalgamated Society of Engineers* v *The Adelaide Steamship Co Ltd* ('*Engineers Case*') (1920) 28 CLR 129.
27. Arthur Dean, *A Multitude of Counsellors: a history of the bar of Victoria* (Cheshire for the Bar Council of Victoria, 1968), 151.
28. R W Bentham, 'The Bench and Bar in Ireland' (1959) 1(2) *University of Tasmania Law Review* 209, 217.
29. Herbert Vere Evatt, 'Mr Justice Cardozo' (1939) 52 (3) *Harvard Law Review* 357, 359.

2.4 Opening of the Australian Bar Conference in Ireland

Editor's note

This address was delivered at a joint conference of the Australian and Irish Bars at Fitzpatrick's Castle, Killarney, Dublin, on 13 July 1987.

Eleven years ago, the first overseas Australian Bar Association tour set off under the leadership of Sir Oliver Gillard. Like the present touring party, it included a cricket team. I think that team played under the same captaincy – Roger Gyles – and among its members were some of the present team: Peter Little, Kerry Cullinane and Jim Webb. The visit to Dublin was then, as it has been and will be on this tour, a highlight. Already two qualities have been identified as common to both Bars: a love of song and a weakness for strong drink!

You have returned to the roots of our common law, especially to the Inns of Court in London and to Trinity College and King's Inn in Dublin. The founders of the legal profession in Australia brought with them the learning which they acquired at these institutions. We have returned to discuss common legal problems and to share the experience of our legal system with those whose legal systems have developed from the same stock. The distinct legal systems of England, Ireland and Australia developed to answer the different needs of the respective societies. The industrial revolution in England, the problems of land tenure in Ireland, the growth of mining, new settlement and industrial relations in Australia, called for distinctive laws in the respective legal systems. And those systems reflect the respective constitutional histories of the three societies. But the three legal systems are derived from a common body of the law at a single point of history. It is a mistake to regard Australian law as simply an antipodean variation of the law of England or of the law of Ireland. There is a common law of each nation, derived from the same common stock. Standing side by side, each legal system reflects the experience and the needs of the people which it serves and governs. The development of our law was, of course, affected by the constitutional status of the Australian colonies and of the Commonwealth of Australia.

Now our constitutional status as a wholly independent nation has emerged. The Australian legal system is as independent as the Irish legal system became 50 years ago as illustrated by the celebrated case of *Moore v. Attorney-General* of the Irish Free State.[1] But independence does not mean isolation. In today's complex society it is increasingly important to understand how the problems arising in one part of the common law world are solved in another. That understanding does not come fully from reading the bare pages of the Law Reports.

Law shapes and is shaped by the society it serves. It is a statement of the values of that society, a definition of the freedoms enjoyed by citizens and a framework of the institutions of the society. It is impossible to understand a nation's laws completely without an appreciation of its culture; equally, an appreciation of its culture is defective without an understanding of its laws. As a medium of cultural exchange, the legal system provides a peerless focus and synthesis of a society's values and institutions. A Conference of the Bars of Ireland and Australia is both cultural exchange and an opportunity to learn from the practitioners of another system and to be challenged by the differences discovered.

The presence of the Australian Bar Association in Dublin is also an institutional acknowledgment of the contribution of Irish-Australians to the foundation of the Australian legal system and to the values which infuse professional practice in Australia. That contribution has been made in part by Irish lawyers who practised their profession in Australia, in part by Australian lawyers of Irish ancestry and tradition.

One of the early Justices of the High Court was Henry Bournes Higgins, who was born in Ireland. He was a considerable leader in the movement for federation, a liberal political figure, a judge of the highest calibre and an architect of our industrial law. Then there is the remarkable family of Sir Charles Gavan Duffy, a noted Irish politician who became Premier of Victoria. One of his sons was Sir Frank Gavan Duffy, a Justice of the High Court from 1913 to 1931 and Chief Justice from 1931 to 1935; another son, George, who was half-brother to Frank, became President of the High Court of Ireland. These two distinguished lawyers of the same family exemplify the close links between the professions of the two countries.

The most notable colony of Irish-born lawyers settled in Victoria. The first three barristers to sign the Bar Roll in Victoria were Irishmen. From 1857 to 1935 there was an unbroken line of Irish Chief Justices; Stawell, Higinbotham, Madden and Irvine. In addition, there were the distinguished Judges, Sir Redmond Barry and Sir Robert Molesworth. Sir Redmond's contribution extended far beyond the law, and Sir Robert is properly honoured as the chief judicial influence on the development of mining law in Australia.

In New South Wales, Roger Therry was the tenth barrister on the roll; he was joined by his friend John Plunkett. They were regarded as the leading barristers of their day. Both were graduates of Trinity College. In New South Wales there have been two Irish Chief Justices, Martin and Darley.

In Queensland, Mr Justice Real of the Supreme Court was Irish born. Judge Blakeney of the District Court, another Irishman, was the second name on the Queensland Bar Rolls. In South Australia the first Chief Justice was Sir John Jeffcott. He arrived in April 1837 but in December of that year he was drowned in a boating accident at the mouth of the Murray. A colourful figure, he had had the unenviable distinction of being indicted for murder after the death of his opponent in a duel. He was acquitted. A more conventional judge, and a most distinguished one, was Mr Justice Crawford. A most notable Irish contributor to the legal system in South Australia – indeed, to the legal systems in many parts of the common law world – was Sir Robert Torrens who devised the Torrens system of land registration.

In Western Australia, Sir Walter Dwyer was a Supreme Court judge of Irish birth. In Tasmania a Chief Justice, Sir Valentine Fleming, was born in England but came from a Tuam family and was a graduate of Trinity College. These are distinguished Irishmen, but I suspect that the greater part of the Irish contribution to the Australian profession came from the children of Irish immigrants.

The journey to Australia undertaken by Irish immigrants in the 19th century was different from the journey which we have experienced in returning. We have travelled far, but we have travelled at speed and in comfort. If we have suffered on the journey the odds are that we have indulged ourselves not wisely but too well. What a contrast with the journey of those immigrants from Ireland who travelled in the opposite direction slowly under sail – for steam was late coming on the Australian run – in incommodious conditions. We come to Ireland as visitors; they went from Ireland as the builders of a new nation. Few would have gone so far with the intention of returning, and few who had committed themselves to the development of the institutions and lands of the new country would have wanted to turn their backs on their life's work to go back to their original home in their later years.

The children of these immigrants found in the Bar a congenial profession. Entry to the Bar was relatively easy. It was attainable by industry, though its standards were high. Ability, not rank or wealth, was the criterion of entry; it was also largely the criterion for success. The majority of Irish immigrants were poor, and the opportunities which opened for their children were limited. The public service, the police and the law were achievable, and the Irish were attracted to these avenues of employment. It has been part of the strength of the Bar that many barristers come from humble origins. It will be a matter for regret if financial barriers keep away future recruits to the

Bar who have the requisite qualifications and character for entry. The Bar has gained both vitality and public esteem from the absence of barriers to entry to its ranks. There is a direct relationship between the ease of entry to the profession and the openness of the doors of the courts to those who require the Bar's services. Apart from the opportunities presented by practice at the Bar to the children of Irish immigrants, the practice of law appealed – and still appeals – to the romantic character of the Celt. The love of language, which is the lawyer's tools of trade, and a fascination with concepts and ideals are qualities to be found in the Irish temperament and in the Bar. The Irish enjoy their robust independence, and that quality is essential both to professional standards and to enjoyment of practice at the Bar. The Bar is attractive to men and women who revel in the keeping of the legal balance between the majority and the minority, between the accuser and the accused, between the State and the citizen, between the powerful and the weak.

The Bar is attractive too to those who enjoy the Irish qualities of companionship, a fondness for good conversation and a modicum of gossip, a penchant for powerful debate and a sense of humour. I remember my friend Vince Fogarty of the Queensland Bar who exhibited all these qualities. One somnolent afternoon he was addressing the jury in Goondiwindi in a cattle stealing case. Though the Crown case was strong, the usual favourable verdict was expected. Nevertheless, Fogarty had to go through the motions. 'Mr Fogarty', said his Honour, with an understandable touch of asperity, 'for all the relevance of what you are putting to the jury you might as well recite "The Green Eye of the Little Yellow God".' 'May it please your Honour', replied Fogarty, 'Were I familiar with the verse, and did I think that its recitation would either entertain your Honour or edify the jury, I should be only too happy to oblige!'

Nowadays the ethnic origins of the Australian barrister is professionally irrelevant, but each of us derives his or her identity from family and ancestral history as well as the profession to which we belong. To return to the ancestral country, to the roots of family and tradition, and to dispel myths which time and distance have engrafted is a delight to those of Irish stock. For those who suffer from – or glory in – a Celtic origin, a visit to Ireland recalls something of our own identity. For us, the welcomes we receive have a special significance for we share some common heritage with those who welcome us. It is expressed, but not explained, in a poem by Frank Sullivan. I was given a copy of this poem by Mr Justice John Kelly of the Australian Capital Territory Supreme Court who is, so far as I know, the only Irish-born Judge presently serving on a Supreme Court in Australia. It is the 'Celtic Lament':

To be a Celt is quite a dreadful thing -
To lead wild melancholy, muzzled on a silken string,
To hear in every silence
High-pitched, distant pipes
Of long-dead warriors marching to defend
The indefensible frontier,
To follow a lost cause as a forsaken lover follows
His disdainful lady
Down dangerous, dark streets;
To love life fiercely, possessive as a lioness her cubs,
And yet – to treat it as a merest trifle
To be wasted, squandered, thrown away,
If God, or country, or truth, a friend, or even
If a very special joke requires it.
To be a Celt is quite a dreadful thing,
For no heart breaks as easily or often
As does a Celtic heart,
Which tears itself apart,
At every parting from a friend
And yet -
though dreadful-danger being Celt begot
how much more dreadful
to
be
not.

---

1. [1935] IR 472; [1935] AC 484.

2.5 Ethics and the Advocate

Editor's note

This address was delivered to the Bar Association of Queensland Conference on 3 May 1992.

On reading the notes I prepared for this talk, I had the impression that I shall be reading a lecture telling the Bar and barristers what they should or should not be doing. That is not what I wish to do. Of course, ethics are normative of conduct at the Bar but, more importantly, the free acceptance of the Bar's code of ethics is the cement that binds the Bar together and unites it with the Bench in the common objective of securing justice according to law for the community we serve. So, I do not want to read a lecture on conduct so much as to discuss the role which the Bar must play in attaining that objective.

The first, and perhaps the most important, thing to be said about ethics is that they cannot be reduced to rules. Ethics are not what the barrister knows he or she should do: ethics are what the barrister does. [1] They are not so much learnt as lived. Ethics are the hallmark of a profession, imposing obligations more exacting than any imposed by law and incapable of adequate enforcement by legal process. If ethics were reduced merely to rules, a spiritless compliance would-soon be replaced by skilful evasion. There is no really effective forum for their enforcement save individual acceptance and peer expectation. However, among those who see themselves as members 'of a profession', peer expectation is sufficient to maintain the profession's ethical code. Ethics give practical expression to the purpose for which a profession exists, so a member who repudiates the ethical code in effect repudiates membership of the profession. It follows that if we are to gain an understanding of the ethics of the Bar, we must first ask ourselves whether the Bar is truly a profession and ascertain the purpose for which it exists. Only then can we see whether and how the ethics of the Bar express that purpose.

If the media can be taken to express at least a substantial segment of public opinion, not all Australians regard the Bar as a profession. So perhaps we need to go back to fundamentals to identify what is meant by a profession and thereby to ascertain the true status of the Bar. I imagine that most of you are familiar with the definition of a profession offered by Sir Owen Dixon: 'It is the essence of a profession that its members master and practise an art. The art must depend on a special branch of organized knowledge and be indispensable to the progress or maintenance of society, and the skill and knowledge of the profession must be available to the service of the State or the community.'[2]

Sir Owen went on to say why it is essential that a profession should maintain high ethical standards: 'Experience has shown in every age that a profession cannot proceed without high professional standards. Special knowledge is always suspected by those who do not share it. Unless high standards of conduct are maintained by those who pursue a profession requiring great skill begotten of special knowledge, the trust and confidence of the very community that is to be served is lost and thus the function itself of the profession is frustrated.'

Note the elements of the definition: mastery of an art, based on special knowledge indispensable to progress or maintenance of society. Those elements describe professional expertise. They are applicable to a barrister, a solicitor, a doctor; but they are equally applicable to a foreign exchange dealer, a computer programmer or a manufacturer of footwear. In a technological society, expertise is not restricted to members of a profession.

The expertise of the Bar covers several fields but, at its core, is the expertise of the advocate before courts and tribunals: an expertise in the marshalling and presentation of facts, in the ascertainment, analysis and application of rules of law and in delimiting and identifying the factors relevant to the exercise of a discretion. It is no part of the Bar's function to judge but it assuredly is part of the Bar's function to present the material on which judgment is based. The function of the Bar is thus essential to the efficient performance of the judicial function of doing justice according to law. Without the services of the Bar, the members of society would be without effective access to justice and courts and tribunals would be unable efficiently to administer justice according to law. The Bar's function is truly indispensable to the progress and maintenance of society.

Where the progress or maintenance of society would be prejudiced by sub-standard service in a given field, a licensing regime must be created to exclude those who do not possess the required knowledge and skill. But the monopoly thus created is conferred on terms: the monopolists must provide the service required. Hence the remaining element in the Dixon definition: 'the skill and knowledge of the profession must be available to the service of the State or the community'. Sir Owen does not say that the service must be available without fee; no substantial service can be continually provided without remuneration to the provider. But fees have a different significance for professions from the significance they have in trade and commerce, as Lord Macmillan pointed out:

> The difference between a trade in a profession is that the trader frankly carries on his business primarily for the sake of pecuniary profit while the members of a profession profess an art, their skill in which they no doubt place at the public service for remuneration, adequate or inadequate, that which is truly an end in itself. The professional man finds his highest rewards in his sense of his mastery of his subject, in the absorbing interests of the pursuit of knowledge for its own sake, and in the contribution which, by reason of his attainments, he can make to the promotion of the general welfare.[3]

It is all very well to quote distinguished jurists of a bygone age but, you may ask, do their lofty sentiments have any relevance in the practical life of the Bar today? Isn't it time to face the realities of modern practice with high overheads, expensive technology, escalating cost of books and of access to data bases, and the need to cope with a large volume of work in order to defray the expenses incurred before the barrister begins to earn his or her take home pay? Of course, these realities must be faced, but that is merely to say that the Bar is under considerable financial pressure in struggling to keep itself in the professional category. The struggle is not solely of the Bar's making. Consensus morality has lost much of its normative influence over social conduct and relationships, and the law and legal process have been invoked to make up the shortfall. The community, and particularly the political branches of government, rely increasingly on legal controls though they have not come to terms with the reality that legal controls, however efficient, are labour intensive and therefore costly. Though tempting in the short term, it would be fatal for the Bar's professional status to capitalize on the demand for legal services, and to weaken its endeavours to provide its services to those who need them but who cannot afford to pay the fees offered by the affluent.

A powerful contemporary reminder of the importance of ensuring the general availability of the Bar's services comes from the Supreme Court of the United States which is concerned with a society more complex than our own and arguably more motivated by the acquisition of wealth. In *Shapero* v *Kentucky Bar Association* O'Connor, with the concurrence of Rehnquist CJ and Scalia J said:

> One distinguishing feature of any profession, unlike other occupations that may be equally respectable, is that membership entails an ethical obligation to temper one's selfish pursuit of economic success by adhering to standards of conduct that could not be enforced either by legal fiat or through the discipline of the market. There are sound reasons to continue pursuing the goal that is implicit in the

> traditional view of professional life. Both the special privileges incident to membership in the profession and the advantages those privileges give in the necessary task of earning a living are means to a goal that transcends the accumulation of wealth. That goal is public service.[4]

The public service which is the goal of the Bar as a profession is no less than the obtaining of justice under the law. As Kitto J. said in *Ziems v The Prothonotary of the Supreme Court of NSW*:

> The Bar is no ordinary profession or occupation. These are not empty words, nor is it their purpose to express or encourage professional pretensions. They should be understood as a reminder that a barrister is more than his client's confidant, adviser and advocate, and must therefore possess more than honesty, learning and forensic ability. He is, by virtue of a long tradition, in a relationship of intimate collaboration with the judges, as well as with his fellow-members of the Bar, in the high task of endeavouring to make successful the service of the law to the community.[5]

To make that service successful, the Bar's ethical code must aim at making justice according to law as accessible as the Bar can reasonably make it and at ensuring that the judge or other decision-maker has the material at hand to do justice according to law. These are the broad objectives which, being shared by all members of the profession, guarantee its status and theirs and, more importantly, its and their satisfaction with the work they do.

Accepting briefs

The 'cab rank' rule is uncompromising: special circumstances apart, the barrister is bound to accept any brief in the courts or tribunals in which he or she professes to practise at a reasonable professional fee. The 'cab rank' rule is, of course, easy to circumvent. Even if 'special circumstances' be narrowly confined, the barrister may find ostensible justification for refusing a brief which is distasteful or relatively poorly paid or for passing on such a brief when a better brief can be got.

The Bar, as every experienced member of it knows, is a chancy business. There is no goodwill saleable on retirement, no sick leave, no long service leave, no superannuation or financial security except such as the barrister pays for himself or herself. Briefing patterns are sometimes fickle. Case lists wax and wane. It is not surprising that the financial insecurity of the Bar leads some barristers to regard briefs primarily as a kind of bankcard docket against which a solicitor will pay. The high-sounding rhetoric of professional duty may find little resonance in concerns about family responsibilities, chamber expenses and the provision of some financial security against death, age or disability.

Yet the 'cab rank' rule is fundamental to the professional status of the Bar. Without it, access to justice would be at the discretion of individual counsel; legal rights would be liable to defeat for reasons of distaste or avarice; the minorities, the poor, the powerless, the unpopular – those who most need the protection of the law – would have to go without representation or to find their advocates among those who would build their own reputations on others' misfortune. In such a situation, the law would become an instrument of oppression, and the courts would lose the confidence of the community. You may think that, to some extent, that has already happened.

There is no reason to think that the cab rank rule will not be fully honoured by providing representation for unpopular clients or causes. The concern about the 'cab rank' rule arises because of the setting of fees at levels which are often thought to be unreasonable. In the boom years of the economy, the Bar did well and it may be that the 'cab rank' rule did not receive too much attention when the demand was for stretch limousines. The pattern of litigation changed during those years and a greater proportion of commercial litigation and litigation involving governments and corporations was found in the lists. The courts suffered some erosion of their popular base among the litigants with less financial strength and in litigation about issues of smaller financial value.

These circumstances make it more imperative that the Bar be consciously oriented to providing service to those who need it. In recent times, the steps which have been taken in some Bars to organize pro bono work so that burden is fairly distributed and so that professional skills can be matched to the client's needs have been steps in the right direction. Most leaders of the Bar, – especially those who are entitled to command the largest fees, have been accustomed to provide their services at no fee or a reduced fee when there is a justifiable call on their services by litigants who cannot afford to pay their usual fees. If there were any diminution in the readiness of the leaders to give this leadership and, indeed, to insist on the general observance of the 'cab rank' rule, I should fear for the future of the Bar.

Perhaps the attitude that needs most careful fostering affects the approach of individual barristers to the fixing of fees. At the Bar, it is not easy to keep fees in proper perspective. In part, a barrister measures his or her progress and standing in the profession by reference to the fees which he or she can command, and it takes a degree of confidence to formulate and adhere to a fee policy which ensures that his or her services will be available at reasonable rates or to a reasonable extent to those who need them. Yet the availability of professional services cannot be unduly restricted by insistence on fees which the State and the community cannot reasonably afford. I suggest that it is not acceptable to approach the fixing of a fee by asking: what will the traffic stand? Or what do I need to charge to maintain an income of $X? Rather, the question must be: having regard to the expected length and difficulty of the case and forming as best I can an estimate of the knowledge and skill I can offer, what is a reasonable fee for my services? And, if only a lesser fee can be afforded, should I accept the brief lest the legitimate interests of the client be unrepresented? I venture to suggest that no counsel who adopts that approach need have the slightest ground for misgiving as to his or her progress or standing in the profession.

The 'cab rank' rule is, paradoxically, the chief security of the Bar for its professional future. If the public can perceive that the Bar's services are truly available to anybody who is in genuine need of those services on payment of a reasonable fee, the Bar may expect to gain the respect, if not the affection, of the public. And reasonable remuneration for the rendering of the service will not be begrudged. Of course, the public will find the fees of eminent leaders to be high. But an assurance that fees do not necessarily stand in the way of representation in cases where the Bar can reasonably provide the service needed will commend a fee system which allows for graduations according to knowledge, skill and experience. Such a system demands, of course, that there be no rigid fee classifications either by scale or by tacit understanding. It is obvious, however, that if the professional aspiration of providing services to those who need them is subordinated to the maximising of income, public opinion will be contemptuous of the legal monopoly, the courts will be hobbled in their appointed task of doing justice equally, the relationship of Bench and Bar will be sundered, and the function of advocacy will come to be entrusted, by default, to modestly paid employees of the State. In such a situation, the third branch of government would lose its robust independence which relies, in the ultimate analysis, on the availability to the public of access to justice.

Preparing and presenting cases

The efficiency of the courts depends largely upon the skill and industry of counsel in identifying and submitting issues for decision, whether in original or in appellate jurisdiction, and presenting the case on the relevant issues economically and accurately. This requires not only a careful consideration of the facts and the relevant law, but a resolute exclusion of issues which are immaterial, unsupported or of marginal relevance.

A barrister is expected to have the knowledge and the skill required by a brief. If the barrister does not have the knowledge and skill and cannot by diligent research make up the deficit, the brief should not be accepted. It is a fraud upon the client and, in the case of a brief on trial, an imposition upon the court, to accept a brief beyond counsel's capacities to work up, or to accept a brief which counsel is unwilling or unable to prepare adequately. Of course, there are times when another night's research would be welcome or when the case before lasts longer than expected, but it is not acceptable for a counsel to go into court without knowing the essential facts relevant to the issues and the legal frames of reference upon which the decision in the case will turn.

Once accepted, a brief imposes an obligation to work it up as well as to appear subject, of course, to supervening circumstances which make it necessary to return the brief – and in good time. A brief is not a piece of property to be flicked to a friend when the barrister has double-booked or has been offered a better brief or is too tired to do the work.

When the case is in court, counsel must remember through the dust of conflict that his or her primary duty is to the court. In *Giannarelli v Wraith*, in a passage which summarizes the duty of the advocate in court, Mason CJ said:

> The performance by counsel of his paramount duty to the court will require him to act in a variety of ways to the possible disadvantage of his client. Counsel must not mislead the court, cast unjustifiable aspersions on any party or witness or withhold documents and authorities which detract from his client's case. And, if he notes an irregularity in the conduct of a criminal trial, he must take the point so that it can be remedied, instead of keeping the point up his sleeve and using it as a ground of appeal.
>
> It is not that a barrister's duty to the court creates such a conflict with his duty to his client that the dividing line between the two is unclear. The duty to the court is paramount and must be performed, even if the client gives instructions to the contrary. Rather it is that a barrister's duty to the court epitomizes the fact that the course of litigation depends on the exercise by counsel of an independent discretion or judgment in the conduct and management of a case in which he has an eye, not only to his client's success, but also to the speedy and efficient administration of justice.[6]

Within the limits imposed by the duty to the court, the barrister's efforts must be devoted to the success of the client's cause. The basic limitation is not to mislead the court. Misleading covers not only the tendering of evidence that is known to be false or the making of submissions that are known to be wrong (in the sense of not reasonably arguable) in fact or in law; misleading includes the advancing of propositions which are true in literal terms, but which imply what is known to be false or wrong. But nothing false or wrong is implied by failing to prove facts relevant to issues which the client does not have to prove. Under the adversary system, the function of putting the court into possession of the material for decision-making rests primarily with counsel and, in relation to all matters of fact, rests entirely with counsel. But, where counsel appears for a party on whom no onus of proof rests, there is no misleading of the court in putting the other party to proof. Hence, in criminal cases, even a confession made by a prisoner to counsel during the trial does not prevent counsel from putting the Crown to proof provided cross-examination and submissions are not inconsistent with the facts confessed.

The second limitation on the duty to the client – not to cast unjustifiable aspersions on a party or witness – flows from the function of counsel as an independent contributor to the administration of justice. This limitation does not impose a duty to be diffident or timorous in advocating a client's cause. Counsel is entitled, sometimes bound, to advance an argument relevant to an issue in the strongest terms consistent with the evidence, whether or not the argument prejudices the reputation of others.[7] But no allegation of moral or legal turpitude against an opposite party should be made in pleadings without a prima facie case being disclosed by the facts and no such allegation should be made in the hearing against any person without evidence to support it. Counsel is not an amanuensis or spokesperson for a client who wishes to place irrelevant or unsupported and scandalous material on public record under cover of privilege. For this reason, no issue should be submitted merely because of a client's desire to raise it. On the other hand, there can be no refusal to submit an issue, however unpalatable or unpopular, which will, if the issue is resolved in the client's favour, advance the client's cause. There may be a relevant issue the raising of which would reflect adversely upon the client's reputation, in which case counsel may decline to plead the issue without specific instructions to do so.

The third limitation is not to withhold documents and authorities which detract from the client's case. The injunction against withholding documents relates, of course, to documents which must be produced either to comply with an order for discovery or to prevent any misleading of the court by the tendering of evidence which the document qualifies. There is, I think, another situation in which a document needs to be produced. Even if there has been no order for discovery, counsel who is aware of a document which relates to an issue the onus of proving which rests on the opponent, but which establishes that issue in favour of the opponent and destroys the client's case, cannot proceed on the footing that the client is entitled to succeed.

The duty of counsel not to withhold authorities which detract from the client's case flows from counsel's duty to assist the court to apply the relevant law. To allow the court to decide a case in favour of a client without knowledge of a contrary authority is tantamount to misleading the court. Of course, it is not misleading to advance a legal argument contrary to authority provided the argument is reasonably open and provided the court is put into possession of the authorities relevant to the problem including authorities contrary to counsel's submission.

Counsel who, through industry and candour, earns the respect of the courts before he or she appears is a powerful advocate of a client's legitimate interests. Sir Owen Dixon, whose lecture on 'Professional Conduct'[8] should be compulsory reading for every barrister, said that 'it is a paradoxical if cynical truth which needs no elaboration that in advocacy candour is a weapon.' When a counsel who has earned a judge's respect is known to be appearing, it is a fact – perhaps a judicial weakness, but nonetheless a fact – that the judge approaches the case with a sense of tranquillity, knowing that the issues for determination will be clearly and accurately defined with the material for determination at hand.

Conclusion

The ethics of the advocate serve a number of purposes. Chief among them is directing the contribution which the Bar makes to the administration of justice, both in respect of its availability and its quality. Next, because of a barrister's ethical responsibilities in court, an immunity from suit is conferred on him or her. Perhaps I should recall a few sentences of what I wrote in *Giannarelli v Wraith:*

> If the immunity of counsel were abrogated, the assistance which the courts obtain from the advocacy of an independent profession would be imperilled. But there is a corollary. If counsel generally were to fail to adhere to the standards of advocacy which the courts expect and on which they rely, there would be no justification for the immunity. That has not happened. Hopefully it never will.[9]

Immunity is not the only advantage gained by adherence to the Bar's ethics. The status of the Bar as a profession, the monopoly rights which the Bar enjoys and the remuneration it derives all depend in the long run on the maintenance of high ethical standards. And perhaps the most immediate advantage which those standards confer is the sense of collegiality in the day to day work of the Bar. A barrister in good standing, without consciously adverting to rules, lives his or her professional life in the camaraderie of a group devoted to justice and to law, jealous of its standards and of the great privileges which it exercises in service of the public. It is not surprising that those of us who have left active practice at the Bar have a nostalgia for the years in which that camaraderie was enjoyed and a certain pride in our continued relationship with an institution held in both affection and respect.

---

1. See *Clyne v The New South Wales Bar Association* (1960) 104 CLR 186, 200.
2. 'The Profession of Accountancy', Melbourne, 4 April 1960, reproduced in Sir Owen Dixon, *Jeting Pilate* (Law Book Co, 1965), 192.
3. Lord Macmillan, 'Law in history' Edinburgh, October 1934, reproduced in Lord Macmillan *Law and Other Things* (Cambridge University Press, 1937), 118, 127.
4. 486 US 466 (1988) 488-489; 100 L Ed 2d 475, 494.
5. (1957) 97 CLR 279, 298.
6. (1988) 165 CLR 543, 566.
7. See, as to pleading the *Statute of Frauds*, *Charlick* v *Foley-Bros.* (1916) 21 CLR 249, 251- 252.
8. Sir Owen Dixon, *Jesting Pilate* (LawBook Co, 1965) 134.
9. (1988) 165 CLR 543, 579-580.

2.6 The Duties of the Advocate

Editor's note

This was an address to the T C Beirne School of Law at the University of Queensland delivered on 4 October 1999.

This discussion of the duties of an advocate relates to the function performed by barristers and solicitors in appearances before courts, commissions, boards and tribunals on behalf of lay clients. We should start by considering the duty to accept a retainer – a duty which the Bar knows as the 'cab rank' rule. It was stated by Lord Reid in *Rondel v Worsley:* 'It has long been recognised that no counsel is entitled to refuse to act in a sphere in which he practises, *and* on being tendered a proper fee, for any person however unpopular or even offensive he or his opinions may be, and it is essential that that duty must continue : justice cannot be done and certainly cannot be seen to be done otherwise.'[1]

The duty to act is put squarely on the role of the advocate as a necessary participant in the administration of justice. Note the very restricted qualifications on the duty to act: 'the sphere in which he practises' – not whether he wants to do that sort of work but whether he does it. 'A proper fee' – not one that equals his top level of charging but one which is reasonable having regard to the difficulty of the brief, the time it is likely to take, the importance of the case and the standing of the advocate. Once the retainer is accepted, duties are owed to the client but also, indeed primarily, to the court.

Although much of what follows deals with the duties owed to the court or, it can be said, to the court and the public, there are two basic duties owed to the client which, unless qualified by the primary duty owed to the court, are binding on the advocate. The first is the duty to apply his or her professional skills and ability in doing whatever the client could lawfully do for himself to procure a favourable judgment. Lord Brougham's dictum that an advocate 'knows but one person in all the world and that person is his client' is too absolute but it is a salutary reminder that the advocate must not have any conflict of interest in representing the client whose retainer has been accepted. Indeed, the fiduciary relationship that is established by the acceptance of a retainer precludes the advocate from acting in the future for another party if there be ' a real prospect that the confidential information obtained from the former client would influence, at least subconsciously, the conduct of the legal practitioner when acting for the new client.'[2] *A fortiori*, the retainer may well preclude the advocate from acting against his client in future litigation. In *D and J Constructions Pty Ltd v Clayton Utz*, Bryson J said: 'Where confidential information has been communicated by a client to a solicitor and is relevant to litigation in which the client is now engaged and still available to the solicitor, the Court should take a cautious approach to any proposal that it should allow the solicitor to act against that client. ... Cautious conduct by the Court is appropriate because the spectacle or the appearance that a lawyer can readily change sides is very subversive of the appearance that justice is being done.'[3]

The second duty owed to the client is to respect the client's confidence and not to divulge without the client's instructions or permission any information acquired under the mantle of professional privilege. However, as we shall see, privileged information may limit the scope of what the advocate may properly do in representing the client.

To understand the duties of an advocate, it is necessary to understand the nature and purpose of the proceeding in which the advocate is retained to appear. The jurisdiction and rules of procedure of courts and tribunals prescribe the issues for their determination, the material on which they are to determine the issues and the manner in which they are to reach a determination. The advocate's function is to assist the courts in the administration of justice according to law by submitting on behalf of a client the evidence and the arguments which can properly be submitted in the client's interests or in accordance with the client's instructions, by making those submissions competently, fearlessly and economically. The proper scope of the submissions depends on the jurisdiction that is invoked and the procedural rules which have to be followed.

The duties of an advocate are not obligations of mere courtesy, albeit courtesy is an important aspect of the manner in which curial proceedings are conducted. The duties of advocacy are not devised by the committee of an elite club to be the indicia of professional gentility. They are canons of conduct framed in response to the rules which govern the jurisdiction and procedure of the courts and tribunals in which advocacy is practised. If those canons are not observed, the law which the court or tribunal is appointed to administer will not be properly administered. Then the outcome of the particular transaction might diverge from the outcome which the law commands and, to that extent, the advocate's failure to observe the relevant canon of conduct will have caused justice to miscarry. I have referred only to advocacy before courts, but the same observations apply, *mutatis mutandis*, to advocacy before commissions, boards and tribunals.

The advocate's function is to produce relevant material and to submit lawful argument in order to persuade the court to determine the issues in conformity with the interests or the instructions of the client. But the advocate is not a gun for hire to shoot at whatever target the client selects; rather, the advocate is a professional participant in the work of the courts and tribunals which administer justice according to law. In *Ziems v The Prothonotary of the Supreme Court of New South Wales,* Kitto J said that counsel: 'is more than his client's confidant, adviser and advocate, and must therefore possess more than honesty, learning and forensic ability. He is, by virtue of a long tradition, in a relationship of intimate collaboration with the judges, as well as with his fellow-members of the Bar, in the high task of endeavouring to make successful the service of the law to the community. That is a delicate relationship, and it carries exceptional privileges and exceptional obligations.'[4]

The primary duty of the advocate is to assist the court to do justice according to law. Other obligations, including the duty to the client are qualified by this primary duty.

I venture to repeat what I said in *Gianarelli v Wraith*: 'If a duty owed to the client were seen to be separate from the primary duty of assisting to do justice according to law, the two duties might not be wholly compatible. No duty to a client which stands apart from the primary duty can be allowed to impair performance of the primary duty.'[5]

Within the proper limits of the advocate's function, he or she is not subject to direction by the court or tribunal in the way in which the proceeding is conducted. And the advocate is ordinarily clothed with immunity from suit, whether by the client or by a third party.

Even if the retainer is to advise rather than to engage in advocacy, the focus must be on the jurisdiction and procedure of the court in which the correctness of the advice can, and potentially will be, put to the test. Why is this? The answer is twofold. First, because that focus demands an analysis of the issues, an accurate appreciation of the strength of the client's case and a realistic appreciation of the likelihood of a favourable or unfavourable determination should the advice be contested. In other words, that focus concentrates on the issue and gives an assurance of the quality of the advice given. In modern practice, there is sometimes a tendency to give the advice which the practitioner thinks will be the advice that the client would wish to have or which the practitioner, without adequate research and hard thinking, hopes to achieve for the client. Whether or not that approach to advice is conducive to the building of good client relationships, it is not the approach which fulfils the obligations of a retainer to give legal advice. The professional adviser is retained because of his or her competence and independence, in order to give impartial advice. The second reason why the focus must be on the jurisdiction and procedure of the relevant court is that that focus defines for the advocate the scope of his or her authority – what the advocate may legitimately do and seek to achieve in advocacy or what legal advice the advocate might properly give in fulfilment of his or her retainer. If the advocate exceeds the proper scope of his or her professional function, the consequence, either in the short term or the long term, will be a failure to command professional respect and a poor professional reputation.

Understanding the basis on which the duties of the advocate rest, we can examine the specific duties under a number of heads. Those heads follow from the nature of the judicial process, a process at the core of which is a syllogism as Kitto J pointed out in the *Tasmanian Breweries Case:* 'the process to be followed must generally be an inquiry concerning the law as it is and the facts as they are, followed by an application of the law as determined to the facts as determined'.[6]

The applicable principles – 'the law as it is' – provide the major premiss; 'the facts as they are' provide the minor premiss; and judgment follows inexorably by applying 'the law as determined to the facts as determined'. In each step of this process, the rules, whether of law or practice, are calculated to ensure that public confidence in the administration of justice is maintained. In the first two steps – the inquiry concerning the law as it is and the facts as they are – the advocate has a critical role to perform.

The duty to assist in the application of the law

Every court is bound to apply the law in the exercise of its jurisdiction. If it fails to do so, justice is not done according to law. The process has miscarried. The advocate, whose duty it is to assist in the doing of justice according to law, can neither abstain from ascertaining the governing law in the particular matter nor refrain from informing the court of the relevant law if the court appears to require that assistance. The duty to find the relevant law is owed both to the court and to the client. The advocate who accepts a retainer to advise or to appear on behalf of a client and who does not undertake the research reasonably necessary to discover the relevant law is negligent. To go into court without having undertaken that research means that the advocate is either hoping to bluff his or her way through or is careless as to whether the outcome is correct in law or not. The advocate who does not know what to do or why he or she is doing it will command no confidence in the submissions made on the client's behalf. An advocate's want of preparation, especially if it be manifested by blustering, impedes the administration of justice. To have the opportunity to undertake research that is reasonably necessary and to pass up the opportunity is incompetence which, if it results in the incurring of unnecessary costs, could be visited with an order to pay the costs personally.[7]

Of course, there are occasions when the brief arrives too late on counsel's desk or when the client of the solicitor-advocate brings the problem in too late to permit the necessary research to be carried out. If adjournment be impossible or undesirable, and if it appears that assistance with the law is sought by the court or is probably required, no more can be done than to inform the court that the advocate is unfortunately unable to give that assistance. The court or tribunal should not be left with the understanding that the advocate's silence is a knowledgeable confirmation of the correctness of the course which the court is taking.

If the advocate, having undertaken the necessary research or otherwise being familiar with the relevant law, perceives that the court or tribunal is proposing to take a course that is inconsistent with the settled law or that may be affected by an authority which the court or tribunal might find to be binding or persuasive, it is the duty of the advocate to ensure that that law or authority is brought to notice. That is one of the primary duties of the advocate, and it prevails over any duty to the client. Even if the authority is adverse to the client's interest, the duty must be discharged. Lord Birkenhead LC, speaking for the House of Lords said[8] that: 'the withholding from their Lordships of any authority which might throw light upon the matters under debate was really to obtain a decision from their Lordships in the absence of the material and information which a properly informed decision required; it was, in effect, to convert this House into a debating assembly upon legal matters, and to obtain a decision founded upon imperfect knowledge. The extreme impropriety of such a course could not be made too plain.'

Kitto J's phrase 'the law as it is' needs a little expansion in a time of rapid social change. Certainly, the advocate is under a duty to ensure that the court is aware of relevant binding authority but that authority may be distinguishable on the facts of the instant case. The advocate is not at liberty to refrain from bringing the authority to the court's notice merely because he or she thinks the distinction is arguable. Unless the distinction is so clear as to make the authority irrelevant, the advocate's duty is to ensure that the court is aware of the authority and to argue the distinction. If the literal application of a precedent would yield a decision that is unjust by contemporary standards, it may be that the precedent is no longer applicable or no longer applicable without qualification. One cannot give an a priori definition of what is or is not unjust – notions of justice cannot be expressed exhaustively – yet the appearance of injustice is the instigator of legal development. It is the warning light that some new factor has entered and may require either the distinction of existing precedents or the development of the law to do justice to the case in hand. In appropriate cases, it is necessary for the advocate to propose a new rule or a reformulation of a rule. That is a familiar challenge to counsel appearing in the higher appellate courts, especially the High Court, but the advocate at first instance may have to formulate the novel proposition in order to keep the question open if, or when, the matter reaches appeal.

However, the judicial development of the law is not freewheeling.[9] Its starting point is existing principle and the organic development of new rules requires that they be fashioned consistently with other rules of the legal system. The technique of development is important, for orderly development of legal principle is essential to the preservation of public confidence. Sir Owen Dixon has noted that in the 'classical' period of English law:

> Principles were not only used, they were developed. There was a steady, if intuitive, attempt to develop the law as a science. But this was done not by an abandonment of the high technique and strict logic of the law. It was done by an apt and felicitous use of that very technique and, under the name of reasoning, of that strict logic which it seems fashionable now to expel from the system.[10]

I suspect that many advocates have not yet appreciated their creative and difficult role in the ascertainment of the law as it is in the present day, yet recent decisions have manifested the need for structured and sophisticated research. Cases such as *Legione v Hateley;*[11] *Burnie Port Authority v General Jones Pty Ltd;*[12] *Rogers v Whittaker;*[13] *Garcia v National Australia Bank;*[14] *David Securities Pty Limited v Commonwealth Bank of Australia*[15] come to mind. Without the assistance of counsel, the judges in these and many other cases would have been less adequately equipped to develop the law.

The second step – The facts as they are

The curial method of dispute resolution is the adversary process. Other methods, adopted by tribunals, boards and commissions may be less formal, more inquisitorial. First, consider the duty of the advocate in the adversary system. Here the role of the judge is essentially passive. The judge decides between the parties on the material they place before the court. The judge sits above the arena lest his vision be clouded by the dust of conflict[16] and leaves the parties to produce the evidence on which the facts are to be found.[17] Not only is the judge kept out of the arena of conflict to give him the appearance of an impartial arbiter; he must be impartial in fact, and there can be no reasonable apprehension to the contrary: 'The view that a judge shall not sit to hear a case if in all the circumstances the parties or the public might reasonably suspect that he was not unprejudiced and impartial, and that if a judge does sit in those circumstances prohibition will lie, is not only supported by the balance of authority as it now stands but is correct in principle.'[18]

So rigid is this view that a decision made by a judge in an earlier case may disqualify the judge from sitting. If a judge has already expressed 'clear views either about a question of fact which constitutes a live and significant issue in the subsequent case or about the credit of a witness whose evidence is of significance on such a question of fact', he ought to refrain from sitting unless it is necessary for him to sit to constitute a court, or the parties consent to his sitting or some extraordinary circumstances intervene: *Livesey v New South Wales Bar Association*.[19]

So, the assembling and presenting of relevant evidence is left to the parties and their advocates. The importance of this responsibility is hard to overstate. Due diligence in obtaining relevant evidence and proper appreciation of its significance is needed not only to discharge the advocate's duty to the client but also to avoid miscarriages of justice, so that public confidence in the trial process is maintained. The case should be prepared for trial as economically and quickly as possible.[20] The introduction of case management rules to reduce delays in hearings may affect applications for adjournments if the case is not prepared.[21]

In adversary litigation, advocacy is partisan but it must be honest and fair. Some aspects of that rule are easy of application: it is clear that a judgment which is obtained by deception in a material matter will be set aside[22] and that counsel must not knowingly adduce evidence to deceive the court.[23] Particular applications of the rule may require anxious consideration.

An obligation not to mislead the court must be distinguished from a legitimate reliance on the onus of proof to resist an opponent's case. That distinction is relevant in both criminal and civil litigation. In a criminal case, as the prosecution bears the onus of proving all the elements of the offence save the defence of unsoundness of mind, the accused is entitled to be acquitted if the prosecution evidence is insufficient to discharge the onus. It follows that a person charged with a criminal offence is entitled to put the prosecution to proof[24] and that an advocate who is retained to act for the accused is under a duty 'both to his client and to the court, to press such rational considerations as the evidence fairly gave rise to in favour of complete acquittal or conviction of manslaughter only'.

That was the formulation of the duty by the High Court in *Tuckiar v R*.[25]

However, since advocacy must be honest, an advocate who *knows* that the accused is guilty of the offence charged cannot make submissions inconsistent with that knowledge. In this context, knowledge is not a judgment formed on hearsay materials; the advocate is not to assume the mantle of a judge. For guilt to be known, it must be the only conclusion which can reasonably follow from the facts personally known by the advocate or accepted by the accused. The classic example is a confession of guilt made to the accused's legal advisers. Such knowledge places a real restriction on advocacy but, in my view, such knowledge does not justify refusal of a retainer to act for the accused unless the advocate is instructed to suggest what the advocate knows to be untrue. There was – and may still be – a contrary view that knowledge of guilt justifies refusal of the retainer[26] but I venture to suggest that that course would merely indicate to the accused that another advocate, not burdened with the knowledge, would be able to enhance the prospects of acquittal by false suggestions of innocence. Of course, if the accused withdraws the retainer because of the limited defence which the advocate can give, professional confidence would preclude the advocate from divulging to others any knowledge acquired under professional privilege.

Similarly, in civil proceedings, an advocate is under no duty to inform an opponent who bears an onus of proof of the evidence by which that onus may be discharged. Conversely, the advocate is under a duty not to conduct the case so as to suggest that the facts are different from what the advocate knows them to be or, if the advocate has no personal knowledge, different from the facts disclosed by the client's instructions. Thus, if the client produces to the advocate a document which destroys the client's case, the advocate must insist on its production to the court.[27] Where instructions are inconsistent with the advocate's knowledge, either the retainer should be refused or, if accepted, the instructions should be refused. The professional advocate is not a mere mouthpiece for the client; he or she must act with personal honesty.

Although it is said that an advocate for one party is not obliged to disclose evidence to an opposing party in civil litigation, that proposition is subject to two important qualifications. The first is that, when a party has any evidence which would put a false complexion on the case made by that party, that evidence must be disclosed, lest the falsity be taken for the truth. That is simply because the suppression of the truth may amount to the suggestion of a lie. Thus, in *Meek v Fleming*,[28] the non-disclosure of the demotion for misconduct of a former Chief Inspector of Police who was called as a witness led to the setting aside of the judgment for the party who called him.

The second qualification relates to cases which are not truly adversarial. The prime example is the application for an ex parte injunction where the respondent is not heard and the court must rely on whatever material is placed before it by the applicant. A recent judgment of the Federal Court[29] has adopted a statement of the relevant principle in *Tate Access Floors Inc v Boswell*:[30]

> No rule is better established, and a few more important, than the rule, 'the golden rule', that a plaintiff applying for ex parte relief must disclose to the court all matters relevant to the exercise of the court's discretion whether or not to grant relief before giving the defendant an opportunity to be heard. If that duty is not observed by the plaintiffs, the court will discharge the ex parte order and may, to mark its displeasure, refuse the plaintiff further inter partes relief even though the circumstances would otherwise justify the grant of such relief.'[31]

There are other cases which, though adversarial in some respects, are not strictly adversarial in nature. Then different rules apply with respect to the disclosure of information. For example, proceedings relating to the welfare of a child.[32] The court places the interests of the child above the interests of parties contesting custody or access and require disclosure of the child's whereabouts.[33] It appears that a similar view is taken with respect to the disclosure of material facts in property disputes between spouses.[34] In submissions in mitigation of sentence, a prisoner's advocate should not suppress material which is peculiarly within the prisoner's knowledge and is relevant to the judge's assessment of the appropriate sentence.

In appearances before commissions or tribunals, as in curial appearances, the advocate is under a duty not to misrepresent the facts or to mislead the commission or tribunal into assuming a falsity to be a fact. But where the procedure is not strictly adversarial, the function and powers of the commission or tribunal determine the nature of the advocate's duty. There is a duty to disclose the law when disclosure is needed – especially if the commission or tribunal might otherwise mistake the extent of its powers or the function which it is to perform. There may or may not be a duty to disclose information unfavourable to the client's interests or instructions. For example, where a tribunal must determine a client's entitlement to a statutory benefit on the basis of material in the client's possession, it would be wrong to disclose only favourable material and to suppress relevant material that is unfavourable. On the other hand, where the client is in effect a respondent to an adverse application, there may be a duty not to disclose material damaging to the client's interests without the client's instructions. The observance of client confidentiality may be extremely important in such instances. An obvious instance is an inquiry into a client's guilt of a criminal offence.

Mr Justice Ipp, in an extensive article in the *Law Quarterly Review*,[35] cites *Vernon v Bosley (No 2)*[36] as 'an instance of the growing trend of courts to require cases to be determined in accordance with the objective "truth" rather than on evidence adduced solely for reasons of perceived tactical advantage.' I would respectfully caution against too ready an acceptance of that trend. Rules of Court and orders made thereunder relating to discovery and case management may well compel disclosure of material which, in earlier times, may have been kept properly confidential. Nevertheless, subject to changes of that kind, the adversary system remains. Provided the advocate is punctilious in observing the duty not to misrepresent or mislead – and *Vernon v Bosley (No 2),* like *Meek v Fleming, might* fall under that rubric – the advocate is not only entitled but bound to observe client confidentiality. Legal professional privilege is the privilege of the client and it is for the client to waive that privilege. It is not to be waived by the advocate without the client's instructions.

Discretionary decision-making

The syllogistic model of 'the law as it is' being applied to 'the facts as they are' does not adequately describe the making of discretionary decisions. The nature of these decisions is diverse and the duty of an advocate to disclose information relevant to the exercise of the discretion cannot be broadly formulated. What can be said is that misrepresentation of fact or misleading conduct is a breach of duty and that an obligation to disclose information without the instructions of the client must be found, if at all, in the statute prescribing the powers and procedure of the court, commission or tribunal.

Duty in representing the client

In *Gianarelli v Wraith,* Mason CJ observed:

> The performance by counsel of his paramount duty to the court will require him to act in a variety of ways to the possible disadvantage of his client. Counsel must not mislead the court, cast unjustifiable aspersions on any party or witness or withhold documents and authorities which detract from his client's case. And, if he notes an irregularity in a criminal trial, he must take the point so that it can be remedied, instead of keeping the point up his sleeve and using it as a ground of appeal.
>
> It is not that a barrister's duty to the court creates such a conflict with his duty to the client that the dividing line between the two is unclear. The duty to the court is paramount and must be performed, even if the client gives instructions to the contrary. Rather it is that the barrister's duty to the court epitomizes the fact that the course of litigation depends on the exercise by counsel of an independent discretion or judgment in the conduct and management of a case in which he has an eye, not only to his client's success, but also to the speedy and efficient administration of justice.[37]

That primacy of the advocate's duty is the reason why the advocate is immune from suit for in-court negligence.[38]

Insistence on the primacy of duty to the court should not chill the performance of the advocate's duty to his or her client. Indeed, a precise and complete discharge of the duty to the court strengthens the effectiveness of submissions made on behalf of the client. In 1953 Sir Owen Dixon reminded the law students of Melbourne University that: 'The obligation of candour rests on simple moral grounds. But at the same time, it is a paradoxical if cynical truth which needs no elaboration that in advocacy candour is a weapon.'[39]

Candour inspires judicial confidence in the advocate and strengthens the advocacy. So does independent and fearless advocacy provided there is no loss of courtesy in presenting submissions. These are robust qualities in an advocate; they command respect. Sometimes, especially in the presence of a forthright or efficient judge, advocates adopt a submissive attitude in order to avoid the need to challenge a view which they believe the judge to have. But it should be kept steadily in mind that, subject to the duties owed to the court, the advocate's duty is to advance the interests of his or her client by all legitimate means, irrespective of the difficulties that might lie in the way.[40] The advocate has an independent and important role to play in litigation, and the advocate may on occasions be called on to remind an opponent, a witness, or even the judge that the advocate must be free to play that role without undue interference and without adverse personal comment.

Respectfulness in argument is not inconsistent with strong and independent advocacy. Litigation, though adversarial, is a courteous procedure. Even if emotional issues are canvassed, the judicial process is always essentially cerebral. So powerful language may be employed, proved misconduct may be roundly condemned and shiftiness and prevarication may be pilloried, but personal abuse is not acceptable. Every party in a curial procedure, including the accused in a criminal trial, is entitled to his or her personal dignity even when their conduct is a subject of the litigation.

Therefore, in cross-examination of a witness, an advocate must not put questions which are calculated only to insult or annoy. Nor should evil conduct be imputed unless the cross-examiner has reliable information for thinking that the imputation is true.[41] Nor should a serious allegation against an opposing party be made in court unless the advocate making it has and intends to adduce evidence in proof.[42] Sometimes those grounds will appear from evidence given in the case; sometimes they must be found, if at all, in other sources.

The judgment, the client and the media

After the close of advocacy comes the judgment. That is the completion of the syllogism. The writing or pronouncing of the judgment is the exclusive function of the judge. Whether the advocate and colleagues regard the judgment to be a forensic triumph or an erroneous disaster, it is no part of the advocate's function to make public comment upon it. It is inconsistent with the function of advocacy to express an opinion to the client, much less to the media, which imputes incompetence or bad faith to the author of the judgment. Of course, the advocate's opinion may be sought and given as to the prospects of appeal. Judgments may be the result of error, whether of law or fact or in the exercise of a discretion – the books are full of successful appeals – but mere error is no ground for imputing incompetence or bad faith. The error may have followed from the advocate's failure to dispel the mistaken concept from the judicial mind. Whatever be the cause, blaming the judge when the advocacy has failed is no part of the advocate's function.

In recent times, a practice seems to have developed in some quarters for the media to seek out the legal representatives of the parties to obtain quotable comment on the outcome of a case. In my opinion, the provision of such comment is wholly inconsistent with the role of the professional advocate. That role is to seek the doing of justice according to law by the rendering of a judgment. To comment publicly on the judgment is to hold up for public revision (whether for good or ill) the judgment which was the subject of the advocate's submissions. It was for the judge to evaluate those submissions; it is not for the advocate to evaluate the judge's judgment. How can a court place any reliance on the independence, candour and integrity of an advocate when the advocacy is a prelude to some public comment on the judgment after it is given?

Enduring reputation as an advocate is not made on street corner interviews. It is made in the faithful and competent performance of the advocate's function in the interests of the client in the court room, the commission or the tribunal. It is an honourable function on which the maintenance of the rule of law largely depends. Those who engage in that function will find it a continuing challenge, an intellectual stimulus, a warming experience of the human condition, a source of friendships and a life-long satisfaction. Those who contemplate advocacy as a career must be aware of the burdens they will have to bear: heavy responsibility, long hours, anxious efforts. But if they have an ambition to pursue that career, nothing should deter them.

---

1. [1961]1 AC 191, 227.

2. See *Complete Technology Pty Ltd v Toshiba (Australia) Pty Ltd* (1994) 53 FCR 125 (Hill J).
3. (1987) 9 NSWLR 118, 124-125.
4. (1957) 97 CLR 279, 298. 8
5. (1988) 165 CLR 543, 579.
6. See *The Queen v Trade Practices Tribunal; Ex parte Tasmanian Breweries Pty Ltd* (1970) 123 CLR 361.
7. See *Kooky Garments Ltd v Charlton* (1994) 1 NZLR 587, 591.
8. In *Glebe Sugar Refining Company, Ltd v Trustees of the Port and Harbours of Greenock* [1921] WN 85.
9. But note the wide variety of factors which Mr Justice Cardozo treated as relevant to the judicial development of the law: 'My analysis of the judicial process comes then to this, and little more: logic, and history, and custom, and utility, and the accepted standards of right conduct, are the forces which singly or in combination shape the progress of the law. Which of these forces shall dominate in any case, must depend largely upon the comparative importance or value of the social interests that will be thereby promoted or impaired.' (Margaret Esther Hall (ed), *Selected writings of Benjamin Nathan Cardozo* (Fallon Law Book Co, 1947), 153.)
10. Sir Owen Dixon, 'Concerning Judicial Method' in Sir Owen Dixon *Jesting Pilate* (Law Book Co, 1956), 157; and see *Myers v Director of Public Prosecutions* [1965] AC 1001, 1021. (Lord Reid).
11. (1983) 152 CLR 406.
12. (1994) 179 CLR 520.
13. (1992) 175 CLR 479.
14. (1998) 194 CLR 395.
15. (1992) 175 CLR 353.
16. See *Yuill v Yuill* [1945] P15, 20.; *Jones v National Coal Board* [1957] 2 QB 44, 63-64.
17. Save in the most exceptional circumstances in a criminal trial: *R v Apostilides* (1984) 154 CLR 563 – though this case was not decided under the *Criminal Code Act 1899* (Qld).
18. See *R v Watson; Ex parte Armstrong* (1976) 136 CLR 248, 262.
19. (1983) 151 CLR 288, 300.
20. See the English cases refered to by Mr Justice Ipp: David Ipp, 'Lawyers Duties to the Court' (1998) 114 *Law Quarterly Review* 63, 65.
21. See *Haset Sali v SPC Ltd* (1993) 67 ALJR 841; but cf *State of Queensland v JL Holdings Pty Ltd* (1997) 189 CLR 146.
22. See *Meek v Fleming* [1961] 2 QB 366, 379.
23. See *Re Gruzman; Ex parte Prothonotary* (1968) 70 SR (NSW) 316, 323.
24. See per Lord Diplock in *Saif Ali v Sydney Mitchell & Co* [1980] AC 198 at 220.
25. (1934) 52 CLR 335, 346.
26. See the discussion in G N Williams, *Harrison's Law and Conduct of the Legal Profession in Queensland* (Lawyer's Bookshop, 2nd ed, 1984), 78-80.
27. See *Rondel v Worsley* [1969] 1 AC 191, 282 (Lord Upjohn).
28. [1961] 2 QB 366.
29. See *Dorissa Pty Ltd v Schwob's Swiss Pty Ltd* [1998] FCA 398 (17 April 1998).
30. [1991] Ch 512, 532-533.

31. See *Brink's Mat Ltd v Elcombe* [1988] 1 WLR 1350 and *Behbehani v Salem (note)* [1989] 1 WLR 723. See https://www-iclr-co-uk.eu1.proxy.openathens.net/ic/1981000423.]
32. See *Re L (A Minor)* [1997] AC 16.
33. See *R v Bell; Ex parte Lees* (1980) 146 CLR 141.
34. See *Jenkins v Livesey* [1985] AC 424, 437; *In the matter of Morrison and Morrison* [1995] FLC 92-573.
35. David Ipp, '*Lawyers Duties to the Court*'(1998) 114 *Law Quarterly Review* 63 at 68-69.
36. (1997) 3 WLR 683.
37. (1988) 165 CLR 543 at 556. See also *Rondel v Worsley* [1969] AC 191, 282 (Lord Upjohn).
38. See *Gianarelli v Wraith* (1988) 165 CLR 543 at 557, 570, 579, 594, 596.
39. Sir Owen Dixon, 'Professional Conduct' in Sir Owen Dixon, *Jesting Pilate* (Law Book Co, 1965), 134.
40. See *Rondel v Worsley* [1969] 1 AC 191, 227 (Lord Reid).
41. See *Clyne v New South Wales Bar Association* (1960) 104 CLR 186, 199.
42. Ibid 200.

2.7 Strength and Perils: The Bar at the Turn of the Century

Editor's note

This was the Inaugural Sir Maurice Byers Lecture delivered on 30 November 2000.[1] Maurice's widow, Patricia was in attendance. She wrote to Brennan on 3 December 2000 saying, 'The very first of the Sir Maurice Byers Memorial Addresses delivered by Sir Gerard Brennan was a triumph. An inspiration for me. Your percipience of Maurice is remarkable.'

Maurice Byers was one of the towering figures of the Bar. His distinguished career included a remarkable decade as Solicitor-General for the Commonwealth. When he died, leaders of the profession, as well as the media, paid eloquent tributes to his record of advocacy. He was described as 'the finest lawyer never to have been appointed to the High Court'.[2] Though there were good grounds for expecting on more than one occasion that an appointment was imminent, 'strategically located smaller minds', Gareth Evans said, 'made its attainment impossible'.[3] The High Court was his milieu. He knew its members well – indeed, he had led several of us at the Bar. He knew its cast of mind and, I suspect, its internal dynamics. His enjoyment of advocacy there evoked a corresponding judicial response. His forensic triumphs were notable. May I repeat the estimate I made from the bench on an earlier occasion: 'His participation in the work of this Court was perhaps no less on that side of the Bar table than it would have been on this'.[4]

His professional eminence and success do not explain why the Bar Association of New South Wales commissioned his portrait to hang in these rooms and created an annual lecture to be delivered in his honour. Professional eminence and success are not alone sufficient to produce, or are even conducive to the production of, the fond response of colleagues. That response reflects a peer group's appreciation of a mind and manner and disposition which commanded affection as well as a profound respect. Tom Hughes identified these qualities in an obituary in which he said that Maurice was –

> the quintessential barrister ... possess[ing] a combination of admirable and lovable qualities seldom found together in one individual and, unlike many others in his profession, his intellectual interests extended well beyond the law... He had the gift of urbane charm; he was suave without being slippery. He was of a kindly disposition and had a gently mischievous sense of humour. He had the blessing of a

> happy marriage and a close-knit family.... He was endowed with a deep, but not unquestioning, religious faith which he practised throughout his life.[5]

Byers came to the Bar in 1944, without the professional or familial connections that might have eased his entrance to this most competitive of professions. Sir Anthony Mason has told us that Byers 'had to make his own way at the Bar, relying on work from less fashionable and smaller firms of solicitors whose clients needed a clever but responsible counsel to argue a legal point when very often that was all that there was to go on. '[6] He was available to appear for anybody who had need of his services. It would seem that his clients of that time were not the large corporations. His talents were sharpened on the intricacies of the *Fisheries and Oyster Farms Act 1935 (NSW)*[7] and on the law which the authorities believed to be inimical to the sale of liquor at the Black Tulip Restaurant.[8] He took silk in 1960, before the risks of that step were minimised by the abolition of the two counsel and two-thirds rule. As with many of the towering figures of the Bar, the quest for financial security was suppressed in favour of the passion for advocacy. That was a symptom of the rugged individualism which is characteristic of the Bar's leaders. Chief Justice Gleeson has noted that 'Maurice Byers belonged to the legal profession before some people gained the insight that it would serve the public better if it were a business.[9]

Rugged individualism is essential to the barrister's assumption of personal responsibility for the advice given or the course of advocacy pursued. David Bennett, sometime Byers' junior and now his successor as Solicitor-General, tells of the occasion when he suggested to his leader that they should take instructions on some question of policy that would be affected by the litigation. Byers' reply was: 'I don't take instructions – I give them'. His constitutional arguments in the High Court were developed according to his view of the *Constitution*, whether or not that view was preferred by the government of the day. Gareth Evans, then Attorney-General for the Commonwealth, speaking at a testimonial dinner on Byers' retirement from the office of Solicitor-General, acknowledged that Maurice, in his role as Second Law officer of the Commonwealth had 'displayed outstanding qualities of objectivity and courage'. The Attorney no doubt had in mind Byers' appearance before the Senate Committee into the Loans Affair. There he displayed a great deal of courage in refusing to disclose the secret counsels of the Crown – but, as Simos QC (as he then was) observed at the Bench and Bar Dinner in honour of Byers in 1994 'such courage is characteristic of our guest of honour'.[10]

Of course, objectivity and courage are esteemed in a barrister because they are conducive to the giving of advice that is correct and to advocacy that is relevant, cogent and persuasive. What the Bar offers to its clients – both solicitor and lay clients – is a high level of expertise in the provision of advisory and advocacy services. That calls for a complex of capacities in the practising barrister: knowledge of the law, a facility for research, analytical skill, tremendous commitment and energy and a familiarity with the courts before which the barrister appears and with modes of judicial thinking. Byers exhibited these capacities to an outstanding degree. Simos knew him to have a phenomenal and detailed memory of decided cases and to have been a prodigious worker.[11] Justice Gummow remembers that his submissions were 'preceded by reflection and speculation' and were calculated to draw the Court into the heart of the matter. Alan Robertson speaks of his intellectual curiosity which led him to look radically at each problem and to re-examine the fundamentals.

And he remembers Maurice seeking to enlist the support of a waitress in a French restaurant in Canberra for the proposition that French was the language of reason – a proposition which elicited only a look of profound consternation. He was an agreeable and entertaining companion whose conversation ranged over music and philosophy and a notion of the cosmic God. Byers' curial arguments, delivered with a 'mellifluous voice' and 'courtly gestures',[12] were always directed to 'the critical grey area of the case'.[13] As Sir Harry Gibbs noted, Byers identified 'the point or points on which the decision … will rest and … advance[d] clearly and strongly, but without undue repetition, the arguments directed to those points, keeping to the main road and not wandering off into side tracks and blind alleys, however attractive they may seem from a distance.'[14] Byers' own opinion was 'the isolation of the matter [for decision] is the most demanding and the most essential of all legal skills. Presenting it clearly, concisely and attractively is the summit of oral advocacy'.[15] Of course, as Gareth Evans remarked: 'The counterpoint to brevity, that which sets it off … is style and that's a quality that Maurice has in abundance.' Sir Anthony Mason remembers a style of his advocacy which Byers described to a junior counsel: 'Put the ball into the scrum and let the politics of the court take over.' Sir Anthony comments that 'he apparently omitted to tell the junior that in feeding the scrum he put the ball into the second row'.[16] Although Byers was a consummate practitioner of the arts of advocacy, the practice of these arts was only a means to his end. Chief Justice Gleeson remembers him as 'a man who hungered, and thirsted, after justice'.[17] It was a concatenation of capacities and personal qualities that endeared Maurice to the Bar and earned him the plethora of accolades that accompanied him in life and on his death – capacities and qualities that commanded the affectionate respect of his clients, who to use Gareth Evans' words, 'valued enormously the wisdom, experience, integrity and objectivity of Maurice Byers'.[18]

Not every barrister can exhibit the style and affability of Byers, not every barrister will be as easily available for his or her fellows as Byers was for other barristers who sought his advice. Not every barrister will be blessed with the same acuity of mind or will burn with the same passion for the constitutional truths which he was briefed to advance. But there are some capacities and qualities which are characteristic of the Bar and which maintain public confidence in the institution. They are objectivity and competence in legal advice, skill and effectiveness in legal advocacy, fearless independence and a commitment to justice according to law. These are the strengths on which the Bar's institutional reputation depends. They are sustained by the structure of the justice system and by the Bar's rules and practices.

The public administration of justice by the courts ensures that advocacy is open to critical evaluation and the validity of legal advice is publicly tested. The fearlessness and independence of the barrister – qualities that stand high in public estimation as Mortimer's Rumpole demonstrates – can be assessed by court and client and, significantly, by peer group. So can the barrister's commitment to justice according to law. Publicity and individual responsibility produce the competition which stimulates a high level of professional service.

The strengths of the Bar are buttressed by its rules and practices. Partnerships have not been acceptable at the Bar, so that each barrister must take individual responsibility for his or her advice and advocacy. The conventional view has been that solicitors facilitate the objectivity of the barrister by providing a *cordon sanitaire* which keeps the barrister at a certain distance from the lay client. A brief is not accepted if the advice or advocacy for which the barrister is retained would be compromised by personal or commercial relationships or by knowledge acquired elsewhere. The confidentiality and commitment which are offered by a barrister to a client are secured by more than a Chinese wall.[19]

Touting for work has been frowned upon and the barrister's remuneration has been confined to payment for specific work done on the solicitor's instructions. In the jurisdictions where an independent Bar has been established, whether by law or in practice, the remuneration of the practising barrister has never been a wage paid by a solicitors' firm or a proportion of the firm's profits.[20] The piecework nature of the solicitor-barrister relationship relieves the barrister from an ongoing concern about the lay client's non-legal objectives. The barrister's attention is focussed on the application of the law, not on the consequences of the law's application. Hence the duty in advocacy is to assist the court to a conclusion that is legally correct, even to the disadvantage of the client. The duty in advising is to be legally objective, not to furnish an opinion which gladdens the client's heart. And when a person who offers a reasonable fee, seeks the barrister's services in an area in which the barrister ordinarily practises, the barrister must accept the brief even though he or she would not wish to do so. That is the cab-rank rule which secures both the reasonable availability of the Bar's services and the independence of its individual members.

These are not merely the rules and practices of an exclusive club. They are calculated to ensure that the barrister is able to perform, efficiently and with objectivity, the function of assisting in the administration of justice according to law. The lofty words of Lord Eldon are worth repeating, if only to restate the reason why the Bar exists:

> He lends his exertions to all, himself to none. The result of the cause is to him a matter of indifference. It is for the court to decide. It is for him to argue. He is, however he may be represented by those who understand not his true situation, merely an officer assisting in the administration of justice, and acting under the impression, that truth is best discovered by powerful statements on both sides of the question.[21]

The sentiment was echoed when Byers responded to his toast at the Bench and Bar Dinner in 1994:

> When we appear before the courts we are engaged in the administration of justice and thus owe to the courts in this ministerial undertaking a duty which prevails over our duty to our client. The practice of the law is thus radically and essentially different from the practice of other professions or callings. We participate and they do not in the administration of justice to the same extent as the judge, though our function differs.[22]

A separate and independent Bar provides not only an organized structure in which individuals can conveniently and efficiently carry on their practices. The primary purpose of an organized Bar is to ensure the existence of a college of advisers and advocates who act in the belief that their chief function is to assist in the administration of justice according to the law. Without that collegial ethos, the individual barrister is hard put to characterize himself or herself as a professional. And were that character to be forsaken, the objectivity of advice and the efficacy of advocacy would be lost, to the disadvantage of client and community alike.

The rules and practices of the Bar that buttress its professional objectives are still the respected modes of professional behaviour and have great attractive force for those who, for whatever reason (or for no good reason at all) seek to practise in this most competitive, uncertain and sometimes cruel profession. But now, facing the reality of a rapidly changing society, is the Bar able to – indeed, does it wish to – retain the character it has had and about which it has boasted in the past?

As the worth of a barrister's services has come to be appreciated by the commercial community, the work of the Bar has changed from what it was in the days when Byers commenced practice. The private litigant is represented by a barrister in the Criminal Court and often in the Family Court and in other jurisdictions in which legal aid is available, but private litigants do not now constitute the same proportion of a barrister's lay clientele as in earlier times. In the lesser cases of earlier times – the fencing disputes, the minor statutory offences, the applications for testator's family maintenance in small estates, the run of the mill accident cases – the barrister built up a large constituency of goodwill. The services of the Bar have been increasingly devoted to service of the corporate and government sectors. The soaring cost of litigation has removed a large part of the public constituency of the Bar. Perhaps it has also given the Bar the image of an institution of and for the affluent. That is an image cultivated by the media as they focus on the fees of the most distinguished or fashionable leaders. Regrettably, the pro bono work of the barrister, especially the pro bono work of the leaders, receives little publicity and lacks the recognition it deserves. I fear that the Bar has lost some of the public support it once enjoyed and, however illogically, that could reduce the high conceit which the Bar holds of its professional standing and could lead some barristers to suspect that (to adapt Chief Justice Gleeson's phrase) 'it would serve the public better if [the Bar] were a business.'

The strength, indeed, the very viability, of an independent Bar depends primarily on its internal ethos. If its members are conscious that they are participants in the high social function of doing justice according to law, the community of the Bar is bonded by a common sense of public service and by mutual respect among its members. Of course, the noble aspiration of justice for all is never fully achieved but, if the aspiration be forsaken, the professional character of the barrister's work would be lost. It would then be a business, the chief purpose of which would be the efficient delivery of advisory and advocacy services to the economic advantage of the practitioner. Then public service would be subordinated to self-interest except to the extent that the rendering of some public service would be deemed to enhance the goodwill of the business. Pro bono work would cease to be a professional obligation and a necessary element of practice.

The limitation on fees, imposed by the reasonableness requirement of the cab-rank rule, would cease to apply. Indeed, the cab-rank rule would lose its obligatory force. Nor would there be an incentive to assist the court on issues of either law or fact if the assistance might prejudice the barrister's business connections. The courts would question their faith in the integrity of a barrister's submissions, to the detriment of the administration of justice.

The differences between a profession and a business may not always be obvious to the superficial observer; nevertheless, the distinction is substantial. True, a rough measure of a barrister's progress in the profession is the volume and importance of the briefs delivered and his or her ability to command a higher fee. Those would be the criteria of success in a business also. In a profession, however, they are the consequence not only of technical competence but also of the judicial and peer group's appreciation of the barrister's adherence to the ethical standards of the Bar. Again, competent and efficient service of a client's interests is or should be the outcome of a barrister's work, whether the barrister is conducting a business or a profession, but in a profession that service is only a particular instance of, and is qualified by, a wider public service that ensures the due application of the law to all aspects of a free and ordered society. And the professional barrister provides that service from time to time to those who, being unable to afford representation, would or might suffer significant injustice if representation is denied them. The expansion of the independent Bar in every state and territory indicates not only the economic viability of a barrister's practice but the attractive force of the Bar's professional standards and the collegiality of Bar membership.

However, the development of new technology may force some contraction of Bar numbers and could require further consideration of the Bar's rules and practices. The implications of technological development are, I venture to think, greater than the Bar or other sections of the legal profession presently appreciate.

When Lord Woolf conducted his inquiry into Access to Justice, he had as an Information Technology Adviser Professor R E Susskind, legal scholar, editor of the *International Journal of Law and Information Technology* and author of several texts including *The Future of Law.* In that book, the author points out that, with the advent of print, the quantity of legal materials was increased and was capable of widespread dissemination. In that milieu, the doctrine of precedent developed. With the advent of massive data bases, the available bodies of law have become more complex and the specificity and detail of the mass of material often renders the law impenetrable. Current technology has been devoted to data processing giving access to this mass, which needs then to be sifted and analysed by experienced legal practitioners. There is much work to be done by the practising lawyer, but developing technology is directed not only to data processing; it is directed also to knowledge processing so that the user is able to pinpoint *all but only* the material relevant to the solution of a problem. When that technology is combined with the public's ability to seek information by operating a television set interactively, there is likely to be a significant alteration in what might be termed the advisory market.

Susskind foresees massive investment, perhaps by legal publishers, in the development of legal information products and services which will provide solutions to many legal problems. Lawyers will be employed as legal engineers, engaged because of their analytical skills and specialist knowledge, in the creation of programmes from which advice can be obtained. The programmes will be cost effective, for the advice will not be sought by, and given to, a single client but will be devised for and sold to many. The legal engineer will be called on to think in more general terms than the adviser to a particular client but the programmes will be sufficiently detailed to resolve specific legal issues. If simple-to-operate but technically complex and legally sophisticated information services become the most familiar way in which the public obtains legal advice, situations which presently lead to litigation may be prevented from arising or may be solved without litigation. Court lists may well contract. One can foresee that much advisory work of the simpler kind will no longer require the services of the Bar.

However, technology cannot cope with the infinite variety of human situations which might call for a legal solution. Susskind points out that computers deal only with natural language which may be ambiguous and in which unspoken implications may reside. Priorities between possible solutions may have to be determined and there will always be lacunae which can be filled only by displaying what Susskind describes as 'the creativity, individuality, intuition, and common sense that we expect of judges acting in their official role.' As moral and ethical judgments will always have to be made about the circumstances of individuals or the interests of society more generally, judges of 'integrity, knowledge and experience acting as impartial arbiters' will always be needed. And if they be needed, the objective barrister of integrity, knowledge and experience will be needed to participate helpfully in the judicial function. There may be a change in the number of barristers needed and in the skills they will require to perform their function. New legal questions may arise from the use of technology. For example, if information services utilise knowledge processing technology, will the general use of a programme over a period give it some force as an authority? What will be the effect on the doctrine of precedent and the manner in which previous authorities are cited to and considered by a court?

The court lists of the future, from which the simpler cases will probably have disappeared, will contain a greater proportion of cases the solution of which is legally problematic. If these be cases which are too sophisticated for the legal information service to solve, they will be cases calling for familiarity with the underlying principles of the relevant law, precise analysis and a sensitivity to the values which can inform the development of new legal principle. The courts' need for the Bar's assistance will certainly be no less than it is today. Whatever may be the cost-effectiveness of new technology in the delivery of legal services, I cannot conceive of a transformation which would eliminate the demand for the functions presently discharged by the independent Bar.

But will those functions continue to be discharged by an independent Bar or will they be an aspect of the functions of large firms or corporations? Will the comparatively meagre resources of the individual barrister withstand the competitive pressures of firms or corporations that can offer the lay client a range of interlocking services including, but not limited to, legal advice and advocacy? That question must cross the mind of many in the legal profession who read the recently-issued discussion paper published by the Law Council of Australia entitled *Multi-Disciplinary Practices: Legal Professional Privilege and Conflict of Interest.*[23] The Law Council's paper observes:

> The perceived dichotomy between business and the professions is regarded by many as being outdated, and the legal profession is recognising that ethical and commercial issues can and must be dealt with simultaneously.
>
> As commercial transactions become increasingly complex, the need to establish multidisciplinary teams is growing. Clients are increasingly demanding more integrated professional services to meet their financial and legal needs. Big firms (and governments) are streamlining their staffing down to 'core business' functions and outsourcing entire programs.

The movement towards Multi-Disciplinary Practices, or MDPs, is widespread and, many would say, commercially irresistible. The Report of the American Bar Association's Commission on Multi-Disciplinary Practices reached this conclusion:

> The forces of change are bearing down on society and the legal profession with an unprecedented intensity. They include: continued

> client interest in more efficient and less costly legal services; client dissatisfaction with the delays and outcomes in the legal system as they affect both dispute resolution and transactions; advances in technology and telecommunications; globalization; new competition through services such as computerized self-help legal software, legal advice sites on the Internet, and the wide-reaching, stepped-up activities of banks, investment companies, and financial planners providing products that embody a significant amount of legal engineering; and the strategy of Big Five professional services firms and their smaller-size counterparts that has resulted in thousands of lawyers providing services to the public while denying their accountability to the lawyer regulatory system.

One of the 'Big Five', Price Waterhouse Coopers, is said to have 1600 lawyers employed in 42 different countries.[24] Anderson Legal and Pricewaterhouse Coopers Legal are now the third and fourth biggest legal firms worldwide.[25] England and Canada are moving in the direction of multi-disciplinary practices and, as you know, New South Wales is perhaps leading the movement with the enactment of the *Legal Profession Amendment (Incorporation of Practices) Act 2000* (NSW).

If this is the general movement of the legal profession in common law countries, can an independent Bar reasonably anticipate a long-term future? The individual barrister is poorly resourced in comparison with the large solicitors' firms of today; the poverty of those resources will be far more dramatic in comparison with those of the large multi-disciplinary partnerships of tomorrow. The large legal firms of today offer expert advice and, if the members of the Bar were to join the firms, would offer advocacy at the highest level of expertise. The one-stop shop for clients must have great attraction, particularly if the shop is a department store rather than a small boutique. And, for the overworked barrister, the prospect of a partnership and shared responsibility might have both financial and life-style advantages. Those advantages would be the greater if the reasoning in *Gianarelli v Wraith*[26] were to yield to the reasoning of the House of Lords in *Arthur J. S Hall & Co v Simons (AP)*.[27] As you know, their Lordships held that a barrister is liable in damages for in court negligence, whether in criminal or in civil proceedings. A minority of the House would not have withdrawn the immunity in relation to criminal cases, but the majority thought that so long as a conviction stood, an action by the convicted person would usually be an abuse of process. I would not presume to speculate on whether the High Court would reconsider *Gianarelli v Wraith*, but I would draw attention to the speeches in *Arthur JS Hall & Co v Simons* in which their Lordships estimate the effect of that judgment on some of the fundamental rules and practices of the Bar.

Although Lord Steyn regarded it as 'essential that nothing should be done which might undermine the overriding duty of an advocate to the court', he thought that in the world of today 'there are substantial grounds for questioning whether immunity is needed to ensure that barristers will respect their duty to the court.'[28] Lord Hoffman did not think that a loss of immunity would tempt barristers to ignore their duty to the court. After all, he said, most are 'honest, conscientious people ... [who] wish to enjoy a good reputation among [their] peers and the judiciary' and '[i]t cannot possibly be negligent to act in accordance with one's duty to the court.'[29] These were the leading majority judgments and others of their Lordships agreed with the general approach. Lord Steyn accepted that the cab-rank rule is a valuable professional rule '[b]ut its impact on the administration of justice in England is not great. In real life a barrister has a clerk whose enthusiasm for the unwanted brief may not be great and he is free to raise the fee within limits.'[30] Lord Hoffman dismisses the argument that the imposition of liability for a barrister's in court negligence would affect the operation of the cab-rank rule by saying that the argument is 'incapable of empirical verification' and, in any event 'vexatious actions are an occupational hazard of professional men and... we are improving our ways of dealing with them.'[31]

Of course, if the Bar did not subject the duty to the client to an overriding duty to the court and if the cab-rank rule were abandoned, the argument against barristers' immunity would be extremely powerful, but their Lordships do not contemplate that the Bar's standards in those respects will be affected. The confidence which their Lordships place in the ability of barristers to adhere to traditional ethical standards – standards which are essential to the maintenance of the rule of law and the administration of justice – even though the traditional safeguard of immunity be withdrawn is a tribute to the English Bar.

Their Lordship's confidence in the Bar's ability to adhere to its trad-itional obligations despite the loss of immunity is exceeded by the Law Council's confidence in the ability of lawyers generally to adhere to their traditional obligations while practising in partnership with other professions. The Law Council proposes Model Rules which state:

1. A lawyer practising within an MDP, whether as a partner, director, employee or in any other capacity, shall ensure that any legal services provided by the lawyer are delivered in accordance with his or her obligations under the applicable legal practice legislation and professional conduct rules.
2. No commercial or other dealing relating to the sharing of profits shall

> diminish in any respect the ethical and professional responsibilities of a lawyer.[32]

The Issues Paper contains three 'principles [which] enshrine the Law Council policy', the first two of which are:

> a) that the regulatory regime should be directed to the individual lawyer who is bound by ethical obligations and professional responsibilities;
> b) that regulation of business structures should no longer be regarded as critical or necessary to the maintenance of professional standards.[33]

Of course, ethical obligations and professional responsibilities can be maintained by an individual lawyer in any environment, just as religious convictions can be maintained by an individual even in a hostile environment. The Colosseum was witness to thousands who did so, though the number of those who survived the lions was small indeed. The structures of a profession may differ from the structures of a business precisely in order to facilitate the maintenance of ethical and professional responsibilities. And that seems to be acknowledged by the third of the Law Council's principles.

> c) that individual lawyers should be free to choose the manner and style in which they wish to practice law, including the right to choose to practice at an independent Bar, which requires practice as a sole practitioner and adherence to the cab-rank rule, recognising the important of the sole practice rule in the administration of justice.[34]

In other words, the unique structure of the independent Bar can be preserved and its preservation will continue to assist in the administration of justice.

The objectivity of an independent barrister's advice or advocacy will not be influenced by the commercial or other aspects of a client's interests which might be the overall concern of a multi-disciplinary partnership. Nor will the barrister be influenced by the commercial interests of such a partnership. There will be no risk of a barrister acting for conflicting interests or breaching the confidentiality of any client's communication. The barrister will accept individual responsibility because he or she will be free of relevant commitments to anybody other than court and client.

The Law Council's recognition of the survival of an independent Bar is to be welcomed for another reason. Although the work of the independent Bar is symbiotically related to the work of the courts, the barrister is independent of the judge. Ill-temper or petulance, arrogance or ignorance or self-indulgence on the part of a judge will be met by calm, courteous but unyielding insistence by the barrister that such judicial conduct be rectified. And the stalwart protection of a client's legal interests even in unpopular causes against unprofessional demands by a client, overreaching by an opponent or even unacceptable conduct by a judge will strengthen in a barrister that courage which equips him or her to assume in due course the responsibilities of an independent and impartial judge. The maintenance of an independent Bar will be essential to ensure a training ground for at least a majority of an independent and fearless judiciary.

I suggest that the functions of an independent Bar will be more significant in the future than in the past. If multi-disciplinary partnerships become the norm and an increasing proportion of lawyers are engaged in those firms and as legal engineers, the need for an independent Bar will be the greater. Its numbers may be fewer than today, its work more complex and sophisticated. Yet it will be a more important participant in the work of the courts and in the administration of justice according to law. Its capacity to perform those functions depends on the maintenance of its own standards, on the strengthening of its collegial ethos and fidelity to its rules and practices. If the independent Bar, forgetful of Lord Eldon's definition of its purpose, were to think that its strength could be measured solely in commercial terms, its privileges would rightly be short-lived and its very existence would be in jeopardy. This was the view of Maurice Byers who, responding as Guest of Honour at the 1994 Bench and Bar Dinner said this: 'An independent Bar has become an essential feature of the administration of justice in every court, State or federal. If we maintain our rights, accept our responsibilities and realise that accountability for what we do is the price of control of our destiny, all will be well.'[35]

Indeed, the Bar is right to honour his memory.

---

1. The lecture was first published in 2000, see Sir Gerard Brennan, 'Strengths and perils: the Bar at the turn of the century (2000 Summer) *Bar News: Journal of the NSW Bar Association*, 32. It also appears in, Nye Perram and Rachel Pepper (eds), *The Byers Lectures 2000-2012* (The Federation Press, 2012) 4-17.
2. See *The Age* (Melbourne, 27 January 1999).
3. Speech at the Attorney-General's dinner in honour of Sir Maurice Byers, 8 February 1984.
4. (1988) 193 CLR v, vi.
5. See *The Australian (*26 January 1999).
6. Sir Anthony Mason, 'Vale Sir Maurice' in *Nye* Perram and Rachel Pepper (eds) *The Byers Lectures 2000 – 2012* (Federation Press, 2012) 300 – 301.
7. Speech by Jacqueline Gleeson at the Bench and Bar Dinner, 17 June 1994 at which Sir Maurice Byers was the guest of honour: see Sir Maurice Byers, Jacqueline Gleeson, Theodore Simons, 'A Living National Treasure —Sir Maurice Byers CBE, QC' (1994 Spring/Summer) *Bar News: Journal of the NSW Bar Association*, 19.

8. McHugh QC (as he then was) at the Attorney-General's dinner in honour of Sir Maurice Byers, 8 February 1984.
9. Gleeson CJ as quoted in Pat Brazil and Douglas Hassall, 'Obituaries – Sir Maurice Byers', (1999) 73 *Australian Law Journal* 380, 382.
10. Sir Maurice Byers, Jacqueline Gleeson, Theodore Simons, 'A Living National Treasure —Sir Maurice Byers CBE, QC' (1994 Spring/Summer) *Bar News: Journal of the NSW Bar Association*, 18.
11. Ibid 18.
12. Gummow J as quoted in Pat Brazil and Douglas Hassall, 'Obituaries – Sir Maurice Byers (n 9), 382.
13. Sir Anthony Mason 7 as quoted by Pat Brazil and Douglas Hassall, (n 9), 381.
14. Attorney- General's dinner in honour of Sir Maurice Byers, 8 February 1984, 17.
15. Sir Maurice Byers, 'From the other side of the Bar table: An Advocate's view of the Judiciary (1987) 10 (1) *University of New South Wales Law Journal* 179, 180.
16. Michael Coper, *Encounters with the Australian Constitution* (CCH Australia, 1987) 195.
17. Gleeson CJ as quoted by Pat Brazil and Douglas Hassall, 'Obituaries – Sir Maurice Byers' (n 9) 382.
18. Attorney-General's Dinner in honour of Sir Maurice Byers, 8 February 1984, 7.
19. Compare *Fruehauf Finance Corporation Pty Ltd v Feez Ruthning (a firm)* [1991] Qd R 558 and *Bolkiah v KPMG* [1999] 2 AC 222 with *Australian Commercial Research and Development Limited v Hampson* [1991]1 Qd R 508.
20. Cf the position of 'in house' counsel discussed in *Law Society of the Australian Capital Territory v Lardner and Andrews* [1998] ACTSC 24.
21. Reported as a note in *Ex parte Elsee* (1830) Mont 69,70n, 72.
22. Sir Maurice Byers, Jacqueline Gleeson, Theodore Simons, 'A Living National Treasure -Sir Maurice Byers CBE, QC' (1994 Spring/Summer) *Bar News: Journal of the NSW Bar Association*, 23.
23. Joanna Mullins (for the MDP working group), 'Multidisciplinary Practices: Legal Professional Privilege and Conflict of Interest: Issues Paper' (Law Council of Australia, 2000) hereafter 'LCA/MDP'.
24. Ibid, Appendix to Report, section C (1).
25. 'LCA/MDP', 10 quoting *Business Review Weekly* (18 February 2000), 76.
26. (1988) 168 CLR 543.
27. (2000) UKHL 38; (2000) 3 WLR 543.
28. [2002] 1 AC 615, 680.
29. Ibid 692
30. Ibid 678.
31. Ibid 696-7.
32. National Profession Taskforce Multi-Disciplinary Practices Working Group, 'Multi-disciplinary practices: legal professional privilege and conflict of interest' (Law Council of Australia, Issues Paper, September 2000) 31-2.
33. Ibid, 4.
34. Ibid, 4.
35. Sir Maurice Byers, 'A Living National Treasure– Sir Maurice Byers CBE, QC' (1994) (Spring/Summer) *Bar News*: *Journal of the NSW Bar Association* 17, 24.

2.8 The Role of the Legal Profession in the Rule of Law

Editor's note

This was an address delivered at a conference which was an initiative of the Law Council of Australia, the Queensland Law Society, the Bar Association of Queensland and LAWASIA. The conference was held in the Banco Court of the Supreme Court of Queensland on 31 August 2007 exploring the theme: 'The Rule of Law: Challenges of a changing world'.

Chief Justice, Mr President, delegates, ladies and gentlemen,

I commence by acknowledging the traditional Aboriginal owners of the land on which we are meeting this morning. That acknowledgment is a reminder of the role which law played in the traditional societies of Australia's indigenous people. Years ago, when the people of north-eastern Arnhem Land claimed an entitlement to their land to protect their heritage, Blackburn J, in a judgment which was constrained by the law as it was then understood, commented that: 'The evidence shows a subtle and elaborate system highly adapted to the country in which the people led their lives which provided a stable order of society and was remarkably free from the vagaries of personal whim or influence. If ever a system could be called "a government of laws, and not of men", it is that shown in the evidence before me.'[1]

His Honour's finding identifies the indicia of the rule of law. It is a system which is appropriate to serve the people of a society, it provides a stable order, it is free from the vagaries of personal whim or influence. Power is controlled not by the dictates of powerful people but by 'a subtle and elaborate system'. Western societies boast of the rule of law but traditional societies may also be governed by the rule of law although colonization and the impact of western civilisation have reduced the number of traditional societies and have replaced or at least modified their legal systems. Legal systems necessarily vary from place to place, from people to people, for each system must respond to local culture and conditions. But whatever be the character of a legal system, the rule of law is the underpinning of peace, order and freedom.

Today's Conference on the rule of law is timely. It is time to understand what it is and what it does, to appreciate the institutions which are responsible for applying the rule of law and to identify the characteristics of the rule of law which ensure its support and continuance. It is time to examine these issues to correct misunderstanding.

A misunderstanding which is sometimes heard is that the rule of law is a mere catch-cry uttered by lawyers in some fictional contest for power between the Judiciary and the Executive. It is nothing of the sort. The Judiciary does no more than apply the law to the Executive government as it does and as it is bound to do to every other element in the community. In the *Communist Party Case*, Dixon J observed that among the traditional conceptions in accordance with which our *Constitution* is framed 'it may fairly be said that the rule of law forms an assumption.'[2] There is no contest for power. There may often be tension between those branches of government, and so there should be. If it happens, as it sometimes does, that the Executive government exceeds or misapplies its power and the unlawful exercise of its power is set aside by an order of a court, the Executive government may well feel frustrated, but that is simply the effect of the law. Judges no less than the executive and its agents, are subject to the rule of law. The tension between the executive and the judiciary is not a solely Australian phenomenon. Lord Bingham of Cornhill, the senior Law Lord, in a wide-ranging analysis of the rule of law[3] stated the British experience:

> Some sections of the press, with their gift for understatement, have spoken of open war between the government and the judiciary. This is not in my view an accurate analysis. But there is an inevitable, and in my view entirely proper, tension between the two. There are countries in the world where all judicial decisions find favour with the government, but they are not places where one would wish to live. Such tension exists even in quiet times. But it is greater at times of perceived threats to national security, since governments understandably go to the very limit of what they believe to be their lawful powers to protect the public, and the duty of the judges to require that they go no further must be performed if the rule of law is to be observed. This is a fraught area, since history suggests that in times of crisis governments have tended to overreact and the courts to prove somewhat ineffective watchdogs.[4]

If the rule of law is the basis on which the Judiciary reviews administrative action as well as the foundation of order in our society, we should understand what the term means. AV Dicey gave this as the primary meaning 'the absolute supremacy or predominance of regular law as opposed to the influence of arbitrary power ... Englishmen are ruled by the law, and by the law alone; a man may with us be punished for a breach of law, but he can be punished for nothing else. It means, again, equality before the law or the equal subjection of all classes to the ordinary law of the land administered by the ordinary law courts; the "rule of law" in this sense excludes the idea of any exemption of officials or others from the duty of obedience to the law which governs other citizens or from the jurisdiction of the ordinary tribunals.'[5]

The law regulates complex relationships – relationships between people and relationships between the people and the state. In a society governed by the rule of law, special knowledge and skills are needed to administer a 'subtle and elaborate system'. Competence, as well as authority, was the concern of Lord Coke's famous rejection in the case of *Prohibitions Del Roy* of King James I's pretensions to judge: 'His Majesty was not learned in the laws of his realm of England, and causes which concern the life, or inheritance, or goods, or fortunes of his subjects, are not to be decided by natural reason but by the artificial reason and judgment of law, which law is an act which requires long study and experience, before that a man can attain to the cognizance of it: that the law was the golden met-wand and measure to try the causes of the subjects; and which protected His Majesty in safety and peace.'[6]

That is why lawyers are essential to the rule of law. The basic assumption of the rule of law is that the law is truly defined. Under the common law system, definition of the law is the ultimate responsibility of the courts. In the familiar words of Chief Justice Marshall in *Marbury v Madison,* 'It is emphatically the province and duty of the judicial department to say what the law is'.[7] One may add 'the judges assisted by the legal profession'. Or, as Lord Bingham pointed out in *A v Secretary of State for the Home Department* : '... the function of independent judges charged to interpret and apply the law is universally recognised as a cardinal feature of the modern democratic state, a cornerstone of the rule of law itself.'[8]

The declaration of the law is a basic, but not the only, element in the operation of the rule of law. Much depends on the terms in which the law is framed and on the manner in which it is applied. A literal application of laws which trample on basic human rights may be the very antithesis of the rule of law. Some of Hitler's heinous policies were implemented in accordance with German law as it then was. There is a difference between the rule of law and rule by law. In a recent speech, the British Attorney-General, Lord Goldsmith QC, said that the rule of law 'is not simply about rule <u>by</u> law. Such a proposition would be satisfied whatever the law and however unfair, unjust or contrary to fundamental principles, provided only that it was applied to all. Instead, it seems to me clear that the rule of law comprehends some statement of values which are universal and ought to be respected as the basis of a free society.'[9]

That requires a commitment to the rule of law by the legislature and the executive as well as by the judiciary. So much was recognized by Lord Goldsmith who added 'In my view all the organs of state – the executive, legislature and judiciary – have a shared responsibility for upholding the rule of law. This is not to down play the responsibility of the courts – they provide the critical long-stop guarantee – but the rule of law will only have real meaning in practical terms in a society in which all organs of the state are mindful of their obligations to respect it.'

This theme about the content of the law was taken up by Lord Bingham when he said that the rule of law means, inter alia, 'that the law must afford adequate protection of fundamental human rights', although he accepted that there is 'an element of vagueness' about that proposition.

In this country, in the absence of a constitutional Bill of Rights, fundamental human rights are susceptible to extinction by statute. It is surely the function of lawyers to be able to identify laws which have that effect, to seek to have them narrowly applied and to contribute to any public consideration of the necessity for enacting or retaining such laws. There must be an overriding justification of public interest to warrant a denial of any person's fundamental human rights. That proposition presents today's lawyers with a significant challenge to keep the law respectful of human rights so far as is compatible with the national interest.

A peaceful and ordered society needs the rule of law but it also needs to be secure against disruption from both external and internal sources. How are these two needs to be satisfied or, if not satisfied, reconciled; or, if not reconciled, balanced? Perhaps the answer is to be found in what it is that sustains the rule of law. Most lawyers are familiar with the danger created by ordinary criminal conduct and, over the years, the courts and the legislature have prescribed the steps to be taken in detecting and punishing crime and the procedures and penalties which are intended to suppress it. But lawyers generally do not know the true nature and extent of the threat posed by terrorism today and, like many others, are uncertain about the steps which should be taken to suppress it. What lawyers do know, however, is what laws, practices and procedures provide the safeguards which maintain public confidence in the rule of law. When the conventional safeguards of law and the legal process are dismantled or reduced so that the public sense that justice according to law is no longer assured to all people within the jurisdiction, public confidence in the rule of law is lost or diminished. That weakens the unity and fabric of society and exposes us to danger from those who do not share a respect for the rule of law.

Lawyers should be, and often are, involved in the process of making our laws. Apart from their engagement in politics, they can explain how the rule of law is impaired by dismantling or reducing the conventional safeguards of law and the legal process. The lawyer's public role, I suggest, is to advocate the importance of preserving the safeguards of the rule of law unless it is tolerably clear that any proposed abrogation of the traditional laws, practices and procedures is necessary to protect the community, that the abrogation is proportionate to the apprehended harm and has a substantial prospect of achieving the desired protection.

Let us then reflect on some of the key features of our system which establish and sustain the rule of law. It matters not that the public does not consciously advert to some of these features; after all, we do not consciously think about the air we breathe. But if any of us were caught in the toils of a system which denied the rule of law, we would surely be conscious of what we had lost. By reminding ourselves of characteristic features of the rule of law, we can identify the risk to our freedom which is posed by any law or practice which eliminates or diminishes those features.

Public promulgation of laws made by the democratic process

To maintain confidence in the rule of law, the laws must be publicly promulgated. Retrospectivity is incompatible with the rule of law. It denies the freedom which individuals are entitled to enjoy subject to conformity with the law. It unbalances the relationship between the government and the governed. If we accept that the moral authority of the law comes from the people, the people must have the ability to reject the laws by changing the lawmakers. The rule of law is not possible, in my view, if the people cannot change the law. In a democracy, a dissident minority agrees to be bound by laws from which that minority dissents and that minority is free to express dissent. Absent that right, dissent festers until expressed in disruptive protest.

The right to peaceful dissent is not merely something to be tolerated. It is an important safeguard of peace and order; it is a feature of a free society under the rule of law. Subject to the ordinary laws governing the limits of free speech, restriction on the freedom to dissent or to contribute fairly to political discussion[10] is an impairment of the rule of law.

The public administration of the law

The public requires assurance of the proper application of the law, so the courts must conduct their proceedings in public. In 1913, the High Court said that the admission of the public to attend proceedings is 'one of the normal attributes of a court'.[11] Stephen J (as Sir Ninian then was) in *Russell v Russell* said that 'a tribunal which as of course conducts its hearings in closed court is not of the same character as one which habitually conducts its proceedings in open court'.[12] Public scrutiny of curial proceedings gives the assurance of integrity in the application of the law. The administration of the law is a public function and secret trials lead inevitably to injustice. To quote Sir Frank Kitto:

> The process of reasoning which has decided the case must itself be exposed to the light of day, so that all concerned may understand what principles and practice of law and logic are guiding the courts, and so that full publicity may be achieved which provides, on the one hand, a powerful protection against any tendency to judicial autocracy and against any erroneous suspicion of judicial wrongdoing and, on the other hand, an effective stimulant to judicial high performance. Jeremy Bentham put the matter in a nutshell ... when he wrote: 'Publicity is the very soul of justice. It is the keenest spur to exertion and the surest of all guards against improbity. It keeps the judge himself while trying on trial'.[13]

The application of the law must be, and be seen to be, impartial

Impartiality is the supreme judicial virtue.[14] It regulates the conduct of the proceedings, the evaluation of evidence, the conclusion of facts and the analysis and application of legal rules. It guarantees that equality of treatment which is at the heart of the rule of law. It is a fundamental precept that the courts must act impartially between the parties.[15] Professor Winterton, commenting on the *Communist Party Case*,[16] said that it 'demonstrated that our freedom depends upon impartial enforcement of the rule of law, of which courts are the ultimate guardians. Although, of course, not infallible, impartial and fearless courts determined to exercise their proper powers are our final defence against tyranny.'[17]

The appearance of impartiality is as critical to the confidence reposed in the courts as impartiality itself. Lord Devlin pointed out that '[t]he Judge who does not appear impartial is as useless to the process as an umpire who allows the trial by battle to be fouled or an augurer who tampers with the entrails.'

No unsuccessful party should be left with any reasonable apprehension of bias affecting the decision. Nor should the public have any ground for concern on that score. For that reason, the courts themselves have laid down the rule[18] that a challenge to a decision on the ground of bias will succeed if 'in all the circumstances the parties or the public might entertain a reasonable apprehension that the judge might not bring an impartial and unprejudiced mind to the resolution of the matter before him'.[19] To ensure impartiality it is essential that a judge be independent – independent of those who can confer a benefit or cause a detriment, independent of politics or power, independent of influences that might inappropriately affect the performance of the judicial function.

Natural justice must be observed

In *Leeth v The Commonwealth,* the majority observed that 'it may well be that any attempt on the part of the legislature to cause a court to act in a manner contrary to natural justice would impose a non-judicial requirement inconsistent with the exercise of judicial power'.[20]

The observance of natural justice, or procedural fairness, is not an obligation imposed only on the exercise of judicial power. We are familiar with this requirement in the review of administrative action and, to the legal professional, it is axiomatic. Natural justice requires, inter alia, that a party whose interests might be affected by a decision must be heard before the decision is made and must have an opportunity to answer any adverse material which might affect the decision to be made When statute exempts any repository of power from the obligation to observe natural justice, an exercise of the power is attended with the risk of injustice – injustice which is not curable by judicial intervention and which may not even be revealed if the repository of the power does not have to disclose the material on which he or she acted.

Justice must be done according to law

The judicial function is not merely to interpret but also to apply the law. The judicial method of reasoning is calculated to ensure that, in the application of the law, justice is done as far as is consistent with the law. The rules of statutory interpretation, for example, are designed to preserve fundamental human rights so far as is consistent with the language of the statute. The freedoms and immunities recognized by the common law are not denied unless the language of the statute so demands. This approach led a Cambridge academic, RWM Dias, to comment that, in the application of legal rules –

> ... it is commonplace that ... [the judges] are guided by their sense of values according to which they balance the interests in dispute.
>
> This explanation, brief as it is, makes it possible to relate judicial independence to the 'rule by law'/'rule of law' dichotomy. Where 'rule by law' obtains, the judiciary is a tool of government, which, along with others, reflects and implements official policies and interests. Where 'rule of law' obtains, judges are free to decide on values of their own, and the check on power derives from their being able to hold governmental interests in balance against others. In this way the British judiciary has built up its tradition of independence over the centuries. By and large judges have contrived to preserve as much balance of power in society as they could by siding with the weaker side whenever the balance tilted against it.[21]

Dias is mistaken in his phrase 'values of their own': Judges do not purport to apply their idiosyncratic values, but rather to give expression to those deep and enduring values of the community which, in large measure, inform the common law. An exercise of the leeway which judges have in applying the law requires as much assistance from the legal profession as the ascertainment of a legal rule.

The law must be applied universally

The law must be applied to all, subject only to exceptions that are justified by a relevant and reasonable ground of differentiation. If it were otherwise, the distinction between those covered by the law and those who are not would be a source of discontent, if not oppression. The law would not rule, that is, it would not govern the conduct of all or order the relationships of individuals or of individuals with the State. In the Supreme Court of the United States, Justice Jackson observed that:

> The framers of the *Constitution* knew, and we should not forget today, that there is no more effective practical guaranty against arbitrary and unreasonable government than to require that the principles of law which officials would impose upon a minority must be imposed generally. Conversely, nothing opens the door to arbitrary action so effectively as to allow those officials to pick and choose only a few to whom they will apply legislation and thus to escape the political retribution that might be visited upon them if larger numbers were affected. Courts can take no better measure to assure that laws will be just than to require that laws be equal in operation.[22]

The law must apply equally to all since, as John Locke pithily observed: 'Where-ever law ends, tyranny begins.'[23]

Thus, it has been held that the criminal law applies equally to all, including those who purport to act in breach of the law under the authority of the executive government.[24]

If the rule of law is to apply universally, the jurisdiction of the courts to judicially review an exercise of administrative power is essential. To the extent that the courts are denied jurisdiction to review judicially an exercise of administrative power, the power is beyond control by operation of law. If the courts are denied jurisdiction to enforce the law governing the exercise of power, the repository of the power can refuse to obey the law with impunity and the rule of law is negated. By reason of s 75(v) of the *Constitution*, however, decisions taken in exercise of federal power cannot be totally exempt from judicial review. As the High Court pointed out in *Plaintiff S157/2002,* the jurisdiction conferred on the High Court by that provision –

> ... is a means of assuring to all people affected that officers of the Commonwealth obey the law and neither exceed nor neglect any jurisdiction which the law confers on them. The centrality, and protective purpose, of the jurisdiction of this Court in that regard places significant barriers in the way of legislative attempts (by privative clauses or otherwise) to impair judicial review of administrative action. Such jurisdiction exists to maintain the federal compact by ensuring that propounded laws are constitutionally valid and ministerial or other official action lawful and within jurisdiction.[25]

The Role of the Legal Profession

I have spoken chiefly of the role of the courts in the maintenance of the rule of law. The ultimate responsibility for maintaining the standards, practices and procedures which are the critical aspects of the rule of law rests with the judiciary. But the courts are the long-stop. The law which rules is the law according to the rulings of the courts, but it is applied in the offices and chambers of the legal profession. It is applied in drafting and advising; in consultations more than in litigation. But, because the courts are the long-stop and because the rulings of the courts determine the way in which the law operates, judicial decision-making is critical to the maintenance of the rule of law. So it is in litigation that the practising legal profession works at the cutting edge of the rule of law. They are the initiators who produce the evidence and frame the issues for determination; they are the principal officers involved in the testing of evidence and honing the issues for judicial consideration; they are the researchers who identify the statutes and the precedents and whose submissions assist in ascertaining the facts and applying the relevant law or, on occasions, in exercising a judicial discretion.

To perform their appointed function, the members of the practising profession must be knowledgeable in the law and competent in its application. It is not sufficient to be mere technicians, familiar with the words of a statute or a precedent. There may be a need to understand the underlying purpose of the statute or the principle to which the precedent is giving effect. The law develops organically and incrementally, and the legal profession usually provides the stimulus to its growth. The advocate, respectful of judge, witness and opponent but fearless in advancing the client's case, is the daily witness to the work of the judiciary. In that role, the advocate is bound not only to assist in the elucidation of relevant fact and law but to ensure and defend the impartial discharge of judicial duty. Misbehaviour by a judge is antithetical to the rule of law and, at whatever cost, the advocate's duty is, firmly but respectfully, to propose a return to judicial propriety. It is a commonplace that judges acknowledge the important role which advocates play in the dispensing of justice according to law. To perform that function, the advocate must be independent of any influence that might tend towards a deviation from an advocate's duty – even the influence of the client to whom a duty is owed, which is a duty subordinate to the duty to the court.

Outside the court, the legal profession has a role to play in the framing of our laws. Individually and institutionally, the legal profession can seek to ensure that the values of the common law are preserved to the extent possible at a time when we are concerned by the threat of terrorism. That is not to suggest that it is the function of the institutional profession to oppose any law simply because it trespasses upon one of the values of the common law. When laws enacted within power do abrogate the ordinary safeguards of the rule of law, it is the function of the practising profession to apply them according to their terms, construing them by established canons of construction. Thus is the rule of law preserved to the extent that it is legally possible to do so. But it should be remembered that, over the centuries, the common law balance of individual freedom and community protection is the balance which the community has accepted as appropriate in an ordered but free society. Only a modicum of freedom can be traded for security without affecting the rule of law. When new incursions are to be made on individual freedom or the values of the common law are to be trespassed upon in some way, some justification must be shown. In recent times, the Parliament has enacted laws which make substantial incursions on individual freedom and the values of the common law.

Under the *Australian Security Organization Act 1979* (Cth),[26] some persons may be detained without any suspicion of their being involved in the commission of any offence; their detention may be authorized on the basis of information of which they have no knowledge; orders can be made in secret without public access or accountability. And the Commonwealth *Criminal Code Act 1995* (Cth)[27] allows the making of control orders against persons who may not have committed any offence if the order is thought to be reasonably necessary to protect the public from a terrorist act. Incursions on the rule of law may be essential to combat the risk of terror but the cautionary words of Justice William Brennan of the United States Supreme Court in 1987 remain pertinent: 'There is considerably less to be proud about, and a good deal to be embarrassed about, when one reflects on the shabby treatment civil liberties have received in the United States during times of war and perceived threats to national security … After each perceived security crisis ended, the

United States has remorsefully realized that the abrogation of civil liberties was unnecessary. But it has proven unable to prevent itself from repeating the error when the next crisis came along.'[28]

The legal profession has an important role in maintaining the rule of law, no less in times of danger as in times of peace. We remember the powerful proclamation of Lord Atkin in his celebrated dissent in *Liversidge v. Anderson* written in one of the darkest periods of World War II: 'In this country, amid the clash of arms, the laws are not silent. They may be changed, but they speak the same language in war as in peace.'[29]

The legal profession is a profession of service. In maintaining the rule of law, it gives vitality to the peace and order, the freedom and the decency, of the society in which we live. Sometimes that may be an anxious duty, sometimes difficult to perform. But that has long been the experience of a robust and proud profession.

---

1. See *Milirrpum v Nabalco Pty Ltd* (1971) 17 FLR 141, 267.
2. See *Australian Communist Party v The Commonwealth* (1951) 83 CLR 1, 193.
3. Lord Bingham of Cornwall KG, 'The Rule of Law', (Sixth Sir David Williams Lecture, Cambridge, 16 November 2006).
4. See Tom Bingham, 'Personal Freedom and the Dilemma of Democracies' (2003) 52 *International Comparative Law Quarterly* 841.
5. Albert Venn Dicey, *Introduction to the study of the law of the Constitution* (Macmillan, 10th ed, 1959), 202-203.
6. (1607) 12 Co Rep 63, 64-65; [77] ER 1342, 1343.
7. 5 US (1 Cranch) 137 (1803, 177.
8. [2005] 2 AC 68; [2004] UKHL 56, [42].
9. Lord Goldsmith, '*Government and the Rule of Law in the Modern Age*' (LSE Law Department and Clifford Chance Lecture series on Rule of Law, 22 February 2006).
10. See *Australian Capital Television Pty Ltd v The Commonwealth* (1992) 177 CLR 106.
11. See *Dickason v Dickason* (1913) 17 CLR 50, 51 (Barton ACJ for the Court).
12. (1976) 134 CLR 495, 532.
13. Sir Frank Kitto, 'Why Write Judgments?' (1992) 66 *Australian Law Journal* 787, 790.
14. See Patrick Devlin 'Judges and Lawmakers' (1976) 39 *Modern Law Review* 1,4, reproduced in Patrick Devlin, *The Judge* (Oxford University Press, 1979), 4,4.
15. See *R v Watson; Ex parte Armstrong* (1976) 136 CLR 248.
16. See *Australian Communist Party v The Commonwealth* (1951) 83 CLR 1.
17. George Winterton, 'The Significance of the Communist Party Case' (1992) 18(3) *Melbourne University Law Review* 630, 658.
18. The rule does not apply when, of necessity, a particular judge must sit on a case.
19. See *Grassby v The Queen* (1989) 168 CLR 1, 20, Dawson J citing *Livesey v New South Wales*

Bar Association (1983) 151 CLR 288 and *R v Watson; Ex parte Armstrong* (1976) 136 CLR 248.

20. (1992) 174 CLR 455, 470 (Mason CJ, Dawson and McHugh JJ).
21. 'Götterdammerung – gods of the law in decline' (1981) 1(1) *Legal Studies* 3, 13.
22. See *Railway Express Agency Inc v New York* 336 US 106, 112-113 (1949), cited by Lord Bingham: see Lord Bingham of Cornwall KG, 'The Rule of Law', (Sixth Sir David Williams Lecture, Cambridge, 16 November 2006).
23. John Locke, *Second Treatise of Government* (1690), Chap XVII, s.202 (Cambridge University Press, 1988), quoted by Lord Bingham: see Lord Bingham of Cornwall KG, 'The Rule of Law', (Sixth Sir David Williams Lecture, Cambridge, 16 November 2006).
24. See *A v Hayden* (1984) 156 CLR 532; *Ridgeway v The Queen* (1995) 184 CLR 19.
25. See *Plaintiff S157/2002 v Commonwealth of Australia* (2003) 211 CLR 476, 513-514 and see *Re Minister for Immigration and Multicultural Affairs; Ex parte Applicant S20/2002* [2003] HCA 30.
26. Division 3.
27. Part 5.3, Division 100.
28. William J Brennan Jr, The Quest to Develop a Jurisprudence of Civil Liberties in Times of Security Crises 18 *Israel Yearbook of Human Rights* (1988) 11 cited by Lord Bingham in the lecture: Lord Bingham of Cornwall KG, 'The Rule of Law', (Sixth Sir David Williams Lecture, Cambridge, 16 November 2006).
29. See *Liversidge v Anderson* [1942] AC 206, 244.

Brennan, on the large drum, in his last year at school participated in a spontaneous victory parade at Downlands College, Toowoomba, on 2 September 1945, the end of World War II.

Brennan was elected to the executive of the National Union of Australian University Students (NUAUS) in 1948 when Peter Durack was President. In 1949, Brennan became President. Here he is meeting with members of the Commonwealth Education Commission.

Brennan presiding at the annual meeting of NUAUS in 1949.

Gerard Brennan and Patricia O'Hara married on 26 May 1953.

As a junior barrister, Brennan practised extensively in criminal law. In 1960, he appeared in the famous Mrs Pressler Murder Case. (*Courier Mail*)

Brennan sometimes appeared for Mt Isa Mines in civil litigation. Here he is down the mine in 1964. In 1970, he appeared against Mt Isa Mines in the High Court in the nervous shock case *Pusey v Mt Isa Mines*. He later worked on the corporate restructure of Mt Isa Mines.

Brennan and his family were given a traditional welcome to Fiji when he was briefed by the Fijian Alliance Party to appear for sugar cane growers in the 1969 arbitration by Lord Denning.

Brennan led a team of local lawyers in the Denning arbitration. He was later asked to be Chief Justice of Fiji, but declined as all his seven children were still at school in Australia.

The Commonwealth briefed Brennan in 1972 to lead the prosecution of 13 Tolais charged with the murder of Jack Emanuel, the District Patrol Officer. The trial was held in Rabaul. The defendants were individually represented by barristers from the Sydney and Melbourne Bars.

Chapter 3

The Role of Judges

3.1 New Growth in the Law – the Judicial Contribution

Editor's note

This was the 8th Wilfred Fullagar Memorial Lecture delivered on 11 September 1979 at Monash University when Brennan was a judge of the Federal Court and President of the Administrative Appeals Tribunal.[1]

The work of a judge is usually appraised by the litigants in the cases over which he presides, and by the profession-practising, academic and employed-in the judgments which he writes. On either of those assessments, Sir Wilfred Fullagar achieved mightily. There is yet another way in which a judge's work may be assessed, namely, by the influence which he has upon the following generation of lawyers. This evening, I pay my humble and respectful tribute to a judge who made manifest to me and to my generation that a profound humanity emanates from a great judge, though he be sitting on high and seized of questions of great moment. With gentle voice and twinkling eye, he coaxed out of counsel whatever they had to offer and submitted the offering to an intellect which displayed both mastery of law and a deep understanding of his times. He sat on two great benches-the Supreme Court of Victoria and then the High Court of Australia-and it does not diminish the stature of either court to say that it was enhanced by his presence.

He was a finder and a teacher of the law, and it is appropriate in this forum to consider how judges make the law to grow, and then to divine, if it be possible, how judicial methods may bring forth new law to respond to the needs of our time.

Judicial development of law

Springtime is now upon us, the season of new growth. The established bushes of the garden put forth new shoots from the old wood and the newer bushes grow with a wild profusion. In the garden of the law it is perpetual spring: both old and new jurisdictions continually send forth new growth from the precedent principles, sometimes to fill in the small interstices in a lattice of established law, sometimes sprouting urgently and luxuriantly to cover an area bare of legal principle. The manner and the extent of the growth of new law is largely in the hands of the judges, and their function is attracting increasing attention as they define new principles and find new application for principles already established.

Judicial development of the law is not, of course, an undertaking of choice: it is a function performed of necessity in order to answer the imperative demand of novel cases. Judges do not choose the facts of the cases which they decide-the facts have a life of their own, grouping and rearranging themselves around the litigants in an infinite variety of ways, and adding new elements drawn from the contemporary social milieu. A pattern may emerge from time to time, but the law reports bear testimony to the stubborn refusal of facts to confine themselves within a Procrustean bed of principle, or to exhibit an enduring homogeneity from year to year.

And so, the established principles of the law must be adjusted one with another, and extended to cover facts to which they had not previously been applied, and thus the instant case is made soluble. 'Our common-law system', said Baron Parke, 'consists in the applying to new combinations of circumstances those rules of law which we derive from legal principles and judicial precedents.'[2]

The system requires the ascertainment of the relevant rule of law which, when applied to the particular facts, will syllogistically yield the conclusion.[3]

The judicial method is to search for an established principle, to develop it according to the exigencies of the case, and to apply it to the facts as found. The starting point is a reference to the body of established legal principles. So far as those principles extend, they provide a foundation for judgment, as Sir Owen Dixon said:

> At every point in an argument the existence is assumed of a body of ascertained principles or doctrine which both counsel and judges know or ought to know and there is a constant appeal to this body of knowledge. In the course of an argument there is usually a resort to case law, for one purpose or another . . . for the most part it is for the purpose of persuasion; persuasion as to the true principle or doctrine or the true application of principle or doctrine to the whole or part of the legal complex which is under discussion .... The presupposition is that there exists a definite system of accepted knowledge or thought and that judgments and other legal writings are evidence of its content.[4]

He goes on to add that the search for principle, in the classical period of English law, was accompanied by its development. 'There was', he says, 'a steady, if intuitive, attempt to develop the law as a science. But this was done not by an abandonment of the high technique and strict logic of the common law. It was done by an apt and felicitous use of that very technique and, under the name of reasoning, of that strict logic which it seems fashionable now to expel from the system.'[5]

When a principle is found, developed and applied by a court, it settles not only the instant dispute, but other and future controversies of a like kind. The doctrine of stare decisis confers upon the court a law-making power-as broad as the principle which the case demands and with the authority which the court's position in the hierarchy confers. A moment's reflection will show that the solving of a new and difficult case is an occasion of defining a new rule for future application. And this is so whether the jurisdiction is statutory or not. Lord Diplock, speaking of the 'Courts as Legislators', had no illusions as to the law-making effect of judicial decisions in the less obvious revenue appeals:

> Do not let us deceive ourselves with the legal fiction that the court is only ascertaining and giving effect to what Parliament meant. Anyone who has decided tax appeals knows that most of them concern transactions which Members of Parliament and the draftsman of the Act had not anticipated, about which they had never thought at all. Some of the transactions are of a kind which had never taken place before the Act was passed: they were devised as a result of it. The court may describe what it is doing in tax appeals as interpretation. So did the priestess of the Delphic oracle. But whoever has final authority to explain what Parliament meant by the words that it used makes law as much as if the explanation it has given were contained in a new Act of Parliament. It will need a new Act of Parliament to reverse it.[6]

The law-making effect of judgments is not reasonably open to doubt, and any attempt to sterilize it is bound to failure. If the courts were unable to develop a principle, their jurisdiction would have to be restricted to cases fitting precisely within the established principles. Or, if a court were given jurisdiction to determine a novel point, but its decision was denied effect in future cases, unevenness and perhaps caprice in judgment would be the inevitable and unacceptable result. So, the courts are lawmakers – not by desire or by an elective assumption of power, but as a consequence of the due performance of their function.

Of course, the scope for law-making activity varies greatly from case to case and, more significantly, between one area of jurisdiction and another. What is of interest is the 'strict logic and high technique'[7] which the judges use-whether consciously or not-in exercising their legislative powers, for the role which our society would confide to the judiciary depends largely upon the suitability of that technique to devise the normative solutions to contemporary problems. Mr Justice Cardozo has described the technique in essays of classical authority.[8] The judge must first 'extract from the precedents the underlying principle, the ratio decidendi; he must then determine the path or direction along which the principle is to move and develop, if it is not to wither and die.'[9]

The high technique of intellects sensitive to legal principle is called for in the extraction of underlying principle from its wraps in the learning of the past. Nice discrimination in stripping away the inessential dicta exposes the precise proposition which carries the imprimatur of precedent. And when that proposition stands exposed, the judge must choose whether to apply it precisely, whether to develop it to suit the needs of the case in hand, or whether to reject it. How he makes that choice is a question to which I shall presently come. But for the moment, consider the significance of the first step of exposing the proposition.

This step in the process furnishes the point of new departure, and it is a point embedded in the trunk or branches of existing law. A body of principle which starts from the existing law cannot be wholly alien to the needs of the society governed by it. No society changes so rapidly that it can sever connection with its history and its laws. Judicial law-making thus commences from a point, the legitimacy of which is axiomatically assured. One may say, and say truly, that such a technique is inevitably conservative, but one cannot say that it is unduly conservative. It so restricts the law-making options which are open to the judiciary as to ensure that new law is grafted on to, and is compatible with, the established legal system. New growth must come out of the old wood, and be sustained by the sap of principle which is common to all branches.

After extracting an available legal principle, the judge decides what to do with it. In the day to day work of the courts, that decision is simple enough. Where the principle was laid down by a superior court and it governs entirely the case in hand, it is the judge's duty to apply it, even though the result is unsatisfactory. Equally, when the available principle, though not binding, governs satisfactorily the facts of the case in hand, the judge does apply it.

Moreover, there is a presumption in favour of extending an established principle to new cases, and the presumption serves two purposes. First, it avoids the necessity for the judge himself to formulate a rule to govern the instant case, and thus the presumption tends to remove the subjective element from judgment. The manifest convenience of this policy has enabled the judiciary to maintain the confidence of the community, without which no curial system could survive. The justice done in the courts is justice according to principle, and not justice according to the idiosyncratic opinions of the judge.

Second, the presumption serves to satisfy the craving of the human mind for consistency and order in the abstract conceptions of the law. This is not a mere aspiration to philosophical elegance. If a principle, which has achieved justice in a variety of cases, finds expression and unifies the reasons for judgment in those cases, the principle may be presumed to be practical and sound, and some cause should be shown if it is not to be extended to the instant case. The presumption secures like results in comparable cases, an essential feature of a system of justice.

The presumption is defeasible, however. Indeed, if the presumption might be applied to two principles which would on extension to the instant case produce differing results, the presumption is self-defeating and a choice must be made between the principles. The choice is that which serves the public interest. Geoffrey Lane LJ had such a choice to make in *R v Secretary of State for Home Affairs; Ex parte Hosenball*, a case concerning the deportation of an alien: 'The alien certainly has inadequate information upon which to prepare or direct his defence to the various charges which are made against him, and the only way that could be remedied would be to disclose information to him which might probably have an adverse effect on the national security. The choice is regrettably clear: the alien must suffer, if suffering there be.'[10]

No principle of general application is likely to be so perfect in its operation as to avoid every injustice that time and the rich variety of human activity may produce. Although a judge is not at liberty to choose between applying his personal view of the justice of the case and a principle which binds him to a contradictory solution, a principle which is found to work injustice in case after case is not immune from modification or rejection. It may take time, but the modification emerges and becomes a new stock of descent. Thus, it was nearly forty years after *Re Polemis*[11] when Manning J announced in *The Wagon Mound (No 1)* his inability to apply it 'with any degree of confidence to a particular set of facts'.[12] The time for change had come, and his observation moved Viscount Simonds, speaking for the Judicial Committee, to say: 'This *cri de coeur* would in any case be irresistible, but in the years that have passed since its decision *Polemis* has been so much discussed and qualified that it cannot claim, . . . the status of a decision of such long standing that it should not be reviewed.'[13]

The pace of change may be unsatisfying, but judicial changes of principle, cautiously made, profoundly affect legal relationships. Mr Justice Cardozo observed: 'This work of modification is gradual. It goes on inch by inch. Its effects must be measured by decades and even centuries. Thus measured, they are seen to have behind them the power and the pressure of the moving glacier.'[14]

Modification may eradicate a principle or develop it; the judges may resect an earlier growth, or extend it for future use. In either case, there is a judgment to be made and it is not a judgment of a syllogistic kind. Whether the modification is needed because of an inherent defect in the old rule, or whether there is some other reason why the old rule will not satisfactorily serve to solve the case in hand, the modification of the rule is an occasion of judicial law-making. The rule then pronounced governs the resolution of cases of a like kind, whether their constituent facts occurred before or after the new definition. In every case where a judge is not constrained by precedent, the judge is entitled to ask whether the application of a precedent available for application will work injustice in the instant case. More, he is bound to determine that question.

In final courts of appeal, the extent of judicial power to modify the law attains its greatest dimension. In the High Court of Australia, the present Chief Justice declared in *Mutual Life & Citizens' Assurance Co Ltd v Evatt*:

> the common law is what the Court, so informed, decides that it should be, ... For, where no authority binds or current of acceptable decision compels, it is not enough, nor indeed apposite, to say that the function of the Court in general is to declare what the law is and not to decide what it ought to be. In such a case, in my opinion, the common law is as much in gremio judicis as ever it was, assisted and instructed now no doubt by all that has happened through the years of its growth: and thus in such a case the two positions of what is and of what should be are in reality coincident. But, of course, the Court is not to depart from what it realizes the common law would provide in order to arrive at some idiosyncratic solution. So to do is to attempt to legislate and to tread forbidden ground.[15]

Lord Reid, avowing that he had never taken a narrow view of the functions of the House of Lords, defined the approach to be taken. He said: 'The common law must be developed to meet changing economic conditions and habits of thought. ... But there are limits .... If we are to extend the law it must be by the development and application of fundamental principles.'[16]

The choice made by a court in the development and application of principles is not made in a vacuum. It is made with the wisdom of past experience, and with the concrete illustration of the way in which the principle would work in the instant case. The court is informed by empirical data, and its formulation of the rule is restricted by the material which is to hand. Lord Diplock asserts that judicial law is made by a method peculiarly suited to the task:

> Judge-made law on the other hand, because litigation is concerned with what is part and incidental, is based upon actual experience of what human beings have in fact done and what were in fact the consequences of their doing so. The courts have thus the material to piece together a rule of conduct by induction from particular instances of how men do in fact behave in particular circumstances, none exactly the same though common elements in each can be discerned. Such a rule of conduct based on the recognition of the common elements in the actual behaviour of men in their environment is one which potentially is flexible not rigid, adaptable to changing circumstances, not fixed for ever in the fetters of the past.[17]

In the long term, the judicial process is inductive, testing the utility of given principles in the crucible of contemporary experience. Statute apart, the law is not proof against the demands of justice in a changing society though the step of questioning the justice of applying a principle, and modifying the principle according to the public good often goes unremarked, perhaps not perceived; or perhaps subconsciously perceived, but not consciously acknowledged. Yet it is one of the most important aspects of judicial activity. In the particular case, it allows right to be done; in point of precedent, it is the stimulus to new growth. Though it is a commonplace of the judicial process, particularly in appellate courts, the question of justice or injustice is not itself amenable to resolution by rule or precedent. Justice and injustice are concepts which are as valuable as they are intangible, and they colour judicial thinking on any occasion when precedent does not precisely and coercively chart the course of decision.

What is just and what is unjust in a given case may appear differently to different minds, and even experienced ministers of the law may be brought into sharp controversy in propounding the just solution in a given case. No doubt the life and experience of a judge contribute the influences which form his values and determine his opinion. And although divergence of opinion among judges is diminished by their common exposure to the values which the law expresses and protects, differences in background and experience, and natural variations among men, ensure that there will be differences in deciding whether justice or injustice would be done if a precedent available for application were applied in a given case.

And thus, the cold mechanics of the syllogism do not exhaust the function of judging. Indeed, it is precisely in those cases where the major premise of the syllogism does not bind the court or does not exhaustively cover the facts of the minor premise, that the serious business of judging begins.

It is then that the search goes behind the words of the precedent judgment to the basic principle which underlies it, and the true dimension and purpose of the principle is ascertained in order to see whether the principle extends, or ought to be extended, to the instant case; or whether the principle reflects a value which is no longer suited to the governance of contemporary social relations.

The court is guided by factors which Mr Justice Cardozo enumerated: 'My analysis of the judicial process comes then to this, and little more: logic, and history, and custom, and utility, and the accepted standards of right conduct, are the forces which singly or in combination shape the progress of the law. Which of these forces shall dominate in any case, must depend largely upon the comparative importance or value of the social interests that will be thereby promoted or impaired.'[18]

With these elements at legitimate play, it is not surprising that Professor Cross warned that 'the part played by rules of law in a legal system is a great deal more limited than is sometimes supposed'.[19]

How is this to be squared with the notion that rights and obligations depend upon known and existing law, and not upon the discretion of the judge before whom the case is tried? Only by judicial sensitivity to the importance of constancy in the development of legal principle, and judicial skill in stripping away the detritus of comment from the substance of underlying principle. The high technique of the judges consists not in knowing the minutiae of the myriad cases which instance the several applications of a principle, but in seeing the underlying purpose of the principle – the public good which the principle has been developed to protect and advance. The nice adjustments in the common law of libel and slander are fine examples of judicial balancing of the interests of reputation and of free speech, and the cases which this area of the law has spawned reveal the judicial search for the values which the weapons of the law were then forged to protect.

The great judge is a bold judge, not because he chances his arm, but because he so perceives the philosophy and history of the law that he can sweep aside the incidental and reach for the essential, and fashion and refashion the basic principles so that they serve the society of his time. Boldness is a function of both understanding and courage: understanding of the deepest values of society, and courage in rejecting the applications of principle which serve an incompatible value, perhaps current at an earlier time.

And so the significant contribution which judges are able to make to the society of their time is not confined to the application of principles, but includes more importantly the modification of principles to suit the public good of that time. The high technique and strict logic is not restricted to the deductive process. The vitality of the judicial contribution is in the inductive process, deriving the rules for contemporary application from the history and contemporary functioning of society. It goes so often unacknowledged, as Mr Justice Holmes observed:

> The very considerations which judges most rarely mention, and always with an apology, are the secret root from which the law draws all the juices of life. I mean, of course, considerations of what is expedient for the community concerned. Every important principle which is developed by litigation is in fact and at bottom the result of more or less definitely understood views of public policy; most generally, to be sure, under our practice and traditions, the unconscious result of instinctive preferences and inarticulate convictions, but none the less traceable to views of public policy in the last analysis. And as the law is administered by able and experienced men, who know too much to sacrifice good sense to a syllogism, it will be found that, when ancient rules maintain themselves..., new reasons more fitted to the time have been found for them, and that they gradually receive a new content, and at last a new form, from the grounds to which they have been transplanted.[20]

Perhaps it is only in the great judges that we find familiarity with principle, confidence in understanding the needs of contemporary society, and courage to go back and prune out or modify the principles which will no longer serve the public good.

Sir Wilfred Fullagar was such a judge. His legal genius did not consist in his undoubted syllogistic skills, but in his ability to give expression to principles in harmony with his time, wisely governing the relations with which he was judicially concerned.

There are three situations where a judge reasons inductively. The first is where an available principle appears to be no longer apposite, if it ever was. Here, the opinion must be formed that the principle, though available for application directly or by logical extension, should not be applied. The false growth is judicially resected.

The techniques of resection are well known. Cases are held either to have misapplied a basic principle and on that account they are discarded as erroneous, or they are held to be distinguishable from contemporary cases and are left to wither into irrelevant obsolescence, or they are held to mean something different from what they literally said.[21] Resection of precedent to a basic legal principle, stripping away the wilderness of single instances and exposing the fundamental principle, is essential if the law is not to be confined in archaisms by the particular cases which have teased out extensions of the basic principle to circumstances of limited relevance, and if the vitality of the underlying values is to send forth new solutions to problems newly arising.

The second is where an available principle does not precisely cover the case, or where a precedent which is not binding does not appear to yield a just result. A decision is made as to whether the principle should be extended, or a modification made.

The third is where precedent fails and statute is silent or gives inadequate guidance, yet the power to make a decision is committed to judicial judgment. On such occasions, the court fashions a rule from whatever sources are available to it. In their dissenting judgment in *United Engineering Workers Union v Devanayagan* Lord Guest and Lord Devlin said: 'Experience shows that out of a jurisdiction of this sort there grows a body of principles laying down how the discretion is to be exercised and thus uniformity is created in the administration of justice. In this fashion, as was said in *Moses v Parker* there emerges inevitably a system of law.'[22]

How is a new rule fashioned? Lord Shaw gave the answer 'The *casus improvisus* is always with us: and in ninety-nine cases out of a hundred it must be settled before Parliament can act. The appeal is not made to laws, for there are none, but to law: call it what you like – the common law, the principles of jurisprudence-anything from the *jus divinum* to common sense, from *recta ratio* to a square deal: it is on and by and with that stuff that judges have to work, and they must do so not as bondmen but as free.'[23]

The raw material is fashioned in the hands of a legal craftsman. He seeks the kind of reference point which gives legitimacy to the rule devised. If the question be the criterion to guide the exercise of unfettered discretion which affects the interests of parties – say, a discretion to extend time – he interests of the parties are the primary reference points in fashioning the criterion. If the question be the content of the rules of natural justice to be implied as a condition upon the exercise of a statutory power, a wide range of relevant circumstances falls for evaluation.[24]

Judicial law-making, often associated with the names of the great jurists, is undertaken in the daily work of courts manned by judges who do not pretend to eminence – judges who dutifully decide the cases before them by a familiar procedure.[25] What are the features of this procedure?

The first feature has already been noted: the occasion for making new law is not of the judge's choosing. The law is made when the case assigned to him requires it. Some judges, to be sure, have a sharper eye for a legal point, and are more readily intrigued by a concept than others; but none may move himself to declare the law, unless it be for the purpose of deciding the case in hand. Judges do not seek the power to make law; they accept it when it is needed for the discharge of their functions. This feature of judicial law-making enables Parliament and the public to maintain confidence in the judges as unconcerned with the extent of their own domain.

Next, the judges answer the questions which are asked of them. Even if the delay be longer than the judges and litigants would wish, at least an answer is always forthcoming. No other branch of government is so invariably responsive. And when the answer is given, it is disciplined by the obligation to expose the reasons for it, so that subjective considerations are minimized and made manifest, and the answer is made referable to an objective standard. Detachment is the hallmark of judicial decisions, and it is essential to achieve the fairness which commends those decisions and gives them authority.

The ultimate stage of the judicial method is syllogistic, so that once the facts are found, the judgment depends solely upon the rule selected to govern the case. Unless there be some rule to guide, if not to govern, the power to decide does not bear a judicial character. Where no rule is, or can be made, available to govern or guide a decision, the making of the decision has not been seen as a judicial function. Thus, in the *Tasmanian Breweries Case*,[26] the High Court rejected the submission that the Trade Practices Tribunal exercised judicial power, Kitto J observing that the question committed to the Tribunal for determination did 'not depend upon the application of any ascertainable criterion', and that the issue for determination depended ultimately upon the Tribunal's 'own idiosyncratic conceptions and modes of thought'.[27]

The essence of the judicial method is the application of a rule derived from an external source. The rule may be a binding precedent, a modified principle derived from a precedent, a statute, or a rule constructed from other sources; but it is a rule which does not grow endogenously. The judges so cling to the syllogistic method, they so seek to avoid the exercise of power according to their own idiosyncratic notions, that they devise and express a rule from whatever sources are available, and they thus supply the major premise for judgment.

Before adopting the rule, they entertain open advocacy on behalf of adversaries in litigation. This procedure tends to expose the implications of choosing one rule or another and allows the implications of an adverse consequence to be put powerfully and to be considered deeply before a rule is chosen for application.

For present purposes, perhaps the most significant feature of judicial law-making is that it has grown and been developed in litigation concerning, for the most part, the adjustment of private rights and liabilities. The courts have been comfortable in determining questions of private law, and curial procedures have developed in a symbiotic relationship with private law.

Judicial method and Public Law

A question which now arises is whether the judicial method can and should be applied to the adjudication of issues which arise in the exercise of powers conferred by public law. The question is important, for the rights and liabilities of citizens (whether natural or corporate) depend increasingly upon the exercise of administrative power. Entitlement to a social security benefit, assessments to various taxes, permission to drive a car or build a house, the payment of bounties, acquisition of citizenship, licensing of professions and trades, quotas, permits and licences granted in respect of importing and exporting-the list of administrative controls and activities is large and expanding. Sometimes administrative power is fettered by the statute which creates it; sometimes there are partial fetters upon its exercise; and sometimes it is quite at large.

When the power is precisely defined, the legal issues which have to be decided are indistinguishable from the issues which a court would determine. The several Taxation Boards of Review are engaged day by day in the construction and application of the *Income Tax Assessment Act 1936* (Cth). The questions which the Administrative Appeals Tribunal determines as to the classification of imports and the application of the Customs Tariff are questions which used to be litigated before the High Court. Clearly enough, the judicial techniques of law-making are applicable to cases of this kind.

Statutes which confer administrative power are not the familiar paths through which lawyers are accustomed to roam, and often there are thickets of administrative practice which have overgrown the statute beneath. Large areas of administration await the exercise of the familiar judicial skills of statutory interpretation: defining the nature and the extent of powers, spelling out the conditions which attend their exercise. We have long gone past the time when statutes were regarded as unwelcome intruders upon the fields of common law and equity, but the statutes which have claimed our attention are those which have to do with private law. A fuller judicial contribution to the illumination of statutes relating to public law will not be made unless the courts are vested with an appropriate jurisdiction.

Of course, the ordinary jurisdiction to grant a prerogative writ, to make a declaration or to issue an injunction may be invoked in proceedings which involve the construction of statutes relating to public law, but that jurisdiction usually gives infrequent, if valuable, opportunity for judicial exegesis.

At least until recent times, and then only in some areas of jurisdiction, the judicial method has not been invoked to control the exercise of discretionary administrative powers. The courts have denied a jurisdiction to control the exercise of a discretion beyond confining the extent of the discretion to its proper scope and object. In *Swan Hill Corporation v Bradbury,*[28] Dixon J referred to the legislature's reasons for the creation of discretionary powers and charted the limits of judicial control of powers conferred in general terms. He said:

> The reason for leaving the ambit of the discretion undefined may be that legislative foresight cannot trust itself to formulate in advance standards that will prove apt and sufficient in all the infinite variety of facts which may present themselves. On the other hand, it may be because no general principles or policy for governing the particular matter it is desired to control are discoverable, or, if discovered, command general agreement .... But courts of law have no source whence they may ascertain what is the purpose of the discretion except the terms and subject matter of the statutory instrument. They must, therefore, concede to the authority a discretion unlimited by anything but the scope and object of the instrument conferring it. This means that only a negative definition of the grounds governing the discretion may be given. It may be possible to say that this or that consideration is extraneous to the power, but it must always be impracticable in such cases to make more than the most general positive statement of the permissible limits within which the discretion is exercisable and is beyond legal control.[29]

In the forty years which have intervened, there has been some change in sentiment. Perhaps the high-water mark was reached when Lord Denning zestfully construed[30] the judgments of the House of Lords in the *Padfield*[31] and *Tameside*[32] cases as showing that 'when discretionary powers are entrusted to the executive by statute, the courts can examine the exercise of those powers to see that they are used properly, and not improperly or mistakenly.' By '"mistakenly"', said Lord Denning, 'I mean under the influence of a misdirection in fact or in law'.

Whether or not the administrative oyster is to be prised open by a knife fashioned by the judiciary, an extra-curial sentiment has been developing which would commit to the judiciary the control of many administrative powers. The importance and growth of administrative powers has stimulated the development of that sentiment.

Parliament may, of course, select repositories of administrative power as it sees fit. In theory, the exercise of administrative power is subject to Ministerial control. (I except independent administrative boards). In theory, a chain of responsibility exists: Administrator to. Minister to Parliament. But in fact, the Minister leaves the day-to-day exercise of the powers to administrators who frequently develop a familiarity with administrative problems exceeding that of their Minister.

The reality is that a large concentration of power, affecting a broad spectrum of activities, is vested in administrators who are largely immune from scrutiny in the particular exercise of that power. It is not surprising that there have been calls for judicial intervention, for the experience of man is that the exercise of power in camera[33] and without effective external review is at risk of miscarrying and doing injustice to those affected by its exercise. The call has become more pressing as the ambit of administrative power increases. Foremost in the invocation of judicial intervention has been Lord Scarman. In the 1964 Hamlyn Lectures, which he entitled 'English Law, the New Dimension',[34] he pointed to the importance of the new areas of legal concern. He said:

> To satisfy the conscience of the nation the state has had to move into the empty spaces of the law, the deserts and hill country left uncultivated by distributive justice, and there to make provision for society as a whole, and for those not strong enough to provide for themselves. Thus the welfare state is challenging the relevance, or at least the adequacy, of the common law's concepts and classifications. Fault, trespass, property, even marriage, are now seen to be an insecure base for the development of a law suited to the needs of our society. [35]

And he urged that we seek: 'a new constitutional settlement that makes use of judicial power ... to use the rule of law in resolving the conflicts that will arise between the citizen and the state in the newly developed fields of administrative legal activity upon which the quality of life in the society of the twentieth century already depends.'[36]

Lord Scarman returned to his theme of a constitutional resettlement of powers recently, when he wrote on 'The Judge – A Man for All Seasons' and sought an extended role for the courts:

> The change of season, . . .calls for a constitutional resettlement-in the sense of a review of the distribution of the decision-making processes in our society. The courts must emerge from their world of private law, that is. the common law, and accept the responsibility of adjudication in disputes between state and citizen and between one decision-making authority and another. If in place of a single legislative sovereign there is to be an interlocking system of legislative, and other decision-making authorities, disputes must be so formulated and the courts system so organised that the judges can adjudicate between one authority and another. There would be no invitation to the judges to decide policy, but a recognition that in a conflict situation the judges can help to avoid disorder by adjudication.[37]

In Australia, a similar view has been expressed. Sir Laurence Street observed: 'We are not being re-equipped with the requisite jurisdiction to fulfil our basic role. ... Instead of seeing our main court system moulded to service these new dispute situations we have seen over some years past the setting up of a multiplicity of special courts and tribunals to handle particular dispute situations.'[38]

Since 1968, the New Zealand Supreme Court has been vested with a jurisdiction to determine on the merits certain appeals from administrative tribunals. An Administrative Division of the Court was created, with jurisdiction to hear and determine specified administrative appeals.[39] The jurisdiction to hear and determine appeals against tribunal decisions on the merits was conferred with caution.[40] According to the Report of the Royal Commission on the Courts, that jurisdiction is a useful one. They said:

> We believe the High Court has a vital and important role to play in this regard. We appreciate that, to some extent, this may involve the court in matters of policy as well as law, and that in theory there are some risks involved. We believe, however, that the protection of the citizen is of paramount importance and that the successful

> operation of the Administrative Division to date has demonstrated how well the judges are able to cope with the problems.[41]

In Federal areas, a different solution has been essayed by the Commonwealth Parliament, and jurisdiction to review a broadening range of administrative decisions on the merits has been conferred upon the Administrative Appeals Tribunal.

I am not here concerned to discuss the form of the reviewing Tribunal, but rather to examine the question of substance: are the judicial techniques of law-making satisfactory to develop the rules which might govern or guide the exercise of some administrative power? And, as a corollary, are judges fitted to perform the function which a constitutional resettlement of power would confide to them?

Perhaps, out of an abundance of caution, I should add that I am not here concerned to deal with the problems of fact-finding in administrative proceedings which bear upon, but are distinguishable from, the definition of those rules which govern or guide the exercise of administrative power.

But first, let me define what a constitutional resettlement of power may involve. It would not be merely an improvement in the procedures of judicial review. It would interpose the courts (or the judiciary, for I use the terms interchangeably) to control the exercise of some administrative powers, with jurisdiction to set right decisions affecting the interests of citizens which the courts think are wrong decisions, or not the preferable decisions in the circumstances of particular cases. The courts would have the power to substitute their own decisions for the decisions of the administrators.[42]

It is clear that judicial control could be suited only to a limited range of decisions, but the range may be nonetheless significant. The extent of that range depends upon the appropriateness of the judicial method (perhaps modified to deal with the novel subject matter) to resolve disputes between the citizen and the state under statutes relating to public law. The controlling power is now vested for the most part in Ministers of the Crown, but circumstances have conspired against their using it except when the pressures of politics or the anguish of a particular plea promote its exercise. Unlike judicial power, the controlling power is not exercised in response to every application in that behalf. Ministers and their departments rightly develop a relationship which, though respectful of each other's proper sphere, has a commitment of loyalty and support. Neither Ministers nor administrators may choose to abandon the existing distribution of controlling power, and the judiciary will be involved only if Parliament (no doubt with the concurrence if not at the behest of the Executive) thinks it right to do so.

The judiciary itself will not seek the power to resolve public law disputes, for judges are, by an appropriate tradition, the passive repositories of power which others confer upon them. The warrant for conferring power to control administration lies in the safeguarding of the individual as he deals with the anonymous complexity of the modern bureaucracy, and the assistance to the bureaucracy which external judicial review can provide. But does the judiciary possess the experience and skills which might accord fair weight to the public purposes to be served by administrative decision-making? Adjudication seems incompatible with the pursuit of policy so that an attempt to marry both functions in a controlling jurisdiction might create 'a position of unstable equilibrium between the judicial and political processes'.[43]

It is a tantalizing dilemma. The judiciary, accustomed to standing between the citizen and the state, between the weak and the powerful; of maintaining the unique dignity of the individual; of balancing interests with great nicety; of independence and detachment-that judiciary seems suited to control the growing and important administrative powers. Yet the assumption of that function is thought to expose the very institution of the judiciary to risk, by requiring it to make its judgments by political rather than legal criteria; by political or economic sentiment rather than by the high technique and strict logic which have been the hallmark of judicial activity and the foundation of public confidence. But the dilemma is partial, and it may be escaped by means which open up new opportunities for judicial development of the law affecting the exercise of the powers of the state.

The risk to the institution of the judiciary arises because, it is thought, cases would have to be decided according to political and economic policies, and policies of that kind are, by common assent, not the business of the judiciary. In *American Federation of Labour v American Sash Co* Frankfurter J limited the functions which courts might properly undertake, saying: 'Courts can fulfill their responsibility in a democratic society only to the extent that they succeed in shaping their judgments by rational standards, and rational standards are both impersonal and communicable. Matters of policy . . . are by definition matters which demand the resolution of conflicts of value, and the elements of conflicting values are largely imponderable.'[44]

Professor Jaffe comments:

> This overstates the case. The policy choices available in applying an authoritative text can be rationally stated and their potential consequences rationally described. But one must admit that, after the ground is rationally surveyed, the choice among competing

> values will involve a personal element. Nor can we avoid the dilemma by the argument that the judges can find purely objective answers in prevailing political, moral, and economic postulates.[45]

And Lord Scarman, anxious though he is to have the judiciary 'help to avoid disorder by adjudication', baulks at the judges deciding policy. These warnings should be heeded. All are supported by the wisdom of experience, and a keen appreciation of the functions for which the judiciary is suited. Yet it seems to me – and I say so timorously – that they appear to diminish the true genius of the judicial method and, in some degree, to mistake the nature of the task which would be confided to the judiciary if it be assigned the duty of controlling the exercise of discretionary administrative power.

The judicial method secures its legitimacy by seeking an appropriate rule from an authority external to the judge deciding the case. So long as the courts are restricted to determining cases dealing with the rights and liabilities of the parties litigant, the search is for an externally derived rule of law, that is, a rule of universal application. But when the question submitted for determination is the exercise of a discretion, the search is not for a rule of law, but for a rule to guide the exercise of a discretion; a rule not of universal application, but of presumptive application. The search for such a rule is not to be carried out in the hiding places of the law. It is not awaiting expression in a yet unwritten appendix to the statutes. Just as a legislative authority is an external authority for the making of rules of law, so an executive authority is an external authority for the making of rules to guide the exercise of discretionary administrative power. And thus if there be a policy to be applied, it is formed by the hands of him who has power to make it. The source of the discretionary rule is different from the source of the legal rule, but nonetheless it is amenable to discovery and application.

Lord Scarman's reservation was about the judge deciding policy, but not about his applying policy decided by others. Indeed, it is difficult to see how one might, settle administrative disputes by adjudication if the judge were precluded from deciding any case in which there was some policy element.

The technique of searching for an applicable policy would be different from the technique of ascertaining a rule of law. The policy may not be found in the books, but in material of a more diffuse kind. One of the parties before the court, however, would be the administrator who would rely upon an existing policy as supporting his decision, and the onus of demonstrating its existence and establishing its terms should not prove impossible to discharge.

In the traditional model, where a precedent is not necessarily binding, the judge must ask whether the rule to be found in the precedent should be applied, or whether it should be extended to apply, to the instant case. Where an administrative discretion has been exercised, the same question would have to be asked. In either case, the answer must depend upon whether the application of the rule would lead to injustice in the instant case.[46]

Of course, minds may differ on so open a question as injustice, but the possibility of difference does not mean that the judicial technique is inapplicable or that the enunciation of a guiding rule is likely to be an apparent, rather than a real, exercise of judicial authority. Take a case where a judicial discretion has been exercised, and a question arises as to whether the exercise accords with the principles judicially defined to govern its exercise. Such a case was *Ellis v Leeder*, where, as the High Court pointed out, principles had been developed to govern the exercise of a discretion under the *Testators Family Maintenance and Guardianship of Infants Act 1916* (NSW): 'That Act confers a discretionary jurisdiction, but it is one controlling substantive rights in property. It is a jurisdiction the exercise of which is determined by settled principles and its purpose is to ensure as far as may be that the needs of the testator's family are justly provided for.'[47]

Confidence in reasoned judgment is not shattered merely because other minds in the Judicial Committee took a different view as to the appropriate order.[48]

In cases where the application of a rule is inconvenient but not unjust, prudence may determine whether the respective kinds of rules should be applied. Judicial prudence requires caution in declining to apply a legal principle derived from a judicial precedent, for certainty in the law is a desirable objective of the common law system. The same consideration does not necessarily affect the reception and application of a rule of policy. A refusal by a judge to apply a rule of policy would tend to defeat the policy, even though the policy-maker insisted on maintaining the rule. Exceptions could become the rule, and thus the ultimate policy power could, in a sense, be susceptible of exercise by the judge rather than by the policy-maker. This seems at first sight to lead the judge into making policy, and indeed, into setting up his policy as the effective alternative to that of the policy-maker. The appearance is deceptive. The question for the judge would be whether the operation of the policy is productive of injustice in the instant case, a confined and pragmatic question. It is the question which is customarily raised in the inductive process of judicial law-making, and there can be few areas of possible judicial activity where the question could be more usefully asked and more appropriately answered. A policy-maker may have wide experience, but once the policy is formed, and it is applied administratively in case after case, it is not readily responsive to change. The genius of the common law system has been its responsiveness to empirical data in determining whether injustice is occasioned by applying a particular rule.

Again, to quote Mr Justice Cardozo:

> Every new case is an experiment; and if the accepted rule which seems applicable yields a result which is felt to be unjust, the rule is reconsidered. It may not be modified at once, for the attempt to do absolute justice in every single case would make the development and maintenance of general rules impossible; but if a rule continues to work injustice, it will eventually be reformulated. The principles themselves are continually retested; for if the rules derived from a principle do not work well, the principle itself must ultimately be re-examined.[49]

In the control of administrative decisions, the court would focus on the particular effect of policy in a given case, not for the purpose of enquiring whether the policy is good or desirable in some political or economic sense, but to answer the question whether it is productive of injustice. If the exceptions were to become so numerous as to become the rule, the cause would be the intrinsic injustice of the policy. The policy would be rejected because it is unjust, not because it is unsound on some political or economic ground other than justice. True, experience in judicially determining the existence of administrative injustice is lacking, but it may not be fanciful to expect that a judge will be able to recognize it when it is encountered, even if it is not definable in advance. And if one seeks justification for refusing to apply a sound political or economic policy because it works an injustice in an individual case, the justification is found in the indulgence which a confident and stable society allows itself in order to accord a unique importance to each of its citizens.

No doubt there are some administrative discretions which are not guided by a defined policy upon which a court might rely, and those discretions thus fall to be exercised at large. A discretionary rule may not be available either because the power is not amenable to structuring by rule, or because there has been default in the development of a rule.

In the former situation, the power is unsuited to judicial control. For example, the granting of landing rights to a foreign airline may depend upon factors so unforeseeable in advance of a particular case that no rule could be devised to guide a decision-maker. An inability to guide a discretion by rule is not necessarily an argument against the width of the discretionary power. Not all wide discretions should be eliminated nor should every exercise of power be justiciable. Every civilized society blends a measure of law and a measure of discretion in its government. And thus, Professor K C Davis speaks of 'a government of laws and of men'.[50] Nevertheless, he insists that rules, where they are practicable, furnish a safeguard against administrative injustice: '... how can we improve the quality of justice for individual parties; how can we reduce injustice? Over the centuries, the main answer has been to build a system of rules and principles to guide decisions in individual cases. That is a good answer, as good for the future as for the past. The continued development of rules and principles is both desirable and inevitable.'[51]

The devising and proper use of a rule devised do not, of course, either fetter a discretion which is not to be fettered, or prevent the consideration of the circumstances and merits of particular cases.[52] The courts may think it beyond their capacity to devise a policy rule where a policy rule is needed to guide the exercise of a discretionary power in a particular case it is not always so. The practice of the courts has been to develop a rule for application according to the experience gained in particular cases; to adopt the inductive method before resorting to the deductive consequence; to discover the major premise before applying it. It may be said that the ascertainment of rules affecting the public welfare is beyond the capacity of the courts, and in respect of some rules that proposition is undeniable. Nevertheless, if the courts are true to the basic traditions of the common law, they will retain their capacity to devise a rule for the public good, at least where the rule is not one best left to Parliament or the Executive.[53]

It is only partially true to say that a political question does not cease to be a political question when it is submitted to judicial determination, though the judges may find difficulty in grappling with the relevant concepts. By the very submission of the question to the judiciary, its mode of solution changes. The process of analysis, and analogy, and induction play their part in devising a rule which, in a political context, may be attained by a more intuitive method. Section 92 of the *Constitution* evoked the observation from the Judicial Committee in the *Banking Case*: 'The problem to be solved will often be not so much legal as political, social, or economic, yet it must be solved by a court of law.'[54]

That the courts have solved questions of wide dimension is manifest from the development of the common law rules in respect of contracts in restraint of trade. Indeed, the transition from a feudal economy to the post-industrial revolution economy was accompanied by a development of the law matching the change in trade and business conditions, and until the end of the 19th century the development was substantially unaided by the legislature.[55] A reference to the judgment of Lord Macclesfield in *Mitchel* v *Reynolds*[56] shows the extent to which social and economic factors were consciously referred to in the framing of legal principle.

The experience of the Trade Practices Tribunal and of the Restrictive Practices Court has demonstrated the appropriateness of modern judicial methods in dealing with issues of wider dimension than those usually submitted to judicial determination. There is no reason to surmise that some questions of the same dimension, submitted to the courts in a different context, should not receive a like analysis and solution.

The limiting factor is not so much the width of the issues for determination, as the importance of ensuring that the functions of the judiciary and of the executive do not overlap or conflict. If the executive be acknowledged as the source of policy, so that the judiciary is constrained to develop policy only where there is none to hand to solve the instant case, or where the executive policy would be productive of injustice in the instant case, the constitutional resettlement will leave to the executive so much of the policy power as the executive chooses to exercise. At the same time, the resettlement would remit to the courts many of the adjudicative tasks of administration.

In the course of exercising that jurisdiction, the new law, meaning thereby the rules which protect against administrative injustice, would grow and be so moulded as to cover the empty spaces of discretionary power.

Though the judiciary may, without departure from the basic common law tradition, undertake a jurisdiction controlling the exercise of some administrative powers, those powers do not exhaust the entire field of administration. Some administrative powers should be exercised subject only to such control as the Executive or the Parliament reserves. Judicial control is not a panacea for all administrative injustice, nor yet desirable in all areas of administration.

What I have been concerned to demonstrate is the ageless vitality of the common law tradition, which entrusts the judges with an awesome function and equips them with the means to fulfil it. It is a function of doing justice to an individual, of having regard to the particular circumstances of his case, of striving to ensure that the greatest good as perceived by the greatest number is not achieved by injustice to the few. The means are the application of rules, whether derived from external authority, or ascertained by study of the subject in the light of history and tradition. The notion that justice is the purpose of law pervades the judicial process, preserving it from aridity and summoning forth new growth to respond to the human condition of the age.

1. The lecture was first published in the *Monash University Law Review*: see Justice Gerard Brennan, 'Eighth Wilfred Fullagar Memorial Lecture: New Growth in the Law – The Judicial Contribution' (1979) 6 (1) *Monash University Law Review* 1.
2. See *Mirehouse v Rennell* [1833] 1 Cl & F 527, 546; 6 ER 1015, 1023.
3. See Kitto J in *R* v *Trade Practices Tribunal; Ex parte Tasmanian Breweries Pty Ltd* (1970) 123 CLR 361, 374.
4. Sir Owen Dixon, 'Concerning Judicial Method' in Sir Owen Dixon, *Jesting Pilate* (Law Book Co, 1965) 155-6.
5. Ibid 157.
6. Brian Harvey, *The Lawyer and Justice* (Sweet and Maxwell, 1978) 270.
7. Maitland's phrase, quoted by Sir Owen Dixon in Sir Owen Dixon, *Jesting Pilate* (Law Book Co, 1965) 153.
8. Margaret Esther Hall, *Selected Writings of Benjamin Nathan Cardozo* (Fallon Book Company, 1947).
9. Ibid 116.
10. See *R v Secretary of State for Home Affairs; Ex parte Hosenball* [1977] 1 WLR 766, 784.
11. [1921] 3 KB 560.
12. See *Mort's Dock and Engineering Co Ltd v Overseas Tank Ships (UK) Limited (The 'Wagon Mound')* (1961) 61 SR (NSW) 688, 715.
13. See *Overseas Tankship (UK) Ltd* v *Morts Dock and Engineering Co Ltd (The 'Wagon Mound'*) [1961] AC 388, 415.
14. Hall (n 8) 115.
15. (1968) 122 CLR 556, 563 (Barwick CJ).
16. See *Myers* v *Director of Public Prosecutions* [1965] AC 1001, 1021.
17. Brian Harvey, *The Lawyer and Justice* (Sweet and Maxwell, 1978) 277.
18. Hall (n 8) 153.
19. Rupert Cross, *Precedent in English Law* (Clarendon Press, 1968) 216.
20. Oliver Wendell Holmes, *The Common Law* (Little Brown & Co, 1881) 35-36.
21. See *Cartledge v Joplin* [1963] AC 758, 772.
22. [1968] AC 356, 384.
23. Lord Thomas Shaw, *Legislature and Judiciary* (University of London Press, 1911), 13-14, quoted in Louis Leventhal Jaffe, *English and American Judges as Lawmakers* (Clarendon Press, 1969) 21.
24. See *Salemi v Minister for Immigration and Ethnic Affairs* (1977) 14 ALR 1, 19 (Gibbs J).
25. See Judge Learned Hand, 'Mr Justice Cardozo' (1939) 52 *Harvard Law Review* 361.
26. (1970) 123 CLR 361.
27. Ibid 376.
28. (1937) 56 CLR 746.
29. Ibid 757-8.
30. In *Laker Airways v Department of Trade* [1977] QB 643.
31. See *Padfield v Minister of Agriculture, Fisheries and Food* [1968] AC 997.

32. See *Secretary of State for Education and Science v Tameside Metropolitan Borough Council* [1977] AC 1014.
33. See *McPherson v McPherson* [1936] AC 177, 200.
34. See 1964 Hamlyn Lectures: Lord Scarman, *English Law, the New Dimension* (Stevens, 1974).
35. Ibid 70-1.
36. Lord Scarman (n 340) 75.
37. (1977) 267 *Round Table* 230, 233-4.
38. Sir Laurence Street, 'Address to the 22nd Annual Industrial Relations Conference Dinner', 15 September 1978.
39. See *Judicature Amendment Act 1968* (NZ).
40. For an early analysis of the problems of this kind of jurisdiction, see Kenneth J Keith, 'Appeals from Administrative Tribunals' (1969) 5 *Victorian University of Wellington Legal Research* 123.
41. See *New Zealand Report of the Royal Commission on the Courts* (1978) 93 par 312(d).
42. Cf s 43 *Administrative Appeals Tribunal Act 1975* (Cth).
43. Geoffrey Marshall, 'Justiciability' in Anthony Gordon Guest (ed), *Oxford Essays in Jurisprudence: A Collaborative Work* (Oxford University Press, 1961) 1st series, 265.
44. 335 US 537, 557 (1948).
45. Louis Leventhal, *English and American Judges as Lawmakers* (Clarendon Press, 1969), 44.
46. See *Re Becker and Minister for Immigration and Ethnic Affairs* (1977) 1 ALD 158, 162-3.
47. (1951) 82 CLR 645, 653 (Dixon, Williams and Kitto JJ).
48. See *Leeder v Ellis* [1953] AC 52.
49. Hall (n 8) 114.
50. Kenneth Culp Davis, *Discretionary Justice* (Louisiana State University Press, 1970) 17.
51. Ibid 215.
52. See *R v Port of London Authority* [1919] 1 KB 176, 184 (Bankes LJ); Ex *parte Forster; Re University of Sydney* (1963) 63 SR (NSW) 723, 732; *R v Rotherham Licensing Justices; Ex parte Chapman* [1939] 2 All ER 710, 712-13.
53. See D J Galligan, 'The Nature and Function of Policies within Discretionary Power' [1976] *Public Law* 332.
54. See *Commonwealth of Australia v Bank of New South Wales* [1950] AC 235, 310.
55. See Lord Wilberforce, et al, *The Law of Restrictive Trade Practices and Monopolies* (Sweet and Maxwell, 2nd ed, 1966) 5.
56. Then Parker CJ, (1711) 1 P Wms 181; 24 ER 347.

3.2 Judicial Qualities of a Different Kind

Editor's note

When United States Supreme Court member Justice Sandra Day O'Connor presented a paper entitled 'The United States Supreme Court and Individual Rights' to the 23rd Australian Legal Convention with the theme 'Destinations in Law' on 6 August 1985, Brennan offered this commentary.

It gives us pleasure again to welcome to an Australian Legal Convention a member of the Supreme Court of the United States. Justice Sandra Day O'Connor's visit to the 23rd Australian Legal Convention also serves to remind us of some themes of enduring importance to those of us who live under a written constitution, especially a federal constitution: the function of judicial review of legislative and executive action; the judicial techniques employed in performing that function; the need for a composition between stability and change; the experience, skills and cast of mind that are required of or acquired by the judges.

Sir Owen Dixon perceived a difference between the outlook of the United States Supreme Court and United States lawyers upon their constitutional problems and the outlook of the High Court of Australia and Australian lawyers upon our constitutional problems.[1] He thought we had a 'much more legalistic' point of view. He attributed this to three causes. The first is the difference in the nature of the constitutional problems arising from the respective texts of the two Constitutions. The second is the fact that the High Court of Australia is a court of general appellate jurisdiction, deciding cases in the constitutional field by a form of reasoning that is akin to the form of reasoning applied to ordinary appeals. The third is the High Court's method of hearing a full oral argument. I do not pause to consider the latter two factors, but I would draw your attention to the difference in the nature of the constitutional problems with which the two courts are concerned.

A comparison of our two Constitutions reveals much that is common to both: the separation of federal legislative, executive and judicial power, a full faith and credit clause, provisions for regular democratic elections and the conferring of specific powers on the federal legislature. But the comparison reveals much that is different. Most significantly, the Bill of Rights and the *14th Amendment* deny to governments of the Union and of the States powers which might be exercised to overreach the individual rights, privileges or immunities which those provisions protect. Those rights, privileges and immunities are expressed in general terms which judges must construe. In this country, one of the most intractable constitutional problems has been the meaning of the term 'absolutely free' in reference to trade commerce and intercourse among the States. In the United States, terms of that kind are used in reference to conceptions of an even broader nature: free exercise of religion, freedom of speech and of the press, peaceable assembly, unreasonable search and seizure, due process of law, cruel and unusual punishments, equal protection of the laws.

The duty of construing such terms and applying them in the review of legislative and executive action of governments is the chief duty of the Supreme Court. Out of those broad and uncertain terms, the Court is required to construct precise principles to guide governments in giving effect to what they see as the public interest and to define for individuals the interests which governments may not infringe. The constitutional disputes in this country are of a different kind. Typically, the disputes relate to the scope of a power granted to the federal legislature, not to a provision which cuts down what would otherwise be included in the grant or which denies the validity of a State's exercise of its residuary powers. The principles applied in construing our *Constitution* and, I suspect, in construing the original articles of the *Constitution* of the United States, owe much less to the contemporary values and aspirations of society than the principles applied in construing the Bill of Rights and the *14th Amendment*. Justice Frankfurter pointed to the nature of the Supreme Court's jurisdiction when he stated some general propositions which, he said, were never denied in the Supreme Court:

> That the Constitution contains within itself the formulated past but was also designed for the unfolding future; that it is a source of governmental energy no less than of governmental restriction; that in the most difficult areas of adjudication the issues which come before the Court do not Primarily present questions as to the meaning of words but invite judgment upon Ultimate issues of society which in the now Classic language of Mr Justice Holmes 'must be considered in the light of our Whole experience and not merely in that of what was said a hundred years ago' *[Missouri v. Holland* 252 U.S.416,433 (1920)] – these are generalities to which fealty is never denied. [2]

The founding fathers of our *Constitution*, despite the century of experience of the United States *Constitution*, did not repose in the federal judiciary the same function of striking the balance between government and the individual. The rights, privileges and immunities of the individual were entrusted to the protection of the common law and were amenable to alteration by the legislature. Judgment upon the 'ultimate issues' of society were reserved to the political branches of government, branches more sensitive to public sentiment than the unelected judiciary. The wisdom of that constitutional disposition of power has not been universally accepted. In Australia some legislative measures have been passed – and more extensive measures proposed – reposing in the judiciary, and removing from the legislature, powers which have a more legislative flavour than the powers which judges in this country have been accustomed to exercise. The creation of a new jurisdiction, to be exercised according to judicial interpretation of words or phrases of chameleon meaning, works a substantial redistribution of power from the political branches to the judicial branch. It requires judicial qualities of a different kind – some would say of a more sophisticated kind – than the qualities which we have looked for in this country as appropriate for our judges.

The Supreme Court of the United States has, for nearly two centuries, exercised its wide constitutional powers to weld together the Union, to guide its development and to contribute substantially to its ethos. Those functions have required not only a high degree of judicial sensitivity to the values and aspirations of the time but also the development of particular techniques. The articulation and orderly growth of legal principle demands more than the expression of an individual philosophy. A judge's authority, as Judge Learned Hand said, depends: 'upon the assumption that he speaks with the mouth of others: the momentum of his utterances must be greater than any which his personal reputation and character can command, if it is to do the work assigned to it – if it is to stand against the passionate resentments arising out of the interests he must frustrate'.[3]

For a court to perform its functions, especially if it assumes a leading role in the moulding of a nation, the court must have the fullest confidence of the people. The functions which a court performs, and the way in which a court performs them, must correspond broadly with public understanding and public expectation. Manifestly public opinion in the United States assigns to the Supreme Court the broad role which it performs. The Court's authority has been maintained by the reduction of issues of great political significance to issues amenable to a special kind of judicial analysis.

I am sure that Australians wish the courts to protect important individual rights and freedoms. I am not sure whether Australians would wish judges to be the final arbiters between the public interest as the legislature perceives it and private interests, if judgment is to turn on individual judges' appreciation of where the balance is to be struck. We have developed neither a jurisprudence of social values nor a calculus of social priorities which might serve to govern the drastic power of judicial review of legislation on the ground that the legislation infringes individual rights. Of course, the common law is permeated by values that are fundamental to our society and effect is given to them, but in the final result it is for the Parliaments of the Commonwealth, the States and the Northern Territory to say whether the public interest should prevail.

If a Bill of Rights were to work a redistribution of powers between the courts and the political branches of government in this nation, it would be necessary to encourage our judges to give consideration to issues which they have been trained largely to ignore. That is a fairly radical change. But the more radical change would need to be not in the judges but in the public understanding of the way in which judges do their work. It is one thing that supremacy in the exercise of a governmental power be assigned by judicial decision to the Commonwealth or to the States; it is another thing that governmental power be denied altogether or for its exercise to be denied by judicial decision where the meaning of the controlling constitutional text is uncertain.

We have been privileged today to be given a valuable insight into the working of one of the great institutions of the common law world, a court whose work testifies to the regard which the people of the Union have for the judicial method and to the genius and technical skills of generations of judges. Justice O'Connor is a significant appointment to a bench of traditional distinction and we thank her for her presence and her paper.

---

1. Sir Owen Dixon, 'Two Constitutions Compared' in Sir Owen Dixon, *Jesting Pilate* (Law Book Co, 1965) 104.
2. Justice Frankfurter, 'Mr Justice Cardozo and Public Law' (1939) 52 *Harvard Law Review* 461.
3. Judge Learned Hand, 'Mr Justice Cardozo' (1939) 52 *Harvard Law Review* 361.

3.3 Courts, Democracy and the Law

Editor's note

Brennan delivered the Blackburn Lecture to the Law Society of the Australian Capital Territory on 7 August 1990.[1]

This evening, we gather again to do honour to the memory of Sir Richard Blackburn. Those who knew Dick Blackburn bear his memory in affection and respect, for his friendship sat lightly and his sense of duty was profound. He was an outstanding judge: a man of undoubted integrity, patient and courteous, industrious, with a capacity for dispassionate analysis of fact and a deep love for and understanding of the law, a helpful colleague who held a high yet humble conceit of the importance of the judicial office. He was one of my first judicial colleagues, and one of the best. I owe him a great personal and professional debt which I acknowledge with gratitude and some pride.

The subject of 'Courts, Democracy and the Law' is not a dry topic of interest merely to constitutional lawyers. It is a subject of critical importance to the political life of this country. It concerns the protection available to women and men who believe themselves to be oppressed by government. It concerns the balance between the governors and the governed, between the powers of the majority and the rights of minorities. It concerns the pivotal role of the courts in the maintenance of a free but ordered society.

We are the inheritors of a Constitution (partly written) which we accept, without too much reflection, as appropriate to secure and preserve our freedom. Our faith is born of a long history, marked by a series of compacts designed to limit the powers of government by creating legal checks and balances by one branch of government upon the functions of the others. Three hundred years ago, the *Bill of Rights* of 1689 declared that the Crown could not lawfully suspend the laws without Parliament's consent and could not lawfully levy taxes except by grant of Parliament. Parliament, to the exclusion of the executive government, was to have the power to make or unmake the law and to keep control of the purse of government. By law, Parliament acquired ascendancy over the executive. Shortly afterwards, by the *Act of Settlement* of 1701 the judiciary's immunity from interference either by the Crown or by Parliament was secured. Judicial independence was achieved by two measures: first, by conferring on the judges tenure of their office during good behaviour, so that they were irremovable by the King save upon an address of both Houses of Parliament. Secondly, by fixing judicial salaries. By ensuring the independence of the courts, the *Act of Settlement* ensured that the administration of the law could not thereafter be affected by the influence of either of the political branches of government. The supremacy of the law was established as the basis of government and the arbitrary power of the executive government, which had proved destructive of freedom under the Stuart kings, was dismantled.

In the early eighteenth century, the personnel of the three branches of government were separated, each branch performing its proper function: law-making and the grant of supply were for the Parliament, maintenance of the law and the exercise of the prerogative were for the Crown, administration of the law was for the courts. The executive government was subject to political supervision by Parliament and legal supervision by the courts. The doctrine of the separation of powers, championed by Montesquieu in 1748 in his De l'Esprit des Lois, had great influence on the framers of the American Constitution. In 1788, Hamilton, writing in The Federalist Papers, described the judiciary as 'the least dangerous' of the three branches of government to the political rights of the people:

> The executive not only dispenses the honours but holds the sword of the community. The legislature not only commands the purse but prescribes the rules by which the duties and rights of every citizen are to be regulated. The judiciary, on the contrary, has no influence over either the sword or the purse; no direction either of the strength or of the wealth of the society, and can take no active resolution whatever. It may truly be said to have neither FORCE nor WILL but merely judgment ....[2]

Government in the United States maintains a more rigorous separation of powers than government under the Westminster system. In nineteenth-century England[3] and, after early colonial days, in Australia, the members of the executive government were generally members of the elected Parliament who retained executive office only so long as they commanded the confidence of Parliament or of the elected House of the Parliament. This was the system of responsible government. Representative government was said to come with the popular franchise, though it should not be forgotten that women did not have the vote at the time of Federation and more than 60 years passed before Australia's Aboriginal people were enfranchised.[4]

The system of representative and responsible government as we know it was substantially the system whose virtues were extolled by the influential constitutionalist, Professor A V Dicey.[5] Political sovereignty, he declared, resided in the people, or at least in the electors of the House of

Commons. Legal sovereignty, which Dicey defined as the power to make laws unrestricted by legal limit, resided in Parliament. But he asserted that there could be no conflict between political and legal sovereignty, because generally 'the permanent wishes of the representative portion of Parliament can hardly in the long run differ from the wishes of the English people, or at any rate of the electors. That which the majority of the House of Commons command, the majority of the English people usually desire'.[6]

As Parliament was both representative and supreme, Dicey expected it to reflect the spirit of freedom espoused by the people and to translate that spirit into every aspect of government. The tolerant bridle of democratic sentiment would guide the horse of State, for Parliament was the rider and Parliament was the alter ego of the people. Parliament posed no threat to freedom and the executive was subject to Parliament's control. One learned commentator has observed that: 'This beatific vision of legal and political harmony was to prove short-lived and may never in reality have existed at all.'[7]

Dicey's portrait of an ideal constitutional arrangement was completed by the courts which, independent of the other branches of government and possessing no legislative or executive power save what was incidental to the performance of their own functions, would faithfully administer the law in individual cases.

This was the ideal to which the Australian *Constitution* gave expression. The representative character of the Commonwealth Parliament was provided for by ss 7 and 24. Although responsible government was not expressly prescribed by the *Constitution*, there is no doubt but that responsible government was the form of government intended by the framers of the *Constitution*. Thus s 64 precludes a Minister from holding office for more than three months unless she or he is or becomes a Senator or a Member of the House of Representatives. In the *Boilermakers' Case*, it was said that: '[p]robably the most striking achievement of the framers of the Australian instrument of government was the successful combination of the British system of parliamentary government containing an executive responsible to the legislature with American federalism.'[8]

The *Constitution* secured the independence of the judiciary by the same measures as those which had first been adopted by the *Act of Settlement*, 200 years earlier: security of tenure, so that judges are removable only on an address from both Houses of Parliament for proved misbehaviour, and remuneration which cannot be diminished during continuance in office.[9] Chapters I, II and III separated the three divisions of power, the repositories being, respectively, the Parliament, the Governor-General (that is, the executive government) and the courts.

The political and economic events of the 90 years since Federation have exposed the fallacies of Dicey's theory or made much of it obsolete. If it ever were a valid theory that the mind of the people would inform and determine the mind of the legislature and that the mind of the legislature would control the acts of the executive, the theory is valid no longer. In the last 90 years, the balance of power has reverted decisively to the executive government. The reasons are various. Government has become more complex, the economy has become increasingly the focus of government attention and political decision-making has had to rely increasingly upon the advice and support of the public service. The exigencies of national defence in two world wars led the community to accept the need to confer a mass of power on the executive government and its bureaucracy. Although powers which had been ceded by Parliaments to executive governments during times of war were resumed to some extent by Parliaments in times of peace, societies living under the Westminster system had grown accustomed to a powerful executive.

Concurrently with the growth of executive power, the tightening discipline of political parties and the predilection of the media for individuals on whom to concentrate attention tied the political fortunes of the members of the Parliament to the political status and reputation of party leaders. Members in the governing party became increasingly dependent on the Ministry for their chances of re-election; backbench members of the Opposition became increasingly dependent on shadow cabinets for their chances of governing. The theory of responsible government, which made the fate of an executive government dependent upon the confidence of the Parliament was, so to speak, turned on its head by the political dependence of the majority members of the Parliament on the executive government. Policy formulation became primarily an executive function. As the pressure on legislative time intensified, a virtual monopoly over initiatives for legislation passed to the executive government. The influence of Ministers in debate, whether in the party room or in Parliament, was enhanced by the support they could command from the public service. These developments virtually destroyed the Diceyan theory. Writing in the *Law Quarterly Review* in January 1990, Professor Paul Craig said: 'Parliament's legitimacy [has] continued to be derived from the electorate. In this formal sense, authority could still be perceived as flowing from the bottom upwards. In substance, our constitutional system became one dominated by the top, by the executive and the party hierarchy.'[10]

The risk to democratic freedom is obvious. It was stated by Locke, who said it may be 'too great temptation to human frailty, apt to grasp at power, for the same persons who have the power of making laws to have also in their hands the power to execute them, whereby they may exempt themselves from obedience to the laws they make'.[11]

Lord Hailsham of St Marylebone, for long Lord Chancellor of England, has said that the powers of government within Parliament are 'now largely in the hands of the government machine, so that the government controls Parliament and not Parliament the government.'[12]

Seeing that Parliament's unlimited legislative power places a vast pool of power in the hands of the Executive, he concluded: 'We live under an elective dictatorship, absolute in theory if hitherto thought tolerable in practice.'

His Lordship's view is broadly stated, but it contains no novelty. Nearly 50 years ago, Joseph A Schumpeter defined, or re-defined, the democratic method in these terms: 'that institutional arrangement for arriving at political decisions in which individuals acquire the power to decide by means of a competitive struggle for the people's vote.[13]

The proposition that 'the electorate controls as well as installs' is misleading '… since electorates normally do not control their political leaders in any way except by refusing to re-elect them or the parliamentary majorities that support them ….'[14]

This is a more realistic view of democracy in our time, but it calls for a reappraisal of our constitutional safeguards of freedom. As the wind of political expediency now chills Parliament's willingness to impose checks on the executive and the executive now has a large measure of control over legislation, the courts alone retain their original function of standing between government and the governed. The late Lord Radcliffe expressed his view of the contemporary relationship between the three branches of government in these terms:

> In the seventeenth century this country turned its back on the idea of a strong central executive, and we have taught ourselves to be proud of the achievement ever since. There was a settlement under which the Commons in parliament and the judges in the courts, working independently, were to be guardians of the rights and liberties of the individual citizen, as then understood, and each was to have power to block any attempt by the executive to trench upon those rights and liberties. Whatever the law courts did or did not do in the next 200 years, they did carry out this part of the bargain, and men valued them accordingly. We have come back, unavoidably, to a strong central executive, and we live by order, decree and regulation and by act of parliament. Parliament and the executive have gone into

> alliance, and the law courts are pushed more and more into a corner of national life.[15]

I presume his Lordship meant that the courts were being pushed into a corner of national life by attempts to exclude the courts from some areas of jurisdiction. That is borne out by the record. He could hardly have meant that the courts were becoming irrelevant to society. The courts continue to apply a check on the exercise of power. And, as power is a threat to freedom, a check on power is an important – and sometimes the only – safeguard of freedom.

In so saying, I would not wish to diminish – much less to overlook – such political checks as Parliament imposes on the executive, nor to pass over the real influence which Parliament brings to bear on the executive. There are some regrettable and notorious exceptions, but the passage of a Bill in Parliament has not generally become a mere ritual, especially when the Government of the day does not command the support of a majority of the Senate or Upper House. Apart from legislative debates, Parliament's continuing contribution to democracy is its holding of the executive to public accountability. Moreover, it scrutinises proposed appropriations and delegations of power and reviews subordinate legislation. The popular spirit of freedom and democracy has been sufficiently lively to encourage Parliament or the party room to seek to restrain, so far as lies within their respective political power, any tendency on the part of an executive government to overreach the rights and the legitimate aspirations of most of our people. But the capacity of Parliament to place a check on executive action is limited by the press of business and the day-to-day exigencies of politics. Inevitably, there are cases where the rights and aspirations of individuals and minorities are disregarded. In that event, the courts and some independent quasi-judicial bodies, notably the Commonwealth Administrative Appeals Tribunal, are the only sources of relief. They apply the law and the law determines the ultimate measure of our rights, our privileges and our freedom. It is the universality and equality of legal remedies that distinguish them from the political process.

The checks imposed by the courts on the actions of the political branches of governments have been seen by some as anti-democratic, for the judges are not elected by the people. That view misconceives what is involved in the exercise of judicial power. The courts do not seek to interfere with lawful policy: that is the proper domain of the political branches. But the courts are concerned to subject the political branches of government to the rule of law, for that is the constitutional imperative which binds all branches of government. It can hardly be anti-democratic to restrain Parliament to its constitutional power, nor to constrain the executive to conform to the *Constitution* and the laws enacted by Parliament.

The real question to ask is: are the courts today fitted to provide an effective check against any oppressive exercise of power by the other branches of government? I leave aside problems of access to the courts by those who seek its remedies and the necessity for funds to maintain the proper functioning of the courts – not because these problems are marginal, but because I wish to address the structural arrangements which affect the courts' capacity to discharge their responsibilities.

The fundamental factor is, of course, the state of the law. The supremacy of the law underpins our constitutional arrangements, and the courts are bound by the limitations which the law itself imposes on the protection which the courts may afford. The Australian *Constitution* confers no jurisdiction to declare an Act of Parliament invalid, except under some few provisions, notably those designed to divide legislative powers between the Commonwealth and the States, to secure freedom of trade, commerce and intercourse among the States and to secure freedom of religion and equality of treatment of out-of-State residents. Nor do the Constitutions of the several States confer jurisdiction to review Acts of Parliament. Therefore, the courts apply the laws enacted by Parliaments within their respective constitutional authority. If Parliament enacts oppressive legislation, the courts are bound to apply it. If the Executive secures statutory authority for its actions, the courts must acknowledge the legal validity of those actions, even if they be oppressive or the statutory authority for them be obtained retrospectively. The courts are helpless to remedy injustice in the face of unjust legislation enacted within power.[16]

Nevertheless, the rule of law ensures that the text of a statute is interpreted, so far as possible, with respect for the values of the common law.[17] Parliament's sovereignty is expressed solely in the words of the statute,[18] and it is for the courts to interpret and apply the law thus expressed. In *Marbury v Madison* Chief Justice Marshall declared: 'It is, emphatically, the province and duty of the judicial department to say what the law is.'[19]

And, as Lord Wilberforce has said, 'the judicial function of statutory interpretation is an essential part of the constitutional process by which subjects are brought under the rule of law.'[20]

The values of the common law inform the rules of statutory interpretation.[21] There is an inclination, where the language permits – a presumption, if you like – against construing an Act to have a retrospective operation, especially if the Act creates a criminal offence; against the creation of a criminal offence or the conferring of a right to seize or search by language which is ambiguous; against the expropriation of property; indeed, against the disturbance of common law rights and privileges. Interpreting statutes in this way, the courts are 'a mediating influence between the executive and the legislature on the one hand and the citizen on the other.'[22]

Sometimes the rules of statutory interpretation may throw up a construction of an Act opposed to the intention of its promoters, but it is no function of the courts to give effect to intentions that have not been translated into the language of the Act. This was reaffirmed by the High Court in *Clunies-Ross v The Commonwealth*:

> It would be an abdication of the duty of this Court under the *Constitution* if we were to determine [this] important and general question of law ... according to whether we personally agreed or disagreed with the political and social objectives which the Minister sought to achieve. ... As a matter of constitutional duty, [the] question must be considered objectively and answered in this Court as a question of law and not as a matter to be determined by reference to the political or social merits of the particular case.[23]

The absence of any power in the courts to invalidate Acts of Parliament that are oppressive of human rights is seen by some to be the Achilles heel of a society which aspires to constitutionally protected freedom. Two solutions have been proposed to arm the courts with legitimate weapons for the task. The first is the entrenching of a Bill or Charter of Rights in our *Constitution*; the second is the exhumation of a proposition advanced by Chief Justice Coke in *Dr Bonham's Case* nearly 400 years ago, namely, that 'the common law will control Acts of Parliament, and sometimes adjudge them to be utterly void: for when an Act of Parliament is against common right and reason, or repugnant, or impossible to be performed, the common law will control it, and adjudge such Act to be void'.[24]

This is not the occasion to rehearse the many arguments for and against a constitutional *Bill of Rights*, but I would refer to one important consideration. Judicial interpretation of a *Bill of Rights* expressed, as it necessarily would be, in terms of broad generality, would require the translation of political and social values into the *Constitution*. The judiciary would be equipped with a political power – albeit a power to be exercised in a structured and reasoned way – to override the power of the political branches of government. The judiciary would be politicised. Whether our society is better served by an apolitical judiciary possessing limited though often effective powers to protect individuals and minorities from overreaching by a majoritarian government, or by a politicised judiciary possessing more direct and extensive powers to confer that protection is a question which I leave to others to answer.

The second suggestion for investing the courts with a jurisdiction to review Acts of Parliament has led to a re-examination of the proposition that the common law will control Acts of Parliament. In New Zealand, the more modest form of the proposition would deny that Parliament has power substantially to alter the tripartite distribution of functions. After all, the doctrine of the sovereignty of Parliament must itself be found in the common law which first distributed among the three branches of government their respective functions. Sir Robin Cooke would go further. In *Taylor v New Zealand Poultry Board,* he said: 'I do not think that literal compulsion, by torture for instance, would be within the lawful powers of Parliament. Some common law rights presumably lie so deep that even Parliament could not override them.'[25]

The Supreme Court of Israel embraced a jurisprudence of judicially protected individual rights though Israel has no *Bill of Rights*.[26] These views have found no Australian resonance, but there are many instances of judicial rejection of attempts to overreach individual rights by exercise of dictatorial power. A prime example is the courts' resistance to attempts on the part of the political branches of government to acquire uncontrolled power by legislative exclusion of the courts' ordinary jurisdiction. Sir William Wade has commented:

> to exempt a public authority from the jurisdiction of the courts of law is, to that extent, to grant dictatorial power. It is no exaggeration, therefore, to describe this as an abuse of the power of Parliament, speaking constitutionally. This is the justification, as I see it, for the strong, it might even be said rebellious, stand which the courts have made against allowing Acts of Parliament to create pockets of uncontrollable power in violation of the rule of law. Parliament is unduly addicted to this practice, giving too much weight to temporary convenience and too little to constitutional principle. The law's delay, together with its uncertainty and expense, tempts governments to take short cuts by elimination of the courts. But if the courts are prevented from enforcing the law, the remedy becomes worse than the disease.[27]

So much for judicial checks on Acts of Parliament. By contrast, no doctrine of sovereignty precludes judicial review of executive action. To the contrary, the doctrine of legislative supremacy requires the courts to determine whether any exercise of executive power – including the power to enact rules and regulations – falls within Parliament's grant. In performing this duty, the courts apply the notions of the common law in protection of individual rights and legitimate expectations.[28] The courts insist that executive and administrative power be exercised in good faith according to law and for the purpose for which it was conferred, having regard to all relevant considerations and to none which are irrelevant, that natural justice be done in exercise of power, and that an exercise of power must not be so unreasonable that no reasonable repository of the power could have so exercised it. These are important constraints on the arbitrary exercise of power and, on occasions, they no doubt frustrate what is seen as its efficient exercise. That is the price which must be paid by a society which lives under the rule of law.

It would be tedious to describe the myriad ways in which the law protects freedom and the ways in which courts, as the administrators of the law, extend its protection over the community. It suffices to say that there are two basic functions which the courts must perform: settlement of disputes between individuals or between individuals and the Government, and declaration of the law as it applies to the settlement of disputes. By the courts' performance of these functions, the rule of law is made to govern, alienation of individuals or powerless groups from mainstream society is avoided, self-help and revolt are made unnecessary, the infrastructure of trade and commerce is secured, an ordered society founded on law applying equally to all is established and governments are constrained by law in the exercise of political power. The list could go on, but it can be summed up by saying what is obvious: that the functioning of the courts is essential to the peace, order and good government of society. To the extent that the courts cannot, or do not efficiently, perform their basic functions, to that extent injustice is done and the cohesion of society is at risk. The risk to society may not be apparent immediately, but injustice compounds on itself and saps confidence in the rule of law on which the stability of society depends.

In the long history of the common law, some values have been recognised as the enduring values of a free and democratic society and they are the values which inform the development of the common law and help to mould the meaning of statutes. These values include the dignity and integrity of every person, substantive equality before the law, the absence of unjustified discrimination, the peaceful possession of one's property, the benefit of natural justice, and immunity from retrospective and unreasonable operation of laws. To ensure that effect is given to these values when they stand in the way of an exercise of power, especially the power of governments, a judiciary of unquestioned independence is essential. The judge stands in the lonely no-man's-land between the government and the governed, between the wealthy and the poor, the strong and the weak. She or he can identify with neither, for partisanship robs the judge of the authority essential to discharge the judicial office.

The spirit of independence is deeply ingrained in the judiciary but it would be folly to believe that it is not susceptible to attrition at the hands of government. Governments, preoccupied with the pressing problems of the day and having little knowledge of and less sympathy with the judicial method, often fail to see that the courts are, and must be seen to be, separate from the other branches of government. Their independence must be respected – not for the sake of some foolish notion of status but in order that they may perform their necessarily lonely function. A free and democratic society could not be long maintained if governments were to seek to impose on the courts controls of the kind properly imposed upon the Departments of State. It would be a cautionary reflection for any government that was minded to do so that, should they come into opposition, the precedent that they had set might rob them of the law's protection.

The judges who constitute the courts must have the knowledge to apply the principles of the law in a great variety of cases. They need experience and a wisdom that do not come in books to make judgments in harmony with the values of the common law as those values are applied in the daily workings of the courts. These are demanding qualifications, but nothing less will do. The judiciary must be appointed as an élite, not to create delusions of social hauteur, but in order that each judge, in the necessary isolation of her or his office, may be supported and, if need be, constrained by collegiate standards of competence and integrity. Yet governments seem not to be alive to the fragility of the attraction of judicial office, which is damaged by any appointment that does not command the respect – I do not say the assent – of judicial colleagues. Let one improvident appointment be made and a well-qualified appointee will be harder to attract to the next vacancy; let two or three such appointments be made and the bench will not recover its attraction or its status for a generation.

Nor do governments always understand judicial insistence on, indeed judicial preoccupation with, the preservation of the twin pillars of independence: tenure and conditions of service that the executive cannot touch. A government, used to the competitive atmosphere of the market, may see these issues merely as the concerns of a pressure group. That is profoundly wrong. The concerns are both constitutionally fundamental and practical. The reality is that, if tenure be not protected against unjustified complaints of unfitness, the fearless and impartial discharge of judicial office will be impaired by fear of personal consequences. The tenure of federal judges is secured by the *Constitution*; the tenure of state judges is not. I do not venture to predict how the tenure of judges of proposed courts of the Australian Capital Territory may be secured. Tenure is one thing; conditions of service is the other. It should be clearly understood that the structural problem of judicial conditions of service is not the level of remuneration. I do not – indeed, I would not – express the least opinion on the level of remuneration. The problem relates to the isolation of judges from influence by government, whether the influence be by generosity or parsimony. The problem, which could have arisen at any time under an unwritten constitution, now exists under the *Constitution* of the Commonwealth because inflation and the nominalistic theory of money have placed judicial remuneration back in the hands of the executive. The problem is not merely that executive control is contrary to constitutional history and intent. The power to fix from time to time the conditions of judicial service is an inappropriate power to entrust to an executive government with the capacity to translate its decision into law. It gives rise to a misgiving of some relationship between the executive government's periodic decisions on conditions of service and judicial conformity to governmental aspirations of judicial conduct or even judicial decision-making. What is essential, in both Commonwealth and State, is machinery for fixing judicial conditions of service that is as independent of political influence as the courts themselves.

While the capacity of the courts to perform their function of applying the law in preservation of a free and democratic society depends in large measure upon the quality of judicial appointments, security of tenure and the removal of conditions of service from executive control, it is clear that the courts' traditional functions must be expanded if they are to discharge efficiently their duty of settling disputes. In a society ruled by law – indeed, in a society whose values and moral standards are increasingly derived from the law – the courts must be fitted to provide efficient and available mechanisms to settle legal disputes. Yet that is not the case. Even when a litigant has the capacity to prize open the doors of the court, the dispute may be solved preferentially by private mediation or arbitration at the litigant's expense. The courts, the state instruments of dispute resolution, are not yet equipped to provide the same services – cheap, speedy, flexible and, if desired, informal – which many potential litigants now find it advantageous to provide for themselves. It is to be hoped that public mechanisms for efficient dispute resolution at reasonable cost will be developed to supplement the traditional formal procedures. Dispute resolution is not a discretionary service offered by the Government; it is an essential part of government. Without it, the rule of law becomes a platitude to which lip-service may be given in the period before it is rejected outright.

If we ask again the question 'are the courts fitted to provide an effective check against any oppressive exercise of power by the other branches of government?' the answer is not an unqualified yes or no. To some extent the capacity of the courts to perform their function depends on the standards adopted by governments in the appointment of judges, but there are also structural weaknesses affecting the maintenance of judicial independence and the facilities available for dispute resolution. If judicial review of Acts of Parliament is thought desirable, some change in our constitutional law is required. The judicial branch of government is still the least dangerous branch to the political rights of the community and the most constant protector of those rights, but its strengthening is critical to the democratic freedom of which we boast and to the peace, order and good government that are the birthright of future generations.

---

1. The lecture was first published in Gerard Brennan, 'Courts, Democracy and the Law' (1991) 65 (1) *Australian Law Journal* 32.
2. See *The Federalist Papers* (The New American Library of World Literature, Inc, 1961).
3. William Searle Holdsworth, *History of English Law* (Sweet & Maxwell, 1964), Vol XIV, 279.
4. Peter Hanks and Bryan Keon-Cohen (eds), *Aborigines and the Law* (George Allen & Unwin, Australia, 1984) 22–24.
5. In his books, Albert Venn Dicey, *Lectures Introductory to the Study of the Law of the Constitution* (Macmillan & Co, 1885), and *Lectures on the Relation Between Law and Public Opinion in England* (Macmillan & Co, 1905).
6. Albert Venn Dicey, *Lectures Introductory to the Study of the Law of the Constitution*, (Macmillan & Co, 1885) 77.
7. Paul Craig, 'Dicey: Unitary, Self-correcting Democracy and Public Law' (1990) 106 *Law Quarterly Review* 105.
8. See *R v Kirby; Ex parte Boilermakers' Society of Australia* (1956) 94 CLR 254, 275.
9. Section 72 of the *Constitution.*
10. Craig, 'Dicey: Unitary, Self-correcting Democracy and Public Law' (n 7) 131.
11. Locke, *Second Treatise of Civil Government*, Ch XII, par 143, cited by Geoffrey Marshall, *Constitutional Theory* (Clarendon Press, Oxford, 1971), 101.
12. In the 1976 Richard Dimbleby Lecture, see Lord Hailsham, *Elective Dictatorship* (British Broadcasting Commission, 1976).
13. Lord Schumpeter, *Capitalism, Socialism and Democracy* (George Allen & Unwin, 3rd ed, 1950), 269.
14. Ibid 272.
15. Lord Ratcliffe, *Not in Feather Beds* (The Quality Book Club, 1968), 34.
16. See Lord Scarman, 'English Law – The New Dimension' (Stevens, 1974) 15 (*Hamlyn Lectures*, 26th series).
17. TRS Allen, 'Legislative Supremacy and the Rule of Law' (1985) 44(1) *Cambridge Law Journal* 111, 134.
18. See *Black-Clawson Ltd v Papierwerke AG* [1975] AC 591, 638 (Lord Diplock).
19. (1803) 1 Cranch 137, 177 ; 5 US 87, 111.

20. See *Black-Clawson Ltd* (n 18) 629–630.
21. See Sir Anthony Mason, 'Future Directions in Australian Law' (1987) 13 (3) *Monash University Law Review* 149, 162–163.
22. See *Stock v Frank Jones (Tipton) Ltd* [1978] 1 All ER 948, 953 (Lord Simon).
23. (1984) 155 CLR 193, 204.
24. (1612) 8 Co Rep 113b, 118a; 77 ER 646, 652.
25. [1984] 1 NZLR 394, 398.
26. Aharon Barak, 'Constitutional Law without a Constitution: The Role of the Judiciary', in Shimon Shetreet (ed), *The Role of the Courts in Society* (Dordrecht, 1988) 448-466.
27. Sir William Wade, *Constitutional Fundamentals* (Stevens for the Hamlyn Trust, 1980), 83–84 Hamlyn Lectures, 32nd series.
28. The basis of judicial review is not free from controversy: compare *Haoucher v Minister for Immigration and Ethnic Affairs* (1990) 169 CLR 648 with *Attorney-General for New South Wales v Quin* (1990) 170 CLR 1.

3.4 The Impact of a Bill of Rights on the Judiciary

Editor's note

Brennan delivered this paper at a Human Rights Conference convened by Professor Philip Alston at University House, Canberra on 16 July 1992. The conference offered comparative perspectives on promoting human rights through bills of rights. Brennan gave an Australian perspective.[1] He offered observations on the Canadian experience of their *Charter of Rights and Freedoms* which was the subject of a paper by Robert J Sharpe who was Dean of the Faculty of Law at the University of Ontario.

Since the abolition of the last avenues of appeal from the courts of this country to the Privy Council, we have broadened our focus of interest in the laws and courts of countries in the common law tradition. The heritage of the common law allows each country to draw on the experience of others, especially when their societies are similar in culture and their constitutional institutions are comparable. Australia therefore has a particular interest in the Canadian experience of the last decade, when the courts of Canada have been administering the *Canadian Charter of Rights and Freedoms*. Not only is Canada a federal democracy operating under a system of representative and responsible government; it was, at the time when the Charter came into force, a society whose legal institutions operated in much the same way as do our legal institutions.

The Diceyan tenet of Parliamentary supremacy was accepted by Canadian courts then, as it is accepted by Australian courts now, as a fundamental postulate of the legal system. Each country has a written Constitution which distributes legislative powers between central and provincial legislatures. The courts of each country are accustomed judicially to review the exercise of legislative and executive power and to strike down any purported exercise which is beyond the power conferred upon the repository by the Constitution. But, most importantly, the courts of Canada deferred, as Australian courts defer, to the political judgment of the political branches of government in the exercise of their respective powers. The Charter has introduced a massive constitutional change which, as Dean Sharpe has demonstrated, has evoked a corresponding change in judicial function and judicial method.

Dean Sharpe is uniquely qualified to describe and evaluate the administration of the Charter. The analytical and critical skills of a distinguished academic lawyer are combined with the practical and demanding experience of working with the Supreme Court as its Executive Legal Officer. The result is the informative and incisive paper that we have had presented to us this morning. If Dean Sharpe is 'cautiously optimistic' about the prospects of judicial articulation of a coherent vision of the Charter that protects human rights and fundamental freedoms without undue interference with legislative judgment, then there are substantial grounds for optimism in considering a constitutionally entrenched Bill of Rights for Australia. If Canada and Canadian judges could cope with – indeed, revel in – the change, surely Australia and Australian judges might do the same. Moreover, the only Bill of Rights which has thus far been exposed for public examination in Australia was that modelled on the Canadian Charter and proposed by the Constitutional Commission in 1988. If such a provision were entrenched in our Constitution, the judicial experience of Canada and the careful development of *Canadian Charter* jurisprudence would give to the Australian courts an advantage which the Canadian courts had to acquire by their own labours. We could introduce a Bill of Rights and have it administered by our existing courts, but would Australians wish that to be done? The voting at the last referendum suggests that the answer is resoundingly negative. However, non-party political interest in and discussion of the *Constitution*, in the last decade of this century, restores the question to the agenda. I do not propose an answer to the question, for reasons which I shall mention. The question is essentially political and should be answered by reference to the political needs that might be satisfied by an entrenched Bill of Rights and the burdens which might be imposed by its introduction.

The question should not be answered generally; it should be answered by reference to a specific proposal tailored to the particular political needs of the Australian people. But, in whatever terms an Australian Bill of Rights be cast, it would contain guarantees of rights which, though expressed in unqualified terms, would not be absolute. No individual rights can be pushed so far as to deny the rights of others: the right to life itself cannot be held to protect the murderous assailant against necessary self-defence by his victim. And liberty, if absolute, is the enemy of equality for it leaves the powerful free to oppress the weak. The scope of an entrenched right is necessarily left for definition in the administration of the entrenched provisions. In whatever terms a Bill of Rights be cast, it calls for what Dean Sharpe describes as a weighing of the collective interest against the right of the individual and an adjustment of broadly-expressed individual rights *inter se*.[2]

This is a function which the Fathers of our *Constitution*, fully alive to the United States Bill of Rights and the 14th Amendment, consciously left to the political branches of government.[3] If the exercise of political power is to be subjected to constitutional Bill of Rights, there is no institution to which the administration of those provisions can be entrusted save the

Courts. The Courts, in supervising the exercise of political power, would be constrained to base their decisions on political considerations. This is foreign to our present conception of judicial function. In *Clunies-Ross v The Commonwealth* the High Court said:

> It would be an abdication of the duty of this Court under the *Constitution* if we were to determine [this] important and general question of law ... according to whether we personally agreed or disagreed with the political and social objectives which the Minister sought to achieve. ... As a matter of constitutional duty, [the] question must be considered objectively and answered in this court as a question of law and not as a matter to be determined by reference to the political or social merits of the particular case. [4]

If the courts are to decide issues on their political and social merits, the courts will have to be given, as the Canadian courts were given, 'a deliberate push away from the cautious and highly deferential posture they exhibited'[5] in cases governed by statute law. Constitutional entrenchment is required to project the courts onto the political stage. Hitherto, under the influence of Diceyan theory, the courts have distanced themselves from the political branches of government.

Diceyan theory, which has informed much of the rhetoric about our democratic system, assumes that the legislative will expressed in statutory form expresses the permanent – or long-term - wishes of the electors.[6] The courts then interpret and apply the legislative will. The theory is no longer tenable. The greater bulk of legislation today consists of statutory instruments which Parliamentary committees may endeavour to supervise, but which Parliament itself cannot hope to consider. Much legislation emanates from the permanent bureaucracy rather than from the elected representatives of the people. More importantly for present purposes, two factors have combined to expose human rights and fundamental freedoms to danger from an exercise of power by the political branches of government. First, our society has become more diverse in its ethnic, cultural, religious, and economic composition. Or, to put it another way, there are more minority groups whose particular interests are liable to be overreached by the exercise of legislative or executive power. The control of the political process by political parties favours the creation of poll-driven policies which will appeal to the majority of the electorate whether or not they unjustifiably discriminate against minority groups or against the weak. There is a consequent risk that factors which justify special consideration of the position of a minority or special support of the weak will be disregarded. A Bill of Rights is seen as a protection of minorities and the weak against a discriminatory exercise of power by the political branches of government. Lord Scarman advances this as the chief political argument for a Bill of Rights in the United Kingdom: 'if you are going to protect people who will never have political power, at any rate in the foreseeable future (not only individuals but minority groups with their own treasured and properly treasured social customs, religion and ways of life), if they are going to be protected it won't be done in Parliament – they will never muster a majority. It's got to be done by the courts and the courts can only do it if they've got the proper guidelines.'[7]

A further danger to human rights and fundamental freedoms is posed by the dominance of the Executive Government, supported by its bureaucracy, over the Parliament. This dominance has undermined the theory that the Westminster model of responsible government effectively guarantees democratic control of executive power, to the extent that Lord Hailsham concluded that '[w]e live under an elective dictatorship, absolute in theory if hitherto thought tolerable in practice'.[8] A Bill of Rights is seen as a protection against the oppressive exercise of this enormous mass of power. As Sir Anthony Mason put it: 'Human rights are seen as a countervailing force to the exercise of totalitarian, bureaucratic and institutional power – widely identified as the greatest threats to the liberty of the individual and democratic freedom in this century. One result has been the widespread entrenchment of fundamental rights in constitutions throughout the world.'[9]

If the exercise of political power is no longer subject to effective checks and balances which protect human rights and fundamental freedoms then, so the argument goes, new checks and balances are needed. A Bill of Rights, which exposes the exercise of legislative and executive power to review, will bring a new and dominant force into the political process. If the risk of discriminatory exercise of power to the disadvantage of minorities and the weak and the risk of oppressive exercise of power by the political branches of government are sufficiently grave, and if there is no other means available to avoid or diminish those risks, then a case can be made for casting on the courts a supervisory role, albeit a role which is radically different from the role which courts have been accustomed to exercise. Over time, the function and significance of the third branch of Government will be substantially changed and the relationship between the courts and the political branches of government will be altered. Before Australia commits itself to a Bill of Rights, we should consider the impact a Bill of Rights would have on the role of the judiciary. After all, the very object of a Bill of Rights is to create a new role for the judiciary – by exercise of a new jurisdiction, the courts are to protect human rights and fundamental freedoms. But what effect would a new jurisdiction have on the exercise of the jurisdiction now vested in the courts?

If a Bill of Rights were entrenched in the *Constitution*, new judicial skills would be required. A Bill of Rights, drawn in open-textured terms, necessarily requires individual human rights to be defined with a content specific to the case in hand. In other words, the court must define whether a particular right or immunity exists and ought to be protected by curial order. And, insofar as individual human rights are not always capable of simultaneous unqualified enjoyment, a Bill of Rights evokes a determination of a priority of rights or values by reference to which the human rights in competition with each other may be adjusted. Once the right is defined, the court must weigh the collective interest against the right of the individual. This is the stuff of politics, but a Bill of Rights purports to convert political into legal debate, and to judicialize questions of politics and morality.

Decision-making under a Bill of Rights starts, no doubt, with a construction of the relevant provisions of the Bill. But a Bill of Rights is merely the key that opens the door of jurisdiction: once inside, the question is whether the law or the exercise of executive power which would otherwise result in one verdict or order should be held obnoxious to the relevant provisions of the Bill of Rights so that another verdict should be returned or another order made. What would otherwise be enforced as legal rights and legal liabilities are qualified by the Bill of Rights, and are enforceable only to the extent that they are, and are held to be, consistent with its terms. Of course, a decision once made would have the value of a judicial precedent but, in cases where there is no binding precedent precisely applicable, the trial must expand to encompass the issues raised by the Bill of Rights. The major premiss of the syllogism which leads to judgment must be ascertained not merely by reference to legislation and the common law but also by reference to the diverse and difficult issues created by the Bill of Rights.

These issues – which I shall call human rights issues, though human rights issues may arise independently of a Bill of Rights – must be resolved by methods which are different from the methods used to resolve other issues in a case. In the first place, the ordinary procedure of adducing evidence simply will not do. The rules of evidence govern the proof of the facts of a particular case – the minor premiss in the judicial syllogism. They do not necessarily apply to the determination of the legal rule which is relevant to the case – the major premiss.

The issues under an entrenched Bill of Rights are constitutional issues and the decision affects the powers of Government and the interests of all who live under the *Constitution*: such issues cannot be made to depend upon the choice or the capacity of the parties to adduce the evidence necessary for the making of an informed decision. The evidence may be quite complex, for the effect of striking down a law or an executive act which has been passed or done in the collective interest must be ascertained. It is no light thing to strike down a law or an executive act which one of the political branches of government, armed with information and experience much wider than the court can muster, has deemed to be justifiable.

The advocacy of human rights issues must range over wider fields than advocacy of other issues. Political, sociological and ethical considerations which impact on the existing legal system can be handled only with an appreciation of both the law and those other considerations. Professor Ferguson, reflecting on the Canadian experience, observed that the Charter has had– 'a dramatic and, for many lawyers, a very stimulating effect on their work. The enactment of the Charter has provided lawyers with a sumptuous smorgasbord of new arguments. One effect, of course, is that a lawyer's research and trial preparation time has increased, which ultimately raises the cost of litigation.'[10]

The cost of litigation is a matter of no small moment. As constitutional issues and the powers of Government are necessarily involved, provisions must be made for governments to intervene to uphold the validity of laws or executive actions which are attacked as obnoxious to a provision of the Bill of Rights. Though the underlying purpose of a Bill of Rights is the protection of individual interests, few individuals could afford to fund the major litigation which would be launched by raising one of its provisions. If an individual litigant succeeded at first instance by relying on such a provision, the prospects of appeal would surely be substantial. Of course, corporate litigants may seek to rely on Bills of Rights provisions in order to achieve a commercial or other advantage unrelated to the interests which the Bill of Rights protects,[11] and interest groups may use litigation as a means of advancing their political, social or ethical objectives.[12] Individuals may take the benefit of decisions given in litigation funded by others, but civil litigation under a Bill of Rights is hardly a practicable means for an individual to protect his or her individual rights against overreaching by Government. However, Bill of Rights litigation may be frequently conducted in the criminal jurisdiction where the cost may be borne by public funds. By whomsoever the cost of Bill of Rights litigation is met, it is likely to be substantial.

Nor should the effect of such litigation on court lists be underestimated. Court congestion, particularly in the criminal lists, would be aggravated by such litigation. Delay in the delivery of judgments, if the Canadian experience is any guide, is likely to grow.[13] And, in the High Court, a flow of Bill of

Rights litigation could be accommodated only by shedding a corresponding volume of non-Constitutional civil and criminal cases. The court would be confined substantially to Constitutional cases. With such a fascinating diet, the court would in time have a diminished appetite for the pedestrian issues of the law.

At the end of the litigating day, the translation of political, social and ethical values into legal principles must be articulated by the judge. He or she cannot avoid giving effect to his or her values in determining whether an impugned law or executive act is obnoxious to a Bill of Rights and unjustifiable in the collective interest. What the judge can and, if required, will do is to expose the reasoning which leads to the conclusion and to articulate a legal rule which gives effect to the conclusion.

It is the very process of open consideration of the issue arising under a Bill of Rights, its formalised debate between adversaries in the cool dignity of the courtroom, the exposure of reasons and the articulation of the applicable legal rule that commends the courts as the repositories of a supervisory power over the political branches of government. A new judicial role under a Bill of Rights has attractions not only for those who would challenge the actions of Government, but for Government itself. There are some issues which, in a pluralist and divided society, are the subject of such controversy that no political party wishes to take the responsibility of solving them. The political process may be paralyzed. If Governments can create a situation where such issues are submitted to curial decision, political obloquy can be avoided by Governments, though it is sometimes transferred to the courts, as the continuing controversy over *Roe* v *Wade*[14] illustrates. However, the judicial method commands a broader acceptance than the political process, and the courts, in exercise of a jurisdiction under a Bill of Rights, can sometimes cut a political Gordian knot. The desegregation decisions of the Supreme Court of the United States provide the classic example.

As the powers conferred on the courts under a Bill of Rights are powers to make political, social and ethical decisions affecting the whole community, the training and selection of judges must be accommodated to the additional functions they perform. That is because the effect of a Bill of Rights depends much more on the attitudes of the judges who interpret it than on the words themselves. Sir Harry Gibbs pointed out

> It is because of this that some apprehend that the adoption of a bill of rights will cause some dangers for the judiciary. It is not unnatural for a government to think that it is justifiable to appoint judges who will be sympathetic to its views. It is a short step to the appointment of judges who, the government believes, will carry

> out its wishes. The danger of the appointment of judges on purely political grounds is the greater if the government strongly holds a policy which may be advanced or frustrated depending on how the bill of rights is interpreted.[15]

The exposure to public gaze of judicial personalities and beliefs is to be expected, if not welcomed, if a Bill of Rights were introduced. The Canadian experience is described by Madame Justice McLachlin: 'The advent of the Charter in Canada has elevated judges from a position where they once toiled in relative obscurity, to the level of media figures. Now, more than ever before, the contributions made by the courts are seen to impact so directly and profoundly on the everyday life of the country that judgments of the Supreme Court on the Charter receive regular and extensive attention from the news media.'[16]

Whether the Australian people wish to alter the role the judiciary now performs is a matter of speculation. It is clear that the Australian judiciary could not perform a role under a Bill of Rights unless the Australian people consciously cast that role upon them. And it is only if the Australian people are made aware that a Bill of Rights will involve changes in judicial modes of thought, in the function of the courts, in the magnitude and cost of some classes of litigation and in the projection of the Courts into the political dynamic that an informed decision can be made as to the desirability of a Bill of Rights and the terms in which it should be cast. It will be necessary to determine what rights need to be constitutionally entrenched in order to protect minorities and the weak from discrimination; what rights need to be constitutionally entrenched in order to prevent the oppressive exercise of legislative or executive power. That calls for an assessment to be made of the present capacity of the political process to prevent the excesses against which protection is sought and an assessment of the extent to which the courts are presently incapable of extending the needed protection, even if aided by statute. An Act of Parliament may suffice, for example, to ensure that a person suspected of crime is protected in a particular respect – say, in respect of a failure to bring the suspect to trial within a reasonable time. The New Zealand Court of Appeal has recently accorded a substantial operation to a statutory Bill of Rights to enhance the rights of a suspect under interrogation.[17] Constitutional entrenchment is not necessary unless there is an apprehension that a law will be directed or will operate against a minority group or against the weak in a discriminatory fashion or will vest in the Executive Government powers which can be exercised oppressively without the possibility of adequate supervision by the ordinary processes of judicial review. Of course, where there is a real risk of legislative sanction of state oppression, incapable of effective remedy by the existing political processes, or where there is a real risk of state discrimination incapable of remedy by the existing legal processes, a Bill of Rights offers a solution. The magnitude of the risk is a matter for the informed judgment of the Australian people.

In a very real sense, it does not matter what the impact of a Bill of Rights will be on judges; what is important is the impact of a Bill of Rights on the role of the judiciary. If the role be limited to the role hitherto discharged by the judiciary, the impact of a Bill of Rights will be to impair the capacity of the judges to perform that role. On the other hand, human rights issues, however arising in litigation, give the courts a new relevance to the society they serve. The reason why the courts might be required to assume a new relevance was stated by Sir Anthony Mason:

> the nature of society and place of the individual within it has changed markedly over the last hundred years. The common law of the 19th century was directed primarily at governing the relationships between individuals. Landlord/tenant and contract law come to mind. The common law, a body of rules crafted by judges and susceptible to modification by legislatures, was well suited to regulating these relationships. However, the emergence of the omnipresent welfare state throws up problems of a different complexion. Government is now a major source of wealth and it participates in nearly every facet of social and economic life. [18]

A new jurisdiction would be unattractive to many judges; to others, the heady powers conferred by a Bill of Rights would present a welcome challenge and an opportunity to sweep aside legislative and executive action which impedes the doing of justice in the instant case. To all judges, however, the introduction of a Bill of Rights would bring a burden of decision-making far heavier than the burden of applying the existing law.

However, it would be a mistake to think that judges are wholly unfamiliar with considerations of policy and are not affected – albeit to a strictly limited extent – by political, social or ethical values in the decisions which they render under the existing constitutional regime. This Conference is considering other papers which canvass the ways in which courts may, without Constitutional entrenchment, give effect to human rights and fundamental freedoms. In interpreting statutes, in judicially reviewing administrative action, in ascertaining the connection between a law of the Commonwealth and a head of Constitutional legislative power and in declaring the common law the courts do not operate in a valueless vacuum. The decisions of the courts of this country during the last decade owe much to judicial appreciation of human rights and fundamental freedoms. It is likely that, particularly under the influence of the First Optional Protocol to the *International Convention on Civil and Political Rights*, concepts drawn from the developing international law of human rights and fundamental freedoms will find a reflection in the municipal law of this country. That said, there remains the question whether the courts should be more fully equipped to stand between the power of the modern state and individual rights and interests and should be required to assume a supervisory role of a particular kind over the exercise of political power. In short, the question is whether the arming of the courts with an additional Constitutional weapon is desirable to assist in the creation and maintenance of a free and just society.

The answer to this question does not depend on some simplistic or doctrinaire view about the respective roles of the three branches of Government. The answer must depend on a number of factors. The first is whether the political processes of this country leave open a risk of state discrimination against minority groups or against the weak or a risk of oppressive exercise of executive power that cannot be supervised adequately by judicial or other independent review, for example, review by the Administrative Appeals Tribunal or a Human Rights Commission. The next factor for consideration is the capacity of courts and tribunals, either in exercise of existing jurisdiction or in exercise of a jurisdiction that could be conferred satisfactorily by statute, to reduce the risks to an acceptably low level. Then, having assessed the extent of the otherwise irremediable risk, the desirability of entrenching a Bill of Rights must be balanced against the inevitable change which the entrenching would bring in the role of the judiciary.

The question of an entrenched Bill of Rights or no is a political question in the broadest sense, though the Constitutional lawyer has a great deal to contribute to the debate. But, as the papers being delivered at this Conference reveal, the question requires an assessment of the operation of our existing Constitutional institutions and an examination of the way in which they do or can be made to protect human rights and fundamental freedoms. We are benefited by the Canadian experience and the excellent analysis of it that Dean Sharpe has provided. And I would hope that, if the Australian people should cast on Australian courts the responsibility of administering a Bill of Rights in this country, the courts may win the respect which the decisions of the Supreme Court of Canada have earned for that distinguished tribunal.[19]

---

1. This paper was first published in Philip Alston, *Promoting Human Rights Through Bills of Rights: Comparative Perspectives,* (Oxford University Press, 1999) 454 – 464.
2. Robert J. Sharpe, 'The Impact of a Bill of Rights on the Role of the Judiciary: A Canadian Perspective', in Philip Alston, *Promoting Human Rights (*n 1) 431, 444

3. See the comments of Sir Owen Dixon, 'Two Constitutions Compared' in Sir Owen Dixon, *Jesting Pilate* (Law Book Co, 1965) 102.
4. (1984) 155 CLR 193, 204.
5. Robert J Sharpe (n 2) 435.]
6. Albert Venn Dicey, *Lectures Introductory to the Study of the Law of the Constitution* (Macmillan & Co, 1885), 77.
7. Lord Scarman, 'Britain and the Protection of Human Rights' (1984) *New Zealand Law Journal* 175, 177.
8. 1976 Richard Dimbleby Lecture: Lord Hailsham, *Elective Dictatorship* (British Broadcasting Corporation, 1976).
9. Sir Anthony Mason, 'A Bill of Rights for Australia?' (1989) 5 *Australian Bar Review* 79, 79-80.
10. Gerry Ferguson, 'The Impact of an Entrenched Bill of Rights – the Canadian Experience' (1990) 16 (2) *Monash University Law Review* 211, 219.
11. As in the case of *R* v *Big M Drug Mart Ltd* [1985] 1 SCR 295; 18 DLR (4th) 321.
12. As in *Operation Dismantle* v *The Queen* (1985) 18 DLR (4th) 481.
13. See Gerry Ferguson, 'The Impact of an Entrenched Bill of Rights – the Canadian Experience' (1990) 16 (2) *Monash University Law Review* 211, 218.
14. 410 US 113 (1973); see in this respect the judgment of Scalia J in *Webster* v *Reproductive Health Services* 492 US 490 (1989), and the conflicting opinions in *Planned Parenthood of Southeastern Pennsylvania* v *Casey (*1992) 60 USLW 4795.
15. Sir Harry Gibbs, 'Eleventh Wilfred Fullagar Memorial Lecture: The Constitutional Protection of Human Rights' (1982) 9 (1) *Monash University Law Review* 1, 8.
16. Beverley McLachlin, 'Southey Memorial Lecture: The Canadian Charter and the Democratic Process' (1991) 18 (2) *Melbourne University Law Review* 350, 355.
17. See *R* v *Kirifi* (1991) 7 Crim Rep NZ 427.
18. Sir Anthony Mason, 'A Bill of Rights for Australia?' (1989) 5 *Australian Bar Review* 79, 85-86.
19. See, for example, ER Alexander, 'The Supreme Court of Canada and the Canadian Charter of Rights and Freedoms', (1990) 40 *University of Toronto Law Journal* 1, 40, cited by Gerry Ferguson, 'The Impact of an Entrenched Bill of Rights – the Canadian Experience' (1990) 16 (2) *Monash University Law Review* 211, 227.

3.5 Law, Politics and Public Life

Editor's note

Brennan delivered the George Higinbotham Lecture in Melbourne on 27 November 1992 commemorating the centenary of the death of Higinbotham who had been Attorney-General and Chief Justice in Victoria.

A Centenary is a time for celebration; a time for reflection; a time for looking to the future. We are celebrating the life of George Higinbotham who was, according to Sir Ninian Stephen, 'of all Victorian public figures of the last century, the most widely admired and loved'.[1] By all accounts, he was a man of immense dignity, but he was not distant. He was in demand as a barrister, but his chambers were the resort of the destitute. He was Chief Justice of the State, but he rejected the personal honours and special emoluments which were the incidents of the office. He was a devout follower of Christ, but not of Christ's followers. Alfred Deakin who thought him to be 'the greatest of Australian orators and of Australian Liberals, the noblest nature and the most refined',[2] wrote of him: ' His practical career whether at the Bar, in the Assembly or on the Bench was never an unqualified success in the ordinary acceptation of that term. His standards were too high, his temper too unbending, his scrupulousness too indiscriminating to render him a colleague whom it was easy to co-operate with or to understand. Just to a hair's-breadth, and generous to a fault, he was yet tyrannical as duty itself and uncompromising as chastity in little as well as great affairs.'

His integrity was a by-word in both his public and his private life. His courtesy was unfailing, his generosity unstinted. Manning Clark says: 'He was a man with Christ-like qualities who spent much of his time with lawyers and accountants, a gentle spirit who found himself with the measurers, an enlarger surrounded by straiteners.'[3]

His contemporaries' admiration of his judicial qualities was virtually unbounded, though they paid tribute to his legal competence rather than to his legal genius. His biographer cites an innominate lawyer's comment: 'If I had ever been before Higinbotham as a litigant, I should probably have felt a doubt as to his law. I often did. I think he was too great a man to be a great technical lawyer. He could not lose sight of the object in the instrument. But I should have had no feeling of soreness.'[4]

This may be an ungenerous estimate of Higinbotham as a technical lawyer, especially when the criticism is based on his adopting of a purposive approach to the interpretation of instruments. On his death, tribute was paid to his great familiarity with case law.[5] His monumental work of consolidating the statute law of Victoria, first in the years 1863 to 1865 when, as Attorney-General, he directed and supervised the consolidation and again in 1890 when, as Chief Justice, he performed much of the work himself, gave him an unrivalled familiarity with the statute law in force in the Colony. His judgments in the *Victorian Law Reports* of the time[6] are expressed with elegant precision and copious citation of authority. It would be erroneous to compare his judgments with the great British judges of the time: his diet of work was more pedestrian than the rich variety of work in London and his capacity to develop the law was constricted by English precedent – not only the precedents of the Privy Council or the House of Lords but also the precedents of lesser Superior Courts.

Nevertheless, a number of his judgments are progressive in outlook[7] and reveal a precise legal mind.[8]

Perhaps his most celebrated judgment was his dissent in *Toy v Musgrove*[9] where, with Kerferd J, he upheld the validity of the refusal of Musgrove, the Collector of Customs, to allow Toy, a Chinese citizen, to land in Victoria. The ground on which he upheld Musgrove's refusal was that Musgrove had acted in obedience to an instruction by the Minister who, under the *Constitution of Victoria,* was authorized to exercise the Crown's prerogative power to exclude aliens. On the approach he took, the Chief Justice had an opportunity to declare that *The Constitution Act 1885* (Vic)[10] passed by the Legislative Council of Victoria and given Royal assent, conferred responsible government on Victoria, that the Government and the Parliament, modelled on Westminster, were designed 'to aid each other in establishing and maintaining plenary rights of self-government in internal affairs for the people of Victoria' and that the executive government of Victoria possessed functions 'similar to, and co-extensive, as regards the internal affairs of Victoria, with the functions possessed and exercised by the Imperial Government with regard to the internal affairs of Great Britain'[11] . Thus Higinbotham gave judicial force to resolutions of the Legislative Assembly in 1869 asserting the existence of self-government in internal affairs which he had moved.[12] And, for good measure, he held a number of the Imperial instructions to the Governor to be void.[13] In doing so, he confirmed his objections to the form of those instructions which he had set out in a letter, written as Chief Justice, to the Secretary of State for the Colonies, in the previous year.[14] When the case went on appeal to the Privy Council, the conclusion supported by the Chief Justice was upheld but on the grounds that the power of exclusion had been conferred by a local Act and that an alien had no legally enforceable right to enter British territory.[15] His views on the *Constitution*, judicially expressed in

Toy v Musgrove, had been a fervent article of faith throughout his political life. He was an undeviating Empire Loyalist, but an implacable opponent of meddling by Downing Street in the internal affairs of the Colony. Sir Kenneth Bailey,[16] who attributed the growth of self-government in Australia to the force of Higinbotham's character, commented 'Able, eloquent, inflexible, doctrinaire, incorruptible, Higinbotham became the exponent of a definite logical theory of responsible government, to the realisation of which, with ... "a knotty consistency", he thenceforward devoted himself.'

His constitutional principles led to his being passed over for appointment as Administrator during the Governor's absences, for he declared that he would not communicate with Downing Street on any matter of internal Victorian concern.[17]

The liberality of his social opinions was well known. At a time when 'the judiciary [was regarded] as the bastion of the status quo',[18] his sympathies were with the colonial labour movement. A visitor reported: 'The greatest doubter about human perfectibility could not be faint-hearted as to the future of labour after he had been for a few minutes under the optimistic spell of the Victorian Chief Justice. He revelled in the fact of the growing solidarity of labour, which served to checkmate the grasping employer when he sought to call in the glutted wealth of one part of the world to aid him in crushing the rising tide of working-class emancipation [in] another'.[19]

His sympathies with labour led to his memorable and controversial contribution to the strike fund in 1890 when he judged the continuance of a disastrous strike to be due to an intransigent refusal by the Employers' Union to confer with the Trades Hall Council. He wrote, using the title of his office, the following letter: 'The Chief Justice presents his compliments to the President of the Trades Hall Council, and requests that he will be so good as to place the amount of the enclosed cheque of £50 to the credit of the strike fund. While the United Trades are awaiting compliance with their reasonable request for a conference with the employers, the Chief Justice will continue for the present to forward a weekly contribution of £10 to the same object.'[20]

The Chief Justice had horrified the Melbourne Establishment. His action was the subject of severe criticism by some, of affectionate admiration by others.[21]

He served on the Supreme Court from 1880, first as a puisne Judge and, after the retirement of Chief Justice Stawell in 1886, as Chief Justice until his death. It is hard to document the influence which Higinbotham's uncompromising integrity, his competence and his exhausting devotion to duty had upon the Supreme Court of Victoria and upon the perception which Government and the people had of that institution. In an institution where the estimate of peers is the greatest source of encouragement and a stern discipline, the presence of such a Chief Justice was an inspiration. On Higinbotham's death, Mr Justice Hodges declared that: 'Britain may have greater lawyers; Britain may have greater statesmen; Britain may have craftier politicians; but Britain has no son with a stronger, gentler, firmer, more tender, nobler nature than the man who lately presided in this court'.[22]

His opinions on constitutional questions were, in his time, idiosyncratic but, as Bailey observed, 'statesman rather than lawyer, Higinbotham had the future with him'.[23] We therefore have much to admire and celebrate in the life of George Higinbotham. It is a life to be celebrated for the contribution he made to the institutions of his day, for the standards he set that strengthened those institutions and for his ideas which have helped to fashion our history.

Reflection

In the 100 years since Higinbotham's death on the last day of 1892, whatever sense of novelty there may have been in his views on responsible government in the Colonies and on the scope of colonial power has been dissipated.

Imperial instructions to the Colonial Governor were amended to meet his objections in 1892.[24] The necessity to devolve power on the developing colonies of a far-flung Empire, made more imperative by the aspirations of colonialists whose primary loyalties were local, led to the recognition of full responsible government for local affairs in most British colonies. Legal orthodoxy now recognizes not only that, subject to the *Colonial Laws Validity Act 1865* (Imp), the pre-Federation colonies enjoyed responsible self-government but also that statutes enacted by Colonial Parliaments at that time had extra-territorial operation.[25]

When Alfred Deakin sought the Chief Justice's opinion on a draft of a *Constitution* during the 1891 Federal Convention, Higinbotham criticized the draft for leaving the Governor-General subject to the control of the Imperial Government. John Waugh has speculated[26] that his opinion may have contributed to the inclusion in s 64 of the *Constitution* of the phrase 'and shall be the Queen's Ministers of State for the Commonwealth'. In some matters, his Empire loyalty curiously put him at odds with the nationalist aspirations of the federal movement. He found fault in the 1891 proposal to arm the Federal Parliament with powers over external affairs and trade; he regarded those powers as proper to be retained by the Imperial Government. [27]And he was critical of the proposal to limit appeals to the Privy Council.[28] Those views did not prevail, but his views were influential. Deakin's estimate was this: 'Federalist heart and soul (though his position as Chief Justice sealed his lips upon the question), it was he who imparted to the Federal Cause in Victoria a special note of undeviating loyalty to the Empire.'[29]

I venture to suggest, however, that his great contribution to the history of Australia was not in the judicial definition of constitutional principle nor in the 'knotty consistency' of his extra-judicial advocacy of responsible self-government nor in his influence on Federation. Rather, it was in the model of judicial service which was his legacy to the judicial branch of government.

The efficacy of a legal system depends largely on the authority of the courts. Unless a losing party accepts the *authority of* the court to decide the case against him, the court's decision does not effectively settle the dispute. The possibility – or, in criminal cases, the certainty – of enforcement is a necessary sanction for the court's authority but an efficient legal system requires acceptance of curial decisions, not merely their enforcement. It is only by general acceptance of the authority of the courts that the peace and stability of society is secured. The judicial branch of government, as Alexander Hamilton pointed out in *The Federalist Papers*, 'has no influence over either the sword or the purse ... It [has] neither FORCE nor WILL but merely judgment'.[30] And the power of judgment rests on the confidence of the people in the work of the court. The courts, no less than the political branches of government, draw their authority from the confidence of the people – not because curial decisions satisfy a popular clamour, but because it is in the courts that the people expect justice to be done, and to be seen to be done, according to law. If Sir Ninian Stephen be right to say that, before Higinbotham, the Supreme Court was seen to be a bastion of the status quo, Higinbotham's invaluable contribution was to demonstrate that justice is not the captive of a class, that the holders of office are not necessarily the protectors of the status quo, that a profound respect for office held is not to be confused with a self-important conceit and that the authority of a court is derived from absolute integrity and from an unremitting pursuit of justice according to law. Higinbotham was, and was seen to be, a judge of independence, integrity, competence, industry and experience. He inspired his colleagues; he was their exemplar in the manifestation of these judicial qualities. The beneficiaries of such judicial qualities are the people whom the courts serve – the powerful and the weak equally, the rich and the poor equally, those in office and those aspiring to office equally. Perhaps the protection of the law is most important to those who will never have nor even aspire to power or riches or office, for they have no other protection of their interests and their dignity. But the judge stands in the lonely no-man's-land between the powerful and the weak, between the rich and the poor, between the government and the governed, applying indifferently and precisely the law of the land. She or he can identify with neither, for partisanship robs the judge of the authority essential to discharge the judicial office.

Over the years, the Supreme Court of Victoria prided itself on its elite tradition of service. At whatever personal cost to the judges, the work of the Supreme Court commanded the confidence of the legal profession, of the litigants and of the general community.

It is hard to overstate the importance to the community of this tradition. The ultimate purpose of the courts is to secure peace, stability and freedom. This is achieved by giving a public hearing to an affected party in every case, by ensuring that no justiciable dispute brought to a court goes unresolved, by applying the law to accord legal rights and afford legal protection and by stating the reasons for decision. It is essential that the judges be, and be seen to be,[31] judges of independence, integrity, competence, industry and experience. A society which does not have an authoritative mechanism of this kind for settling disputes between its citizens is unstable, for then the law's writ does not run and the individual is driven to self-help. A government which does not submit itself to an authoritative mechanism of this kind for settling disputes between it and its citizens is totalitarian. The law's writ must run in a free society, else power goes unchecked.

These propositions are so obvious that we seldom think of them. The appointment of judges to constitute our courts goes unremarked. The assumption is that the judicial tradition is strong enough to ensure that any appointee will conform to its high standards. This is a tribute to the Higinbothams of our history and, for the most part, the assumption has proved to be valid. But a judge's quality affects the morale and standing of his or her court. Defects in judicial quality, unless remedied during the tenure of office, can disrupt the operation of law and weaken public confidence in its administration as well as working injustice in particular cases. A poor judicial appointment erodes the strength of peer standards and deters other potential judges from accepting appointment. The quality of judicial appointments is arguably of more significance to peace, stability and freedom than the appointment of officers to any other branch of government. Governments should exercise the greatest care in making judicial appointments. The judicial office must never be an office of patronage, for patronage would quickly diminish the authority of the courts.

I suspect, and I regret the suspicion, that the function of the courts is not fully understood in our society. That is not surprising. Governments and the media take the courts for granted; their routine work does not impinge on the political and economic debates of the day. And, in applying the law, the courts are accustomed to work with an unattractive – sometimes needlessly unattractive – precision of language to express the law's balance of competing duties and immunities. Such language and the nicety of legal reasoning can lend themselves to misunderstanding, if not misrepresentation. Some judgments need expert explanation to be understood by the legal laity. But whether the work of the courts is fully understood or not, it measures the extent to which our society is governed by law. Hence judicial insistence on independence from influence by the political branches of government and judicial interest in the quality of appointments to judicial office. Of course, the problems confronting a government in making judicial appointments are greater than they were 100 years ago.

The volume of litigation has created a demand for legal services then undreamt of and appointments to all courts, federal and state, has increased to meet that demand. When Higinbotham was Chief Justice, he presided over a Supreme Court of six judges. Today in Victoria there are 25 Supreme Court judges, 10 resident Federal Court judges, 11 Family Court judges, 46 County Court judges and a bench of 90 Magistrates who, by reason of their qualifications, jurisdiction and case load, constitute a vital component of the court system. The numerical increase in the Victorian judiciary is representative of the position throughout Australia. It has been found necessary to appoint judges to superior courts whose experience, if not more limited in volume than their predecessors, is more confined in scope. And the conditions of judicial service have been substantially diminished. The selection of judges has become a difficult task. The difficulty in recruiting judges is a matter of particular concern for courts whose jurisdiction includes judicial review of administrative action.

As the powers of the executive government have increased relatively to the powers of the Parliament during the last century and as areas of administrative activity have expanded, litigants affected by administrative action have resorted increasingly to the courts for relief. The courts have responded by developing and refining the law which governs the exercise of administrative power and the jurisdiction to review. The exercise of this jurisdiction has sometimes been regarded as officious intermeddling in the administration of government but it is no more than the precise application of the law. So long as we live under the rule of law, the impediments which judicial review, precisely applied, place in the way of implementing government policy must be accepted. Administrative review is but one of the growth areas of jurisdiction which require the resolution of disputes between powerful institutions and less powerful litigants. When litigation of that kind is before a court, it is manifestly important that the judge be, and be seen to be, possessed of the judicial qualities which Higinbotham displayed.

The standards which he set for judicial conduct have been an example for judges in this country to follow and have made a massive contribution to the authority of the courts. Those standards remain valid as the courts grapple with new problems flowing from rapid changes in our society.

The future

The province of law today is immeasurably greater than it was 100 years ago. The complexity of modern society is reflected in the exponential growth of statutory law, especially of delegated legislation. The common law (in which for this purpose I include equity) has been expanded by judicial decision to give relief in cases that were left without remedy in earlier times. The conditions of Australian society have evoked the development of an indigenous law, free of the fetters which bound us to English law but informed by its wisdom. As a moral consensus has fallen away or has failed to form, law has been pressed into becoming a source of substitute morality – especially in commercial life and in the field of bio-ethics. The courts have thus acquired an extended charter, not of their own seeking but of necessity. The explosion of law and of litigation creates new problems as to the role which the courts should play in the development of the law and as to the capacity of the courts to settle the multitude of disputes that require the application of law.

It is trite to say that it is the duty of the courts to apply the law. But what is the law to be applied? To the extent that the law is defined by the *Constitution* or by statute, the text of the *Constitution* or of the statute governs. The function of the courts is interpretation of the text. If and to the extent that constitutional or statutory text does not govern the case in hand, the court must ascertain the law from precedent and from analogy to precedent where precedent is binding. Where there is no binding precedent or, in the case of an ultimate court of appeal, no acceptable precedent,[32] the law must be derived from more diffuse sources which Mr Justice Cardozo broadly identified: 'logic, and history, and custom, and utility, and the accepted standards of right conduct, are the forces which singly or in combination shape the progress of the law. Which of these forces shall dominate in any case, must depend largely upon the comparative importance or value of the social interests that will be thereby promoted or impaired.'[33]

The need, and hence the proper scope, of judicial creativity thus depends on the source and the nature of the law to be applied to the case in hand.

The task of constitutional interpretation is not a charter for judicial amendment – that is a power which is reserved to the people in the case of the Commonwealth *Constitution* and to Parliaments in the case of State

Constitutions. But occasionally, old interpretations which have been proved to be without foundation in the constitutional text[34] or unworkable in practice[35] have to be revised. Under a *Constitution* which confers limited powers on the Commonwealth, the courts – and particularly the High Court – have the function of determining the validity of laws passed by the Parliament and regulations made by the executive. Constitutional review of validity is not, though it is sometimes portrayed as, an exercise of judicial power over the power conferred on the political branches of government. It is and can be no more than an application of the law which governs all branches of government. There can be no adventures with judicial power in the constitutional field – only the careful task of textual analysis, reference to history, consideration of precedent and, if there be truly competing interpretations open on the text of the constitutional law, an evaluation of which interpretation most closely corresponds with the values which the Court perceives to be underlying the relevant provision. The same task confronted the Court in *Toy v Musgrove.* The basic judicial technique is not novel. To be sure, the economy of the constitutional text leaves much work for the judicial interpreter to do, but a court is not armed with a power to mould the *Constitution* to its liking. In federal constitutional matters, no branch of government is.

In the application of statute law, the courts are similarly constrained. The courts cannot refuse to apply a law validly passed by the Parliament or a regulation validly made in exercise of statutory power, though the validity of regulations is a question for the courts for they are responsible for ensuring that the repositories of statutory power do not exceed the legal limits of their authority.

In interpreting statute law, the courts apply some presumptions, the most important being that the law-maker does not intend, in the absence of express words to the contrary, to infringe the fundamental human rights of the people to whom the law applies.[36] When the courts attribute a narrow operation to a statute in order to preserve human rights, executive governments may find that the interpretation frustrates their purposes in the same way as judicial review of administrative action may frustrate those purposes. It must be accepted that the jurisdiction of the courts is not conducive to the most efficient or cost-effective implementation of government policies, but that is the very purpose of a system of checks and balances in a democratic society governed by law.

The third category of law which the courts administer is the common law. Sometimes the common law is spoken of as though it is an immutable body of principles embodying and reflecting eternal values. It is, of course, an absurdity to regard principles as immutable if they are to serve the changing needs of a living society. The principles of the common law were developed over the centuries by judges who were alive to the values of their contemporary societies, some of which are enduring from generation to generation – such as the principle of *audi alteram partem* – and some of which reflect the prevailing social values of a period – such as the rule of common employment. And so changes must be made to keep the law in a satisfactory state of repair to serve the contemporary community. Intermediate Courts of Appeal may be restrained by precedent but an ultimate Court of Appeal has more latitude. However, changes in the common law are made only in response to a perceived need to do justice and to enhance the efficiency of the law. To quote Mr Justice Cardozo again: 'Every new case is an experiment; and if the accepted rule which seems applicable yields a result which is felt to be unjust, the rule is reconsidered. It may not be modified at once, for the attempt to do absolute justice in every single case would make the development and maintenance of general rules impossible; but if a rule continues to work injustice, it will eventually be reformulated. The principles themselves are continually retested; for if the rules derived from a principle do not work well, the principle itself must ultimately be re-examined.'[37]

In times of rapid social change, it should come as no surprise that changes in the common law will be more frequent than in times of social equilibrium. But the common law is not changed to conform to an idiosyncratic opinion. The factors to which Mr Justice Cardozo referred have their parts to play and there must be an appreciation of the origin and operation of the existing rule and an awareness of the manner in which any proposed change will affect interlocking principles of the law.

In the years since World War II, the law has been more finely tuned to take account of the variety of situations to which it must apply; it has grown more complex. The reporting of decisions has proliferated, stimulated by commercial opportunity rather than restrained by a professional discretion. The consequence is that while the law has become more finely tuned, it has become more unpredictable[38] as Holdsworth foretold 65 years ago:

> The law is likely to be burdened with so great a mass of decisions of different degrees of excellence, that its principles, so far from being made more certain by the decisions of new cases, will become sufficiently uncertain to afford abundant material for the infinite disputations of professors of general jurisprudence....English lawyers have hardly realized that [a limitation in the number of reported cases] was a condition precedent for the satisfactory working of our system of case law.[39]

The more uncertain the law, the greater are the costs involved and the more difficult is access to justice. If the courts open their doors to admit litigation which only a few can afford, they become more remote from the community on whose confidence they depend. There is a paradox in the growing complexity of the law. Unless the law be adjusted to do justice in new situations, the law becomes an instrument of injustice, but if adjustments must be made or defined by litigation, many rights will go unenforced and much legal protection will be insubstantial. Perhaps we need to re-examine some of the methodology of the law.

Do we need to modify the doctrine of precedent, to restrict citable authority, to accept minor inconsistencies in the application of precedent? Certain it is that we do not need to find new law in every case. One way of reducing the cost of litigation is to reduce the burden of research – not to conceal the principles, but to exclude their myriad applications. Apart from precedent, the rules of procedure must be applied to achieve efficiency in litigation. Yet the frequency of interlocutory appeals suggests that an even tighter rein over procedure is required to prevent unnecessary or inefficient applications for mere procedural relief. After trial, a litigant should be limited to one appeal unless the public interest justifies the expense involved and the deployment of judicial resources for the purpose. The absence of constraints on advocacy warrants re-examination. The advice of older advocates that there is usually only one, sometimes two, points in a case worth contesting seems often to be ignored. On appeals, where the results of research can be effectively conveyed in writing, there is much to be said for focussing oral argument by restricting the time allocated to each party. Indeed, even in trial courts, the focussing of an advocate's examination and cross-examination on the real issues in dispute might benefit from some judiciously-applied limitations.

Courts are not the only, or necessarily the desirable, forum for resolving some disputes. We have become familiar with independent tribunals, of varying degrees of cost and formality, which have jurisdiction to review the merits of administrative decisions. When it is proposed to create new rights or impose new obligations by statute, it is desirable that the right or obligation be so defined as to be enforceable in practice, either by a court or by a tribunal. It is futile to create a right or obligation which is enforceable only by litigation disproportionate to the value of the right or obligation. Perhaps the most significant development in the administration of the law in the foreseeable future will be the growth of tribunals which, independently of government, will see to the administration of those laws conferring rights or imposing obligations of limited value which nevertheless bear closely on the quality of the lives of individuals. The expertise and independence of these tribunals will have to be carefully protected for they are no less a part of the apparatus of justice than the courts.

There is the possibility of using the artificial intelligence of computers to resolve a large proportion of the cases to which modern statute law applies. May it not be possible, by consultation between Parliamentary counsel and computer experts, to draft legislation in terms that facilitate the making of decisions in large-volume areas simply by the entry of data? And may not computers be used to transmit records from trial courts to courts of appeal? And is it not likely that, by extremely competent analyses of case law data bases by legal engineers, computers can extract relevant principles from the mass of unusable data base material? No doubt there are other and perhaps better ways of coping with the burden of modern litigation.

The vast proliferation of legal literature, the involvement of teams in litigation, the mounds of paper wheeled into and out of courts, the lengthening time of trials and the frequency of appeals suggest that there are problems in the system of administering the law that need to be addressed.

Whatever innovations be adopted, the core of the system must be courts that work in the traditional judicial way either by determining the issues or by reviewing the determinations made by other decision-makers. The authority of these courts will continue to rest on the independence, integrity, competence, industry and experience/of the judges who constitute them, for those are the qualities which underpin a peaceful, stable and free society.

---

1. Ninian Stephen, *Daniel Mannix Memorial Lecture: George Higinbotham,* (1983) 2 (unpublished).
2. Alfred Deakin, *The Federal Story* (Robertson & Mullens,1944) 7-8.
3. Manning Clark, *A History of Australia, Volume 4* (Melbourne University Press, 1978), 109.
4. Edward Ellis Morris, *A Memoir of George Higinbotham,* (Macmillan, 1895) 261.
5. Ibid 312.
6. Volumes 6 to 18.
7. See, for example, *Fergusson v Union Steamship Co* (1884) 10 VLR (L) 279 and *Reg v Martin* (1884) 10 VLR (L) 343 considered in *Barton v The Queen* (1980) 147 CLR 75.
8. See, for example, *Athoness v Anderson* (1888) 14 VLR 127, followed in *Jack v Smail* (1905) 2 CLR 684. Sir Ninian Stephen collected other cases: Daniel Mannix Memorial Lecture, 42-43.
9. (1888) 14 VLR 349.
10. 19 Vict.
11. (1888) 14 VLR 349, 396-397.
12. Morris (n 4) 160-161.
13. (1888) 14 VLR 439, 381-385.
14. The letter of 28 February 1887 is reproduced by Quick & Garran, *The Annotated Constitution of the Australian Commonwealth* (Angus & Robertson, 1901) 396-398; and see *Attorney-General (Cth) v T & G Mutual Life Society-Ltd* (1978) 144 CLR 161, 194 (Aickin J).
15. [1891] AC 272. Their Lordships endorsed reasons which were 'involved in the very able

judgment of Mr Justice Kerferd, with which their Lordships gather that the Chief Justice concurred': at 283.

16. See K H Bailey, 'Self-government in Australia, 1860–1900' in Holland Rose, Newton, Benians (eds), *The Cambridge History of the British Empire* (Oxford University Press, 1933) Vol VII, Part 1, Chapter 14, 395.
17. See *Australian Dictionary of Biography*, (1851-1890) vol. 4, Melbourne University Press, 1972, 391, 394; Bailey (n 16), 396.
18. Stephen (n 1) 35.
19. Morris (n 4) 233.
20. Morris (n 4)285.
21. The *Australian Dictionary of Biography* (n 17) 395 records : 'Diehards demanded that the artillery should drag him from the Supreme Court and shoot him, and critics accused him of impropriety in using his official title in his letter to the Trades Hall, but to this day the Seamen's Union lays a wreath on his statue on each anniversary of his death.'
22. Morris (n 4) 313.
23. Bailey (n 16), 397.
24. Australian Dictionary of Biography, (n 17) 394; John Quick and Robert Randolph Garran, *The Annotated Constitution of the Australian Commonwealth* (Angus & Robertson, 1901) 398-400.
25. See for example *Union Steamship Co of Australia Pty Ltd v King* (1988) 166 CLR 1.
26. J Waugh, 'George Higinbotham on the Constitutional Bill' (1991) 2 (3) *Public Law Review* 156-159.
27. Bailey (n 16), 396.
28. Letter, Higinbotham to Deakin, April 4 1891, J Waugh, 'George Higinbotham on the Constitutional Bill' (1991) 2 (3) *Public Law Review* 1158-159.
29. Deakin (n 2) 8.
30. (1788), No. 78
31. As Lord Devlin wrote in 'Judges and Lawmakers' (1976) 39 (1) *Modern Law Review* 1, 4: 'The Judge who does not appear impartial is as useless to the process as an umpire who allows the trial by battle to be fouled or an augurer who tampers with the entrails.'
32. See *Mutual Life & Citizens Assurance Co Ltd v Evatt* (1968) 122 CLR 556, 563 (Barwick CJ).
33. Margaret Esther Hall, *Selected Writings of Benjamin Nathan Cardozo* (Fallon Book Company, 1947) 153.
34. As revealed in *Amalgamated Society of Engineers v Adelaide Steamship Co Ltd* ('*the Engineers Case*') (1920) 28 CLR 129.
35. As revealed in *Cole v Whitfield* (1988) 165 CLR 360.
36. See *Nationwide News Pty Limited v Wills* (1992) 177 CLR 1, 34 (Mason CJ); Brennan J, 42-3 (and cases there cited); see also *Australian Capital Television v Commonwealth* (1992) 171 CLR 106, 183 (Dawson J).
37. Hall (n 33) 114.
38. See the dispiriting analysis by Marc Galanter, 'Law Abounding: Legalisation Around the North Atlantic,' (1992) 55 (1) *Modern Law Review* 1, especially 18-19.
39. William Searle Holdsworth, *Some Lessons from Our Legal History* (Macmillan Co, 1928) 22.

3.6 The Courts and Culture

Editor's note

As Chief Justice, Brennan participated in the 6th Conference of Chief Justices in Asia and the Pacific held in Beijing on 17 August 1995. Brennan had always been a strong advocate for the Australian judiciary contributing to ultimate Courts of Appeal in the region. Addressing the 18th Australian Legal Convention back in 1975, before his appointment to the bench, he had said: 'The newly emerging countries often times demand that they should have courts of their own creation as the final Court of Appeal. Does this mean that we cannot offer any contribution to the judicial work of these countries even though they may wish to have it? Is it impossible for us to take the initiative in inquiring whether these countries would like to avail themselves of the judicial strength that we and other Common Law countries could provide? Not by way of providing an ultimate Court of Appeal sitting here for them, but by way of providing judges from Australian courts to sit upon their ultimate Courts of Appeal. It seems to me, that this type of international co-operation is something which might well bear a closer examination from the Australian profession, and from the profession of other countries in this region. We have already seen an example in Fiji, where the Court of Appeal draws upon the services of New Zealand judges. In Papua New Guinea, under the constitution soon to become effective, there is a final Court of Appeal in the Supreme Court of Papua New Guinea. At the moment that Court is constituted largely by members of the profession cradled in this country. I wonder whether it is impossible for us to continue to provide services of that kind, not by way of providing an appellate Court structure, but by way of providing the services of judges on an ad hoc basis for the solution of national disputes within the borders of the nation concerned.'[1]

A conference of judges is not like a conference of political leaders or leaders of commerce. We have no responsibilities for the making of treaties or the important diplomatic discussions that foster international peace. We negotiate no commercial transactions; we have nothing to buy and sell. We have nothing to trade but ideas; no agreements to make except the agreement of friendship and mutual respect. But the ideas we have to exchange are concepts of the laws of our countries and those laws are the expression of the culture of our peoples. We come from the nation States of Asia and the Pacific and we are drawn from a variety of cultures and systems of government. While every society at formative stages of its history looks to the experience and systems of other societies and adopts features which suit its particular conditions, every society nevertheless generates a distinctive political and legal system.

Every legal system evolves to meet the different challenges within its particular society. So the ideas we have to exchange will be different one from the other.

Of course, we learn that there are common problems: the pressure of pending cases awaiting hearing and decision, increasing complexity of trading arrangements, the control of drug related crime. We learn of solutions adopted in some countries that may be useful in our own: mediation, alternative dispute resolution, computer assistance, judicial training institutes. We hope to derive benefits from our discussions and to strengthen the mutual respect which each national court system should entertain for the court systems of other nations. But those benefits will be diminished and that respect will not be given unless we appreciate the differences in the conceptions of law and the functions of the courts which distinguish the legal systems of the region.

Some societies insist that there be a division between religion or morality on the one hand and law on the other, although the law can be formulated so as to produce minimum inconsistency between the two; other societies deny the validity of endeavouring to separate those concepts. Some societies regard the primary purpose of the law to be the moulding of individual conduct so as to be conducive to the maximum benefit of the community; others regard the law's primary purpose to be the protection of the rights of individuals against the demands of the community. These trends can be seen in tension in every legal system. The secular-religious tension can be seen in the common law countries in the laws relating to blasphemy and obscenity. The balance between community protection and individual freedom in commercial matters is struck by the laws of every country. The balance between objectives of the legal system that are in tension are struck differently by each legal system. Nevertheless, we are here to exchange ideas and there is nothing so infectious as the contagion of ideas.[2] Roman Law entered Germany not by any edict of a king or legislature but by an appreciation on the part of German judges that the logic of Roman Law answered the needs of the time.[3] Legal ideas which grow and bloom in one garden can be transplanted into other gardens where the soil of tradition and the political and economic climate are similar. Or they may undergo a mutation where conditions, though similar, are not the same. Our gardens are not all planted with the same plants, and the plants of the same genus may flower differently in different gardens. In the long run, the law must accord with the culture of the peoples of our respective countries or our societies would break down. Law necessarily reflects basic human values, but cultures differ and the systems of government differ. Those differences are reflected by laws which govern us.

We are drawn from countries which have different systems of government and, even amongst those countries which have similar systems of government, the dynamics of domestic culture may produce differing conceptions about the manner in which power may be exercised. For those who belong to the tradition of the common law operating under a written Constitution, the division of power among the legislative, executive and judicial branches of government is taken for granted. That division of power and, in particular, the jurisdiction of the judicial branch of government to ensure that the executive branch exercises its powers in accordance with law, are governed by particular and well-known rules. We have a conception of law as an abstract body of principles which stand independently, and govern the exercise, of the powers of the three branches of government. The legislature and the judiciary are each given a function of adding to or qualifying the body of law but ultimately it is the law itself, considered as an abstract body of rules, which governs our societies. The courts are the ministers of this law. The advantages of that system for the societies it serves may be as difficult to appreciate for those living under a different system and coming from a different culture as their system is difficult to appreciate for those living under a written constitution enlivened by the tradition of common law. The laws and the function of the courts differ from country to country because the expectations of the people and the system of government of each country dictate that the law should be so administered as to govern society in different ways.

It is not for judges, each of whom must be faithful to the laws of his or her own country, to pass judgment on the culture of another people or on the functions assigned to the courts by the system of government of another country. International comity demands a respect for the differences as well as for the similarity of functions. When there is a disparity in conceptions as to the nature and source of law, the respective systems cannot be the same. The relationship between the courts and the other branches of government will not be the same. It would therefore be erroneous for the judges of one system to find a ground of criticism of judicial work which, though faithful to its system, is different from our own. If criticism is to be made, it must be criticism of the system itself and that is a matter of high policy for consideration and discussion by the governments concerned. That does not mean that any of us must concede the superiority of a foreign system of law. For myself, I am proud of the capacity of Australian law to serve the interests of the Australian people in a free and confident society and to protect the multicultural values of our nation. In this international year of tolerance it is incumbent on the judges of each nation to endeavour to understand the legal systems of other nations and the assumptions which underlie them. In that way misunderstanding is avoided and mutual respect is fostered. In that way also respect is given to the international integrity of each state's own culture and system of government.

There are, however, some requirements of a judicial system which are universal. The courts, as the judicial branch of government, must apply the law equally to all who come within its terms; they must ascertain the facts of each case as fairly as the rules of procedure permit; and they must reach a decision in the case without allowing themselves to be influenced or controlled by those who do not have the legal responsibility for the rendering of the decision. The duty to apply the law equally includes procedural equality in the practical administration of the law. It involves the right of an accused person to a fair trial in which he has as substantial an opportunity effectively to challenge the prosecution as the prosecution has to assemble and present its case. If the courts fail in any of these essentials, they forfeit not only the respect of their international colleagues but they fail to perform their solemn duty to the people whom they are appointed to serve. I do not suggest that these requirements exhaust the expectations of the international legal community but they are, I suggest, the minimum indicia of any institution that claims the judicial character. At gatherings of this kind, the resolve of judges of good faith to serve their people faithfully according to the laws by which they are governed can be strengthened by contact with other judges of like mind.

Although there are differences in our legal systems, the growth of international law points the way to the common aspirations for the legal system which are shared by human kind. Domestic law and international law will, through a process of dialectic, infuse all our domestic legal systems with principles which, once adopted, will diminish tensions between nations and promote a greater understanding of the aspirations of all the diverse peoples who populate this planet. This may be an exercise proceeding at a glacial pace, but its onward movement is irresistible if we are to survive as the human family, respecting the dignity and the cultural differences of all its members.

In the centuries of the new millennium our societies will inevitably be drawn closer together. Differences may become more noticeable, perhaps more abrasive, as we come to learn more about one another. But the disappearance of the fences in our global village will benefit all nations if we start with a respect for the culture and the genius of our neighbours.

We are indebted to his Excellency Mr Ren Jianxin for bringing together such a stimulating and useful meeting. He has the ultimate responsibility for administering justice to nearly a quarter of this planet's population. That is a task which those of us from smaller countries can hardly contemplate. In the midst of those onerous duties we are grateful for the opportunity that he has given us to meet and get to know each other personally and to exchange our views. Our laws are the distillation of the culture and genius of our societies. A growth in understanding of those laws offers no threat to any nation. It controls no market. It produces no power but it is a cogent instruction about the world in which we live.

---

1. Francis Gerard Brennan, 'Where Now?' (1975) 49 *Australian Law Journal* 672, 677.
2. A phrase of Sir Owen Dixon in 'Concerning Judicial Method' reproduced in Sir Owen Dixon, *Jesting Pilate* (Law Book Co, 1965) 154.
3. Oskar Bulow 'Gesetz und Richeramt' (1885) published as 'Statutory Law and the Judicial Function' (1995) 39 *American Journal of Legal History* 71, 85.

3.7 Courts for the People – Not People's Courts

Editor's note

Brennan delivered the inaugural Deakin Law School Oration on 26 July 1995.[1]

Alfred Deakin, while a Minister and even while Prime Minister, was an anonymous contributor of articles on Australian affairs to the *London Morning Post.* An article which appeared in that journal on 16 November 1903 spoke of the difficult passage which the *Judiciary Act 1903* (Cth) had had through the Parliament of the Commonwealth. Deakin, who was then Attorney-General, wrote:'No measure yet launched in the Federal Parliament was so often imperilled, skirted so many quicksands, or scraped so many rocks on its very uncertain passage.'[2]

The *Judiciary Act 1903* (Cth) marked the fulfilment of Deakin's legislative ambition for the creation of the High Court as the ultimate constitutional tribunal for the Australian Commonwealth. Deakin had fought for this in the movement for federation. He had been a protagonist for clause 74 of the draft Bill for the *Commonwealth of Australia Constitution Act* which would have eliminated appeals to the Privy Council in constitutional matters while allowing appeals in other matters subject to limitation by the Commonwealth Parliament.[3] While the Australian delegates were in London to secure the passing of the Bill, a divisive battle raged over the inclusion of clause 74.[4] Chamberlain's government, in coalition with some colonial representatives, were for deleting clause 74 entirely. Deakin recalls in *The Federal Story* that the 'Conservative classes, the legal profession and all people of wealth desired to retain the appeal to the Privy Council and had heartily and openly supported Chamberlain's proposed abolition of clause 74'. The most significant colonial Government to support the deletion of clause 74 was Queensland, influenced by Sir Samuel Griffith, then Chief Justice of the Colony. However, it was he who made the suggestion that appeals to the Privy Council in inter se matters should depend on leave to be granted by the High Court itself and that suggestion, says Deakin, 'provided the golden bridge over which the delegates passed to union'.[5] Deakin, Barton and Kingston had stood firmly in favour of clause 74 throughout the controversy. Ultimately, they salvaged what became s 74 of the *Constitution*. That section contains the legislative power which was exercised in time to abolish all appeals from the High Court to the Privy Council.[6]

Deakin's second reading speech on the Judiciary Bill, delivered in the year before its final passage, was immediately hailed in the House as an example of his 'great ability and eloquence'.[7] Much of what he said is as true today as it was 93 years ago. Indeed, it states the basic conceptions on which a federation under the rule of law operates. 'What are the three fundamental conditions to any federation authoritatively laid down?' he asked rhetorically. He answered:

> The first is the existence of a supreme Constitution; the next is a distribution of powers under that Constitution; and the third is an authority reposed in a judiciary to interpret that supreme *Constitution* and to decide as to the precise distribution of powers. ... The Constitution is to be the supreme law, but it is the High Court which is to determine how far and between what boundaries it is supreme. The federation is constituted by distribution of powers, and it is this court which decides the orbit and boundary of every power. Consequently, when we say that there are three fundamental conditions involved in federation, we really mean that there is one which is more essential than the others – the competent tribunal which is able to protect the Constitution, and to oversee its agencies. That body is the High Court. It is properly termed the 'keystone of the federal arch'.[8]

He took that descriptive phrase from another eloquent speaker, Josiah Symon, the chairman of the judiciary committee of the Constitutional Convention meeting in Adelaide in 1897. Symon said that 'unless you have not only a powerful High Court but a High Court which shall be constituted under such a Constitution that it will maintain its fortitude under all conditions, you will damage what is really the keystone of the federal arch.'[9]

The founding fathers clearly saw an independent High Court to be essential to the existence of the proposed Australian Commonwealth. The hard-fought compromise over appeals to the Privy Council could not have been achieved if it were not for the confidence that was then reposed by all parties in the competence and integrity of the judiciary of the Australian colonies. Without that confidence, it is unthinkable that Chamberlain's government would have permitted any limitation of appeals to the Privy Council or would have allowed the Commonwealth to limit the matters in which leave to appeal to the Privy Council might have been asked. It is not without significance that the final great issue that stood in the way of Federation was the finality of the jurisdiction to be allowed to the Courts of this country. As we approach the centenary of Federation, it is useful to consider the importance of public confidence in the courts of the Commonwealth, States and Territories and the means by which that confidence is maintained.

The rule of law depends on and is perhaps synonymous with confidence in the courts. If we regard the law as the expression of the values of our civilization, to govern the conduct and the relationships of powerful and weak, rich and poor, government and governed, the majority and a minority, there must be an arbiter whose authority will be accepted by all parties. The law would not be effective if conformity to its precepts depended on force or the imminent threat of force. Such a situation would consume the resources of the nation if it did not first destroy the nation itself. And, in such a situation, what would happen if the State, the enforcing power, refused to accept the arbiter's decision? No, the rule of law must rest on a surer foundation than force or the imminent threat of force. It must rest on the common acceptance by all who are subject to the jurisdiction of the courts of the authority of the courts to determine cases and controversies. The rule of law in a free society can be maintained only if, in the event of dispute, it is accepted that curial judgments will prescribe the norm to which all parties will conform.

The rule of law assumes its equal application. The principle of equality under the law is based on respect for the equal dignity of every person. By equal application of the law, the rule of law is made to govern every case, so that justice according to law is administered. It is a corollary of the principle of equality that no person is so powerful or so privileged as to avoid the law to which that person is subject. These principles can operate in practice only if there be such a degree of public confidence in the courts that neither power nor riches, nor political office nor numerical superiority can stand against the weight of the court's authority.

To destroy public confidence in the courts is to destroy the foundation of the rule of law. Without the rule of law as we know it, we would experience tyranny and oppression. Professor Winterton, commenting on the *Communist Party Case*,[10] said that it 'demonstrated that our freedom depends upon impartial enforcement of the rule of law, of which courts are the ultimate guardians. Although, of course, not infallible, impartial and fearless courts determined to exercise their proper powers are our final defence against tyranny.'[11] Of course, we take the rule of law for granted. We do not perceive a risk to the capacity of our courts to exercise their allotted jurisdiction. Ours is a settled and secure society. That, at least, is the public rhetoric and the private assumption. Reflecting on the factors which inspire public confidence and those which sap it, history demonstrates what can be done to create and sustain it, but some contemporary phenomena reveal a risk to its maintenance. Public confidence in the courts arises from the public perception that judges are men and women of competence and unshakeable integrity.

Judicial competence

The rule of law is effective only if its true terms are discovered and applied. You need competent people to do that. Competence, as well as authority, was the concern of Lord Coke's famous rejection in the case of *Prohibitions Del Roy* of King James I's pretensions to judge:

> then the King said, that he thought the law was founded upon reason, and that he and others had reason, as well as the Judges: to which it was answered by me, that true it was, that God had endowed His Majesty with excellent science, and great endowments of nature; but His Majesty was not learned in the laws of his realm of England, and causes which concern the life, or inheritance, or goods, or fortunes of his subjects, are not to be decided by natural reason but by the artificial reason and judgment of law, which law is an act which requires long study and experience, before that a man can attain to the cognizance of it: that the law was the golden met-wand and measure to try the causes of the subjects; and which protected His Majesty in safety and peace.[12]

Back to the time of Edward I, so Holdsworth tells us, the bench was 'recruited from among those who had passed their lives practising at the bar.'[13] This training ground of the judiciary produced judges who were learned in the law so that, as Maitland pointed out, the qualities that saved the common law in the Tudor age were 'strict logic and high technique, rooted in the Inns of Court, rooted in the Year Books, rooted in the centuries'.[14] Recruiting from the ranks of barristers of proved competence went a long way towards ensuring that the judges would not only know the law but also would have the practical ability to try cases expeditiously and to determine the relevant facts on the evidence adduced.

Not all the British colonies were as fortunate as the Mother Country. Anthony Stokes, writing in 1783, noted that: 'Wherever a salary is annexed to the office of [a colonial] Chief Justice, and the income is sufficient to induce a man of abilities to accept of it, a proper person is appointed from England to fill such office; but ... the Assistant Judges are, in general, appointed [by] the Governor, and are almost always unacquainted with the law.'[15]

He instanced some gross miscarriages of justice as the result.

Familiarity with the sources of law not only ensures that a judge can apply the law; it enhances the judge's ability in controversial cases to speak with the authority which inspires public confidence in the court's application of the rule of law. Thus, Judge Learned Hand said in his tribute to Justice Cardozo: 'His authority and his immunity depend upon the assumption that he speaks with the mouth of others: the momentum of his utterances must be greater than any which his personal reputation and character can command, if it is to do the work assigned to it – if it is to stand against the passionate resentments arising out of the interests he must frustrate.'[16]

The need for judicial competence increases with the increasing complexity of the law. When I first practised at the Bar, the assessment of damages for personal injury was a relatively simple matter. Actuarial calculations would then have been regarded as clever attempts to confuse what was essentially a matter of impression. By the time I sat on *Todorovic v Waller*,[17] the significance of discount rates had been explored at appellate level on many occasions. Today's plethora of statutes and statutory instruments, the contemporary appellate development of the law in various fields, the surfeit of published decisions from all courts and tribunals and the explosion of legal sources on computer data bases tax the ability of any lawyer to ascertain confidently the law to be applied in a problematic case. In *Grant v Downs*, the Court spoke of the law as 'being a complex and complicated discipline'.[18] There is practically no field of law within the jurisdiction of superior courts today in which problems drawn from other fields of law do not intrude.

A judge who is incompetent in finding his or her way through the areas of law touching the jurisdiction to be exercised is a bull in the judicial china shop. Not all the broken pieces can be put together on appeal and, even if they be restored, the pecuniary and personal cost is unacceptable. Sometimes, in discussions about judicial appointments, the criterion of professional merit seems to receive mere lip service. Yet, since it is one of the critical factors in the capacity of the courts to maintain the rule of law, it is one of the most important factors on which public confidence in the courts depends. Competent, well-furnished lawyers, with the experience and capacity to preside over trials of complex issues are needed to constitute the benches of the trial courts. They are in short supply and many who are fitted for judicial appointment decline or defer acceptance for years.

Judicial integrity

Confidence in the courts would be destroyed if judicial integrity were suspect. Judicial integrity in a system that applies the rule of law equally to all is manifested by impartiality between the parties, procedural fairness and a rigorous application of the law. Impartiality, as Lord Devlin remarked, is the supreme judicial virtue. The Judge must not only be but also appear to be impartial. Lord Devlin commented: 'The Judge who does not appear impartial is as useless to the process as an umpire who allows the trial by battle to be fouled or an augurer who tampers with the entrails.'[19]

Want of impartiality poisons the stream of justice at its source; an appearance of partiality dries it up.

Judicial impartiality is not a quality that is picked up with the judicial gown or conferred by the judicial commission. It is a cast of mind that is a feature of personal character honed, however, by exposure to those judicial officers and professional colleagues who possess that quality and, on fortunately rare occasions, by reaction against some instance of partiality. Impartiality may produce a peaceful and courteous demeanour in court, but it produces more than demeanour. This indefinable quality governs the conduct of the proceedings, the evaluation of evidence, the conclusion of facts and the analysis and application of legal rules.

The appearance of impartiality is as critical to the confidence reposed in the courts as impartiality itself. No unsuccessful party should be left with any reasonable apprehension of bias affecting the decision. Nor should the public have any ground for concern on that score. For that reason, the courts themselves have laid down the rule[20] that a challenge to a decision on the ground of bias will succeed if 'in all the circumstances the parties or the public might entertain a reasonable apprehension that the judge might not bring an impartial and unprejudiced mind to the resolution of the matter before him'.[21]

The second aspect of judicial integrity is procedural fairness. That is a fundamental postulate of the common law[22] on which the courts insist. In an adversary system, the parties must be left to conduct their cases as they see fit, but the procedure must be such that each party has a fair opportunity to present his or her case.[23] And, in the case of an unrepresented person on trial for a criminal offence, a further duty is imposed on the trial judge: the judge must inform the accused of his procedural rights.[24]

Judicial integrity also calls for a rigid application of the relevant rule of law. In the lower courts, the relevant rule of law must be ascertained in strict accordance with the decisions of courts higher in the curial hierarchy. But, in the higher appellate courts and particularly in the High Court, the relevant rule of law must be ascertained in strict accordance with the judicial method. The judicial method allows for some development of legal principle, but it is subject to clear limitations. No court is authorized to change a rule of law fixed by the *Constitution* of the Commonwealth or the Constitution of a State or fixed by a valid statutory provision. Those areas apart, the higher appellate courts have the authority – indeed, the responsibility – by analogical reasoning and by reference to the enduring values of the society which the law is designed to serve, of maintaining the rules of law in a state which commands the respect of the contemporary community. That is not to say that the outcome of particular cases will be pleasing to all or even to a majority of the community. But it does mean that a fair and informed analysis of the principles which have determined the outcome will be found to be in accord with enduring values. Enduring values are not to be equated with popular opinion on some issue of transient interest. Enduring values are the bonds of a civilized society that lives in peace; lesser values are the stuff of controversy within such a society, settled if need be by the political process.

This is not the occasion to expound the scope of the jurisdiction of appellate courts to develop the law. It is sufficient to rebut the notion that courts which develop the law or reveal the implications of a constitutional or statutory text are exceeding their proper function. There is a natural tension between maintaining the certainty of the law and developing the law to answer contemporary needs, but that has to do with the desirable pace of change and the weight attributed to different factors relevant to legal reasoning. That tension is not unique to this country. Activism and self-restraint are the descriptions given to the differing approaches of courts in the common law world. It is interesting to note that the tension between them has been experienced in Europe as a Judge of the Court of Justice of the European Community recently remarked:[25] 'In Europe the problem was not dressed up as activism/self-restraint; because of different historical circumstances, it remained as a problem of respect for the separation of powers.[26] However, the historic necessity came to Europe too, with the Community, and rendered the activism of the Court of Justice expedient ...'[27]

In 1902, Deakin did not envisage the function of the High Court to be the exposition of the static content of the *Constitution*. He saw the Court as an interpreter of the *Constitution* as an organic instrument, answering the needs of the nation as it grew and changed. In his second reading speech on the Judiciary Bill, a passage appears which, despite its length, is worth remembering 93 years later:

> the nation lives, grows, and expands. Its circumstances change, its needs alter, and its problems present themselves with new faces. The organ of the national life which preserving the union is yet able from time to time to transfuse into it the fresh blood of the living present, is the Judiciary ... It is as one of the organs of Government which enables the Constitution to grow and to be adapted to the changeful necessities and circumstances of generation after generation that the High Court operates. Amendments achieve direct and sweeping changes, but the court moves by gradual, often indirect, cautious, well considered steps, that enable the past to join the future, without undue collision and strife in the present.[28]

Mr Conroy interjected: 'But we cannot read into the Constitution something which is not there.'

To this, Deakin replied:

> Perfectly true. Yet if he takes the doctrine of implied powers as developed by the Supreme Court of the United States, I will undertake to say that the ablest of its earliest lawyers – even Hamilton or Madison – could not have discovered the faintest evidence of the existence of a power which now authorises many of the greatest operations of its government, and which has been of incalculable advantage to the United States. Why? Because the law, when in the hands of men like Marshall or those trained in his school, or of the great jurists of the mother country, becomes no longer a dead weight. Its script is read with the full intelligence of the time, and interpreted in accordance with the needs of time. That task, of course, can be undertaken only by men of profound ability and long training. It is to secure such men that we desire the establishment of a High Court in Australia.

It is not for me to say whether the present Court, which happily includes a distinguished woman in its membership, answers that lofty description. But when activism is paraded as a ground of criticism, it is as well to remember that, from a time before its creation, the Court was intended to speak with a voice that interpreted the spare text of the *Constitution* for each generation of the nation. In today's changing world, the courts would forfeit their integrity if they failed to exercise their legitimate jurisdiction to declare the general law in terms which, while truly giving effect to organic and statutory law, accord with the enduring values of our society.

So long as the judges are impartial, procedurally fair and rigorous in the application of the law, the judiciary has done what it can to preserve that confidence in the courts which ensures that our society enjoys freedom under the rule of law.

Of course, that does not guarantee, nor should it guarantee, immunity from criticism. Nor do judges expect to be immune from criticism. Sir Frank Kitto, in his splendid paper 'Why Write Judgments? said: 'Every Judge worthy of the name recognises that he must take each man's censure; he knows full well that as a Judge he is born to censure as the sparks fly upwards; but neither in preparing a judgment nor in retrospect may it weigh with him that the harvest he gleans is praise or blame, approval or scorn. He will reply to neither; he will defend himself not at all.'[29]

That is a statement of prudence; it is also a statement of the resoluteness of a judge. Every judge is conscious that, at some time, a judgment will be unpopular with the powerful, or hurtful to one whom the judge would not needlessly hurt, or satisfying to a cause with which the judge has no sympathy. The foresight of such consequences cannot be permitted to influence the judgment. Independence from improper influences is, in the first place, something that each judge must consciously and self-confidently achieve. Nevertheless, if our system is to buttress the fortitude of mind expected of a judge, it must afford the judge some protection against external influences. Chief among these influences is the power of the political branches of government.

External influences

Hamilton, observing that the judicial branch of government did not command the force of the executive or the power of the legislature, held the judicial branch of government to be 'the weakest of the three departments of power'.[30] He thought 'that all possible care is requisite to enable it to defend itself against [the] attacks [of the other two departments]' and that 'from the natural feebleness of the judiciary, it is in continual jeopardy of being over-powered, awed, or influenced by its co-ordinate branches'. The safeguards devised to protect the judiciary from the executive branch of government and, at the same time, to facilitate the exercise of judicial power independently of other alien influences were put in place by the *Act of Settlement 1701*.

Prior to that time, English judges were appointed by the Crown during the Crown's pleasure. Those judges who opposed the Crown were often dismissed. The Crown consulted the judges on forthcoming cases, particularly if they were of a political nature. In 1637 in *Hampden's Case*[31] the judges upheld the Crown's power to exact ship money in the exercise of the Royal prerogative without the authority of Parliament. But a compliant judiciary was the harbinger of revolt. Holdsworth regards the judgment in *Hampden's Case* as containing the most logical expression of the theory of sovereign prerogative power just before its final overthrow.[32] Then, after the Bill of Rights reined in the prerogative, s 3 of the *Act of Settlement* provided that upon the Hanoverian accession: 'Judges commissions be made *quamdiu se bene gesserint*, and their salaries ascertained and established; but upon the address of both Houses of Parliament it may be lawful to remove them.'

Tenure and conditions of service conferred security and independence on the judiciary. Elsewhere[33] I have described tenure and conditions of service as the 'twin pillars' of independence. Tenure and an irreducible salary are secured for Federal judges by s 72 of the *Constitution*. The tenure of State and Territory judges of superior courts is not constitutionally entrenched except in New South Wales.[34] In recent times, security of tenure has been legislatively undermined. Nominal tenure of judicial office has been preserved in some cases while the jurisdiction of the court to which the judge was appointed has been removed. Examples can be found in the statutes of both the Commonwealth and the States.

The undermining of security of judicial tenure by this device has been attributable to the desire of governments either to strip a particular appointee of jurisdiction or to redistribute a specialist jurisdiction. In other words, governments have sought to undo decisions which have proved unsatisfactory to the government of the day. Government decisions on the creation of specialist courts, on the vesting of particular jurisdictions and on the appointment of judges have a long life. If judicial independence is to be maintained as a cornerstone of our society, these decisions, once made, must be recognized as beyond recall. They must therefore be made with all due deliberation. They should not be undone by interfering with the security of tenure which is essential to the protection of judicial independence. The risk of such interference for the impartial application of the rule of law is manifest.

Of further concern is the want of an adequate mechanism for determining judicial remuneration. Inflation was not a concern when the Commonwealth *Constitution* precluded the reduction of judicial salaries. But the recent report on remuneration by Professor Winterton for the Australian Institute of Judicial Administration[35] has demonstrated that the political branches of government have acquired what they were denied by the *Act of Settlement*, namely, financial power over the judiciary. The Report cites[36] a Canadian Commission on Judicial Remuneration which remarked: 'the mere appearance of the judges having to negotiate with the executive branch would only erode the public perception of judicial independence.'[37]

The AIJA Report proposes an independent tribunal to review remuneration annually.[38] That proposal seeks to reconcile judicial independence with Parliament's control over appropriation. That would remove the possibility, not unreal, that satisfaction with a court's decisions by the executive or by those who influence the executive might be a condition of updating remuneration.

Judicial immunity

At the same time as English judges acquired security of tenure under the *Act of Settlement 1701*, the judges of the superior courts of record developed a common law immunity from civil suits[39] for an act done judicially in good faith and in the belief that there was jurisdiction to do it.[40] If a judge were subject to civil liability in respect of his or her judicial acts, the judge would be tempted – and, where the aggressive and powerful were involved, the temptation would be hard to resist – to decide cases in such a way as to eliminate or reduce the risk of being sued. The equal application of the rule of law would be impossible generally to maintain.

The maintenance of public confidence

This is a brief and incomplete review of the factors which, on the one hand, maintain public confidence in the courts and, on the other, present some risk to the maintenance of public confidence. Public confidence depends both on the reality and the perception of a judiciary that is competent, of unshakeable integrity and isolated from influences that might improperly affect the administration of justice according to law. Its awesome powers must be exercised always in the service of others. It must always respond to any application duly made to it. And it must account publicly and to the parties for the reasons for its decisions. It is a judiciary for a society living under the rule of law. Its standards must be, and be seen to be, unimpeachable.

Our traditions and our system know nothing of decisions reached according to mass opinion or popular acclaim. If mass opinion or popular acclaim were the reference points, courts could trim their decisions to accord with public sympathy or outrage, or the policies of the government of the day, or popular political opinion, or the pontifical pronouncements of the columnists. But they could not maintain the rule of law. In our courts, popularity of decisions is no criterion of the true discharge of judicial duty. The rule of law must stand, when needed, against the power of public opinion and those who might influence it. That is not to discount the enduring values of society but it does mean that the true accord between society and the law by which it is ruled is to be found in the principles of law expounded in a court's reasons for judgment – not necessarily in the result.

The reasons for judgment give a public account for the exercise of judicial power. The judge, who is bound by the law and by the facts of the case but who is accountable to no government, must expose the reasons for judgment to public examination and criticism. To quote Sir Frank Kitto again:

> The process of reasoning which has decided the case must itself be exposed to the light of day, so that all concerned may understand what principles and practice of law and logic are guiding the courts, and so that full publicity may be achieved which provides, on the one

> hand, a powerful protection against any tendency to judicial autocracy and against any erroneous suspicion of judicial wrongdoing and, on the other hand, an effective stimulant to judicial high performance. Jeremy Bentham put the matter in a nutshell ... when he wrote ... 'Publicity is the very soul of justice. It is the keenest spur to exertion and the surest of all guards against improbity. It keeps the judge himself while trying on trial'.[41]

Given the safeguard of publicity, the exercise of judicial power according to law can command the continued confidence of the community. Of course, publicity is not always accurate and criticism is not always informed. That must be accepted. Judges are not fitted to promote or defend themselves or their decisions. Not for them are information agencies, confidential briefings or personal relationships with the moulders of public opinion. They have neither talent nor time to seek public favour for decisions reached in discharge of their duty. Even if there be a scandalous disparagement of a court or judge, the judge will regard 'the good sense of the community [as] a sufficient safeguard'.[42]

Perhaps there are risks in that sanguine approach, for it would be an injury to society itself if the courts were so portrayed as to lose public confidence or if misleading publications disheartened the judges in discharging their lonely duty. Inaccuracy of reporting, trivialising of issues, misunderstanding of principle or a desire to subject a remote judiciary to the buffeting of public opinion could erode public confidence in the courts. But that stage has not been reached. To be sure, there are some petulant or pusillanimous annoyances from time to time but these are seen by the community and by the judiciary alike to be insubstantial. Far more important are the large debates on issues of principle. These debates are to be welcomed. When they are fostered by informed reports, the community gains an interest in the legal principles which govern important aspects of our lives and relationships. By such debates, Australians have been informed about native title, the treatment of refugees, the power to impose taxes, the operation of corporations, the investigation and punishment of crime and the awarding of compensation for loss. It is a sign of vigour in the judicial branch of government that informed discussion on the administration of justice is, and always has been, a feature of Australian life.

After a lifetime in the law, I count myself fortunate to have known the Australian judiciary as an institution who, by their competence and unshakeable integrity, have given the nation its confident freedom under the law. That is the aspiration which Deakin entertained for the Australian courts. It is an aspiration which the graduates of the Deakin Law School may entertain as they place their talents and their training at the service of the nation.

---

1. The lecture was first published in the Deakin Law Review: Sir Gerard Brennan 'Courts for the People – Not People's Courts' (1995) 2 (1) *Deakin Law Review* 1.
2. Reproduced in JA La Nauze (ed), *Federated Australia – Selections from Letters to the Morning Post 1900-1910 by Alfred Deakin* (Melbourne University Press: Cambridge University Press, 1968), 119.
3. See cl 74 in the final draft Bill in the *Official Record of Debates of the Australasian Federal Convention*, Vol 5, (Legal Books, 1986) 2536.
4. Alfred Deakin, *The Federal Story – The Inner History of the Federal Cause* (Robertson & Mullens, Melbourne, 1944) 156.
5. Ibid 156.
6. See *Privy Council (Limitation of Appeals) Act 1968* (Cth); *Privy Council (Appeals from the High Court) Act 1975* (Cth).
7. Commonwealth, *Parliamentary Debates,* House of Representatives, 18 March 1902, 10989 (Alfred Deakin, Attorney-General).
8. Ibid 10966-10967.
9. See *Official Record of Debates of the Australasian Federal Convention,* Adelaide 1897, volume 3, 950.
10. See *Australian Communist Party v The Commonwealth* (1951) 83 CLR 1.
11. George Winterton, 'The Significance of the *Communist Party Case* (1992) 18 (3) *Melbourne University Law Review* 630, 658.
12. (1607) 12 Co Rep 63, 64-65; [77 ER 1342, 1343].
13. William Searle Holdsworth, *History of English Law* (Sweet & Maxwell, 1964), vol ii, 229.
14. Selden Society Year Book Series, vol I, xviii; cited by Sir Owen Dixon in 'De Facto Officers' in Sir Owen Dixon, Jesting Pilate (Law Book Co, 1965) 229.
15. Anthony Stokes, *A View of the Constitution of the British Colonies in North-America and the West Indies* (1783) 264-265.
16. Learned Hand, 'Mr Justice Cardozo' (1939) 52(3) Harvard Law Review 361.
17. (1981) 150 CLR 402.
18. (1976) 135 CLR 674, 685.
19. Lord Devlin, 'Judges and Lawmakers', (1976) 39 (1) *Modern Law Review* 1, 4.
20. The rule does not apply when, of necessity, a particular judge must sit on a case.
21. See *Grassby v The Queen* (1989) 168 CLR 1, 20 (Dawson J) citing *Livesey v New South Wales Bar Association* (1983) 151 CLR 288 and *Reg v Watson; Ex parte Armstrong* (1976) 136 CLR 248.
22. See *Cooper v Wandsworth Board of Works* (1863) 14 CB (NS) 180,194; 143 ER 414, 420.
23. See, for example, the procedural steps insisted on in *Smith v New South Wales Bar Association* (1992) 176 CLR 256.
24. See *MacPherson v The Queen* (1981) 147 CLR 512.
25. Judge C N Kakouris, during the ceremony of his nomination for an honorary Doctorate of Laws at the University of Athens, ms par 25.

26. 'Constitutional courts were established in Europe only after World War II. In Germany and Italy initially, as a reaction to totalitarian regimes. And their activism – without the term – was observed mainly in connection with human rights, together with the renaissance of natural law. The German Bundesverfassungsgericht, however, did mention activism in its judgments.'
27. The Judge notes that 'the Court of Justice is not bound by its previous judgments, unlike the Supreme Court [of the United States] with its stare decisis, which constitutes some limitation. Another method of self-restraint is the so-called "political question doctrine", which is reminiscent of the doctrine of acts of government in Europe.'
28. Commonwealth, *Parliamentary Debates*, House of Representatives, 18 March 1902, 10967-10968 (Alfred Deakin, Attorney-General).
29. Delivered 1973, published: Sir Frank Kitto, 'Why write judgments' (1992) 66 *Australian Law Journal* 787, 790.
30. The Federalist Papers, No 78 (1961 Mentor ed), 465-466.
31. (1637) St Tr 825.
32. William Searle Holdsworth, *History of English Law* (Sweet & Maxwell, 1964), vol.vi, 28.
33. Gerard Brennan, 'Courts, Democracy and the Law' (1991) 65 *Australian Law Journal* 32, 40-41.
34. See *Constitution Act 1902 (NSW)* s 53, entrenched by s 7B after the 1995 referendum.
35. George Winterton, 'Judicial Remuneration in Australia' (Australian Institute of Judicial Administration, 1995).
36. Ibid 77.
37. See *Report and Recommendations of the 1989 Commission on Judges' Salaries and Benefits/ submitted to the Minister of Justice of Canada* (5 March 1990) 6.
38. Winterton (n 35) 81-84.
39. William Searle Holdsworth, *History of English Law* (Sweet & Maxwell, 1964), vol.vi, 234.
40. See *Sirros v Moore* [1975] 1 QB 118.
41. Sir Frank Kitto, 'Why Write Judgments?' (1992) 66 *Australian Law Journal* 787, 790.
42. See *Gallagher v Durack* (1983) 152 CLR 238, 243; *Nationwide News Pty Ltd v Wills* (1992) 177 CLR 1, 33.

3.8 Why be a Judge?

Editor's note

Brennan delivered this paper on 12 April 1996 to the New Zealand High Court and Court of Appeal Judges' Conference held in Dunedin.[1]

To ask, 'Why be a judge?' in a paper given at a Conference of judges is at least a work of supererogation, for each of us has addressed that question when the offer of judicial appointment was made. We have given a variety of answers to ourselves and our families when the offer of appointment was accepted. Now, with the benefit of judicial experience and with the wisdom that hindsight confers – as we know, judicial wisdom depends heavily on hindsight – each of us can see whether his or her decision to be a judge was the right or preferable decision. But retrospection is not the chief reason to address the question 'Why be a judge?'. The contemporary public scrutiny of judges and their functions invites us to state for ourselves what we do and how and why we do it.

Once upon a time, judges were revered and invested with an aura of infallibility. That was in days when social institutions were never questioned and the work of the judiciary was not generally understood. You may remember Lord Devlin's observation that '[t]he English judiciary is popularly treated as a national institution, like the navy, and tends to be admired to excess'.[2] The differences between Lord Devlin's England of 20 years ago and the society we know and the doubtful naval analogy should deter us from taking too much comfort from that statement or, for that matter, from the statements of eminent judges in jurisdictions in which social conditions and cultural attitudes are different from our own.

I understand that popular respect for the judiciary in New Zealand is at a high level. It may be that the opinion recently expressed by the distinguished Canadian jurist, Madam Justice McLachlin, that 'the public has never held the judiciary in higher esteem' applies in New Zealand.[3] But, whether Madam Justice McLachlin's assessment is correct or not, she is surely right to conclude that 'Judging is not what it used to be. Judges are more important now; judges are more criticised. And judges face more difficult tasks than they ever have before faced in the history of the Commonwealth.'[4]

Criticism and difficulty in performing tasks are hardly the attractive features of any vocation and yet judges accept appointment. It can hardly be to gain personal acclaim, or an easy lifestyle or affluence. If these are not the incidents of judicial office, is it right to say that society esteems judges to be 'more important now'? Perhaps we should start by considering the essential judicial functions and the manner in which they are performed. We begin with the raison d'être of the judiciary: the maintenance of the rule of law in a free society.

The Rule of Law

It is axiomatic that peace and order in society can be maintained only by the rule of law. Peace and order exist when there is general conformity with *a priori* rules, breaches of which result in penalties, nullifications, or other disadvantages imposed by the State. If the miscreant goes unpunished by the State, the victim will take the remedy into his own hands. So will the unpaid creditor, the wronged spouse, the injured casualty and the disgruntled citizen. To achieve peace and order, a government must provide laws that, broadly speaking, tend to diminish injustice and a mechanism to redress injustice by application of those laws. The provision of such a mechanism is not an optional benefit which parties in dispute must obtain for themselves and at their own expense. To the extent to which the machinery of government does not provide for the application of law in the binding resolution of disputes, the rule of law is jeopardised. The resolution of disputes then depends upon the actions taken by the disputants: the choice between resolution by raw force or by fairer methods depends on the election of the more powerful party or the desperation and opportunities of the more oppressed. The most basic, the most important and, happily, the least remarkable function of the judiciary is the binding resolution of disputes according to law.

Of course, disputes could be resolved by a judge who, with or without a hearing, would decide the case in accordance with State policy untrammelled by any law which is not compatible with the interests of the State or the policy of its government. Such a totalitarian resolution of disputes would have to be imposed by force, for the judicial *ipse dixit* would carry no authority of its own. It is the hallmark of a free society that disputes are resolved according to law by courts whose authority depends not so much upon the force available to the State as upon popular (if not universal) acceptance of the authority of their decisions. The authority of the courts at all levels is accepted in our society because they are recognized as the dispensers of justice according to law. It is recognized that freedom – not only peace and order, but freedom – depends, as Professor Winterton has said: 'upon impartial enforcement of the rule of law, of which courts are the ultimate guardians. Although, of course, not infallible, impartial and fearless courts determined to exercise their proper powers are our final defence against tyranny.'[5]

Popular respect for the administration of justice by the courts is essential to peace, order and good government in a free society based on the rule of law. Popular respect has been earned by steady and manifest adherence to the judicial method. In practical terms, that means simply that confidence is inspired by the way in which the judges do, and are seen to do, their work.

The Judicial Method

There are four elements of the judicial method relevant to our present discussion: impartiality, procedural fairness, pursuit of justice in accordance with law and exposure to public scrutiny.

The fundamental postulate of the judicial method is that the judge is impartial. Impartiality is the supreme judicial virtue.[6] And it must not be reasonably open to doubt. Subject to necessity, the rule is that a challenge to a decision on the ground of want of impartiality will succeed if 'in all the circumstances the parties or the public might entertain a reasonable apprehension that the judge might not bring an impartial and unprejudiced mind to the resolution of the matter before him' or her. [7] This is a high standard that precludes any real possibility of judicial conflict between the judge's interests and his or her duty.

Impartiality has two aspects. First, the judge must be free of relationships that might improperly influence the determination of the case or might be perceived reasonably to do so. We can leave aside the more obvious relationships of influence as requiring no comment, save this: sometimes a judge withdraws from a social situation to avoid any prospect of embarrassment in the discharge of his or her duties. It is regrettable that this self-denying ordinance is sometimes construed as a haughty remoteness. It is one of the aspects of the loneliness of judicial life. Apart from obvious relationships of embarrassment, there are other relationships, especially with government, that might give rise to subtle and impermissible influences. Sometimes it is hard to draw a bright line by which to divide the relationships which must be avoided from relationships that are permissible. For that reason, judges of the Supreme Court of Victoria (which follows a policy expressed in what is known as the 'Irvine memorandum'[8]) generally decline to accept an invitation to perform non-judicial functions. Lord Cooke of Thorndon has taken a more robust view: 'Wherever judicial qualities are called for – that is to say, typically, a calm and objective factual judgment on evidence – in my opinion a judge should be willing to serve. The essential corollary is a judicial approach.'[9]

In Australia, I think it would be right to say that judicial experience has shown that the undertaking of some non-judicial functions can embarrass the exercise of the judicial function or suggest to the public too close a connection between the judge and the government. Much depends upon the manner in which the judge is selected, the nature of the non-judicial function, its political significance, the ongoing nature of the task and the extent of interaction with Ministers and their Departments. If non-judicial functions are to be performed by a serving judge, the involvement of the Chief Justice of the court in the selection of the judge may provide a measure of protection for both the judge and the court from undue Executive interference.

The second aspect of impartiality is the cast of mind with which the judge approaches the case. He or she will consciously seek to ensure that every party is treated equally before the law, whoever the parties may be, whatever the facts may be and whatever interests will be advanced or defeated by the judgment. But prejudice based on race, religion, ideology, gender or lifestyle may unconsciously affect the mind of a judge as it affects the minds of others. Unless the basis of prejudice might be material to the merits of the case, the prejudice must be recognized and consciously disregarded. This is easy to say; not always easy to achieve. Indeed, it is sometimes difficult to be sure where the wisdom of human experience ends and prejudice begins. Programs to raise judicial consciousness of the possibility of impermissible bias are commendable. But, in the enthusiasm to extirpate impermissible prejudice, there is a risk of over-reaction to attitudinal bias, which is at least as dangerous as the risk of bias. Perhaps that is why judges are sceptical of expressions designed to give an assurance of attitudinal correctness.

The next element in judicial method is procedure. Procedural fairness, a fundamental postulate of the common law,[10] governs the work of the courts and, with rare and limited exceptions,[11] governs the performance by judges of any non-judicial functions. Courts not only give the parties a full opportunity to be heard; they are also usually under a duty to state their reasons for decision.[12] No other branch of government is so responsive to every application that is made to it. Every litigant gets a response – though oftentimes, and regrettably, after a lengthy and costly proceeding. But a reasoned response is ultimately forthcoming.

The third element is the pursuit of justice according to law. The finding of facts, or the giving of directions to a jury with respect to facts, calls for great experience of the human condition. The notion that judges are immured in an ivory tower, shut off from the activities, emotions, virtue and vice of ordinary life is sheer nonsense, as any observer of the sittings of a trial court would testify. Moreover, judges, most of whom have been successful advocates in litigation practices, have gained an unrivalled capacity to appreciate the facts and the nuances of those situations that arise in litigation in their chosen field.

The facts being fairly found, the law must be applied. As Lord Bridge of Harwich has observed: 'The maintenance of the rule of law is in every way as important in a free society as the democratic franchise. In our society the rule of law rests upon twin foundations: the sovereignty of the Queen in Parliament in making the law and the sovereignty of the Queen's courts in interpreting and applying the law.'[13]

The general thrust of this observation can be accepted, but the interpretation and application of the law – even statute law – is not the function of a mere automaton. Nor is it a function in which the demands of justice play no part.

In a Parliamentary democracy, it would not be just for the courts to hold the law to be different from that laid down by Parliament;[14] but neither should the Parliament be easily taken to have intended to create an unjust rule. Accepting statute law as enacted by Parliament, the courts endeavour to give a just interpretation to a statute so far as its terms admit. And the common law is developed and declared so as to do justice in the conditions of contemporary society. Sometimes, abstract justice competes with, and triumphs over certainty which is itself a material element of justice. Sir Stephen Sedley put the position dramatically: 'Law spends its life stretched on the rack between certainty and adaptability, sometimes groaning audibly but mostly maintaining the stoical appearance of steady uniformity which public confidence demands.'[15]

This tension calls for a complex of skills in the modern judge. The simple propositions of a student text book may suffice in some cases, but not in others. The modern judge possesses not only a general knowledge of the law but also skill in the interpretation of statutes and of the judgments of superior courts, awareness of the existence and limits of the leeway in judicial decision making, appreciation of community standards and, on occasion, appreciation of enduring community values and the susceptibility of legal rules to their influence. Enduring community values is not a term masking a judicial assumption of legislative power. Though the term cannot be exhaustively defined, its content in a particular context is not reasonably open to controversy. For example, an enduring value of our contemporary community is that every person should be treated by the law with substantive equality, not merely formal equality. Another enduring value is that a person should not be liable to criminal punishment unless his conduct has breached an existing law and the person had some moral responsibility for that conduct. If their terms permit, statutes are construed to accord with enduring community values[16] and common law rules that are inconsistent with those values are liable to be overruled.[17] The public expectation is that the law will be just. The judicial method reduces any antinomy between justice and law to a minimum and thereby seeks to fulfil that expectation.

Finally, the judicial method requires that, subject to narrow exceptions, every word that is uttered from the opening sentence of a case to the closing words of an appellate judgment be open to scrutiny. Nothing must be hidden.[18] Justice is not a cloistered virtue. In *Russell* v. *Russell*[19] Gibbs J [20]expressed a long-standing doctrine when he said of the rule requiring proceedings to be conducted 'publicly and in open view':[21]

> This rule has the virtue that the proceedings of every court are fully exposed to public and professional scrutiny and criticism, without which abuses may flourish undetected. Further, the public administration of justice tends to maintain confidence in the integrity and independence of the courts. The fact that courts of law are held openly and not in secret ... distinguishes their activities from those of administrative officials, for 'publicity is the authentic hall-mark of judicial as distinct from administrative procedure'.[22]

Sir Frank Kitto, when he delivered his classic paper on 'Why Write Judgments?' to an Australian Supreme Court Judges' Conference, said: 'The process of reasoning which has decided the case must itself be exposed to the light of day, so that all concerned may understand what principles and practice of law and logic are guiding the courts, and so that full publicity may be achieved which provides, on the one hand, a powerful protection against any tendency to judicial autocracy and against any erroneous suspicion of judicial wrongdoing and, on the other hand, an effective stimulant to judicial high performance.'[23]

Quoting Bentham, he added: 'Publicity is the very soul of justice. It is the keenest spur to exertion and the surest of all guards against improbity. It keeps the judge himself while trying on trial.'

But the finding or holding of the judge may be exposed publicly to be erroneous by an appeal court or by a majority of a collegiate bench; it may be condemned by the powerful interests it offends or by commentators who find it at odds with opinions that they assert with an assumed authority. Those criticisms must be borne with such fortitude as the judge can muster.

It is by manifest adherence to the basic elements of the judicial method – impartiality, procedural fairness, the pursuit of justice in application of the law and exposure to public scrutiny – that judges have commanded the confidence of the community they serve.

Public confidence

The earning of public confidence evokes skills and qualities of a high order: unquestioned integrity of character, human understanding, intellectual capacity especially in analysis, knowledge of the law, social awareness, wisdom, patience, industry, and a willingness to expose one's every judicial word and action to public observation and comment. Those who, possessing the necessary judicial skills and qualities, are appointed to be judges are an elite. I do not mean, of course, an elite demanding social rank. I mean an elite because of their pivotal role in securing a peaceful and free society governed by the rule of law. Membership of that elite is no passport to an easy lifestyle. Judging is a lonely life. When the evidence is heard and the argument is over, when the books have been read, we come to the point of judgment. No conscience other than the judge's own can be the guide. No pen but the judge's own can write the reasons for decision or sketch the summing up. No expression of satisfaction can satisfy the judge unless the judge's own standards be satisfied. If the work be done properly, it earns the accolades – albeit seldom expressed – of colleagues who command our respect. The accolades of others, if forthcoming, may give encouragement according to our estimate of their insights.

The dispiriting criticisms that are sometimes offered have led some judges to think that they should undertake a public relations exercise to enhance the judicial image. I suggest that that is a mistake. In the first place, it is difficult to avoid responding to media inquiries that touch upon the decision of actual cases. In responding to such inquiries, a judge may commit himself or herself to a view on a topic that might arise for evaluation in a case for hearing. It is not for a judge to disqualify himself or herself from the full performance of duty by prior public comment. And, at a practical level, few judges have either the skills or the inclination to maintain a relationship with the media which preserves judicial dignity and appropriate reticence while communicating an insight into the work of the courts.

It is one thing to inform the community of the service which the courts provide in securing justice according to law and the way in which they provide that service. That is an objective which enhances public understanding of the courts to the benefit of the community. It is another thing to seek publicity in the hope that media coverage will create a favourable image either for a judge, a court or the judiciary as a whole. Such a hope would be quickly detected by both the media and public. Public confidence must be earned by the regular work of judges in the court room. It is the reality, not the image, which must sustain public confidence.

When ephemeral and unjustified criticism is made of a judge personally or of the judicial institutions to which he or she belongs, it is right to recall what Lord Denning MR said when the then Mr Quintin Hogg QC MP launched a broadside in the press against a judgment of the Court of Appeal:

> It is the right of every man, in Parliament or out of it, in the Press or over the broadcast, to make fair comment, even outspoken comment, on matters of public interest. Those who comment can deal faithfully with all that is done in a court of justice. They can say that we are mistaken, and our decisions erroneous, whether they are subject to appeal or not. All we would ask is that those who criticise us will remember that, from the nature of our office, we cannot reply to their criticisms. We cannot enter into public controversy. Still less into political controversy. We must rely on our conduct itself to be its own vindication.
>
> Exposed as we are to the winds of criticism, nothing which is said by this person or that, nothing which is written by this pen or that, will deter us from doing what we believe is right.[24]

I do not suggest that judges should shut their ears when criticism is raised, whether in the media or otherwise. Judicial capacity does not include imperviousness to criticism that deserves attention. On the contrary, judicial capacity includes a willingness and an ability to learn from other views, irrespective of the source and irrespective of the terms in which the views are expressed.

Of course, if the public scrutiny of judges is used as the plaything of controversy to destroy public confidence in the administration of justice according to law, an enormous disservice is done to society generally. It should be a sobering thought for captious critics that, if the criticism erodes that confidence, it erodes the protection of the critics to make it. And it should be a comforting thought for the judiciary that the occasions of unjustified criticism are few and that public confidence in the courts is so abiding that those occasions do little to erode that confidence.

However, the burden of heavy caseloads, the tyranny of reserved judgments and the difficult conditions in which some courts operate may depress the judicial spirit. When Governments seem to place little store by the performance of the judicial function, or when media criticism seems to denigrate the judicial office or, particularly, when other judges or the practising profession give some support to these attitudes – whether tacitly or overtly – the judge's perception of the high social importance of his or her work is hard to maintain. At such times, the attraction of judicial office is dimmed. The question 'Why be a Judge?' is likely to produce a cynical response. Why be a judge whose every professional word or deed is open to public scrutiny and criticism? Why be a judge who cannot reply to critics lest the appearance – if not the reality – of impartiality be lost? Why be a judge who, under the pressure of work, foregoes other delights of intellectual life – not to mention the demands of family life and the abbreviation of recreational or other extra-curricular activities?

In those quieter moments that we allow ourselves for reflection, we know that the dignity and the fulfilment of the aspirations of free men and women in our complex society depend on the faithful performance of judicial duty. In a complex society, justice would be unattainable without the sophisticated skills and unquestioned integrity of the judiciary. The high importance of the judicial office makes it a privilege to be invited to the bench; the responsibilities of the office create a continuing challenge to proper performance. The trust reposed by the community in the judiciary is an enduring comfort. The stimulus of judicial work is enhanced and its burdens lightened by the support of other judges whose character, intellect and industry command our unfeigned respect. The satisfactions of judicial life of necessity flow from an inner conviction of the service of society in a pivotal role, from the satisfaction of the aspirations of litigants, of the profession, of the public and most importantly, of oneself, and from the mutual esteem of judicial colleagues. These are the considerations, I suggest, that give the true answer to the question: 'Why be a judge'?

---

1. This paper was published in (1996) 14 *Australian Bar Review* 89.
2. Lord Devlin, *The Judge* (Oxford University Press, 1979), 25.
3. Of the Supreme Court of Canada in her paper: 'The Role of Judges in Modern Commonwealth Society', delivered at the 10th Commonwealth Law Conference, Cyprus, 1993 and published: Justice B McLachlin, 'The Role of Judges in Modern Commonwealth Society' (1994) 110 *Law Quarterly Review* 260, 261.
4. Ibid 269. Justice J B Thomas chronicles some changes in Circuit courtesies in Queensland in his 'Epistle from a Judge on Circuit' published in (1987) 10 (1) *UNSW Law Journal* 173.
5. George Winterton, 'The Significance of the Communist Party Case' (1992) 18 (3) *Melbourne University Law Review* 630, 658.
6. See Lord Devlin, 'Judges and Lawmakers' (1976) 39 *Modern Law Review* 1, 4, reproduced in Lord Devlin, *The Judge* (Oxford University Press, 1979), 4.
7. See *Grassby v The Queen* (1989) 168 CLR 1, 20 (Dawson J) citing *Livesey v New South Wales Bar Association* (1983) 151 CLR 288 and *R v Watson; Ex parte Armstrong* (1976) 136 CLR 248; *E H Cochrane Ltd v Ministry of Transport* [1987] 1 NZLR 146, 152-153.
8. Letter of 14 August 1923 from Sir William Irvine to Sir Arthur Robinson, quoted in McInerney 'The Appointment of Judges to Commissions of Enquiry and Other Extra-Judicial Activities', a paper delivered to the 1974 Annual Judicial Conference.
9. Sir Robin Cooke, 'The Courts and Public Controversy' (1983) 5 *Otago Law Review* 357, 365.

10. See *Cooper v Wandsworth Board of Works* (1863) 14 CB(NS) 180, 190, 194; 143 ER 414, 418, 420.
11. See *Grollo v Palmer* (1995) 184 CLR 348.
12. See *Deakin v Webb* (1904) 1 CLR 585, 604-605; *Public Service Board of NSW v Osmond* (1986) 159 CLR 656 at 666-667; *De Iacovo v Lacanale* [1957] VR 553 at 558-559. And see *Potter v New Zealand Milk Board* [1983] NZLR 620, 624-625 (Davison CJ).
13. See *X Ltd v Morgan-Grampian Ltd* [1991] 1 AC 1, 48.
14. Cf the views of Cooke P in *New Zealand Drivers' Association v New Zealand Road Carriers* [1982] 1 NZLR 374, 390; *Fraser v State Services Commission* [1984] 1 NZLR 116 at 121; *Taylor v New Zealand Poultry Board* [1984] 1 NZLR 394, 398.
15. Sir Stephen Sedley, 'Human Rights: a Twenty-First Century Agenda' (1995) *Public Law* 386, 387.
16. See *He Kaw Teh v The Queen* (1985) 157 CLR 523.
17. See *Mabo v Queensland [No2]* (1992) 175 CLR 1.
18. See Lord Devlin, *The Judge* (Oxford University Press, 1979), 26-27.
19. (1976) 134 CLR 495; and see *Dickason v Dickason* (1913) 17 CLR 50, 51; *H (falsely called C) v C* (1859) 29 LJ (P & M) 29, 30.
20. (1976) 134 CLR 495 at 520.
21. See *Scott v Scott* [1913] AC 417 at 441. See *Skope Enterprises Ltd v Consumer Council* [1973] 2 NZLR 399.
22. See *McPherson v McPherson* [1936] AC 177, 200.
23. (1973), published: Sir Frank Kitto. 'Why Write Judgments' (1992) 66 *Australian Law Journal* 787, 790.
24. See *R v Commissioner of Police of the Metropolis; Ex parte Blackburn (No 2)* (1968) 2 QB 150, 155.; see *Attorney-General v Blundell* [1942] NZLR 287, 289.

3.9 Judicial Independence

Editor's note

Brennan delivered this address to the Australian Judicial Conference at University House, Canberra, on 2 November 1996.

I should like to take as a theme for these remarks the first object of the Australian Judicial Conference. It is stated in these terms: 'in the public interest to ensure the maintenance of a strong and independent judiciary as the third arm of government in Australia'. To your ears and mine, and perhaps to the ears of many of our fellow Australians, that seems a fairly bland statement of a desirable and non-contentious object. And so it is. But the implications for our society are profound. Judicial independence does not exist to serve the judiciary; nor to serve the interests of the other two branches of government. It exists to serve and protect not the governors but the governed. But, you may ask, if that is so, why do we see so much ill-informed criticism of the judiciary? There are many answers to this question, but it cannot be doubted that one answer is this: there is a lack of awareness of the extent to which the peace and order of our society depend upon the maintenance of a strong and independent judiciary as the third arm of government. The subject which you have chosen for this symposium belongs primarily in the public domain, not in legal corridors or in academic halls. It is of chief concern to the public rather than to the judiciary or the legal profession. Of course, it is right that the techniques of maintaining a strong and independent judiciary should be discussed by those with primary responsibility for the task, but the discussion should be followed by giving an account of those techniques to the public. And that would be a task worthy of the mettle of the Australian Judicial Conference.

The reason why judicial independence is of such public importance is that a free society exists only so long as it is governed by the rule of law – the rule which binds the governors and the governed, administered impartially and treating equally all those who seek its remedies or against whom its remedies are sought. However vaguely it may be perceived, however unarticulated may be the thought, there is an aspiration in the hearts of all men and women for the rule of law.

That aspiration depends for its fulfilment on the competent and impartial application of the law by judges. In order to discharge that responsibility, it is essential that judges be, and be seen to be, independent. We have become accustomed to the notion that judicial independence includes independence from the dictates of the executive government. Lord Coke's denial of the King's right to judge cases and the provisions of the *Act of Settlement* are landmarks in the development of that notion. But modern decisions are so varied and important that independence must be predicated of any influence that might tend, or be thought reasonably to tend, to a want of impartiality in decision-making. Independence of the executive government is central to the notion but it is no longer the only independence that is relevant.

Appearance, no less than the reality, of independence is essential. The judiciary, the least dangerous branch of government,[1] has public confidence as its necessary but sufficient power base. It has not got, nor does it need, the power of the purse or the power of the sword to make the rule of law effective, provided the people whom we serve have confidence in the exercise of the power of judgment. In earlier times in this century, that confidence was undoubted. Then institutions were not questioned and the work of the judiciary was not well understood. Judges were the revered symbols of justice. You may remember Lord Devlin's observation that '[t]he English judiciary is popularly treated as a national institution, like the navy, and tends to be admired to excess'.[2] That is no longer the position in Australia. As Madam Justice McLachlin said at a recent Commonwealth Law Conference: 'Judging is not what it used to be. Judges are more important now; judges are more criticized. And judges face more difficult tasks than they ever have before faced in the history of the Commonwealth.'[3]

I respectfully agree. Today the community looks to the courts to adjudicate disputes in areas extending far beyond the areas of jurisdiction invoked 50 years ago. Reposing that function in the judiciary, the community examines judicial performance of the function more critically than hitherto. Of course, this development demonstrates the confidence of the community in the judicial branch of government: a confidence that is not misplaced so long as independence from impermissible influences is jealously maintained.

Impermissible influences may be of different kinds.

First, take the changes that have occurred in the distribution of political power. The Diceyan theory which translated the political sovereignty of the people into the legal sovereignty of the Parliament and thus into laws which corresponded with the wishes of the electorate[4] may have been a logical construct rather than a description of political reality. But, however that may be, the political machinery of today led Lord Hailsham to describe the modern democratic system as 'an elective dictatorship, absolute in theory if hitherto thought tolerable in practice'.[5] It is beyond question that the contemporary form of Westminster government keeps the Parliament in line with Executive policy, rather than the reverse. And the exigencies of administration coupled with the demands of political success expose the interests of minorities and individuals to risk. That leaves the courts in a singular position. Lord Radcliffe summed up the transition:

> In the seventeenth century this country turned its back on the idea of a strong central executive, and we have taught ourselves to be proud of the achievement ever since. There was a settlement under which the Commons in parliament and the judges in the courts, working independently, were to be guardians of the rights and liberties of the individual citizen, as then understood, and each was to have power to block any attempt by the executive to trench upon those rights and liberties. Whatever the law courts did or did not do in the next 200 years, they did carry out this part of the bargain, and men valued them accordingly. We have come back, unavoidably, to a strong central executive, and we live by order, decree and regulation and by act of parliament. Parliament and the executive have gone into alliance, and the law courts are pushed more and more into a corner of national life. [6]

That seems to be an overstatement. The community looks to the courts for the protection of minorities and individuals against the overreaching of their legal interests by the political branches of government.

In other parts of the common law world, courts have been expected to protect minority and individual rights in situations that were once not thought to be justiciable. In Canada, the Charter of Rights and Freedoms has conferred on the courts a wide jurisdiction touching issues that were once reserved to the political branches of government. In New Zealand, a nation with a unitary Constitution, an appellate judge has suggested that '[s]ome common law rights presumably lie so deep that even Parliament could not override them'. [7] In India, the long record of activism on the part of the Supreme Court has entrenched it firmly in the affectionate confidence of the people. In Australia, the High Court's approach has been more cautious, although its declaration of an implied freedom of political discussion has stimulated judicial and public discussion of the validity of a variety of laws.

Judicial review of executive action has blown the wind of legal orthodoxy through the silent corridors of the bureaucracy, ensuring that powers whose exercise is apt to affect individual interests are constrained by requirements of procedural fairness. In the construction of statutes, the courts have sought to find in the text propositions that accord with the values of the common law and thus to be what Lord Simon has called 'a mediating influence between the executive and the legislature on the one hand and the citizen on the other'.[8]

In these and in other areas of jurisdiction involving the citizen and government, the impartial application of the rule of law demands independence of the judicial branch of government from the political branches of government. And, of course, that independence continues to be essential to the due administration of the criminal law. If that independence were, or were thought by the litigants or the public to be, put at risk, the rule of law would be imperilled and the peace and order of society would be problematic.

Independence is necessary not only from the political branches of government nor only to safeguard the impartial administration of public law. The courts have been invested with jurisdiction to determine private law issues under open-textured or non-exhaustive laws that leave much to be filled in by judicial reasoning. Trade practices and unfair contract legislation often call for the making of judgments by reference to values rather than by reference to detailed rules. Oftentimes one party to the litigation will be a comparatively powerful corporation; the other, an individual either in his or her own interest or as a representative of a consumer, industrial or other interest group. The entrusting of jurisdictions of these kinds to the courts proceeds on the footing that judges are independent of the interests represented by either side of the controversy. Although in earlier times similar interests were arrayed against each other in litigious battles, there was less room for judicial opinion to determine the outcome. Nowadays, open-textured criteria of reasonableness, fairness, justifiability or proportionality are statutorily employed to cast on the courts the responsibility of forming value judgments that have, or might have, significant economic or social effects.

Perhaps the independence that is most difficult for a judge to achieve is independence from those influences which unconsciously affect our attitudes to particular classes of people. Attitudes based on race, religion, ideology, gender or lifestyle that are irrelevant to the case in hand may unconsciously influence a judge who does not consciously address the possibility of prejudice and extirpate the gremlins of impermissible discrimination. Such gremlins are not extirpated by mere declaration. Indeed, too vocal a judicial protest of impartiality may bespeak an overreaction to prejudice in one direction by forming a prejudice in the other. Or it may indicate a failure to employ that worldly wisdom which permissibly takes account of differences that are relevant for some purposes but irrelevant for others.

Independence of the modern judiciary has many facets. The external factors that tend to undermine independence are well recognized by the judiciary but perhaps not so well recognized by the political branches of government or by the public. Some of the structures that preserve independence are well established. I need not canvass the twin constitutional pillars of judicial independence – security of tenure and conditions of service that the executive cannot touch – except to say this: if either of these pillars is eroded, in time society will pay an awful price.

Judicial independence is the priceless possession of any country under the rule of law. The public are entitled to insist on its observance by the judges and on its protection by the Parliament and the Executive. But in the ultimate, judicial independence rests on the calibre and the character of the judges themselves. Judicial independence is not a quality that is picked up with the judicial gown or conferred by the judicial commission. It is a cast of mind that is a feature of personal character honed, however, by exposure to those judicial officers and professional colleagues who possess that quality and, on fortunately rare occasions, by reaction against some instance where independence has been compromised.

The importance of symposia of the kind which is now to take place is twofold: it confirms the ethos and the commitment to independence of the Australian judiciary and it reflects upon the means by which that independence can be protected and enhanced in the interest of the public whom we serve. Justice is administered by human institutions; they can be fallible, but they should never be perverse. Being human institutions, continual vigilance is needed to ensure that they are isolated from impermissible influences and strengthened by the pressure of a peer group devoted to impeccable standards of independence.

I offer my respectful congratulations to the Australian Judicial Conference, the Faculty of Law of Griffith University and the Research School of Social Sciences at the Australian National University on the organization and conduct of a symposium on a topic of such public importance.

---

1. See *The Federalist Papers* No 78 by Hamilton (1788).
2. Lord Devlin, *The Judge* (Oxford University Press, 1979) 25.
3. Justice B McLachlin, 'The Role of Judges in Modern Commonwealth Society' (1994) 110 *Law Quarterly Review* 260, 269.
4. Albert Venn Dicey, *Lectures Introductory to the Study of the Law of the Constitution* (Macmillan & Co, 1885), 77.
5. Lord Hailsham, *Elective Dictatorship,* 1976 Richard Dimbleby Lecture (British Broadcasting Corporation, 1976) 2.
6. Lord Radcliffe, *Not in Feather Beds* (The Quality Book Club, 1968) 34.
7. Sir Robin Cooke P (as he then was) in *Taylor v New Zealand Poultry Board* [1984] NZLR 394, 398.
8. See *Stock v Frank Jones (Tipson) Ltd* [1978] 1 All ER 948, 953.

3.10 The Role of the Judge

Editor's note

Brennan delivered this address to the National Judicial Orientation Program held in Wollongong on 13 October 1996.

I must begin by offering to each of the newly-appointed judges my congratulations – not, as is ordinarily said, on your elevation but on your acceptance of an office which is of pivotal social importance and your willingness to expend much of your time and energy and all your talents in performing its duties. You have been appointed to your respective courts because you have demonstrated the capacities which are needed to be a judge and your attendance at this programme of induction is a tribute both to your desire to fulfil your office with distinction and to that humility of mind that is essential to your being able to do so.

I suppose you have all experienced the sense of novelty in sitting when others stand, in presiding rather than participating and in finding yourself alone with your own thoughts when the time for decision arrives. Sometimes the new judge finds the transition too rapid, forgetting for the moment his or her position on the other side of the bar table. As you know, those incidents give the profession a good story or, in cases where the judge keeps on the mantle of the advocate, grounds for much headshaking and mutterings of foreboding.

In the following sessions of this seminar, there will be papers on practical aspects of the judicial function. I was given as a topic for this address the subject 'The Role of the Judge', so I shall start by saying something about the general approach to judicial duties. I understand that you have access to – I do not assume you have read – what I said to the Supreme and Federal Court Judges' Conference on 'Why be a Judge?'. I shall not repeat what is in that paper, except in one important respect.

A judge's role is to serve the community in the pivotal role of administering justice according to law. Your office gives you that opportunity and that is a privilege. Your office requires you so to serve, and that is a duty. No doubt there were a number of other reasons, personal and professional, for accepting appointment, but the judge will not succeed and will not find satisfaction in his or her duties unless there is a continual realisation of the importance of the community service that is rendered. Freedom, peace, order and good government – the essentials of the society we treasure – depend in the ultimate analysis on the faithful performance of judicial duty. It is only when the community has confidence in the integrity and capacity of the judiciary that the community is governed by the rule of law. Knowing this, you must have a high conceit of the importance of your office. When the work loses its novelty, when the case load resembles the burdens of Sisyphus, when the tyranny of reserved judgments palls, the only permanently sustaining motivation to strive onwards is the realisation that what you are called on to do is essential to the society in which you live.

You are privileged to discharge the responsibilities of office and you are obliged to leave it unsullied when the time comes to lay it down. What you say and what you do, in public and to some extent, in private, will affect the public appreciation of your office and the respect which it ought to command. The running of the risk of being .06 while driving home from a dinner party or a minor understatement of income in a tax return could have public significance. The standards of Caesar's wife are the standards that others will rightly apply to what you say and do and, having a high conceit of your judicial office, they are the standards you will apply to yourself. These standards apply to matters great and small. In some respects, the management of petty cash or the acquittal of expenditure can be a matter of great moment.

Hand in hand with a high conceit of the office is a humility about one's capacity to live up to the standards set by one's predecessors and expected of the present incumbent. There are few judges who are sufficiently self-confident not to entertain a doubt about their ability to achieve the expected level of performance – and, so far as I know, none of those possessed of that self-confidence has done so. Of course, with growing experience the anxiety about one's capacity to perform the duties of office abates. But this is not attributable so much to self-satisfaction as it is to a realistic acceptance of the limits of one's capacity. Provided one does one's best, anxiety about any shortfall in capacity can be counter-productive. Intellectual humility (even if it does not show), a sense of duty and self-esteem, the exposure of every step in the judicial process to public examination and peer group pressure are the factors which inspire a judge to the best achievement of which he or she is capable.

The first role of the judge is to preside and to hear. It is your court and, unless you are sitting on a collegiate bench, the atmosphere of the court is chiefly in your hands. From time to time, you will experience a mounting frustration as a bumbling counsel fails to tell you what the case is about, or a witness prevaricates, or the key issue in the case is missed or some idiosyncrasy of counsel, party or witness proves bothersome. At such times, judicial sang froid is sorely tested. You may find it helpful quietly to set yourself a test: can I stay calm, or shall I yield to the temptation to put an end to the source of the frustration? The desirable answer is obvious, but the technique of how to achieve it depends on the individual personality of the judge. A sense of humour helps. I do not mean the *bon mot* that extracts a dutiful show of mirth from counsel nor the flippancy that might lead a litigant to think that the trial is regarded as a mere entertainment. I mean a sense of humour that allows the mind to concentrate on the issues without taking oneself and one's preconceptions too seriously. If humour fails, the situation is ameliorated by a certain remoteness created by the physical separation of the bench from the well of the court and the wearing of the judicial robe. Although both of these features undergo critical evaluation from time to time, I doubt whether *curial decorum* could be so easily preserved without them.

It is not necessary for a judge to demonstrate mastery of the issues by the making of informed comments on the running of the case. The hearing is for the purpose of informing the judicial mind about the material required for judgment, not for the purpose of staging a debate or providing a public and privileged platform. That is not to say that judicial silence should mask the issues on which the judgment might turn; it is to say that exchanges should have some point and that silence is the appropriate alternative if they do not.

A second, and more important, point can be made about the function of presiding at a trial. A trial – including a criminal trial – is not the occasion for diminishing the dignity of any person in the courtroom. It is an occasion for the dispassionate finding of facts and application of law, not for the humiliation of any of the trial's participants. At the end of the trial – even a trial in which an accused has been convicted and sentenced – the participants in the trial should be able to leave the courtroom with their dignity unaffronted. That is not to say that a judge should not comment, and comment forcefully, on the conduct of a participant in the proceedings as revealed in the courtroom where such a comment is relevant to the imposition of a sentence, the credibility of a witness or the professional conduct of an advocate, provided the comment does not exceed what is necessary for the purpose of the decision and the object of any adverse comment has been given an opportunity to deal with the ground of criticism.

As you know, unrepresented litigants constitute an increasing percentage of those appearing in the courts. The trend is likely to continue. Unrepresented litigants often present a real obstacle to the efficient disposition of the court's lists, as the judge must take additional care to ensure that, even if they be incapable of adequately advancing their own case, no points of merit are buried in what is oftentimes a mass of distracting irrelevancies. There is a tendency to want to even the scales by assisting the unrepresented litigant to develop his or her case or to attack the opponent's case. That is a tendency to be detected and resisted. The judge's role is to keep the ring, not to enter the fight. By all means let the relevant rules be understood, but then the judicial duty is to retreat to the calm isolation of the judgment seat.

When the hearing is complete, the lonely moment of decision-making has arrived. Nobody but you can make the decision or frame the reasons. Yours is the sole responsibility. Help may be sought from more experienced or more learned judicial colleagues but ultimately there is only one judicial mind that must assent to each step in the reasoning and to each part of the order made. In formulating the reasons for decision, you give a public account of the reasons which have led you to exercise the coercive powers of the State – the powers which the State has vested in you – by making the orders on which you have decided. Of course, the parties are those most immediately interested in your reasons, and the unsuccessful party is the one who is primarily entitled to a fair statement of the reasons why you have exercised your powers against that party's interests or contentions. Read, and be comforted by, Sir Frank Kitto's article 'Why Write Judgments?'.[1] There are two passages that bear repetition in this context. The first is this: 'The process of reasoning which has decided the case must itself be exposed to the light of day, so that all concerned may understand what principles and practice of law and logic are guiding the courts, and so that full publicity may be achieved which provides, on the one hand, a powerful protection against any tendency to judicial autocracy and against any erroneous suspicion of judicial wrongdoing and, on the other hand, an effective stimulant to judicial high performance.'[2]

Later, Sir Frank said 'Every Judge worthy of the name recognises that he must take each man's censure; he knows full well that as a Judge he is born to censure as the sparks fly upwards; but neither in preparing a judgment nor in retrospect may it weigh with him that the harvest he gleans is praise or blame, approval or scorn. He will reply to neither; he will defend himself not at all.'

The finding of facts is perhaps the most difficult aspect of judgment. What is needed is a finding on every constituent element of the charge, the claim or the defence which is not conceded expressly or impliedly. It is no use reciting the submissions on either side without reaching the conclusion. That might give an impression that the judge was attending to the argument, but it is not judging. Be cautious in the use of the umbrella phrases: 'I prefer the evidence of X to the evidence of Y where their evidence conflicts'. That smacks more of a formula than it does of reasoning, especially when the real choice may be – `as it often is – between two defective recollections. There are some tell-tale phrases that can alert you to a part of the judgment that requires further consideration: 'clearly' is a word that contains more of an assertion than a reasoning to a conclusion, and the assurance that 'after giving the matter earnest consideration, I have come to the conclusion that' says nothing about the reasons for the conclusion. Rather, it conveys an uneasy impression of a failure to give the matter the consideration it deserves.

Provided the essential facts of charge, claim or defence are found, a lengthy judgment is seldom required. To be sure, an argument that is being rejected should be rejected with reasons, but a distinction should be drawn between a judgment and an academic exposition of the law. There are occasions, especially in courts of appeal, where extensive examination of authority is required or desirable, but that is seldom the situation in a trial court. Thinking, rather than writing and, even more, rather than dictating, is the critical factor in judgment.

The competent and conscientious performance by judges of the duties of their office is the most effective way to maintain respect for the rule of law. It is hard and not glamorous work, but judges are not public relations officers and it is a false priority to try to put the fostering of our public image ahead of the sheer hard work of judging. There is no prohibition against a judge giving, or authorising the giving, to the media and the public information about the function of judging provided, of course, the discussion does not trespass upon the decision of a particular case or an issue that might have to be judicially decided. And, I should add, provided the discussion is not an exercise in self-promotion. Judicial inability to control editorial treatment of an interview and to engage in media controversy may point towards a prudent reticence, but that is a matter of discretion. Because the media are often willing to report a judge's observations on matters of contemporary interest, some few judges choose to make public statements on subjects outside their judicial expertise. If they be experts on other subjects, their expertise in those subjects may warrant the making and publication of the statements, but if their authority derives solely from the judicial office and the judicial office is used as a descriptive badge of authority, the privileges of the office are misused.

I should say something about impartiality, the supreme judicial virtue, and the appearance of impartiality. They can be impaired in a variety of ways, some of which are too obvious to require comment. Those ways include too close a connection with, or expressions of support for, causes – albeit the causes are laudable. Impartiality and its appearance can be impaired by such an intellectual predilection for one view of an issue falling for determination as precludes, or appears to preclude, a fair consideration of contrary argument. And beware of expressions that emphasise forward-looking, right-thinking or politically-correct attitudes, for such expressions might be thought to trim a judgment to the breeze of public or political approval.

A bastion of impartiality is independence – independence not only from the executive government but from other centres of power. I need not dwell on that topic. Independence is not only essential to the judiciary; it is one of its greatest attractions. Nothing to fear, nothing to gain by the performance of the judicial office. That leads me to say something about the prospects of judicial promotion. There is nothing dishonourable about hoping for promotion when an appropriate vacancy occurs; but it is dishonourable actively to seek a promotion. Ambition and its twin, envy, can corrode a character and destroy the harmony of a court. Judicial appointment is not a stepping stone in a career; it is prima facie a dead-end job of the highest importance.

If promotion should come, it should be supported by those who have had an opportunity to form an opinion on the quality of the work done and the judicial demeanour manifested in doing it.

Finally, I should mention intra-curial relationships. Although each judge should have and retain a fierce sense of personal independence and be prepared to accept the consequences and the criticisms of his or her own judgments, a court cannot operate efficiently without a shared objective of getting the work done to a standard that enhances public confidence in the court as a whole. Life on the bench is a sheer delight when one's colleagues command unfeigned respect. Let there be the gravest divisions of legal opinion, or of judicial style, of expedition or even of native ability, among the members of a court provided only that each member is genuinely respectful of each other and extends co-operation and camaraderie to those who share the burden of the court's caseload. None of us chooses his or her judicial colleagues; that is the prerogative of the executive government. But overall, the executive governments of this country have appointed judges with the requisite competence and experience, and for that we may be truly grateful. Sometimes you may think another judge is not up to standard. Then it is necessary to remember that one's own reputation is not advanced by derogating from the reputation of another judge of the court; rather, individual reputation is enhanced with the enhancing of the reputation of the court to which the judge belongs.

Be not uncaring about the small courtesies and conventions of judicial life. They are the natural incidents of a civilised elite who are conscious of the importance of their service to the community and who desire to give and to receive the respect which their office demands and which their efforts merit. You have joined or you are joining that elite – an elite of service, not of social grandeur – and your membership of it can be a source of great personal satisfaction and no little pride. You will not grow affluent on the remuneration that you will receive; you will work harder and longer than most of your non-judicial friends; your every judicial word and action and some other words and actions as well will be open to public criticism and the public esteem of the judiciary may be eroded by attacks that are both unjustified and unanswered. But if, at the end of the day, you share with colleagues whom you highly esteem a sense of service to the community by administering justice according to law, you will have a life of enormous satisfaction. Be of good and honourable heart, and all will be well. You have made a major decision. On behalf of the institution of the judiciary, I thank you for your commitment. It will be for you, in the fullness of time, to decide whether you have made the right decision. I am sure you will find that it was.

---

1. (1992) 66 *Australian Law Journal* 787.
2. Ibid 790.

3.11 Exchange of Letters with Deputy Prime Minister Tim Fischer

Editor's note

The Liberal/National Party Coalition won the 1996 federal election which was held on 2 March 1996. The Coalition had been elected with a commitment to winding back key provisions of Paul Keating's *Native Title Act 1993* (Cth) which was the Parliament's response to the High Court's 1992 *Mabo* decision. Just weeks prior to the 1996 election, the Wik peoples from Cape York had received a judgment in the Federal Court in relation to their claim that native title could co-exist on pastoral leases. Three weeks after the election, the State of Queensland applied to have the legal proceedings removed to the High Court for determination. The National Party was very upset that native title might be found to co-exist on pastoral leases. Tim Fischer, the Leader of the National Party, was outspoken about the court delays. After the High Court delivered judgment in Wik on 23 December 1996, Chief Justice Brennan wrote to Deputy Prime Minister Fischer.[1]

---

3 January 1997

The Honourable T Fischer, MP

Deputy Prime Minister

Parliament House

CANBERRA ACT 2600

Dear Mr Fischer,

I have delayed writing this letter until the judgment of the Court in the *Wik* Case was delivered.

The Australian of 28 November carried a headline and article 'Fischer lashes High Court for delay in *Wik* decision'. This was the second attack you have made upon the Court suggesting an unwarranted delay: the first was in relation to the date of hearing, the second in relation to the date of judgment. It is as well that you should be acquainted with the facts of the case. The *Wik Case* judgment was delivered by Justice Drummond of the Federal Court on 29 January 1996. The Federal Court granted the Wik and Thayorre Peoples leave to appeal to the Full Court of the Federal Court on 22 March 1996. On 27 March 1996, the State of Queensland and another party filed notices of motion in the Brisbane office of the High Court seeking removal of those appeals into the High Court pursuant to s 40 of the *Judiciary Act 1903* (Cth). Removal of such cases is not automatic. Because of the urgency of the matter, the application was expedited by being inserted into the list for the next day of hearing applications for special leave to appeal, namely, 15 April. The order for removal was made on that day. On 6 May, I held a directions hearing to identify the issues and to give directions for the preparation of this complex matter. The parties, who co-operated efficiently, prepared lengthy written submissions and accepted time limits on oral argument. The matter was advanced in the High Court hearing list and came on for hearing on 11 June. The hearing was completed on 13 June.

The appeal books consisted of 17 volumes, containing 263 documents covering 3,036 pages. There were seven volumes of legislation contained in 338 documents covering 1,971 pages. The written submissions of the parties and of the interveners covered 714 pages with 915 pages of attachments. 98 Australian and 155 overseas cases were cited. The transcript of oral argument covered 266 pages.

This mass of material involving novel and difficult questions of law is an indication of the length of time that each of the Justices was required to spend to form his or her view on the answers to be given to the questions of law that arose in each of the appeals. That time had to be found while the Court continued to sit and to deal with the cases listed for hearing during the balance of the year. To say that there was any unwarranted delay in the delivery of this judgment is quite unjustified. The practice of this Court is to deliver a judgment as soon as can conveniently be done after all Justices have written their judgments. This was the practice followed in the *Wik* case. Judgment was delivered on 23 December 1996.

This Court has never attracted criticism for a failure to discharge its enormous burden. On the contrary, during my time on this Court, the only comment on this score that has been made by those who are familiar with its working is amazement at its capacity to produce judgments of erudition in the variety of fields covered by its caseload. Perhaps some indication of the Justices' devotion to their duty is that the members of this Court, alone amongst other courts and, for that matter, other branches of government, have for many years been unable to take the leave to which they are entitled, sabbatical or other, during their tenure of office.

I am sure that you are no stranger to long hours of work. Neither are the Justices of this Court. You will the more readily appreciate that attacks of the kind that you have made, emanating from a Deputy Prime Minister, are damaging to this Court. You will appreciate that public confidence in the constitutional institutions of government is critical to the stability of our society. By a convention which is based in sound practice, judges do not (and certainly should not) publicly attack the members of the political branches of government, and the members of the political branches of government do not (and certainly should not) attack the judges except on a substantive motion in the Parliament. This convention does not restrict criticism of court judgments, but it does restrict criticism of judicial integrity or devotion to judicial duty.

Neither the co-operation that is required among the branches of government nor the dignity of this Court would be advanced by my making a public statement to repel the attacks which you have made. Indeed, courts are not capable of responding – nor would they wish to respond – to media attacks. I ask you to bear this in mind and to consider whether the making of attacks on the performance by this Court of its constitutional functions is conducive to good government, even if an attack can gain some temporary political advantage.

Yours sincerely,
(Signed: Gerard Brennan)

* * * * *

13 January 1997

The Hon. Sir Gerard Brennan

Chief Justice High Court of Australia

PO Box E435

KINGSTON ACT 2604

Dear Chief Justice Brennan

I acknowledge your letter of 3 January and I have carefully noted your comments.

In my public statements I have at all times sought to acknowledge the separation of powers between the executive government and the judiciary. This separation of powers was referred to in The Australian article of 28 November 1996.

My comments were made against the background of incorrect advice I had received which predicted that the Wik decision would not be handed down by the High Court until calendar year 1997. My intentions were neither to engineer the headline printed in The Australian, nor was it to gain 'some temporary political advantage'. Short or long term political advantage and/or disadvantage would only have resulted, in my view, from a far more robust comment than those I made.

Ironically, I am currently under attack for placing too much faith in the judiciary in the context of debate concerning the *Constitution*, and one option proposing a non-discretionary extra role for the Chief Justice in relation to the Governor General.

I readily acknowledge the huge and difficult workload before the High Court of Australia. I also strongly concur with your view that 'public confidence in the constitutional institutions of government is critical to the stability of our government'. I have made a point of saying on the ABC 'AM' program and elsewhere recently, that I respect the amount of work being processed by the High Court.

I should add I also particularly note your comment that court judgments may be criticised as a separate matter from judicial integrity and devotion to duty, the Sydney Morning Herald of 11 January 1997 falls into that category although it was somewhat exaggerated.

Thank you for writing to me and please accept my best wishes for 1997.

Yours sincerely,
(Signed: Tim Fischer)

* * * * *

14 January 1997

The Hon. Tim Fischer, MP
Deputy Prime Minister
Parliament House
CANBERRA ACT 2600

Dear Mr Fischer,

Thank you for your letter of 13 January 1997. I appreciate the speed and terms of your response.

Yours sincerely,
(Signed: Gerard Brennan)

---

1. The letters were published in full in (1997) 100 *Victorian Bar News* 7-8.

3.12 The State of the Judicature 1997

Editor's note

It was customary for the Chief Justice of the High Court to deliver the State of the Judicature address at the Australian Legal Convention. Brennan's address on 19 September 1997 at the opening of the 30th Australian Legal Convention in Melbourne attracted significant attention as it followed upon the High Court's decision in the *Wik* Case. The Deputy Prime Minister, Tim Fischer had been very critical of the High Court's decision, and the Attorney-General, Daryl Williams made it clear that he did not think it part of the role of the Attorney-General to defend the courts from criticism by members of parliament.[1]

Every society has a judicature – the dictatorship as well as the democracy, the simpler societies of earlier centuries as well as the sophisticated societies of the modern day. It is the institution which avoids self-help in resolving disputes and controls excesses of power. Its decrees give concrete effect to the laws of the state. What the Judicature does or does not do largely determines the character of the society in which we live. So, the State of the Judicature is the concern not only, nor even chiefly, of the officers of the judicature; rather it is the concern of the people of Australia who are protected by, and are subject to, its jurisdiction.

What are the functions which the Australian people expect the Judicature to perform? That question is hard to answer unless we have answers to some even more fundamental questions: should there be protection against excesses of governmental power, including the police power? how far should a majority's will or a majority's interest prevail over the will or interest of a minority? should the powers of a democratically-elected legislature be limited? should the policies and actions of an executive government be subject to judicial review or control? should there be any regulation of economic and industrial power other than the market? The answers which most Australians would give to these and other fundamental questions all point to the obvious conclusion that Australians, like every civilized society, wish to be ruled by law, not by popular clamour or by raw power. Australia has no place for the police State, the show trial, the oppression of minorities, unfettered and arbitrary governmental power, or the tyranny of officialdom or great economic or industrial might. The law, impartially and competently administered, is the infrastructure of our society and the protector from conduct that would disrupt it. It is our assent to the rule of law that makes us a free and confident nation.

If we are to be governed by the rule of law, we must have a Judicature to administer it. The characteristics of that Judicature reflect the functions it is charged to perform. First, it must be a Judicature that is and is seen to be impartial, independent of government and of any other centre of financial or social power, incorruptible by prospects of reward or personal advancement and fearless in applying the law irrespective of popular acclaim or criticism. Second, it must be a competent Judicature; there must be judges and practitioners who know the law and its purpose, who are alive to the connection between abstract legal principle and its practical effect, who accept and observe the limitations on judicial power and who, within those limitations, develop or assist in developing the law to answer the needs of society from time to time. Third, it must be a Judicature that has the confidence of the people, without which it loses its authority and thereby loses its ability to perform its functions. Fourth, it must be a Judicature that is reasonably accessible to those who have a genuine need for its remedies.

These being the criteria of a Judicature required to maintain the rule of law in a free and confident nation, they are the reference points for considering the state of the Judicature.

Impartiality

Impartiality is the supreme judicial virtue.[2] Partiality and the appearance of partiality are both incompatible with the proper exercise of judicial power. The one poisons the stream of justice at its source; the other dries it up. Lord Devlin commented that 'The Judge who does not appear impartial is as useless to the process as an umpire who allows the trial by battle to be fouled or an augurer who tampers with the entrails.'[3]

That is why judges and lawyers place such emphasis on judicial independence. In July this year, the American Bar Association Commission's *Report on Separation of Powers and Judicial Independence* noted that 'Judicial independence is not an end in itself but is a means to promote impartial decision-making and to preserve the supreme law of the land'. Chief Justice Lamer of Canada acknowledges that the fundamental purpose of judicial independence is the maintenance of the rule of law but, he observes - 'There is an unfortunate tendency on the part of some to characterize judicial independence as a principle that enures primarily if not exclusively to the benefit of the judiciary itself. While it would be disingenuous to deny that the judiciary benefits from security of tenure and financial security, it must be emphasized that the primary beneficiary of the principle of judicial independence is society as a whole.'[4]

One of the most important doctrines to emerge in recent times is the doctrine of constitutional incompatibility which precludes federal judges from being appointed to perform functions incompatible with the holding of judicial office.[5] No occasion has arisen for determining whether a similar doctrine applies in relation to state judges.

In April of this year, the Chief Justices of the states and territories drew pointed attention to the threat to judicial independence in the appointment of acting judges 'to avoid meeting a need for a permanent appointment'. And they objected to the appointment by the executive government of a serving judge to any position of seniority, administrative responsibility, increased status or emoluments where continuance in the office was in the discretion of the executive government. Judicial independence is at risk when future appointment or security of tenure is within the gift of the executive. Notwithstanding the clear intent of the Chief Justices' declaration, it seems that economic considerations induce governments to make acting appointments. However, the increasing volume of litigation must lead ultimately to permanent appointment sufficient to cope with the workload. In New South Wales, there are currently five acting judges on the Supreme Court and over 30 on the District Court. These appointments are said to be necessary to dispose of a temporary backlog.

In Canada, judicial independence has been held to require what the Supreme Court has called 'institutional independence', that is 'the institutional independence of the court or tribunal over which [a judge] presides, as reflected in its institutional or administrative relationships to the executive and legislative branches of government.'[6] Chief Justice Dickson said: 'The role of the courts as resolver of disputes, interpreter of the law and defender of the *Constitution* requires that they be completely separate in authority and function from all other participants in the justice system.'[7]

The theory behind the concept is not hard to discern. It is the same theory that underlies the Australian doctrine of incompatibility. The courts must not be permitted to be too closely associated with or affected by the political branches of government. But some association is involved in the obtaining of resources. A government which effectively controls the administrative and financial resources required by a court could, if it were ill-advised enough to do so, withhold what the court requires if the decisions of the court were unpalatable to that government. A decision taken on those grounds would, of course, be a blatant attempt to influence judicial decision-making.

The concept of institutional independence presents some jurisprudential difficulties. The *Constitution* reposes the power of appropriation[8] in the

Parliament on a recommendation by message from the head of the executive government.[9] Similar provisions govern appropriation of funds for state courts. It has always been the practice – indeed, an essential constitutional convention – that executive governments, both of the Commonwealth and the states, seek an appropriation and Parliament appropriate sufficient funds to permit the courts to perform their constitutional functions. In times of financial stringency, there is a risk that governments might regard the courts simply as another executive agency, to be trimmed in accordance with the executive's discretion in the same way as the executive is free to trim expenditure on the functions of its own agencies. It cannot be too firmly stated that the courts are not an executive agency. The law, including the laws enacted by Parliaments or by executive regulation and including executive orders affecting the government of the country, goes unadministered if the courts are unable to deal with ordinary litigation. It is insufficiently appreciated that laws, regulations and orders, which may give effect to high government policy, would be mere points for argument if the courts were not giving them effect in ordinary litigation.

The courts cannot trim their judicial functions. They are bound to hear and determine cases brought within their jurisdiction. If they were constrained to cancel sittings or to decline to hear the cases that they are bound to entertain, the rule of law would be immediately imperilled. This would not be merely a problem of increasing the back-log; it would be a problem of failing to provide the dispute-resolving mechanism that is the precondition of the rule of law.

It should never be forgotten that the availability and operation of the domestic courts is the unspoken assumption on which the provisions of our *Constitution* and laws are effected, on which the operation of the entire structure of government depends, on which peace and order are maintained, on which commercial and social intercourse relies and on which our international credibility is based. Constitutional convention, if not constitutional doctrine, requires the provision of adequate funds and services for the performance of curial functions.

Courts, being labour intensive, draw on the public purse for their maintenance. So do the political branches of government, the Parliament and the executive. Governments have been attracted to the notion of 'user pays' in order to assist in the defraying of the costs of the judicial branch, seemingly disregarding the fundamental importance of ensuring the effective enforcement of the rule of law. Sir Richard Scott, head of the Chancery Division in England, in a recent speech said 'the civil justice system is an integral and indispensable part of the structure of administration of justice that must be put in place by every State in which public and private affairs are to be conducted in accordance with the rule of law; and ... a policy which treats the civil justice system merely as a service to be offered at cost in the market place, and to be paid for by those who choose to use it, profoundly and dangerously mistakes the nature of the system and its constitutional function.'[10]

Recently, the English Divisional Court judicially reviewed the Lord Chancellor's Order which increased the scale of Court fees and repealed provisions that had previously relieved litigants in person who were in receipt of income support from the obligation to pay fees. In declaring the repeal to be unlawful, Laws J said: 'Access to the courts is a constitutional right; it can only be denied by the government if it persuades Parliament to pass legislation which specifically – in effect by express provision – permits the executive to turn people away from the court door.'[11]

The Lord Chancellor did not appeal. 'User pays' is consistent with the rule of law only to the extent that every genuine would-be user can pay. 'User pays' puts a premium not on genuine need for legal protection but on financial power.

The passage of legislation which adds to a court's caseload is not always matched by an increase in the court's resources. In modern times, when so many personal and social problems have been thought to be amenable to legal solution, Parliaments have created what are deemed to be appropriate rights or liabilities and thus curial jurisdiction has been extended. The impact of these laws on the Executive and its agencies may be factored into the legislative decision, but the increase in caseloads seems to be a less pressing consideration. If economic stringency invites reconsideration of the funding levels for courts, the first question that arises is: what laws must be repealed or what special provisions must be enacted to lighten the court's caseload?

The executive government is not the only threat to judicial independence, though the executive's powers of appointment and preferment and its influence, if not control, over judicial remuneration and judicial resources make independence from Executive influence a continual concern for the judiciary. Judges are conscious of other influences that may appear to affect their impartiality. To avoid any such appearance, judges often withdraw from political, financial or social contacts which they would otherwise enjoy. Sometimes prudence and a high regard for the judicial office are regrettably misinterpreted as a withdrawal to an ivory tower.

An embarrassing erosion of judicial impartiality can originate from a judge's expression of a view touching either a political issue or an issue that might arise in the course of litigation. If such a view is expressed in a speech, the judge has obviously thought about the topic and become publicly committed to the view. But judges must not become committed to views which might disqualify them from sitting. The public perception of judicial impartiality has been nurtured by a traditional reticence in speaking publicly on many topics. Clearly judges must refrain from intruding into political matters and from expressing committed views on matters of public controversy. The desirable policy was expressed by my distinguished predecessor, Sir Anthony Mason, in these terms:

> Putting to one side the exceptional case which requires an exceptional response, I favour a cautious approach. Judicial reticence has much to commend it. It preserves the neutrality of the judge; it shields him or her from controversy. And it deters the more loquacious members of the Judiciary from exposing their colleagues to controversy. [12]

Chief Justice Lamer has drawn attention to another matter which, if not properly understood and developed, would pose some threat to judicial impartiality. He speaks of 'social context education' which is 'designed to make judges both more aware of and better able to respond to the many social, cultural, economic and other differences that exist in the highly pluralistic society in which ... judges now perform their important duties.' [13] The Chief Justice welcomes the availability of programmes of this kind. And so do I. The Australasian Institute of Judicial Administration Seminar on Equality and Justice in October 1995 sharpened judicial awareness of the need to guard against stereotypes or assumptions based on gender, aboriginality and cultural awareness. But, the Chief Justice warns, it is essential that the ultimate control of the design of such programs remain with the judiciary. Again, I respectfully agree. No instruction or advice about judging, however seemingly innocuous it may be, can be accepted by judges from the executive government. It is equally inappropriate to permit non-governmental interest groups to control the design of judicial educational programs touching their own special interests, especially when those interest groups are likely to appear in litigation or to stimulate litigation to promote their agenda.

Judicial and practitioner competence

The level of competence among practitioners who appear before the courts is sustained by professional structures, especially by the professional and financial independence of barristers who continue to perform most of the work of advocacy. That independence is conducive to the discharge of the advocate's duty to the court on which the efficient disposition of cases depends. However, a recently emerging phenomenon occasions some misgiving. Some advocates have assumed the role of public relations officers for their clients, making their client's case to the media and offering comment on the court's judgment. That role is inconsistent with the advocate's duty to the court. The court can have no confidence that such an advocate will fairly and candidly assist the court on both fact and law. And the accolade or lament that the advocate presumes to express about the court's judgment belittles the court's authority. It is commendable for advocates to provide journalists with information to assist in the accurate reporting of a case, so far as the material is on the public record, but if court proceedings were the postscript or the prelude to counsel's media release or court door interview, the courtroom becomes a mere backdrop to counsel's media performance.

The competence of the judiciary has not hitherto given grounds for concern. Nevertheless, the Council of Chief Justices of Australia and New Zealand encouraged an initiative on the part of the Australian Institute of Judicial Administration (AIJA) to establish a National Judicial College. The project was examined but was abandoned for want of funding. The AIJA, in conjunction with the Judicial Commission of New South Wales, has instituted a highly successful and much appreciated Judicial Orientation Course. It has the support not only of the Council of Chief Justices but also of some of the Pacific courts which have nominated newly-appointed judges to attend. The availability of places and the frequency of courses are limited by the available resources.

In recent times and with comparatively few exceptions, the professional skills of the judge have been adequate for the discharge of his or her judicial duties. Of course, stories of judicial idiosyncrasies abound in the common rooms of the Bar, but the proportion of cases in which judicial incompetence has been the cause of a failure to do justice according to law has been small. For the most part, executive governments of Commonwealth and state have been conscious of the need to make judicial appointments on merit, although infrequently political or personal commitments by governments have raised a doubt about a particular appointee.

Judicial competence is not instantly acquired. It is the product of long professional study and experience. The call for more judges to deal with increasing caseloads and the diminished attractions of judicial office now give some ground for concern about the ability of governments to continue to recruit judges possessed of the desirable levels of scholarship and experience. Where are those judges to be found?

Leading advocates have traditionally been the source of judicial recruitment and, in my opinion, rightly so. That status gives an assurance that the appointee is qualified in the opinion of the court in which he or she usually practises to research, identify and refine the principle of law applicable to a case and to deal efficiently with evidentiary questions, that the appointee is accustomed to subordinate personal convenience to legal duty, that the appointee is accustomed to act in a public forum, to be exposed to criticism in the event of a failure to live up to high professional standards and has demonstrated an independence of mind and conduct that will stand him or her in good stead in a judicial office.

The need for practical experience is not restricted to the trial courts. In the appellate courts, where there is more room for development of the law than in the courts of first instance, knowledge of legal authorities and a capacity for logical analysis are not a sufficient warrant of competence. Experience and the elusive quality of wisdom are needed to develop and articulate legal principle consonant with the enduring values and practical needs of society. Efficiency, no less than independence, requires that the judges of every level of courts be accustomed to the sophisticated dialogue between fact and law, between principle and practice.

But, you may ask, how can the judicial recruiting of leading advocates be maintained? The attractions of judicial office have diminished in recent years. The problem is not merely financial, although that has been significant enough. The disparity between the earnings of experienced advocates and the remuneration of judges has been notorious and governments have often been unable to obtain the services of those who are most qualified for judicial office. Practitioners are being invited to accept appointment at a younger age – an age when they are at the peak of their earning capacities and when the costs of educating their children and meeting their mortgage commitments are at a maximum. Nevertheless, many were prepared to accept the honour of judicial appointment for two reasons. First, there was the security of an indexed pension which conferred on the appointee and his spouse a security that might have been missing in the practice of the profession. Secondly, and perhaps more significantly, appointment was accepted because of the public respect shown to, and the status of, the office of a judge. The attractive force of both of these inducements has been diminished.

The Commonwealth Government is proposing in future to subject judicial pensions to a 15 per cent reduction, on the footing that the reduction is analogous to the impost on funded superannuation schemes. I note, however, that the Senate Select Committee on Superannuation published a Report earlier this month which concluded:

> that the judicial pension scheme does indeed have a greater role than

> just being part of a remuneration package. The Committee recognises that judicial independence is a guarantee of the impartiality of the judiciary, which underpins the federal nature of the Commonwealth, and the protection of individual rights. The Committee shares the widespread view that secure and adequate remuneration, during retirement as well as during service, is essential to judicial independence.[14]

In consequence the Committee's unanimous recommendation maintains with some improvement of benefits the provisions of the Judges' Pensions Act 1968 (Cth) which applies to federal Judges.

A reduction in the non-contributory judicial pension otherwise than by the imposition of the general tax on income would create a belief that the financial security of judicial office is chancy. That would compound the problems of judicial recruitment and of premature judicial retirement. These are problems that are of real concern for the maintenance of a highly-qualified judiciary. A contrary approach was taken in Singapore, a highly-commercialised society. Terms and conditions of judicial service were raised to a level sufficient to induce professional leaders including those practising in commercial fields to accept appointment to the Bench, judicial strength was increased to match the caseload and modern technology was introduced to assist court administration. The policy was pursued to secure a highly-qualified judiciary so as to foster, inter alia, investment, commerce and international trade.

The respect for, and status of, the office of a judge was and, to a great extent, still is an inducement to accept judicial office. But it is clear that intemperate and ill-informed attacks on particular members of the judiciary, the trumpeting of criticism by commentators who have little knowledge of the judicial method and the absence of effective defence of judicial institutions by the political branches of government have damaged that respect and status to some extent. I shall refer to these factors in connection with public confidence in the judiciary. In the present context, the significance of these developments is that it becomes more difficult to attract practitioners who value both their reputation and their privacy.

The result is that it can no longer be said that leading advocates will necessarily regard an offer of judicial appointment as the fulfilment of a professional ambition. Consequently, there is a risk that governments will seek or will be forced to seek recruitment from sources that may not yield judges of the same competence as the judiciary of earlier times. That is not to say that competent judges have not been appointed from among the ranks of practising solicitors, academics and government lawyers but, as Sir Anthony Mason says, the 'problem is to identify the lawyers from a different background who have the capacity to adapt',[15] especially in those jurisdictions in which complex evidentiary or procedural problems require speedy disposition.

Suggestions are sometimes made that the judiciary is not properly representative. In some respects, that is true. There are too few women judges and too few from what might be termed an 'ethnic' background. That under-representation reflects the under-representation of women and minorities among our leading advocates. The real question is how to remove the obstacles and attitudes that restrain the under-represented groups from advancing to the ranks of the leading advocates and thence to judicial appointment. Particular and valuable insights are contributed by competent judges drawn from groups that are now under-represented. Other things being equal, it would strengthen the judiciary to have an increase in the proportion of women judges and judges drawn from minority groups.[16] Yet it would be an erroneous policy, demeaning of an appointee's dignity, to appoint a judge on grounds other than merit. The judiciary cannot be appointed to represent a class or interest; it is appointed to find the facts accurately, to apply the law impartially and to exercise judicial discretions reasonably, irrespective of the class or interest to which any litigant belongs.

Public Confidence

Perhaps there is no more significant issue affecting the State of the modern Judicature than the issue of public confidence in the Judiciary. Twenty years ago, the Judiciary was revered as a treasured institution – 'like the navy ... admired to excess' said Lord Devlin.[17] But Madam Justice McLachlin of the Supreme Court of Canada is close to the modern mark when she says: 'Judging is not what it used to be. Judges are more important now; judges are more criticized.'[18]

Recent criticism has often been focused on the judge personally, not on the judge's decisions much less on the reasons for the judge's decision. And if the critic is criticized, the criticism is defended on the ground that judges must be 'accountable'. Clearly the time has come when some ground rules should be spelt out.

In the first place, there can be no inhibition on proper criticism of court judgments. Judgments are too important to be exempt from public discussion, especially judgments which have significance for the wider community. It would be absurd to suggest that the *Mabo*[19], *Wik*[20] and *Ha and Hammond*[21] judgments of the High Court could not and should not be subject to critical examination. They affect interests far wider than those of the particular parties and decide controversial issues touching the very nature of our society. If judges pronounce judgments of that significance, should they not be accountable for the exercise of their powers? Of course they should. And they are. They spend their days and nights giving an account of the exercise of those powers. The account is called 'Reasons for Judgment'. A full account of the exercise of judicial power must always be given for the reason that Sir Frank Kitto so clearly stated: 'The process of reasoning which has decided the case must itself be exposed to the light of day, so that all concerned may understand what principles and practice of law and logic are guiding the courts, and so that full publicity may be achieved which provides, on the one hand, a powerful protection against any tendency to judicial autocracy and against any erroneous suspicion of judicial wrongdoing and, on the other hand, an effective stimulant to judicial high performance.'[22]

Reasons for judgment in important and difficult cases cover page after page, statute after statute, precedent after precedent. They are often technical, because they are judgments 'according to law'. What else should they be? Judgments to suit the government of the day? Judgments to earn popularity or to satisfy the demands of those with power and influence? Judgments that will attract the accolades of the media? Not at all. The rule of law is most valuable when it protects the vulnerable and the unpopular.

Sometimes judges are reproached for exercising power without having been elected to do so. The suggestion is that judges should be accountable to the electorate as politicians are accountable. The duties of the judiciary are not owed to the electorate; they are owed to the law, which is there for the peace, order and good government of all the community.[23] Change that view of judicial duty and you have destroyed your own security. I recall again the words which Robert Bolt has Thomas More saying to Roper in *A Man for All Seasons* 'This country's planted thick with laws from coast to coast ... and if you cut them down ... d'you really think you could stand upright in the winds that would blow then?'[24]

The real problem of accountability for the exercise of judicial power is not the giving of the account, it is the reporting and critical appreciation of the account that is given.

Some courts have appointed media officers to assist the media in the reporting of decisions. No doubt that has proved to be of assistance, especially in cases at first instance where the facts are found and a single set of reasons is delivered. A media officer can ensure that every reasonable and lawful request for assistance in reporting the work of the courts is met; but a media officer is not an advertising agent, seeking to influence favourable publicity or issuing releases designed to put a favourable spin on court decisions. The prerogative of and the responsibility for reporting and offering interpretation and criticism of court decisions must rest with the media. That is one of the great services that the media perform. It is the means by which the judiciary's account for the exercise of their powers reaches the people. So regarded, legal reporting and comment are necessary elements in our constitutional arrangements. They call for a high level of journalistic skill.

By employing an informed and critical faculty, the media justifies its freedom; conversely, ill-informed criticism abuses that freedom. Of course, there are often two stories to be written about an important case. One story is the account given by judges for the decision that the court has reached: that will often be a dreary and technical story, even though it is the story in which any unwarranted departure from the rule of law would be found and in which the principle that will govern future cases could be stated. The other story is the political, financial or social fall-out of the decision. This is more familiar territory to the majority of journalists and, of course, to politicians. When the case is important, both stories could and should be run. But that brings me to the second ground rule: the restriction on political criticism of court decisions.

From time to time, strident and sustained criticism is made of court decisions, usually decisions on sentencing or decisions in cases of major public significance. Sentencing is one of the most anxious of judicial functions, so much depending on the particular facts of each crime and of each criminal. Community interests and standards are taken into account but the judge has to distinguish those standards from an ephemeral cry for vengeance or a stimulated wave of concern about offences of a particular kind. Political capital about sentencing can be earned by speeches on a law and order theme and public feeling can be aroused by reports which fail to disclose all the facts, especially any circumstances of mitigation. It is difficult for judges in the criminal courts to perform their duty calmly, impartially and in accordance with law if politicians and special interest groups arouse public feeling about the level of sentences generally, ignoring the unique circumstances of each case. The safety valve for manifestly inadequate sentencing is the Crown's appeal against sentence.

Over recent years, politicians and other interested parties, showing little interest in the court's function of administering the law but versed in the techniques of political struggle, public controversy and media relations, have criticized the courts, not for their reasons for decision but for the decisions they have made. Criticism which pays little or no attention to the reasons for decision may be politically successful because, as surveys have shown, the public generally are not familiar with the *Constitution* and with the powers which are distributed under it. Even less is the public familiar with statute law and less again with the common law. Nor is the public familiar with the step by step reasoning that leads a judge to a conclusion in accordance with his or her understanding of the law. But the public is accustomed to the cut and thrust of political debate. Consequently, if no defence is made to a political attack on a court, some will regard the attack as unanswered or unanswerable. No effective answer can be given by the courts themselves. The courts cannot be advocates to plead their own cause in justification of their judgments. If they were, they would be induced to temper their judgments to protect their own interests. Impartiality would be gone, traded for protection from attacks. To quote Sir Frank Kitto again: 'Every judge worthy of the name recognises that he must take each man's censure; he knows full well that as a judge he is born to censure as the sparks fly upwards; but neither in preparing a judgment nor in retrospect may it weigh with him that the harvest he gleans is praise or blame, approval or scorn. He will reply to neither; he will defend himself not at all.'[25]

In earlier days, attacks on courts or judges with reference to their decisions brought an immediate response from the Attorney-General. And attacks by members of the political branches of government were almost unknown. That is no longer the case. Attorneys-General, both federal and state, have been singularly quiet in defence of the courts at times when the courts have been subject to the most acute and often ill-informed criticisms. Of course, the Attorneys-General of today are seen and apparently see themselves as political figures rather than as Ministers with a peculiar responsibility for the judicial branch of government. The consequence is that they are politically hamstrung in the response that they can make or are willing to make when one of their political colleagues launches a political attack on the Courts or the judges. The Federal Attorney-General, Mr Daryl Williams, AM QC, a distinguished lawyer whose resolute integrity is not open to doubt, has recently accepted this position: 'In essence, I do not believe that the public perceives that the Attorney-General acts independently of political imperatives. An Attorney-General cannot be a wholly independent counsel who rushes to the defence of the judiciary when under attack. This is particularly the case when the attack comes from the executive arm of government.'[26]

He had earlier written that 'it is more compatible with the independence of the judiciary from the executive government, and more compatible with being so seen, that the judiciary not rely on the attorney-general to represent or defend it in public debate in the media. The judiciary should accept the position that it no longer expects the attorney-general to defend its reputation and make that position known publicly.'[27]

Mr Williams rightly seeks the best way of keeping the courts out of the political arena. I venture to suggest that an Attorney's silence is not the way.

The courts do not need an Attorney-General to attempt to justify their reasons for decision. That is not the function of an Attorney-General. But why should an Attorney not defend the reputation of the judiciary, explain the nature of the judicial process and repel attacks based on grounds irrelevant to the application of the rule of law? Can an Attorney not explain publicly that courts must apply the law whatever the consequences, that the facts of each case and not some unbending policy must govern the exercise of judicial discretions including sentencing discretions, that the courts have no political agenda, that the only valid ground of criticism is an error in the facts that the court has found or in a step in the legal reasoning or in the exercise of a judicial discretion? It has been suggested that the Judicial Conference of Australia might be the defender of a court against an attack on a court's decision. But no Conference spokesman, if a judge, could presume to defend another judge's or another court's decision. The Conference, which seeks to foster an understanding of judicial independence is neither intended nor equipped to respond to such attacks. And, if the attack is from a political source, the response must be from a political identity.

If it be politically unrealistic to expect an Attorney publicly to defend the integrity of the judicial process, it must be because governments now perceive the courts to be players in the political game. That is a false perception but – frightening though the thought may be – governments have the power to make that perception a self-fulfilling prophecy. Political attacks on courts will inevitably lead some judges into political responses. Treating courts as political players will lead politicians to make political appointments, to offer personal or institutional rewards for judicial conduct that is politically desirable and to impose penalties for decisions that are politically unacceptable. Mutual understanding of and respect for the functions of each branch of government is essential to rebuild and preserve an appropriate relationship between the judicial and the political branches. The American Bar Association, speaking of 'An Independent Judiciary' has pointed out that 'The key to managing interbranch tension and maintaining the essentially sound state of judicial independence and accountability in a system of separated powers is mutual restraint.'[28]

The third ground rule relates to the substance and character of legitimate criticism. Exceptional and scandalous cases aside, any valid ground for criticism of a court or judge in relation to a judgment must be found in the reasons for judgment or in some blemish in the conduct of the proceedings. These are on the public record. If the record shows that the facts have been properly found, that the law has been properly applied and that any discretion has been properly exercised, it is beside the point that the result is unpalatable. If the critic does not consult the public record or does not understand it, the criticism is mischievous. That said, there is ample room for reasoned criticism. Every dissenting judgment in an appeal court will reveal tenable grounds for criticizing the majority judgment. If the criticism relates to supposed defects in legal reasoning, the critic must distinguish between reasoning which interprets the *Constitution*, reasoning which interprets a statute and reasoning which develops the common law. Only in the last case is there room for judicial policy to affect the reasoning[29] and for criticism about the wisdom – as distinct from the correctness – of a judicial development of the law.

Recent criticisms of decisions of the courts, especially decisions made in sentencing offenders and in constitutional and native title cases, have seldom referred to, or even revealed any acquaintance with, the relevant facts or the reasons for judgment. Postures have been adopted and declarations have been made as to what the decisions ought to have been in order to satisfy some non-legal criterion which the critic embraces. Such criticism does not reveal a valid ground for attack on a Court or the judge or judges who constitute it. By all means let defects in applying the judicial method be criticized – trenchantly criticized if need be – but unless the rule of law has been misapplied, criticism of a decision is destructive of public confidence in the institution on which the rule of law depends.

Access to justice

Access to justice is the immediate concern of those with a genuine need for the law's protection. Two factors affect the availability of legal remedies. The first is the need for expert advice and assistance; the second is the practice and procedure that govern the obtaining of legal remedies.

Advice and assistance for those who cannot afford to retain lawyers of their own choice depends largely on government funding supplemented by pro bono work undertaken by the profession. Shop front legal services and legal aid schemes have allowed a legal system of increasing complexity to serve many members of the public who otherwise would have been denied justice. Moreover, these services and schemes have contributed greatly to the ability of the courts to dispose of cases efficiently. Apart from anecdotal evidence, concern about the denial of justice is raised by a survey of Victorian practitioners conducted in November 1996 by the Federation of Community Legal Centres – a survey which was not fully processed and may not be statistically accurate. But it is said to have shown that '26 per cent of respondents – [legal practitioners] – indicated that clients had been forced to plead guilty to criminal charges inappropriately'.[30] If that is accurate, it is truly disturbing. Anecdotal evidence from the registries of the courts indicates that an increasing proportion of registry time is spent in managing the matters involving litigants in person. In the High Court, the estimate of that time is 25 per cent. The Australian Law Reform Commission's Background Paper on 'The Unrepresented Party' points to the consequences of parties being unrepresented. Increased judicial, courtroom and registry time is taken in dealing with litigants in person. In *Cachia v Hanes*, the majority said: 'Whilst the right of a litigant to appear in person is fundamental, it would be disregarding the obvious to fail to recognize that the presence of litigants in person in increasing numbers is creating a problem for the courts'.[31]

Procedural changes have to be made in all courts not only to assist litigants but to assist the courts to cope with the burden of litigation in which one or more of the parties is unfamiliar with the practice and procedure of the court and even with the nature of the issues which the court has jurisdiction to determine. In the High Court, the rules relating to the seeking of special leave were amended to require the filing of summaries of argument identifying the facts and propositions relied on or contested and by imposing a time limitation on oral argument. These rules abrogate the special rules which previously governed applications by litigants in person but impose a greater burden on registry staff in advising litigants of the court's requirements.

Of course, the major cost of litigation for the privately funded litigant is usually professional fees. It cannot be otherwise. Professional work must be properly remunerated and litigation is labour intensive. As you know, various proposals for limiting professional costs have been advanced and some criticism has been made of the current level of professional fees, especially those charged by the leaders of the profession. Some of those proposals are matters for government policy – for example, the abolition of tax deductibility of litigation expenses – and on those I would not comment. But two professional practices should be mentioned. The first is the 'cab rank' rule which obliges a barrister, if available, to accept any brief in a field in which he or she ordinarily practises if a reasonable fee is offered. Reasonableness is a matter of assessment but it should be remembered that professional remuneration is earned within the framework of professional rules.

Next, the practice, now widespread, of charging out on a time basis seems to raise two questions worthy of consideration. First, does it not place a premium on inefficiency? And, secondly, does it involve a conflict of interest and duty to the client? I am sure most practitioners would resolve that conflict in favour of the client, but experience in the law teaches that conflicts of interest and duty are best avoided. I respectfully agree with Justice Geoff Davies of the Queensland Court of Appeal who writes: 'It is not that lawyers' fees are generally too high for the work which they do. I do not believe that generally either the rate at which lawyers are paid is too high or the incomes of lawyers are too high. My main concern is rather that our system in general and our costs system in particular discourage efficiency and, on the contrary, offer incentives to inefficiency and over servicing.'[32]

The solution which his Honour advances is 'a costs system based on the amount of work which should be performed, or best practice, and which will make costs more predictable.'[33] The Federal Review of Scales of Legal Professional Fees on which the profession is represented has engaged the Business School of Melbourne University to advise. No doubt the method of charging for litigious work will receive consideration. It is a question which warrants continued consideration also by the relevant professional bodies.

Finally, I pass to the procedural changes which the courts have introduced to streamline the handling of cases.

In the great majority of trial courts, mediation has been introduced as part of the court process. The form of mediation varies: in some courts mediation is performed by court officers and is free; in others it is performed by persons outside the court system, but appointed by a judge, at the parties' cost. The latter form is not objectionable in principle, unless the payment of the mediator's fees is a condition of being allowed to proceed. Where that is the case, there are two in principle objections. Access to justice is denied unless a fee is paid to a third party – that is one objection – and the third party who is to receive the fee is nominated by the judge – that is another.

Some state courts also provide a system of case appraisal which allows an experienced practitioner to make an informal assessment of the likely result of a trial. The parties may accept that assessment as binding or proceed to trial at a risk of costs in the event of not achieving a better result than that assessed.

In some courts, discovery, which can be a major cost in commercial actions, is limited to documents directly relevant to an issue in the proceeding. New rules also ensure easier access to opponents' documents. Interrogatories have been abolished in many jurisdictions except by leave. Again, in some jurisdictions a wide discretion has been conferred on judges to admit evidence otherwise inadmissible and evidence is taken by video link or telephone. In Western Australia there are now rules giving judges control over the form (whether oral or in writing) and length of evidence, power to limit examination-in-chief and cross-examination and control over the length and form of addresses.

Case management, in one form or another, exists in most trial courts. Case management varies, as you know, from a system of fairly automatic triggering events through to intensive individual management by judges.

In the Federal Court, after extensive investigation and expert advice and after introduction of a pilot scheme in the Melbourne Registry, an individual docket scheme has been introduced. Cases will be allocated randomly to particular judges who will monitor their cases to conclusion. Fixed but few conferences will ensure, inter alia, compliance with directions and the diversion of appropriate cases to non-curial assisted dispute resolution (ADR). Special panels of judges will be constituted to deal with cases requiring particular expertise.

Extensive case management is not universally accepted as desirable in all classes of litigation[34] but it is probably true to say that all courts and their registries are now more actively engaged in managing their case flows and the preparation of complex cases for trial than they were in earlier times. The Family Court, with an enormous caseload and with an especial concern for litigants in person, has been a leader in introducing mediation and user-friendly procedures. Mega litigation has also produced technologically assisted responses. The *Rothwells* litigation in Western Australia, the *Fairfax* litigation in New South Wales and the *Estate Mortgages* litigation in Victoria demanded the creation of courtrooms equipped with sophisticated electronic technology.

Information technology has been embraced by Australian courts. The judgments of the High Court of Australia are available on the internet minutes after they are handed down in Court. So are the judgments of the Federal Court, the Family Court, and the Supreme Courts of New South Wales, South Australia, Tasmania, the Australian Capital Territory and the Northern Territory. High Court transcripts are available shortly after a matter is heard. The High Court home page will be providing information relating to the progress and listing of cases. All of these services are provided free of charge. In March the council of Chief Justices of Australia and New Zealand gave in principle support to the concept of 'media-neutral' citation, which will enable reference to electronic reports of the decisions in the courts as well as to the hard copy reports.

The Council of Chief Justices is currently sponsoring work on an Electronic Appeals Project designed to reduce the necessity to reproduce masses of printed material from trial courts and to permit the standardising of the printed and electronic material in all appellate courts including the High Court. Appellate court rules are under review at the same time.

Courts and judges have been active in seeking ways to improve the efficiency of the courts and thereby to improve access to justice. With respect to other and grander studies about the justice system and the way it operates, I wonder whether better results can be achieved than those which are devised by practical and hard-nosed practitioners and administrators (in which I include judges) with experience in the justice system.

It is beyond the time I should have asked you to sit to hear of the State of the Judicature. At base, the State of the Judicature means the quality of the judges and their ability to perform their functions. Judges, from the viewpoint of a practitioner, may be a varied group. Mostly polite in court, some judges may be sharp; mostly quick and industrious, some judges may not always reveal it; mostly with a generous view of human nature, sometimes a more straitened view emerges. But in the years, I have been privileged to be a judge, I have not known a corrupt judge; none has sought to do anything except justice according to law as he or she honestly saw it; none would yield to improper pressure that might impermissibly tilt the scales of judgment. The Judicature is, and has been, in a good state. But that state has not been achieved by accident or by mere good fortune. It is the consequence of the structures, the traditions and the values of the judiciary and the profession – recognized, if not articulated – and enforced by the pressure of an honourable peer group.

As the work of the judiciary impacts more on public than on private issues, there will be danger to the impartiality and the competence of the judiciary and to public confidence in the institution. As society and the law become more complex, obstacles to public access to justice will grow. Those dangers will be contained, and the State of the Judicature will be strengthened, only if governments and the public generally and the profession in particular understand the fundamental significance of the Judicature to Australian society and the conditions which must be maintained in order that it can continue to serve the Australian people.

---

1. This address was published in (1998) 72 *Australian Law Journal* 33.
2. Lord Devlin 'Judges and Lawmakers' (1976) 39 *Modern Law Review* 1, 4.
3. Ibid.
4. Right Honourable Antonio Lamer, PC, 'The Tension Between Judicial Accountability and Judicial Independence: A Canadian Perspective' Singapore Academy of Law Annual Lecture (1996) 4.

5. See *Wilson v Minister for Aboriginal and Torres Strait Islander Affairs* (1996) 189 CLR 1; 70 ALJR 743; 138 ALR 220.
6. See *Valente v The Queen* [1985] 2 SCR 673, 687; *The Queen v Beauregarde* [1986] 2 SCR 56, 70; see Ian Greene, 'The Doctrine of Judicial Independence Developed by the Supreme Court of Canada' (1988) 26 (1) *Osgoode Hall Law Journal* 178.
7. See *The Queen v Beauregard* [1986] 2 SCR 56, 72.
8. See *Constitution*, ss 53, 83.
9. See *Constitution*, s 56.
10. Cited by Lord Ackner in United Kingdom, *Parliamentary Debates,* House of Lords, 14 July 1997, 865; see also Sir Richard's interview reported in *The Times*, 2 December 1996.
11. See *R v Lord Chancellor; Ex parte Witham* [1997] 2 All ER 779.
12. Sir Anthony Mason, 'Judicial Independence and the Separation of Powers – Some Problems Old and New', *The Leon Ladner Lecture*, (1989) 21 and published in (1990) 13 (2) *UNSW Law Journal* 173, 181.
13. Lamer (n 4) 9.
14. Conclusion 1.43, 25th Report of the Senate Select Committee on Superannuation, *The Parliamentary Contributory Superannuation Scheme & The Judges' Pension Scheme*, September 1997, 46.
15. Sir Anthony Mason, *Fragile Bastion: Judicial Independence in the Nineties* (Judicial Commission of New South Wales, 1997) 3.
16. As Sir Anthony Mason commented four years ago in the last 'State of the Judicature' Address, (1994) 68 *Australian Law Journal* 125, 131-132.
17. Lord Devlin, *The Judge (*Oxford University Press, 1979) 25.
18. Justice Beverley McLachlin, 'The Role of Judges in Modern Commonwealth Society'(1994) 110 *Law Quarterly Review* 260, 261.
19. See *Mabo v Queensland [No 2]* (1992) 175 CLR 1.
20. See *Wik Peoples v Queensland* (1996) 187 CLR 1.
21. See *Ha v New South Wales; Walter Hammond & Associates Pty Ltd v New South Wales* (1997) 189 CLR 465; 71 ALJR 1080; 146 ALR 355.
22. Sir Frank Kitto, 'Why Write Judgments? (1992) 66 *Australian Law Journal* 787, 790.
23. Lamer (n 4) 6.
24. Robert Bolt, *A Man for All Seasons*, London: Heinemann, 1969, Act 1, 39.
25. Sir Frank Kitto, 'Why Write Judgments? (1992) 66 *Australian Law Journal* 787, 790; see also Lord Denning in *Reg v Commissioner of Police of the Metropolis; Ex parte Blackburn (No 2)* [1968] 2 QB 150, 155 and Myers CJ in *Attorney-General v Blundell* [1942] NZLR 287, 289.
26. Williams had intended to publish an article 'Who will Defend the Courts?'in the *Australian Bar Review*. As editor of these papers, I have not been able to trace it.
27. Collection of Papers from a National Conference, "Courts in a Representative Democracy", Canberra, 11-13 November 1994 at 192.
28. 'Report of the Commission on Separation of Powers and Judicial Independence', 4 July 1997.
29. As I have explained in *Theophanous v Herald & Weekly Times Ltd* (1994) 182 CLR 104, 142-144.

30. 'Justice for All', the Federation's 'Report into the Impact of Legal Aid Guideline Changes since March 1996', 3 par 4.
31. (1994) 179 CLR 403, 415.
32. Justice Geoffrey Davies, 'Justice Reform: A Personal Perspective', (1997) 15 *Australian Bar Review* 109, 114-115.
33. Justice Geoffrey Davies, 'Managing the Work of the Courts', AIJA Asia-Pacific Courts Conference, Sydney, 22 August 1997, 3.
34. See, for example, the observations of Davies JA in 'Managing the Work of the Courts', AIJA Asia-Pacific Courts Conference, Sydney, 22 August 1997, 8-9.

3.13 The Courts and Human Rights

Editor's note

This is an edited version of the paper delivered by Brennan at the Introduction to Human Rights Law Seminar conducted by the Judicial College of Victoria on 19 February 2007. Victoria had enacted its *Charter of Human Rights and Responsibilities Act 2006* (Vic). Brennan took the opportunity to highlight some possible jurisdictional issues which might arise.[1]

Introduction

Twenty years ago I was privileged to attend a conference of the Canadian Institute for Advanced Legal Studies held in Cambridge. It was opened by Sir John Donaldson, then Master of the Rolls. He spoke about the Canadian Charter of Rights and Freedoms which had come into force five years earlier. In the course of his address, he said 'Look at the problem how you may, I can see no escape from the conclusion that the courts and the judges are being pitched into a political battle in which, if it was an English court, it would be gravely wounded and which it could not win.'

His dismal prognosis was not welcomed by the Canadian judiciary. Nor, I think, has been it fulfilled in the intervening years. It was undoubtedly true that the Canadian Charter, like the American Bill of Rights, reposed in the judiciary a novel power which had hitherto been reserved to the political branches of government. But that was the result of legislative action and it was the duty of the Canadian judiciary to exercise the jurisdiction which had been reposed in their respective courts.

So, it is in Victoria. Whatever be the views of individual judges, or even of a majority of judges, it is no longer judicially relevant to consider the arguments for or against the introduction of the *Charter of Human Rights and Responsibilities Act 2006* (Vic). Assuming its constitutional validity, the Charter is a law enacted by the Parliament awaiting application according to its terms by all branches of government and public institutions including the courts of Victoria.

The courts will have an important role to play in effecting the protection of individual interests, as the legislature intends. The spare terms in which rights and responsibilities are defined in the Charter will have to be fleshed out by judicial decision case by case. Thus, will the jurisprudence of the Charter emerge. That jurisprudence will depend on concepts or principles determined by the judiciary – and particularly by the Supreme Court – to be appropriate having regard to the common law, the laws and conventions in force in Victoria, the text and structure of the Charter and the values and standards of the contemporary Victorian community. The concepts and principles which are open to the judiciary to adopt are indeed diverse and, in a seminar of this kind so soon after the Charter has come into force, it is tempting to offer definitions of the content of the several rights conferred by Pt 2 of the Act. But, while I shall endeavour to locate some of the significant areas of decision-making, I must be careful not to trespass upon the role of the Victorian judiciary by proposing specific interpretations of the Charter rights. The responsibility for interpreting the Charter and determining its application in particular cases or to particular issues rests with the judiciary and is to be discharged in a judicial manner – that is, after a public hearing of submissions from the respective parties on the meaning and operation of applicable Charter provisions and having regard to the circumstances of the case, and by a process of reasoning which satisfies the judicial mind and which is then articulated in published reasons. A recent example is the decision of King J in *R* v *Williams*.[2]

The Charter will have a broad significance. It is of general application, which means that it may have an effect whenever the circumstances attract its operation. The experience in Canada, as one of that country's senior judges told me, was that the Charter operated as a kind of juristic vacuum cleaner, sweeping up the miscellany of cases that lay in its path and laying them before courts in every jurisdiction without waiting for the development of guiding precedent. Victoria may have the same experience with challenging issues arising in cases that appear, at first sight, to be mundane or even run of the mill. The burden of judging may increase, and appeals may be frequent. The issues will be challenging, but that will give judicial life an additional fascination.

Judges will probably experience the novel sensation of becoming a public news item from time to time. The advent of the Charter will tend to focus more public attention on the judiciary as it exercises its new statutory authority. Madam Justice McLachlin, now Chief Justice of Canada, said in 1991 'The advent of the Charter in Canada … elevated judges from a position where they once toiled in relative obscurity, to the level of media figures. Now, more than ever before, the contributions made by the courts are seen to impact so directly and profoundly on the everyday life of the country that judgments of the Supreme Court on the Charter receive regular and extensive attention in the news media.'[3]

There may be other changes to the ordered anonymity of judicial life. The possibility of some of these changes has left me, I confess, with a rather ambivalent view about charters or bills of rights. I should confess this ambivalence so that you may determine for yourselves the validity of any subsequent comments that I offer. I have feared the politicisation of the judiciary and the adoption of political criteria for the selection of judges. This fear was confirmed by Dean Griswold, sometime Solicitor-General of the United States and Dean of the Harvard Law School. We were discussing the nomination of Robert Bork to the Supreme Court of the United States, when Dean Griswold opined that the American procedure of publicly vetting candidates for appointment before a Committee of the Senate was warranted by a Constitution which reposed political power in that Court.[4] On another occasion I heard a Canadian academic observing that, once you enact a charter of rights, the consequences are rather like the experience of dancing with a gorilla: you do not have an option about when to stop. I had concern also about the expertise of a judiciary in exercising power which has been traditionally political and, like Sir John Donaldson, I had some concern about public acceptance of a judiciary entering fields ordinarily reserved to the political branches of government. On the other hand, it has become increasingly clear that the fundamental aspirations of justice, equity and human dignity are often neglected or overlooked in favour of more venal or politically expedient objectives and a charter of rights was likely to stimulate a political sensitivity about those aspirations and to foster a community culture which insists on individual human dignity. It can be understood that, entertaining these contradictory views and acknowledging the responsibility of the judiciary to administer the Charter, I would favour a liberal interpretation of the rights conferred by the Charter when needed to preserve justice, equity and human dignity, but I would be cautious about judicial interventions of a more adventurous kind lest the judiciary should overplay its hand and risk damage to public confidence in, and the authority of, the courts.

In interpreting the spare terms of the Charter, the courts will naturally tend to follow the customary judicial method of seeking for a persuasive precedent. Apart from the intellectual assistance thus obtained, that method safeguards the judiciary from any suggestion of idiosyncrasy, a suggestion which might readily be made when open textured terms are to be interpreted. As Learned Hand observed '[a judge's] authority and his immunity depend upon the assumption that he speaks with the mouth of others: the momentum of his utterances must be greater than any which his personal reputation and character can command, if it is to do the work assigned to it – if it is to stand against the passionate resentments arising out of the interests he must frustrate.'[5]

Therefore, the Victorian courts will look to the experience of other jurisdictions with similar Charters for guidance in developing the jurisprudence of the Victorian Charter. Indeed, s 32(2) expressly provides that the judgments of other courts and tribunals 'may be considered in interpreting a statutory provision'. No doubt the industry and enthusiasm of counsel will ensure that the vast reservoir of human rights material is tapped in the course of argument on the provisions of the Charter, but I venture to suggest that caution is needed in treating the judgments of overseas courts as influential precedents in applying the Charter provisions in the context of the laws of Victoria. I shall explain presently why I suggest a cautious approach but, for the moment, I note that the Victorian judiciary has had placed upon it a considerable responsibility and is offered a considerable challenge. It is to craft the jurisprudence of human rights in and for Australia.

True, the Australian Capital Territory has a similar Charter, but the volume and complexity of litigation in that jurisdiction is likely to be far less than the volume and complexity of litigation that will fall for decision in Victoria.

The effect of the Charter is, of course, subject to the operation of s. 109 of the *Constitution* of the Commonwealth. A law of the Commonwealth may override the operation of the Charter. That is a question that will be resolved case by case dependent on the operation attributed to the Commonwealth law. In theory, the laws of the Commonwealth and of the other States and Territories are not affected by the enactment of the Charter. Nevertheless, an interesting question could arise if a law, uniformly incorporated in and enacted as a law of the several States, were said to be inconsistent with the requirements of a Charter right. Would the Charter apply to such a law or would the operation of the Charter be excluded by an implied necessity to preserve uniformity? If the interpretation of a uniform statutory provision is affected by operation of s 32 of the Charter, the effect of the Charter will extend beyond the boundaries of the State.

I turn to an examination of the Charter and its terms.

General conspectus of the Charter

The main purpose of the Charter is stated by s 1(2) to be the protection and promotion of the civil and political rights set out in Pt 2 of the Act. Those are in substance the rights specified by the *International Covenant on Civil and Political Rights* (1966), ('ICCPR'), although the language of the ICCPR is said to have been modernised and 'modified as required for the Victorian context'.[6] These rights are defined in the familiar, open-textured, manner appropriate to a condition generally enjoyed by natural persons living in a 'free and democratic society'.

The rights defined by Pt 2 of the Charter are vested in every natural person (s 6(1)) and no person, entity or public authority (other than Parliament or courts and tribunals acting judicially) has any right to limit or destroy a person's human rights (s 4(1)(i), (j) and s 7(3)). The notion of a personal right limiting the general operation of a public law is unusual and it may give rise to unusual difficulties. When, prior to *Cole v Whitfield*,[7] s 92 of our *Constitution* was construed as conferring a personal right of free interstate trade rather than a limitation on legislative and executive power, the 'judicial exegesis of the section … yielded neither clarity of meaning nor certainty of operation'.[8] The problem is inherent in an attempt to reconcile a provision which confers a personal right or a personal immunity from legislative interference and a statutory provision which, in terms or in operation, would deny the right or infringe the immunity.

If the personal right is constitutionally entrenched, it is a limitation on legislative power; if it is not entrenched, reconciliation with an infringing statute is a question of interpretation, a question of ascertaining the legislature's intention. In one case, the judiciary must determine the extent to which the parliament may give effect to what it sees as the public interest; in the other case, 'parliamentary sovereignty' is intact and the judiciary ascertains what the Parliament intends. The distinction is significant when we come to s 7(2) of the Charter.

Although the several rights defined by Pt 2 are expressed in unqualified terms, s 7(2) permits their limitation under law to an extent that can be 'demonstrably justified in a free and democratic society'. This provision does not seem to prescribe the limits on the authority of a maker of the limiting law, but rather to accept that some statutory provisions which limit a defined right may be found to be compatible with the Charter, despite the limitation. Curiously, the progenitor of s 7(2) is s 1 of the *Canadian Charter of Rights and Freedoms*, which is constitutionally entrenched. It was copied by s 5 of the New Zealand Bill of Rights, which is not constitutionally entrenched, and has migrated across the Tasman.

The Act provides a series of mechanisms to protect the rights defined in Pt 2. Legislative procedure is changed to require a Minister or Member of Parliament introducing a Bill to table a statement of compatibility with those rights or the nature and extent of any incompatibility (s 28). Then the Scrutiny of Acts and Regulations Committee is to consider and report on the compatibility of any Bill with the Pt 2 rights (s 30). Parliamentary power is not limited by Pt 2, however, and the Parliament expressly reserves power to make a declaration that the provision of any Act is to have effect despite any incompatibility with Pt 2, although the intention is that such a declaration will be made only in exceptional circumstances (s 31). 'Parliamentary sovereignty' is not affected by these provisions, as the Charter itself provides that non-compliance with s 28 or the key provisions of s 31 with respect to a Bill in the Parliament does not affect 'the validity, operation or enforcement' of the resultant Act.

Of course, these protective mechanisms affect only future legislative activity. But all enactments, past as well as future, are subject to the interpretative provisions which are at the heart of the Charter. At the outset, s 1 declares that the purpose of protecting and promoting human rights is to be effected by, inter alia:

> 1(2)(b)
>
> ensuring that all statutory provisions, whenever enacted, are interpreted so far as is possible in a way that is compatible with human rights; and
>
> (c)
>
> imposing an obligation on all public authorities to act in a way that is compatible with human rights.[9]

And by:

> conferring jurisdiction on the Supreme Court to declare that a statutory provision cannot be interpreted consistently with a human right and requiring the relevant Minister to respond to that declaration.[10]

To the extent that statutes can be interpreted 'in a way that is compatible with human rights', the purpose of the Charter is to amend all prior statutory provisions and to provide an additional canon of statutory construction to govern the interpretation of future provisions. Unless the Parliament makes an express override declaration, the interpretative canon of compatibility is to be applied to the legislative text. What is critical, however, is the determination of how far it is possible to interpret statutes compatibly with human rights where the statute would not otherwise be interpreted in that way. As this question raises issues of particular difficulty, I focus on questions of interpretation of statutory provisions, leaving other applications of the Charter to be resolved according to the circumstances of the particular case and the scope attributed to the relevant Charter right.

Statutory interpretation

The provisions of the Charter which confer jurisdiction on the courts of Victoria are ss 32(1) and 36(2). These provisions correspond substantially with paras (b) and (e) of s 1(2) the section which declares the Charter's purpose. Section 32(1) is directed to all courts, the latter to the Supreme Court alone. Section 32(1) provides 'So far as it is possible to do so consistently with their purpose, all statutory provisions must be interpreted in a way that is compatible with human rights.'

Section 36(2) provides 'Subject to any relevant override declaration, if in a proceeding the Supreme Court is of the opinion that a statutory provision cannot be interpreted consistently with a human right, the Court may make a declaration to that effect in accordance with this section.'

There is a curious variation of language between the two paragraphs of s 1(2) relating to interpretation and the subsections which contain the substantive provisions relating to interpretation. The two substantive provisions seem to be complementary one to the other. Thus, if 'it is possible' to interpret a statutory provision 'in a way that is compatible with human rights', it must be so interpreted; but if it 'cannot be interpreted consistently with a human right', a declaration of inconsistent interpretation may be made. An interpretation which it is 'possible' to make under s 32(1) is the antithesis of an interpretation that 'cannot' be made under s 36(2). An interpretation which is not consistent 'with a human right' under s 36(2) is presumably not 'compatible with human rights' under s 32(1). If this be a correct construction, no declaration of inconsistency with a human right can be made in respect of a statutory provision unless the Supreme Court is satisfied that it is not possible to interpret the provision in a way that is compatible with human rights, that is, with all the rights set out in Pt 2 of the Charter modified, if need be, by s 7(2). The primary judicial function, therefore, is prescribed by s 32(1). It is to determine whether 'it is possible' to interpret a statutory provision 'in a way that is compatible with human rights' but 'consistently with [the statutory provision's] purpose'.

The phrase 'consistently with their purpose' does not appear in s 1(2), nor is it expressed (though it may be implied) in s 36(2). But if that phrase qualifies the direction to interpret statutory provisions consistently with human rights, Victorian courts must address the question of compatibility between the purpose of a statutory provision and the exigencies of the defined human rights. Under the Victorian Charter, that question may well be found to be central to the application of the Charter.

It will be noted that what is required is compatibility with the purpose of a statutory provision, not simply with its text. The meaning of the text is ascertained in its context which includes the existing state of the law and the mischief which the statute is intended to remedy.[11] And s 35 of the *Interpretation of Legislation Act* (Vic) (*Interpretation Act*) demands that a construction of a statutory provision which 'would promote the purpose or object underlying' the provision should be preferred to a construction which would not promote that purpose or object. The purpose is ascertained primarily from the text and structure of the provision, but s 35(b) of the *Interpretation Act* authorises consideration to be given also to Hansard, explanatory memoranda and preliminary reports on the legislation. On its face, s 32(1) of the Charter does not purport to affect this canon of construction. Indeed, s 32(1) seems to take the *Interpretation Act* purpose of a statutory provision as the linchpin of its interpretation, for a human rights' interpretation of the provision is possible only if it is consistent with that purpose.

Although the Parliament has changed its procedure to ensure that future legislation is measured against the Charter rights, it nevertheless intends that the enforcement of Charter rights should not frustrate its purpose in enacting any piece of legislation, past or future. Coupled with the provisions which maintain the validity, operation and enforceability of statutory provisions despite any incompatibility with Charter rights or a failure to adhere to the procedure governing Bills in the Parliament, the legislative intention appears tolerably clear. It is to maintain untrammelled the legislative authority of the Parliament and the executive but to allow the benefit of Charter rights that are consistent with the purposes of the lawmaker.

On this approach, the first step in applying s 32(1) to a statutory provision is to ascertain the purpose of the provision without reference to the Charter. Only then is it necessary to ascertain whether there is a 'human rights' interpretation of the provision which is consistent with what has been ascertained to be its purpose. The second step raises the question of the scope of a Charter right, a question which will often be open to debate. So s 32(1) raises, as distinct and difficult questions:

1. What is the purpose of the statutory provision?
2. What is the content of the Charter right relied on?
3. Is it possible to construe the statutory provision consistently with the purpose of the statutory provision and with the content of the Charter right?

The Victorian requirement that the construction placed on statutory provisions must be 'consistent with their purpose' is a major point of distinction from the corresponding provision in the *Human Rights Act 1998* (UK). That Act substantially incorporates the *European Convention on Human Rights* – not merely as a text for adoption in domestic legislation but as an instrument binding on the UK. The whole objective of that Act was to ensure conformity with the UK's obligations under the Convention, the terms of which were expressly included (subject to the UK's derogations and reservations) in the

Act. Jurisdiction under the Convention is vested in the European Court of Human Rights, sitting in Strasbourg, a court whose decisions were sometimes embarrassing to the UK. The *Human Rights Act* contains no provisions for the parliamentary scrutiny of legislation. Section 3(1) of that Act contains the simple command: 'So far as it is possible to do so, primary legislation and subordinate legislation must be read and given effect in a way which is compatible with the Convention rights.'

The course of judicial decision under this provision, which contains no requirement of compatibility with statutory purpose, has provoked from Professor Conor Gearty a comment: 'The judges are being sent two apparently contradictory messages: on the one hand, apply these broadly based and generalized human rights whose meaning is not at all self-evident in a wide-ranging way, if necessary by distorting Parliament's intention in specific instances; on the other hand, always respect parliamentary sovereignty.'[12]

The Victorian Parliament seems to have settled that dilemma if, on its true interpretation, s 32(1) forbids any departure from the purpose of Victorian statutory provisions, ascertained as prescribed by the *Interpretation Act*. It follows that the question whether the Charter effects a great or small change in the meaning of a provision depends in part upon the purpose of the provision and in part upon the scope attributed to the relevant human rights.

If the scope of a statutory human right goes no further than an interest protected by the common law, s 32(1) of the Charter would not have effected any change in interpretation of that provision. That is because the courts assume that statutory provisions are not intended to abrogate human rights and fundamental freedoms in the absence of clear language to the contrary.[13] And if a statutory provision which is otherwise ambiguous is capable of being construed consistently with a treaty ratified by Australia (including the *ICCPR*), that construction is adopted.[14] But if the statutory human right is construed as extending beyond the interest protected by the common law and there is no ambiguity to be resolved by reference to the *ICCPR*, it is necessary to determine the effect which s 32(1) might have on the statutory provision under consideration. Decisions on similar issues in other jurisdictions may throw some light on these questions, but only if the statutory context and social conditions of those other jurisdictions are relevantly similar to the statutory context and social conditions affecting the interpretation of the Charter.

In examining cases from other jurisdictions, it is helpful to distinguish between two issues: first, the way in which the foreign court ascertains the scope of a human right and, second, the effect which the court attributes to the human right in its interpretation of statutory provisions or in its application to executive action. In ascertaining the scope of Charter rights, so far as they are expressed in language which is identical with, or substantially similar to, the language of the *ICCPR*, reference has to be made to the meaning of those rights in international law.[15] It may not be easy, however, to derive a settled meaning from the numerous decisions of various tribunals which have sought to apply the Convention provisions. It may be even more difficult to derive from foreign decisions a uniform approach to the way in which a human right, defined by a domestic statute, affects the interpretation of other statutory provisions.

The United Kingdom

We have noted one critical distinction between the Charter and the *Human Rights Act 1998 (UK)*. The latter Act does not make the purpose of a statutory provision the governing factor in its interpretation. In enacting the UK Act, the Parliament at Westminster addressed considerations that have no resonance in the Antipodes. In *Ghaidan* v *Godin-Mendoza*, Lord Steyn pointed out: 'In enacting the 1998 Act Parliament legislated "to bring rights home" from the European Court of Human Rights to be determined in the courts of the United Kingdom … The mischief to be addressed was the fact that Convention rights … could not be vindicated in our courts. Critical to this purpose was the enactment of effective remedial provisions.'[16]

And he attributed to s 3(1) of the Act (which he described as 'the linch-pin of the legislative scheme') an effect of considerable constitutional significance:

> [S]ection 3(1) applies even if there is no ambiguity in the language in the sense of it being capable of bearing two possible meanings. The word "possible" … is used in a different and much stronger sense. [The section] imposes a stronger and more radical obligation than to adopt a purposive interpretation in the light of the [Convention]. The draftsman of the Act had before him the model of the New Zealand Bill of Rights Act which imposes a requirement that the interpretation to be adopted must be reasonable. Parliament specifically rejected the legislative model of requiring a reasonable interpretation.[17]

Lord Hope of Craighead has said the Act 'will subject the entire legal system to a fundamental process of review and, where necessary, reform *by the judiciary*'.[18]

In *R* v *A [No 2]*, his Lordship said: 'The rule of construction which s 3 lays down is quite unlike any previous rule of statutory interpretation. There is no need to identify any ambiguity or absurdity.'[19]

That is now the settled approach to the application of s 3. The courts in the UK are not restrained by the purpose of a statutory provision when there is an inconsistent Convention right. In *R v A [No 2]*, Lord Steyn said:

> [T]he interpretative obligation under s 3 of the 1998 Act is a strong one. Parliament specifically rejected the legislative model of requiring a reasonable interpretation ... Undoubtedly, a court must always look for a contextual and purposive interpretation: [but] s 3 is more radical in its effect. It is a general principle of the interpretation of legal instruments that the text is the primary source of interpretation: other sources are subordinate to it ... Section 3 qualifies this general principle because it requires a court to find an interpretation compatible with Convention rights if it is possible to do so ... it will sometimes be necessary to adopt an interpretation which linguistically may appear strained. The techniques to be used will not only involve the reading down of express language in a statute but also the implication of provisions. A declaration of incompatibility is a measure of last resort.[20]

The extent to which the UK courts will go in applying s 3 is highlighted by the majority and minority speeches in *Ghaidan*. Under the *Rent Act 1977* (UK), a surviving spouse of a tenant was entitled to a statutory tenancy of the premises. By an amendment, 'a person who was living with the original tenant as his or her wife or husband' was to be treated as a spouse. Prior to the *Human Rights Act*, the House of Lords had held that the amendment did not cover a homosexual couple. That view was reversed by majority in *Ghaidan*. Lord Nicholls identified two questions: first, whether the amendment drew a distinction on the grounds of sexual orientation so as to infringe the applicant's Convention rights and, secondly, if so, whether the amendment could be 'read and given effect to' so as to comply with the Convention. The first question was unanimously answered in the affirmative; the second question was affirmed by majority. Lord Nicholls found no 'justification for the difference in treatment of homosexual and heterosexual couples' and held that the court's 'role is one of review' but 'it will reach a different conclusion from the legislature only when it is apparent that the legislature has attached insufficient importance to a person's Convention rights'.[21]

Lord Millett's dissent emphasised the words 'read and given effect to' as showing that the court's function was one of interpretation, not legislation.[22] He asserted that '[i]t must be possible, by a process of interpretation alone, to read the offending statute in a way which is compatible with the Convention'. Accordingly, 'the court must take the language of the statute as it finds it and give it a meaning which, however unnatural or unreasonable, is intellectually defensible ... But it is not entitled to give it an impossible [interpretation] however much it would wish to do so.'[23]

It is difficult to attribute a merely interpretative function to s 3(1). The 'cardinal constitutional principle', as Lord Nicholls has described it, is that 'the will of Parliament is expressed in the language used by it in its enactments'.[24] But the courts of the UK are required to exercise a new role which, his Lordship said 'is fundamentally different from interpreting and applying legislation'.[25] The difference has inspired Professor Conor Gearty in writing *Principles of Human Rights Adjudication* to propose broad principles of civil liberties, legality and respect for human dignity in order to answer 'the myriad of questions raised by this unique piece of British legislation'.

The cases under the *Human Rights Act* reveal the UK's reliance on the decisions of the Strasbourg court[26] to determine the scope of the human rights defined in the European Convention and they show dramatically that, in applying the Convention domestically, the courts will depart from the purpose of the legislature as revealed by a purposive interpretation of the text if the legislature has given insufficient importance to a person's Convention rights. It is arguable – I hesitate to put it any higher – that these considerations warrant considerable caution in accepting UK precedent relating to human rights in the interpretation of Victorian statutory provisions. Let me reiterate, however, the importance of determining the meaning and operation of the Charter only by and after due judicial process.

Canadian authority

The *Canadian Charter of Rights and Freedoms* is, of course, part of the *Canadian Constitution*.[27] Dickson CJC observed that '[i]n Canada, we have tempered parliamentary supremacy by entrenching important rights and freedoms in the Constitution'.[28] In determining the constitutional validity of Canadian laws, the question arises under s 1 of the Charter whether a statute which infringes a Charter right goes beyond 'such reasonable limits prescribed by law as can be demonstrably justified in a free and democratic society.' That is not a mere question of interpretation. The Court has to determine 'which government objectives are of sufficient importance to warrant overriding a constitutionally protected right or freedom'.[29] The answer to that question is not dictated by the terms of the statute under review; the Court must make a value judgment. That is a different function from attempting to give effect to a statute conformably, if possible, with defined human rights.

In construing the rights and freedoms protected by the *Canadian Charter*, Dickson J pointed out in *Hunter v Southam* that: 'The task of expounding a constitution is crucially different from that of construing a statute ...[A constitution] must be capable of growth and development over time to meet new social, political and historical realities often unimagined by its framers.'[30]

The Supreme Court views the provisions of the Charter as 'a living tree capable of growth and expansion within its natural limits',[31] a metaphor used by the Privy Council to support a dynamic interpretation of federal powers under the *BNA Act*.[32] Whether the metaphor is appropriate to the interpretation of rights and freedoms that are restrictive of legislative power has been questioned.[33] The Court has rejected decisions under the statutory Bill of Rights which preceded the Charter as binding authority in interpreting the Charter.[34] In performing its constitutional function, the Supreme Court often draws on US authority. These factors may justify some caution in applying Canadian decisions to the Victorian Act.

New Zealand

The *Bill of Rights Act 1990* (NZ) is not part of a written Constitution. Although s 1 affirms the rights and freedoms contained in the Act, s 4 denies that any inconsistency with its provisions impliedly repeals, revokes, invalidates or makes ineffective any enactment or makes its provisions inapplicable. But s 6 provides that a meaning consistent with the statutory rights and freedoms is to be preferred if the enactment 'can be given' that meaning. This provision is radically different from the UK provision, for it 'only authorises consistent meanings that can be "reasonably" or "properly" given, or that are "fairly open" and "tenable". Conversely, it does not authorise a "strained interpretation" or authorise a Court to "legislate".'[35]

Parliamentary sovereignty is maintained, as it is under the Victorian Charter. In this context it is curious that the Act, reproducing s 1 of the *Canadian Charter*, purports to limit infringement of protected rights and freedoms to what can be "demonstrably justified in a free and democratic society" (s 5). The interaction of these provisions was explained by Tipping J:

> if there are two tenable meanings, the one which is most in harmony with the Bill of Rights must be adopted. Section 5 when read with s 6 fulfils a similar role. An enactment which limits the rights and freedoms contained in the Bill of Rights should be given such tenable meaning and application as constitutes the least possible limitation. Where an unjustified and unreasonable limitation nevertheless results, because no other meaning or application is tenable, such limitation, while constituting a breach of s 5, nevertheless prevails by dint of s 4.[36]

Thus, the regime prescribed by the New Zealand Act is neither constitutional nor affected by the factors which account for the jurisprudence of the English and Canadian courts. Moreover, the social conditions of New Zealand may seem attractively similar to the social conditions in which the Victorian Charter operates. The decisions of New Zealand courts may prove to be of more assistance than the decisions of courts of other nations. However, the decision in *Baigent's Case*[37] illustrates the differences between jurisdictions in their approach to charters of rights. There the Court of Appeal held that there is a public law remedy which may sound in damages against the Crown – albeit not a remedy in tort – for infringement of the statutorily protected human rights. Section 39(3) of the Victorian Charter denies such a remedy.

Other jurisdictions

The cases decided by the European Court of Human Rights cover the spectrum of human rights under the European Convention and examine numerous situations in which the Convention rights are invoked. Its careful methodology can be seen in decisions such as *Odievre* v *France*[38] in which the Grand Chamber examined the history of the French provisions for anonymity in the adoption of children. The Annual Report of the European Court contains a useful survey of the cases decided in the year under review.

Hong Kong is a jurisdiction in which the courts are accustomed to the citation of authority on human rights from other jurisdictions. Although Hong Kong has been, since 1 July 1997, a Special Administrative Region of the People's Republic of China, the *Bill of Rights Ordinance*,[39] which was in force prior to that date,[40] was continued in force by the Basic Law[41]– in effect, the Hong Kong Constitution. It provides for the implementation of the *International Covenant on Civil and Political Rights* by local law.[42] Thus the human rights which are protected by Hong Kong law have constitutional force[43] and are applied by the Court of Final Appeal in determining the validity and operation of domestic statutes.[44]

Declarations of inconsistency

A declaration of inconsistency with a human right can be made only in a proceeding in which a question of law arises relating to the application of the Charter or the interpretation of a statutory provision in accordance with the Charter.[45] The jurisdiction to make such a declaration is conferred only on the Supreme Court, either in proceedings in that Court or on a reference under s 33 by another court or by a tribunal.[46] To adapt the interpretation of the now repealed s 40A of the *Judiciary Act 1903* (Cth), such a question arises if and when it appears that judgment cannot be pronounced without a decision being given upon the question, but 'it is immaterial that the possibility has not been exhausted of deciding other questions in such a way that a judgment may be pronounced which will dispose of the cause without the [Charter] question having had to be decided.'[47]

If a reference is made under s 33, the court or tribunal must not make a determination while the referral is pending.[48]

The Attorney-General and the Human Rights Commission are entitled to notice of proceedings in the Supreme Court if a Charter question arises there or there is a s 33 reference. The Attorney is given a right to intervene if a Charter question arises in any other court or tribunal. If the Attorney intervenes, he may be taken to be a party to any appeal. If the Supreme Court is considering the making of a declaration of inconsistency, it must ensure that proper notice is given to the Attorney and the Commission.

A declaration of inconsistency does not create any legal right, give rise to any civil cause of action or affect in any way the validity, operation or enforcement of the relevant statutory provision. It does impose an obligation on the relevant Minister to make a response, lay it before the Parliament and publish it in the Gazette. An issue that will arise if a declaration of inconsistency is being considered is the operation of s 7(2). If the court is satisfied that the relevant human right is limited in conformity with the requirements of that subsection, a declaration of inconsistency with an unlimited human right seems hardly justified. If that is correct, the scope of a human right relied on must be determined in the light of s 7(2) when it is being taken into account in interpreting a statutory provision under s 32.

Jurisdictional issues

As a law of Victoria, the Charter must be given effect by all Australian courts and tribunals under the full faith and credit clause of the *Constitution*.[49] Thus when, for example, a Victorian statute is relied on in proceedings in the Federal Court, that Court will necessarily construe the statute in accordance with s 32 of the Charter. If that Court did not find it possible to construe the statute consistently with the Charter, it could not make a declaration of inconsistency under s 36. Rather, it would be for that Court to resolve whether it could and should, in its federal jurisdiction, make a declaration in similar terms. There would be a question whether an application for such a declaration would constitute a 'matter' within the meaning of Chapter III of the *Constitution*.

In the event of the Attorney-General or a party seeking to appeal to the High Court from the making of a declaration of inconsistency, there would be a preliminary question whether the subject of the appeal would constitute a 'matter'. Professor Geoffrey Lindell favours the view that it does[50] but, if there be no issue affecting the rights, duties or liabilities of the parties, the question is not beyond argument. In a sense, such an appeal would be collateral to the issues in the litigation. However, even if the High Court were to hold that an appeal against a declaration of inconsistency did not constitute a 'matter' within Chapter III of the *Constitution*, that Court will no doubt be entertaining appeals in which the effect of the Charter on the interpretation of Victorian statutory provisions will be in issue. A new era of litigation has opened up.

Conclusion

The *Charter of Human Rights and Responsibilities 2006* (Vic) is not without its difficulties. It will call for a knowledge of, if not a familiarity with, a huge and ever-growing literature, a critical appreciation of differences among collateral jurisdictions and a sensitivity to social conditions. It will be an intellectually challenging journey, similar to but not identical with the journey which has been travelled by judges in other western democracies. In blazing a parallel path for Australian jurisprudence, I wish you well.

---

1. The edited paper was first published at (2007) 81 *Australian Law Journal* 248.
2. [2007] VSC 2
3. Beverley McLachlin B, 'Southey Memorial Lecture: The Canadian Charter and the Democratic Process' (1991) 18(2) Melbourne *University Law Review* 350, 355.
4. See William Brennan, 'Why have a Bill of Rights? (1989) 9 *Oxford Journal of Legal Studies* 425, 434-435.
5. Judge Learned Hand, 'Mr Justice Cardozo' (1939) 52 *Harvard Law Review* 361.
6. See *Report of the Human Rights Consultation Committee*, Recommendation 6; see Second Reading Speech – Victoria, *Parliamentary Debates*, Legislative Assembly, 4 May 2006, 1291 Mr Hulls, Attorney-General).
7. See *Cole v Whitfield* (1988) 165 CLR 360.
8. Ibid 384.
9. See *Charter of Human Rights and Responsibilities Act 2006* (Vic), s 1(2)(b), (c).
10. Ibid s 1(2)(e).
11. See *CIC Insurance Ltd v Bankstown Football Club Ltd* (1997) 187 CLR 384, 408.
12. Conor Gearty, *Principles of human rights adjudication* (Oxford University Press, 2004) 24.
13. See *Re Bolton; Ex parte Beane* (1987) 162 CLR 514, 523; *Potter v Minahan* (1908) 7 CLR 277, 304; *Wheeler v Leicester City Council* [1985] AC 1054 at 1065; *Nationwide News Pty Ltd v Wills* (1992) 177 CLR 1, 43.
14. See *Chu Keng Lim v Minister for Immigration, Local Government & Ethnic Affairs* (1992) 176 CLR 1, 38.
15. See *Koowarta v Bjelke-Petersen* (1982) 153 CLR 168, 265. Whether this meaning is to be ascertained in accordance with *Vienna Convention on the Law of Treaties*, Art 31, or

in accordance with a domestic *Interpretation Act* may not be settled: see *Applicant A v Minister for Immigration & Ethnic Affairs* (1997) 190 CLR 225, 252 fn 93 (McHugh J).

16. [2004] 2 AC 557, 574 [42]; [2004] UKHL 30.
17. Ibid 575 [44]-[46].
18. See *R v Director of Public Prosecutions; Ex parte Kebeline* [2000] 2 AC 326, 374-375 (emphasis added).
19. [2002] 1 AC 45,86; [2001] UKHL 25.
20. Ibid 67 [44].
21. Ibid 564, 568 [7], [18], [19].
22. Ibid 579 [63].
23. Ibid 580 [66], [67].
24. See *Wilson v First County Trust [No 2]* [2004] 1 AC 816, 843 [67] (sub nom *Wilson v Secretary of State for Trade & Industry* [2003] UKHL 40.
25. See *Wilson v First County Trust [No 2]* [2004] 1 AC 816, 842 [61].
26. European Court of Human Rights.
27. See *Constitution Act 1982* (UK); enacted as Sch B to the *Canada Act 1982* (UK), Ch 11.
28. See *Wilson v First County Trust [No 2]* [2004] 1 AC 816, 838 [39].
29. See *R v Big M Drug Mart Ltd* [1985] 1 SCR 295, 352 [40]; (1985) 18 DLR (3d) 321.
30. [1984] 2 SCR 145, 155 [17].
31. See *Gosselin v Quebec* [2002] 4 SCR 429 at [82]; (2002) 221 DLR (4th) 257 McLachlin CJC, citing *Edwards v Attorney General of Canada* [1930] AC 123, 144-145 (Sankey).
32. See *British North America Act 1867* (UK) (now the *Constitution Act 1982* (UK)).
33. Robert Sharpe, 'The Impact of a Bill of Rights on the Role of the Judiciary: A Canadian Perspective' in Philip Alston (ed), *Promoting Human Rights through Bills of Rights* (Oxford University Press, 1999) 438; Grant Huscroft, 'The Trouble with Living Tree Interpretation' (2006) 25(1) *University of Queensland Law Journal* 3.
34. See *R v Oakes* [1986] 1 SCR 103, [38]; (1986) 26 DLR (4th) 200.
35. See *Hansen v The Queen* [2005] NZCA 220, [23] (citations of authority omitted).
36. See *Moonen v Film and Literature Board of Review [No 1]* [2000] 2 NZLR 9; [1999] NZCA 329 (17 December 1999); see also the comment on Tipping J's 'five step approach' in *Moonen v Film and Literature Board of Review [No 2]* [2002] 2 NZLR 754; [2002] NZCA 69.
37. See *Simpson v Attorney-General* [1994] 3 NZLR 667.
38. See *Odievre v France* [2003] ECHR 86.
39. *Hong Kong Bill of Rights Ordinance 1991*, Cap 383.
40. For the history of the period before 1997, see A Byrnes, 'The Experience of Hong Kong's Bill of Rights' in Philip Alston (ed) *Promoting Human Rights through Bills of Rights* (Oxford University Press, 1999) 318.
41. Basic Law, Arts 8, 18; see *Re Kong Wah Holdings Ltd* [2004] HKCFI 865, [39]; [2005] HKEC 780.
42. See *Hong Kong Bill of Rights Ordinance*, s 8.
43. See, inter alia, *So Wai Lun v HKSAR* [2006] HKCFA 68; [2006] 3 HKLRD 394.
44. For an example of Hong Kong's consideration of the ICCPR, see the *Flag Desecration case*: *HKSAR v Ng Kung-siu* (1999) 2 HKCFAR 442; [1999] 3 HKLRD 907; [2000] 1 HKC 1.

45. See *Charter of Human Rights and Responsibilities Act 2006* (Vic), ss 33(1), 36(1)(a), (c).
46. Ibid s 36(1), (2).
47. See *Lansell v Lansell* (1964) 110 CLR 353 (Kitto J). This interpretation was driven by a 'high policy' of reserving for the jurisdiction of the High Court the solution of inter se questions (at 358 per Kitto J). A similar policy of reserving Charter questions to the Supreme Court can be seen in s 33.
48. See *Charter of Human Rights and Responsibilities Act 2006* (Vic), s 33(2).
49. Ibid s 118.
50. Geoffrey Lindell, 'The statutory protection of rights and parliamentary sovereignty: Guidance from the United Kingdom?' (2006) 17 *Public Law Review* 188, 204 et seq.

Chapter 4

Administrative Law Reform

4.1 The Challenges of Administrative Law Reform

Editor's note

Brennan was appointed the first President of the Administrative Appeals Tribunal (AAT) and the first President of the Administrative Review Council (ARC) on 1 July 1976. He was appointed a founding judge of the Federal Court of Australia which commenced on 1 February 1977. Increasingly, he found a conflict in the roles and was convinced that the new conceptual thinking required to shape the new administrative law would take place in Federal Court appeals rather than through the initial rulings of the AAT. He also found the workload and strain on family unbearable. He had known Michael Kirby well since their days together on the Australian Law Reform Commission (1975-1977). Kirby had urged him to maintain his roles on the AAT and the ARC. On 2 September 1979, he wrote this letter to Kirby explaining the reasons for his decision to resign from the AAT and the ARC which he then did, being replaced by Daryl Davies on 1 December 1979. The letter highlights the tensions between judicial and political aspects of administrative law reform.

Administrative Review Council

GPO Box 9955

Canberra 2600

President

The Hon. Mr Justice F G Brennan

2 September 1979

Dear Michael

It is Sunday evening, and I have spent the weekend cogitating on the views you expressed and the advice you gave me on Friday, respecting my future work. I am aware – I hope, not boastfully – that I have been able to contribute something of value to the new administrative law system, and I am acutely aware that that system (particularly the AAT part of it) is not only important now, but will be so important in the future that it can carry democracy in a complex society into the 21st century. It involves a resettlement of powers, and a shift of power from the executive to the judiciary. So I have no illusions as to the importance of the work on which I am engaged in the AAT/ARC.

The new system can be brought to its full fruition, however, only by the political decisions to shift power in the several areas of jurisdiction. Those decisions will be made in the light of the statutory and judicially imposed function of the AAT. I have, with one exception, chartered the dimension of the tribunal's function, and laid down the manner of its exercise: its procedures are firmly in the curial mould, adversarial in form to the extent needed to allow the tribunal to form an impartial and detached judgment, canvassing the whole of the elements of the decision – law no less than fact, and asserting a power over policy. Expertise is drawn on, but does not dominate decision-making; the parties are masters of their own cases, and if any would say that the atmosphere is too court like, none will assert that they have not been fully heard and fairly treated. The one exception to the judicial formation of the tribunal, I am about to deal with, viz, the way in which the tribunal will exercise its power to review policy: the rehearing of *Drake's case* is listed before me on 24 September.[1] (Needless to say, I hope for good argument on this).

The further major developments depend upon the political decisions of government and the bureaucracy: who shall be given the power and who shall be subject to its exercise? What resources will be provided? I have lately been seeking the jurisdictions which Parliament (Export Grants) and the Executive (Social Security) have said the AAT is to have, but to do so is to engage in a kind of lobbying – discreet and proper lobbying, but lobbying nonetheless. I've been seeking power which I and my tribunal are to exercise. This is not judicial activity, and soon the ARC will want to protest the non-vesting of jurisdiction (unless the members of the ARC, solicitous for the present powers and procedures of the bureaucracy, prevail upon their fellow council members to cry off the hunt).

Work of the court, on the other hand, is judicial – which is not to say non-constructive. In *Heffernan*[2], the court's decision was sought on appeal from the AAT before amending legislation was introduced; in *Drake*[3] the court confirmed (as *Becker*[4] could not confirm, though it could assert) the AAT's policy powers; in *Brian Lawler*,[5] the definition of powers in jurisdictional questions is to be found in the court's judgments, not in mine; in *Sullivan*,[6] the measure of the obligation to state reasons is derived from the ancillary judgment (not a slighting reference) of Fisher J. The work of judicial, as distinct from political, development of the tribunal rests with the court. Moreover, the development of the court itself is a task which I have taken some part in. Its manner of proceeding and the quality of its work are a source of some satisfaction, and the creation of a viable federal judiciary – viable in the sense of professional and public acceptability – is a task worthy of some effort.

Hitherto, I have tried to combine these activities as you know. And in addition, to give some supervision to the ARC and to write or speak on topics in which the audience has an interest directed to the new judicial activity in administration. It has reached the stage now where it is impossible to continue these masses of activities.

When we met on Friday, I did not speak to any extent of the burden which all of this is placed on my family. They were subjected to the disruption of the move to Canberra – not that it was unwelcome in general, though some of the children disliked it, and the sheer physical task was immense. Since then, Patricia and the children who have been at home have had me as an occasional husband and father. Others have had holidays free of care, ours have been abbreviated and marked by my preoccupations and punctuated by interruptions. Frequent travel was accepted, but constant exhaustion and preoccupation with problems –most of them of an administrative or political kind – has been a burden which should not have been borne. For the last 18 months, I have been begged by the children away from home to change the family's lifestyle. I thought that the family and I simply had to bear it, but that decision was wrong. They and I are exhausted.

So, I have to choose: Court or AAT? Judiciary or politics? The latter is more exciting, but at base I love the law and the work of the courts. When I was first approached, I made it a condition of appointment that I should have commissions to the Supreme Courts of the Territories. I was unwilling to part from the curial disciplines, and it would not have been wise to do so. I feel the dissipation of curial skills and welcome an opportunity to regenerate them.

You may say that I have chosen the wrong option. I do not think so, for the flag which you accuse me of deserting is one to be kept at the masthead by politicians and bureaucrats – those who have the power which is the subject of transfer to the AAT. It is not to be kept there by the judges.

The power may be only nominally transferred, if the AAT is restricted to recommendations, or if its procedures so approximate the administrative procedures that the primary decision maker can perceive no basic difference. Neither of these courses commend themselves to me, yet the recent discussions on AAT procedures, the comments on the cost, the querying of the basic notions of AAT review make it clear that the political/bureaucratic reaction is in full swing. The solution is political. I have said what can be said. I do not have the talent or the stomach for controversy at that level. But most importantly, I will not compromise my judicial work in order to keep the political ring.

Two weeks ago, I found myself doing just that. Judgments were not being written, or not written well. It is time to change. I'm sorry to have taken so much of your time to explain my own ratiocinations, but be assured that this a*pologia pro vita mea* was inspired by your comments and advice. I am grateful for your provoking me to state the reasons for an action which I am sure is right.

If I must bear the criticism of deserting that which I have largely formed, of neglecting the creature of my efforts, I shall do so with sadness. But I trust that you will accept that the decision is made – whether right or wrong – with as much care as I can devote to it.

I know I'm quite unmoved by any thoughts of consolidating my personal position on the Federal Court, and you may put that matter aside.

Thank you for seeing me – your stimulus is ever as welcome as your friendship.

Sincerely,

Gerard Brennan

---

1. The original hearing was *Drake and Minister for Immigration and Ethnic Affairs* (1979) 2 ALD 60. Brennan conducted the rehearing: *Drake and Minister for Immigration and Ethnic Affairs (No 2) (*1979) 2 ALD 634.
2. The original AAT decision is *Heffernan and Defence Force Retirement and Death Benefits Authority* (1978) 1 ALD 220. The Federal Court decision *is Defence Force Retirement and Death Benefits Authority & Another v Heffernan* [1978] FCA 63.
3. See *Drake v Minister for Immigration and Ethnic Affairs (*1979) 24 ALR 577.
4. See *Becker and Minister for Immigration and Ethnic Affairs* (1977) 1 ALD 158.
5. Brennan's decision in the AAT is *Brian Lawler Automative Pty Ltd and Collector of Customs, New South Wales* (1979) 2 ALD 1. The Federal Court decision is *Collector of Customs, New South Wales v Brian Lawler Automative Pty Ltd* (1979) 24 ALR 307.
6. See *Sullivan, Delegate of the Secretary Department of Transport* [1978] FCA 48.

4.2 Review on the Merits: A New Frontier or Beyond the Pale?

Editor's note

Having been the first President of the Administrative Appeals Tribunal and the first Chair of the Administrative Review Council, Brennan was then a foundation judge of the Federal Court before being appointed to the High Court in February 1981.He was invited to address the annual Supreme Court Judges Conference in Canberra in January 1983. By this time the conference was being attended by Judges from the Supreme Courts and the Federal Court. He took the opportunity to look back on the introduction of the administrative law reforms and to highlight some of the unresolved issues.

This paper is to speak of current problems, not current solutions, in Administrative Law. And so, I am relieved of responsibility for furnishing solutions to the problems I shall mention.[1] An important problem, perhaps the most important, arises from the involvement of judges in reviewing administrative decisions on the merits. I had the privilege of participating in the establishment of the Administrative Appeals Tribunal (the AAT), and the problems posed by the exercise of its jurisdiction may be of assistance in charting the course of future judicial activity in the field of administrative law. Judicial involvement in administration has increased for a number of reasons, and the proper role of the judiciary is not easy to determine. The importance of the subject is hard to overstate. The rights and obligations of individuals have come to depend increasingly upon the exercise of powers and discretions by the executive government and its officers. The worth of the title to *Blackacre* has become a function of planning permission; freedom of contract has been hedged about with proscriptions enacted to safeguard the public interest, exemption from the operation of which must be sought from a public functionary who is a stranger to the contract; the production of a farm is affected by quotas; the price and competitiveness of an imported article is determined largely by its tariff; the use of capital is affected by several provisions relating to internal and foreign trade; entitlement to benefits or bounties depends upon administrative decision.

In 1971 the Kerr Committee noted:

> In recent times in Australia, as in other countries, there has been a considerable expansion in the range of activities regulated, and in the volume and range of services provided, by government and

> statutory authorities for the benefit of the public. This expansion has been accompanied, as it must be, by a substantial increase in the powers and discretions conferred by statute on Ministers of the Crown, officers of the administration and statutory authorities. The exercise of these powers and discretions involves the making of a vast range of decisions and recommendations which affect the individual citizen in many aspects of his daily life. [2]

The list of administrative controls and activities is large and expanding. The law and its institutions, which have coped so well with many of the problems of property, must be made to cope well with the problems of the exercise of administrative power. In the 1964 Hamlyn Lectures, Lord Scarman said:

> To satisfy the conscience of the nation the state has had to move into the empty spaces of the law, the deserts and hill country left uncultivated by distributive justice, and there to make provision for society as a whole, and for those not strong enough to provide for themselves. Thus the welfare state is challenging the relevance, or at least the adequacy, of the common law's concepts and classifications. Fault, trespass, property, even marriage, are now seen to be an insecure base for the development of a law suited to the needs of our society.[3]

The legal framework of the welfare, or regulated, state is extra-ordinarily complex and its statutory provisions are frequently ill-drafted or in a sad condition of statutory disrepair. The administrators are not, for the most part, trained lawyers. In theory, however, administrative decisions are subject to scrutiny to ensure that they are properly made. In theory the exercise of administrative power (other than that reposed in independent administrative boards) is subject to ministerial control, and a chain of responsibility exists: Administrator to Minister to Parliament. When the exercise of a power bears significantly upon the community at large, political structures are often effective to supervise its exercise. But neither Parliament nor the upper echelons of government has time or opportunity to supervise effectively the large volume of decision-making which, though it may be of great importance to individuals, has little political significance. The reality is that powers affecting a broad spectrum of activities are vested in administrators who are substantially immune from scrutiny in the particular exercise of that power.

The perception of a divergence between the Westminster theory of government and the absence in practice, of ministerial responsibility for much departmental decision-making led Lord Scarman to urge: 'a new constitutional settlement that makes use of judicial power…to use the rule of law in resolving the conflicts that will arise between the citizen and the state in the newly developed fields of administrative-legal activity upon which the quality of life in the society of the twentieth century already depends.'[4]

The public confidence in judges and the judicial process explains in part the suggestion that judges should move into the areas for which ministers are not in truth responsible or which they are unable to scrutinize effectively. But the late Professor de Smith, it will be remembered, delivered a warning about unrestricted judicial review:

> Judicial review of administrative action is inevitably sporadic and peripheral. The administrative process is not, and cannot be, a succession of justiciable controversies. Public authorities are set up to govern and administer, and if their every act or decision were to be reviewable on unrestricted grounds by an independent judicial body the business of administration could be brought to a standstill. The prospect of judicial relief cannot be held out to every person whose interests may be adversely affected by administrative action.[5]

From the viewpoint of the judiciary, the expansion of the traditional administrative law caseload already poses a problem of resources: judges, registry, courtrooms, court reporters. To some extent, the technicalities of the old prerogative writs helped to keep the flood of litigation to a trickle, but the statutory simplification of procedures in some jurisdictions has facilitated access to the courts in administrative cases.

In the United Kingdom, Order 53 of the Rules of the Supreme Court was redrawn in 1977 to provide for applications for judicial review in lieu of mandamus, prohibition, certiorari or a statutory form of quo warranto; in *Victoria the Administrative Law Act 1978* (Vic) achieved much the same result; and the *Administrative Decisions (Judicial Review) Act 1977* (Cth) (hereafter the '*ADJR*' *Act*) created a new system of judicial review of Commonwealth administrative decisions supplementary to the Constitutional jurisdiction of the High Court. In the opinion of some commentators, the *ADJR Act* modified the traditional grounds for granting prerogative writs. These reforms seem to be generally accepted as beneficial. But it is noteworthy that the United Kingdom and Victorian reforms contain a significant barrier, to be overcome before the application can be made. Order 53 r 3 requires the leave of the court to be obtained before an application for judicial review is made. The application for leave is made on affidavit and may be determined by a judge without a hearing. Under the Victorian Act, an order for review (the modern counterpart of the order nisi) is made ex parte on affidavit and may be refused if the court or judge is satisfied 'that no matter of substantial importance is involved or that .... such refusal will impose no substantial injustice upon the applicant' (s 4). There is no similar barrier in the *ADJR Act*. I do not suggest that there should be one, or that such a barrier, if created, should apply to all applications. However, by raising the level of professional awareness of, and familiarity with, the procedure for seeking judicial review the new laws will probably lead to a large increase in administrative law litigation. That seems to be the emerging pattern in the Federal Court of Australia. In 1981, 84 applications were filed seeking an order under the *ADJR Act*; in 1982 (to mid-December) 145 applications were filed. Whether some screening procedure should be introduced is a problem which may arise, but it will be a difficult problem to solve if the screening criterion were to require more than the showing of a prima facie case. But. if a right of appeal to a quasi-judicial tribunal exists or if there is a right of appeal from such a tribunal to a court, it may be reasonable to exclude judicial review unless special circumstances are shown.

Although resource problems may follow upon the simplification of the procedure for obtaining judicial review, those problems are not as grave as they would be if the judiciary were empowered generally to review administrative decisions on the merits. This is, of course, the jurisdiction of the AAT with respect to the administrative powers specified in the enactments which confer its jurisdiction. The AAT has now been in existence for 61 years and its experience is at once an indicator of the need for – or, if there be a difference, the popularity of judicial review on the merits, and an indicator of problems which such a jurisdiction brings in its train.

A brief conspectus of its origins, jurisdiction and workload will aid in explaining some of the problems to which this innovative institution has given rise. The AAT is one of the elements in the new federal administrative review structure for which statutory provision has been made during the last seven years. The AAT and the ARC,[6] were brought into existence pursuant to the *Administrative Appeals Tribunal Act 1975* (Cth). The AAT came into existence on 1 July 1976. The next element was the office of the Commonwealth Ombudsman, created by the *Ombudsman Act 1976* (Cth). Professor Richardson was appointed on 1 July 1977. This was followed by the passing of the ADJR Act in 1977, though the Act (as amended) did not come into force until October 1980. Finally, the *Freedom of Information Act 1982* (Cth) came into force in December 1982.

The new administrative review structure seeks to strike a balance between the purposive activity of the bureaucracy and the individual interests of the citizen. It provides, independently of the executive, for three kinds of review in respect of most Commonwealth administrative decisions: judicial review by the Federal Court to ensure that administrative decisions have been made in accordance with law;[7] administrative review by the AAT on the merits;[8] and review by the Ombudsman who, though not empowered to change an administrative decision, has been given a wide-ranging jurisdiction to investigate and to report upon complaints of maladministration in practically all areas of federal administration.[9] The jurisdiction of the High Court to grant relief by way of a writ of mandamus or prohibition or an injunction against an officer of the Commonwealth[10] remains unaffected by the new legislation.

Perhaps the most revolutionary step,[11] a step for which there was no precedent elsewhere in the common law world, was the creation of the AAT. Pursuant to ss 25 and 26 of its Act, the AAT has jurisdiction to review decisions made in the exercise of powers conferred by particular enactments. [12] Though the number of such enactments continues to grow, a relatively small group of statutes has accounted for the bulk of the cases.[13]

Statistics showing the caseload of the AAT over the period from 1976-1977 to 1981-1982 are attached as Appendix A. These show an enormous increase in the number of applications for review in the last two years, arising from the extension of the jurisdiction of the AAT to the review of decisions made by the Director-General of Social Security and decisions made by the Commissioner for (Commonwealth) Employees' Compensation.[14] This explosion in the AAT's caseload raises a problem not merely of the burden of litigation but of the role of the AAT. How is a duplicate bureaucracy to be avoided? In part the answer is pragmatic: only a proportion of reviewable decisions actually give rise to a review. In part the problem is self-solving because of the normative effect of AAT decisions on primary administration. When jurisdiction was originally conferred on the AAT to review the triennial valuation of land in the Australian Capital Territory for rating purposes, a large number of ratepayers applied for review. The valuation system was significantly altered as the result of AAT review. There were substantially fewer applications for review in the next triennium. In part the solution is structural. An application to the AAT initiates an intra-departmental review and, if grounds of dissatisfaction persist, the AAT arranges a preliminary conference.[15] It is not unusual for such a conference, together with a statement of reasons, to give entire satisfaction to a dissatisfied citizen.

The AAT is not itself a primary decision-maker. It is not the original repository of powers and discretions under an enactment.[16] Nor are its powers limited to assisting or advising an administrator in making a decision. It has power, in most cases,[17] to affirm the decision under review, to vary it: to set it aside and substitute its own decision in lieu, or to remit it to the primary administrator with or without directions or recommendations.[18] These powers are exercisable not only in respect of a decision of the primary administrator made in a valid exercise of his powers, but also in respect of a decision made in purported – albeit invalid – exercise of his powers.[19] And so the jurisdiction vested in the AAT allows it to give forthwith the relief which might otherwise be obtained only by judicial review and further consideration by the original decision-maker. The AAT jurisdiction is thus a useful complement to the jurisdiction of the Federal Court under the ADJR Act.

Though the AAT has a number of curial features,[20] its powers, conformably with constitutional constraints,[21] are administrative, not judicial.[22] But it exercises its power in the place of and independently of the primary administrator. It hears the case de novo, without any presumption as to the correctness of the decision under review.[23] The question facing the AAT is not whether the decision of the primary administrator was the 'correct or preferable' one on the material before him. The question is whether that decision is the 'correct or preferable' one on the material before the AAT.[24]

In *Drake v Minister for Immigration and Ethnic Affairs*, Bowen CJ and Deane J pointed to the distinction between the function of the AAT in reviewing a decision and the traditional function of a court:

> In that review, the Tribunal is not restricted to consideration of the questions which are relevant to a judicial determination of whether a discretionary power allowed by statute has been validly exercised. Except in a case where only one decision can lawfully be made, it is not ordinarily part of the function of a court either to determine what decision should be made in the exercise of an administrative discretion in a given case or, where a decision has been lawfully made in pursuance of a permissible policy, to adjudicate upon the merits of the decision or the propriety of the policy. That is primarily an administrative rather than a judicial function. It is the function which has been entrusted to the Tribunal.[25]

In performing its functions, the AAT finds facts, applies the law and, in appropriate cases, exercises discretions. These are familiar enough functions for a judge, but the differences in the manner of performing these functions define some of the current problems of administrative law. If efficient decision-making by the AAT requires modification of, or even departure from, judicial techniques, what lessons may be learned? If judicial techniques are not effective for review of administrative decisions on the merits, either the courts ought not to accept a jurisdiction which requires the application of those techniques or, accepting the jurisdiction, the techniques will have to be modified or discarded. I use techniques here as a term descriptive of the ordinary course of curial procedure. The dichotomy is not absolute. Some areas of jurisdiction could be covered quite effectively without departure from curial techniques; some techniques can be, and are, modified or discarded in the course of ordinary litigation without affecting the effectiveness of the judicial process.

The obvious point, however, is that review on the merits of some classes of administrative decisions is not a jurisdiction which, constitutional limitations apart, the courts are ready willing and able to accept. To the extent to which the courts ought not, or do not, modify or discard the techniques presently employed, it will be necessary to vest jurisdiction to review on the merits in other tribunals. That is no novelty, but it is an important consideration when Parliaments wish to expose an increasing range of administrative decisions to review on the merits. It is also an important consideration in determining whether, and to what extent, the services of judges should be made available to constitute or to preside in tribunals in which such jurisdiction has been vested.

The techniques in which differences may be detected between the courts and the AAT may be considered under headings corresponding with the elements of a decision: fact, law and discretion.

Fact finding

The Tribunal is, of course, bound by the rules of natural justice. Apart from rare exceptions, it therefore -

- ensures that a party has notice of the case to be met;
- permits a party to confront and cross-examine opposing witnesses; and
- allows a party an opportunity to rebut the opposing case.

The second of these rules marks the clearest departure from the administrative to the judicial model. It is at the heart of the procedure by which conflicts of evidence or challenges to its truth are resolved. It is a curial procedure. Though one cannot predicate of every case that cross-examination must be permitted, in the kinds of cases with which the Tribunal has been dealing hitherto, it has not denied a party the opportunity to cross-examine.[26] Indeed it might be wrong to deny a party the right of cross-examination if there was no other way in which he might meet the opposition case.[27] However, the AAT is not bound by the rules of evidence, but may inform itself on any matter in such manner as it thinks appropriate.[28]

In several of the recent deportation cases the AAT has admitted material which, though relevant, would not have been admissible in a court of law, including 'Royal Commission reports, statistical material on migrant crime and oven a journalistic description of social conditions in Turkey'.[29] Its eventual decision must nevertheless be based on material which is logically probative.[30]

The 'adversarial' production and testing of evidence gives the-AAT a greater capacity than the primary administrator to resolve evidentiary conflicts and challenges. Fact finding is improved. But at a price. Where the decision is likely to affect the individual in a substantial way (for example, cases of deportation), the benefit of fully judicial fact finding justifies the cost involved. In other cases, the cost may be excessive and an abbreviated procedure for fact finding may be justified. The cost of fact finding was a point taken up by the President of the Constitutional Court of West Germany, Professor Dr W Zeidler, in his paper 'Evaluation of the Adversary System: As Comparison, Some Remarks on the Investigatory System of Procedure' which he concluded by saying 'Nowadays in Germany we tend to place the courts and their decision-making in the field of quasi-public utilities which means that in the final analysis the dispensing of substantive and procedural justice may in the end become a problem of 'finite judicial resources', or, to put it from another viewpoint, a problem of a limited availability of justice.'[31]

As the AAT is required to conduct its proceedings with as little formality and with as much expedition as the relevant legislation and the exigencies of the hearing permit,[32] the procedures are variable within certain limits. The AAT is developing flexible procedures (for example, preliminary hearings, telephone conferences) reflecting differences in the issues, in the importance of cases, and in the representation of the parties.[33]

Where specialist skills or knowledge are required, experts of distinction in their respective fields, are appointed as part-time ordinary members to sit on cases appropriate to their expertise.[34] Thus, experienced actuaries or officers of insurance companies are appointed to sit in cases where the licensing of insurance companies is in question; experienced aviators where questions of airmanship are involved; businessmen and retired senior administrators in cases of customs classification; and so forth.

Hitherto, the problems of fact-finding have not loomed large in judicial review; but in review on the merits the means of finding facts becomes a problem of central importance.

Application of the law

Power to decide any question of law arising in proceedings before it is a necessary concomitant of the AAT's power to review on the merits.[35] That an administrator may fall into error in defining his own function is quite understandable. Many of the enactments which it falls to the AAT to consider have rarely if ever been examined by a court. Moreover, both the pressure of administrative business and the administrator's isolation from legal advice may cause him to stumble from the path of statutory duty. The pursuit of a policy objective or a departmental guideline may tend to divert his steps entirely from that path.

An appeal on a question of law lies from the AAT to the Federal Court[36] and the AAT may, with the concurrence of its President, refer a question of law to that Court.[37] On the hearing of such an appeal or referral, a member of the Court who is also a presidential member of the AAT is frequently invited to sit.

By laying down general principles in the course of deciding particular cases, the AAT performs a normative function designed to guide primary administrators. Primary administration is thus more exposed to correction of legal error than it was when the only remedies were prerogative writs, injunctions or declarations. This role is, of course, eminently suited to the judiciary.

Discretion

It is in the formation of discretionary judgments that the AAT most clearly diverges in function from the curial model. Nowhere is this divergence more apparent than in cases where the discretion involves consideration of government policy. Discretions are conferred on administrators in order that they might balance the public interest against the individual interest, the desirability of consistency in the treatment of individuals against the ideal of justice in the individual case.[38] An independent exercise by the AAT of a discretion can ensure that the interests of an applicant are not unduly overridden by the objectives of government or its bureaucracy. Reciprocally, independence means that the objectives of government and its bureaucracy are susceptible to frustration by the AAT. How is the balance to be struck? When a case turns upon the application of a policy and the policy applied by the primary administrator is lawful, but the policy does not commend itself to the AAT, should the AAT apply that policy without question – as would seem to have been the expectation of both the Kerr and the Bland Committees[39] – or should it reject it, or should it give it some weight? And what is the appropriate weight?

These questions have arisen principally – and perhaps unfor-tunately[40] – in deportation cases.[41] In each case a statement of policy prepared under the direction of the Minister had been tendered in the AAT proceedings.[42] In *Drake v Minister for Immigration and Ethnic Affairs*, Bowen CJ and Deane J said:

> Where the tribunal is not under a statutory duty to regard itself as being bound by that policy, the Tribunal is entitled to treat such government policy as a relevant factor in the determination of an application for review of that decision ... On the other hand, the Tribunal is not, in the absence of specific statutory provision, entitled to abdicate its function of determining whether the decision made was, on the material before the Tribunal, the correct or preferable one in favour of a function of merely determining whether the decision made conformed with whatever the relevant general government policy might be.[43]

In the subsequent rehearing of *Drake's Case* before the AAT, I affirmed the Tribunal's independent statutory role:

> In fulfilling its function, the Tribunal, being independent of the Minister, is free to adopt reasoning entirely different from the reasoning which led to the making of the decision under review. But it is not bound to do so ...
>
> If the Tribunal applies ministerial policy, it is because of the assistance which the policy can furnish in arriving at the preferable decision in the circumstances of the case as they appear to the Tribunal.[44]

Under the Westminster system of government, however, a Minister is politically responsible to the parliament for the policy adopted to guide the exercise of his discretionary power, and so administrative policies – necessarily amenable to revocation or alteration on political grounds – are best formed and amended in a political context.[45] Substantial revocation or alteration of policy by the AAT would deny to Parliament its ability to supervise the content of the policy guiding the discretion which Parliament itself has created. Thus, it seemed to me that, notwithstanding the independence of the AAT from the executive, 'there are substantial reasons which favour only cautious and sparing departures from Ministerial policy, particularly if parliament has in fact scrutinized and approved that policy'.[46] Indeed the very independence of the AAT demands that it be apolitical:

> The Tribunal is not linked into the chain of responsibility from Minister to government to parliament, its membership is not appropriate for

> the formulation of broad policy and it is unsupported by a bureaucracy fitted to advise upon broad policy. It should therefore be reluctant to lay down broad policy, although decisions in particular cases will impinge on or refine broad policy emanating from a Minister.[47]

These considerations led me in *Re Drake (No 2)* to recommend the-adoption by the AAT of the following practice:

> When the tribunal is reviewing the exercise of a discretionary power reposed in a Minister, and the Minister has adopted a general policy to guide him in the exercise of the power, the Tribunal will ordinarily apply that policy in reviewing the decision, unless the policy is unlawful or unless its application tends to produce an unjust decision in the circumstances of the particular case. Where the policy would ordinarily be applied, an argument against the policy itself or against its application in the particular case will be considered, but cogent reasons will have to be shown against its application, especially if the policy is shown to have been exposed to parliamentary scrutiny.[48]

Not long after that statement was made a new deportation policy was promulgated by the Minister, and it was thought to be very severe in its application to all categories of drug offenders. My saving exception relating to an unjust decision in a particular case proved too pallid to satisfy a robust judiciary. Smithers J attacked the new policy head on. With characteristic vigour, he characterized the policy as 'Draconian' and 'oppressive'.[49] Later, Deane J was to describe the policy as 'callous'.[50] The policy has been given varying weight,[51] and it seems that the judges give such weight to the policy as it appears to deserve in the circumstances of the particular case.

Commenting on the trend emerging from the cases, Mr Justice Kirby (an ex officio member of the ARC and a perceptive critic of the system) said:

> The Federal Court in *Drake* declined to state any general rule as to how far the AAT should go in its review of clearly stated government policy. But if there are no clear limits in law, save those that must be drawn by inference from the nature and functions of the AAT, the scope of the AAT to question, criticize, elaborate, vary and depart from government policy, openly and lawfully stated is very great indeed.[52]

Mr Justice Kirby thought that the AAT may occasionally, by its reasoned judgment, lead officials and even Ministers to the point of modifying or even abandoning lawful and strongly held policy.[53] In a sense this has occurred with deportation policy, three separate policies having been produced in as many years, though the modifications therein became progressively more 'Draconian'. However, Mr Justice Kirby considered that more frequently:

'the response is likely to be a frustration with the AAT, a feeling that it has over-stepped the – proper bounds of an unelected body and a determination to retaliate either by limiting its jurisdiction to inconsequential matters (largely free of policy) or even, in the migration area, by rejecting its decisions, framed as they are in the form of a recommendation.'[54]

It is in the area of policy, of course, that the surefooted judicial process is left behind and judges find themselves without adequate guidance. This is an area into which judges do not seek entry. And yet there are many – classes of administrative decisions which, though involving some policy element, call for the employment of judicial skills in fact-finding and legal analysis. Some classes of administrative decisions are clearly suitable for submission to judges for determination; some classes are, equally clearly, unsuitable. When the conditions governing the exercise of administrative power are precisely defined by the statute which creates the power, the issues which fall to be decided are indistinguishable from the issues which a court would determine in the ordinary exercise of the judicial function. The several Taxation Boards of Review are engaged day by day in the construction and application of the *Income Tax Assessment Act 1936* (Cth). The questions which the AAT determines as to the classification of imports and the application of the customs tariff are questions which used to be litigated before the High Court. Clearly enough, judicial techniques are applicable and appropriate to cases of this kind. A relaxation of the hearsay rule might be entirely consistent with judicial techniques.

Where an administrative decision turns principally on questions of fact or law – and a large proportion of decisions do so turn[55] – the practice of the curial virtues most securely guarantees an improvement in administrative justice. And who better to practice the curial virtues than judges, long accustomed to standing, independent and detached, between the citizen and the State, between the weak and the powerful; to maintaining the unique dignity of the individual?

But does the judiciary possess the experience and skills which might accord fair weight to the public purposes to be served by administrative decision-making? And does the assumption of that function expose the institution of the judiciary to risk by requiring it to make judgments by political rather than legal criteria, by political or economic sentiment rather than by the high technique which has been the hallmark of judicial activity and the foundation of public confidence? Neither question is easy of determination. It has been said that a judge who gives a judgment without applying rules already defined to some extent, is making a decision beyond the pale of curial activity. In the *Boilermakers' Case*, Williams J said: 'Purely administrative discretions governed by nothing but standards of convenience and general fairness could not be imposed upon [the courts]. Discretionary judgments are not beyond the pale but there must be some standards applicable to a set of facts not altogether undefined before a court can hear and determine a matter.'[56]

On the other hand, in *R v Joske; Ex parte Australian Building Construction Employees*, Barwick CJ considered that judicial power had a capacity to resolve questions according to criteria of significant breadth: 'The determination whether some activity or its result is oppressive, unreasonable or unjust is not something which is foreign to the exercise of judicial power.'[57]

It is arguable that the width of an administrative discretion is not necessarily a bar to a judge undertaking the review of a decision on the merits. Even though there may be no principle at first available to guide the exercise of such a discretion, principles emerge from analysis, debate, and the need to assign reasons for decision. These are at the heart of the judicial process, and the development of principles to govern relationships is a function which judges are accustomed to perform. But there must surely be an unacceptable risk to the judiciary and to the system of government if the questions remitted to judicial determination are, in the broad sense, political. Some of the reasons why political questions ought not to be determined by judges were stated by Brennan J in *Baker v Carr*:

> Prominent on the surface of any case held to involve a political question is found a textually demonstrable constitutional commitment of the issue to a co-ordinate political department; or a lack of judicially discoverable and manageable standards for resolving it; or the impossibility of deciding without an initial policy determination of a kind clearly for non-judicial discretion; or the impossibility of a court's undertaking independent resolution without expressing lack of the respect due co-ordinate branches of government; or an unusual need for unquestioning adherence to a political decision already made; or the potentiality of embarrassment from multifarious pronouncements by various departments on one question.[58]

No doubt the good sense of the judges has kept them at a safe distance from political policy,[59] and there is much to be said for the view that the courts, left to themselves, will keep judicial involvement in the administrative process within the appropriate, but not overly conservative, bounds. The extent to which the courts will go is a matter of what is called nowadays 'judicial policy'. Professor Wade in his 1980 Hamlyn Lectures 'Constitutional Fundamentals' said:

> Today no apology is needed for talking openly about judicial policy.

> Twenty or thirty years ago judges questioned about administrative law were prone to say that their function was merely to give effect to the will of Parliament and that they were not concerned with policy. In reality, they are up to their necks in policy, as they have been all through history, and nothing could illustrate this more vividly in our own time than the vicissitudes of administrative law. In the period of their backsliding they declined to apply the principles of natural justice, allowed ministers unfettered discretion where blank-cheque powers were given by statute, declined to control the patent legal-errors of tribunals, permitted the free abuse of Crown – privilege, and so forth. Then in the 'sixties, when the public reaction against administrative injustice had become too strong to be ignored, the judges executed a series of U-turns which put the law back on course and responded to the- public mood. The choice of policies before them was wide indeed.[60]

The vitality – some might think the adventurous quality – of contemporary judicial review denies an untoward reserve when it comes to ensuring that administrative injustice is remedied.[61]

But weapons are missing from the traditional judicial armoury. Whether Miss Green, after the declarations made by Stephen J in *Green* v *Daniels*[62] ought to have received payment of her unemployment benefit was not a matter for the courts. Recently Lord Hailsham LC in *Chief Constable* v *Evans*,[63] disapproved of passages in the judgments in the Court of Appeal which his Lordship considered 'might be read as giving the courts carte blanche to review the decision of the authority on the basis of what the courts themselves consider fair and reasonable on the merits'.[64] The Lord Chancellor said: 'The purpose of judicial review is to ensure that the individual receives fair treatment, and not to ensure that the authority, after according fair treatment, reaches on a matter which it is authorised by law to decide for itself a conclusion which is correct in the eyes of the court.'[65]

Lord Brightman (with whom Lord Fraser and Lord Roskill agreed) stated the restriction on judicial power: 'Judicial review is concerned, not with the decision, but with the decision-making process. Unless that restriction on the power of the court is observed, the court will in my view, under the guise of preventing the abuse of power, be itself guilty of usurping power.'[66]

So long as that restriction is observed, there will be a cordon sanitaire to safeguard the judiciary from political infection. Equally, there will be an incapacity in the courts fully to supervise the exercise of administrative power which will be without effective scrutiny if there is default in ministerial supervision.

The nature of the problem has been clearly perceived. In his essay on 'Justiciability', Geoffrey Marshall wrote:

> Attempts at 'crystallization' of policy may sometimes be inappropriate and occasionally the use of a tribunal form of decision may signal deliberate departure from, rather than obedience to, principle. An administrative tribunal is in a position of unstable equilibrium between the judicial and political processes. It faces the potential criticism that if its decisions involve discretion of a policy kind its work might be more properly done by responsible administrators. On the other hand, if its decisions are fairly narrowly defined matters, involving the interpretation of statutes and regulations, it may be criticized as not being judicial enough.[67]

On the other hand, if the courts and judges are unable to engage in the supervision of administrative decision-making on the merits, administrative decisions may prove to be what Denis Galligan describes as 'variable and sectional':

> ... if conceptions of the public interest within these areas of discretion are variable and sectional, and dependent upon the assessment of the administrative official, then questions for the legal order arise. To what extent can these areas of power be subject to traditional notions of law with its emphasis on fixed and continuing principles with general application, and upon a particular method of reasoning on the part of legal institutions? The risk is that courts with their characteristic methods of control and accountability are either pushed to the margin of public affairs and become ineffectual, or that the exercise of legal control itself becomes discretionary, sectional and subjective in the same way as the institutions that it seeks to control.[68]

The problem is not susceptible of an entirely satisfying solution. But that is no novelty.[69] It is a problem which is likely to be solved pragmatically and piecemeal.

I should like to add a brief reference to the opening up of the traditionally cloistered administrative process. [70] A statement of reasons may be requested by a person whose interests are affected by a decision[71] reviewable under the *Administrative Appeals Tribunal Act 1975* (Cth).[72] A statement must be furnished and, if an Application to the AAT ensures, the material documents must also be produced.[73] In *Pochi*, Deane J said of these provisions:

> The *Administrative Appeals Tribunal Act 1975* (Cth) did not directly impose upon decision makers, whose decisions it made subject to review, any substantive or procedural obligations to be observed in

> the making of such decisions. It did, however, effect a quiet revolution in regard to such decisions. The Act lowered a narrow bridge over the moat of executive silence in that, subject to limited exceptions, it conferred upon a person entitled to apply to the Tribunal for a review of a decision, the right to be supplied with a statement in writing prepared by the person who made the decision and setting out the findings on material questions of fact, referring to the evidence or other material on which those findings were based, and giving the reasons for the decision ...[74]

Similar provisions are to be found in the *Administrative Decisions Judicial Review Act 1977* (Cth). Subject to the exceptions set out in ss 13A and 14, a person entitled to make an application for review under s 5 may, by notice in writing, request the decision-maker to furnish 'a statement in writing setting out the findings on material questions of fact, referring to the evidence or other material on which those findings were based and giving the reasons for the decision'.[75] The provision does not however apply to an application under s 7 to review a failure to make a decision.

The *Freedom of Information Act 1982* (Cth) came into force in December 1982. The key provision of that Act is s 11:

> Subject to this Act, every person has a legally enforceable right to obtain access in accordance with this Act to -
>
> a document of an agency, other than an exempt document; or
>
> an official document of a Minister, other than an exempt document.

The Act is expressed to apply to courts[76] and to certain tribunals[77] in respect of administrative matters. There are however a large number of exempt and partially exempt agencies,[78] and a large number of exempt documents,[79] including documents affecting the enforcement of law and tie protection of public safety, documents affecting personal privacy, documents subject to legal professional privilege, documents containing material obtained in confidence, and disclosure of which would be in contempt of Parliament or contempt of court.

The new federal administrative law has not, simplified administration. Nor was it intended to. Its great achievement to date has been to modify the anonymous activities of government so that they are more responsive to the needs of the individual.

---

1. I should like to acknowledge the assistance of Mr Justice Davies, President of the Administrative Appeals Tribunal, in furnishing me with some of his recent writings on the topics raised in this paper. However, none of the views expressed should be assumed to represent his Honour's views.

2. Commonwealth Administrative Review Committee, of which the Honourable Mr Justice Kerr, CMG (as he then was) was the Chairman.
3. Lord Scarman, *English Law – the New Dimension* (Stevens, 1974) 70, 71, Hamlyn Lectures, 26th series.
4. Ibid 75.
5. Stanley Alexander De Smith and John Marix Evans, *De Smith's Judicial Review of Administrative Action* (Stevens, 4th ed, 1980) 3.
6. An advisory body to oversee the whole structure and to make recommendations as to the classes of case in which jurisdiction should be conferred upon the Administrative Appeals Tribunal and other bodies: see *Administrative Appeals Tribunal Act 1975* (Cth), s 51.
7. See *Administrative Decisions (Judicial Review) Act 1977* (Cth), ss 5, 6, 7; note however the exclusions in Sch 1 of the 1980 amendment.
8. See *Administrative Appeals Tribunal Act 1975* (Cth), ss 25-27, 29, 42, 43.
9. See *Ombudsman Act 1976* (Cth), ss 5-8, 15-18.
10. See *Constitution* (Cth), s 75(v).
11. See *The Seventh Annual Report of the Law Reform Commission of Canada* (1977-8), 14 referred to the new Australian legislation as having taken 'an awesome leap'.
12. A wide meaning is given to 'decision' by s 3(3) of the *Administrative Appeals Tribunal Act 1975* (Cth). However, in *Director-General of Social Services v Chaney* (1980) 31 ALR 571, the Federal Court held that an impugned ruling of the Director-General was not a 'decision' but was merely a step in the review process which would ultimately lead to the making of a decision; see also *Re Lawson and Director-General of Social Services* (1980) 3 ALD 58, where the AAT held that a proposed course of action was not a 'decision' until a decision had been made to implement that course.
13. The principal caseload of the Tribunal has come from the *Customs Act 1901* (Cth) the *Insurance Act 1973* (Cth), the *Migration Act 1958* (Cth), the *Superannuation Act 1976* (Cth), the *Defence Forces Retirement and Death Benefits Act 1973* (Cth), *the Air Navigation Act 1920* (Cth), the *Home Savings Grant Act 1976* (Cth), the *ACT Rates Ordinance,* the *Export Market Development Grants Act 1974* (Cth), the *Export Expansion Grants Act 1978* (Cth), the *Repatriation Act 1920* (Cth), the *Compensation (Commonwealth Government Employees) Act 1971* and the *Social Security Act 1947 (Cth)* Cases under the *Insurance Act 1973* (Cth) have occupied a large number of sitting days.
14. See SR 1980 No 62 and Act No 74 of 1981 respectively.
15. See *Administrative Appeals Tribunal Act 1975* (Cth), s 34.
16. See *Brian Lawlor Automotive Pty Ltd v. Collector of Customs (NSW)* (1978) 1 ALD 167, 175.
17. The notable exception is in the deportation cases. The power of the AAT is to affirm the order of the Minister or to recommend that it be reconsidered: see *Migration Act 1958* (Cth), s 66E (3); *Minister for Immigration and Ethnic Affairs v Pochi* (1981) 36 ALR 561.
18. See *Administrative Appeals Tribunal Act 1975* (Cth), s 43.
19. See *Collector of Customs (NSW) v Brian Lawlor Automotive Pty Ltd* (1979) 24 ALR 307, 314-316,3 39 (FCA); see also *Deputy Commissioner of Patents* v *Board of Control of Michigan Technological University* (1979) 28 ALR 551, 561, 569, 572 (FCA).
20. For example, the requirement that the hearing be public (s 35), the right of representation (s 32) and the fact-finding procedures referred to in this paper.
21. See *R v Kirby; Ex parte Boilermakers Society of Australia* (1956) 94 CLR 254; [1957] AC 288; *R v Trade Practices Tribunal; Ex parte Tasmanian Breweries Pty Ltd* (1970) 123 CLR 361.

22. See *Drake v Minister for Immigration and Ethnic Affairs* (1979) 24 ALR 577, 583-585, 589; see also Enid Campbell, 'The Choice between Judicial and Administrative Tribunals and the Separation of Powers', (1981) 12(1) *Federal Law Review* 24.
23. See *Ladybird Childrens' Wear Pty Ltd. and Department of Business and Consumer Affairs* (1976) 1 ALD 1, 5; cf. *Re Control Investments and Australian Broadcasting Commission* (1981) 39 ALR 281, 317, 392.
24. See *Re Becker and Minister for Immigration and Ethnic Affairs* (1977) 1 ALD 158, 161; *Drake v Minister for Immigration and Ethnic Affairs* (1979) 24 ALR 577, 589; see also *Minister for Immigration and Ethnic Affairs v Pochi* (1981) 36 ALR 561, 671, 683.
25. (1979) 24 ALR 577, 589.
26. See *R v War Pensions Entitlement Appeal Tribunal; Ex parte Bott* (1933) 50 CLR 228, 244, 249.
27. See *TA Miller Ltd v Minister of Housing and Local Government* [1968] 1 WLR 992, 995 (Denning MR).
28. See *Administrative Appeals Tribunal Act 1975* (Cth) s 33(1)(c); see generally R K Todd, 'Administrative Review before the Administrative Appeals Tribunal – A Fresh Approach to Dispute Resolution?' (Part II] (1981) 12 (1) *Federal Law Review* 95.
29. Justice Michael Kirby, 'Administrative Review: Beyond the Frontier marked "Policy – Lawyers Keep Out"', (1981) 12 (2) *Federal Law Review* 121, 148; see also 138, 139,141,143.
30. See *Minister for Immigration and Ethnic Affairs v Pochi* (1981) 36 ALR 561, 689, 690.
31. (1981) 55 *Australian Law Journal* 390, 400.
32. See *Administrative Appeals Tribunal Act 1975* (Cth) s 33 (1) (b).
33. See A N Hall, 'Administrative Review before the Administrative Appeals Tribunal – A Fresh Approach to Dispute Resolution? (Part I)' (1981) 12 (1) *Federal Law Review* 71, 91.
34. See *Administrative Appeals Tribunal Act 1975* (Cth), s 7(3); there are presently 26 such members.
35. See *Drake* (n 22) 584,585.
36. See *Administrative Appeals Tribunal Act 1975* (Cth), s 44.
37. Ibid s 45.
38. 'Inconsistency is not merely inelegant: it brings the process of deciding into disrepute, suggesting an arbitrariness which is incompatible with commonly accepted notions of justice': *Re Drake (No 2)* (1979) 2 ALD 634, 639. 'On the other hand, while consistency may properly be seen as an ingredient of justice, it does not constitute a hallmark of it': *Nevistic v Minister for Immigration and Ethnic Affairs* (1981) 34 ALR 639, 647.
39. See Parliament of Australia, *Commonwealth Administrative Review Committee Report,* August 1971, 87-90; Parliament of Australia, *Committee on Administrative Discretions Final Report*, October 1973, 32,33.See Dennis Pearce, 'Courts, Tribunals & Government Policy' (1980) 11 (2) *Federal Law Review* 203, 219.
40. See Dennis Pearce, 'Courts, Tribunals & Government Policy (1980) 11 (2) *Federal Law Review* 203, 219.
41. See Justice Michael Kirby, 'Administrative Review: Beyond the Frontier marked "Policy - Lawyers Keep Out"', (1981) 12 (2) *Federal Law Review* 121, 131-145 for a review of these cases, and see 131,132 for a list of other reported deportation cases.
42. Ibid 131.
43. (1979) 24 ALR 577, 590.

44. See *Re Drake (No 2)* (1979) 2 ALD 634, 643.
45. Ibid 643,644.
46. Ibid 644.
47. Ibid
48. Ibid 645.
49. See *Gungoor* (1980) 3 ALD 225, 228 230.
50. See *Nevistic v Minister for Immigration and Ethnic Affairs* (1981) 34 ALR 639, 649.
51. See for example, Fisher J in *Re Vincenzo Barbaro and Minister for Immigration and Ethnic Affairs* (1980) 3 ALN No 31 and *Re Jeropoulos and Minister for Immigration and Ethnic Affairs* (1980) 2 ALD 891; Davies J in *Re Sergi and Minister for Immigration and Ethnic Affairs* (1979) 2 ALD 224, *Re Saverio Barbaro and Minister for Immigration and Ethnic Affairs* (1980) 3 ALD 1, Nevistic (1980) 3 ALN No 9 and *Re Piscioneri and Minister for Immigration and Ethnic Affairs* (1980) 3 ALN No 8; McGregor J in *Re* Tombuloglu and Minister for *Immigration and Ethnic Affairs* (1980) 3 ALN No 13; Gallop J in *Re Gallo and Minister for Immigration and Ethnic Affairs* (1980) 3 ALN No 12.
52. See Justice Michael Kirby, 'Administrative Review: Beyond the Frontier marked "Policy - Lawyers Keep Out"', (1981) 12 (2) *Federal Law Review* 121, 144.
53. Ibid 147.
54. Ibid 147.
55. 'The reasoned decisions of the AAT, now over a period of more than four years disclose that a great many cases involve little or no element of government policy. Many of them follow perfectly orthodox lines with which lawyers are well familiar. Most turn on the fuller ascertainment of facts, in which the AAT frequently has decided advantages over the administrator. Many depend upon the clarification of the law': Justice Michael Kirby, 'Administrative Review: Beyond the Frontier marked "Policy - Lawyers Keep Out"', (1981) 12 (2) *Federal Law Review* 121, 145.
56. (1956) 94 CLR 254, 315; and see *R* v *Trade Practices Tribunal; Ex parte Tasmanian Breweries Pty Ltd* (1970) 123 CLR 361, 376, 377 (Kitto J).
57. (1974) 130 CLR 87, 94.
58. 369 US 186, (1962), 217.
59. Cf *R v Anderson; Ex parte Ipec-Air Pty Ltd* (1965) 113 CLR 17, 192, 199, 205; *British Oxygen Company Ltd. v. Minister of Technology* [1971] AC 610, 624, 625; *Salemi (No 2) v Minister for Immigration and Ethnic Affairs* (1977) 14 ALR 1, 6.
60. Willam Wade, *Constitutional Fundamentals* (Stevens for the Hamlyn Trust, 1980) Hamlyn Lectures, 32nd series, 61, 62
61. 61 See *re Toohey; Ex parte Northern Land Counci*l (1981) 38 ALR 439; *FAI Insurances Ltd v. Winneke* (1981) 41 ALR 1.
62. (1977) 13 ALR 1; 51 ALJR 463.
63. [1982] 1 WLR 1155.
64. Ibid 1160.
65. Ibid 1161.
66. Ibid 1173.
67. Geoffrey Marshall 'Justiciability' in Anthony Gordon Guest (ed), *Oxford Essays in Jurisprudence* (0xford University Press, 1961) 265, 285.

68. D J Galligan, 'Judicial Review and the Textbook Writers', (1982) 2 (2) *Oxford Journal of Legal Studies,* 257.
69. See Justice Else-Mitchell, 'The Place of the Administrative Tribunal in 1965', Third Commonwealth & Empire Law Conference, Sydney 1965, 65.
70. See *McPherson* v *McPherson* [1936] AC 177, 200.
71. See *Administrative Appeals Tribunal Act 1975* (Cth), ss 27(1), 30(1A); see *Re Control Investments (No 1)* (1980) 3 ALD 74, 79 applying *Re McHatten and Collector of Customs (NSW)* (1977) 1 ALD 67, at 69,70.
72. See *Administrative Appeals Tribunal Act 1975* (Cth), s 28.
73. Ibid s 37.
74. See *Minister for Immigration and Ethnic Affairs v Pochi* (1981) 36 ALR 561, 685,686.
75. See *Administrative Decisions Judicial Review Act 1977* (Cth), s 13 (1). The section expressly excludes the decisions specified in Schedule 2 or those to which s 28 of the *Administrative Appeals Tribunal Act 1975* (Cth) applies.
76. See *Freedom of Information Act 1982* (Cth), s 5.
77. Ibid s 6.
78. Ibid s 7, Schedule 2
79. Ibid ss 12,13,32-47.

4.3 The Purpose and Scope of Judicial Review

Editor's note

Brennan delivered this paper at a seminar organized by the Legal Research Foundation Inc at the University of Auckland on 20 February 1986.[1]

Judicial review, being concerned with the making of decisions and the taking of actions by the executive branch of government, is an institution of fundamental constitutional importance. The political legitimacy of judicial review depends, in the ultimate analysis, on the assignment to the courts of that function by the general consent of the community. The efficacy of judicial review depends, in the ultimate analysis, on the confidence of the general community in the way in which the courts perform the function assigned to them. Judicial review has no support other than public confidence. Alexander Hamilton, writing one of the *Federalist Papers*, held the judiciary to be the branch of government 'least dangerous to the political rights of the Constitution... The judiciary . . . has no influence over either the sword or the purse; no direction either of the strength or of the wealth of the society, and can take no active resolution whatever. It may truly be said to have neither force nor will but merely judgment; and must ultimately depend upon the aid of the executive arm even for the efficacy of its judgments.'[2]

One could hardly rely on the executive arm of government to give efficacy to judicial review if community confidence were lacking. Of course, all branches of government seek community confidence and, in a stable society, are given it. Yet our traditions and contemporary sentiment subject the exercise of executive power to limited review by the courts.

The investing of the ordinary courts with authority to strike down the decisions and actions of the executive is not a universal mechanism for subjecting the executive branch of government to legal rules. Not all legal systems find it expedient to repose in the judiciary a power to review the actions of the executive. In the People's Republic of China, for example, the People's Congress is charged with the responsibility of reviewing the function of the other three branches of Government: the executive, the judiciary and the procuratorate. Each of those branches must act independently of the others. Subject to congressional supervision, the laws governing the function of each of those branches is administered by the branch in question, the higher echelons controlling the lower. The continental droit administratif provides for the administrative hierarchy itself to test the legality of administrative action.

Such a system is more efficient than ours in achieving the objectives of the executive. As hierarchical controls within the executive branch do not need to distinguish too closely between the laws which govern and policies which guide executive decisions and actions, legal rules do not bite so hard upon executive policy as they sometimes do under our system. Judicial review, under our system, is and is intended to be a fetter on the executive's pursuit of its policies; it is intended to make the courts the arbiter of legal propriety in the processes of administration. Ours is a system of inevitable, if not intended, inefficiency. Some inefficiency in achieving the objectives of the executive is the price we pay for assigning to the courts the function of declaring and applying the law as well to government as to the citizen. But we do not assign the exercise of executive power to the courts and we would not accept the straitjacketing of executive power so that its exercise is made to conform with the court's view of what is correct or preferable.

The boundary between judicial review and executive freedom is determined by law but, being a matter of law, that boundary is determined by the courts. In recent times the courts have moved the boundary, sometimes aided by the legislature, and we can perceive an increment in the scope of judicial review responding to a diminution in legislative control over executive power.[3] Parliament no longer stands as a counterweight to executive power. Nowadays Parliament is the ally of the executive, giving effect to the executive's programs and policies. The rigid party system and the transference of much important public debate from the chamber to the party room have led to a simplistic identification of the Parliament with the government of the day. There is little incentive for Parliament to review the exercise of executive power and, such is the press of parliamentary business, less opportunity to do so. The doctrine of the supremacy of Parliament, a central doctrine in our constitutional law,[4] is now a buttress of executive power, for the members of the executive government, on whose political skills the fortunes of the parliamentary majority greatly depend, control the allegiance of that majority.

I do not suggest, of course, that the Parliament does not have a lively interest in and some influence on the functions of the executive. But the inhibitions on parliamentary review of the exercise of executive power leave the mass of administrative decision-making without any real supervision by members of Parliament or even by Ministers. Nowadays the bureaucracies of government departments and public authorities are the real repositories of executive power. Day to day administration is in their hands whether or not they are the nominal repositories of power. They are responsible to their Minister for implementing the policy of the executive government, but the other elements in administrative decision-making — the ascertainment of the relevant facts and the application of the relevant law — is left largely in their hands. And this at a time when the significance, volume, and complexity of executive power grow as the statute book expands.

It is not surprising that the courts have expanded their jurisdiction to review administrative action (in which I include administrative decisions and omissions to take administrative action) whereby they supervise the bureaucracy's functions of ascertaining the relevant facts and applying the relevant law. The courts in their appellate jurisdiction are accustomed to the task of supervising the finding of facts and the application of law by a primary judge and they are accustomed too to the protection of individual rights against overreaching by governments. So, it is fitting that the review of the factual and legal elements of administrative decision-making should be undertaken by the courts. But what of the element of policy?

The process of administrative decision-making is often quite different from the syllogistic process of judicial decision-making. In the first place, judicial decision-making usually has only two basic elements: law and fact (the major and minor premises). If discretion or evaluation plays a part, the part is well confined. No broad policy elements intrude. But policy is often an integral part of administrative decision-making, denying the application of the syllogistic method. A decision-maker who has mistaken a fact or made an error in law may nevertheless make the correct or preferable decision if he legitimately applies a policy wide enough to require the same decision whether or not there be a mistake of fact or an error of law. Some administrative action is not based upon the existence of a fact but on the apprehension of the possibility that the fact exists.

Secondly, the terms of a policy may determine whether a fact is material to the making of an administrative decision. In judicial proceedings, the facts in issue are confined by the legal elements of the cause of action or the defence, but the facts which fall for consideration in administrative decisions may be diffuse. Their materiality may depend upon the terms of a policy which is not expressed in statute and is not itself susceptible of proof. A policy may, so to speak, reverse the onus of proof so that administrative action is to be taken unless a particular fact exists rather than if that fact exists.

Administrative decision-making is different from curial decision-making when policy is an element. The courts have neither the capacity nor the procedures appropriate to the review of policy. In its application to particular cases, policy calls for the balancing of the interests of an individual and the interests of the community at large. The court is not equipped to assess the interests of the community at large as against the interests of the litigant before the court: the adversary system is not designed for that purpose.[5] The courts do not have the resources or techniques for assessing the worth of policy, and they may be quite mistaken about the effect of exempting a particular case from the application of a policy. On the other hand, the balancing of individual and community interests is the stuff of the political branches of government. If policy hardens into law, the courts do not have to balance individual against community interests: the law determines how the balance is struck. However, in widening areas of government activity, the law is not prescribing how the balance between individual and community interests is to be struck: that function is remitted to the bureaucracy subject to direction by government policy.

The most rapidly growing and socially significant concentrations of power in our community are vested in administrative agencies, whose distinguishing feature, as Professor Bernard Schwartz notes, is their 'power to determine, either by rule or by decision, private rights and obligations'.[6] Some kind of adjudication – however formal or informal – is involved in the exercise of their power. There is no novelty in this. It is simply 'not true that the function of adjudication is either by common law or by the course of modern legislation confined to courts'.[7] But the creation of numerous and varied administrative agencies – Ministers, departments of government, statutory authorities and officials – and the range and complexity of the powers reposed in them give impetus to the task of developing laws to regulate administrative adjudication which affects the interests of individuals.[8]

It seems an elementary proposition that the function of the courts is not to assume the powers conferred by Parliament on administrative agencies. But there is no shortage of advocates of judicial activism, urging the courts on to do so. Who better? they ask. Much the same as the courts have always done, they say. To the timid – or cautious – who say that the courts are not concerned with policy, there is the rough rejoinder that the judges 'are up to the necks in policy, as they have been all through history'.[9] Those are the words of Professor Wade who reproaches the courts for a supine refusal to intervene when, in the years before *Ridge v Baldwin*,[10] he suggests that administrative injustice went unchecked:

> In the period of their backsliding they declined to apply the principles of natural justice, allowed ministers unfettered discretion where blank-cheque powers were given by statute, declined to control the patent legal errors of tribunals, permitted the free abuse of Crown privilege, and so forth. Then in the 'sixties', when the public reaction against administrative injustice had become too strong to be ignored, the judges executed a series of U-turns which put the law back on course and responded to the public mood.

The pendulum has undoubtedly swung towards increased judicial intervention and it is reasonable to surmise that that swing coincides with public sentiment, the sentiment of Parliament and the sentiment of at least some sections of the executive. The problem is to determine how far judicial intervention should go.

The scope of judicial review has been extended piecemeal, in the way of the common law and largely by judges. But there are limits to judicial activism, especially when a contemplated reform is calculated to enlarge the powers of the courts over a co-ordinate branch of government which is expected to forge and apply policy. There are two deeply held (if seldom articulated) expectations which affect the judicial reform of administrative law. The first is that the courts ought to protect individual interests but ought to leave policy to governments; the second is that judicial lawmaking must follow the judicial method, so that settled law is not simply discarded (though it may be modified). New legal rules evolve from past experience. The first of these factors gives rise to a critical problem of contemporary administrative law; the second dictates the technique by which that problem must be solved. We shall have to examine the problem, but in the light of the techniques which can be employed in solving it. If the judicial method of lawmaking cannot yield the desired solution, we cannot risk destruction of public confidence in the legal system generally in order to solve a problem which needs to be solved by legislation. Public confidence in the whole legal system would be impaired if judicial activism outstrips the consensus of the community and becomes what Lord Devlin castigated as 'judicial dynamism'.[11]

Judicial dynamism, as Lord Devlin defined it, is antithetical to public confidence in the legal system. Let me remind you of his distinction between activist and dynamic lawmaking:

> In activist lawmaking the idea is taken from the consensus and demands at most sympathy from the lawmaker. In dynamic lawmaking the idea is created outside the consensus and, before it is formulated, it has to be propagated. This needs more than sympathy: it needs enthusiasm. Enthusiasm is not and cannot be a judicial virtue. It means taking sides.[12]

That view echoes what Lord Radcliffe said:

> We cannot run the risk of finding the archetypal image of the judge confused in men's minds with the very different image of the legislator. We cannot run the risk that an institution which societies such as ours have never yet known how to do without should be destroyed merely through an untimely eagerness to be all

> things to all men, to be at the head and the rear and the centre of the column all at one time. There is no sufficient compensation in human benefit. The truth is, in my belief, that the image of the judge, objective, impartial, erudite and experienced declarer of the law that is, lies deeper in the consciousness of civilisation than the image of the lawmaker, propounding what are avowedly new rules of human conduct. Each has a separate authority, and the appeal of each for men's obedience is fundamentally different.[13]

Much has been done by judges in expanding judicial review to answer the community's expectations. Much remains to be done. The balance between too much and too little intervention must be fixed in principle and made effective by laws as precise as the subject matter allows.

The interpretation and application of the express terms of a statute are clearly within the scope of judicial review. But intervention on grounds other than the application of express terms of the statute can give rise to controversy. Then the court's authority to declare the common law enables it to declare the legitimacy of its own decision to intervene. Thus, in *Council of Civil Service Unions* v *Minister for the Civil Service*, Lord Scarman said:

> I believe that the law relating to judicial review has now reached the stage where it can be said with confidence that, if the subject matter in respect of which prerogative power is exercised is justiciable, that is to say if it is a matter upon which the court can adjudicate, the exercise of the power is subject to review in accordance with the principles developed in respect of the review of the exercise of statutory power.[14]

Bold assertions of jurisdiction can be traced back to the claims made by Coke in 1616 when the Privy Council ordered the court to desist from issuing certiorari and mandamus. The Royal authority, Coke asserted, had been irrevocably invested in the courts and only Parliament could 'shake' their jurisdiction.[15] But the fact that Coke's pungent proclamation of the court's jurisdiction sufficed to establish judicial review in a primitive form gives no guarantee that the judicial ipse dixit is sufficient to expand the scope of judicial review in the modern day. If the courts simply declare that the common law authorizes intervention on conditions that have not previously been held sufficient to authorize intervention, the declaration adds no patina of historical authority to what is a modern extension of judicial review. The extension itself must be founded on legal principles earlier established so that the increment in jurisdiction is no more than a judicial development – albeit an activist development – of the law. The legitimacy and strength of judicial development of the law is derived from the settled law – whether statute or case law – out of which it grows. The method is described by Benjamin Cardozo: 'A stock of juridical conceptions and formulas is developed, and we take them, so to speak, ready-made. . . . These fundamental conceptions once attained form the starting point from which are derived new consequences, which, at first tentative and groping, gain by reiteration a new permanence and certainty. In the end, they become accepted themselves as fundamental and axiomatic.'[16]

The judicial method is restrained, as it must be, by respect for precedent which, as Lord Devlin pointed out, is exacted 'not only to keep the law in good shape, but primarily as a safeguard against arbitrary and autocratic decision-making'.[17] For the most part, the modern developments of the grounds of judicial review have been founded on precedent, the expectations of the community being met by expansion of principles earlier confined to particular classes of cases. But the court must not be eager to expand its control over administration. As Mr Justice Frankfurter acknowledged in *Trop v Dulles*: 'All power is, in Madison's phrase, "of an encroaching nature." . . . Judicial power is not immune against this human weakness. It also must be on guard against encroaching beyond its proper bounds, and not the less so since the only restraint upon it is self-restraint.'[18]

The object of expanding the scope of judicial review is to enhance the protection of individuals. The object has been, or is in course of being, achieved by courts in different parts of the common-law world. Active development of the law relating to standing to seek judicial review, to the kinds of decisions amenable to judicial review, to the procedures to be followed by administrative agencies and to the reasoning leading to an administrative decision, has secured to the courts a wide supervisory jurisdiction, though the rules governing the exercise of the expanded jurisdiction have not been fully developed.

Standing to sue

The movement is all one way, that is, towards relaxing earlier restrictions on standing to sue. In *Australian Conservation Foundation v Commonwealth*[19] and *Onus v Alcoa of Australia Ltd*,[20] the High Court of Australia, building on what had been said in *Boyce v Paddington Borough Council*,[21] held that public law duties may be enforced at the suit of persons who have a special interest in the subject matter of the action though they have no private right to enforce. The interest must be 'special' in comparison with the interest of the public at large. A legal right or obligation is not essential to standing. The same general criterion has been applied to determine who is 'a person who is aggrieved' – the statutory criterion of standing to sue under the *Administrative Decisions (Judicial Review) Act 1977 (Cth) (ADJR Act)*. In *Tooheys Ltd v Minister for Business and Consumer Affairs*,[22] Ellicott J construed the term in a way that has been accepted by subsequent decisions of the Federal Court of Australia. He said 'I am satisfied from the broad nature of the discretions which are subject to review and from the fact that the procedures are clearly intended in part to be a substitution for the more complex prerogative writ procedures that a narrower meaning was not intended. This does not mean that any member of the public can seek an order of review. I am satisfied, however, that it at least covers a person who can show a grievance which will be suffered as a result of the decision complained of beyond that which he or she has as an ordinary member of the public.'[23]

A person may seek review under the *Administrative Law Act 1978 (Vic)* if he is a 'person affected', that is, a person 'whose interest (being an interest that is greater than the interest of other members of the public) is or will or may be affected, directly or indirectly, to a substantial degree by a decision' (s 2). The same general criterion appears in *Attorney-General of The Gambia v N'Jie*, where Lord Denning said that, although the words 'person aggrieved' do not include a mere busybody, 'they do include a person who has a genuine grievance because an order has been made which prejudicially affects his interests'.[24]

In England, another strand of thinking has appeared in connection with the criterion of standing to seek judicial review prescribed by Order 53 of the *Rules of the Supreme Court*: a 'sufficient interest in the matter to which the application relates' (a formula which appears to deny the necessity for a legal right or obligation). In *R* v *Inland Revenue Commissioners; Ex parte Federation of Self-Employed and Small Businesses Ltd*, Lord Diplock, going further than the other members of the House of Lords, said: 'It would, in my view, be a grave lacuna in our system of public law if a pressure group, like the federation, or even a single public-spirited taxpayer, were prevented by outdated technical rules of locus standi from bringing the matter to the attention of the court to vindicate the rule of law and get the unlawful conduct stopped.'[25]

The Court of Appeal in New Zealand derived 'guidance' from this case in *Environmental Defence Society Inc* v *South Pacific Aluminium Ltd (No 3)*. There Cooke J said:

> The Crown contended that the societies did not have standing to bring these proceedings. We did not regard this contention as precluding the court from examining whether the Order in Council was lawfully made and, if we had held that it was not, we would not have refused relief on this ground. . . .

> Moreover the proceedings challenge the legality of government action. It is unrealistic to expect the Attorney-General to do this and we see no reason why it must be left to individuals directly affected to undertake the burden. In the exercise of the court's discretion responsible public interest groups may be accepted as having sufficient standing under the National Development Act. We are not concerned in this case with questions of standing under other Acts. [26]

Each of these two strands of thinking – one looking to the interest affected by the impugned action, the other looking to the need to enforce the law – focuses on the statute creating the relevant power. The interest apt to be affected by, or the illegality of, an exercise of the power supports standing to impugn the action taken. Neither strand of reasoning suggests that review may be refused merely because the impugned exercise of the power affects an interest less than a legal right or legal obligation.[27] If standing to seek judicial review comes to be determined by a single criterion – which it appears to be under the *ADJR Act*, but perhaps not under the *Judicature Amendment Act 1972* (NZ) as amended[28] – and some personal qualification is required, the affection of an interest (whether or not a legal right or obligation) distinct from the interest of the public at large seems to be emerging as that criterion. That criterion expands the scope of judicial review to protect individual interests not amounting to legal rights and obligations.

Such a criterion is not very precise, and the absence of precision may give rise to new problems. How is the 'mere busybody' to be distinguished from the person with a special interest if the statute creates a public right to be enjoyed by all?[29] Can a mere intellectual or emotional interest ever amount to a special interest if the statute creates a power that is apt to affect intellectual or emotional interests?[30] And a question remains as to the correspondence between special interest and what Lord Denning called a 'legitimate expectation'[31] when an applicant seeks judicial review on the ground that he has been denied natural justice.[32] These are by no means all the questions awaiting judicial determination.

Review of the exercise of prerogative power

In *Council of Civil Service Unions* v *Minister for the Civil Service*,[33] it was held that, dependent on subject matter, a Minister might be under a duty to act fairly and his action might be subject to judicial review though he acts in pursuance of the prerogative and not under a statutory power. This case, following on *R* v. *Criminal Injuries Compensation Board; Ex parte Lain*[34] – itself a 'landmark case' according to Lord Scarman[35] – rejects the necessity to find legislative warrant for the jurisdiction judicially to review administrative action. Lord Diplock said: 'My Lords, I see no reason why simply because a decision-making power is derived from the common law and not a statutory source, it should for that reason only be immune from judicial review.'[36]

If that view be right, it is no longer necessary to pay lip-service to the notion that the jurisdiction judicially to review administrative action depends upon the intention of Parliament. The law of judicial review can be seen as an autonomous part of the common law. The judicial supremacy inherent in this approach departs from the traditional view which Professor Bora Laskin expressed in this way:

> We may well feel that judicial supremacy is the highest of all values under a democratic regime of law, and a value to which even the legislature should pay tribute. But we have not enshrined it in any fundamental constitutional law or in our political system. On the contrary, the cardinal principle of our system of representative government, inherited from Great Britain, has been the supremacy of the legislature. . . . We must not then delude ourselves that judicial review rests on any higher ground than that of being implicit in statutory interpretation.[37]

The traditional view serves well enough when the relevant power is statutory, and in most cases it may be of little practical importance whether the grounds of judicial review are derived from the implied intention of Parliament or from an autonomous common law rule. If the traditional view can provide no warrant for judicial review of the exercise of prerogative power, however, it will be an open question in jurisdictions not bound by decisions of the House of Lords whether this extension of the scope of judicial review can be effected by judicial decision.

The theory of an autonomous common law of judicial review is conducive to the development of general principles governing all administrative action, irrespective of the source of the power purportedly exercised. It may tend to shift the statutory provision which creates or confers the power away from the focus of analysis. It raises, of course, the interesting questions whether there are any prerogative powers exempt from judicial review and, if so, what is the criterion of exemption?

Natural Justice: *audi alteram partem*

When Lord Reid in *Ridge* v *Baldwin* showed that the rules of natural justice applied to agencies having 'legal authority to determine questions affecting the rights of subjects'[38] – the duty to act judicially being inferred from the nature of the authority – the content of the rules of natural justice had to take account of the great variety of agencies exercising authority of that kind and of their differing capacities to adopt curial procedures. Curial analogy could not be taken too far. It has long been recognized that the content of the principles of natural justice is variable, and variable content is essential if some legal rule of fairness is to be applied to a diversity of administrative actions. The content of the principles of natural justice depends on 'the circumstances of the case, the nature of the inquiry, the rules under which the tribunal is acting, the subject-matter that is being dealt with, and so forth', to quote the well-known judgment of Tucker LJ in *Russell* v *Duke of Norfolk*.[39]

And so the application of the principles of natural justice to administrative agencies whose statutory charter precludes the adoption of court-like procedures may require the adoption of some non-curial procedures designed to secure fairness in the exercise of their powers.[40] The flexibility of the principles of natural justice requires the court to decide whether the repository of a power failed to take any procedural step which the repository was bound to take in the particular exercise of the power under review. The court must examine the particular, perhaps unique, circumstances of each case and the statute creating or conferring the relevant power. The definition of fair procedures to govern the making of every determination affecting the interests of an individual is a formidable task. Indeed, the almost infinite variety of factors precludes an a priori definition of precise procedures to guide every administrator in the exercise of his power in every case. Some agencies have power to summon witnesses, some do not. Some can compel the production of documents and the giving of information, some cannot. Some are bound by constraints of confidentiality, some are not. Some administrative decisions depend on clearly defined facts, some require a rather diffuse inquiry. Some decisions owe little to policy, some owe a lot. Some administrative decisions are made at leisure, some must be made on the moment. Across the broad spectrum of administrative decision-making, the principles of natural justice require that the procedure 'be fair in all the circumstances'.[41] Is 'natural justice' no more than a high-sounding expression?[42] It is an expression which has had some concrete effects in particular cases, though it must be allowed that there is imprecision in the notion and that its content is not always ascertainable until the impugned administrative action has been reviewed. Thus, in *Kioa* v *West*,[43] the High Court of Australia considered yet again the question whether the principles of natural justice govern the exercise of a power to order deportation of prohibited immigrants under the *Migration Act 1958* (Cth). A negative answer to this question had been given in *Salemi* v. *Mackellar (No 2)*[44] and in *R* v *Mackellar; Ex parte Ratu*,[45] but in *Kioa* an affirmative answer was given. The different answer can be attributed to amendments made to the statute since the previous cases. The 'broad and flexible concept of fairness', as Cooke J described it,[46] no doubt creates some uncertainty in administration. I suspect it inspires administrators to judicialize their procedures in order to protect the validity of their actions, despite judicial deprecation of 'over-judicialising' administration.[47] The imprecision in the content of 'natural justice' and the ex post facto declaration of that content is one of the unsolved problems of administrative law and practice.

However, the courts have largely abjured judicial review on the grounds of natural justice when the relevant power is legislative in nature. The line between powers whose exercise is exempt from the requirements of natural justice because they are legislative and the powers whose exercise is governed by the principles of natural justice is not always clear, but the distinction between them seems to depend on whether an exercise of the relevant power is apt to affect distinctively the interests of individuals rather than the interests of the public at large or a large segment of the public.[48] The courts assume jurisdiction to review procedures when individual interests are involved but the processes affecting the interests of the public at large are left to political control.

Review on the merits

In *Daganayasi* v *Minister of Immigration*,[49] Cooke J sought to establish a wide scope for judicial review. 'Fairness need not be treated as confined to procedural matters' his Honour said, and posed the question: 'has the applicant been treated fairly?' Answering that question in the negative, he said 'what has been done in good faith has produced an injustice'. Cooke J embraced the wide scope of judicial review by admitting mistake of fact as a ground of review. However, the majority of the Court of Appeal reserved their opinion on the availability of the ground of mistake of fact, and the case was decided on more traditional grounds. Shortly afterwards, in *Chief Constable* v *Evans*, Lord Denning MR asserted a jurisdiction to review on the ground of unfairness in the decision: 'Not only must he be given a fair hearing, but the decision itself must be fair and reasonable. That is the protection afforded to every servant who is employed under a contract of service. He is protected against unfair dismissal.'[50]

The House of Lords unanimously rejected that statement which, according to Lord Brightman[51] would transform, and wrongly transform, the remedy of judicial review. Lord Hailsham of St Marylebone stated the purpose of judicial review to be 'to ensure that the individual receives fair treatment, and not to ensure that the authority, after according fair treatment, reaches on a matter which it is authorised by law to decide for itself a conclusion which is correct in the eyes of the court.'[52]

If the wide scope of the jurisdiction to review were established, the court would be in a position to control the exercise of a discretionary power conferred on an administrative agency. An appellate court which entertains an appeal from a lower court by way of rehearing is usually empowered to give such judgment as the court below ought to have given in the first instance, but the jurisdiction of a court entertaining an application for judicial review is more limited. It cannot substitute its decision for the decision under review. It can set aside the decision under review and direct a further exercise of the relevant power, but the power must be exercised by the agency in which it is reposed. Therefore, it has been thought that the agency, not the court, is the judge of what is the correct or preferable decision to make. It is one thing for the court to insist that an administrative agency should act fairly in ascertaining the facts of the case. It would be another thing for the court to assume the function of directing the exercise of a discretionary power conferred on an administrative agency. It is for the legislature alone to consider whether review on the merits is appropriate in a given area of administration and, if it is, to prescribe the person or tribunal to whom a review function should be entrusted. The legislature alone can confer jurisdiction to exercise on 'appeal' a discretionary power reposed in an administrative agency.

Review of the reasoning process in administrative decisions

If the courts see an injustice, their inclination is to remedy it. But they must have the tools at hand. An injustice by administrative action can be undone if there has been an excess of jurisdiction in doing the injustice. For this reason, the concept of ultra vires is central to administrative law. The widening of the range of factors which deny jurisdiction to an administrative agency extends the scope of judicial review; conversely, a narrowing of the scope of judicial review effectively widens the jurisdiction of the administrative agency.[53] An injustice can also be undone though it is done within the jurisdiction of an administrative agency if it is done by an error of law and the error is one of which the court may take cognizance: an error on the face of the record. But an injustice that is done not by excess of jurisdiction or by error of law on the face of the record is more difficult to undo.

An injustice arising from a wrong finding of fact, or an unjust policy could be undone if it were possible to set aside the finding of fact or the policy. It is possible to set aside findings of fact when the exercise of a power is conditioned on the existence of the fact, rather than on the finding.[54]

And that is so even when the existence of the fact can be ascertained only after consideration of policy.[55] But when the fact is not one on which jurisdiction depends, different considerations apply. The facts and policies on which an administrative agency acts are what constitute the merits of the case, and a court cannot review administrative action merely because it would make a different finding of fact or apply a different policy. Then the court can intervene only if the finding of the fact or the application of the policy is either beyond the powers of the administrative agency or an error of law on the face of the record.

The path to expansion of judicial review following the judicial method is thus to perceive the errors of law which attend errors in the finding of facts or in the application of policies, and to characterize errors of law as errors either going to jurisdiction or on the record. The courts have not all been in step as they walked this path. And in the wilderness of cases the terminology is not uniform. If we were able to draw an analogy between appeals and judicial review, we would say that there is no error of law when a finding of fact is made on conflicting evidence but an error of law is made when a finding is made without evidence. I am not sure that the analogy can always be drawn, because the differences between a judicial finding of facts in issue and administrative consideration of material relevant to the exercise of a discretion are significant. Professor de Smith regarded 'no evidence' as a well-established error of law,[56] but the absence of evidence has frequently been treated more as a foundation for inferring the existence of another error of law than as an independent error of law. It cannot be accurate to regard absence of evidence of any fact as an independent ground of review. Thus, the grounds of review under the *ADJR Act* include the ground (s 5(1)(h)) 'that there was no evidence or other material to justify the making of the decision', but the ground is taken to be made out only if—

> (a) the person who made the decision was required by law to reach that decision only if a particular matter was established, and there was no evidence or other material (including facts of which he was entitled to take notice) from which he could reasonably be satisfied that the matter was established; or
>
> (b) the person who made the decision based the decision on the existence of a particular fact, and that fact did not exist. (s 5(3)).

A finding of fact without evidence of it by a commission of inquiry appointed to find whether the fact exists has been held to be contrary to natural justice. In *Mahon* v *Air New Zealand*[57] the Judicial Committee espoused this view, holding that a finding of such a fact must be based upon evidence that has some probative value. In the Court of Appeal, the majority judgment had reserved the question of the connection between an absence of probative evidence and natural justice.[58] It was thought that the question might arise again in *Re Royal Commission on Thomas* case,[59] but it did not.

Even if it is not right to treat absence of evidence in all circumstances as an error of law, and even though a finding of fact against what the court regards as the weight of evidence is not an error of law, an examination of the factual material on which the administrative agency has acted may lead the court to infer that an error of law has affected the administrative decision under review: the agency may have failed to address the right question,[60] it may have failed to take account of matters which ought to have been taken into account, it may have taken account of matters which it ought not to have taken into account, or it may have exercised its powers for a purpose foreign to the purpose for which the powers were conferred. An error of law inferred from the material before the agency is so closely related to the merits of the case that a court having a general jurisdiction to review for error of law has authority to exercise a substantial degree of control over the reasoning process of the administrative agency as well as over its procedures. To assert a general jurisdiction to review for error of law therefore raises a fundamental problem: is there any immunity from review of decisions involving errors, either of fact or law, made within jurisdiction? The courts have drawn a distinction between errors going to jurisdiction and errors within jurisdiction, the latter not being amenable to review unless the error appeared on the face of the record. That distinction, now largely eroded in some countries,[61] is maintained in Australia, as Gibbs CJ recently pointed out:

> There is a well recognized distinction between an error made by a tribunal in the course of deciding a matter, on the one hand, and an absence or excess of jurisdiction on the other. . . However, the question on which side of the line a particular case should fall may be a very difficult one. . . . Since *Anisminic Ltd* v *Foreign Compensation Commission* . . . it has been more clearly understood that an error of law may amount to a jurisdictional error even though the tribunal which made the error had jurisdiction to embark on its inquiry. [62]

In England it seems that *Anisminic*[63] had a more profound significance. Lord Diplock said:

> The break-through made by Anisminic . . . was that, as respects administrative tribunals and authorities, the old distinction between errors of law that went to jurisdiction and errors of law that did not, was for practical purposes abolished. Any error of law that could be

> shown to have been made by them in the course of reaching their decision on matters of fact or of administrative policy would result in their having asked themselves the wrong question with the result that the decision they reached would be a nullity.[64]

This view was substantially repeated by his Lordship in *O'Reilly* v *Mackman*[65] where it commanded the support of the other members of the House of Lords. This may prove to be an extreme view of the effect of errors of law, but it may not be every error of law which nullifies an administrative decision. In *Bulk Gas Users Group* v *Attorney-General*,[66] Cooke J approved Lord Diplock's exposition as applicable in New Zealand, though his Honour thought that an exception might be made in 'cases in which an error of law by an administrative tribunal is not significant enough in the context of the tribunal's reasoning as a whole to lead a reviewing court to intervene.'[67]

Apart from error of law going to jurisdiction, Australian courts applying the common law still refuse relief when there is no error on the record.[68] But the *ADJR Act*, applicable to federal administrative action, eliminates the distinction, providing for review subject to the court's discretion[69] when 'the decision involved an error of law, whether or not the error appears on the record of the decision'.[70] If judicial review follows on any error of law involved in an administrative decision, the standard of administrative decision-making will have to be raised to the standard expected of the courts. That may be a desirable if unattainable objective; but it may also be too costly to pursue. The problem must be resolved as a matter of judicial policy.

If the pendulum continues its swing in favour of the protection of individual interests, administrative decision-making which falls short of the curial standard will lead the courts to intervene freely, the courts will be astute to perceive in administrative decision-making errors of law which the courts are authorized to correct. If the pendulum swings back towards increased autonomy for administrative agencies, the courts will be slower to perceive errors of law, more selective in the errors which they are authorized to correct or more discretionary in allowing the remedy of judicial review. The course which the courts will take may be affected by their success in isolating the element of policy.

The Courts and Policy

The courts are kept out of the lush field of administrative policy,[71] except when policy is inconsistent with the express or implied provisions of a statute which creates the power to which the policy relates or when a decision made in purported exercise of a power is such that a repository of the power, acting reasonably and in good faith, could not have made it. In the latter case, 'something overwhelming' must appear before the court will intervene.[72] That is, and ought to be, a difficult onus for an applicant to discharge. The courts are not very good at formulating or evaluating policy. Sometimes when the courts have intervened on policy grounds, the court's view of the range of policies open under the statute or of what is unreasonable policy has not won public acceptance. On the contrary, curial views of policy have been subjected to stringent criticism.[73] In the world of politics, the court's opinions on policy are naturally less likely to reflect the popular view than the policies of a democratically elected government or of expert administrators. The court does not have the resources either to develop or review the merits of a general policy; its procedure focusses its concern on the interests of the individual litigant rather than on the interests of the public at large; and it may not see the instant case in the context of the mass of cases to which the policy applies.

The considerations by reference to which the reasonableness of a policy may be determined are rarely judicially manageable. For this reason, the court is slow to intervene when injustice has been done to individual interests by what may appear to be an unjust policy. To undo such an injustice, the court must reject the view of the public interest which is held by the political branches of government, and that is a course from which the courts must refrain except in the clearest cases.

It is largely because of this limitation on the scope of judicial review that it is desirable to create what, in Australia, is called the Administrative Appeals Tribunal, exercising jurisdiction to review on the merits, administrative decisions of specified classes. Such tribunals, adopting flexible procedures which do not always require servicing by lawyers, and which develop an internal expertise to produce consistency in the exercise of discretionary powers, are valuable complements to judicial review.[74] Indeed, their remedies are alternatives to judicial review, often more cost-efficient and accessible.

An Administrative Appeals Tribunal, being armed with authority to apply whatever policy it thinks appropriate[75] may, by the publication of its reasons, engage in a constructive dialogue with the Minister or other authority formulating the guiding policy. It can ensure that the policy to be applied is capable of doing reasonable justice to individual interests or, at least, that the policy has been exposed to public discussion and has not been disapproved by Parliament.[76] So lively a role in policy formation is not for the courts.

The path of further development

The contemporary scope of judicial review has been achieved by adopting a standard technique of the judicial activist: eliciting from a number of particular cases, each of which is restricted to its particular facts and governed by a rule of limited application, some underlying principle which accounts for the court's jurisdiction to grant a remedy in all those cases. The principle emerges as an all-embracing rule shorn of the limitations applied in the particular cases, leaving the court with a discretion whether and to what extent the expanded jurisdiction should be exercised in new cases falling within the principle. As the court's discretion hardens into law, new limits appear different from the limits imposed by the superseded rules and more appropriate to the conditions of contemporary society. And when new limits are established, the rule is ripe to undergo yet another transformation. By a kind of dialectic between general principles and concrete cases, the common law makes its compromise between certainty and contemporary relevance.

The law has now developed so that the court has the theoretical tools by which to intervene freely in the taking of administrative action. The rules governing judicial review are broad indeed. Lord Diplock, in *Council of Civil Service Unions*, felt able to identify the grounds of judicial review as 'illegality', 'irrationality' and 'procedural impropriety', perhaps shortly to be supplemented by 'the principle of proportionality'.[77] These criteria are too broad for practical use in hard cases. But it is clear that there is much room for judicial discretion or evaluation in ascertaining the content of natural justice in a particular case, or the material on which a decision-maker could reasonably act, or whether an error of law is involved in a decision, or whether the error goes to jurisdiction, or whether a policy is consistent with the statute and is reasonable. It is inevitable that the courts will refine the applicability of the general grounds for review case by case. As Denis Galligan says:

> The restrictions on the scope of natural justice have been removed so what is left uncertain is its content; the decision has been made to look into the reasoning process of officials exercising discretionary power with a view to testing reasonableness, the propriety of purposes, and the relevance of considerations; restrictions on the reviewability of errors of law have been largely cast off; similarly issues of fact can be scrutinized under the developing requirement of a foundation of evidence. . . . Once these and other heads of review are opened out in this way, the second step becomes important: that is, how are the discretionary assessments, necessary in applying the heads of review, to be made? [78]

The courts will have to answer that question from case to case. The answer will depend on the balance which the courts strike between the interests of individuals (which the court is concerned to protect) and the interests of the community at large (which the political branches of government are concerned to advance). An answer is needed. One of the important purposes of judicial review is the definition of principles to govern administration. But that is not its primary purpose. The primary purpose of judicial review may be stated under Lord Diplock's broad headings: it is the safeguarding of individual interests against affection by illegal or irrational administrative action or by administrative action taken without proper procedures. The tension between the purpose of safeguarding individual interests and the purpose of defining principles to govern administration produces some uncertainty in the scope of judicial review. There has to be a composition between flexibility and certainty in the law, and the law is not settled.

The scope of the remedy may not be determined effectively by judicial decision alone, but the imaginative responses of the courts to the problems created by the explosion in administrative power in the last twenty years affirms the vigour of the common law and its capacity to retain public confidence in the institution of judicial review.

---

1. The paper was published in the *Australian Bar Review:* see Sir Gerard Brennan 'The Purpose and Scope of Judicial Review (1986) 2 *Australian Bar Review* 93.
2. No 78.
3. See Lord Radcliffe, 'The Place of Law Courts in Society' in Lord Radcliffe, 'Not in Feather Beds. Some collected papers' (Hamish Hamilton, 1968) 34.
4. See the discussions by TRS Allan in 'Legislative Supremacy and the Rule of Law: Democracy and Constitutionalism' (1985) 44 *Cambridge Law Journal* 111, and TRS Allan, 'The Limits of Parliamentary Sovereignty' [1985] *Public Law* 614.
5. See JAG Griffiths, 'Judicial Decision-Making in Public Law' (1985) *Public Law* 564; and *Kioa v West* (1985) 159 CLR 550.
6. Bernard Schwartz, *Administrative Law* (Little Brown, 1976) 6.
7. See *State of New South Wales v Commonwealth* (1915) 20 CLR 54, 63 (Griffiths CJ).
8. Procedural reform has been effected by legislation in some places: see *Judicature Amendment Act* 1972 (NZ) and *Judicature Amendment Act* 1977 (NZ); *Administrative Decisions (Judicial Review) Act 1977* (Cth); *Administrative Law Act 1978* (Vic).
9. Sir William Wade, *Constitutional Fundamentals* (Stevens for The Hamlyn Trust, 1980), Hamlyn Lectures 32nd series, 62.
10. [1964] AC 40.
11. Lord Devlin, 'Judges and Lawmakers' (1976) *Modern Law Review* 1, 5, 8; reprinted in Lord Devlin, *The Judge* (Oxford University Press, 1979), 5, 9.
12. Ibid 5.

13. Lord Radcliffe, 'The Lawyer and his Times', a 1967 address to Harvard Law School published in Lord Radcliffe, *Not in Feather Beds. Some collected papers* (Hamish Hamilton, 1968) 271-2.
14. [1985] AC 374, 407.
15. Louis Jaffe and Edith Henderson, 'Judicial Review and the Rule of Law: Historical Origins' (1956) 72 *Law Quarterly Review* 345 especially 361, 362.
16. Benjamin Cardozo, *The Nature of the Judicial Process, Selected Writings* (Yale University Press, 1921), 47-8.
17. Lord Devlin, *The Judge* (Oxford University Press, 1979), 181.
18. 356 US 86 (1957), 119.
19. (1980) 146 CLR 493.
20. (1981) 149 CLR 27.
21. [1903] 1 Ch 109.
22. (1981) 36 ALR 64, 79.
23. See *Safadi v Minister for Immigration and Ethnic Affairs* (1981) 38 ALR 399, 403; *Ricegrowers Co-operative Mills Ltd v Bannerman and Trade Practices Commission* (1981) 38 ALR 535, 539-40; *Doyle v Chief of General Staff* (1982) 42 ALR 283, 287-8; *Lamb v Moss* (1983) 49 ALR 533, 554; *Dalton v Deputy Commissioner of Taxation (NSW)* (1985) 60 ALR 783, 790, 794, 796-7.
24. [1961] AC 617, 634.
25. [1982] AC 617, 644. Cf Lord Roskill.
26. [1981] 1 NZLR 216, 220.
27. See the discussion in *Wall v Livingston* [1982] 1 NZLR 734.
28. See *Paterson v Dunedin City Council* [1981] 2 NZLR 619, 621; but cf *Consumers Co-operative Society v Palmerston North City Council* [1984] 1 NZLR 1.
29. See *Lonrho Ltd v Shell Petroleum Co Ltd* [1982] AC 173, 185.
30. See *Australian Conservation Foundation* v *Commonwealth* (1980) 146 CLR 493 and *Onus* v *Alcoa of Australia Ltd* (1981) 149 CLR 27.
31. See *Schmidt v Secretary of State for Home Affairs* [1969] 2 Ch 149, 170.
32. In *Kioa* v *West* (1985) 159 CLR 550 at 617-8, I thought that the notion of legitimate expectations seems to be ill fitted to do the work assigned to it. But that is not the present point.
33. [1985] AC 374.
34. [1967] 2 QB 864.
35. See *Council of Civil Service Unions* v *Minister for the Civil Service* [1985] AC 374, 407.
36. [1985] AC 374, 410.
37. Bora Laskins, 'Certiorari to Labour Boards: The Apparent Futility of Privative Clauses' (1952) 30 (10) *Canadian Bar Review* 986, 990. Cf Hudson Janisch, 'Bora Laskin and Administrative Law: An Unfinished Journey' (1985) 35 UTLJ 557, 572.
38. See *Ridge v Baldwin* [1964] AC 40, 74-9.
39. [1949] 1 All ER 109, 118.
40. See *FAI Insurances Ltd* v *Winneke* (1982) 151 CLR 342, where the principles of natural justice were held to apply to the exercise of a statutory power by the Governor of a State.
41. See *Wiseman* v *Borneman* [1971] AC 297, 308 (Lord Reid).

42. See *Local Government Board* v *Arlidge* [1915] AC 120, 138 (Lord Shaw of Dunfermline) .
43. (1985) 159 CLR 550.
44. (1977) 137 CLR 396.
45. (1977) 137 CLR 461.
46. See *Daganayasi* v *Minister of Immigration* [1980] 2 NZLR 130, 145. Cf David Mullan, 'Natural Justice and Fairness — Substantive as well as Procedural Standards for the Review of Administrative Decision-Making?' (1982) 27 *McGill Law Journal* 250.
47. See, for example, Lord Diplock in *Bushell v Environment Secretary* [1981] AC 75, 97.
48. See *Attorney-General of Canada* v *Inuit Tapirisat of Canada* (1980) 115 DLR (3d) 1, 19.
49. [1980] 2 NZLR 130, 136.
50. [1982] 1 WLR 1155, 1173.
51. Ibid 1174.
52. Ibid 1161.
53. See *R* v *Coldham*; *Ex parte Australian Workers' Union* (1983) 153 CLR 415, 418, 419.
54. See, for example, *Stewart* v *Invercargill City Corporation* [1976] 2 NZLR 362.
55. See *Secretary of State for Education and Science* v *Tameside Metropolitan Borough Council* [1977] AC 1014.
56. See Stanley Alexander de Smith and John Marix Evans, *Judicial Review of Administrative Action* (Stevens, 4th ed, 1980) 133.
57. [1984] AC 808, 820.
58. See *Re Erebus Royal Commission; Air New Zealand Ltd* v *Mahon* [1981] 1 NZLR 618, 664.
59. [1982] 1 NZLR 252, 273.
60. See *Anisminic Ltd* v *Foreign Compensation Commission* [1969] 2 AC 147; *Sinclair* v *Maryborough Mining Warden* (1975) 132 CLR 473.
61. See J A Smillie, 'Judicial Review of Administrative Action — A Pragmatic Approach' (1980) 4 *Otago Law Review* 417.
62. See *Re Gray; Ex parte Marsh* (1985) 62 ALR 17, 32; 59 ALJR 804, 812.
63. [1969] 2 AC 147.
64. See *In re Racal Communications Ltd* [1981] AC 374, 383.
65. [1983] 2 AC 237.
66. [1983] NZLR 129, 134.
67. [1983] NZLR 129, 136.
68. See *Hockey* v *Yelland* (1984) 56 ALR 215; 59 ALJR 66.
69. Section 16(1) gives the court a discretion.
70. Section 5(1)(f).
71. Lord Diplock, in *Ex parte Federation of Self-Employed and Small Businesses Ltd* [1982] AC 617, 644, held the departments of government accountable to Parliament for policy and to the courts for lawfulness. But the lawfulness of policy is for the courts, and the dichotomy between policy and lawfulness is difficult to maintain.
72. See *Associated Provincial Picture Houses Ltd* v *Wednesbury Corporation* [1948] 1 KB 223, 230.
73. See John Aneurin Grey Griffith, *The Politics of the Judiciary* (Fontana Press, 3rd ed, 1985) 129 ff.

74. As I described in the article, Gerard Brennan, 'The Future of Public Law — The Australian Administrative Appeals Tribunal' (1979) 4 *Otago Law Review* 286.
75. See *Drake* v *Minister for Immigration and Ethnic Affairs* (1979) 2 ALD 60.
76. See *Re Drake and Minister for Immigration and Ethnic Affairs (No 2)* (1979) 2 ALD 634.
77. [1985] AC 374, 410.
78. Denis Galligan, 'Judicial Review and the Textbook Writers' (1982) 2 *Oxford Journal of Legal Studies* 257, 263.

4.4 20th Anniversary of the Administrative Appeals Tribunal

Editor's note

Having been the first President of the Administrative Appeals Tribunal, Brennan, as Chief Justice of the High Court was invited to address the Administrative Appeals Tribunal Twentieth Anniversary Conference on 21 July 1996.

It was a cold, crisp Canberra morning on Thursday 1 July 1976 when my wife and I walked down Northbourne Avenue and around London Circuit to the Wales building. The doors of the Administrative Appeals Tribunal (AAT) were opened without ceremony. The bare space was interrupted by the occasional desk and powerpoint. The AAT name was on the noticeboard downstairs but months would pass before anybody needed to find it. Ron Mills, prised away from the Attorney-General's Department and his favoured Treasury, was on hand to command the Registry. So was Dianne Smith who, apart from her other talents, had a way with African violets, tea and cake. So, we celebrated the opening of the Administrative Appeals Tribunal. I was escorted to my new chambers and met the efficient Delcia von Brandenstein, whose presence was a tribute to her sense of adventure and to the sense of self-sacrifice of her previous boss, Frank Mahony, the Deputy Secretary of the Attorney-General's Department.

There was enthusiasm within that Department for this new creature, the AAT. Sir Clarrie Harders, the redoubtable permanent head, decided to expose me at lunch at the Commonwealth Club to the inspection of Sir Frederick Wheeler of Treasury and Sir Alan Cooley of the Public Service Board. As one who came from practice at the Bar to a tribunal charged with the review of administrative decisions on the merits, I encountered a steep learning curve. I had barely stepped upon its lowest point when we lunched that day. Sir Frederick Wheeler asked me how the tribunal would review a decision of the kind he was then contemplating, namely, a recommendation to his Minister to make an ex gratia payment. I had no idea whether the tribunal had any jurisdiction in such a matter but I knew that the Act required a decision-maker to state his reasons. So, I responded weakly that, if there were jurisdiction to review such a decision, he would have to state his reasons and we would look at them and do the best we could!

The incident provided a valuable lesson. It showed that the AAT was bound first to ascertain its own jurisdiction and then it had to acquire sufficient experience or wisdom to review usefully primary decisions made by experienced officers who had the strength of departmental culture and research behind them.

Some time passed before the existence, much less the utility, of the AAT dawned on the community, particularly the legal community. In the early days, Ron Mills spoke to several interested groups – notably an association of customs agents – to inform them of the availability of the new jurisdiction to challenge particular classes of administrative decisions. In time, the customs jurisdiction was readily invoked and the Customs Tariff, which had previously been the subject of litigation only in the High Court and then only infrequently, became a regular subject of decision by the AAT. But the first case came across the registry counter in Brisbane. A tax agent, Mr Adams, challenged the cancellation of his registration by the Tax Agents' Board.[1] One ground for challenging the decision was that the relevant provision of the *Income Tax Assessment Act 1936* (Cth) was invalid. To challenge the validity of a Commonwealth statute before an administrative tribunal was a brave step but, after all, the exercise of any power by an executive agency depends upon the validity of the law conferring power. The question raised by *Adams' Case* illustrated the curious position of the AAT and its uneasy straddling of the divide between the exercise of executive power and the exercise of judicial power.

The fact that the AAT straddled that divide meant that there were two models available for the AAT to follow. It could follow the administrative model and become, so to speak, a higher tier in the bureaucracy. Or it could follow the judicial model which would mark it as something standing outside the bureaucracy and beyond ministerial power to prescribe the policy it was to follow. It is no secret that the AAT followed the judicial method, nor that the period of my presidency was one in which that model was adhered to closely – perhaps too closely. At this time, on the 20th Anniversary of the AAT's foundation, we may reflect on whether the AAT has evolved in a way that, irrespective of the model, practically answers the needs of the community and of government administration.

Having been away from the coalface of the AAT for 17 years, I do not presume to pontificate on what or, more significantly, who the AAT should be today. But the singularity of the functions which it performs makes it a subject of continuing interest and enhances that lively concern for its continued vitality which I acquired with high hopes 20 years ago. So, I shall indulge myself with some reflections that may be trite or out-of-date or irrelevant to the focus of today's Tribunal. But I excuse myself for taking this indulgence on the ground that the problems addressed by the *Administrative Appeals Tribunal Act 1975* (Cth) and by the Tribunal in its early years must be enduring problems because of the nature of the AAT's function. And this Conference is devoted to reflection on those functions in the light of 20 years' experience.

The model adopted by the AAT necessarily reflected the functions committed to it. At the beginning, Professor Harry Whitmore, who had been a member of the Kerr Committee, was an advocate of the administrative model. He had envisaged the AAT as a shopfront reviewer of administrative decisions in the large volume as well as small volume areas, righting the wrongs suffered by individual members of the public. Professor Whitmore did not envisage a high-powered institution engaged in statutory construction and the time-consuming enunciation of reasons for decision. But there were practical impediments to the implementation of an AAT based on the shop-front model. Shop-fronts would have been required in every part of the Commonwealth, staffed by persons on whom AAT powers had been conferred. It would have required a degree of training and sophistication on the part of all of those persons to equip them to deal with a variety of decisions and to do so with some show of tolerable consistency. Although the Tribunal was advantaged by the extraordinary administrative skills and bureaucratic capacity of Sir Clarrie Harders, Mr Frank Mahony and Mr Lindsay Curtis of the Attorney-General's Department, the resources required for the creation of such an AAT would not have been obtained in 1976. I doubt whether they would be obtained today.

More significantly, the Act gave a clear indication of the quasi-judicial character of the Tribunal envisaged by the Parliament. The reason why the Parliament gave the Tribunal this character can best be understood by reference to the five deficiencies that Sir Anthony Mason identified as distinguishing administrative from judicial decision making:

> Experience indicates that administrative decision-making falls short of the judicial model – on which the AAT is based – in five significant respects. First, it lacks the independence of the judicial process. The administrative decision-maker is, and is thought to be, more susceptible to political, ministerial and bureaucratic influence than is a judge. Secondly, some administrative decisions are made out in the open; most are not. Thirdly, apart from statute, the administrator does not always observe the standards of natural justice or procedural fairness. That is not surprising; he is not trained to do so. Finally, he is inclined to subordinate the claims of justice of the individual to the more general demands of public policy and sometimes to adventitious political and bureaucratic pressures.
>
> The five features of administrative decision-making which I have

> mentioned reveal why it is that administrative decision-making has never achieved the level of acceptance of the judicial process in the mind of the public. [2]

As to independence, s 7(1) of the *Administrative Appeals Tribunal Act 1975* Cth) provided, as it continues to provide, that the President must be a Judge of the Federal Court. At first, the only presidential members of the Tribunal were Judges of the Federal Court. There was no provision for senior members. They were quickly introduced. Mr Keith Edmonds accepted appointment as a part-time senior member and gave the AAT the benefit of his experience both as a Judge of the Supreme Court of Papua New Guinea and as a senior member of the bureaucracy.

Other members had to have, as they are still required to have,[3] specialist qualifications. These members were to serve part-time and were to constitute the tribunal with a presidential member in reviewing classes of decisions within their expertise.

The members of the Tribunal had to possess high qualifications and be independent of the influence of the parties to decisions under review. The Act did not prescribe independence as a requirement for appointment, but the practice was established of entrusting appointments to the Attorney- General, not to the Ministers of the departments whose decisions were to be subject to review.

The Tribunal thus had the authority of independent members of undoubted experience, knowledge and skill in the particular field. The presidential members would have the weight of their judicial office to support their determinations of questions of law and their enunciation of principles or policies that would ensure consistency in the reviewing of decisions even if no doctrine of strict precedent applied. The senior members would be lawyers of acknowledged capacity and independence. And so it proved to be.

Openness of decision-making was achieved by requiring the AAT ordinarily to hear matters in public: s 35. Reasons for decision could be obtained from a primary decision-maker by a person affected by the decision: s 28. And the AAT's obligation to state its reasons was spelt out by s 43(2) and (3) which, in 1976, read as follows:

> (2) The Tribunal shall give reasons in writing for its decision and those reasons shall include its findings on material questions of fact.
>
> (3) The Tribunal shall cause a copy of its decision to be served on each party to the proceeding.

The AAT's obligation to accord natural justice was supplemented by an express statutory requirement to ensure that every party has an opportunity to present his case and make submissions: s 39. And, as to Sir Anthony's fifth point of distinction, the balance between the individual interest and public, political or bureaucratic interests was to be assured, so far as could be, by the openness and accountability of the procedure.

Applicants for relief had to be persons whose interests are affected by the decision to be reviewed. The Tribunal was empowered to summon witnesses. It had to state the reasons for its decisions on review. Its decisions were then subjected to appeal on a question of law to the Federal Court to which the AAT might, if it chose, refer a question of law for determination. The model of the Tribunal was thus statutorily identified. It was to interpret and apply the relevant law. It was to ascertain the facts from witnesses in a court-like procedure. And its obligation to state reasons for decision was similar to the obligation of courts to state their reasons for judgment.

Although the AAT, like any other officer of the Commonwealth within the meaning of that term in s 75(v) of the *Constitution*, was subject to prerogative writs issued by the High Court, its decisions were also amenable to appeal on questions of law. It had no leeway for the making of decisions which, though erroneous in point of law, were within jurisdiction. Any decision that was made by the tribunal had to accord both to the applicant and to the decision-maker their precise legal entitlements and be based on their precise legal obligations.

The quasi-judicial nature of the Tribunal was emphasized by the conferring of a power to stay a decision – a power similar to that exercised by a judge granting an injunction. In the very earliest days, when I was the only member of the AAT, I amused my wife by telephoning periodically as we were moving by road from our home in Brisbane to the frosty atmosphere of Canberra to see whether any applications had been made for urgent stay orders. 'It would be wrong', I would say, 'if an elephant were destroyed on a wharf because of an administrative error by the quarantine service!' No elephant was ever at risk, as far as I know. In those earliest days, the likelihood is that the only persons with knowledge of the AAT's jurisdiction were the members of the public service whose superannuation entitlements were to be protected by review by the AAT under s 154 of the *Superannuation Act 1976* (Cth). That section was proclaimed to come into effect on 1 July 1976.

If the AAT be reproached for judicialising administrative decision-making, it can be said that the Act required decision-making by the AAT to become more acceptable than primary decision-making by adopting some judicial characteristics. Of course, the rules of evidence were not to be binding and the AAT's procedures could and should be as informal and flexible as the nature of the case permitted (s 33) but the basic requirements of the Act could not be short-cut by the adoption of a procedure that brought into the review process the summary, and sometimes unsatisfactory, aspects of administrative decision-making.

However, a judicial model could not be adopted for the AAT without qualification. Courts declare and enforce existing rights and obligations; administrative decisions create or modify rights and obligations. Courts exercise their powers upon findings of fact made on evidence governed by legal rules; the AAT exercises its powers upon findings of fact made by reference to wider sources of information. But courts and the AAT are both bound by, and bound to apply, the law and to apply it precisely. The major distinction between courts and the AAT is that, generally speaking, the courts are not concerned with administrative policy whilst administrative policy is a core concern in some areas of AAT jurisdiction.

From the viewpoint of the judiciary, the participation of judges in the work of the AAT was a radical innovation – not so much because judges were asked to find facts or to apply law for the purpose of reviewing administrative decisions but rather because in making administrative decisions which were wholly or partly discretionary, they were involved in applying an administrative – sometimes ministerial – policy. Judges were accustomed to the exercise of judicial discretions, but such discretions were exercised by reference to ascertainable criteria supplied by the legislature[4], not according to broad policies which, if not idiosyncratic, were derived from or influenced by the will of the government of the day.

True, administrative policy must be consistent with the relevant statute but the policies which presented novel problems for the judicial mind were policies that were not prescribed by, or implied in, a statute. How could a series of decisions consistent one with another be made when consistency depended upon the application of such a policy? Should the judge accept a ministerial statement of policy? That would be an unusual step for a judge to take. Or should the tribunal without the benefit of administrative knowledge and experience and without that breadth of view which comes from a political balancing of contending interests endeavour to formulate a policy for itself?

Logically, the tribunal's jurisdiction to determine issues involving policy makes it an anomaly in our system of government. The theory of the system is that administrative policy is a matter for which ministers are responsible and for which they must accept political responsibility, answering for their policies before the Parliament. The courts, on the other hand, must have some ascertainable benchmark by which to make a decision, albeit some element of discretion is involved. Absent the unifying influence of policy on decision-making, there is a risk that inconsistency brings the decision-making process into disrepute. In *Drake* v *Minister for Immigration and Ethnic Affairs*[5] the Full Court of the Federal Court held that in cases where the relevant statute permitted a primary decision-maker to take account of government policy, the AAT was entitled to have regard to government policy. However, Bowen CJ and Deane J said:

> the Tribunal is not, in the absence of specific statutory provision, entitled to abdicate its function of determining whether the decision made was, on the material before the Tribunal, the correct or preferable one in favour of a function of merely determining whether the decision made conformed with whatever the relevant general government policy might be.
>
> It is not desirable to attempt to frame any general statement of the precise part which government policy should ordinarily play in the determinations of the Tribunal. That is a matter for the Tribunal itself to determine in the context of the particular case and in the light of the need for compromise, in the interests of good government, between, on the one hand, the desirability of consistency in the treatment of citizens under the law and, on the other hand, the ideal of justice in the individual case.[6]

I attempted in the AAT hearing following this decision, that is, in *Re Drake (No 2)*,[7] to adopt a ministerial policy provisionally as a guide to AAT decision-making in order to provide both a benchmark for consistency and a recognition of ministerial and parliamentary authority in the definition and approval of executive policy. But, as subsequent experience has shown, the attempt could not produce consistency to the same degree as might be produced within a department under ministerial control. Nor should it do so. The 'ideal of justice in the individual case' is a weightier factor than consistency.

Although policy has presented difficulties to the AAT, some benefits have resulted. By exposing ministerial or administrative policy to critical examination, a useful dialectic can be commenced between the Tribunal and the executive government. At the same time, rigidities that would otherwise be productive of injustice in individual cases can be relieved by the Tribunal's authority to make the correct or preferable decision in the instant case even though the decision runs counter to existing policy.

The AAT was thus armed with authority to review every aspect of administrative decision-making: fact, law and discretion including policy. It is not surprising that the decisions reached by the AAT were frequently different from the decisions made by primary decision-makers. AAT decisions depended on evidence given before the Tribunal, and were frequently different from the information available to the primary decision-maker. And departmental opinions about or evaluations of particular facts were sometimes found to be deficient when exposed to the more open and authoritative views of the specialist members. Specialist qualifications, in fields as diverse as airmanship and actuarial assessment, contributed to the quality of AAT decision-making and the authority of the Tribunal. And, if I may add a personal note, the knowledge of the President was broadened and the pleasure of sitting was enhanced by working with varied groups, all of whom commanded respect.

The AAT was charged with the responsibility of blowing the winds of legal orthodoxy through the corridors of administrative power. Departmental culture and practice and departmental handbooks were to be brought into conformity with the governing statute, truly interpreted. Discretions which had become atrophied or distorted by departmental tradition were again to be exercised in cases contemplated by the legislature. In some areas of administration, the governing Act had become no more than a footnote to divergent practice. The AAT was intended not only to give better administrative justice in individual cases but also to secure an improvement in primary administrative decision-making. This had to be achieved by the quality of the AAT's reasoning. Departments, like any organised human activity, tend to have an inward focus and the corporate culture tends to be the most powerful influence on the conduct of individuals engaged in that activity. External review is only as effective if it infuses the corporate culture and transforms it. The AAT's function of inducing improvement in primary administration would not be performed merely by the creation of external review. Bureaucratic intransigence would not be moved unless errors were clearly demonstrated and a method of reaching the correct or preferable decision was clearly expounded. AAT decisions would have a normative effect on administration only if the quality of those decisions was such as to demonstrate to the repositories of primary administrative power the validity of the reasoning by which they, no less than the AAT, were bound. Any effect that the AAT might produce in primary administration would depend upon the reasoning expressed in the reasons for AAT decisions.

The AAT was not needed to supply, nor would it have supplied, management skills. Those skills, essential to an efficient public service, were not discounted by the introduction of external merits review. The skills that were introduced were legal and specialist skills – by specialist skills, I mean skills in the particular discipline relevant to the diverse areas of jurisdiction.

They were to be exercised in a procedure following a judicial model by members independent of the influence of the Department making the decision under review.

Now, all of this is probably all too familiar to the present audience. I am conscious that the problems of procedure, legal analysis, fact finding and policy application have been refined in the last twenty years. I am not competent to comment on those developments except to pay my respects to those whose insights I have detected by a skimming of the huge volume of material that has emerged. But I refer to the concepts that commanded attention at the beginning because the problems that were then encountered are the natural concomitants of vesting power in an independent tribunal to review on the merits administrative decisions made by Ministers or their departments in a Westminster system of government. It is the contemporary lessons, however, which are of present concern. I mention four topics: membership, jurisdiction, procedure and management.

Membership

First, membership of the AAT. For the reasons just stated, the AAT is not strengthened by the addition of mere management skills. Managers may have other specialist skills that commend them for appointment but an ability to manage a diversity of programs is a skill which, however valuable in administration generally, adds little to the ability of the AAT to perform its functions. I venture to suggest that the AAT should never be, or be seen to be, either a promotion or retirement opportunity for managers who do not possess the skills which really are relevant to the AAT's function. Let me give you an example. Two of our early part-time members were Messrs Vic Skermer and Mr Reg Stock. One had been Auditor-General; the other, a captain of commerce. Both had managerial skills but their contribution to the AAT lay in their understanding of the issues with which we had to deal, such as the Brussels *Convention on the Valuation of Goods for Customs Purposes*.[8]

The judicial membership of the AAT has, I suspect, become more attenuated than in earlier times. That was to be expected. Judicial participation in the work of the AAT was secured for two reasons. The first was to secure lawyers of judicial capability to contribute to the elucidation of legal principles. For that reason, a judge was usually asked to sit on the Tribunal in the first case that arose in a new area of the jurisdiction. The second, and associated, reason, was that the status, independence and authority of the judicial officer was thereby lent to decisions on the interpretation of statute and the limitation of powers arising under it. It needed judicial authority, albeit exercised in a non-judicial tribunal, to expose and correct errors which had formed part of departmental culture or practice or which were to be found in departmental manuals.

With the growing authority of the tribunal and its acceptance as a normative influence on decision-making in the executive branch of government, it was possible to reduce the demands made on the Federal Court. Presidential members have been appointed from among the judges of the Family Court and permanent presidential members came to be appointed without judicial status. At this point I would like to pay a tribute to Messrs Alan Hall and Robert Todd, who not only carried enormous burdens as senior members and later as presidential members but demonstrated that non-judicial presidential members, if selected with the requisite qualifications and experience, would perform the functions of that high office with efficiency, courtesy and conspicuous ability.

Although judicial influence in the tribunal has been diminished, the need for a high level of competence in decision-making in a judicial manner is in no way diminished. If legal rules are loosely or inaccurately stated, if their application is problematic or if their expression is unclear, the Tribunal will quickly lose the authority that has been gained by the assiduous application of the legal method. If departmental culture or practice or the departmental manual were to assume a paramountcy over the law enacted by the Parliament or prescribed under legislative authority, one of the main purposes of the *Administrative Appeals Tribunal Act 1975* (Cth) would be frustrated.

The legal method involves not only skill and knowledge; it involves independence and impartiality. These are qualities of mind and character which are not necessarily developed in the non-judicial branches of government as they are in the judicial branch. When the focus of occupational interest is on the management of programs, individual interests and aspirations are not factors of compelling weight. There is an inevitable tension between protecting the public purse and securing benefits for individuals under programs that are funded by the public purse. An officer who has been accustomed to the development of programs beneficial to the majority of the Australian community may not be as attuned to the interests of individuals or of a minority as those who have been devoted professionally to the protection of individual interests. A fortiori, a mind which has been devoted to the achievement of ministerial goals will not find it easy to reach decisions which are out of kilter with government policy. One of the great purposes of the AAT is to strike a balance between the interests of the public and individual interests. That balance requires, on the one hand, sufficient flexibility in program policies to cope with the almost infinite variety of circumstances that affect individuals and, on the other, vigilance to ensure that individuals do not undermine the protection or the benefits which a program is intended to confer on the community generally by receiving greater protection or more benefits than the program is intended to afford or bear. Independence, skill and impartiality of mind are essential to this task.

The Administrative Review Council Report No 39 'Better Decisions: Review of Commonwealth Merits Review Tribunals' contains the startling recommendation that 'Save for the President, legal qualifications should not be a prerequisite for appointment' to a new unified tribunal.[9] The Council believes that some members of a new, unified tribunal would have legal qualifications[10] and it proposes that legal expertise can be contributed by persons whom Robert Todd has described as 'barefoot lawyers',[11] or by the tribunal's legal or research staff[12] or even by assistance from the President.[13]

As Robert Todd has pointed out, the recommendation bespeaks a fundamental lack of appreciation both of the functioning and of the dynamics of external review as experienced by the AAT. The Council's recommendations in this respect would deny to the proposed tribunal the capacity to provide – and the continued assurance that the tribunal would provide – coercive correction if a primary administrator were to follow departmental guidance that does not conform to legal principle. If that capacity were lost, much of the *raison d'être* of external review is gone.

If legal expertise be discounted, perhaps management personnel with their ability to cover many fields would be offered as the presiding members. That would be an inversion of the conception of the AAT. Presiding officers with legal training – I do not say merely with legal qualifications – are (or ought to be) alert to the difference between legal rules which lie within their province and expertise which lies within the province of specialist members and pertains to issues of fact. Would presiding officers without legal training be comfortable with that division of function? Or would the contribution of the specialist members be depreciated by the universal skills of the managers?

As to specialist members, it is difficult to overstate their importance to the success of the AAT. Although the presiding members of the Tribunal are expected to possess the capacity to articulate reasons for a decision, the expertise of the specialist members contributes to the reasoning that has to be expressed. The Administrative Review Council has already noted:[14]

> 4.4 ... that satisfaction with a tribunal's performance appears to be highly correlated with opinions as to the quality of its members,[15] and this point has been reinforced during the inquiry.

> 4.5 Applicants and the broader community must have reason to be confident that the members of review tribunals both have the skills required to provide merits review and will consider the merits of their cases in an impartial way, and make a different decision to that of the relevant government agency where they consider that appropriate.

The recommendation I have criticized is more surprising in the light of this statement. Unless the specialist members are seen to be contributing their expertise to the functions of the AAT, the confidence in decisions of the AAT will be seriously diminished.

Jurisdiction

With increasing experience of review in particular areas of jurisdiction, the need for frequent exposition of legal principle is diminished. With the expansion of AAT jurisdiction into large volume areas, fact-finding became an increasingly dominant function of the AAT. That does not mean that legal skills became irrelevant.

But the vesting of large volume jurisdictions raises a troublesome question. Is the AAT too high-powered, too expensive, too legalistic a tribunal to deal with essentially factual issues in cases such as social security or veterans' entitlements in which relatively small amounts of money are usually involved? A variety of filters can be contemplated to respond to this problem: lower-level tribunals such as the SSAT with more expeditious, less judicialised procedures is one solution. Internal review, required as a condition of a right to appeal to the AAT, is another. And, of course, mediation and preliminary conferences. Filtering mechanisms of these kinds must be provided, not only to effect economies of personnel and resources but also to ensure that the jurisdiction of the AAT is reserved for cases that warrant its intervention. As the ultimate tribunal for review on the merits, its intervention is needed when a decision will have a normative effect on primary administration. If the AAT were seen to be no more than a tribunal concerned with a wilderness of single instances, its ethos would grow closer to that of the departments; and questions would arise as to whether resources would be better channelled into departmental decision-making rather than to the AAT.

In large volume areas of jurisdiction, consistency in decision-making is an enduring problem. Where there is a large measure of discretion there will always be some unevenness in decisions by differently constituted tribunals; where such decisions are made in large volume, the unevenness is capable of undermining the confidence in tribunal decision-making. It is important that the AAT caseload be sufficiently limited to permit the development of principles or guidelines that will yield substantial consistency between decisions in similar cases in a given area.

At a time of economic constraint, the need to save costs is likely to inspire proposals which maximise the throughput of cases without too nice a regard for the means and mechanisms that have been previously adopted to improve the standard of administrative justice. In particular, the two features of AAT decision-making which gave the Tribunal its authority may be targeted for unacceptable reduction: the expertise of the legal members and the expertise of the specialist members.

I venture to suggest that, if those expedients of cost-cutting be adopted, the distinction between the functions of the AAT and the functions of the primary administrator will be blurred and, in time, the authority of the AAT will be diminished. That would be a consequence which the AAT could not long survive, for it is of the essence of AAT decision-making that it contributes acknowledged independence and expertise to administrative decision-making.

In selecting areas of jurisdiction for the AAT, the criterion cannot be merely the importance of an exercise of the relevant power to the individual. The awarding of a multi-million dollar defence contract to an offshore contractor will be of immense importance to the contractor but the AAT is not fitted to review either the assessment of tenders or the political considerations that may affect the decision. The importance of a decision to the individual is one factor, but the critical factors are the elements that go into the making of a decision. The finding or evaluation of facts, the need for a clear application of legal principle and the scope and nature of any discretion are the factors that must be given the most careful attention.

The AAT has been immensely successful, and it would be regrettable if its utility were prejudiced by the conferring of jurisdiction in areas that are not appropriate to external review. It would be equally regrettable if the resources of the AAT were insufficient to allow it to exercise the jurisdictions vested in it. Far better that jurisdictions be withdrawn than that the quality of AAT decision-making, and hence its authority, be compromised.

If the AAT is thought to be too expensive, too high-powered to deal with a given area of jurisdiction, and resources are too scarce to allow of an efficient exercise of the AAT jurisdiction, would it not be better to channel such resources into internal review at a lower level than to provide a statutory pretence of higher level external review?

Procedure

The disadvantage of the judicial model is that curial procedure is presented as the natural means of fact-finding. Of course, some of the trappings or indicia of curial proceedings were easily dispensed with. The traditional description of a case as being one party versus another was not adopted; a hearing room in the round with a minimum elevation of the bench was created. But, more significantly, the variety of decisions falling for review by the AAT quickly broke down the traditional curial procedure. The statutory admonition to provide each party with a reasonable opportunity to present a case required some formality but new, less formalized, procedures were devised in and before hearings, particularly during the distinguished and innovative presidency of my successor, Justice Daryl Davies.

However, informality, when it comes to fact-finding, can be taken only so far or it will start to infringe upon the requirement of natural justice. It must be kept firmly in mind that the issue in an AAT appeal is inevitably one in which an applicant's interests are affected by the decision under review: that is the criterion of an entitlement to apply. If the decision is defended there is a conflict of interest and adversaries are, to that extent, created. If that cannot be avoided, the importance of the preliminary conference is obvious. A sense of grievance arises often from sheer misunderstanding and an opportunity for explanation given in an impartial atmosphere is likely to remove a large proportion of the contest that would otherwise have to be determined. Preliminary conferences, unlike hearings, are not intended to have a normative effect on administration. They need only the moderating influence of a mediator who, whether legally qualified or not, is familiar with the field.

Management

The growth of large volume jurisdiction has necessarily produced a bureaucracy of the AAT itself. I notice from the *AAT Annual Report 1994-1995* a diagram of the large bureaucracy under the control of the Registrar. No doubt, having regard to the heavy caseload which the AAT now bears (as the statistics for that year demonstrate), a large bureaucracy spread throughout Australia is required. I hope that the need for this core of personnel and the inevitable closeness of their working relationship with the members, especially the permanent members, is not conducive to a cast of mind that subjects the independence of the members to the corporate memory or knowledge or advice of the AAT bureaucracy.

On looking back over these pages, I can see that I have been guilty of the offence committed by parents and grandparents: giving advice to those who are living their own lives, over whom the adviser has no authority and for whom he or she bears no responsibility. Forgive me as I offer an explanation or, at least, an excuse. The AAT occupies a precarious and, to some extent, anomalous position in our system of government. The Kerr and Bland Committees conceived it as a brilliant solution to the problems of the rapid expansion of administrative decision-making in a complex society. Its success depends on the maintenance of nice distinctions between the departmental lines of ministerial responsibility and the interventionist function of external merits review. I readily acknowledge that the experience of 20 years ago is inadequate to determine the functions and methodology of external review today. But that experience threw up the issues I have mentioned and which, I suggest, require principled responses in the conditions of 1996.

---

1. See *Re Adams and The Tax Agents' Board* (1976) 1 ALD 251.
2. Sir Anthony Mason, 'Administrative Review: The Experience of the first Twelve Years' (1989) 18 *Federal Law Review* 122, 130.
3. s 7(2).
4. See *R* v *Trade Practices Tribunal; Ex parte Tasmanian Breweries Pty Ltd* (1970) 123 CLR 361, 376-377 (Kitto J).
5. (1979) 24 ALR 577.
6. (1979) 24 ALR 577, 590-591.
7. See *Re Drake and Minister for Immigration and Ethnic Affairs (No 2)* (1979) 2 ALD 634.
8. See *Re Renault (Australia) Pty Ltd and Bureau of Customs* (1977) 1 ALD 19.
9. Administrative Review Council Report No 39 'Better Decisions: Review of Commonwealth Merits Review Tribunals', (1995) Recommendation 91, 149.
10. Ibid para 8.32.
11. Robert Todd, 'The Structure of the Commonwealth Merits Review Tribunal System' (1996) 7 AIAL Forum 33.
12. Administrative Review Council Report No 39 'Better Decisions: Review of Commonwealth Merits Review Tribunals', (1995) par 4.14.
13. Ibid par 4.19.
14. Ibid par 4.4.
15. Parliament of Australia, *Administrative Review Council Review of Commonwealth Merits Review Tribunal – Discussion Paper*, (Australian Government Publishing Service, Canberra, 1994), par 4.53.

4.5 The Mechanics of Responsible Government

Editor's note

Brennan delivered the 1998 Sir Robert Garran Oration at the Institute of Public Administration Annual Conference in Hobart on 25 November 1998. Having retired from the High Court in May 1998, he had the opportunity to address senior public servants about administrative law matters, spared the constraints or judicial reserve.[1]

Robert Garran was Premier Reid's legal and constitutional adviser at the Premiers' Conference in Melbourne in 1899. If Alfred Deakin is to be believed,[2] Garran there performed in classical fashion the duties of the competent administrator. Out of sight in an adjoining room, he and a financial adviser, Mr Coghlan, awaited Premier Reid who would withdraw from the conference room from time to time for consultation with his advisers. Then Reid would return 'freshly primed to re-open the debate' presumably stating the propositions with which he had been recently furnished. In later years his scholarly and incisive work on the *Constitution* was a source of sound advice to all those concerned to understand the workings of the organic law under which we live. I acknowledge my debt to his work and I am honoured to deliver an Oration that bears his name.

Sir Robert's reputation stands high among both administrators and lawyers but that is not to attribute to him a duality of skills. His genius was to combine the skills of both professions and to perceive that sound law and sound administration are not only compatible but essential one to the other. It is fitting at this Conference to raise for your critical reflection some of the legal issues that affect the delivery of services to the community. The legal framework of any undertaking, as Garran so clearly recognised, gives it substance and shape.

Supervision of the delivery of public sector services and supervision of governmental measures governing the delivery of services by the private sector is the province of public law. Otherwise, the delivery of services is governed by private law, in particular (except in the case of charities) the law of contract. The outsourcing of governmental functions raises new and interesting questions as to the mechanism for supervising the delivery of outsourced services, a topic to which I shall return. But first let us reflect on the public law mechanisms.

Legal supervision of the delivery of public sector services consists chiefly in the review of the exercise of powers by the executive government or its agencies. In considering the mechanisms for the review of decisions to exercise executive or administrative power, it is necessary to refer briefly to the history and theory of their development. In this paper I refer to Commonwealth power partly to avoid the need to examine the several constitutions and laws of the states and territories, partly to draw attention to some issues that arise under the *Constitution* of the Commonwealth and partly to deal specifically with issues current in the revision of the administrative law of the Commonwealth.

The Constitutional Framework

The *Constitution* provides for both political and judicial review of executive power: political review by the Parliament under a system of responsible government, judicial review by the High Court to give effect to the rule of law. The *Constitution* has been held repeatedly in the High Court to mandate a system of responsible government of the Commonwealth.[3] In the *Engineers Case* in 1920, the majority judgment recalled the speech of Lord Haldane, when a member of the House of Commons, in speaking to the Bill for the enactment of the Commonwealth *Constitution*. He said: 'The difference between the *Constitution* which this bill proposes to set up and the *Constitution* of the United States is enormous and fundamental. This bill is permeated through and through with the spirit of the greatest institution which exists in the Empire, … – I mean the institution of responsible government, a government under which the executive is directly responsible to – nay, is almost the creature of – the legislature.'[4]

That view was accepted by the Court in 1920 and has never since been put in question. Sections 7, 24, 28, 53, 64 of the *Constitution* are consistent only with the view that, under our system of government, the executive government is responsible to the Parliament. Whether or not responsible government in the states is constitutionally entrenched by s 106 of the *Constitution,*[5] the recent decision of the High Court in *Egan v Willis*[6] shows that, for all practical purposes, responsible government can be taken to be a characteristic of state Constitutions.

The doctrine of responsible government reposes in the Parliament a general authority over the Executive. In *FAI Insurances Ltd v Winneke,* Mason J said:

> In passing I should observe that ministerial responsibility means (1) the individual responsibility of Ministers to Parliament for the administration of their departments, and (2) the collective responsibility of Cabinet to Parliament (and the public) for the whole conduct of administration.[7] The principle that in general the Governor defers to, or acts upon, the advice of his Ministers, though it forms a vital element in the concept of responsible government, is not in itself an instance of the doctrine of ministerial responsibility.

> It is a convention, compliance with which enables the doctrine of ministerial responsibility to come into play so that a Minister or Ministers become responsible to Parliament for the decision made by the Governor in Council, thereby contributing to the concept of responsible government. [8]

In the same case, I referred to a quotation by Alpheus Todd[9] of an observation by Earl Grey who described as the 'distinguishing feature' of Parliamentary government the practice which requires the powers belonging to the Crown to be exercised by ministers who possess the confidence of Parliament. By making the executive accountable to the Parliament, the doctrine of responsible government gives a measure of democratic control over the exercise of power by the executive.

Judicial review of the executive's exercise of power is provided for by s 75(v) of the *Constitution*. That provision confers on the High Court jurisdiction in all matters in which a writ of mandamus or prohibition or an injunction is sought against an officer of the Commonwealth. By means of those remedies, the Court can ensure that no purported exercise of power by the executive exceeds the power actually conferred and that no power is exercised otherwise than in accordance with the conditions governing its exercise. Although both political review by the Parliament and judicial review by the High Court are crucial safeguards of a free society under the rule of law, those supervisory mechanisms proved to be inadequate to cope with the massive growth of executive power since 1901, a growth that was stimulated by the two World Wars. New mechanisms were proposed by a series of reports commissioned thirty years ago and were introduced by consequential legislation that was identified collectively as the new Commonwealth Administrative Law.

Of course, Parliamentary scrutiny of executive action remained the basic mechanism for review. When decisions are taken on issues of high policy affecting the community at large, there is really no other appropriate mechanism. Political issues must be determined in the political forum. But many powers, especially statutory discretionary powers, that are vested in Ministers, their departments or agencies are not suited to Parliamentary scrutiny, either because the matters that the repository of the power has to consider do not lend themselves to review by the Parliament or because the Parliament, or even the Minister, simply does not have the time to review all decisions taken in exercise of the power.

In 1969, the Commonwealth Administrative Review Committee was commissioned to advise on additional mechanisms of review. That Committee was chaired by Mr Justice Kerr, as he then was, and included Mr Justice Mason, subsequently Chief Justice of Australia, Mr RJ Ellicott QC, the Solicitor-

General of the Commonwealth and Professor Harry Whitmore. The Kerr Report was the seminal document in the creation of the new Commonwealth Administrative Law. It expressed the underlying reasons for the new law in these terms:

> [W]hen there is vested in the administration a vast range of powers and discretions the exercise of which may detrimentally affect the citizen in his person, rights or property, justice to the individual may require that he should have more adequate opportunities of challenging the decision which has been made against him, not only by obtaining an authoritative judgment on whether the decision has been made according to law but also in appropriate cases by obtaining a review of that decision.
>
> [T]he very existence of machinery for review of [the] kind [proposed] is likely to produce a greater efficiency and correctness in the making of those decisions. It will be seen that our detailed proposals have been designed to achieve balance between justice to the individual and efficient administration.[10]

The work of the Kerr Committee was supplemented by Sir Henry Bland's Committee on Administrative Discretions and by Mr Ellicott's Committee of Review of Prerogative Writ Procedures.

The new Commonwealth Administrative law had many facets. Together they were designed not only to provide review mechanisms that lay beyond the practical capacity of the Parliament and the High Court but also to overcome perceived deficiencies which are inherent in the administrative process. These deficiencies were identified by Sir Anthony Mason:

> Experience indicates that administrative decision-making falls short of the judicial model … in five significant respects. First, it lacks the independence of the judicial process. The administrative decision-maker is, and is thought to be, more susceptible to political, ministerial and bureaucratic influence than is a judge. Secondly, some administrative decisions are made out in the open; most are not. Thirdly, apart from statute, the administrator does not have to give reasons for his decision. Fourthly, the administrator does not always observe the standards of natural justice or procedural fairness. That is not surprising; he is not trained to do so. Finally, he is inclined to subordinate the claims of justice of the individual to the more general demands of public policy and sometimes to adventitious political and bureaucratic pressures.[11]

The new Commonwealth Administrative Law sought to provide remedies in the event that any of these deficiencies produced injustice in an individual case. An overall non-coercive mechanism of review was provided by the *Ombudsman Act 1976* (Cth). Reasons for decision were required by s 28 of the *Administrative Appeals Tribunal Act 1975* (Cth) ('the *AAT Act*') and by s 13 of the *Administrative Decisions (Judicial Review) Act 1977* (Cth) ('the *ADJR Act*'). Information on which decisions are based could be elicited subject to exceptions under the *Freedom of Information Act 1982* (Cth). Judicial review was simplified by the *ADJR Act* and the novel provisions of the *AAT Act* permitted merits review of prescribed categories of decisions. All this is, of course, old matter but its relevance lies in the comparison to be drawn between the new Commonwealth Administrative Law and the proposals currently under consideration for changing it.

The ADJR Act

This Act prescribed the grounds on which a court is authorised to review judicially decisions made under Commonwealth law. Unnecessary technicalities in the law were removed and the review jurisdiction was vested in the Federal Court. That Court was also given jurisdiction[12] substantially concurrent with the jurisdiction of the High Court, in matters in which mandamus, prohibition or injunction is sought against an officer of the Commonwealth. Jurisdiction to judicially review exercises of Commonwealth power, whether corresponding with the jurisdiction of the High Court or with the jurisdiction of the Federal Court under the *ADJR Act*, was denied to State Courts.[13] Recognising that the High Court's other functions and its workload precluded its exercise of the day to day review jurisdiction, the Parliament intended the Federal Court to be the specialist repository of the judicial review jurisdiction to the exclusion of all other courts except when the High Court thought it appropriate for particular reasons itself to hear and determine cases under s 75(v) of the *Constitution*. Review cases became a large and significant proportion of the Federal Court's case list.

The AAT Act

Judicial review for excess of power or legal error could not ensure that executive or administrative decisions were the correct or preferable decisions. The way chosen to ensure that executive power was exercised independently, openly, with reasons given and natural justice accorded and without subordinating the claims of individual justice to governmental policies and pressures – in short, the way chosen to overcome the deficiencies in administrative decision-making identified by Sir Anthony Mason – was to create an independent tribunal with authority to review prescribed decisions on their merits. The Administrative Appeals Tribunal was created accordingly, and the Administrative Review Council was appointed to monitor, and to advise Government on, the new package.

The package was piloted through the Parliament by the Attorneys – General of the time, Mr Enderby, Mr RJ Ellicott QC and Senator Peter Durack QC, assisted by three formidable members of the bureaucracy: Sir Clarrie Harders, Mr Frank Mahony and Mr Lindsay Curtis. The first measure, the *AAT Act*, was proclaimed to come into operation on 1 July 1976.

The new system necessarily gave rise to some tensions between primary decision-makers and the new review bodies. That was foreseen. In a foreword to the Second Annual Report of the Administrative Review Council, I said: 'The objective of these reforms is to make administration responsive to the interests of the individuals affected by it; but some may see these innovations as intrusions into an orderly process of administration – a process which (in constitutional theory) is already responsible to a Minister and through him to the Parliament. Both of these propositions are true. They are not contradictory, but neither can be pushed too far.'

The difficult question was, and is, how to strike the balance between response to the claims of individuals affected by the exercise of power and the exercise of that power in an orderly, efficient and economical way. Obviously new resources had to be employed. Merits review would be no more than an irritant to primary administrators if merits review were not based on a more adequate finding of the relevant facts or a more accurate exposition of the relevant law or a sounder exercise of the relevant discretion.

The AAT was equipped with powers to gather evidence that the bureaucracy does not have; it was staffed with experienced lawyers to preside over hearings; it had expert part time members available who could bring their skills to the evaluation of the circumstances and the exercise of any discretion. In cases that were subjected to AAT review, both the primary decision-maker and the AAT had to state his, her or its reasons for decision. Provided the AAT clearly articulated the reasons for departing from an original decision when it did so, the AAT's reasons ought to have had a helpful normative effect on primary decision-making. But the intersection of the lines of bureaucratic authority by external review on the merits always contained the seeds of dissatisfaction on the part of the bureaucracy. Criticism, overt or covert, was to be expected on the ground of cost and complexity or on the ground that the external reviewer espoused an alien and inappropriate culture. Sir Anthony Mason commented: 'The attraction of judicial review and of tribunal review on the merits is that they offer justice to the individual by means of independent adjudication. The real thrust of the objection is a distaste for genuinely independent review and a preference for departmental decision-making because it is weighted in favour of the government viewpoint.'[14]

However, if the heavy artillery of the AAT were to be directed at comparatively small administrative cases, there was likely to be a waste of firepower. And, as the AAT's jurisdiction was enlarged and its remedial powers became known, the caseload increased extensively. Costs mounted and the quasi-judicial methods of the AAT which exposed the complexity of the issues that sometimes fell for determination in the exercise of administrative power were time consuming. Flexibility in AAT procedures and the conferring of jurisdiction on less high-powered Tribunals diminished this problem, though it did not entirely avoid it. Then, under financial constraints, an increased proportion of matters was determined by single member Tribunals without the benefit of the services of the specialist part-time members.

The normative effect of AAT decisions on primary decision making was one of the benefits expected of the system of merits review. And so, it was. Yet, from time to time, criticism on the ground that the AAT espoused an alien and inappropriate culture was quite strident, notably when decisions exposed the government to unexpected expenditure. There seem to have been uneven responses by departments to the reasoning of the AAT. This may have been due to departmental or ministerial opposition to the approach taken by the AAT in particular cases. However, that may be, unless there were departmental encouragement to make primary decisions accord with the approach of the AAT, the normative effect of the AAT's decisions would be problematic.

In September 1995, the Administrative Review Council (the 'ARC') submitted to the Minister a report entitled '*Better Decisions*'. The Report recommends the creation of an Administrative Review Tribunal ('ART') to incorporate not only the AAT but several other Tribunals, and the organisation of the ART into several specialist Divisions. The Government has accepted that recommendation. No white paper has been issued for public discussion of the proposed Tribunal, though some features of the proposal can be gleaned from a brief press release by the Attorney-General in February 1998 and an address by a government spokesperson in June 1998.[15] If the forecast features are carried into execution, the ART will be a different Tribunal from that which the Government brought into existence in 1976.

The first point of distinction arises from the 'Better Decisions' Report itself, which proposed that legal qualifications should be a prerequisite for appointment of the President alone.[16] This recommendation was supported by the observation that 'Tribunal members are … generally able to access specialised advice from their tribunal's legal or research staff, as well as through informal liaison with other members.'[17] If a tribunal on which the President is not sitting cannot confidently make a decision as to legality, the Tribunal must entrust the decision on legality to some official who has not heard the matter. The Tribunal might be unable to appreciate the force of all the submissions made in the course of a hearing. It is of the nature of an independent review that the Tribunal that hears the matter, not some unidentified official, should render the decision which affects the applicant's interests. Moreover, to repeat what I said on another occasion:

> If legal expertise be discounted, perhaps management personnel with their ability to cover many fields would be offered as the presiding members. That would be an inversion of the conception of the AAT. Presiding officers with legal training – I do not say merely with legal qualifications – are (or ought to be) alert to the difference between legal rules which lie within their province and expertise which lies within the province of specialist members and pertains to issues of fact. Would presiding officers without legal training be comfortable with that division of function? Or would the contribution of the specialist members be depreciated by the universal skills of the managers? [18]

An important function of external merits review is to ensure that decisions are not made in excess of the power of the decision-maker and are made in accordance with conditions which govern the exercise of the power. One of the achievements of the AAT was to blow the winds of legal orthodoxy through the corridors of power and to secure consistency between departmental manuals and traditions and the relevant statutory requirements. The Council's recommendation would deny the ART this continuing capacity.

Sir Anthony Mason has warned that a sub-standard tribunal system would be a 'passport to disaster' and would stimulate wider judicial review.[19] The stimulus would be twofold: a person dissatisfied with a primary decision would go to the courts for judicial review more readily than he, she or it would have done were there a tribunal of high standing; and the absence of legal expertise in the review tribunal would lead to more appeals against, or applications for judicial review of, the Tribunal's decisions.

Next, the Government has proposed administrative measures relating to Divisions of the new Tribunal which have excited the concern of the President of the AAT. The Government spokesperson explained the funding arrangements for the several Divisions as follows:

> It is proposed that the ART will be funded largely by resource agreements between the President of the ART and the Departments with significant review jurisdictions, (as is currently the arrangement

> for funding the SSAT and the Veterans' Review Board). Under these arrangements, the ART will negotiate with each Department as to the level of funding necessary to provide review of portfolio decisions within agreed standards of timeliness. As workload increases or decreases, the amount of funding that the Department is required to provide to the ART will increase or decrease. …
>
> Concerns have been expressed in some media reports that these arrangements will undermine the independence of the ART. The Government, however, has stressed that the funding arrangements will be clearly linked to workflow and caseload and will not be used as a vehicle for executive interference in ART decision making. …

The President of the AAT, Justice Matthews, noted that the proposal as to funding of the ART by the Departments whose decisions are to be reviewed is in direct opposition to the Administrative Review Council's approach to funding and, she adds: 'Not only does this involve a very significant independence issue, at least in perception and possibly also in practice, but it threatens to create a bureaucratic nightmare.'[20]

The Government spokesperson outlined a proposal for the appointment of members of the Tribunal: 'Recommendations for appointment will be made to the Governor-General by the portfolio Minister responsible for the Division in which the Member is to have his or her primary duties.'

The President expressed concern 'that giving line portfolio ministers the power to appoint ART members might well have an adverse effect upon the actual and perceived independence of the appointment process and therefore of the Tribunal itself'. But her most serious concern related to a government proposal that '… the qualifications for ART membership should usually be the same as those for primary decision-makers in the relevant jurisdictions. This reflects … the fact that members are administrative decision-makers not pseudo judges.'[21]

The President asks rhetorically where will there be any improvement in primary decision-making?

These are substantial criticisms and need to be addressed. I note a further ground for concern. In February 1998, the Attorney-General announced that the management of the ART would include 'liaison with portfolios to facilitate improvement in primary decision-making'. The Government spokesperson later amplified the Attorney's statement: 'The focus of the merits review system should be on promoting and encouraging the right decision at the earliest possible stage. This aim underlies the efforts of Government and the existing tribunals to improve primary decision making by a variety of means, including communication and liaison between review tribunals and portfolio Departments.'

It appears that the AAT does in fact convene regular liaison meetings with agencies.[22] If the liaisons proposed by government are merely to facilitate the processes of review or take the form of open tri-partite discussions between representatives of clients or applicants, of the agency and of the Tribunal[23], there could be no objection. But if the proposed 'liaison' were to have the purpose or the effect of securing conformity by the ART to the culture of the department that appoints the members and funds their engagement by the ART, the independence of the ART would be compromised. There is, of course, a desirable dialogue of ideas exchanged by the medium of tribunal decisions on the one hand and the announcement of ministerial or departmental policies on the other. In the '*Better Decisions*' Report, the Council was alert to the need for communication between the ART and primary decision-makers. It recommended that: 'All agencies should actively promote the potential beneficial effect of review tribunal decisions on the general quality of the agencies' decision-making. As an important aspect of this, agencies should make a visible, formal and real commitment to promoting that effect. Agencies should ensure that their organisational structures are such as to maximise the potential beneficial effect of review tribunal decisions on the quality of agency decision-making.'

In the event of an Agency failing to respond adequately to a review tribunal's decision, the Council recommended: 'Review tribunals should be encouraged to raise with the relevant minister or agency head, or with the Ombudsman, concerns they may have about agency responses to tribunal decisions.'[24]

These recommendations, if adopted, would place *on the agency* the responsibility for bringing agency practice into conformity with the Tribunal's approach. But, if the proposed liaison were intended to enhance the authority of departmental culture in the making of review decisions, there would be little point in seeking to enhance the effect of ART reasons on agency practice.

The proposals for the creation of the ART warrant serious reflection. Justice Matthews expresses the concern that the Government's proposals, if implemented, will produce 'very limited benefit to the community and very great cost, in terms of both the quality and the independence of external merits review'.[25] I share that concern.

There are two chief justifications for providing a system of external merits review: first, the decisions on review are the product of more mature abilities and greater powers than those possessed by the group of primary decision-makers and can reflect a more detached consideration than that which can be given by the primary decision-makers; secondly, the independence of a review tribunal satisfies the individual applicant that perceived injustice at the hands of government can be rectified or at least a fair hearing can be had. If the proposed ART were to lack the status of the AAT, not to possess the same legal strengths nor to exhibit expertise higher than that possessed by primary decision-makers, to be constituted by members appointed on the recommendation of the Minister whose department's decisions are to be reviewed and to be funded to the extent that that department determines, its utility would be much less than that of the AAT.

Judicial Review

There is a core jurisdiction that cannot be reduced by legislation, namely, the jurisdiction conferred on the High Court by s 75(v) of the *Constitution*. Any further Commonwealth judicial review jurisdiction must be invested in a court selected by the Parliament.[26] But the general review jurisdiction can be exercised in practice only by the Federal Court. The High Court's constitutional jurisdiction, though exercised from time to time chiefly in constitutional cases, cannot be exercised generally, given the caseload and broad constitutional functions of the High Court.

It is therefore of the highest importance that the Federal Court's jurisdiction be unimpaired. The purpose and extent of judicial review is to enforce 'the law which determines the limits and governs the exercise' of administrative power.[27] It follows that, if the courts are denied jurisdiction to enforce the law relating to particular powers or cannot enforce some of the rules governing the exercise of power, the repository of the power can refuse to obey the law or observe the rules. Absent judicial review, executive power may be abused with impunity. To the extent that the courts are impeded from exercising judicial review of administrative decisions, the rule of law is negated.

In recent years, Parliament has withdrawn jurisdiction from the Federal Court jurisdiction to review certain decisions made under the *Migration Act 1958* (Cth).[28] And there is a more significant denial of jurisdiction. Although a decision might have been taken unlawfully in the sense that natural justice was not accorded, or the decision-maker took irrelevant considerations into account or failed to take account of relevant considerations or exercised his or her discretion in bad faith or exercised his or her power so unreasonably that no reasonable person could have exercised the power in that way, the Federal Court is denied jurisdiction to review any decision under the *Migration Act* on any of those grounds.[29] A charter of arbitrariness is thereby created. The Parliament has made a conscious incursion upon the rule of law. It is no answer to say that some grounds of judicial review are left standing or to point to the High Court's jurisdiction under s 75(v) of the *Constitution* that lies beyond the reach of the Parliament.

The policy of withdrawing jurisdiction from the Federal Court can only produce embarrassment for the High Court which, as is commonly known, is already overburdened by its case load and the need to discharge the appellate and constitutional functions imposed upon it by the *Constitution*. The rule of law is not maintained by burdening the High Court with an impossible caseload. Administrative expediency must not undermine the foundational principle on which a free society depends. If, in particular cases, it be thought that a judge of the Federal Court has overreached his or her jurisdiction in setting aside a decision made under the *Migration Act*, the remedy is to appeal, not to endeavour to immunise all decisions under that Act from operation of the rule of law. Indeed, it is unacceptable in a society governed by the rule of law to deny jurisdiction to enforce the law in a particular area to the court fitted to exercise jurisdiction in that area knowing that the capacity of the only court with jurisdiction is already fully extended. It is even more unacceptable when the known consequence of the withdrawal is to prejudice the capacity of the High Court to perform with due deliberation its constitutional and appellate duties that are essential to the rule of law throughout the Commonwealth.

Regrettably, it seems that the executive government contemplates further legislation to withdraw from the Federal Court even more jurisdiction to review decisions under the *Migration Act*.[30] Governments generally are peculiarly sensitive to review of migration decisions, but it is earnestly to be hoped that mature reflection on the implications of the proposed legislation will lead to its discard and to a repeal of the jurisdiction denying provisions.

Limits of External Review

Decisions that are subject to external review are made in exercise of statutory power by Ministers, their departments and agencies in the public sector. Information about the functions they perform is obtainable by the Parliament and its Committees or by FOI requests or by statements of reasons for decision. Persons affected by those decisions are protected by public law remedies in the courts or by merits review where that is available. But when the delivery of Government services is contracted out or some other function that Government once performed is privatised, different supervisory mechanisms apply.

Contract, the legal servant of the entrepreneur, takes the place of governmental chain of command. Ministers and the heads of departments or agencies lose the power to control and command and are relegated to the seeking of contractual remedies in the event of non-performance. Contractual remedies consist ordinarily in an award of damages to the innocent party to the contract, although sometimes the innocent party may be entitled to a decree of specific performance. But if the government's contractor fails to perform a contract for the delivery of services to the public or the performance of some function for the benefit of the public, the ordinary contractual remedies are inappropriate to ensure that a disappointed member of the public receives the service or the benefit of the function. Members of the public are not parties to the contract.

Moreover, FOI procedures or a statutory requirement for Ministers or their departments or agencies to give reasons for decision cannot be used by a member of the public to elicit information from a private contractor as to the contractor's performance of its contractual obligations. Can the contractor be made accountable to members of the public? This is a subject for legal speculation. I venture to suggest that this issue will find its way into the courts. Privity of contract might be stretched to admit members of the public to contractual remedies or public law remedies might be extended (no doubt with modification) to the review of decisions taken in the discharge of contracts designed for the service or benefit of the public. Some solution will be sought to protect members of the public who are entitled to a service or benefit from government against the consequences of failure by the government's contractor to provide the service or perform the functions that have been contracted out.

Ministerial accountability to Parliament is another question. Concern has been expressed about the Parliament's ability to acquire information relating to outsourcing contracts and Parliaments have met with some resistance when they have sought 'commercial in confidence' information. The Auditor General of South Australia stated the problem in his 1997 comments on 'Government Contracts':

> Whilst the convention of Ministerial responsibility does not make Ministers personally responsible for all acts performed by their subordinates, nonetheless, it does require Ministers to be accountable to answer on behalf of their departments, to ensure that reasonable administrative structures are in place, and to impose remedies when faults come to light.[31] Such responsibility entitles Ministers, or senior public servants acting on their behalf, to intervene at any point in the departmental/statutory authority hierarchy and implement remedial arrangements if such are deemed necessary.[32]

> Contracting out, however, imposes a break in this chain of oversight and accountability. Ministers are no longer accountable for the day-to-day administration of service provision because their role and rights of intervention are limited to the terms of the contract. Day-to-day accountability of individual private service providers is to their private sector employers not to the department or the Minister.

The doctrine of responsible government to which I referred at the beginning of this paper can hardly be undermined by contract. And the recent decision of the High Court in *Egan v Willis* eloquently asserts the aspect of accountability that gives the Parliament access to information:

> A system of responsible government traditionally has been considered to encompass 'the means by which Parliament brings the Executive to account' so that 'the Executive's primary responsibility in its prosecution of government is owed to Parliament'.[33] The point was made by Mill, writing in 1861, who spoke of the task of the legislature 'to watch and control the government: to throw the light of publicity on its acts'.[34] It has been said of the contemporary position in Australia that, whilst 'the primary role of Parliament is to pass laws, it also has important functions to question and criticise government on behalf of the people' and that 'to secure accountability of government activity is the very essence of responsible government'.[35] In *Lange v Australian Broadcasting Corporation,*[36] reference was made to those provisions of the Commonwealth *Constitution* which prescribe the system of responsible government as necessarily implying 'a limitation on legislative and executive power to deny the electors and their representatives information concerning the conduct of the executive branch of government throughout the life of a federal Parliament'.[37]

In another passage in the joint judgment,[38] it is clear that there are two aspects to responsible government: one, that the ministry must command the support of the lower House of a bicameral legislature upon confidence motions; the other, that Ministers are liable to the scrutiny of the chamber of which they are members in respect of the conduct of the executive branch of government. Of course, the point that was not and did not have to be decided in *Egan v Willis* is the measure of ministerial responsibility to give an account of the performance of government functions by a private contractor. Nor did the Court consider whether 'commercial in confidence' agreements can stand against the exigencies of responsible government. These are questions that must await another day.

This is a timely conference. There are major issues upon which further reflection is required in relation to the mechanisms for reviewing the decisions taken in the executive branch of government. Of course, the mechanisms of review are but one aspect of the multi-faceted problem of delivering services, but the legal framework is critical to any program. Experience has shown that poorly devised frameworks become, before long, a source of conflict and inefficiencies. When programs enjoy logical and precise statutory and regulatory support, their implementation is the easier, but no degree of political or even public support can ensure order and efficiency when proper statutory and regulatory support is wanting. The work of Sir Robert Garran testifies to this obvious truth. Here, in a Conference of quiet reflection, his successors are gathered to bring their individual and collective experience to bear on current problems. Sir Robert's spirit must hover over such a gathering. I wish you well in your important deliberations.

---

1. This address was first published in *Australian Journal of Public Administration:* Sir Gerard Brennan, 'The Mechanics of Responsibility in Government', (1999) 58 (3) *Australian Journal of Public Administration* 3.
2. Alfred Deakin, *The Federal Story* (Robertson & Mullens,1944), 97-98.
3. See *Nationwide News Pty Ltd v Wills* (1920) 177 CLR 1, 47, 71; *Amalgamated Society of Engineers v Adelaide Steamship Co Ltd* (1920) 28 CLR 129, 147; *Commonwealth v Kreglinger & Fernau Ltd.* and *Bardsley* (1926) 37 CLR 393, 413; *Commonwealth v Colonial Combing, Spinning & Weaving Co Ltd* (1926) 31 CLR 421, 466.
4. (1920) 28 CLR 129, 147.
5. The word 'Constitutions' in s 106 encompasses such of the laws of a State as relate to the designation and form of its government: *McCawley v The King* (1918), 26 CLR 9, 51-52.
6. (1998) 195 CLR 424.
7. Emy, *The Public Service and Political Control* in the Appendix to the report of the *Royal Commission on Australian Government Administration* (1976) vol 1, 16; John Mackintosh, *The Government and Politics of Britain*, (Hutchinson, 4th ed, 1977) 17.
8. (1982) 151 CLR 342, 364-365
9. Alpheus Todd, *Parliamentary Government in England,* Vol 1 (Sampson Low, 2nd ed, 1887) 3.
10. See *Report of the Commonwealth Administrative Review Committee 1971*; Parliamentary Paper No 144 of 1971, paragraph 12.
11. Sir Anthony Mason, 'Administrative Review: The Experience of the First Twelve Years' (1989) 18 *Federal Law Review* 122, 130.
12. See *Judiciary Act 1903* (Cth), s 39B.
13. See *Judiciary Act 1903* (Cth), s 38; *Administrative Decisions Judicial Review Act 1977* (Cth) s 9.
14. Mason, 'Administrative Review – The Experience of the First Twelve Years' (n 11) 131.
15. Renée Leon 'Reform of Federal Merits Tribunals – The Government's Position', *AIAL* 1998 Administrative Law Forum, Melbourne, 18 June 1998.
16. Recommendation 91, Administrative Review Council, *Better Decisions: Review of Commonwealth Merits Review Tribunals*, Report 39, AGPS, 1995, 144.
17. Ibid par 4.14.

18. Opening Address 'The AAT – Twenty Years Forward', The Administrative Appeals Tribunal Twentieth Anniversary Conference (21 July 1976 – 21 July 1996) 15.
19. Sir Anthony Mason, 'Reflection on the Development of Australian Administrative Law' in Robin Creyke and John McMillan (eds) *The Kerr Vision of Australian Administrative Law – At the Twenty-Five Year Mark* (Australian National Centre for International and Public Law, 1998).
20. AIAL Twilight Seminar Address, 5 August 1998 reported 'Verbatim Financial Review' 30 October 1998, AFR Net Services. A report of this address can be found in 'More Questions about the ART', *Social Security Reporter*, Vol 3, No 6, 1998, 90-1.
21. Ibid Matthews J.
22. S Skehill, 'The Impact of the AAT on Commonwealth Administration: A View from the Administration' in John McMillan (ed), *The AAT – Twenty Years Forward* (Australian Institute of Administrative Law, 1998) 56, 61; see also AS Blunn 'The Impact of the AAT on Social Security Administration' John McMillan (ed), *The AAT – Twenty Years Forward* (Australian Institute of Administrative Law, 1998) 99, 106.
23. The format adopted by Ms Joan Dwyer as AAT National Resource Member for Social Security: see '*The Impact of the AAT: A View from the Tribunal*' in *The AAT – Twenty Years Forward* (Australian Institute of Administrative Law, 1998) 64, 70.
24. Recommendation 71, Administrative Review Council, *Better Decisions: Review of Commonwealth Merits Review Tribunals,* Report 39, AGPS, 1995, 113.
25. Matthews J (n 20).
26. See *Constitution*, ss. 71, 75, 76.
27. See *Attorney General (NSW) v Quin* (1990) 170 CLR 1,36.
28. See *Migration Act 1958* (Cth), s 475 (2).
29. See *Migration Act 1958* (Cth) s 476 (2)(3).
30. Statement by the Prime Minister reported in *The Australian*, *The Age* and *The Sydney Morning Herald*, 21 November 1998.
31. See Management Advisory Board/Management Improvement Advisory Committee; Accountability *in the Australian Public Sector* (Canberra, AGPS, 1993).
32. See *Public Sector Management Act 1995* s 15. A Chief Executive of an administrative unit is subject to Ministerial direction other than regarding the appointment etc of a particular person.
33. Kinley, 'Governmental Accountability in Australia and the United Kingdom: A Conceptual Analysis of the Role of NonParliamentary Institutions and Devices' (1995) 18 (2) *UNSW Law Journal* 409, 411.
34. Mill, *Considerations on Representative Government* (1861) 104.
35. Queensland, Electoral and Administrative Review Commission, *Report on Review of Parliamentary Committees*, (October 1992), vol 1, par 2.23.
36. (1997) 189 CLR 520, 561.
37. (1998) 195 CLR 424.
38. (1998) 195 CLR 424, 453.

4.6 Early Issues for the Administrative Appeals Tribunal

Editor's note

Marking the 25th anniversary of the establishment of the Administrative Appeals Tribunal, Brennan offered these observations at a seminar on 1 April 2001.

The Administrative Appeals Tribunal ('AAT') was, and is, both a curial curiosity and a political anomaly under the Westminster system. A curial curiosity in that a tribunal, presided over by a serving Judge and exercising its jurisdiction independently of the executive, reviews governmental policy and overrules administrative decisions made in lawful exercise of statutory power. It is a political anomaly in that the discretionary decisions which it makes are made independently of ministerial direction. The hierarchical echelons of power on which the theory and practice of responsible government depend are intersected by the AAT. From its inception, it was inevitable that tensions would develop between the AAT and the bureaucracy; and it was likely that the judiciary would be wary of the hybrid creature that was seeking to utilize the judiciary's mantle of authority. But the AAT was launched with the constructive support of some redoubtable members of the bureaucracy and was blessed by the encouragement of some senior Judges.

The officers of the Attorney-General's Department who were mainly concerned with getting the new Tribunal operating were Sir Clarrie Harders, Secretary of the Department, Mr Frank Mahony, Deputy Secretary, Mr Lindsay Curtis First Assistant Secretary and Mr Len Glare who was, I think, Assistant Secretary. Clarrie Harders took me to lunch in the Commonwealth Club to meet the mandarins: Sir Frederick Wheeler of Treasury and Sir Alan Cooley of the Public Service Board. They were courteous, of course, and were cautiously supportive of the new venture but they were astute to discover how it would work in practice. 'At the moment', said Sir Frederick, 'I have on my desk a draft submission for the Treasurer as to whether he should authorize the making of an ex gratia payment. How would the Tribunal review a decision of that kind?' I confess I had no idea whether the AAT jurisdiction extended to decisions to make ex gratia payments. Even less idea as to any principles which the AAT might invoke to conduct the review. So, I limply replied: 'If we had jurisdiction to review the decision, you would have to put your reasons in writing and we would do our best to consider them.' The meeting illustrated a number of points: the areas of the AAT's jurisdiction was critical to the prospects of establishing its authority in and over the bureaucracy; the

AAT could not be an effective reviewer of decisions which were essentially exercises of a purely political discretion; and effective review by the AAT would depend on its demonstrating a superior capacity to that of the primary decision-maker. The selection of appropriate jurisdiction remained, for me, a continuing matter of concern during the early years. I shall refer to jurisdiction again but I mention it at the outset because it is, in my view, critical to the utility of a system of external and independent merits review.

It is difficult now to appreciate that the AAT was, at its inception, without any public or professional profile. It was several months after the AAT began that the first application – in *Adams and the Tax Agents Board*[1] – was lodged in the Brisbane Registry. Champagne was broken out in the Wales Centre in Canberra where we were then accommodated. Mr Ron Mills, the founding Registrar of the AAT lifted the profile of the AAT and took steps to inform persons who had an occupational interest in its jurisdiction. Ron had come from the Attorney-General's Department after completing a distinguished degree in law from the ANU. His first love had been Treasury and in later years he returned there to contribute the acuity of his mind to the devising of laws and policies which have, subject to curially approved exceptions, protected our public revenue. Ron organized the administration of the Tribunal and introduced me to the ways and the terminology of the public service. But he also set about addressing meetings of Customs Agents and other interest groups. His evangelization of the administrative heathens bore good fruit. In the early years, the AAT developed its skills and its modus decidendi in customs and other cases which were brought to it by those to whom the gospel of the new system had been preached. In time, the Administrative Review Council successfully recommended that those whose interests were affected by primary decisions should be informed of their right to appeal to the AAT when such a right existed. The case load grew exponentially and the problem was then to ensure that the Tribunal's resources were increased to deal with the increase in its work.

Strangely enough, the legal profession was slow to seize on this new area of professional work. In Canberra, the resident Bar was seldom seen in the Tribunal even after the headquarters of the Tribunal moved from the Wales Centre to the AMP Building in which the Bar had its chambers. But there was one case which dramatically informed the politicians and the public about the existence and the power of the AAT. It was *Re The Hospital Contributions Fund of Australia and the Minister for Health*.[2] HCF appealed against the Minister's refusal to sanction an increase in members' subscriptions. It was a matter of urgency as the reserves of the Fund were being depleted by the month. I fixed the earliest possible date for a hearing – between Christmas and New Year, much to the concern of the counsel who had been retained. It was the silly season for the press and so, when the appeal succeeded on New Year's Eve 1977 and health fund contributions rose, the news was splashed across the headlines of the Sunday papers. The case demonstrated the public significance of the Tribunal and provided another learning experience for the Tribunal as well. It was clear that politically difficult decisions could be left to the Tribunal which, operating in a judicial manner and under a judicial mantle, could wear the consequences of unpopular decisions with impunity.

Of course, the political and public acceptance of the AAT depended on the way in which it exercised its functions. And that in turn depended on two factors: its procedure and the quality of its membership. As has been often said, there were two procedural models open to the AAT – the administrative and the judicial. Clearly the debate about the two models has continued until recent times. The *Administrative Review Tribunal Bill 2000* which the Senate has now rejected clearly sought to terminate the judicial model and to have an administrative model take its place. The ART would not have had to have legally qualified presiding officers, it would have been funded largely by client departments and its members would have been appointed on the nomination of client department Ministers. It would have consulted regularly with client departments. In my respectful opinion, it would have become no more than another, and perhaps unnecessary, tier in the administrative structure. Although Professor Whitmore had favoured an administrative model for the AAT, I do not understand that he would have sanctioned so supine a model as that contemplated by the *Administrative Review Tribunal Bill 2000*. It is well known that I favoured a judicial model – perhaps a model that, at least in later years, was found to be too judicial in its procedure. But I should explain some of the reasons why I favoured the judicial model and sought to ensure that the essential qualities of judicial adjudication should mark the way in which the AAT went about its work.

The *Administrative Appeals Act 1975* (Cth) required the President to be a Judge.[3] It was given power to require reasons for the primary decision,[4] to summon witnesses and to examine them on oath.[5] It was bound to give interested parties an opportunity to be heard[6] and it was obliged to give reasons for its decisions.[7] Its proceedings were generally open to the public.[8] It had no power to execute the decisions it gave but, if a decision of the Tribunal overruled the primary decision, it took the place of the primary decision and was enforced as though it were the primary decision.[9] It was not subject to Ministerial direction or departmental control. These statutory powers and duties were characteristic of the judicial method and distinguished the Tribunal's exercise of its powers from the exercise of power by the ordinary echelons of administration. Moreover, if a departmental decision was defended, there was an adversarial situation on which the Tribunal was bound to adjudicate. And adjudication was most fairly conducted by adopting the judicial model. The Tribunal's procedures were clearly intended to overcome the deficiencies in administrative decision-making which Sir Anthony Mason identified:

> Experience indicates that administrative decision-making falls short of the judicial model – on which the AAT is based – in five significant respects. First, it lacks the independence of the judicial process. The administrative decision-maker is, and is thought to be, more susceptible to political, ministerial and bureaucratic influence than is a judge. Secondly, some administrative decisions are made out in the open; most are not. Thirdly, apart from statute, the administrator does not always observe the standards of natural justice or procedural fairness. That is not surprising; he is not trained to do so. Finally, he is inclined to subordinate the claims of justice of the individual to the more general demands of public policy and sometimes to adventitious political and bureaucratic pressures.
>
> The five features of administrative decision-making which I have mentioned reveal why it is that administrative decision-making has never achieved the level of acceptance of the judicial process in the mind of the public. [10]

The AAT, like the courts, does not have field officers or an investigatory bureaucracy.[11] It was dependent upon the departmental file, any material which was produced to supplement the file and the material placed before it by an applicant.[12] At first some respondents were not fully forthcoming in the production of documents. Ron Mills and his deputy, Jim Jolliffe, were effective instructors in the respondents' statutory duty. The Tribunal was not equipped to conduct an inquisition. On the one occasion when I exercised the extraordinary power to summon a witness whom neither of the parties was willing to call, the witness was left without needed protection. I resolved not to repeat the experiment.

In addition to the statutory framework within which the Tribunal operated, there was a practical incentive to adopt a judicial model. It emphasized the Tribunal's independence from the executive, an independence that was facilitated by the judicial office of the President. The judicial model, by its very remoteness, acquired a certain authority. It would not, I think, have acquired its authority so effectively had its work been done in conformity with an administrative model of decision-making. I remember that, in *Becker and the Minister for Immigration and Ethnic Affairs*,[13] the first deportation case, I asked counsel for the Minister what the policy of the government was about the deportation of aliens convicted of drug offences. Counsel produced some 'Notes for guidance of Officers' which recorded some public statements on the topic by the Minister. Subsequently I received a letter from the Minister setting out a formal statement of the Government's policy. I replied by returning the statement to the Minister and asking that it be provided to the Tribunal and to applicants as part of the departmental papers which came to be described as the 'T' file. The Tribunal was not to be the recipient of confidential communications; the parties before it were to be entitled to deal with the whole of the material on which the Tribunal would make its decision.[14]

Of course, an independent, judicially-modelled Tribunal exercising administrative power would not have acquired the authority needed to ensure obedience to its decisions and to influence primary administration if the personnel of the Tribunal had not been equal to the task. But they were. I was privileged by the appointments made by the Attorney-General's Department during my term of office and – I hope this sounds respectful rather than patronizing – edified, challenged and encouraged by the quality of the work which they did. It is hard to overestimate the significance of the appointments made in the years immediately following 1 July 1976. The first part-time Deputy Presidents were Mr Justice Smithers, senior Judge of the Federal Court (which itself was fully constituted only in February 1977), Mr Justice Fisher, a Judge of the Federal Court based in Adelaide and Sir John Nimmo who had returned to Australia after a term as the first-appointed Chief Justice of the newly independent Dominion of Fiji. The first full-time Deputy President was, as you know, Mr Justice Davies. I shall mention the significance of his contribution in a moment. The Federal Court and its Chief Judge, Sir Nigel Bowen, were generous in the provision of the services of judicial members to the Tribunal but, as the case loads of both the Court and the Tribunal increased, it was right that the AAT should be able to provide presiding members from within its own resources. At the end of 1976, I had requested the then Attorney-General, Robert Ellicott QC, to seek an amendment to the 1975 Act to provide for the appointment of Senior Members. That was effected by the 1977 amendment and Mr Keith Edmonds, formerly an Acting Judge of the Supreme Court of Papua New Guinea and an Assistant Secretary of the Attorney-General's Department, became the first Senior Member. His immense experience and legal ability set a standard for his successors. First, Mr Allan Hall, later Mr Robert Todd. These two gentlemen gave distinguished service as Senior Members and then as Presidential Members. They were not only the workhorses of the Tribunal but reflective and insightful exponents of the laws and practices that newly arose for consideration by the AAT.

Without diminishing the contributions made by other members of the AAT, the quality of the decisions of Daryl Davies, Allan Hall and Robert Todd firmly established the high standards and the high repute of the Tribunal. Daryl assumed a great proportion of the administration of the Tribunal, not only in the listing of cases but in the securing of hearing rooms – not always an easy search – obtaining reporting services and supervising registry services. At the same time, he accepted a substantial case load, especially in the troubling deportation jurisdiction. Allan Hall and Robert Todd proved to be splendid jacks of all trades, whatever the issues in the case might be. They ameliorated the rigour of the judicial hearing, adopting an informal mode whenever that was consistent with preserving the Tribunal's impartiality and dignity. The efficiency and style with which these members presided and disposed of the Tribunal's cases and the clarity of their decisions, were no doubt, the underlying cause of the enormous case load which the AAT was called upon to bear.[15]

The part-time members were outstanding experts in their respective fields.[16] It was both a pleasure and a broadening experience to sit with them. Their great contributions lay in their ability to understand and evaluate the facts in their respective disciplines – for example, in determining the quality of airmanship or lack of it that an applicant had demonstrated, or in assessing the adequacy of provisions to cover the run-offs of liability incurred by an insurer. The experience and wisdom which the part-time members contributed to the Tribunal guaranteed a quality of decision-making that commanded the respect of the parties and the primary administrators as well.

The selection of the primary powers to be subjected to AAT review was critical to its successful establishment. First, it had to have a sufficiently broad jurisdiction so that it would truly be a general administrative appeal Tribunal. The Bland Committee had listed classes of decision which it thought to be appropriate for Tribunal review. The first Annual Report of the Administrative Review Council compared the Bland list with the jurisdiction of the AAT as it stood at 30 June 1977. The Report showed that the initial jurisdiction of the AAT fell far short of the Bland list. But at the time I was not anxious to have the Tribunal loaded with jurisdiction so burdensome that its docket of cases would outstrip the resources available. We had moved into new premises in the AMP Building and constructed our hearing rooms in a somewhat circular design to facilitate exchanges between the Tribunal, the parties and the witnesses. We had not then solved some of the major issues that would inevitably arise as we learnt more about our jurisdiction. The learning curve relating to the procedures and problems of this novel jurisdiction was rather steep, and care had to be exercised in taking on additional case loads in new fields. There was, from early times, a desire by the government to vest in the AAT, jurisdiction to hear appeals by applicants for social security and veterans' benefits. I resisted these approaches. Both areas of jurisdiction would have attracted a numerous case load and I was concerned, not only with the Tribunal's ability to cope with the burden, but also with the prospect that those areas would swamp the other areas of jurisdiction and transform the character of the Tribunal that was then emerging. Although, in retrospect, I do not think that I would recant the view I then expressed, I respectfully agree with the acceptance of these areas of jurisdiction as the AAT grew and became more firmly established. Messrs Lindsay Curtis and Len Glare held fortnightly meetings to review with me the case load, the growth of jurisdiction and the availability of resources in both personnel and facilities. At a time when the financial stringencies of government were not as tight as they seem to be today and when the AAT was enjoying the bloom of favour that attends newly launched government initiatives, the liaison between the AAT and the Attorney-General's Department worked well. One of the contributing factors to this relationship was the active interest of Sir Clarrie Harders as a member of the Administrative Review Council and Mr Frank Mahony's role as his alternate in that forum, as well as the officer with more immediate departmental responsibility for the development of the new administrative law system of the Commonwealth.

The Administrative Review Council (ARC) played an important part in the development of the new administrative law system. It too was well constituted. Its ex officio members were, at the time, the President of the AAT, the Chairman of the Australian Law Reform Commission (Mr Justice Michael Kirby) and, upon his appointment, the Ombudsman (Professor Jack Richardson). In addition, there were senior members of the bureaucracy, of the legal profession, of commerce and industry. Ron Mills undertook the early administration of the Council until Dr GDS Taylor took up his appointment as the first Director of Research. The Council's reports drew attention to areas of jurisdiction which ought to be vested in the AAT and considered and advised upon Ministerial or other legislative proposals, including legislation to vest jurisdiction in the AAT. At this time, the combined duties of Presidency of the AAT and Presidency of the Council had a particular utility, for it was necessary to ensure that proposals to confer new jurisdiction on the AAT were consistent with the development of the Tribunal's expertise and to utilize the AAT's experience in determining the suitability of jurisdiction to be vested in it. But the combination of the AAT and ARC offices was anomalous. It gave the appearance that the President of the Tribunal was avid for jurisdiction and could seek it through the Council. And it placed an additional burden on the work to be done on both the Tribunal and the Federal Court. Ultimately the

Government agreed to amend the Act to provide a President of the ARC other than the President of the Tribunal. There were three significant novel issues to be determined in exercising the AAT's jurisdiction. The first arose from the limited remedies available in deportation cases. These were different from the remedies in other areas of jurisdiction. The AAT could not set aside decisions of the Minister for Immigration but could only recommend reconsideration if the Tribunal was of the opinion that the Minister's decision was not the correct or preferable one.

The second issue was how to regard, to ascertain and to deal with government policy. The third was the scope of the jurisdiction: did it overlap the jurisdiction exercised by the court judicially reviewing a decision? In particular, could the AAT deal with decisions which had been made in excess of, or otherwise outside the power of, the primary decision-maker?

Becker's Case[17] presented the first opportunity to consider both the approach to be taken in deportation cases and the role of policy in AAT decision-making. It was a case in which the decision to deport appeared, on the evidence adduced in the case, to be unwarranted. Nevertheless, the Minister's decision was lawful and he could take a different view. Should that lead the Tribunal to refrain from making a contrary recommendation? Was the AAT merely an adviser to the minister? I said:' [The AAT's] function is to decide appeals not to advise the Executive. The remedies which it awards may be limited or large but the remedies are incidental to the decision at which it arrives. The decision . . . is therefore to be resolved according to its opinion as to the merits of that case.'[18]

To determine whether a deportation decision was the correct or preferable one, it was necessary to determine what, if any, weight should be given to the policies of the Executive government. It was important to stress that the AAT was not bent on the frustration of government policy but sought to play a critical but constructive role in policy development. I said: "Whenever the review of a decision involves consideration of policy, it is essential that the Tribunal be fully informed as to the policy and the reasons for it. Otherwise, the decisions of the Tribunal may, instead of providing a rational analysis of policy and assisting to develop principled yet flexible decision-making, intervene incongruously to disrupt the due course of administration.'[19]

At that time, the question of whether there was a legal obligation on the Tribunal to apply government policy had not been determined. The answer to that question was given by the Federal Court in *Drake v Minister for Immigration and Ethnic Affairs*. Bowen CJ and Deane J said:

> It is not desirable to attempt to frame any general statement of the

> precise part which government policy should ordinarily play in the determinations of the Tribunal. That is a matter for the Tribunal itself to determine in the context of the particular case and in the light of the need for compromise, in the interests of good government, between, on the one hand, the desirability of consistency in the treatment of citizens under the law and, on the other hand, the ideal of justice in the individual case. [20]

Then *Drake (No 2)*[21] presented a full opportunity to consider this critical question. What was said in the reasons for decision in that case was not my view alone, though I accepted, of course, sole responsibility for deciding that case and stating my reasons for decision. But a meeting of Presidential members was held between the time of the hearing and the delivery of the decision and there was no reason why the principles which were expressed in *Drake (No 2)* should not be discussed by those who were responsible for administering the deportation jurisdiction. In the first place, policy was an important element in reducing the risk of inconsistency, and so it was said: 'Inconsistency is not merely inelegant: it brings the process of deciding into disrepute, suggesting an arbitrariness which is incompatible with commonly accepted notions of justice.'

The Tribunal was bound to respect the constitutional authority of the executive to determine a general policy which should guide the exercise of the deportation power but that authority had been statutorily qualified by the jurisdiction of the AAT to do justice in individual cases. These two considerations were reflected in the well-known passage with which all Presidential members agreed:

> When the Tribunal is reviewing the exercise of a discretionary power reposed in a Minister, and the Minister has adopted a general policy to guide him in the exercise of the power, the Tribunal will ordinarily apply that policy in reviewing the decision, unless the policy is unlawful or unless its application tends to produce an unjust decision in the circumstances of the particular case. Where the policy would ordinarily be applied, an argument against the policy itself or against its application in the particular case will be considered, but cogent reasons will have to be shown against its application, especially if the policy is shown to have been exposed to Parliamentary scrutiny.
>
> The general practice of the Tribunal will not preclude the Tribunal from making appropriate observations on Ministerial policy, and thus contributing the benefit of its experience to the growth or modification of general policy; but the practice is intended to leave to the Minister the political responsibility for broad policy, to permit the Tribunal to function as an adjudicative tribunal rather than as

> a political policy-maker, and to facilitate the making of consistent decisions in the exercise of the same discretionary power.[22]

The fact that this approach by the Tribunal was not inimical to the doing of justice in an individual case was clearly demonstrated when Smithers J, whose sense of justice was unerring, refused to follow a new and harsher Ministerial policy in *Gungor and the Minister for Immigration*.[23] He said: it is clear that I consider that there is a danger of inflicting injustice and hardship in cases of various individuals if that policy is applied according to its terms. It is clear also that I consider that deportation in this case would inflict injustice on the applicant and be oppressive.'

His Honour's decision was of a piece with his earlier decision in *Re Chan and Minister for Immigration and Ethnic Affairs* in which he construed a phrase in the policy then current: 'The expression "the best interests of Australia" leaves much open to judgment. It is my view that in the application of policy as stated that expression is to be understood not in a narrow and restricted sense, but as extending to such interests broadly regarded, and embracing, on occasion and according to circumstances, the taking of decisions by reference to a liberal outlook appropriate to a free and confident nation.'[24]

Clearly the AAT was best suited to review discretionary decisions where the manner in which the discretion was to be exercised depended largely on assessment of particular facts rather than on the attainment of policy objectives. If the Tribunal had been required to review the exercise of discretions which depended on political or other objectives, it would have been adrift on a sea of uncertainty without any anchor of either law or fact to keep it within the harbour of its own competence.

In a memorandum to the Administrative Review Council, I requested that, in making recommendations for the vesting of jurisdiction in the AAT, the Council focus on the nature of the decision to be reviewed rather than on the mechanisms of review. I wrote:

> The independence of the reviewing authority is of critical importance, however, when the review is on grounds of discretion. If the discretion requires chiefly a consideration of the special position of the applicant, external review may be justified; but where the exercise of the discretion requires chiefly the evaluation of a general policy, it is difficult to justify external review. Policy is formed by government, and the bureaucracy administers policy in accordance with the directions of government. If the decisions of the bureaucracy are subject to review by an external authority which deals with general policy, there is a bifurcation of policy power and uncertainty as to the policy to be applied by the bureaucracy. Or perhaps, the policy

> powers of government are transferred to the external authority. It is for this reason that I have urged caution in the vesting of discretionary jurisdiction in the Tribunal.[25]

There were strong pragmatic reasons for proceeding cautiously not only in the selection of jurisdiction but in the manner of its exercise. So long as the Tribunal demonstrated care in fact finding and soundness in applying the law, it would earn respect and be able to repel criticism of intrusion into the bureaucratic process. The Tribunal's standing would have been prejudiced if it had been required to exercise discretions without an understanding of policy and the background of policy – factors essential to the formation of a sound judgment.

The scope of the AAT's jurisdiction was quickly tested in two cases: *Adams and the Tax Agents Board*[26] and *Brian Lawler Automotive Pty Ltd and the Collector of Customs (NSW).*[27] In *Adams,* the Tribunal was invited to hold a provision of the *Income Tax Assessment Act 1936* (Cth) invalid and to determine Adams' application accordingly. Clearly the AAT was to act according to law, but it was not seized of jurisdiction judicially to determine validity or invalidity of legislation. The question was resolved in these terms: '[W]hen a decision-maker acts in conformity with his statutory authority, a person whose interests are affected by his act may not obtain relief from this Tribunal upon the ground that the statute is *ultra vires* the Parliament.'[28]

But what of decisions that were taken *ultra vires* the decision-maker? That question was first addressed by Davies J, and Messrs Hall and Borthwick in the second *Hospital Contribution Fund case.*[29] In that case a challenge to the validity of the Minister's decision was raised but dismissed after a close examination of the statutory power. That being so, it was not necessary to address the question whether the Tribunal could grant relief if the Minister had made his decision outside his power. That question arose in *Brian Lawler* where it was held that the decision under review was taken in excess of the power of the decision-maker. On judicial review of such a decision, a court would have held the decision to be void and of no effect. Could the AAT assume jurisdiction to set the decision aside, its order having virtually the same effect as a curial declaration of invalidity? If the AAT could not deal with primary decisions made unlawfully but in purported exercise of a power, many of its cases would have been beyond its jurisdiction. The ability of the AAT to rectify erroneous decisions would have been problematic by reason of a constitutional inhibition on its exercise of jurisdiction. By a majority, the Full Court of the Federal Court upheld the AAT's jurisdiction to review decisions taken in excess of, but in purported pursuance, of a statutory power. Bowen CJ said: '[T]he Tribunal has jurisdiction provided there is a decision in fact and provided further that the decision purports to have been made in exercise of powers conferred by an enactment whether or not as a matter of law it was validly made and whether or not action on the basis there was power to make the decision was right or wrong.'[30]

The resolution of important questions of law was necessary to an understanding of the charter under which the Tribunal was to perform its function. The satisfactory resolution of these questions was necessary also to ensure that the AAT's reputation was sufficient to ensure that the law which it declared, and not some mutation within the bureaucratic culture, governed the exercise of reviewable powers at the primary level. As each new area of decision-making came under review, a close study of the relevant statute and applicable law had to be made and expounded. And once expounded, it was picked up by departments and applied. Oftentimes a clear understanding of the law quelled a multitude of disputes. Thus, the plethora of Australian Capital Territory rating appeals were largely resolved by the decisions of Fisher J in the two *Palmer cases*.[31] Questions about the construction of the Customs Tariff were illuminated by consulting the jurisprudence of other countries for the Australian tariff had engaged the courts only infrequently since 1901. To maintain the capacity for legal research, a substantial library was needed and, after some controversy, was established under the supervision of Ms Ruth McJarrett.

By the end of 1979, the AAT's charter was fairly clear, though there would always be new issues to be resolved. By then, the AAT had been substantially accepted by the public and by the bureaucracy. The Parliament had shown itself ready and willing to vest it with jurisdiction. It was staffed by outstanding personnel and, assuming that the government would appoint Mr Justice Davies as my successor – a fairly safe assumption – it would be led by a Judge who had a proven track record as a fine lawyer of wise judgment, experienced in the work of the Tribunal and in control of its administration. The AAT was enjoying the support of the Attorney-General, Senator Peter Durack QC, and his department. It was time to put a new hand on the tiller as the AAT pushed further out of the safe harbour of small volume jurisdictions. And the workload of the Federal Court was increasing. So, it was time to go. The experience of the AAT was immensely rewarding. The great regret of the separation was the loss of the close contact with its members and of the excitement of seeing new fields of decision-making open out to the rule of law and the light of public examination.

A quarter of a century later, the AAT is entitled to be proud of its civilizing effect in bringing a greater measure of administrative justice to the Australian people. We are all privileged to have been party to the venture.

1. (1976) 1 ALD 251.
2. (1977) 1 ALD 209.
3. Section 7.
4. Section 37; see also s 28.
5. Section 40.
6. Section 39.
7. Section 43(2).
8. Section 35.
9. Section 43(6).
10. Sir Anthony Mason, '*Administrative Review: The Experience of the first Twelve Years* (1989) 18 (3) *Federal Law Review* 122, 130.
11. The 'Kerr Report' had proposed 'a small administrative and research staff' to be shared with the Administrative Review Council. The staff would also be used 'to assist the Commonwealth Administrative Court in appropriate matters.': Sir John Kerr, *Commonwealth Administrative Review Committee Report*, Parliamentary Paper No 144 (Australian Parliament), August 1971, par 292.
12. Sections 37 – 39.
13. (1977) 1 ALD 158; 15 ALR 696.
14. There was provision for treating material confidentially: s 36.
15. The Second Annual Report showed that the number of lodgements for review had increased from 49 in the year 1976-1977 to 275 in the year 1977-1978, although the latter figure was inflated by applications relating to rating notices in the ACT. In 1978-1979, the numbers had plateaued at 263 but with few rating applications and an increase in 'national' jurisdiction areas. See the Third Annual Report of the ARC, par 51.
16. As required by s 7(2).
17. (1977) 1 ALD 158.
18. (1977) 1 ALD 158, 161.
19. (1977) 1 ALD 158, 162-163.
20. (1979) 24 ALR 577; 2 ALD 60, 70.
21. (1979) 2 ALD 634.
22. (1979) 2 ALD 634, 645.
23. (1980) 3 ALD 225.
24. (1978) 1 ALD 55, at 56; (1977) 17 ALR 432, 434
25. See *Some Further Notes on Administrative Review: No 2* (Council document No M2304), pars 25, 35.
26. (1976) 1 ALD 251.
27. (1978) 1 ALD 167; on appeal to the Federal Court (1979) 2 ALD 1.
28. (1978) 1 ALD 251, 257.
29. (1978) 1 ALD 549.
30. See *Collector of Customs (NSW) v Brian Lawler Automotive Pty Ltd* (1979) 2 ALD 1, 7.
31. (1978) 1 ALD 183 and (1979) 2 ALD 209.

When President of the Australian Bar Association in 1975, Brennan joined the Australian Law Reform Commission chaired by Michael Kirby. He enjoyed the academic and political challenges. Here clockwise are Brennan, Gareth Evans, Professor Alex Castles, Michael Kirby, John Cain, and Professor Gordon Hawkins. (Photo: ALRC)

Brennan was appointed a federal judge in June 1976 and a founding judge of the Federal Court in February 1977 and the first sitting of the Federal Court of Australia, Sir Nigel Bowen presiding, and Brennan, the second most junior judge on the right hand end.

Brennan learnt much and was given every opportunity by Sir Nigel Bowen who often sat him on appeals with Justices Deane and Toohey.

Brennan was appointed to the High Court in February 1981 (*Canberra Times*).

Gerard and Patricia moved to Canberra in 1976 when Gerard was appointed the President of the Administrative Appeals Tribunal. They resided there throughout Gerard's 17 year term on the High Court.

When Sir Garfield Barwick retired in 1971, Sir Harry Gibbs was appointed Chief Justice and Brennan joined the court. Standing: Brennan, Wilson, Aickin, Murphy; seated: Stephen, Gibbs, Mason. (Photo: John Leongard, *A Day in the Life of Australia*, 2001).

When Sir Harry Gibbs retired in 1987, Sir Anthony Mason was appointed Chief Justice. Standing: Wilson, Brennan, Gaudron, Deane; seated: Mason, Dawson, Toohey. (Photo: Heide Smith)

Gerard and Patricia being greeting by Sir Zelman and Lady Cowen at Government House. Post-retirement, Brennan and Cowen joined with Sir Anthony Mason recommending that Australia become a republic.

On Mason's retirement in April 1995, Brennan was appointed Chief Justice. Brennan and Mason led the High Court during challenging times. On 8 August 1995, Brennan spoke at the launch of The Mason Court and Beyond. (Photo: Graham Crouch, *Mirror Newspapers*)

Chapter 5

The Federal Court

5.1 Creation of the Federal Court: 40th Anniversary Reflection

Editor's note

On the 40th anniversary of the establishment of the Federal Court, Chief Justice Michael Black invited Brennan as a foundation member of the Court to deliver a lecture in the newly designed main courtroom in Sydney. Brennan delivered his reflection on the Court on 7 February 2017, 40 years to the day after his initial swearing in as a judge of the Federal Court.[1] Brennan noted: 'This reflection relates to a period ending two years after the Federal Court commenced to exercise its jurisdiction, namely, February 1979. A masterly essay covering the first 30 years of the Court (on which I have drawn gratefully) is Chief Justice Black's "The Federal Court of Australia: The First 30 Years" (2007) 31(3) *Melbourne University Law Review* 1. Although this is a personal reflection, I am indebted to Justice Mortimer, a former Associate, whose interest, research and analysis have contributed greatly to this article, especially the biography of Sir Nigel Bowen. She and I acknowledge the assistance of her Associate Glyn Ayres (whose research capacities reflect those of his judge).' Mortimer is now Chief Justice of the Federal Court.

The *Constitution* (s 71) provides that the Parliament can invest Commonwealth judicial power in the Supreme Courts of the States, as well as in the High Court and in federal courts. In the early days of the Federation, it would have been economically and practically impossible to create federal courts exercising broad federal jurisdiction and the 'autocthonous expedient'[2] of vesting the general body of federal jurisdiction in the Supreme Courts of the states became the norm. Some matters were reserved for the exclusive jurisdiction of the High Court and the Commonwealth Court of Conciliation and Arbitration was created in 1904.[3] The volume of litigation was modest at the beginning of the 20th century, so the High Court was able to exercise the original jurisdiction vested in it either by the *Constitution* or by laws enacted by the Parliament without impairing its ability to exercise its appellate and constitutional jurisdictions. State courts had sufficient capacity to accept jurisdiction vested in them by federal laws without impairing their ability to dispose of cases under State law. Until the 1960s, lawyers regarded the Australian judicial hierarchy as substantially linear, with the High Court at the apex directly above the court systems of the States and Territories.

In 1963, Paul Toose QC and Maurice Byers QC revived professional interest in the idea of a federal superior court exercising jurisdiction under federal law.[4] At the 13th Australian Legal Convention, they pointed out that increases in both the volume and complexity of litigation were imposing a heavy burden on the Justices of the High Court in both original jurisdiction and appellate matters and a heavy burden on state courts exercising federal jurisdiction. In several areas, the vesting of federal jurisdiction in state or territory courts seemed to the authors to be inappropriate. The solution they proposed was the creation of a new federal court, taking over the jurisdiction of the Federal Court of Bankruptcy, the Commonwealth Industrial Court, the Supreme Courts of the Territories (other than PNG), and the federal jurisdiction conferred on the Supreme Courts of the States. It would be invested with the same original jurisdiction as the original jurisdiction vested in the High Court under ss 75 and 76 of the *Constitution*. The authors suggested that the new court should have appellate jurisdiction in these matters, thus providing an intermediate appellate court immediately below the High Court. The purposes of the proposal were relief of the burden of work in both the High Court's original and appellate cases, relief of the federal workload of State and Territory courts and federal responsibility for the judicial administration of federal laws, eliminating some anomalies in the differing administrations of some federal laws such as matrimonial causes and bankruptcy.

A proposal for a new court had already been raised for consideration by the government, as the Solicitor-General, Sir Kenneth Bailey, revealed. On 11 December 1962, Cabinet gave approval to the Attorney-General, Sir Garfield Barwick, to proceed with the drafting of a Bill to create a new court, though no decision to proceed was then taken. Mr E G Whitlam, as deputy leader of the Opposition, affirmed to the Convention his support for the solution proposed by Toose and Byers. Although it seemed that there would be political agreement about the creation of a new court, there were differing views about the purpose of the court and about the size and jurisdiction of the court to be created. Sir Garfield Barwick, shortly before his appointment as Chief Justice, acknowledged a general professional consensus that a new federal court would have real utility. 'But', he wrote, 'many of those who share this conclusion reach it for different, and to some extent conflicting, reasons which lead to flatly divergent views as to the jurisdiction that the new court should exercise, and therefore as to its optimum size and the nature of its organization'.[5] Sir Garfield rejected the busy lists of the state courts as a justification for reversing the investiture of state courts with federal jurisdiction unless the relevant law had a 'special element', 'a distinct and separate character', such as bankruptcy and industrial law. But he favoured measures, including the creation of a new federal court to deal with such 'special' matters and to entertain appeals from territory courts. That would relieve the High Court of some of its work.

The proposal did not produce any parliamentary response until Mr Nigel Bowen, then Attorney-General, made a ministerial statement in May 1967. He announced that a Commonwealth Superior Court would be created incorporating the Bankruptcy Court and the Commonwealth Industrial Court and with additional original jurisdiction in taxation, Commonwealth employees compensation, industrial property, the matters specified in s 75(iii), (iv) and s 76(i), (iii), (iv) of the *Constitution* and such other matters as the Parliament might specify. The main purpose of this proposal was to relieve the pressure of original jurisdiction work of the High Court. However, Mr Bowen said that 'the provision of an entire system of Federal courts would be uneconomic' and the government proposed to establish 'a relatively small new federal court of quality and standing'. There would be only four new judges required. The proposal reflected the Barwick suggestion that the Superior Court should deal only with matters having a 'distinct and separate character'. In 1969, Bowen introduced a Bill for the creation of the court but it lapsed when the Parliament was dissolved for a general election. In December 1971, Chief Justice Barwick raised with Prime Minister McMahon (and confirmed in a letter to the Attorney-General, Senator Ivor Greenwood, in January 1972) the 'more than burdensome' work of the High Court in original jurisdiction matters and the desirability of transferring jurisdiction in taxation and industrial property to the Supreme Courts. However, no action was taken to relieve the High Court until 1973 when the Treasurer in the new government, Mr Crean, introduced the *Income Tax Assessment Bill (No 3)* (Cth) to vest in State courts the jurisdiction of single High Court justices in income tax appeals.

In October 1972, Senator Greenwood had announced that the proposal for a new federal court would not be proceeded with.[6] With the change of government, the new Attorney-General, Senator Lionel Murphy, introduced a Bill to establish a Superior Court of Australia. The main purpose of this Bill was to vest exclusively in the new court all federal jurisdiction invested under ss 75 and 76 of the *Constitution*, subject to some exceptions.[7] The new court would also subsume the existing federal courts and the Supreme Courts of the Territories. It would be vested with new federal jurisdiction in administrative and trade practices matters. An internal appeal from single judges was to be available. It was to be organised on a district basis with a chief judge for each district and there were to be six divisions of the court, the judges being assigned to the respective divisions. It was foreseen that the work of the new court could lighten the workload of the High Court but High Court relief – the chief purpose of all Coalition proposals – was not advanced as the purpose of the court's creation.

The Bill excited opposition, not least because the Supreme Courts were to be stripped of considerable federal jurisdiction. The Bill failed to pass the Senate either before or after the double dissolution of 1974. The main grounds of objection were stated by Mr R J (Bob) Ellicott in his Second Reading Speech in the House of Representatives in July 1974. He drew attention to 'the grand design to which this Court is to be constructed' making it 'ultimately the largest court in the country' exercising 'tremendous power over our citizens'. He thought the new court would be unnecessarily divisive, as federal jurisdiction could be exercised appropriately by State courts or by the existing Australian Industrial Court. 'The proposed court', he said, 'would degrade the Supreme Courts, stripping them of their existing jurisdiction'. He was troubled by future growth of federal jurisdiction, asking: 'What will be left of the great common law courts of the States of this country? They will be nothing but property courts with an inferior status.'

A further change of government saw a resolution of the controversy by then Attorney-General Ellicott in 1976. He proposed the creation of the Federal Court of Australia. There had been some changes in the judicial scene since 1973. The Family Court of Australia had been created and was to exercise an exclusive jurisdiction under the *Family Law Act 1975* (Cth). Two major non-judicial tribunals had been established under the *Trade Practices Act 1975* (Cth) and the *Administrative Appeals Tribunal Act 1975* (Cth), each presided over by a federal judge dealing with matters in which points of law might arise and require determination by a court. Further development of federal administrative law was expected.

The Attorney-General, conscious of the need to preserve the status of the State Supreme Courts, proposed that the High Court's original jurisdiction in taxation and industrial property should be taken from the High Court and vested exclusively in the Supreme Courts of the States and Territories. This gave effect to a policy that State courts should be the trial courts in federal as well as State matters and should administer the general body of Commonwealth criminal law. There was to be no diminution in the original jurisdiction of the State and Territory Supreme Courts. The Territory Supreme Courts were to be maintained. The jurisdictions of the Australian Industrial Court and the Federal Court of Bankruptcy were to be transferred to the Federal Court and that Court was to have jurisdiction under the *Trade Practices Act 1974* (Cth) and under the *Administrative Appeals Tribunal Act 1975* (Cth) – jurisdiction which hitherto had been vested in the Australian Industrial Court. The work of the Bankruptcy Court and the Australian Industrial Court was to continue uninterrupted in the Federal Court. The Federal Court was to have appellate jurisdiction from decisions of single judges of that Court, of the Territory courts and of the State courts in taxation and industrial property matters. This was to divert Territory appeals from the High Court to the Federal Court and to ensure uniformity of interpretation in taxation and industrial property law.

The *Federal Court of Australia Act 1976* (Cth) supplemented by the *Federal Court of Australia (Consequential Provisions) Act 1976* (Cth), received the Royal Assent on 9 December 1976. In a 1977 article designed to explain the complex series of 1976 laws, the Attorney-General described the key features of the restructuring of federal jurisdiction and indicated some future developments that were imminent, particularly in administrative law.[8] To complete the establishment of the Court, many administrative matters called for attention: judges, registrars and support staff had to be appointed, rules of practice and procedure had to be promulgated and the workload organised. The Attorney-General's Department marshalled its distinguished team of bureaucrats – Sir Clarrie Harders, Messrs Frank Mahony, Trevor Bennett and Lindsay Curtis. They met in November 1976. Few departmental records of the period survive but there is a note that the appellate work was expected to be 'greater than that of the existing Bankruptcy and Industrial Courts combined'. Registry services were to be provided chiefly by the Bankruptcy registry,[9] then within the Department of Business and Consumer Affairs. Carmel Meiklejohn records:

> Creation of the Federal Court precipitated a tussle over the Registrars in Bankruptcy between the two departments ... The Bankruptcy Branch at this time was severely short-staffed and allocation of staff and resources across the public service generally tight ... It was subsequently negotiated that the Bankruptcy Branch would provide registry facilities for the Federal Court – which had jurisdiction for bankruptcy, industrial law, trade practices and administrative appeals – and for other bodies. By 1978 these included the Administrative Appeals, Trade Practices, Copyright and Courts Martial Appeals tribunals.[10]

The Court's first Registrar was Bernard Foley, who remained with the Court until October 1977. He was followed by Jim Howard, who was in office until the end of 1995. He supervised the expansion of registry services during years when the work of the Court increased greatly. In addition to staff, arrangements had to be made for premises, libraries, the general incidents of court administration and finance.

Appointment of the Chief Judge

The pivotal appointment was, of course, the appointment of a Chief Judge. I imagine that the Attorney, Mr Ellicott, had no difficulty in nominating Sir

Nigel Bowen. Ellicott had read with Bowen and they had worked closely together at the Bar. Ellicott had been appointed Commonwealth Solicitor-General (1969-1973) when Bowen was Attorney-General. At the time of Bowen's appointment, he was Chief Judge in Equity in the Supreme Court of New South Wales. He had been a successful barrister, politician, minister and judge. There were few, if any, who could match either his experience or his reputation.

On 26 May 1911, Nigel Bowen was born in a log cabin in British Columbia, Canada. Shortly afterwards, his family moved to New South Wales. A stint farming sheep in Gunnedah was brought to an end by drought, and the family finally settled in Sydney.[11] Bowen was educated at The King's School in Parramatta and won a scholarship to the University of Sydney, where he graduated in Arts and Law. He played first-grade cricket and rugby. He was also a keen – though less adept – boxer. He competed in the finals of the University's Novice Boxing Championships but was 'soundly thrashed', first tasting fame when his 'battered and bleeding face ... was featured on the front page of the Sydney papers'.[12]

He had greater success at the Bar. He entered the profession in the middle of the Great Depression, one of only three barristers admitted in New South Wales in 1936.[13] However, he quickly established a practice which was interrupted by the outbreak of World War II. He enlisted with the Second AIF.[14] He rose to the rank of captain and served in New Guinea, where his Company included Corporal Ninian Stephen.[15]

He resumed practice in 1946, took silk in 1953, and over the next decade developed an extensive High Court practice.[16] During this time, he led a number of juniors who would later be his colleagues on the Federal Court. Bowen was editor of the *Australian Law Journal* (1946-1958) and served as Vice President of the Law Council of Australia (1957-1960) and Chairman of the New South Wales Bar Council (1959-1961), expressing an underlying political interest that came to the fore in 1964 when he entered the Commonwealth Parliament as member for Parramatta.[17] He subsequently became a prominent political figure, serving as Attorney-General,[18] Minister for Education and Science[19] and Minister for Foreign Affairs.[20] His maiden question in the House of Representatives concerned the establishment of a federal court.[21] As Attorney-General, he shaped the Australian system of justice, introducing the Bill that became the *Privy Council (Limitation of Appeals) Act 1968* (Cth)[22] as well as a Bill which, though discontinued, paved the way for the *Federal Court of Australia Act 1976* (Cth).[23]

As Minister for Foreign Affairs, he played a leading role in galvanising international opinion against the testing of nuclear weapons in the Pacific.[24] He led a delegation that met with representatives of the People's Republic of China in Paris when the question of officially recognising the People's Republic was under discussion in Australia.[25] And he drafted the first piece of legislation responding to a foreign corporate takeover. As Justice Faulks tells it:

> [t]his was in the days before Australia had entered the legislative field to control foreign takeovers ... The time available to prepare the legislation was very limited and the problems involved in moving into an unchartered territory were endless ... [W]hile pessimists were saying it couldn't be done, Sir Nigel was asked when the legislation would be ready. His calm reply was: 'We attend to difficult matters with expedition. The impossible takes a little longer'.[26]

After leaving politics, Bowen J spent four years first as a judge of the New South Wales Court of Appeal and then as Chief Judge in Equity.[27] He later said that, when he was approached to be the first Chief Judge of the Federal Court, he 'was doubtful about accepting': the Court's 'proposed jurisdiction did not seem to be very appealing'.[28] Ellicott knew that he could not take Sir Nigel's acceptance for granted, so he 'took him to the splendid and spacious Chief Judge's chambers on the 21st floor [of the new Law Courts Building] and showed him the view'.[29] We can be glad that it did not disappoint. Bowen's appointment was very well received by the profession. It was a firm indication that the Federal Court was to be a court of high standing.

Appointment of the Judges

There were 19 foundation judges, including the Chief Judge. Those available were sworn in in Court 21A of the Law Courts Building in Sydney on 7 February 1977. With the exception of Keely J who was appointed from the Victorian Bar to assist the Industrial Division of the Court, all the judges were members of existing courts. Six judges were resident members of the Supreme Courts of one or other of the mainland Territories,[30] two were judges of the Bankruptcy Court[31] and nine were judges of the Australian Industrial Court.[32] At that time, of course, all federal judges had life tenure, but the Attorney-General imposed an age limit on appointment of Industrial Court judges to the Federal Court. Two members of the Industrial Court (Dunphy and Joske JJ) exceeded the age limit and were not appointed. A third – the redoubtable Reginald Smithers J – protesting truthfully that his judicial capacities were undiminished by age – was appointed. Twelve judges had been appointed to the General Division of the Court, three to the Industrial Division and the remainder had general commissions to sit in either division, but the Chief Judge could transfer a judge to another division if listing requirements made it desirable to do so. However, some of the judges were engaged in duties which precluded them from participating full time in the work of the Federal Court. Sir Edward Woodward was Director General of Security, Northrop J was President of the Trade Practices Tribunal, and I was President of the Administrative Appeals Tribunal and the Administrative Review Council.

In the first two years, additional judges were appointed. Deane J, then a recently appointed member of the Equity Division of the Supreme Court of New South Wales, was appointed as a judge of the Federal Court and President of the Trade Practices Tribunal. Northrop J became a Deputy President. Toohey J was appointed a judge of the Northern Territory Supreme Court and of the Federal Court. Toohey J, who had been a leading counsel in Western Australia and who had a vast experience of Aboriginal people in legal proceedings, was appointed as the inaugural Land Commissioner under the *Aboriginal Land Rights (Northern Territory) Act 1976* (Cth). McGregor J, a leading member of the NSW Bar, replaced Fox J when the latter became the Ambassador at Large for nuclear non-proliferation and safeguards. Gallop J, a leader of the ACT Bar, succeeded Ward J who died in November 1977. In 1978, three other distinguished leaders of the Bar were appointed: Fisher J from South Australia; Davies J from Victoria (who became a Deputy President of the Administrative Appeals Tribunal); and Lockhart J from New South Wales. After two years, the Court had been accepted as a court of high standing and the judges were, I think, regarded as lawyers of quality well capable of discharging efficiently the functions of both primary and appellate judges.

Court facilities

At the first judges meeting on the afternoon of the swearing in ceremony, the support facilities of the new Court were discussed. The Chief Judge reported on the accommodation then available. In Sydney, courtrooms and judges' chambers were available. In Melbourne, the High Court Building at 450 Little Bourke Street offered court space when the High Court was not sitting in Melbourne and another courtroom was available in the Industrial Court Building at 451 Little Bourke Street for sittings of the Industrial Division. The Industrial Court chambers were retained in 451 Little Bourke Street and three new sets of chambers were to be constructed in 450 Little Bourke Street. Accommodation and library facilities in other State capitals were less adequate, but they sufficed for the time being. Territory courts were available for use by the Federal Court.

Practice and procedure

As Chief Judge, Bowen was 'responsible for the orderly and expeditious discharge of the business of the Court'.[33] The Chief Judge devoted vision and energy in discharging that responsibility. He had a draft set of rules prepared and submitted to the first judges meeting. These were gazetted,[34] followed by an amendment to cover matters arising under the *Administrative Appeals Tribunal Act 1975* (Cth), and ultimately a comprehensive set covering all matters coming before the Court. The Chief was intent on making the procedure as simple and expeditious as possible. An applicant's case was to be stated as part of the initiating process and was to be followed by judicial management of the matter. Cases were not to be allowed to linger until the parties decided to proceed. Under the influence of the industrial judges, the party seeking relief was to be termed 'the applicant', not the plaintiff.

The first judges meeting resolved that for the time being, the Chief Judge should 'take care of the listing of cases'. The Chief Judge also took care of the listing of the judges who should sit on cases. This was a necessary function but it was not free from tension. The Chief Judge was anxious to ensure that the judges were allocated to sit on cases appropriate to their experience. I do not know if it was a general practice, but I remember that he called me in to inquire into my past professional experience and, feeling that I was not well equipped for the industrial jurisdiction, he did not list me to sit in industrial cases unless I was sitting with J B Sweeney and Evatt JJ – two very experienced industrial judges.

Sir Nigel's first Associate, now Richard White J of the NSW Supreme Court, reports that the Chief Judge kept a large sheet on which the names of the available judges would be listed and then allocated to the pending cases. But his allocation was not mere office work. I remember sitting with Deane and Fisher JJ in a Full Court in Court 21A when the Chief Judge unostentatiously made his entrance into the public gallery. I had not known a Chief Justice to visit a sitting court before and I wondered whether we should acknowledge his presence. After hurried and quiet consultation, we decided not to do so. After all, he was merely doing the rounds to see whether his judges were able to do the job! We must have passed muster for we were pleased oftentimes to be listed to sit together again. From time to time, a judge regretted not being listed to sit on a particular case, but overall the judges accepted the Chief's listing as appropriate.

Reaction to the Court's creation

The reaction of Mr F T Burt QC (as he was in 1963) to the Toose-Byers proposal of a new federal court was that 'it would inevitably and seriously reduce the status of the State Supreme Courts' and that was a concern that affected the debate in the following years. Another concern was the risk of a dual system of courts creating confusing and complex jurisdictional disputes. The American system was cited as a warning. Then, as the judicial membership of the new Court was drawn chiefly from the judges of the Industrial Court, there was scepticism about the capacity of the Federal Court effectively to administer its jurisdiction. The jurisdiction of the Federal Court was to extend to areas that were thought to be outside the experience of the Industrial Court and more highly technical than industrial law.

The controversy sparked some feeling. Some comments in the profession were opposed to the creation of the Federal Court, were dismissive of its utility and reflected an element of antipathy towards it. But those sentiments had no apparent effect on the counsel briefed to appear in many of the significant early cases.[35] In the first two years, the Silks appearing in the Court included no fewer than 24 future judges of the Court. Presumably they were satisfied that the Court was achieving the high judicial standard anticipated by the Chief Judge in the swearing in ceremony in February 1977: 'This Court has no history and, as yet, no tradition. At least it has some fine examples. It is my hope that the Court will quickly establish itself as a court of high standing in the eyes of the profession and of the public. It will be the earnest endeavour of the members of this bench to ensure that it does so.'

In December 1977, the Chief Judge explained the rationale for the establishment of the Federal Court, its jurisdiction and workload and its important and necessary role as: 'the primary arbiter in respect of a wide range of matters arising from regulation by the Commonwealth Parliament on an Australia-wide basis of business conduct, the administration of government and the conduct of employer and employee organisations in industrial relations.'[36]

Nevertheless, the concern about the dual system of courts persisted. Even after the Federal Court had commenced its work, the desirability of its continued existence was challenged. In the August 1978 edition of the *Australian Law Journal*, the Chief Justice of New South Wales, Sir Laurence Street, fearful of a system of dual courts, wrote: 'I do not assent to the suggestion that it is too late to turn back … The system of justice is too precious an inheritance to become a pawn in a power struggle between Commonwealth and State. There is no room here for the empire builders to gratify their desires.'[37]

In January 1979, two years after the Court commenced, when its work was available for the profession and the public to evaluate, Sir Nigel delivered a paper entitled 'Federal and State Court Relationships' at the Supreme and Federal Court Judges' Conference in Brisbane.[38] He pointed out that, for the last 70 years, there had been a dual judicial system in which the same issues could be litigated either in the High Court or in the courts of the States, yet 'no significant conflict [had] occurred'. Experience had shown that there were some areas of Australia-wide significance where Federal Court jurisdiction was desirable. He instanced matters in industrial, trade practices, bankruptcy and family law. He recalled that when, as Attorney-General, he proposed the 1968 *Superior Court Bill,* he was 'conscious of the need to avoid, as far as possible, creating a new court which would produce new conflict of jurisdiction problems beyond those which already existed'. He explained that the original jurisdiction of the High Court in income tax, patent and trademark matters had been transferred to State Supreme Courts but, to ensure uniformity in application of the law, appellate jurisdiction had been vested in the Federal Court. Thus, 'the range and importance of the cases in which the State Supreme Courts have jurisdiction has been increased. This should enhance rather than detract from their status'. He commented that the Federal Court was the appropriate repository of jurisdiction in matters of Commonwealth administrative law and appeals from the Territories. His scholarly analysis of the Court's jurisdiction and its constitutional utility was a convincing response to the arguments against the Court's existence. Sir Nigel's conclusion commanded general assent. He said: 'It is in the best interests of the community in general, of the law, and of the judiciary itself, both State and federal, that we, as Judges, do all in our power to enhance and defend the standing and reputation of all courts and of those who serve upon them. If we seek to diminish one another it is inevitable that we shall be ourselves diminished.'[39]

This was not mere rhetoric; it was the voice of a man who was familiar with the *Constitution*, with government and public affairs, a statement by a lawyer of the highest calibre.

The ethos of the Court

The judges of the Court in its early years were conscious of the transformation that the Federal Court might make in the Australian judiciary. On the one hand, there was an obvious need for a court ensuring that the laws of the national Parliament were given a uniform interpretation and were efficiently applied nationally; on the other, the overlapping of jurisdictions applicable to some justiciable controversies raised some nice legal problems. It was a time for reflective analysis, adequate research and clear enunciation of principle. The judges knew that the reputation of the Court and its attractiveness to future appointees of ability depended on the assessment of their judicial work. The listing procedures were designed to ensure no undue delay in disposing of the

Court's lists and the judges decided, in part by force of their Chief's example in part by their own experience and temperament, to be a Court where courtesy was the hallmark and Socratic dialogue between Bench and Bar did not go beyond quiet discussion. This was not the atmosphere of hearings in some courts at the time.

The judges met regularly and a warm collegial spirit was engendered. Personal relationships grew, facilitating co-operation. Draft judgments were circulated among the judges hearing appeals and were returned with corrections or suggestions that were happily received. It was an enjoyable and stimulating environment and we were all aware of our good fortune in being members of a new Court that had new problems for us to address in the company of colleagues whom we respected. I think the satisfaction of repelling some of the arguments that had been raised against the existence of the Court encouraged the judges in their work.

There were features of life on the Federal Court that distinguished that Court from most others: a stimulating variety of work with different groups of judicial colleagues and frequency of travel. From the beginning the Court exercised original jurisdiction in bankruptcy, industrial law, trade practices, and appeals from, or judicial supervision of, federal Tribunals.[40] Its appellate jurisdiction extended to general appeals from the Supreme Courts of the Territories, from single judges of the Federal Court and from single judges of State Supreme Courts exercising federal jurisdiction in industrial property and taxation.[41]

Apart from sitting in the Federal Court, several judges held appointments to the Supreme Courts of the ACT and the Northern Territory, the Administrative Appeals Tribunal, the Trade Practices Tribunal and the Insurance Tribunal. There may have been others. That work provided an interesting smorgasbord of cases adding to the judicial experience. It was fascinating to sit in a tax appeal one day, in crime or contract the day after and then with actuaries or retired bureaucrats or airline pilots the day after that. In the Tribunals, the presiding judge might sit with expert lay members of the Tribunal and this, I discovered, offered an education in fields outside the usual pastures of judicial interest.

Because judges were needed to sit in different jurisdictions in different capitals, they travelled frequently. Judicial mobility facilitated the task of the Chief Judge in the listing of cases. Although this added to the workload, the Federal Court judges had the advantage of meeting, and evaluating the work of, the judges and profession throughout Australia. Most of the Federal Court judges were socially gregarious and enjoyed the contacts with other judges and the profession. And there was pleasure in visiting unfamiliar places. I remember a joyful photo of a Full Court of judges – Lockhart, Gallop and myself – sitting in our swimmers on a log at Berry Springs (before crocodiles migrated there). The Federal Court was a happy Court.

Growth in federal court jurisdiction and its implications

The Federal Court has always been a busy court. Although the workload cannot be estimated merely by the number of judgments delivered, the increases in the number of delivered judgments is some indication of a substantial workload, much attributable to increases in jurisdiction. The number of judgments increased from slightly more than 200 in 1977-1978 to approximately 1,700 in recent years, after a peak of 2,330 in 2007. The present appellate jurisdiction of the Court extends to appeals from judgments of the Federal Circuit Court (other than family law and child support judgments).[42] Additional original jurisdiction specifically invested includes tax[43] and industrial property[44] appeals at first instance, appeals on questions of law from decisions of the Trade Practices Tribunal regarding access to declared services,[45] applications under the *Native Title Act 1993* (Cth),[46] and applications[47] and some appeals[48] under the corporations legislation. Two statutes invested the Court with broad areas of jurisdiction. The first was the *Administrative Decisions (Judicial Review) Act 1977* (Cth) which came into force only on 1 October 1980 and gave the Court jurisdiction to review judicially decisions made under a federal enactment and s 39B of the *Judiciary Act 1903* (Cth), inserted on 20 December 1983,[49] giving the Court the same jurisdiction as that vested in the High Court by s 75(v) of the *Constitution*. Section 39B has been subsequently amended[50] to invest the Court with jurisdiction in any matter: '(a) in which the Commonwealth is seeking an injunction or a declaration; or (b) arising under the *Constitution*, or involving its interpretation; or (c) arising under any laws made by the Parliament, other than a matter in respect of which a criminal prosecution is instituted or any other criminal matter.'

A Full Court held in *Transport Workers' Union* v *Lee* that para (c) 'operates according to its terms as a "general conferral of jurisdiction" and "stands in contrast" to the prior history of limited Act by Act conferral of jurisdiction upon the Federal Court.'[51]

Matters arising under most Commonwealth laws are now within the jurisdiction of the Federal Court. However, s 39B also makes provision for complementary jurisdiction to be exercised by the Family Court or State courts in matters outside Federal Court jurisdiction.

The *Constitution* and federal legislation have precluded the existence of any national court of general jurisdiction. State courts are territorially limited and their jurisdiction does not extend to vast areas of social activity now governed by federal law. Nor does the High Court possess unlimited original jurisdiction. It could not exercise its original jurisdiction without impairing its capacity to perform its key function of determining appeals and constitutional matters. The Federal Court's jurisdiction is Australia-wide and, although it cannot be invested with State jurisdiction,[52] its jurisdiction extends to determining matters which, having a substantial federal element, also involve issues governed by common law or by State laws.[53] It cannot be classified as a court of general jurisdiction but it is a court of very broad jurisdiction. In an age when national borders are of diminishing significance in trade and commerce, it is inevitable that the ascertainment of the rights and liabilities of persons, both natural and corporate, engaged in international trade or commerce and the peaceful resolution of their controversies will present an increasing demand for judicial services. Those services may take different forms: national courts, international courts, arbitrations and mediations. Whatever the appropriate steps might be, it is essential that Australia should have available the judicial services needed for the nation's trade and commerce.

This will place further demands on the Federal Court. It is the Australian court which is best suited in structure and procedure to assume jurisdiction in relation to matters involving Australia's international trade or, indeed, any of Australia's external affairs. For example, as a court vested with jurisdiction in respect of actions *in rem* under the *Admiralty Act 1988* (Cth) (s 10), its procedures facilitate the arrest of a ship anywhere in Australia at any hour of the day or night. It may need additional government support, not only financial; it may have to develop a cadre of non-judicial officers to assist the Court or the parties and to advise on available procedures; it may have to reach agreements with other tribunals to facilitate the obtaining of evidence or the enforcement of orders. The history of the Federal Court from its commencement has shown that its comparative youth gives it the freedom to innovate, that its commitment to scholarship, integrity and courtesy commends it to counsel and litigants and that its internal relations ensure efficient and co-operative disposition of its work. The Court is well placed for the challenges of the times.

---

1. This reflection was published in (2017) 91 *Australian Law Journal* 461.
2. See *R v Kirby; Ex parte Boilermakers' Society of Australia* (1956) 94 CLR 254.
3. *Commonwealth Conciliation and Arbitration Act 1904* (Cth).
4. Paul Toose and Maurice Byers, 'The Necessity for a New Federal Court' (1963) *36 Australian Law Journal* 308.
5. Sir Garfield Barwick, 'The Australian Judicial System: The Proposed New Federal Superior Court' (1964) 1 (1) *Federal Law Review* 1.

6. Commonwealth, *Parliamentary Debates*, Senate, 27 October 1972, 2086 (Ivor Greenwood, Attorney-General).
7. Superior Court of Australia Bill (Cth), cl 37.
8. R J Ellicott, 'The Exercise of Federal Jurisdiction – A Revision of the Federal Judicial Structure' (1977) 1 *Criminal Law Journal* 1.
9. In Melbourne, the Industrial Registry would service the Industrial Division of the Court.
10. Carmel Meiklejohn, Officially Receiving – 80 Years of Australian Bankruptcy Administration, Manuscript as at 30 September 2009 (Attorney-General's Department Library, 2010).
11. Bob Ellicott, 'Tribute to Sir Nigel Bowen AC, KBE' (1995) 69 *Australian Law Journal* 143, 144.
12. Alex Chernov, 'Farewell Sitting for the Hon the Chief Justice' (30 November 1990) 6.
13. Barry O'Keefe, 'Farewell Sitting for the Hon the Chief Justice' (30 November 1990) 10.
14. Bob Ellicott, 'Tribute to Sir Nigel Bowen AC, KBE' (1995) 69 *Australian Law Journal* 143, 144.
15. Ibid 144.
16. Ibid 144-145.
17. The seat of Parramatta was previously held by Sir Garfield Barwick, who vacated it when appointed to the High Court.
18. 14 December 1967 to 12 November 1969; 22 March 1971 to 2 August 1971.
19. 12 November 1969 to 22 March 1971.
20. 2 August 1971 to 5 December 1972.
21. Commonwealth, *Parliamentary Debates*, House of Representatives, 29 October 1964, 2462. The question was addressed to the Attorney-General: 'At the last Australian Legal Convention, held in Hobart, an announcement was made on behalf of Sir Garfield Barwick that Cabinet had authorised him to design a new Federal superior court. I ask the Attorney-General whether he is pursuing this matter. If so, when may we expect a bill to be brought before this House?'
22. Commonwealth, *Parliamentary Debates*, House of Representatives, 28 March 1968, 568 (Nigel Bowen, Attorney-General).
23. Commonwealth Superior Court Bill 1968; Commonwealth, Parliamentary Debates, House of Representatives, 21 November 1968, 3142 (Nigel Bowen, Attorney-General).
24. Commonwealth, Parliamentary Debates, Senate, 10 October 1994, 1314 (Senator Hill); Hon Michael Duffy MP, 'Farewell Sitting for the Hon the Chief Justice' (30 November 1990) 3.
25. Commonwealth, Parliamentary Debates, Senate, 10 October 1994, 1314 (Senator Hill); Bob Ellicott, 'Tribute to Sir Nigel Bowen AC, KBE' (1995) 69 *Australian Law Journal* 143, 144.
26. Justice Faulks, 'Sir Nigel Bowen's Service to the Law and Legal Profession Marked' (1988) 23 (9) *Australian Law News* 25.
27. Bob Ellicott, 'Tribute to Sir Nigel Bowen AC, KBE' (1995) 69 *Australian Law Journal* 143, 146.
28. Sir Nigel Bowen, 'Farewell Sitting for the Hon the Chief Justice' (30 November 1990) 15.
29. Bob Ellicott, 'Tribute to Sir Nigel Bowen AC, KBE' (1995) 69 *Australian Law Journal* 143, 146.

30. Fox, Blackburn and Connor JJ came from the ACT and Forster, Muirhead and Ward JJ came from the NT.
31. Riley and Charles Sweeney JJ.
32. Smithers, Nimmo, Woodward, Franki, J B Sweeney, Evatt, St John, Northrop, Brennan JJ.
33. See *Federal Court of Australia Act 1976* (Cth), s 15.
34. See *Federal Court Rules* 1977 (Cth), SR 20 of 1977.
35. For example, *Trade Practices Commission* v *Milreis Pty Ltd* (1977) 29 FLR 144; *R* v *Trade Practices Tribunal; Ex parte Tooheys Ltd* (1977) 31 FLR 1; *Re Tooth & Co Ltd [No 2]* (1978) 34 FLR 112; *Parish* v *World Series Cricket Pty Ltd* (1977) 16 ALR 172; *Tradestock Pty Ltd* v *TNT (Management) Pty Ltd [No 2]* (1978) 32 FLR 420; *Federal Coke Co Pty Ltd* v *Commissioner of Taxation (Cth)* (1977) 34 FLR 375; *Adamson* v *Western Australian National Football League (Inc)* (1978) 38 FLR 237.
36. Sir Nigel H Bowen, 'The Federal Court of Australia' (1977) 8(2) *Sydney Law Review* 285, 292.
37. Sir Laurence Street, 'The Consequences of a Dual System of State and Federal Courts' (1978) 52 *Australian Law Journal* 434, 437.
38. Sir Nigel Bowen, 'Federal and State Court Relationships' (1979) 53 *Australian Law Journal* 806.
39. Ibid, 816.
40. The Court did not have jurisdiction to hear appeals on questions of law from decisions of the Trade Practices Tribunal, but under *Trade Practices Act 1974* (Cth), s 163A, which had been enacted on 31 August 1976, the Court had jurisdiction to make orders 'by way of, or in the nature of, prohibition, certiorari or mandamus' and declarations 'in relation to the validity of any act or thing done, proposed to be done or purporting to have been done' under the Act, including decisions of the Tribunal.
41. See *Federal Court of Australia Act 1976* (Cth) s 24(1).
42. Ibid,
43. Section 14ZZ of the *Taxation Administration Act 1953* (Cth) inserted by *Taxation Laws Amendment Act (No 3) 1991* (Cth) s 112.This jurisdiction is now exclusive to the Federal Court: *Jurisdiction of Courts (Miscellaneous Amendments) Act 1987* (Cth) s 4.
44. See *Patents Act 1990* (Cth) s 154; *Trade Marks Act 1995* (Cth). This jurisdiction is now exclusive to the Federal Court: *Jurisdiction of Courts (Miscellaneous Amendments) Act 1987* (Cth) s 5, Sch.
45. See *Competition Policy Reform Act 1995* (Cth) s 59, inserting s 44ZR in the *Trade Practices Act 1974* (Cth).
46. See *Native Title Act 1993* (Cth) s 81.
47. See *Corporations Act 2001* (Cth) s 1337B.
48. See *Corporations Act 2001* (Cth) ss 1135, 1321.
49. See *Statute Law (Miscellaneous Provisions) Act (No 2) 1983* (Cth) ss 2(1), 3, Sch 1.
50. See *Law and Justice Legislation Amendment Act 1997* (Cth) ss 2(1), 3, Sch 11, Item 1; *Law and Justice Amendment Act 1999* (Cth) ss 2(1), 3, Sch 10, Item 1.
51. See *Transport Workers' Union of Australia* v *Lee* (1998) 84 FCR 60, 67.
52. See *Re Wakim* (1999) 198 CLR 511.
53. See *Fencott v Muller* (1983) 152 CLR 570.

5.2 The Federal Court 40th Anniversary Dinner

Editor's note

Brennan was invited to deliver the after-dinner speech at the Conference Dinner marking the 40th anniversary of the Federal Court. The dinner took place on 8 September 2017.

You honour me by inviting me to speak at this dinner when we are celebrating 40 years of the Federal Court's life and activity. The invitation is a tribute to my longevity as I think that Ray Northrop and I are the only survivors of those who took their oaths of allegiance and office as judges of the Court under the Chief Judge, Sir Nigel Bowen, on 7 February 1977. I rang Ray to ask him for any pertinent recollections. Now Ray was a devoted advocate of the creation of the Court and he rejoices in this celebration. One of his recollections was the good wishes he received from Lionel Murphy who congratulated him on his successful advocacy. But then I was left with the problem of saying something to the many here tonight who are giving or have given the Court its life and activity for the past 40 years. For nearly half that time I have been retired, freed from what Sir John Nimmo used to refer to as 'the tyranny of reserved judgments'.

Each of you or your partner has a more authoritative knowledge of the Federal Court than I can offer. I asked the Chief Justice to give me a list of some of the more notable judgments of the Court during the last 40 years and he kindly did so. I was tempted to talk about the fine jurisprudential quality of these judgments, for they do indeed show the research, scholarship and incisiveness of the authors but that would merely confirm what is already familiar to you. But then my son in law, Dan O'Gorman, who had attended the ABA Conference in Dublin, lent me his copy of Ruadhan Mac Cormaic's book on the Supreme Court of Ireland – a book which has escalated in the sales charts of that island of saints and scholars. It demonstrates that the life of a court is not exhausted by recounting a court's jurisdiction, the judgments it delivers or the legal principles it has defined. The life of a court involves more than is found in the reports; it involves the personalities of the judges, their relationships one with another and with the members of other branches of government, with the tensions that arise between them, with the sensitivity of the court to the changing culture and values of the community, with the style of advocacy, with the accessibility of the court to potential litigants, with the transparency and facility of the court's procedures and with the atmosphere and architecture of the court room. These are factors which shape the role that a court may play in the history of a nation. Courts have played an influential role in the history of the Australian nation, as we would expect in a nation which boasts adherence to the rule of law. So, I must ramble a little over different aspects of the Federal Court's 40 years, perhaps reminding you of matters that are already familiar but stressing the novel growth of a federal judiciary in our federal Commonwealth.

There have been radical changes in the Australian judiciary since the Second World War, when I first became familiar with the courts and the legal profession. The creation of the Federal Court and the exercise of its jurisdiction have arguably worked the most radical changes, and an evaluation of the life of the Federal Court must be made in the milieu of an age of change. Changes occurred in the administration of the traditional fields of the law: in crime and family law, in tort, contract and equity, in probate and other traditional fields. In those fields, litigation focussed chiefly on rights and obligations arising or existing between individuals including non-government corporations. But in more recent times, rights and obligations arising or existing under statutory or public law have assumed much greater importance and that has created the need for new distributions of judicial power.

That is not to say that the traditional fields have been untouched by change. There have been major changes in the way in which those jurisdictions have been exercised. I can remember when juries, always male only, used to be locked up before they delivered their verdict and when florid advocacy was the style of leading counsel. Mac Cormaic's book opens with the Latin maxim *fiat justitia ruat coelum* – 'Let justice be done though the Heavens fall'. I was reminded that that maxim was painted above the bench in the Roma Courthouse, where some local cynics mistranslated the maxim to 'if justice is done, the heavens will fall'. In that courtroom, I heard the powerful florid advocacy of the legendary Dan Casey, one of the founders of Alcoholic Anonymous. Dan was addressing a jury which included four local members of that estimable organization. 'I know not,' said Casey in this murder trial 'whether any of you gentlemen has suffered the ravages of drink..' The jury returned a verdict of manslaughter. I wonder whether advocacy of that kind would be so effective today. This was a time when undefended divorces were the bread and butter of the junior Bar, and landlord and tenant litigation was a feature of many a fashionable practice. So were personal injury claims but the size of insurers' liabilities led to restrictions on the remedies. A barrister of my generation would be unfamiliar with the daily life of a barrister today. Before 1977, most practitioners were familiar only with the work of the state and territory courts. The High Court's jurisdiction engaged mostly leaders of the profession and was a remote and costly venue. It had a heavy case load in tax. If you look at the first volume of the *Commonwealth Law Reports Index and Digest*, the income tax entries run from pages 381 to 407. By contrast, the heading 'Administrative Law' contains only seven sub-headings, each of which merely refers the reader to other specific provisions. As the years passed statute law opened up new fields and commercial litigation increased. Public law remedies assumed greater significance in the protection of individual interests.

Commonwealth legislation created new areas of federal jurisdiction and the Federal Court, after some controversy, was created to exercise a large part of that jurisdiction. The jurisdiction under some of the new Commonwealth laws had been conferred at first on the Australian Industrial Court or on Commonwealth Tribunals. There were difficulties with this distribution of judicial authority. The Industrial Court itself was not a popular venue. When I became a member of that Court in 1976 in order to preside over the Administrative Appeals Tribunal and the Administrative Review Council (ARC), I found that the Court's case load was extremely light. Indeed, one of my judicial colleagues advised me that if I wanted to sit on a case, I would have to apply to, and be nominated by, the secretary of the Chief Judge. In fact, I sat only twice on that Court – once in the small Bankruptcy Court in Brisbane in order to be welcomed by the Solicitor-General (Sir Maurice Byers) and some of my friends in the Queensland profession. On that occasion, I sat alone. Later, I sat with all my judicial colleagues of that Court for the ceremony on the retirement of the Chief Judge, Sir John Spicer. That ceremony was begun when a senior judge enquired: 'Is there a solicitor here?' whereupon the Solicitor- General rose from his chair.

The procedure was more familiar when we all sat together for the swearing in of the Federal Court on 7 February 1977, but there was no mistaking the novelty of the Court, its membership and its jurisdiction. To start with, Attorney-General, Bob Ellicott had dropped the contentious title of 'Superior Court' – a title which had exacerbated objections to a federal court. He had limited the jurisdiction of the Court so as to avoid impairment of the jurisdiction of the State and Territory Supreme Courts while the jurisdictions of the Territory Supreme Courts, the Bankruptcy Court and the Australian Industrial Court were maintained and transferred to the new Court. Some appellate jurisdiction was invested in the Federal Court and this achieved a number of objectives: uniformity in the construction and application of important Commonwealth laws, substantial hierarchical status for the new Court, judicial work of sufficient difficulty to attract judges of good ability and controversies which were likely to engage the commercial Bar. The creation of the Federal Court transformed the Australian judiciary.

The Federal Court was given in time a general supervisory power over Commonwealth Tribunals and over the exercise of Commonwealth administrative power. From the beginning there were frequent applications to the Court for public law remedies in federal matters. Those cases, by example and precedent, encouraged similar applications to State courts in matters arising under State laws. Administrative law became a fertile field of litigation. Then the open textured *Trade Practices Act 1974* (Cth) gave the Court entry to a vast field of commercial litigation. More jurisdiction has been added in the 40 years of the Court's existence. The significance of the Federal Court's jurisdiction was not recognized immediately. I remember one critic asking me why I had accepted appointment to a Court that had no power. The power of the Federal Court expanded with the rapid expansion of Commonwealth legislative regulation. As you know, the Court became a busy tribunal with a varied case list: trade practices, administrative review, bankruptcy, industrial, corporations, immigration, native title, revenue, intellectual property, admiralty.

To exercise this jurisdiction, a strong bench of judges was needed, led by strong Chief Justices and supported by committed and competent staff. In general, the Court has been fortunate in the appointments made by government. The relationship between a court and the Executive Government, especially the Attorney-General, is critically important. The relationship has reciprocal responsibilities. Government must be solicitous for what a Court needs to perform its functions and must be willing to consult the Court or its appropriate agents, especially the Chief Justice, to determine the necessary resources of both personnel and material. The Court, for its part, must ensure that it uses those resources efficiently and accounts punctiliously for their use; and the court should be understanding of the exigencies affecting the capacities of government.

The appointment of judges is not merely one of the gifts of government. Sometimes a Government may see a vacant judicial office as an opportunity for patronage or reward or the placing of a political sympathiser. That is an abuse of power. Appointment is a power to be exercised in the public interest to ensure that the Court is best able to perform its judicial functions competently, efficiently without fear or favour or ill will. Judicial friendships and political affiliations are equally irrelevant to the selection process. Trust in the integrity and insightfulness of the appointment process is vital not only to avoid risking a misuse of judicial power or a waste of resources, but also to ensure that public confidence in the courts is maintained and that candidates of high standing can be attracted when future appointments are to be made. An Attorney who does not appoint the most qualified candidate for a judicial post damages the very institution for which he or she is responsible. For the most part, the Federal Court has been well served by the appointments made to its bench.

The Chief Justices have been outstanding. The Court was fortunate to have Sir Nigel Bowen as the first Chief Justice. He had precisely the ability and the personal qualities appropriate to establishing the Court as an institution of erudition, innovation, industry and courtesy. His respectful but knowledgeable assessment of his judges' judicial work ensured that we were allocated to the cases that best suited our experience and capacities. And no doubt his standing with the governments of the day ensured that his views on the suitability of candidates for appointment to his Court were given great weight. The standard which he set has been upheld by his successors but, as they are happily still with us, I must not comment on their contributions except in relation to two matters for which Michael Black is chiefly responsible. First, his masterly conspectus of the first 30 years of the Court's life and work published in the *Melbourne University Law Review.*[1] That is an important chapter in our nation's history. Secondly, the Courts and Court Houses in which the Federal Court works in the State capitals. Dignified but not overpowering, practical and efficient and proudly exhibiting fine Australian materials and workmanship. They are attractive venues for litigants, the profession, the judges and the staff. The physical settings provide an ambience that facilitates the working of the Court. However, the Court has sat in other venues. The robed judge sitting under a tree or tent and being addressed by counsel in their robes has become a commonplace in native title cases, however unexpected that scenario would have been 40 years ago. Federal Court judges have not stood on ceremony when some alternative is appropriate. John Toohey's towelling hat was no substitute for a wig but it was suitable cover from the tropic sun when he was sitting as Aboriginal Land Commissioner.

Modern courthouses have fully embraced modern technology. Today's judges conduct hearings and conferences by videolink. And now the Court is moving to paperless filing and exhibition of court documents. The Court has demonstrated an innovative ethos and an aptitude for moulding procedure to identify issues and to find the facts relevant to the instant case. Judicial competence, aided by innovation and by an absence of unnecessary formality, has given the Court an enviable status and reputation. The Court has been well served by staff who share the Court's commitment to useful change. The co-operation between judges and staff has been obvious to observers and has reinforced the appreciation of the Court as a peaceful and efficient institution. That is a tribute especially to the long serving Registrars Jim Howard and Warwick Soden.

Now what of the judges who have constituted the Court for the past 40 years? As that book on the Irish Supreme Court shows, and as each judge of experience can testify, the relationship of judges *inter se* gives a court its vitality and makes judicial life both stimulating and attractive. Of course, I cannot testify to the nature of judicial relationships on the Court after 1981 but I have no reason to think that the integrity and competence, the erudition and humour that I experienced in the early days of the Court has not persisted throughout the following decades. Perhaps the competence of the judges has benefitted from judicial orientation courses which were unknown 40 years ago. Thus, I remember John Lockhart's reply when I enquired how he was going in the difficult trial over which he was presiding. 'Like a duck in a pond', said John. 'Gliding peacefully on the surface and paddling furiously below.' New judges in those days got training on the job. When the Chief Judge wanted me to get some experience in the industrial jurisdiction, he sent me off with Jack Sweeney and Phil Evatt to hear a case about breach of an award. There was a guilty plea and when we retired to consider the penalty, Jack and Phil thought that a fine of $200 and a stiff lecture were called for. Of course, I agreed but I had some concern for Jack. He had a thin voice which might not be suited, I thought, to giving a stiff lecture. How wrong I was! It was one of the most excoriating and minatory lectures I had ever heard, enhanced by the reedy tones in which it was delivered.

I hope the judges still enjoy the rare moments of humour, like the time when Bill Deane, Bob Fisher and I were sitting on a tax appeal in the court room in 450 Little Bourke Street in Melbourne. During the morning, counsel for the taxpayer had regaled us with the outrage felt by Sir Timothy Tolpuddle (as I shall call him) when his corporation had been served with a large assessment to tax. After lunch, as we were about to enter the Court and the Court Crier had commanded all to stand, Bill Deane said – for Bob and me to hear – something along the lines of 'Will Sir Timothy recover his composure? Wait for the next thrilling instalment!' We had to withdraw precipitately to recover our composure. Bill had that mischievous streak. Shortly after I had delivered a judgment in the World Series Cricket saga including a quote, we had been given from *Wisden's Cricketers Almanac*, Bill and I were having breakfast in the Adelaide Club and I observed that the library there stocked a full series of the *Almanac*. 'What?' said Bill, 'you had the gall to quote *Wisden* and you had not read the series?'

Perhaps more important than knowledge of the law is an intuitive sense of justice. Reg Smithers did not have to choose between them – he had both. His judgments reflected his familiarity with the authorities. Indeed, he confided that at night he used to read High Court judgments to his wife, Dorothy. (How

Dorothy, a forthright intelligent woman put up with that entertainment I do not know). But his passion was for justice. I had asked Reg if he would accept appointment as a Vice-President of the Administrative Appeals Tribunal and he had accepted ('Been wanting to get behind the counter for years!' he opined). There he had no hesitation in rejecting government policy on alien deportations if he thought the policy unjust in the instant case.[2] As Reg's judgments showed, a sense of justice is the guide to sound legal analysis, for the law – and the Parliament which enacts a law – are assumed to intend that the application of the law will do justice unless there are clear contrary indications. This assumption sometimes accounts for tensions arising between the courts and government, a tension that confirms the importance of strong and independent judges.

The Federal Court has had a calendar of cases that have affected the history of our country in the last 40 years. Its judges have continued, I believe, to show those qualities which I admired in my colleagues of the early days: integrity and competence, erudition and humour. And thereby they have fulfilled the hope which Nigel Bowen expressed on 7 February 1977: 'It is my hope that the Court will quickly establish itself as a court of high standing in the eyes of the profession and of the public.'

That has been the Court's achievement and, with the other superior Courts of this nation, it maintains the eminence of Australia's judicial system in the common law world.

---

1. Michael Black, 'The Federal Court of Australia: The First 20 Years – A Survey on the Occasion of Two Anniversaries' (2007) 31(3) *Melbourne University Law Review* 1017.
2. There was no error of law in that approach, but it gave full rein to the discretion left in *Re Drake and Minister for Immigration and Ethnic Affairs (No 2)* (1979) 2 ALD 634.

Chapter 6

The High Court and the Constitution

6.1 Three Cheers for *Engineers*

Editor's note

On 31 August 1920, the High Court delivered judgment in *Amalgamated Society of Engineers v Adelaide Steamship Company Limited* (*Engineers Case*).[1] By a majority of 5-1, the Court overruled two doctrines which the court's founding members had propounded: reciprocal intergovernmental immunity and reserved state powers. On the 75th anniversary of the decision, Professors Michael Coper and George Williams at the Australian National University convened a conference, 'How Many Cheers for *Engineers*?' They pithily summed up the judgment: 'effect must be given to the express words of the *Constitution*, which should not be qualified by vague implications derived from extraneous political theory'.[2] On 31 August 1995, Sir Anthony Mason introduced the new Chief Justice, Sir Gerard Brennan to deliver the closing address entitled 'Three Cheers for *Engineers*'.[3]

The celebration of a case, or a commemoration of the occasion of the delivery of a judgment, is justified by two considerations. The first is that the case marks the dawning of legal light by the adoption of a proposition that was theretofore shrouded in darkness. The second is that, having regard to subsequent experience, the proposition has been found to be in accordance with the needs or aspirations of the community. Of course, it is only if the needs or aspirations of the community are met that the proposition adopted in the case will be characterized as luminous.

If the proposition were previously shrouded in darkness, there must have been some intellect which pierced the darkness in order to admit the light. And thus, whenever there is a case to celebrate, there is a kind of legal champion to praise. I suppose Lord Atkin in *Donoghue v Stevenson* is the most noteworthy.[4] Now, in the *Engineers Case*, is the hero Menzies or Starke or Isaacs? Or others as well? The first contender for the accolade must be Menzies.

On 24 May 1920 in Melbourne, Menzies dutifully advanced the argument that the government sawmills in Western Australia were trading rather than government enterprises and, on that account, disentitled to the protection of a state instrumentality. Menzies' version of what happened starts with

Starke J's intervention: 'That argument is nonsense.' Menzies describes what happened next:

> I, in what I later realized to be an inspired moment, replied: 'Sir, I quite agree.' 'Well', intervened the Chief Justice, Chief Justice Knox, never the most genial of interrogators, 'why are you putting an argument which you admit is nonsense?' 'Because'... 'I am compelled by the earlier decisions of this Court. If your Honours will permit me to question all or any of these earlier decisions, I will undertake to advance a sensible argument.' I waited for the heavens to fall. Instead, the Chief Justice said: 'The Court will retire for a few minutes.' And when they came back, he said, 'This case will be adjourned for argument at Sydney. Each government will be notified so that it may apply to intervene. Counsel will be at liberty to challenge any earlier decision of this Court!'[5]

Now that version may be correct. But the suggestion that the attack on the doctrine of the earlier cases was not made until the Sydney hearing does not accord with the entries in the notebooks of Sir Adrian Knox and Sir Isaac Isaacs. Sir Adrian Knox noted an argument by Menzies designed to distinguish the *Railway Servants' Case,* but then he noted a further argument:

> Section 51(xxxv) power is quite unlimited on the face of it and capable of being exercised to bind State governments ... Nothing in the *Constitution* which gives a state operation any protection – any protection must be based on implication – *D'Emden v Pedder.*[6] There is no reciprocal doctrine to protect a State corresponding with rule in *D'Emden v Pedder. Municipalities Case* 26 CLR 508, 532.[7]

At that page in the joint judgment of Isaacs and Rich JJ, the decision in *D'Emden v Pedder* is founded 'on the principle of supremacy, and on nothing else'. Their Honours attributed that principle to s 109 and Covering Clause 5. They said: 'As soon as it is perceived that the principle of the decision is "supremacy," it is manifest that there can be no reciprocity. ... If the power exists, *D'Emden v Pedder* annihilates the opposing enactment; if the power does not exist, the case is inapplicable. The position is simply stated.'[8]

Isaacs and Rich JJ then discussed the notion of the unity of the Crown.

After Menzies referred to the *Municipalities Case,* he put a further argument based on a distinction between governmental and non-governmental functions. That elicited a further mention of the *Railway Servants' Case*[9] by Higgins J.

Isaacs' note is much briefer than the Chief Justice's, but it accords with it: 's 51(31) – quite unlimited – 26/532' (the *Municipalities Case* reference). And thus, it appears that it was at the initial hearing in Melbourne that Menzies first advanced his attack on the *Railways Servants' Case's* notion of reciprocal supremacy. After Isaacs' note of that argument he penned, in shorthand, his suggestion for the course then to be followed. The note is not easily deciphered but it seems to read as follows:

> We think that counsel should have the opportunity of raising the question whether the *Rail Servants* case as far as it concerns this case is correctly decided and upon that argument it will be open to counsel to question any case relevant to the decision of this case. That will give counsel a perfectly free hand on the argument.
>
> We think that notices in this case and the question to be raised should be given to each counsel and every State except Western Australia. They will use their own judgment and this case will be taken on Monday, 26 July in Sydney.

And, perhaps after a brief adjournment, it was so ordered.

When the matter came on for argument in Sydney, the available Justices' notebooks are fairly sparse in their recording of the arguments of any of the counsel. In Isaacs' notebook, the recording of Menzies' arguments is limited to the citation of 12 cases including, however, 25 pages of the *Municipalities Case.* He referred also to the *Steel Rails Case.*[10] The notes run on, briefly, from day to day until Leverrier KC rose on behalf of the Commonwealth. Isaacs J then recorded what is practically verbatim the opening passage of Leverrier's argument as reported in at (1920) 28 CLR 129, 139. He wrote:

> We contend that supremacy in *D'Emden v Pedder*[11] and the rule in *D'Emden v Pedder* merely a branch of supremacy, is a valid rule of law based on the *Constitution* itself. We say that what is called the reciprocal doctrine in *Railway Servants' Case*[12] is not only not derivable from the *Constitution* but is inconsistent with it. The powers of the Commonwealth must be ascertained externally by the ordinary rules of construction applied to the *Constitution* as a *Constitution.* Ordinary rules of construction include surrounding circumstances. Compact with States etc. Supremacy from express words. We rely (1) on sec. V. (Covering) (2) sec. 106 to 109. Sec. 106 standing alone would be sufficient.

It seems quite clear that Menzies lit the fuse in Melbourne, though the main charge for exploding the notion of reciprocal supremacy seems to have been prepared by Isaacs and Rich JJ in the *Municipalities Case.* Yet it was Leverrier's, rather than Menzies' advocacy which seems to have had the greatest impact on the putative author of the majority judgment.

What was the proposition adopted by the *Engineers Case?* Sir Owen Dixon said that, 'stripped of embellishment and reduced to the form of a legal proposition', the proposition established by the *Engineers Case* was simply 'that a power to legislate with respect to a given subject enables the Parliament to make laws which, upon that subject, affect the operations of the states and their agencies'. [13]

Did the decision in 1920, and has it since, satisfied the needs and aspirations of the Australian people? Sir Owen Dixon noted that, as the result of the conditions produced by the First World War, the states had been reduced in stature and the Court itself had been accustomed to the exercise of an all-pervading power by the Commonwealth. He commented:

> The substance of the decision has been hardly impugned, but its result was to reduce still further the power of the State and its importance in the eyes of the community. At the same time the authority of the Court suffered. A tendency grew among the States to look to the Judicial Committee of the Privy Council. Moreover the legal profession for a time appeared to feel that a more stable development of our constitutional law might come from that body. It was a vain hope. [14]

But the legal profession was not the Australian people. Professor Brian Galligan points out that, by adopting a legalist interpretation of the *Constitution*, the Court both accommodated an expansion of federal powers and maintained the integrity and independence of the Court in an atmosphere of extreme political partisanship.[15] Windeyer J in the *Payroll Tax Case* said: 'in 1920 the *Constitution* was read in a new light, a light reflected from events that had, over twenty years, led to a growing realization that Australians were now one people and Australia one country and that national laws might meet national needs.'[16]

And on his retirement, Sir Garfield Barwick warned us 'to be very wary that the triumph of the *Engineers Case* is never tarnished'.[17] So, it seems that judicial opinion at least would give three cheers for *Engineers*.

How was the revolution of the *Engineers Case* (as Sir Robert Garran described it[18]) effected? The majority judgment contains rhetoric that has a modern ring to it:

> The more the decisions are examined, and compared with each other and with the Constitution itself, the more evident it becomes that no clear principle can account for them. They are sometimes at variance with the natural meaning of the text of the Constitution; some are irreconcilable with others, and some are individually rested

> on reasons not founded on the words of the Constitution or on any recognized principle of the common law underlying the expressed terms of the Constitution, but on implication drawn from what is called the principle of 'necessity', that being itself referable to no more definite standard than the personal opinion of the Judge who declares it. The attempt to deduce any consistent rule from them has not only failed, but has disclosed an increasing entanglement and uncertainty, and a conflict both with the text of the Constitution and with distinct and clear declarations of law by the Privy Council.[19]

This passage is similar in both tone and content to what was said in *Cole v Whitfield.*[20] We can readily understand how, as a matter of judicial reasoning, the decision was arrived at in *Engineers.*

The Court did not then rank among its members the Justices who had formulated the doctrine of reciprocal supremacy. O'Connor J had died in 1912, Griffith CJ had left the Court in 1919. He died on 9 August 1920 between the hearing of *Engineers* and the delivery of judgment. Barton, who was disappointed not to have been Griffith's successor, died on 7 January 1920. The Court was then substantially under the influence of Isaacs,[21] the senior Justice and an advocate of Commonwealth power. Higgins, the next most senior Justice, was anxious to resist interventions by the High Court in the work of the Industrial Court.[22] Knox, the comparatively new Chief Justice, had been a leader of the New South Wales Bar. He, Rich and Starke JJ. were lawyers to whom the propounded method of constitutional interpretation was more attractive than a doctrine which owed much to the political history known to the departed members of the Court. Gavan Duffy J dissented and Powers J, it seems, was on leave at the time and did not sit.

The approach in the *Engineers Case* was not only legalist but literalist, seeming to deny the possibility of implications that might limit Commonwealth legislative power. It was left to Dixon J in *West's Case*[23] and in later cases to restore the legitimacy of implications in construing the constitutional text. But I must stop at this point – not only because I have gone too long, but because the nature and scope of limiting implications is a topic of current controversy. Perhaps the third cheer for *Engineers* has been muffled or even silenced by implied limitations. Professor Galligan thinks so. He writes: 'the court needs to jettison the legalistic methodology of *Engineers,* which is antithetical to Australia's federal Constitution. It is quite inappropriate to interpret the Commonwealth's enumerated heads of power in a literal way irrespective of the broader federal architecture of the Constitution and regardless of the centralising effect that such a method produces.'[24]

I presume that has been a proposition fully discussed today. It should delay the festivities no longer.

---

1. (1920) 28 CLR 129.
2. Michael Coper and George Williams (eds), *How Many Cheers for Engineers?* (Federation Press, 1997) xiv.
3. The address was first published in Michael Coper and George Williams (eds) *How Many Cheers for Engineers?* (Federation Press, 1997) 145-151.
4. [1932] AC 562.
5. Sir Robert Gordon Menzies, *Central Power of the Australian Commonwealth* (Cassell, 1967) 38-39.
6. (1904) 1 CLR 91
7. See *Federated Amalgamated Government Railway and Tramway Service Association v New South Wales Railway Traffic Employees Association (Railway Servants Case)* (1906) 4 CLR 488
8. See *Federated Municipal and Shire Council Employees' Union of Australia v Melbourne Corporation* (1919) 26 CLR 508, 533.
9. (1906) 4 CLR 488,539.
10. See *Attorney-General of NSW v. Collector of Customs for NSW* (1908) 5 CLR 818.
11. (1904) 1 CLR 91.
12. (1904) 4 CLR 488.
13. See *Melbourne Corporation v The Commonwealth* (1947) 74 CLR 31, 78.
14. Sir Owen Dixon, 'Aspects of Australian Federalism' in Sir Owen Dixon, *Jesting Pilate* (Law Book Co, 1965) 116-117.
15. Brian Galligan, *Politics of the High Court* (University of Queensland Press, 1987) 97.
16. See *Victoria v. Commonwealth* (1971) 122 CLR 353, 396.
17. (1981) 148 CLR x.
18. Sir Robert Garran, *Prosper the Commonwealth* (Angus and Robertson, 1958) 180.
19. (1920) 28 CLR 129, 141.
20. (1988) 165 CLR 360, 384-385.
21. Max Gordon, *Sir Isaac Isaacs, a life of service*, (Heineman, 1963) 128.
22. John Rickard, *HB Higgins, The Rebel as Judge,* (George Allen & Unwin, 1984) 276-281.
23. See *West v Commissioner of Taxation* (1937) 56 CLR 657, 681- 682.
24. Brian Galligan, *A Federal Republic: Australia's constitutional system of government* (Cambridge University Press, 1995) 188.

6.2 The Mason Court and Beyond

Editor's note

After Sir Anthony Mason retired as Chief Justice, Professor Cheryl Saunders convened a conference at the University of Melbourne on 8-10 September 1995 entitled 'The Mason Court and Beyond'. Brennan gave two papers at the conference, the first of which was this tribute to Sir Anthony Mason. The second was a paper entitled 'Looking to the Future'.[1]

Tradition, at least in the High Court, requires reticence in comment about the judicial work of one's colleagues. The dignity of both the individual justices and the institution is thus ensured. The reasons for judgment must speak for themselves. If they command a concurrence from other members of the Court, the concurrence is on record. If, by reason of principle, or expression, or the desire of each justice to work to a conclusion in his or her own words, a justice's reasons for judgment command no concurrence, no extra curial comment is appropriate. The strength of any judgment and the reputation of its author must depend on the cogency of the concepts it expresses and the manner of their expression. As among the members of a small collegiate court, the ultimate estimate of a judgment must be left to other minds than one's judicial colleagues. The estimate will be made, of course, by the verdict of history. For these reasons, you must hold me excused from framing my tribute to Sir Anthony Mason in terms of particular judgments he has written.

Further, I am bound to say that there is no personality cult in the High Court. The Chief Justice is regarded – in practice, not only in theory – as primus inter pares. As Sir Owen Dixon said when he was sworn into the office of Chief Justice: 'The court is a co-operative institution; the position of the man who presides differs very little from that of any other judge. Perhaps he receives a little more attention from the Bar than he deserves because he announces the conclusions of the court first, but all my judicial experience tells me that a man's influence on the court does not depend on where he sits.'[2]

To describe the Court during Sir Anthony Mason's Chief Justiceship as 'the Mason Court' is a useful shorthand, but it is not a term which accurately describes the dynamics of a Court constituted by justices of robust independence of mind, willing and able to give cogent expression to their own views. That said, I am free to frame my tribute to Sir Anthony in a way which reflects my experience of him as a judicial colleague. I would speak of the themes that informed his judgments, his cast of mind and his relationship with the other members of his Court.

His public law judgments reveal a vision of Australia as an independent nation fully equipped to take its place as a member of the international community.[3] Moreover, he has a passion for free expression which is the natural concomitant of a lively and informed intellect. His judgment in *Commonwealth v John Fairfax & Sons Ltd* contains the memorable and influential observation that '[i]t is unacceptable in our democratic society that there should be a restraint on the publication of information relating to government when the only vice of that information is that it enables the public to discuss, review and criticize government action'.[4] In *Nationwide News*, he described freedom of expression as one of the 'fundamental values traditionally protected by the common law'.[5]

He was concerned to diminish the possibility of abuse of power in what were once the opaque processes of government. As Solicitor-General for the Commonwealth, he suggested to Mr Nigel Bowen (the then Attorney-General) the establishment of the Commonwealth Administrative Review Committee. He became a member of that Committee which launched what became known as the Commonwealth administrative law package: the *Administrative Appeals Tribunal Act 1975* (Cth), the *Ombudsman Act 1976* (Cth), the *Freedom of Information Act 1982* (Cth) and the *Administrative Decisions (Judicial Review) Act 1977* (Cth). Later, in his judgments, Sir Anthony charted and expanded the remedies of judicial review. But he was conscious of the limitations on judicial power. In the *Peko-Wallsend* case he reminded us of the limited role of a court reviewing the exercise of an administrative discretion.[6] Speaking of that case in a subsequent speech, he said: 'Judicial review on the merits of administrative decisions would be difficult to reconcile with the separation of powers.'[7]

Especially in his later judgments, Sir Anthony manifested a concern at the power of the modern State to overreach the individual. Fastening on the proposition that the power of government is derived from the people governed, he sought jealously to protect the governed from any attempts to exceed or to misuse legitimate power. He concluded his Wilfred Fullagar Memorial Lecture with a declaration of the courts' responsibility: 'Our evolving concept of the democratic process is moving beyond an exclusive emphasis on parliamentary supremacy and majority will. It embraces a notion of responsible government which respects the fundamental rights and dignity of the individual and calls for the observance of procedural fairness in matters affecting the individual. The proper function of the courts is to protect and safeguard this vision of the democratic process.'[8]

In considering the validity of an exercise of power, Sir Anthony would not suffer words and formulae to hide the substance. In *Cole v Whitfield,* the s 92 criterion of operation formula was cast aside with these words: 'In truth the history of the doctrine is an indication of the hazards of seeking certainty of operation of a constitutional guarantee through the medium of an artificial formula. Either the formula is consistently applied and subverts the substance of the guarantee; or an attempt is made to achieve uniformly satisfactory outcomes and the formula becomes uncertain in its application.'[9]

In the areas of private law, the Mason judgments were marked by an accurate knowledge of existing authority and a refusal to be bound by a rule of law when, consistently with the judicial method, it could be recast to be more useful or more attuned to contemporary needs. His judgments on waiver and estoppel, on fiduciary relationships, unjust enrichment, negligence and company law have illuminated these fields. It is chiefly in the fields of private law that his avidity for ideas and his search for assistance from other jurisdictions can be detected. For the first time, academic writing was encouraged on cases pending in the High Court. The research capacity of the Court library was strengthened and, more importantly, utilised. In *Waltons Stores*, for example, within four printed pages you will find references not only to the usual sources but also to cases in Massachusetts and Malaysia, New York and New Zealand as well as a number of academic texts. [10] He was willing to open the door more widely to criminal cases. He was anxious to achieve, is possible, clear solutions of principle to be applied by trial judges and to insist upon conditions conducive to the fairness of criminal trials.[11]

Perhaps the most significant feature of his writings is not in the solutions propounded to particular problems but, rather, in his approach to the roles of precedent and policy. Sir Owen Dixon's 'strict and complete legalism', which had served the Court well in shielding it from controversy, could no longer be defended as an adequate explanation of the judicial method. In a final court of appeal, precedent has to pass through informed and critical scrutiny before its authority is fully recognized. Lecturing on 'The Use and Abuse of Precedent', Sir Anthony attacked the transformation of precedent from a judicial policy to a state of mind[12] and he concluded that the problem of stare decisis is not a problem to be solved automatically by the application of precise rules or formulae. He saw stare decisis as 'an exercise in judicial policy which calls for an assessment of a variety of factors in which judges balance the need for continuity, consistency and predictability against the competing need for justice, flexibility and rationality'.[13] If precedent was not automatically to be applied, policy had an overt role to play. So much was not only accepted but welcomed. He wrote:

> Because policy-oriented interpretation exposes underlying values for debate it would enhance the open character of the judicial

> decision-making process and promote legal reasoning that is more comprehensible and persuasive to society as a whole. This development would lead to a better understanding of constitutional judgments and, no doubt, to a greater capacity and willingness to criticize them. But criticism is a small price to pay if the approach is one that contributes ... to a stronger sense of constitutional awareness on the part of the community and a more accurate appreciation of the issues arising for decision. [14]

This was a wind of change. To be sure, controversy was inevitable. Statements of judicial policy would be perceived by some as though they were statements of political policy. Judicial policy, informed by precedent and disciplined by analogy, confines the scope of discretionary judgment. But the risk of confusion between judicial policy and political policy had to be run in order to guarantee the integrity of the judicial process and to bring the influence of contemporary values to bear on modern expositions of legal principle.

His relationship with other members of the Court fostered its collegiate spirit. Suggestions for changes in a draft judgment were freely given or received with full recognition of the independence and intellectual integrity of other justices. It is no wonder that the members of the Court remained on the most agreeable terms, though we often divided on issues of the greatest importance. The atmosphere of mutual respect that was thus engendered was drawn on to the full in the writing of the judgment of *Cole v Whitfield*.[15] This judgment might rightly be considered to stand as testimony to the multiple judicial qualities of Chief Justice Mason. He did not write all of it and, although I do not propose to identify the passages which he did not write, it is easy to identify the most important parts as flowing from his pen. Of more importance, perhaps, was the judicial management of the judgment when differences of expression or even of concept among the justices were negotiated to a united conclusion. Precise appreciation of points of difference and full discussion of implications led to complete satisfaction with the text.

There is another aspect of his time as Chief Justice which, if not controversial, was unusual. He spoke in public about judges and judging. His view has been that, if the courts were not to be misunderstood by the public, the judges have a part to play in cultivating public understanding. Of course, this involves a certain risk. Judges cannot easily justify themselves; nor can they conduct an ongoing controversy. The hustings are not only unfamiliar to judges; they do not have time to mount them. Yet, overall, the innovation was successful, perhaps because he chose the occasion with discrimination while his personality was not submerged in stilted phrases. All of this was carried through with a mischievous twinkle in the eye and a mordant wit which was never designed to offend.

In a period of change, the Court was fortunate to have a Chief Justice who was rooted firmly in the history of the law but who had a vision of the future which allowed for the moulding of old principles to suit new conditions. I borrow from Harlan Stone's tribute to Cardozo in saying: 'He saw in the judicial function the opportunity to practice that creative art by which law is molded to fulfill the needs of a changing social order.'[16]

Freedom is secured by the rule of law and the rule of law is secured by a competent and independent judiciary. Our nation's freedom and the rule of law are more firmly fixed by the service which he gave.

---

1. Both papers are published in Cheryl Saunders (ed), *Courts of Final Jurisdiction: The Mason Court in Australia* (Federation Press, 1996) 10-14, 264-8.
2. (1952) 85 CLR xii.
3. See *Victoria v The Commonwealth and Hayden* ('the *AAP Case*') (1975) 134 CLR 338, 497; *Davis v The Commonwealth* (1988) 166 CLR 79, 94-95; *Koowarta v Bjelke Petersen* (1982) 153 CLR 168, 229; *Commonwealth v Tasmania. The Tasmanian Dam Case* (1983) 158 CLR 1, 124, 127.
4. (1980) 147 CLR 39, 52.
5. See *Nationwide News Pty Ltd v Wills* (1992) 177 CLR 1, 31.
6. See *Minister for Aboriginal Affairs v Peko-Wallsend Ltd* (1986) 162 CLR 24, 40-41.
7. Sir Anthony Mason, 'Administrative Review: The Experience of the First Twelve Years' (1989) 18 (3) *Federal Law Review* 122, 126.
8. Sir Anthony Mason, 'The William Fullagar Memorial Lecture: Future Directions in Australian Law' (1987) 13 (3) *Monash Law Review* 149, 163.
9. (1988) 165 CLR 360, 402.
10. See *Waltons Stores (Interstate) Ltd v Maher* (1988) 164 CLR 387, 399-402.
11. See *Jago v District Court (NSW)* (1989) 168 CLR 23; *McKinney v The Queen* (1991) 171 CLR 468; *Dietrich v The Queen* (1992) 177 CLR 292.
12. Sir Anthony Mason, 'The Use and Abuse of Precedent' (1988) 4 *Australian Bar Review* 93, 106.
13. Ibid 111.
14. Sir Anthony Mason, 'The Role of a Constitutional Court in a Federation: A comparison of the Australian and the United States Experience' (1986) 16 (1) *Federal Law Review* 1, 28.
15. (1988) 165 CLR 360.
16. Harlan Stone, 'Mr Justice Cardozo' (1939) 52 (3) *Harvard Law Review* 353, 354.

6.3 The Parliament, the Executive and the Courts

Editor's note

This article by Brennan was published in the *Bond Law Review* in 1997.[1]

Constitutions are made for a people and for a time. They may be drawn in terms which reflect the history and aspirations of a people, as does the preamble to the Irish Constitution, in terms which prescribe the repositories of the powers of government, as does the Australian *Constitution*, and in terms which limit the powers of government in order to protect personal rights, privileges and immunities, as the United States Bill of Rights or the Canadian Charter of Rights and Freedoms are expressed to do.

After two centuries of constitutional development and one century of Federation, Australia is reconsidering its federal Constitution. We may choose to alter the preamble to our *Constitution*, or to distribute the powers of government in different ways, or to define new limits to the powers of government. Whatever changes are made to the *Constitution*, it must serve not only the present generation, but future generations in a future world dealing with problems that are presently unforeseen.

If those problems could be foreseen, it would be easier to fashion a Constitution that would best serve the Australian people. But the problems that can be foreseen provide only a tantalizing indication of the future while showing with certainty that the world in which we live will be vastly changed before another century has passed. Society will be transformed by technology, science and economics. Artificial intelligence will alter the patterns of employment and diminish the need for human agency in many activities; the influence of the mass media on human values and ways of thought may become even more powerful; interventions in human reproductivity and modifications of the natural span of life may radically affect familial, sexual and social relations; globalization of economies will see the growth of corporate states and a corresponding contraction of the nation state; international agreements will bind the nation states to action in an ever-enlarging variety of subjects; new sources of energy may affect the distribution of wealth and the possession of political and military power; climatic change may affect not only land but peoples; the speed and ease of movement and communication may either assist global peace or enhance the risk of conflict between peoples of different cultures, races and religions. Homogeneous electorates of the old democracies will become increasingly diverse with movements of people from their ancestral homelands. But throughout these changes, humankind will remain the same - with the same mystical spark that gives each a unique dignity and, as those who believe would hold, an eternal destiny; with the same basic concerns for life, liberty, property and human relationships that can be satisfied only in a society governed by law.

As we reach the end of the 20th century, it is helpful to draw on our experience of the institutions of government which have served us in the changing circumstances of our own times and to consider whether those institutions and functions are to be maintained or changed by a Constitution that must cope with the exigencies of the century to come. It is useful to reflect on the roles of the three branches of government under the *Constitution* of the Commonwealth and the extent to which each is or should be immune from external checks on the exercise of its powers. This is familiar territory but we need to identify the aspects of our *Constitution* that can serve us well and the aspects which need to be improved.

The *Constitution* of the Commonwealth brought the Australian nation into existence. It ordained a federal system of government with limited powers. The Constitutions of the erstwhile Colonies became the Constitutions of the States subject to the *Constitution* of the Commonwealth. Ultimately, with the passage of the *Statute of Westminster Adoption Act* (Cth) in 1942 and the *Australia Act* (Cth) in 1986, sovereign power came to be held wholly within Australia. The dual legal regimes of Commonwealth and states were adjusted by the *Constitution*[2] so that Commonwealth, State and Territorial laws are integrated, and the High Court, being a single apex of the hierarchies of the several court systems, is empowered to keep legal principle consistent throughout the Australian legal system. The division of powers between the Commonwealth and States has raised major constitutional issues for determination and still does so. Dispute over the taxation powers of the respective polities is a recent example.[3] That is inevitable under a Constitution which distributes power in a Federation. But I do not pause to consider that division. There is a more basic question for consideration, namely, the suitability for the future of the Westminster system of government as adapted for use by the Commonwealth under our *Constitution*. It is a system which, with variations, defines the organs of government of the States and Territories and distributes their respective powers – legislative, executive and judicial - among those organs.

The common law spelt out the principles governing the exercise of power by the three branches of government under the Westminster system, the theory of which was expounded and the virtues of which were extolled by Professor Dicey.[4] The Diceyan theory attributes political sovereignty to the people, or at least to the electors. The theory assumes that Parliament, being subject to popular election, must adhere to the wishes of the people and that the laws made by delegates of the people in Parliament will accord with the people's will. The executive government, being responsible to the Parliament for the exercise of executive powers, is accountable, albeit indirectly, to the people. Thus, the political branches of government simply give expression to the popular will. The courts apply the statutory expression of the people's will in individual cases. Thus, government by the people is effected through their elected delegates, democracy is secure and the beneficent sentiments of the people protect the life, liberty and property of the individual. Dicey acknowledged that the courts also make law but make it under the constraints of logic and precedent, two factors which distinguish judicial legislation from parliamentary legislation.[5]

The *Constitution* substantially followed the Westminster practice described by Dicey. Popular election of the Parliament is required by ss 7 and 24; s 64 requires that every Minister of State be or become within three months a member of the Parliament. Representative and responsible government is the constitutional model, as the High Court pointed out in *Lange v Australian Broadcasting Corporation*.[6]

Our *Constitution*, influenced by the Constitution of the United States, assigned federal legislative, executive and judicial powers to different repositories: legislative power to the Parliament (s 1); executive power to the Governor-General (s 61) and judicial power to the Courts (s 71). But there is a radical difference between the two Constitutions.[7] Our *Constitution* brings the repositories of legislative and executive power together in the Parliament in order to make the executive government responsible to the Parliament in conformity with the Westminster system. The American Constitution keeps the President, the repository of executive power, separate from the Congress, the repository of legislative power. Ministerial responsibility to the Parliament is at the heart of our system. Despite s 61 of the *Constitution*, which provides that the executive power of the Commonwealth should be 'vested in the Queen and ... exercisable by the Governor-General', executive power is reposed only nominally in the Governor-General. Leaving aside the reserve powers, executive power is exercised by the Governor-General in accordance with the advice of the Executive Council. Hamilton, writing in *The Federalist Papers* 200 years ago, spoke of the then-emerging Westminster system in England: 'Nothing, therefore, can be wiser in that kingdom than to annex to the king a constitutional council, who may be responsible to the nation for the advice they give. Without this, there would be no responsibility whatever in the executive department – an idea inadmissible in a free government.'[8]

Under the American system, the President acquires authority to exercise executive power not from the Congress but from direct election by the people.

Under both the Australian and the American Constitutions, the political branches of government are kept separate from the judicial branch. Montesquieu had pointed out that 'there is no liberty, if the power of judgment be not separated from the legislative and executive powers'.[9] Hamilton, following Montesquieu, described[10] an independent judiciary as 'the best expedient which can be devised in any government to secure a steady, upright, and impartial administration of the laws'.[11] In this country, the separation of judicial from legislative and executive power and the separation of the judges from political activity have been rigorously maintained by the High Court.[12] The separation of the political powers from the judicial power and the repositories of those respective powers from one another guarantees not only the independence of the judiciary but the appropriate responsibility for the exercise of those powers. Let me explain.

Responsibility for the state of the law and its implementation must rest with the branches of government that are politically accountable to the people. The people can bring influence to bear on the legislature and the executive to procure compliance with the popular will. But a clamour for a popular decision must fall on deaf judicial ears. The judiciary are not politically accountable. The courts cannot temper the true application of the law to satisfy popular sentiment.[13] The courts are bound to a correct application of the law, whether or not that leads to a popular decision in a particular case and whether or not the decision accords with executive policy. In *Clunies-Ross* v *The Commonwealth* the High Court said: 'It would be an abdication of the duty of this court under the *Constitution* if we were to determine the important and general question of law ... according to whether we personally agreed or disagreed with the political and social objectives which the Minister sought to achieve. ... As a matter of constitutional duty, that question must be considered objectively and answered in this Court as a question of law and not as a matter to be determined by reference to the political or social merits of the particular case.'[14]

The rule of law would be a hollow phrase if the courts were not bound to ignore popularity as an influence on a decision. Hamilton wrote: 'Considerate men of every description ought to prize whatever will tend to beget or fortify that temper in the courts; as no man can be sure that he may not be tomorrow the victim of a spirit of injustice, by which he may be a gainer today. And every man must now feel that the inevitable tendency of such a spirit is to sap the foundations of public and private confidence and to introduce in its stead universal distrust and distress.'[15]

Some critics of the judiciary, and even some judges, mistake public popularity for confidence. But if the courts were to seek popular acclaim, they could not be faithful to the rule of law. Confidence is based on faithful adherence to the law by the courts which are charged with its declaration[16] and application. Our *Constitution*, rooted in the common law, does not need to express the proposition that the nation is under the rule of law and that the courts are the organ of government responsible ultimately for the enforcing of the rule of law. that is the Constitution's fundamental postulate, inherent in its text, especially in Ch III. As Dixon J said in the *Communist Party Case*, the *Constitution* 'is an instrument framed in accordance with many traditional conceptions, to some of which it gives effect, as, for example, in separating the judicial power from other functions of government, others of which are simply assumed. Among these I think that it may fairly be said that the rule of law forms an assumption.'[17]

Under our *Constitution*, the courts apply the law not only as between private individuals but in proceedings for the control of the other branches of government. In some Constitutions, such as the Constitution of the People's Republic of China, the rule of law is differently understood. It is understood to require the several agencies of government to observe such rules as bind those agencies but the rule of law is not thought to confer any jurisdiction on courts to compel obedience to laws binding other agencies.[18] Under Ch III of our *Constitution*, all federal legislative and executive power is brought under the supervision of the judicial power in order to ensure conformity with the *Constitution* and the laws made under it. No exception is allowed. No immunity of a federal legislative or executive act from judicial review is possible. This is the constitutional guarantee of equality under the law for the minority as well as the majority in their relationship with government; for the underprivileged as well as the powerful, for the unpopular as well as the mainstream. Sir William Wade has written: 'to exempt a public authority from the jurisdiction of the courts of law is, to that extent, to grant dictatorial power. ... The law's delay, together with its uncertainty and expense, tempts governments to take short cuts by elimination of the courts. But if the courts are prevented from enforcing the law, the remedy becomes worse than the disease.'[19]

The courts do not seek to assert some personal supremacy over the other branches of government; they simply discharge their duty of applying the law to them as they apply it to themselves. Precedent, analogy and logic as well as experience confine judicial decision-making in cases of political significance as in cases concerning purely individual rights and liabilities.

The rule of law is the cement of the Westminster system in our federal

Constitution. If the Diceyan theory holds, the legal regime emerging from that system must give effect to the popular will. Parliament is responsive to the popular will, and Parliament initiates the laws that the regime implements and enforces. But the theory of parliamentary initiative in setting the agenda of the regime does not now fit the reality, if ever it did.

Politically, the discipline of the party system, the policy initiatives undertaken by cabinets and shadow cabinets and the media focus on personalities have tied political fortunes to the performance of party-political leaders. In government, the fortunes of the executive and particularly of the Prime Minister determine the fortunes of the government back bench; the fortunes of the shadow executive and particularly of the Opposition Party Leader determine the prospects of return of the Opposition to the government benches. Nowadays, one of the most important functions of members of Parliament is performed in the party rooms when the members caucus as an electoral college for the choice of a leader or leaders to whose fortunes their own fortunes are linked. And circumstances have enhanced the importance of executive functions. The increasing complexity of society, the exigencies of war, the control of domestic economies and international trading relationships have all evoked the exercise of executive power to make speedy and nice adjustments to regulatory regimes. The welfare state has multiplied the range of administrative powers affecting our daily lives.

Executive policy has become the central feature of governmental activity and legislative power is oftentimes seen merely as an adjunct to the implementation of executive policy. The statute book now bulges with Regulations, Proclamations and Orders in Council made not by the Parliament but in reality, by Ministers or their departmental officers under parliamentary authority. In 1995, the Acts of the Parliament covered 5,626 pages and the Statutory Rules covered 3,893 pages. Ministers, faced with the difficult and complex problems of contemporary government, draw upon both legislative and executive powers as needed to implement their policies and to respond to situations requiring governmental action. Parliament's role as the master of governmental initiatives has been diminished. Dicey thought that 'a parliamentary executive [that is, the Ministry] must by the law of its nature follow, or tend to follow, the lead of the Parliament'.[20] A century of change has inverted that proposition. Lord Hailsham of St Marylebone, a former Lord Chancellor, said that the powers of government within Parliament are 'now largely in the hands of the government machine, so that the government controls Parliament and not Parliament the Government.'[21] He concluded: 'We live under an elective dictatorship, absolute in theory if hitherto thought tolerable in practice.'

That is not a completely accurate description of our constitutional workings. Parliamentary committees and an elected Senate that is not necessarily of the same political complexion as the House of Representatives monitor the exercise of some powers by the executive government of the Commonwealth. However, Lord Hailsham's description is close to the mark. It is particularly close to the mark in those states where similar balancing mechanisms are not found.

The model of a powerful executive, responsible to but in substantial control of the Parliament, is familiar to the Australian people. It ensures that any divergence between the policy of the executive government and statute law is kept to a minimum and it provides a concentration of powers to cope with problems of national importance and great urgency. Thus, there is much to be said for retaining the present distribution of political power under the Westminster system. At least it provides a single line of political legitimacy, although the people's access to their local members is not assured of any effect upon the policy of government.

The rejection by the recent Constitutional Convention of the proposal to have the President of a republican Australia elected by popular vote seems to have been based on a concern that political authority should not be divided between a popularly-elected President on the one hand and the executive government responsible to and through the Parliament on the other. Of course, such a division could be avoided if a popularly-elected President were constitutionally constrained to exercise executive powers in accordance with ministerial advice. In essence, that is the way in which the Irish people kept the mass of political power in the hands of an executive responsible to a Parliament while providing for a popularly-elected President.[22] Special provision was made to govern the President's exercise of her powers to summon or dissolve Parliament[23] and to appoint the Taoiseach (the Prime Minister).[24] The constitutionally significant issue is whether executive power (other than reserve powers) is to be exercised in fact solely by Ministers responsible to the people in and through the Parliament (the Westminster system) or whether executive power is to be exercised by a President responsible to the people by direct election (as in the American system).

If our *Constitution* continues to deny the Governor-General (or a republican President) executive power to be exercised independently of ministerial advice – leaving aside the reserve powers – the question we have to face is whether a concentration of such political power in the hands of a Parliamentary executive is desirable to cope with the problems of the century to come. Efficiency in administration and a capacity to deal quickly and confidently with major domestic issues, with the economy, with national security, with foreign relations or with international trade, commerce and intercourse suggest that such a concentration of political power should be retained. But there are dangers in maintaining a structure which lends itself to the concentration of political power in the executive government. There is a risk of efficiency turning into tyranny.

The separation of powers is supposed to preserve freedom by providing checks and balances. It is here that one sees a weakness in the constitutional framework. The traditional checks and balances are inadequate to protect minorities and the interests of individuals. The traditional checks are supervision by Parliament and judicial review by the courts.

The creation of Senate Committees and Committees of the House to examine particular aspects of the exercise of executive power – for example, subordinate legislation – strengthens Parliamentary machinery for supervising the exercise of executive power. But the political ascendancy of the executive government necessarily limits the capacity of the parliamentary committees to deny validity to executive actions that come within their remit. And *Victorian Stevedoring & General Contracting Co Pty Ltd* v *Dignan*[25] has thus far precluded a judicial invalidation of subordinate legislation on the ground of an impermissible delegation by the Parliament of legislative power.

It may be unrealistic to expect any further development of parliamentary supervision of executive action. Indeed, the capacity of a government to govern might be impaired if the political ascendancy of the executive were too severely eroded by parliamentary assertiveness. The executive government of the day should be able to command the political support needed to preserve the national interest in a constantly changing world. The national interest may be endangered in the century to come not only by the military, diplomatic and economic hazards with which this century has been sadly familiar but by the ambitions of the emerging corporate states. Corporations that recognize no geographical boundaries that exist to serve their shareholders' interests and that command economic resources greater than those available to many nation States may pose a threat in the 21st century to the economies, lifestyles and systems of government which we and other parliamentary democracies will wish to preserve. Of course, a powerful executive government which fell captive to an adverse corporate influence would itself be a Quisling to the national interest. But we must surely place our faith in the strong democratic tradition of our nation and the ability of the electors to regard integrity and devotion to the national interest as the chief criteria for election to the Parliament.

Whatever be the further development of parliamentary supervision of the executive, the other traditional check on executive power, namely, judicial review, is and will remain unqualified. In *Brown* v *West*, the High Court said: 'Whatever the scope of the executive power of the Commonwealth might otherwise be, it is susceptible of control by statute.'[26]

It is, of course, susceptible of control by the *Constitution* itself. The law and the *Constitution* must control all branches of government, else freedom is a mirage. So, the executive cannot be immune from judicial review.

The subjection of executive action to judicial review has given rise to some tension between these two branches of government. The tension reaches its height when the court sets aside a politically important decision of the executive government. It is the maintenance of the rule of law in politically charged cases that make it essential that the judiciary be, be seen as, and see themselves as, independent of government and immune from its influence. Traditionally, tenure and irreducible conditions of engagement have been the props of judicial immunity. But inflation and the nominalist theory of money have exposed judicial conditions to executive influence and the provision of resources for the courts remains an unresolved problem. This seems to me to be another area in need of constitutional repair to ensure both independence of the judiciary and its ability to administer the law in a timely and efficient manner.

The tension between the two branches of government is fed sometimes from another source. If a court erroneously classifies a question of fact as a question of law or too readily stigmatizes a decision as unreasonable in the *Wednesbury*[27] sense of a decision that no reasonable repository of the power could make and the court thereby holds itself to have a jurisdiction to set aside an executive decision, the executive government may justifiably be aggrieved. These are cases on which minds may differ as to the true classification. The principle is clear, but this source of tension will remain.

Although in recent times most attention has been given to the control of executive power, the Parliament remains the organ of government which is constitutionally central to our form of government. The *Constitution* made the Houses of Parliament the masters of their own powers, privileges and immunities and of the mode in which those powers, privileges and immunities might be exercised and upheld.[28] No change in these provisions would be consistent with the maintenance of the Westminster system. The powers, privileges and immunities of the Houses of Parliament are the constitutional underpinning of the system of responsible government for they ensure that the manner in which the people's forum exercises its constitutional functions is immune from interference by either the executive or the judicial branch of government.

Although more rigorous political control of the executive government is not to be expected and judicial supervision is limited to ensuring that executive action is lawful, the exercise of some administrative powers – notably those that affect individual interests – needs to be subject to external merits review.

Administrative decision-making affecting individual interests has become so complex and voluminous that it has outstripped parliamentary capacity for effective supervision. The technical procedure for seeking judicial review of administrative action at common law is cumbersome and, in any event, judicial review cannot alter a decision which, though valid, is not the correct or preferable decision that ought to be made in the particular case. Sir Anthony Mason pointed out[29] that administrative decisions were made by officers lacking independence from the executive government and subject to political or bureaucratic influence, that they were not usually made in public, that the reasons for decision were usually unstated, that the requirements of natural justice were not always observed and that the individual's claims of justice were often subordinated to public policy. Acknowledgment of these realities led the Commonwealth to introduce an integrated set of statutory provisions for the review of administrative decisions.[30] The Administrative Appeals Tribunal ('AAT') and the office of the Ombudsman were created, the procedures for judicial review were broadened and simplified and departmental records were opened up under freedom of information legislation.

It will come as no surprise when I say that, in my respectful opinion, a modern Westminster democracy requires an effective means of externally reviewing the merits of some administrative decisions. The model of an independent, highly qualified, AAT possessed of the skills needed to apply the relevant law, to obtain evidence, to evaluate the relevant facts and to exercise the relevant discretions was an admirable advance in administrative law and practice. Constitutionally, the AAT straddles two branches of government: the executive branch, whose powers it exercises in reviewing decisions on the merits, and the judicial branch, which it emulates in its independence, impartiality, skilled application of the law and coercive power to obtain evidence. The tension between the securing of justice in the individual case by the making of the correct or preferable decision and the application of executive policy for which a Minister is politically responsible sometimes poses a difficult problem for the AAT. But that is precisely the problem that is created by the existence of a powerful and active executive government in a society that places great store by individual rights, privileges and freedoms. Again, it will come as no surprise that executive governments and, in particular, their bureaucracies sometimes regard the AAT as an irksome trespasser on their territory – a cuckoo in the administrative nest. And so it is.

And, in my respectful opinion, so it should be. It should also be a constructive participant in the improvement of administration and the refinement of policy. In times of economic stringency, the cost of maintaining a system of external merits review may be more than an executive government (perhaps encouraged by its bureaucracy) wishes to bear, but it is hard to overstate the importance of allowing the citizen an opportunity to meet government on equal terms in matters that affect that citizen.

An important check on possible misuse of executive power – indeed, on the exercise of any power – is publicity. Misuse of power flourishes in the dark; it cannot survive the glare of publicity. It is partly for that reason that the courts adopt the general rule that they must sit in the open and deliver their reasons for judgment in the open. In *Russell* v *Russell*, Gibbs J wrote: 'This rule has the virtue that the proceedings of every court are fully exposed to public and professional scrutiny and criticism, without which abuses may flourish undetected. ... The fact that courts of law are held openly and not in secret is an essential aspect of their character. It distinguishes their activities from those of administrative officials, for "publicity is the authentic hallmark of judicial as distinct from administrative procedure"'.[31]

The *Freedom of Information Act 1982* (Cth) ('FOI Act') provided a mechanism for prizing open the files of government and thus exposing the dealings of government to publicity. Of course, there had to be some limits imposed. The great affairs of state cannot be transacted in a gold fish bowl and too free an access to those transactions could have a chilling effect on communications on subjects of national interest.

The FOI Act has arguably been a useful tool in political debate and has been availed of by the media. The glare of publicity focused by independent and careful media on the transactions of government in all of its branches is one of the most significant protections of a modern Westminster democracy. The safeguarding of the independence of the media must be one of the primary objects of any Government committed to democracy. That is not to say that engagement in media activities is beyond legal control. To the contrary. Control may be needed to safeguard independence from influences which might tend to corrupt the fair and accurate reporting of newsworthy events and situations and which might produce unfairness in emphasis or comment. These journalistic desiderata are themselves encouraged by the laws of defamation.

I have said little about the role of the courts, but it is clear that the competent, independent and impartial application of the rule of law is fundamental to all constitutional government. This was seen by Alfred Deakin, an architect of the Federation who, as Attorney-General speaking on the introduction of the *Judiciary Act 1903 (*Cth), said this:

> What are the three fundamental conditions to any feder ation authoritatively laid down? The first is the existence of a supreme Constitution; the next is a distribution of powers under that Constitution; and the third is an authority reposed in a judiciary to interpret that supreme Constitution and to decide as to the precise distribution of powers. ... The Constitution is to be the supreme law, but it is the High Court which is to determine how far and between what boundaries it is supreme. The federation is constituted by distribution of powers, and it is this court which decides the orbit and boundary of every power. Consequently, when we say that there are three fundamental conditions involved in federation, we really mean that there is one which is more essential than the others – the competent tribunal which is able to protect the Constitution, and to oversee its agencies. That body is the High Court. It is properly termed the 'keystone of the federal arch'.[32]

So long as the fundamental postulate of the *Constitution* continues to be the rule of law in the hands of the courts, the individual can be protected against an unlawful exercise of power. However, the courts are subject to the statutory directions of the Parliament. The consequence is that, if the statute is oppressive, injustice must follow. There can be some amelioration of oppression by judicial interpretation of statutes[33] and development of the common law[34] so as to preserve human rights and fundamental freedoms. But under our present *Constitution*, it would be impermissible to strike down laws simply because they offend human rights and fundamental freedoms. That may be the function of a court armed with a Bill of Rights. Should we have a Bill of Rights?

A Bill of Rights is necessarily drawn in open-textured terms. In essence it requires the courts to apply values rather than rules to the solution of concrete problems and to attribute to values that are in competition a priority as between themselves. Thus, if liberty and equality were both proclaimed in a Bill of Rights, priority might have to be determined, for liberty is antipathetic to equality when the protagonists are of unequal strength. A Bill of Rights invites, indeed, compels the courts to assume a degree of political power. This would require a radical change in the judicial mind set which currently prides itself on its apolitical function. To be sure, a jurisprudence develops to guide its exercise, but the United States and Canadian experience shows that a Bill of Rights transfers considerable power from the political branches of government to the judiciary. A public expectation is fostered that the courts, rather than the Parliament, will be the ultimate protector of the public good and of individual freedoms and interests. Does Parliament seek to pass that role to the courts? Power which is exercised according to values rather than rules inevitably involves the making of decisions affected by personal predilection. And, as every member of the community has his or her own values, the validity of court judgments may be seen to be problematic. Curial impartiality may become suspect.

On the other hand, a Bill of Rights would require the judiciary to protect individual freedoms and interests more fully than they can be protected under the existing *Constitution*. And that protection may be needed if the Parliament is unwilling or unable to provide it. A further consideration in favour of a Bill of Rights is the strengthening of the hands of government against any external attempt to require the adoption of domestic laws or policies antithetical to individual freedoms and interests. Thus far the debate about the desirability of a Bill of Rights has excited controversy as to whether the Parliament, which is responsible to the people at the ballot box, can alone be trusted to protect minorities and the human rights and fundamental freedoms of individuals. Or whether the courts, which are independent of majoritarian support and which are focused on individual cases, should be enlisted to safeguard the individual against incursions on human rights and fundamental freedoms by the political branches of government. In the future, the debate may focus more on the need for a Constitution that, by its own force, forestalls incursions on human rights and fundamental freedoms from any source, governmental or non-governmental, domestic or foreign. The considerations are complex. The answer I must leave to others.

Our *Constitution* is the product of our national experience. It is stable because it has substantially answered the political and legal expectations of the people. And, whatever be the form of our Constitution in the future, its effect will depend on the values and the sentiments of the Australian people.

Democracy and freedom will survive if the people demand it; strong government will protect the national interest if the people support it; the rule of law will secure a peaceful and ordered society if the people have confidence in it. It cannot be taken for granted that the values and sentiments of the people that infuse and inform our *Constitution* will continue to do so. The Constitution of the future must be seen to satisfy the needs and aspirations of a widespread, multi-cultural population. But the peace and order which comes with constitutional stability will remain if the people see their government reflecting their aspirations. And so we look to a Parliament and an executive government which show their commitment to democracy and freedom, to the national interest, to the protection of individual rights and interests and to the securing of an independent media. And we look to an independent, impartial, fearless and competent judiciary to maintain the rule of law. Constitutionally, we are a lucky country. It is for Australia's leaders and its people to determine whether our luck holds.

---

1. This paper was first published in (1997) 9 (2) *Bond Law Review* 136-149.
2. Section 109.
3. See *Ha v New South Wales* (1997) 189 CLR 465.
4. In his *Lectures Introductory to the Study of the Law of the Constitution* (Macmillan & Co, 1st ed, 1885,) and for the 8th edition :(Macmillan & Co, 8th ed, 1915), and *Lectures on the Relation Between Law and Public Opinion in England* (Macmillan & Co, 1st ed, 1905), 2nd ed reprint Macmillan & Co, London, (1924).
5. A V Dicey, *Law and Opinion in England*, London, (1924), 370 note 1.
6. (1997) 189 CLR 520, 557-9.
7. See Hamilton's comparison of the two systems in No 70 of *The Federalist Papers*, New American Library (ed) 423.
8. Ibid 429.
9. Montesquieu, *The Spirit of Laws* (1751), Dublin vol I, Bk XI, Ch 6, 185.
10. No 78 of *The Federalist Papers*, 464.
11. Ibid 465.
12. See *R v Kirby; Ex parte Boilermakers Society of Australia* (1956) 94 CLR 254; *Wilson v Minister for Aboriginal & Torres Strait Islander Affairs* ('*Hindmarsh Island Bridge Case*') (1996) 189 CLR 1.
13. A V Dicey, *Law of the Constitution* (n 4) 71-72.
14. (1984) 155 CLR 193, 204.
15. No 78 of *The Federalist Papers*, 470.
16. See *Marbury v Madison* 1 Cranch 137 (1803); 5 US Reports 87.
17. See *Australian Communist Party v The Commonwealth* (1951) 83 CLR 1, 193.
18. Albert Hung-Yee Chen, *An Introduction to the Legal System of the People's Republic of China* (Butterworths Asia, 1992) 46.
19. Sir William Wade, *Constitutional Fundamentals*, Hamlyn Lectures, 32nd series (Stevens for the Hamlyn Trust, 1980) 83-84.
20. A V Dicey, *Law of the Constitution* (n 4) Appendix, 484.
21. Lord Hailsham, *Elective Dictatorship: The Richard Dimbleby Lecture 1976* (British Broadcasting Corporation, 1976).
22. See *Irish Constitution*, Arts 13.11, 12.2.
23. See *Irish Constitution*, Art 13 2.
24. See *Irish Constitution*, Art 13.1.
25. (1931) 46 CLR 73.
26. (1990) 169 CLR 195, 202.
27. See *Associated Provincial Picture Houses Ltd v Wednesbury Corporation* [1948] 1 KB 223.

28. See *Constitution of the Commonwealth*, ss 49, 50. As to State Parliaments, see *Arena v Nader* (1997) 71 ALJR 1604.
29. Sir Anthony Mason, 'Administrative Review: The Experience of the First Twelve Years' (1989) 18 (3) *Federal Law Review* 122, 130.
30. See *Administrative Appeals Tribunal Act 1975* (Cth), *Ombudsman Act 1976* (Cth), *Administrative Decisions (Judicial Review) Act 1977* (Cth), *Freedom of Information Act 1982* (Cth).
31. (1976) 134 CLR 495 at 520. See also the article by Sir Frank Kitto, 'Why Write Judgments?' (1992) 66 *Australian Law Journal* 787.
32. Commonwealth, *Parliamentary Debates,* House of Representatives, 18 March 1902, 10966 – 1967 (Alfred Deakin, Attorney-General).
33. See, for example, *Coco v The Queen* (1994) 179 CLR 427, 436-438. Cf *Chu Kheng Lim v Minister for Immigration* (1992) 176 CLR 1, 38.
34. See, for example, *Mabo v Queensland* [*No 2*] (1992) 175 CLR 1, 41-42.

6.4 Centenary of the Enactment of the Commonwealth of Australia Constitution Act

Editor's note

This was an address Brennan delivered at the luncheon of the Australia-Britain Society (New South Wales Branch) Inc and Anglo-Australasian Lawyers Association on 10 July 2000.[1]

Today we assemble to celebrate the centenary the first of the three legally significant events which brought the Commonwealth of Australia into existence. On 9 July 1900, Her Majesty Queen Victoria assented to the Bill for the *Commonwealth of Australia Constitution Act 1900* (Imp) which had been passed by the Commons and the Lords. The appending of the Royal signature to the Commission of Assent marked the fulfilment of the aspirations of the Founding Fathers and of the Parliaments and peoples of five Australian Colonies, not then including Western Australia. The immediate effect of the Act was to authorize the Queen to proclaim that 'the people of New South Wales, Victoria, South Australia, Queensland and Tasmania, and also, if Her Majesty is satisfied that the people of Western Australia have agreed thereto, of Western Australia, shall be united in a Federal Commonwealth.'[2] The Queen made the Proclamation on 17 September 1900 at Balmoral[3] – the second of the formal events. She, being satisfied by this time that the people of Western Australia had agreed to unite, declared 1 January 1901 to be the day when the Federal Commonwealth should come into existence. When that day came – the third event – the Commonwealth was created. We have lived in peace and order under our *Constitution* for nearly 100 years. It has been in force for a period longer than most of the world's Constitutions. It is no coincidence that constitutional longevity is a quality shared chiefly by the Constitutions of the common law democracies.

Our *Constitution* has stood the test of that time; it has maintained our institutions through two world wars and other international conflicts; it has sufficed, with some amendment, to support stability and growth in the economy; it has permitted the development of national and international independence; it has seen the transformation and multiplication of the population so that we are now a multiracial, multicultural population of 19 million; it has provided the foundation for a system of social services and, above all, it has underpinned the rule of law. That is a *Constitution* to be celebrated – celebrated for its origin, celebrated for its effects, celebrated for its continuing operation.

First, we celebrate its origin. As we know, the terms of the *Constitution* were, with only one exception of substance, drawn in Australia and adopted by the electorates of the federating Colonies.[4] After Sir Henry Parkes set the movement for federation on its way, the Australasian Federation Conference of 1890 determined that there should be a federation of the Australian Colonies. Then Andrew Inglis Clark and Charles Cameron Kingston produced drafts that drew on the American model and laid those drafts before some of the members of the 1891 Convention. The '*Lucinda*' weekend during the 1891 Convention formulated a basis which, on 9 April 1891, emerged with few changes as a proposed *Commonwealth Constitution Bill*. The proposal languished in the Parliaments of the Colonies. Then the people took a hand directly. The Australian Federation Leagues of the Border towns convened the Corowa Conference of 1893. That Conference and the subsequent devising by Dr John Quick of a machinery Bill to secure the drafting of a Federation Bill and its submission to referendum gave a new impetus to the movement. Ultimately, in March 1897, a new Convention assembled in Adelaide but without representation from Queensland. Kingston, as Premier of South Australia, presided. The Convention worked on the 1891 draft but adjourned after four weeks so that the Premiers could attend Queen Victoria's Jubilee in England. While there, Joseph Chamberlain, the Secretary of State for the Colonies, furnished Sir George Reid, Premier of New South Wales, confidentially with three Memoranda proposing amendments to the Draft Constitution Bill. The first contained seventeen amendments intended to protect imperial interests, including an amendment to a controversial provision restricting Privy Council appeals; the second contained arguments for those amendments; the third contained drafting suggestions. When the Convention resumed in Sydney in September 1897, Reid unobtrusively introduced several of the amendments, nearly half of which found their way into the final draft.[5] Before the Sydney Convention, there were some 286 amendments for consideration proposed by the several Colonial Parliaments. After three weeks, the Convention adjourned to meet for a final session in Melbourne.

The Melbourne Convention met from 20 January to 17 March 1898. A final Bill was produced. At last, the Constitution was ready for submission to the people of the Colonies in referenda. Mr Kingston, in closing the Convention, welcomed the *Constitution* 'as the most magnificent Constitution into which the chosen representatives of a free and enlightened people have ever breathed the life of popular sentiment and national hope.'

In June 1898, Victoria, South Australia and Tasmania voted overwhelmingly for the Bill but in New South Wales the Bill failed to command the prescribed majority. Then the six Premiers met and seven amendments to the Bill were agreed. A second referendum was held in June 1899. Victoria, South Australia and Tasmania voted even more strongly for the Bill. In New South Wales, the second referendum was carried on 20 June 1899 by 107,420 votes to 82,471. Queensland, though unrepresented at the Melbourne Convention, went to the polls on 2 October 1899 and the referendum was narrowly carried there by 38,499 to 30,996. Western Australia held back but the other five Colonies decided to press for the enactment of the Bill. Ultimately, on 31 July 1900, by which time the Act had been passed, Western Australia voted in favour of joining the Federation by a majority of 44,800 to 19,691.

The British Government favoured the federation of the Australian Colonies and, generally speaking, the Colonial Office accepted the Bill which had been drafted to effect the agreement of the people of the federating Colonies 'to unite in one indissoluble Federal Commonwealth under the Crown...and under the Constitution'. But Chamberlain had one great reservation – clause 74 which restricted the right of appeal to the Privy Council. He wished to retain the Privy Council's unfettered power to grant leave to appeal from all Australian courts. Controversy about the British proposal raged both in England and in Australia. The Australian Chief Justices, especially Sir Samuel Griffith, supported Chamberlain's proposal not to restrict Privy Council appeals. Edmund Barton, Alfred Deakin and Kingston stood firm, asserting that the people of the Colonies had resolved on their *Constitution* and that it was not open to change, but Dickson, the Queensland delegate, sided with the British Government. The Bill, which Chamberlain introduced into the Commons on 14 May 1900, omitted clause 74. Debate was adjourned for a week and that evening he invited the Australian delegates to a convivial dinner.

There the seeds of compromise were laid and three days later Barton, Deakin and Kingston met Chamberlain and agreed on a measure which, though clumsily drafted, was acceptable. Deakin reports that: 'When the door closed upon them and left them alone, they seized each other's hands and danced hand in hand in a ring around the centre of the room to express their jubilation.'[6] The compromise itself was then attacked, especially by Queensland and by the legal profession, for interfering with the right of appeal to the Privy Council. Ultimately, said Deakin, a 'suggestion emanating from Sir Samuel Griffith that the High Court might grant leave to appeal from itself or from a subordinate court to the Privy Council provided the golden bridge over which the delegates passed to union'. The Bill, including the new cl 74, passed the third reading in the Commons on 25 June. In the House of Lords, clause 74 was again a matter of debate but it received its third reading on 5

July and received the Royal assent at Windsor Castle four days later. The postscript lies in the piecemeal abolition of appeals to the Privy Council until the last avenue was closed by the passing of the *Australia Act* in 1986.

None of the terms of the *Constitution* was imposed upon the Australian people. It is the product of the labours of Australian founding fathers and the successful advocacy of the delegates who stood firm on the principle of cl 74. Chamberlain described it as 'a monument of legislative capacity.' After the event, as Deakin wrote, 'all history takes in the appearance of inevitableness' but, he observed, '[t]o those who watched its inner workings, followed its fortunes as if their own, and lived a life of devotion to it day by day, its actual accomplishment must always appear to have been secured by a series of miracles.'[7] So well may we celebrate the centenary of those miracles that brought our nation into being.

Secondly, we celebrate the immediate effects of the *Constitution*'s enactment by the Imperial Parliament. It conferred on the new nation two unwritten but inherent and inestimable benefits. The first was the product of the centuries of British constitutional development. Sir Owen Dixon observed that during the 17th and 18th centuries, British constitutional development had reconciled the three juristic conceptions of the supremacy of the law, the supremacy of the Crown and the supremacy of Parliament 'to produce an enduring form of government.' He wrote: 'The splendour of the Crown remained as the legal expression of the sovereignty of the State. The law remained supreme over all organs of government as well as the people. But the legislative power, at any rate when expressed and authenticated in the manner required by the law for the time being in force, extended over the whole field of law.'[8]

These conceptions, which inform our *Constitution,*[9] give us the stability and security of the rule of law, the adaptability and freedom of a democracy and efficiency in the execution of the laws and policies of government. Next, by enacting the *Commonwealth of Australia Constitution Act* in exercise of the authority conferred upon it by the common law, the Imperial Parliament prescribed, without any need to express its intent or the intent of the people of the Colonies, that the common law would be the basic law of the Commonwealth, just as it had been the basic law of the federating Colonies. And as the *Constitution* provided for a centralised final court of appeal, the common law of Australia, unlike the common law of the American States, has been uniform throughout the nation, albeit subject to variation in exercise of local legislative power.[10] The priceless inheritance of the common law has given us the legal culture of freedom, of fairness and of security in person and property.

The common law allows for the interpretation of the *Constitution* as a living instrument, continually serviceable in changing conditions. Inglis Clark foresaw this when he wrote:

> the social conditions and the political exigencies of the succeeding generations of every civilised and progressive community will inevitably produce new governmental problems to which the language of the *Constitution* must be applied, and hence it must be read and construed, not as containing a declaration of the will and intentions of men long since dead, and who cannot have anticipated the problems that would arise for solution by future generations, but as declaring the will and intentions of the present inheritors and possessors of sovereign power, who maintain the *Constitution* and have the power to alter it, and who are in the immediate presence of the problems to be solved. It is they who enforce the provisions of the *Constitution* and make a living force of that which would otherwise be a silent and lifeless document.[11]

And so, Mr Justice Windeyer wrote in 1971: 'In any country where the spirit of the common law holds sway the enunciation by courts of constitutional principles based on the interpretation of a written constitution may vary and develop in response to changing circumstances.'[12]

Thus, to take two examples, the posts and telegraphs power has carried the Commonwealth into the electronic age and the external affairs power has supported Australia's emergence as an independent member of the family of nations and has permitted the legislative discharge of Australia's international obligations.

Thirdly, we celebrate the continuing operation of the *Constitution*. The Australian people do not declare their affection for, or admiration of, the *Constitution*. Being largely unaware of its terms, they would find it difficult to do so. But they are aware of its operation in helping to define the Australian way of life. The government can be changed at an election; the validity of laws and of executive action can be challenged in the courts; nobody can be criminally punished for conduct unless the conduct breaches an existing law and the offender has been tried and found guilty; the government cannot take property without just compensation; there is freedom of religion. The government in Canberra looks after international and most national affairs; the State governments look after more localized concerns. And so the diverse interests of people living in different parts of this wide land can be addressed by the States and Territories while their common interests can be addressed by the Federal Government. Diversity in unity has been possible.

The *Constitution* was never a perfect document – witness the troublesome history of s 92 – but, despite demonstrable shortcomings that a century's experience has shown, generally it has served the nation well. Only eight amendments have been carried at referenda. One of the eight, the 1967 Referendum, remedied the constitutional discrimination against Australia's Aboriginal peoples and affirmed 'the will of the Australian people that the odious policies of oppression and neglect of Aboriginal citizens were to be at an end'.[13] Public opinion polls now seem to show that a majority of Australians would favour a republican form of government if the consequential amendments to the *Constitution* could be resolved to their satisfaction. Amendment of the *Constitution* is in the hands of the people under s 128 and we are the masters of our own constitutional destiny. Whether we seize that destiny and how we shape our nation in the century to come are questions that should concern every Australian mind and stir every Australian heart.

After 100 years, we live in a society vastly different from the society of 1901. We enjoy many advantages – physical, economic, legal and cultural – that are the envy of other peoples, and those advantages impose on us a duty to transmit to the generations of the coming century a nation as full of opportunity and optimism as the nation which was bequeathed to us.

We are a pluralistic, multi-cultural society: let us celebrate diversity, capture its vibrancy and champion its tolerance. We pride ourselves on our egalitarianism: let us have the courage to ensure substantive equality to all Australians, especially the indigenous people of this land and recent immigrants. We have high hopes for our children: let us not neglect the education and research that they need to sustain them in a competitive world and that they can use to improve it. We rejoice in the beauty of our country: let us not deface it for short-term or sectional gain. A majority of Australians are comfortable in their life-style: but let neither narrowness of vision nor fear nor indolence diminish our confidence in our ability to construct a better nation for all our people and to make a real contribution to a better world. Vision and courage, compromise and determination were the virtues demonstrated by the Founding Fathers. We can offer no less.

We celebrate in order to assure ourselves of our resolution not to fail, so that we may on 1 January 2001 echo the sentiments which Professor Helen Irving attributes to our forebears of a century ago: 'When the Inauguration of the Commonwealth was celebrated on the first day of the new century, many things were elevated to the status of national icon. But, above all else, the people celebrated their optimism and their imagination, and in doing so they celebrated themselves.'[14]

We thank the New South Wales Branch of the Australia-Britain Society and the Anglo-Australasian Lawyers Society for the opportunity to join in today's celebration of the passing of the *Commonwealth of Australia Constitution Act* into law. It is a celebration the more important because, I have been told, no official celebration of that event has been held or is to be held in this country, save one: Chief Justice Spigelman, as Lieutenant Governor of New South Wales, held a reception on the evening of 5 July – the centenary of the third reading in the House of Lords – to celebrate a century of our *Constitution*. The centenary of the Proclamation of the Commonwealth on 17 September is likely to be overshadowed by the Olympic Games. But when 1 January 2001 arrives, we must – we will – celebrate our entry into the second century of our Nation – a nation proud of its heritage and confident of its future.

---

1. An edited version of this address was first published in (2001) 75 *Australian Law Journal* 31.
2. Covering Clause 3.
3. No 722 of 1900.
4. See, generally the history of Federation in John Quick and Robert Randolph Garran, *The Annotated Constitution of the Australian Commonwealth* (1901, Legal Books reprinted 1976), 79-261.
5. B K de Garis, 'The Colonial Office and the Commonwealth Constitution' in Allan William Martin (ed) *Essays in Australian Federation* (Melbourne University Press, 1969), 94.
6. Alfred Deakin, *The federal story: the inner history of the federal cause* (Robertson & Mullers, 1944), 155.
7. Ibid 166.
8. Sir Owen Dixon, 'The Law and the Constitution' in Sir Owen Dixon, *Jesting Pilate* (Law Book Co, 1965) 38, 41.
9. See *Lange v Australian Broadcasting Corporation* (1997) 189 CLR 520, 564.
10. See *Favelle Mort Ltd v Murray* (1976) 133 CLR 580, 591; *Lipohar v The Queen (*1999) 200 CLR 485, 505-7. (1999) HCA 65 [44-45,50] 74 ALJR 282, 289-290.
11. A Inglis Clark, *Studies in Australian Constitutional Law* (Charles F Maxwell, 1901) 21-22 cited by Deane J in *Theophanous v Herald & Weekly Times Ltd* 182 CLR 104, 171-172.
12. See *Victoria* v *The Commonwealth* (1971) 122 CLR 353, 396.
13. See *Commonwealth v Tasmania ('The Tasmanian Dam Case')* (1983) 158 CLR 1, 242.
14. Helen Irving, *To Constitute a Nation* (Cambridge University Press, 1997) 196, 211.

6.5 One Hundred Years On: Strengths and Strains

Editor's note

Brennan delivered this as the annual Geoffrey Sawer Lecture at the Australian National University on 18 July 2001.

It was a triumph of vision over short sight; of the popular will over political lethargy; of aspiration over self-interest; of confidence over timidity; of hope over pessimism. It came about in the quietness of the night, the product of law, not of revolution or war. 'It was sought by Australians, not imposed on them'.[1] The Australian people, following the procedures of the times, secured the passage by the United Kingdom Parliament of the *Commonwealth of Australia Constitution Act* and the Proclamation which brought our nation into being at the first moment of the twentieth century and has sustained it in existence ever since. In the *Engineers Case*,[2] the *Constitution* was recognised as 'the political compact of the whole of the people of Australia, enacted into binding law by the Imperial Parliament'. The *Constitution* is, in every sense, the people's *Constitution*. As Deane J observed, 'ultimate authority in this country lies with the Australian people'.[3]

But unless we, the Australian people, take an informed and lively interest in its operation and keep it in good modern repair, it will not serve us as well in the twenty-first century as it has in the twentieth century. The advice 'If it ain't broke, don't fix it!' might apply to plumbing, but not to the Constitution of a nation in a rapidly changing environment. The events of the last 100 years have shown some strengths and some shortcomings, some obsolete and some miscast provisions of our *Constitution*. Perhaps the wonder is that an instrument which was a work of inspired compromise should have served us as well as it has. Our good fortune has been the consequence of three inter-related factors: the common law as the ultimate constitutional foundation, the conventions and constitutional practices which have determined or guided the exercise of constitutional powers and the work of the High Court in interpreting the text and structure of the *Constitution*.

The *Constitution* has provided a stable framework for growth, in war and in peace. During the past century, Australia progressed from the status of a geographical aggregation of dependent colonies to the status of a united and independent nation, charting its own destiny. Massive changes in international relations and defence, in immigration policy, in trade, commerce and industry, in labour relations, in health and social security, in education and in culture have been accommodated under the *Constitution*. With few amendments to the original text, with the adoption of the *Statute of Westminster,* and with the passage of the *Australia Act,* the *Constitution* has proved to be flexible enough to cope with these changes. Australia is now an independent nation and Australians live in freedom under the law in a stable democracy. We seem to regard these conditions as a natural phenomenon, neither liable to disturbance by, nor needing to respond to, changing circumstances. Perhaps that is why the celebration of the Centenary of Federation has failed to capture the public interest to the same extent as do sporting feats and the exploits of the stars of film and television.

The common law

In a memorable paper, Sir Owen Dixon observed that: 'It is easy to treat the written instrument as the paramount consideration, unmindful of the part played by the general law, notwithstanding that it is the source of the legal conceptions that govern us in determining the effect of the written instrument.'[4]

In *Cheatle v The Queen,* the High Court declared it to be 'well settled that the interpretation of [our] *Constitution* is necessarily influenced by the fact that its provisions are framed in the language of the English common law, and are to be read in the light of the common law's history'.[5] It follows that the repositories of constitutional power are subject to the rule of law, that the courts within the limits of their several jurisdictions are empowered to declare what the law is and to give effect to their declarations.

The common law provides a measure of protection against an overreaching of power by government. The strict discipline of the party system and the complexity of modern government have placed the executive government largely in control of the Parliament's powers and in a position to acquire discretionary powers that might be exercised oppressively were it not for two ameliorating factors. First, the common law's basic rules for the interpretation of statutes and the protection of individual rights and liberties; and, second, the vesting in the High Court by s 75(v) of the *Constitution* of an impregnable jurisdiction to issue prohibition and mandamus to officers of the Commonwealth.

In accordance with the common law, the courts construe statutes, statutory instruments and other expressions of executive power where their texts permit so as to maintain our fundamental freedoms.[6] And, 'where two alternative constructions of legislation are open, that which is consonant with the common law is to be preferred'.[7] Acknowledging the *Magna Carta* as 'the groundwork of all our Constitutions', Sir Isaac Isaacs found in its terms three basic principles of the common law's protection of personal freedom:

> (1) primarily every free man has an inherent individual right to his life, liberty, property and citizenship; (2) his individual rights must always yield to the necessities of the general welfare at the will of the State; (3) the law of the land is the only mode by which the State can so declare its will. These principles taken together form one united conception for the necessary adjustment of the individual and social rights and duties of the members of the State. For their effective preservation and enforcement, the courts have evolved two great working corollaries in harmony with the main principles and without which these would soon pass into merely pious aspirations. The first corollary is that there is always an initial presumption in favour of liberty, so that whoever claims to imprison or deport another has cast upon him the obligation of justifying his claim by reference to the law. The second corollary is that the courts themselves see that this obligation is strictly and completely fulfilled before they hold that liberty is lawfully restrained. [8]

It is the common law which leaves 'everybody ... free to do anything, subject only to the provisions of the law' so that one proceeds 'upon an assumption of freedom of speech';[9] it is the common law which gives us the principles of representative and responsible government adopted by the *Constitution*;[10] it is the common law, reflecting the history of the Glorious Revolution, which itself acknowledges the binding authority of statute.[11] And when the High Court in *Nationwide News v Willis*[12] recognised a restriction on legislative power in order to permit freedom of speech, TRS Allan, commented that '[T]he common law not only indicated the existence of limits to legislative power, but provided a *measure* to determine their scope.'[13] It is the common law that gives us our conception of the rule of law and it is one of the strengths of the *Constitution* that the rule of law is ultimately immune from impairment.[14]

Conventions and constitutional practices

While the *Constitution* vests the legislative, executive and judicial powers of the Commonwealth in their respective repositories, it says little about the ways in which those powers are to be exercised. In the United Kingdom, and later in Australia, practices have developed which guide, and in some instances govern, the exercise of these constitutional powers. Many of these practices are called conventions, though the precise meaning and effect of conventions are not always easy to determine.

Professor Sawer observed that, in all the cases in which a practice is said to amount to a convention: 'The common feature ... is the existence of a practice of some duration, reasonably well-illustrated by examples, as to the way in which legal powers are exercised by some organ of government, the practice not being itself prescribed by law. However, the importance of the practice and its legal consequences, if any, can vary enormously.'[15]

Professor Sawer cautions against the description of a practice as a convention, at least when there is no practical sanction for its breach.[16]

Richard McGarvie AC, a former Governor of Victoria and a distinguished former Judge of the Supreme Court of that state, described a constitutional convention 'as an obligation accepted by office-holders as binding them in the way they exercise their legal powers, because it is clearly necessary for the practical achievement of representative democracy and is backed by an effective practical penalty for breach'.[17] This description illustrates the difficulty in adopting the 'practical penalty' criterion for distinguishing a convention from a mere practice. If, for example, the practical penalty is no more than the incurring of public opprobrium, it may prove to be inadequate to maintain a practice which has been thought to amount to a convention. Thus, it may have been a convention that a casual Senate vacancy be filled by a nominee of the same party as that to which the previous incumbent Senator belonged.[18] But, despite some adverse reaction when the putative convention was breached in 1975, a political advantage was obtained by the breach and that was sufficient compensation for the incurring of the opprobrium. To restore the putative convention, it was necessary to entrench it in the *Constitution* by referendum amending s 15.[19]

Although the norms which ordinarily guide the exercise of an office-holder's powers are, generally speaking, accepted by the office-holder, a convention may exist independently of the view of a particular office-holder. A practice can derive normative force from a long and regular adoption of a course of action by office-holders, giving rise to a general expectation that the incumbent office holder will exercise his or her powers in a similar way. Expectations lack both the cogency and the rigidity of law, and may therefore change with changing circumstances. On the other hand, when there are clear external sanctions which can be imposed in the event of departure from a practice, the practice is likely to be slow to change and is more likely to warrant classification as a convention. Even then, the convention lacks the force of law and is amenable to evolution. Although it is difficult to define conventions exhaustively, the *Constitution* would be misunderstood if we were not to take account of convention in the operation of the system of government which the *Constitution* prescribes. Most importantly, the convention which requires the Governor-General to act, and to act only, on the advice of his Ministers has ensured that responsible government based on the Westminster model became the system of government for the Commonwealth. To ignore the significance of conventions is to forget our constitutional history and development.

Take, for example, the conventions which have secured and maintain the independence of the Commonwealth. Australia's growth into independent nationhood was assisted by the convention,[20] which was given statutory recognition,[21] that the United Kingdom Parliament would not legislate for a selfgoverning colony without that colony's consent. That convention has now been superseded by the *Australia Act 1986* (Cth), s 1 of which denies to the Parliament of the United Kingdom any power to legislate for the Commonwealth, its states or territories. Since the Balfour Declaration of 1926 it has been recognised that the Governor-General holds 'in all essential respects the same position in relation to the administration of public affairs as is held by [the Monarch] in Great Britain'. Since 1930, it has been the convention that the Monarch appoints the Governor-General on the formal advice of the Prime Minister[22] after informal consultations between them. By 1983 a report to the Australian Constitutional Convention held in Adelaide was able to recommend recognition of the conventions that: 'The Queen does not intervene in the exercise by the Governor-General of powers vested in him by the Constitution and does not Herself exercise those powers.'[23]

The report was based on established practice. If s 2, which authorises the Queen to assign a function to the Governor-General, or s 59 which empowers the Queen to disallow a law, has any present relevance, neither power would be exercised without the direct advice of her Commonwealth ministers. Royal assent under s 74 was given to the Bills limiting appeals to the Privy Council on the direct advice of Commonwealth Ministers.[24] The Queen acts (or, if the occasion were to arise, would act) on the direct advice of her Commonwealth ministers in any matter of Commonwealth concern.[25] If it were not for these conventions, ultimate control of the exercise of the powers conferred by the *Constitution* would not be in Australian hands.

It was to be expected in 1900 that the United Kingdom Parliament in enacting the *Constitution Act* would repose in the Queen powers which were to be exercised on the advice of the United Kingdom government. The source of that advice was determined by the conventions of the time. Then the United Kingdom government would have offered advice on the appointment of our Governor-General; it could have advised the Monarch on the exercise of power to disallow Commonwealth legislation under s 59; and Her Majesty's pleasure would have been determined by the United Kingdom government in respect of any proposed law to limit appeals to the Privy Council under s 74. But conventions changed in response to the change in relationships between Australia and Britain. As the *Constitution* does not define the manner in which the powers vested in the Queen are to be exercised, basic changes in constitutional practice have been accommodated. Power has shifted from Whitehall to Canberra without constitutional amendment or inter-governmental confrontation. Overall, the absence of codified conventions has been beneficial in allowing the evolution of an independent system of national government. The adaptability of conventions and practices to changing circumstances permits some flexibility in the actual working of government.

The role of the High Court

Deakin's second reading speech on the Judiciary Bill on 18 March 1902 states the basic conceptions on which a federation under the rule of law operates. 'What are the three fundamental conditions to any federation authoritatively laid down?' he asked rhetorically. He answered:

> The first is the existence of a supreme *Constitution*; the next is a distribution of powers under that *Constitution;* and the third is an authority reposed in a judiciary to interpret that supreme *Constitution* and to decide as to the precise distribution of powers. ... The *Constitution* is to be the supreme law, but it is the High Court which is to determine how far and between what boundaries it is supreme. The federation is constituted by distribution of powers, and it is this court which decides the orbit and boundary of every power.[26]

Deakin recognised that an evolutionary approach had to be taken to the interpretation of the spare text of the *Constitution* in order to keep it serviceable in the changing circumstances of national life. In his speech, Deakin went on to say:

> The nation lives, grows, and expands. Its circumstances change, its needs alter, and its problems present themselves with new faces. The organ of the national life which, preserving the union, is yet able from time to time to transfuse into it the fresh blood of the living present, is the judiciary. ... It is as one of the organs of government which enables the *Constitution* to grow and to be adapted to the changeful necessities and circumstances of generation after generation that the High Court operates.[27]

When the Court first sat on 6 October 1903 in Melbourne, the Attorney-General of the day expressed the belief that 'the decisions of [the] court will breathe a living spirit into the dry bones of a parchment *Constitution*'.[28] This expectation was given judicial endorsement when O'Connor J said in *Jumbunna Coal Mine, No Liability v Victorian Coal Miners' Association* that: 'it must always be remembered that we are interpreting a Constitution broad and general in its terms, intended to apply to the varying conditions which the development of our community must involve.'[29]

And later, in *Australian National Airways Pty Ltd v Commonwealth*, Dixon J said: '[I]t is a Constitution we are interpreting, an instrument of government meant to endure and conferring powers expressed in general propositions wide enough to be capable of flexible application to changing circumstances.'[30]

To perform this function, the Court had to be a court of unquestioned authority familiar with the environment in which the *Constitution* operates. The first Court saw itself in that light. In the first great challenge to the ultimate authority of the High Court, the Court described itself as 'an Australian Court, immediately available, constant in its composition, well versed in Australian history and conditions, Australian in its sympathies, ... whose judgments, rendered as the occasion arose, would form a working code for the guidance of the Commonwealth.'[31]

The Court construed the *Constitution* as a statute, but as a statute of a special kind. In 1908, Higgins J in *Attorney-General for NSW v Brewery Employees Union of NSW* (the *Union Label Case*) said: 'although we are to interpret the words of the Constitution on the same principles of interpretation as we apply to any ordinary law, these very principles of interpretation compel us to take into account the nature and scope of the Act that we are interpreting — to remember that it is a Constitution, a mechanism under which laws are to be made, and not a mere Act which declares what the law is to be.'[32]

At first, the founding Justices read the text of the *Constitution* as providing for the cession of clearly limited powers by the six self-governing colonies to the Commonwealth. It was understandable that they should do so. Having experienced the travails of securing colonial agreement to the creation of a Commonwealth, they espoused the doctrine of state reserved powers and implied immunities.

In time, with the First World War, the economic and commercial integration of the states and the growing sense of national identity, the doctrine of reserved powers was discarded in the *Engineers' Case*.[33] Changing conditions exposed the true meaning of the text. Windeyer J, in the *Payroll Tax Case,* explained that the discarding of the doctrine of the implied immunity of state instrumentalities occurred 'because in 1920 the *Constitution* was read in a new light, a light reflected from events that had, over twenty years, led to a growing realisation that Australians were now one people and Australia one country and that national laws might meet national needs'.[34] The Court saw that new circumstances evoke from the constitutional text a new application and that the judiciary must declare the scope of constitutional powers or the limitations on their exercise which might be relevant to those circumstances. The Court looked to the history of the constitutional text to identify the subject to which the language of the troublesome s 92 was directed.[35] It found that as threats to national security waxed and waned, so did the scope of the defence power.[36] The Court has found the principles of representative and responsible government and protection for freedom of speech (subject to tortious qualifications) by an examination of the text and structure of the *Constitution*.[37] It has held that the *Constitution* protects all civilian persons within the jurisdiction in peacetime from punishment except pursuant to due process of law before a court.[38] The Court has responded to the development of technology in communications by holding that the power to make laws with respect to 'postal, telegraphic, telephonic and other like services' extends to the regulation of wireless.[39] Presumably the power would be held to extend to other recently developed means of communication. For the purpose of the requirement of trial by jury in s 80, the Court has accepted that liberalisation in the qualifications or jurors since 1901 to accord with contemporary standards and perceptions does not affect the essential character of the jury.[40]

As a constitutional grant of power to the Commonwealth is given a broader rather than a narrower construction in order to encompass the varying conditions produced by the passage of time,[41] the ambit of activities which fall within the power continually increases.[42] Phenomena which revealed no nexus with a head of Commonwealth power in earlier times may, with changing circumstances, be shown to have a sufficient nexus to support legislation with respect to those phenomena.

Perhaps the external affairs power provides the clearest illustration of the expanding subject matter of Commonwealth legislative power in response to changing external circumstances. The founding fathers, understanding that the 'sole treaty-making power [was] in the Crown of the United Kingdom',[43] amended an early draft of the *Constitution* to exclude treaties as a specific head of Commonwealth legislative power.[44] In time, the treaty-making power was exercised by the executive government of the Commonwealth. It may be that the founding fathers did not distinguish between the power to make a treaty and the legislative power needed to implement the provisions of a treaty. However, that might be, the High Court in a series of cases, has upheld the validity of legislation based on treaty provisions[45] and, as the subject matter of treaties expands, so does the subject matter of Commonwealth legislative power. In addition, as legislation operating on persons, conduct, matters and things external to Australia is supported by the external affairs power,[46] laws may be enacted with respect to a vast range of such issues.

Changing convention warranted the exercise of executive power and judicial interpretation affirmed the legislative power which permitted Australia to take its place as an independent self-governing nation while the text of the *Constitution* remained unchanged.

The federal form of government necessarily installed the High Court as the 'keystone of the federal arch'.[47] In that role the High Court has been the mechanism for keeping the *Constitution* as effective in changing conditions as its text and structure permit.

Another strength of the *Constitution* is the vesting in the High Court of its jurisdiction under s 75(v). The provision for the constitutional writs of prohibition and mandamus, which are aided, when necessary, by the common law writ of *certiorari* and possess in the main the common law incidents of the eponymous writs[48] is critical to the maintenance of the rule of law and to the imposition of constraints on executive power. The High Court has, in exercise of this jurisdiction, kept other courts and tribunals within their legal powers and prevented the executive government and its agencies from either overreaching their powers or failing to perform their legal duties. Parliament and the executive sometimes find judicial review of executive action irksome, especially when administrative action is invalidated because natural justice has not been done. Or when the action is invalidated because the repository of a discretionary power has erred in the factors which the common law prescribes to be taken into account or to be excluded from consideration. But as s 75(v) is constitutionally entrenched, governments which would willingly secure their immunity from judicial review wholly or in part[49] are constrained to act within and in accordance with their legal functions. Recently, the government has regrettably withdrawn much of the review jurisdiction of the Federal Court in migration matters with the result, if not the intent, of forcing applicants to apply under s 75(v) to the High Court, thereby embarrassing that Court's ability to cope with its massive case load.[50] The High Court is, so to speak, the long stop to ensure legality in the exercise of power.

These three factors – the common law, conventions and the High Court's exercise of its jurisdiction – have ensured that, under the *Constitution*, Australia has grown into a free and independent nation under the rule of law, enjoying a democratic form of government and an integrated system of law. The *Constitution* has served Australia well and retains the strengths that have secured that satisfying state of affairs. That is not to say that the *Constitution* either was, or is now, a perfect document. Strains and inadequacies have appeared, expended provisions clutter up the text, and new technologies have emerged which call for national regulation.

Present defects

There are obvious defects in the drafting of some provisions of the *Constitution*. Notoriously s 92, which was drawn in terms of intractable uncertainty, spawned a mass of litigation troubling to the courts and frustrating legislators. Hopefully *Cole v Whitfield*[51] gave a new and clearer direction to the jurisprudence of this section, although some problems remain.[52] Perhaps some uncertainty is inevitable when the *Constitution* seeks to maintain a freetrade zone covering a number of areas under differing legislative control. Section 90 also has been gravely troublesome. The meaning of the term 'duties of excise' was open to such differing interpretations that state revenues were hostage to the rise and fall of various constitutional theories. It has taken a long time for the cases to settle the operation of the section.[53] Whether the operation currently attributed to the section is politically and economically desirable for the future is a question that may stimulate a proposal for constitutional change.

The Corporations power is clearly defective in denying the Commonwealth power to make laws with respect to the formation of trading and financial corporations[54] and, for that matter, with respect to corporations generally. Section 80, which guaranteed trial by jury in trials on indictment for Commonwealth offences, failed to provide that serious offences should be charged on indictment. In consequence, s 80 proved to be a hollow protection and 'has been reduced to a mere procedural provision'.[55] Structurally, the *Constitution* has been found to be defective in denying validity to a scheme for the cross-vesting of federal and state jurisdiction.[56] There is no obstacle to the vesting of federal jurisdiction in state courts: the 'autochthonous expedient' was one of the masterstrokes of the founding fathers. Nor is there any objection to the vesting in federal courts of jurisdiction to determine 'matters' that arise in part under state law where the matter arises also under federal law.[57] But states cannot vest state jurisdiction in courts created by or under Chapter III of the *Constitution*.

Between 1986 and 1988, a Constitutional Commission inquired into the working of the *Constitution*. It was assisted by five Advisory Committees. The Commission and its Committees were constituted by members possessing formidable political, practical and legal expertise. The Commission recommended changes. Yet the Report, pre-empted by a Bill[58] hastily cobbled together and submitted to referendum, was buried in the rubble of the Referendum's failure.

The Commission addressed the defects I have noted above. It recommended that the corporations power be extended to incorporation and to financial, investment and other like services[59] and that the trial of offences carrying substantial penalties, other than contempt and defence force offences, be by jury.[60] It recommended that states and territories be empowered to confer jurisdiction under their laws on federal courts with the consent of the Federal Parliament.[61] It declined to recommend an integration of the court systems of the Commonwealth and the states, contrary to the suggestion by Sir Owen Dixon who regarded the legal system of Australia as a unit and believed that: 'It would … have been … more consistent with this outlook upon the law, and at the same time better for the efficient administration of justice, if our Australian constitution-makers had refused to adopt the American distinction between State and federal jurisdiction.'[62]

The Commission's recommendation would solve most of the jurisdictional issues which have bedevilled the courts without raising the more difficult legal, political and logistical problems that would arise if there were a disruption of the relationships between courts on the one hand and their respective legislatures and governments on the other. The extension of the corporations power and the validation of cross-vesting are required urgently to ensure efficiency in the legal system, especially to provide the infrastructure for commerce and industry.[63] We try to patch up the system rather than make the needed reforms.

Other amendments recommended by the Commission would settle the problems of territory and new state representation in the Parliament,[64] qualifications for members of Parliament,[65] the franchise[66] the Senate's power over money bills,[67] disagreement between the two Houses of Parliament,[68] judicial review jurisdiction of federal courts,[69] the removal of federal judges,[70] conflict of laws[71] and Commonwealth places.[72] Then there are the transitional and obsolete provisions of the *Constitution* which are littered throughout the text, cloud the true nature of the Constitutional framework and impair its readability. The Commission observed that they could be repealed with no practical effect on the operation of the *Constitution*.[73] Dr Helen Irving makes the same plea: '[R]emove the detritus … Send them to a constitutional elephants' graveyard for historians like myself to lament.'[74] The Commission's list of repealable provisions: '*include* sections 26, 41, 52(ii.), 69, 84, 85, 86, 87, 89, 93, 95, 97 and the second paragraph of section 83, the second paragraph of section 90, the second paragraph of section 92 and the introductory words of section 96. Expended words should also be removed from other sections including 3, 15, and 66.'

These are all transitional provisions. The list for repeal could usefully add s 25 which authorises disqualification from the franchise on grounds of race. The Commission would repeal the race power (s 51(xxvi)) and replace it with a power to make laws with respect to Aborigines and Torres Strait Islanders.[75] It is high time to be rid of s 74, the dead letter which still purports to provide for appeals to the Privy Council, and the provisions of ss 58, 59 and 60 which permitted the reservation of a law for the Queen's pleasure and reserved the Queen's power to disallow a law even after it had been assented to by the Governor-General.

Indeed, the provisions which confer powers on the Queen, with one exception, have become anachronistic. The removal of these provisions should not be seen as dependent upon the adoption of a republican form of government. It is an anachronism that the *Constitution* should repose in the Queen powers which are obsolete; it is an anachronism that powers which are exercised only in accordance with the advice of the Ministers of the Commonwealth government should be vested in the Queen rather than in the Governor-General. Removal of the provisions of the *Constitution* which vest such powers in the Queen would better reflect the reality of Australia's present system of government. Dr Helen Irving, wishing to remove misleading provisions of the *Constitution* which wind 'like morning glory vines ... around the branches of the constitutional tree', regards the provisions relating to the Queen to be 'in almost all cases misleading. The Queen simply does not exercise the powers, or engage in the activities that the *Constitution* says she does'.[76] As the Monarch no longer exercises any power other than the power to appoint the Governor-General – and that power is exercised on the advice of the Prime Minister of the Commonwealth – there seems to be little point in retaining these provisions. But the power to appoint the Governor-General cannot be removed unless and until an alternative provision can be inserted for the appointment of a Head of State.

Some of the Commission's recommendations may be too controversial to command the bilateral support or to inspire the electoral enthusiasm required to affirm a referendum proposal. For example, minimum three-year and maximum four-year terms for the House of Representatives;[77] advisory opinion jurisdiction for the High Court[78] and extension of the Commonwealth power to make laws with respect to intra-state trade and commerce,[79] industrial relations generally,[80] defamation[81] and accident compensation and rehabilitation.[82] But the rapid growth of technology in fields that affect human existence (the cloning of humans and genome engineering, for example), the ecosystem (genetic modification of plants and animals) and personal freedom (intrusive eavesdropping) now call for a power to intervene, if necessary, by enacting uniform national laws. The Commission also proposed power to make laws with respect to nuclear material, nuclear energy and ionising radiation.[83] Some of these subjects may fall within the external affairs power if there be international conventions to which Australia is a party but it is preferable to confer the power to make laws with respect to specified areas of technology in order to facilitate laws appropriate to Australian conditions.

A clean up of the *Constitution* is long overdue. If a degree of statesmanship were exhibited by political leaders, the Australian people could be trusted to repair these defects in our *Constitution* at least to the point where the document can operate in the twenty-first century as it was intended to operate at the beginning of the twentieth century. It would take more effort to explain the amendments which are needed to address the problems that are now calling for national attention.

It is time to dust off the recommendations of the Constitutional Commission and to bring our *Constitution* into shape to cope with the scientific and technological problems of the twenty-first century. Surely it is not beyond the capacity of Australia's politicians and their parties to agree on those proposals which can command their unanimous or substantially unanimous support and to propose amendments which can be confidently submitted to referendum. Controversial proposals which command only majority support could, if the government of the day so chose, be put to the people in referenda which were clearly distinguished from the non-controversial proposals.

Politically, of course, the most pressing issue of constitutional reform is the further consideration of an Australian republic, and to that controversial issue I must now turn.

The republic

The recent referendum seeking a change to a republican form of government was defeated by a combination of voters who desired to retain a constitutional Monarchy and voters who desired to elect a President by direct vote on a universal franchise. Some who desired to retain the Monarchy did so by reason of deep attachment to the Queen; others perceived that we enjoy the benefits of representative and responsible government under the present system and were concerned to avoid the possibility of change. On the other hand, the direct electionists were advocating a democratic power to appoint the Head of State: a power which they did not wish to entrust to politicians. The implications of these views should be examined.

The English constitutional scholar, Walter Bagehot, cynical of the sophistication of the English populace of the last century, observed that: 'so long as the human heart is strong and the human reason weak, royalty will be strong because it appeals to diffused feeling, and Republics weak because they appeal to the understanding.'[84]

But that facile comment does not do justice to the strong sense of loyalty to the Queen personally which is felt by many Australians and the tie which many Australians have with Britain. Those sentiments are unlikely to change and they deserve respect. Yet the references to the Queen in the *Constitution* have given rise to a constitutional absurdity. By force of Covering Clause 2, references to the Queen 'extend to Her Majesty's heirs and successors in the sovereignty of the United Kingdom'. The identity of the Australian Head of State is determined for us by the laws of the United Kingdom which is, by Australian constitutional law, a 'foreign power'.[85] By reason of the *Australia Act 1986* (Cth),[86] the future laws of the United Kingdom have no application to the Commonwealth or to any state or territory. So, if the United Kingdom were to amend the provisions of the United Kingdom statute governing succession to the throne – for example, by eliminating male preferences or the requirement of Protestant faith – the amendment would have no effect in Australian law, although it would be effective in determining the Australian Head of State. Loyalty to the Monarch personally and British ties have to be weighed against the constitutional absurdity of having our Head of State selected under the laws of a foreign power.

The argument for the status quo has more practical significance: not because the present system is perfect, but because the *Constitution* provides the fundamental features of representative and responsible government.[87] We, the people, elect the members of both Houses of the Parliament to which the government ministry is responsible for the exercise of executive power. If the *Constitution* were amended by providing for the appointment of a President in place of the Queen and the Governor-General, the provision for the election of the Parliament would remain but the mechanism for keeping the ministry politically responsible to the Parliament would need amendment, at least in most of the models under consideration. That is because responsible government depends not only on the terms of the *Constitution*, but also on convention. Regrettably, in the debate preceding the recent republican referendum, there was little analysis of these elements.

Responsible government is not expressly provided for in the *Constitution*; it was not thought necessary to do so when the Federation was being formed 'under the Crown of the United Kingdom'.[88] The conventions which secured responsible government under the Imperial Crown were assumed to be applicable under the *Constitution*. At the Constitutional Convention of 1898, Mr Josiah Symon said: 'A written Constitution is not exhaustive. We have implanted responsible government in this *Constitution*, but we have not said so in so many words. We must have some regard to the instrument we are framing, and we ought to look upon it as a *Constitution* with plenty of elasticity, under which all the constitutional usages will apply and be interpreted.'[89]

The Constitutional requirement that Ministers be, or become, members of the Parliament[90] clearly indicates an expectation that responsible government in the Westminster model would be the form of government. In the *Engineers Case*[91] in 1920, the majority judgment recalled the speech of Lord Haldane, when a member of the House of Commons, in speaking to the Bill for the enactment of the Commonwealth *Constitution*. He said: 'The difference between the *Constitution* which this bill proposes to set up and the *Constitution of the United States* is enormous and fundamental. This bill is permeated through and through with the spirit of the greatest institution which exists in the Empire, ... – I mean the institution of responsible government, a government under which the executive is directly responsible to — nay, is almost the creature of – the legislature.'

Yet the executive power of the Commonwealth is not vested in the ministry by s 61 of the *Constitution*; it is vested in the Queen and is exercised by the Governor-General. The ministry is responsible for the way in which the Governor-General exercises his power because *by convention* the Governor-General exercises his powers only on the 'advice' of his Ministers, except on those rare occasions when he exercises the so-called 'reserve powers'. Informed by practical experience, former Governor McGarvie observes: 'The basic constitutional convention that binds the Governor-General to exercise powers as advised by Ministers of the elected Government is the essential link between the exercise of those powers and the sovereignty of the people.'[92]

Mason J in *FAI Insurances Ltd v Winneke* explained the role of convention in the system of responsible government:

> The principle that in general the Governor defers to, or acts upon, the advice of his Ministers, though it forms a vital element in the concept of responsible government, is not in itself an instance of the doctrine of ministerial responsibility. It is a convention, compliance with which enables the doctrine of ministerial responsibility to come into play so that a Minister or Ministers become responsible to Parliament for the decision made by the Governor in Council, thereby contributing to the concept of responsible government. 'The principal convention of the British constitution", says de Smith in his *Constitutional and Administrative Law*, 3rd ed. (1977), p.99, 'is that the Queen shall exercise her formal legal powers only upon and in accordance with the advice of her Ministers, save in a few

> exceptional situations'. Comformably with this principle there is a convention that in general the Governor-General or the Governor of a State acts in accordance with the advice tendered to him by his Ministers and not otherwise (Sawer, *Federation under Strain* (1977), p. 142; see also Keith, *Responsible Government in the Dominions*, 2nd ed. (1928), pp.107-108).[93]

The significance of this convention in the republican debate is obvious. Indeed, McGarvie observes that: 'The basic constitutional convention of acting on ministerial advice is so vital to our democracy and responsible government, that it would be reasonable to assume that the first priority of anyone designing a model for head of state in a republic would have been to maintain the convention and its binding effect. Yet for a long time that was generally overlooked.'[94]

If the *Constitution* were to vest executive power in a republican President, would the President be bound by a convention which is the cornerstone of constitutional monarchy?[95] In the United Kingdom, the Monarch has been constrained to act only on ministerial advice since the Hanoverian succession. When George III attempted to exercise power without ministerial advice, he was met by the Commons resolution in 1780 moved by Mr Dunning 'that the influence of the Crown has increased, is increasing, and ought to be diminished'.[96] In the United Kingdom, constitutional monarchy and responsible government are the reciprocal results of history. In Australia, no Governor-General would decline to observe the convention, for it is basic to the accepted system of government. Long established practice would be enforced, if a Governor-General were to breach the convention, by the 'practical penalty' of dismissal on the insistence of the Prime Minister.

The discretionary powers which the *Constitution* confers on the Governor-General include power to appoint and dismiss Ministers,[97] to appoint members of the Executive Council,[98] to submit a Bill for the amendment of the *Constitution* to referendum,[99] to summon and prorogue the Parliament,[100] to dissolve the House of Representatives,[101] to issue writs for a general election of the House of Representatives,[102] to dissolve both Houses of the Parliament;[103] to assent to Bills passed by the Houses of the Parliament;[104] to recommend by message to the Parliament the purpose of an appropriation.[105] The Governor-General exercises these powers on ministerial advice[106] and the Constitutional Commission recommended that that practice should be incorporated in the *Constitution* with respect to most of these powers.[107] If Australia were to become a republic, a President, especially an elected President, with a fixed term of office would feel less constrained than a Governor-General to act only on ministerial advice. If responsible government is to be retained, there should be a new, legal duty, corresponding with the duty which convention imposes on a Governor-General, imposed on the President. The duty should be entrenched in the *Constitution*. If the need should ever arise, the courts could enforce the duty. Imposition of the duty would be desirable to avoid any misunderstanding even if the President, like the Governor-General, were appointed and could be removed by the Prime Minister. The Constitutional Commission so recommended without proposing any change to the Monarchical system.[108]

If the conventional duty were entrenched in the *Constitution*, one of the two main objections to an elected Presidency would be substantially reduced. One objection to an elected Presidency relates to the category of candidates who would be willing to stand for election. But the principal objection to an elected Presidency is the risk – perhaps the likelihood – that the President, armed with the authority of a popular mandate, might exercise executive and, possibly, reserve power to frustrate the policies or impair the powers of the Prime Minister and government. There would be two hands on the tiller of national interest. The rationale of the present convention is that the Parliament represents the people and the Governor-General must act on advice of his Ministers so that Ministers can be held responsible to the people's representatives in the Parliament for the exercise of executive power. But a popularly elected President *is* a representative of the people, with a broader constituency than a Prime Minister or even a government party. If a presidential election were conducted on a platform of policy, would not the President have a mandate to implement the policy even if it were opposed by the Prime Minister? To preserve Ministerial responsibility to the Parliament, it would be essential that the *Constitution* impose on the President the general duty to act, and to act only, on the advice of the Ministry. Of course, that would not give protection against a President's unreasonable exercise of reserve powers; that problem needs to be separately addressed.

Although the convention that the Governor-General should exercise his powers on the advice of responsible ministers and only on that advice is a basic element in the system of responsible government, some provision must be made as against the possibility that a Prime Minister or government may pursue an unlawful course of conduct or govern otherwise than according to the law and custom of the *Constitution*. The so-called reserve powers exist in order to ensure that the Governor-General can act to prevent a failure of the rule of law or a disregard of constitutional law and custom. But an exercise of reserve powers is extraordinary and can be justified only when the exercise is '*absolutely necessary* to preserve the rule of law and protect the operation of responsible government from abuse by the executive' (to adopt Professor Winterton's test).[109]

The Constitutional Commission suggested that 'the reserve powers … that is the powers the Governor-General may exercise without or contrary to Ministerial advice, should be kept to a minimum'. The reserve powers were identified as: 'the power to appoint and to dismiss the Prime Minister (section 64), dissolution of the House of Representatives (section 5), and a double dissolution pursuant to section 57 of the *Constitution*. How the reserve powers should be exercised is, however, regulated to a large extent by constitutional convention.'[110]

A majority of the Commission also recommended that legislation should be enacted to prescribe the circumstances in which a Governor-General might dismiss a Prime Minister.[111] In 1998, the Constitutional Convention Communiqué, which supported in principle that Australia become a republic, proposed that the non-reserve powers be 'spelled out so far as possible' and that a statement be made 'that the reserve powers and the conventions relating to their exercise continue to exist'.[112] It is difficult to spell out conventions prescribing the occasions for exercise of reserve powers. Sir Ninian Stephen, in an address to mark the 75th Anniversary of the *Constitution*, observed that: 'The truly difficult and important part, having once identified the area governed, if at all, only by conventions, is that of determining the content of the constitutional rules that should then apply, and accordingly be reflected in the new constitutional text.'[113]

If the *Constitution* were amended to spell out the powers that can or the powers that cannot be exercised without ministerial advice, and the occasions when powers can be exercised without ministerial advice, the exercise of a power would be justiciable. It has been suggested that the statement of conventions need not be justiciable but that would surely have the doubly unfortunate effect of petrifying the conventions while denying them legal efficacy. However, if the *Constitution* were to spell out either the reserve powers or the conventions governing their exercise, issues that are more political than legal would be litigated. The High Court would be invited to determine whether the political circumstances existing *at a particular time* satisfy the conditions for exercising the reserve powers. The occasions when a President might have to act to enforce the rule of law or to maintain representative and responsible government — occasions when speedy action is likely to be required — would pass by while the litigation proceeded. That is unacceptable where there are reasonable grounds for exercising a reserve power. The political situation may need urgent solution.

A Governor-General or a President can, without ministerial advice, appoint a Prime Minister if there is a vacancy in that office and accept the resignation of a Prime Minister.[114] Allowing for that power,[115] I would think it misconceived to attempt to spell out either the powers that can and the powers that cannot be exercised without ministerial advice. I respectfully agree with former Governor McGarvie, writing of the November 1975 double dissolution, that 'once absolute necessity justifies use of the reserve authority, the Governor-General is free of the inhibition of the basic constitutional convention and has an independent discretion to exercise the reserve power of dissolution given by the *Constitution* independently of ministerial advice'.[116] The powers which would be needed if it became *absolutely necessary* to enforce the fundamental constitutional principles of the rule of law and representative and responsible government – a question of timing as much as substance cannot be identified in advance. Nor can the precise circumstances which might warrant an exercise of the reserve powers be foreseen. For that reason, it would be preferable to prescribe a control mechanism to ensure that reserve powers are exercised only when there is a real assurance that the occasion has arisen when it is absolutely necessary to exercise them. A President who is concerned by a situation which, in her or his view, warrants an exercise of reserve power, should be required first to consult a Constitutional Council and obtain its assessment of the situation. The Council, constituted by, say, three former Governors-General or Presidents or state governors and three former Chief Justices or Justices of the High Court or the Chief Justices of other superior courts – all subject to an age limit – should certify whether or not, having regard to the prevailing circumstances, there are reasonable grounds for the opinion that it is absolutely necessary to exercise the reserve power. A certificate that reasonable grounds exist should be conclusive and the validity of the exercise of the power should be justiciable before the High Court only if the President were to exercise the power without such a certificate.

In this way, the fundamental convention not to act except on ministerial advice would be maintained unless, in the view of the President, it would be absolutely necessary to enforce the fundamental constitutional principles of the rule of law and representative and responsible government and the existence of reasonable grounds for that view is affirmed by the Constitutional Council or, in default, by the High Court. I would propose a new s 2 of the *Constitution* which would eliminate the obsolete provision empowering the Queen to assign powers and functions to the Governor-General and which, together with an amended s 61,[117] would confer powers (in particular, the prerogative powers)[118] and functions on the President and regulate their exercise. Appendix A contains a draft for consideration.

To avoid any misunderstanding, it may be desirable to add to the High Court's jurisdiction under s 75 a provision covering matters affecting the exercise of a reserve power.[119]

With these provisions in place, the system of responsible and representative government should be assured irrespective of the model which might be adopted for the election or dismissal of a President. Even so, the model of direct election could be adopted only at a price, namely, the virtual elimination of eminent, non-political citizens as candidates for the Presidency. The Australian Governors-General who have held office in recent times have fallen into two categories: those who have held political office and have been appointed on the nomination of their political party, and those who have achieved eminence in a non-political field and would have declined any invitation to engage in an electoral campaign for the office. It is unlikely that citizens who fall into the latter category would agree to be nominated to contest an election for the office of President. A choice must be made between that loss and any desire to vote to elect the Head of State. But that is not the principal choice which the Australian people will have to make if they wish Australia to become a republic.

The principal question is: do we wish to retain our Parliamentary system of government with a Prime Minister whose government is responsible to the Parliament and commands the confidence of a majority of the House of Representatives and whose government will fall if it loses that confidence? If we say 'Yes', then we can start to think about the way in which we need to provide for a President without destroying responsible government. Debate has raged about direct election, Parliamentary election and Prime Ministerial appointment as though the mode of election is all-important, but it is only when we decide on the powers which a President should have that we can sensibly discuss the mode of election and the safeguards that must be in place to maintain Parliamentary government as we know it.

Of course, the republic is not the only issue calling for constitutional reform. Perhaps it is the only issue which will command sufficient parliamentary interest to lead to a referendum. But if a referendum is to be held for a republic, it would be a pity if we did not take the opportunity to amend those obsolete and defective provisions which presently encumber the text of the *Constitution*; it would be a pity if we did not incorporate provisions to permit a national response to the issues that developing technology will assuredly raise. Our *Constitution* has served us well. It needs to be refreshed. We should hope that petty politics and inertia do not hobble our nation in the century to come.

Appendix A

Section 2 might read as follows:[120]

(1) The powers which were vested in and functions performed by the Governor-General before the *Constitution Alteration (Republic of Australia) Act* came into force are vested in and may be performed by the President.

(2) Subject to subsection (3), the President shall exercise the powers and functions conferred upon the President by this *Constitution* solely in accordance with advice tendered to the President by the Prime Minister, the Executive Council or, in the case of a statutory power, a Minister of State responsible for the administration of the statute.

(3) The President may exercise her or his powers without the advice prescribed by subsection (2):

  a) in appointing or accepting the resignation of a Prime Minister; or

  b) if the President is of the opinion on reasonable grounds that it is absolutely necessary to exercise a power in order to execute or maintain this *Constitution* and the laws of the Commonwealth and the President has first consulted the Constitutional Council and the Council has had a reasonable opportunity to determine and to certify whether, in relation to a proposed exercise of power, there are reasonable grounds for the President's opinion.

(4) A certificate by the Constitutional Council that there are reasonable grounds for the President's opinion under subsection (3) is conclusive evidence that there are reasonable grounds for the opinion in relation to the proposed exercise of power.

(5) The Constitutional Council shall consist of:

  a) Three citizens who, not having attained the age of 75 years, have served as:

    (i) Governor-General or President of the Commonwealth of Australia, being the three most recently in office who are willing and able to serve as members of the Council; or

    (ii) if fewer than three of those persons be not willing and able to serve, former Governors of a State;

  b) Three citizens who, not having attained the age of 75 years, have served as:

    (i) A Chief Justice of the High Court of Australia, being the three most recently in office who are willing and able to serve as members of the Council; or

(ii) if fewer than three former Chief Justices be not willing and able to serve, a Justice of the High Court; or

(iii) if fewer than three former Chief Justices or Justices of the High Court be not willing and able to serve, a former Chief Justice of the Federal Court of Australia or of the Supreme Court of a State.

(6) The Parliament shall appoint the persons referred to in paragraphs (a) (ii) and (b)(ii) and (iii) in the previous subsection being persons willing and able to serve as members of the Council and may appoint persons in the place of any person so appointed who ceases to be willing and able to serve.

Section 75 (vi) might read as follows:

In all matters:

(vi) in which an order is sought affecting a purported or proposed exercise of power by the President under paragraph (b) of subsection 2 (3) of this *Constitution* the High Court shall have original jurisdiction.

---

1. See *Victoria v Commonwealth* (1971) 122 CLR 353, 395 (Windeyer J).
2. See *Amalgamated Society of Engineers v Adelaide Steamship Co Ltd* (1920) 28 CLR 129, 142.
3. See *Kirmani v Captain Cook Cruises Pty Ltd [No 1]* (1985) 159 CLR 351, 442.
4. Sir Owen Dixon, 'The Common Law as an Ultimate Constitutional Foundation' (1957) 31 *Australian Law Journal* 240, 241; reprinted in Sir Owen Dixon, *Jesting Pilate* (Law Book Co, 1965) 201, 205.
5. (1993) 177 CLR 541, 552.
6. See *Re Bolton; Ex parte Beane* (1987) 162 CLR 514, 523.
7. See *Balog v Independent Commission against Corruption* (1990) 169 CLR 625, 635-636.
8. See *Ex parte Walsh & Johnson; In Re Yates* (1925) 37 CLR 36, 79.
9. See *Lange v Australian Broadcasting Corporation* (1997) 189 CLR 520, 564.
10. See *Victorian Stevedoring and General Contracting Co Pty Ltd and Meakes v Dignan* (1931) 46 CLR 73, 114; *Nationwide News Pty Ltd. v Wills* (1992) 177 CLR 1, 47, 70; *Lange v Australian Broadcasting Corporation* (1997) 189 CLR 520, 557-558.
11. See *British Railways Board v Pickin* [1974] AC 765, 782 (Lord Reid); see also Sir Owen Dixon 'Sources of Legal Authority' in Sir Owen Dixon, *Jesting Pilate* (Law Book Co, 1965) 199-200; 'The Common Law as Ultimate Constitutional Foundation' in Sir Owen Dixon, *Jesting Pilate* (Law Book Co, 1965) 206.
12. (1992) 177 CLR 1.

13. T R S Allan, 'The Common Law as Constitution: Fundamental Rights and First Principles' in Cheryl Saunders (ed), *Courts of Final Jurisdiction. The Mason Court in Australia* (The Federation Press, Sydney, 1996) 146, 154.
14. For an appreciation of the rule of law as protection from despotism, see TRS Allan, 'Legislative Supremacy and the Rule of Law: Democracy and Constitutionalism' (1985) 44 *Cambridge Law Journal* 11.
15. G Sawer, *Federation under Strain* (Melbourne University Press, 1977) 178.
16. Ibid 192.
17. Richard McGarvie, *Democracy – Choosing Australia's Republic* (Melbourne University Press, Melbourne, 1999), 60.
18. Ibid 155.
19. See *Constitution Alteration (Senate Casual Vacancies) 1977*.
20. Sir Owen Dixon, 'Sources of Legal Authority', in Sir Owen Dixon, *Jesting Pilate* (Law Book Co, 1965) 200.
21. See *Statute of Westminster 1931* (UK), s 4; *Australia Act 1986* (Cth), s 1. See also, *Australia Act* 1986 (UK).
22. Declaration of the Imperial Conference of 1930 and the insistence by Prime Minister Scullin that Sir Isaac Isaacs be appointed as Governor-General.
23. Standing Committee D's 4th Report, 4.
24. The Paper prepared by Professor Saunders and Mr Ewart Smith for Standing Committee D summary of conventions, 29 [2] and [3].
25. See Sir Clarrie Harders, 'Conventions associated with the Australian Constitution: the effect of the events of 1973–1975 relating to references and appeals to the Privy Council', (1982) 56 *Australian Law Journal* 132 and the correspondence culminating in the letter from Sir Maurice Byers in (1982) 56 *Australian Law Journal* 316.
26. Commonwealth, *Parliamentary Debates*, House of Representatives, 18 March 1902, 10966-10967 (Alfred Deakin, Attorney-General).
27. Ibid 10967-10968.
28. John Michael Bennett, *Keystone of the Federal Arch: a historical memoir of the High Court of Australia to 1980* (Australian Government Publishing Service, 1980) 11.
29. (1908) 6 CLR 309, 367-368.
30. (1945) 71 CLR 29, 81, 85.
31. See *Baxter v Commissioners of Taxation (NSW)* (1907) 4 CLR 1087, 1118.
32. (1908) 6 CLR 469, 611-612.
33. See *Amalgamated Society of Engineers v Adelaide Steamship Co Ltd* (1920) 28 CLR 129 (*Engineers' Case*).
34. See *Victoria v Commonwealth ('Payroll Tax Case')* (1971) 122 CLR 353, 396.
35. See *Cole v Whitfield* (1988) 165 CLR 360, 365.
36. See *Marcus Clarke & Co Ltd v Commonwealth* (1952) 87 CLR 177.
37. See *Lange v Australian Broadcasting Corporation* (1997) 189 CLR 520, 557-558.
38. See *Chu Kheng Lim v Minister for Immigration, Local Government and Ethnic Affairs* (1992) 176 CLR 1, 36.
39. See *R v Brislan* (1935) 54 CLR 262; *Jones v Commonwealth (No 2)* (1965) 112 CLR 206; *Australian Broadcasting Commission v Industrial Court of South Australia* (1977) 138 CLR 399.

40. See *Brown v The Queen* (1986) 160 CLR 171, 197, 217.
41. See *Jumbunna Coal Mine NL v Victorian Coal Miners' Association* (1908) 6 CLR 309, 368. (O'Connor J).
42. See *Commonwealth of Australia v Tasmania ('Tasmanian Dam Case')* (1983) 158 CLR 1, 221.
43. See *Official Record of the Debates of the Australasian Federal Convention, Second Session,* Sydney, 1897 (9 September 1897) 239.
44. See *Official Record of the Debates of the Australasian Federal Convention, Third Session,* Melbourne, 1898 (21 January 1898) 30.
45. See *R v Burgess; Ex parte Henry* (1936) 55 CLR 608; *Koowarta v Bjelke-Petersen* (1982) 153 CLR 168; *Commonwealth v Tasmania ('Tasmanian Dam Case')* (1983) 158 CLR 1.
46. See *Polyukovich v Commonwealth* (1991) 172 CLR 501 (*War Crimes Act Case*).
47. In the *R v Kirby; Ex parte Boilermakers' Society of Australia* (1956) 94 CLR 254 the majority judgment pointed out that: 'The conception of independent governments existing in the one area and exercising powers in different fields of action carefully defined by law could not be carried into practical effect unless the ultimate responsibility of deciding upon the limits of the respective powers of the governments were placed in the federal judicature.'
48. See *Re Refugee Review Tribunal; Ex parte Aala* (2000) 176 ALR 219.
49. See the *Migration Act 1958* (Cth), s 476; and *Abebe v Commonwealth* (1999) 197 CLR 510, 534.
50. See *Abebe v Commonwealth* (1999) 197 CLR 510; *Re Minister for Immigration and Multicultural Affairs; Ex parte Durairajasingham* (2000) 74 ALJR 405, 407-408 and *Re Refugee Review Tribunal; Ex parte Aala* (2000) 204 CLR 82, 129.
51. See *Cole v Whitfield* (1988) 165 CLR 360.
52. See *Bath v Alston Holdings Pty Ltd* (1988) 165 CLR 411.
53. See now *Castlemaine Tooheys Ltd v South Australia* (1990) 169 CLR 436; *Ha v New South Wales* (1997) 189 CLR 465.
54. See *New South Wales v Commonwealth* (1990) 169 CLR 482 (*Incorporation Case*).
55. Final Report of the Constitutional Commission, 1988, Summary Volume, 35.
56. See *Re Wakim; Ex parte McNally* (1999) 198 CLR 511.
57. See *Fencott v Muller* (1983) 152 CLR 570.
58. See *Constitution Alteration (Rights and Freedoms) Bill 1988*.
59. See *Summary, Final Report of the Constitutional Commission*, AGPS, Canberra, 1988, 66.
60. Ibid 34.
61. Ibid 25.
62. Sir Owen Dixon, 'Sources of Legal Authority' (n 20) 201.
63. The qualified reference of power in a state referring Act (eg, *Corporations (Commonwealth Powers) Act 2001* (NSW)) goes some way towards a resolution but falls short of what is constitutionally preferable.
64. See *Summary, Final Report of the Constitutional Commission*, AGPS, Canberra, 1988, 5-6.
65. Ibid 14-15.
66. Ibid 15.
67. Ibid 9.

68. Ibid 10-11.
69. Ibid 25-26.
70. Ibid 27-28.
71. Ibid 53-54.
72. Ibid 61.
73. Ibid 78.
74. H Irving, 'Australia's Constitutional Identity: A Conundrum for the Twentyfirst Century', *The Barton Lecture,* Parliament House, Sydney, 10 April 2001 (ABC Radio National, 15 July,2001) manuscript, 5.
75. See *Summary, Final Report of the Constitutional Commission,* AGPS, Canberra, 1988, 54-56.
76. Ibid 8.
77. Ibid 7.
78. Ibid 29.
79. Ibid 66.
80. Ibid 67.
81. Ibid 47.
82. Ibid 52.
83. Ibid 47-48.
84. Walter Bagehot, *The English Constitution* (1867 [1963], 1987 Fontana/Collins) quoted by Brian Galligan, *A Federal Republic: Australia's Constitutional System of Government* (Cambridge University Press, 1995) 19.
85. See *Sue v Hill* (1999) 199 CLR 462, 489.
86. Section 1.
87. See *Lange v Australian Broadcasting Commission* (1997) 189 CLR 520, 557-559.
88. Preamble to the *Constitution of Australia Act 1900* (Cth).
89. See *Official Record of the Debates of the Australasian Federal Convention, Third Session,* Melbourne, 1898 (10 March 1898) 2262; reproduced in Correspondence, letter of James A Thompson (1981) 55 *Australian Law Journal* 166.
90. See *Constitution* s 64; and see *New South Wales v Commonwealth* (*'Seas and Submerged Lands Case'*) (1975) 135 CLR 337, 364-365.
91. See *Amalgamated Society of Engineers v Adelaide Steamship Co Ltd ('Engineers' Case)* (1920) 28 CLR 129, 147.
92. See *Constitution* s 64, 61.
93. (1982) 151 CLR 342, 364-5.
94. See *Constitution* s 64, 89.
95. The question was raised by George Winterton, 'Reserve Powers in an Australian Republic' (1993) 12 (2) *University of Tasmania Law Review* 249, 254.
96. TP Taswell-Langmead, *English Constitutional History: from the Teutonic Conquest to the Present Time* (Sweet & Maxwell, 4th ed, 1890) 730.
97. See *Constitution* s 64.
98. See *Constitution* s 62.
99. See *Constitution* s 128.
100. See *Constitution* s 5.

101. Ibid.

102. See *Constitution* s 32.

103. See *Constitution* s 57.

104. See *Constitution* s 58.

105. See *Constitution* s 56.

106. Report of Standing Committee D of the Australian Constitutional Convention (Adelaide 1983) and Report of Structure of Government Sub-Committee Report to Standing Committee D, 1984. However, the Saunders-Smith Paper prepared for Standing Committee D suggests (p 18) that assent may be withheld from a Bill that is 'flagrantly unconstitutional'; and see the intervention of Mr Higgins in the Convention Debates of 31 January 1898. *Official Records of the Debates of the Australasian Federal Convention, Third Session*, Melbourne, 1898 (31 January 1898) 339.

107. The recommendation did not cover the power to submit a Bill to referendum under s 128 as the Commission recommended the elimination of the discretion to submit: see *Summary, Final Report of the Constitutional Commission*, AGPS, Canberra, 1988, 19-20, 75.

108. See the Constitutional Commission Summary, Ibid 19.

109. G Winterton, *The Resurrection of the Republic*, Law and Policy Paper No 15 (Centre for International and Public Law, Australian National University, 2001) 17.

110. Final Report of the Constitutional Commission vol 1, 342 [5.151].

111. Ibid 326 [5.66].

112. Report of Proceedings, vol 1, 45.

113. Reproduced in David Marr, *Barwick* (Allen & Unwin, Sydney, 1980) 303-304.

114. This is not a power to dismiss a Prime Minister who does not resign.

115. The Constitutional Commission recommended the creation of a specific power to appoint a Prime Minister as Head of Government, *Final Report of the Constitutional Commission, Volume 1,* AGPS, Canberra, 1988, 316.

116. See also G Winterton, *The Resurrection of the Republic*, Law and Policy Paper No 15 (Centre for International and Public Law, Australian National University, 2001), 16.

117. Section 61 would simply vest in the President the executive powers vested in the Governor-General, thus: 'The executive power of the Commonwealth is vested in the President and extends to the execution and maintenance of the *Constitution*, and of the laws of the Commonwealth.'

118. See *Barton v Commonwealth* (1974) 131 CLR 477.

119. See a suggested draft in Appendix A.

120. In the drafting of an amendment, it would probably be necessary to provide a separate section to deal with vacancies in Constitutional Council membership, the chair, voting procedures and the like.

6.6 Toast to the High Court

Editor's note

On 13 February 2002, a conference was held at the Australian National University to launch *The Oxford Companion to the High Court of Australia* edited by Professors Tony Blackshield, Michael Coper and George Williams (Oxford University Press, 2001). At the conference dinner, Brennan was invited to propose the toast to the High Court.

Mr Dean, Pro-Chancellor Dr Annabelle Bennett and your accompanying person, Vice-Chancellor, Chief Justice, your Honours, distinguished guests – particularly those who have occupied the highest offices in this nation – former colleagues, ladies and gentlemen. It is an awesome task to be asked to propose a toast to the High Court of Australia.

I think back to the time when I first had contact with the Court. It was at a time when the High Court, going on circuit, used to occupy the chambers of the Justices of the Supreme Courts of the several States. Sir George Rich used to take my father's chambers in Brisbane. I remember going to pick up the mail one day and seeing this elderly figure camped on the step outside the Chambers sunning himself in the Queensland sunshine. I was about to go up and say 'See here my man' when the figure stirred. 'Hello Brennan' he said. Very quickly drawing breath, I said 'Hello Sir George, are you enjoying your stay in Queensland?' 'Oh' he said 'we've had a splendid morning striking down some more regulations!' Which led me to think that the Court was not only a great institution but a human institution as well.

Years afterwards, when I was privileged to join the Court, I discovered again something of the humanity of the institution. A case of great difficulty had been argued – *Todorovic v Waller (*1981) 150 CLR 402- and it had to do with the rate of discount to be used in calculating damages for personal injury causing loss of income. It was necessary for the Court to legislate. A week or two before we had heard a criminal appeal from Western Australia in which a Detective Sergeant of Police was said to have extracted a voluntary confession by, amongst other things, throwing his coat down on the table and saying to the suspect 'Now fess up'. It was a hot day as we sat around the table to discuss the rate of discount. Opinions were sharply divided. Lionel Murphy was a little late in coming. He came in sweating, took off his jacket, as the Detective Sergeant of Police had done, threw it on the table and stated his view. When the laughter subsided, the Court reached consensus at 3%, albeit with some dissenters. Shortly after that when Sir Ninian Stephen was leaving for another place, I heard one Associate say to him 'Come back, Sir Ninian, come back, and we'll agree to 0%'.

When I was asked to propose this toast I learnt, from the Oxford Companion, of the uncertain provenance of the Court's existence. It seems that it has not yet been resolved judicially whether the Court owes its existence to the *Constitution* or to the *Judiciary Act* 1903 (Cth). The question was raised in *Hannah v Dalgarno* (1903) 1 CLR 1, the first case. The authors say 'that Sir Samuel Griffith took the question seriously is remarkable; that he declined to answer it is unsurprising. The gap between ontology and law was unbridgeable'. That is a proposition to which I would assent. They go on, speculating that the *Constitution* establishes Parliament's *procreative* capacity; it is Parliament that procreates the Court and exercises the parental right to determine where the High Court will live. This really puzzles me. I had always thought that for procreation two entities were required and that it was of the nature of procreation that its product should exhibit something of the same essential characteristics as its forbears. Now I would assert that the High Court of Australia has quite distinct characteristics from the Parliament of the Commonwealth, in its purpose, in its powers, in its manner of exercise, in its constitution. Nonetheless the ontological problem has been overcome and the Court's existence can be confidently asserted because, as the authors say, *Judico, ergo sum.*

The existence of the High Court can be celebrated under a litany of titles – perhaps somewhat florid metaphors but nonetheless appropriate for a festive occasion such as this. Guardian of the *Constitution*, keystone of the federal arch, bulwark of our democracy, protector of the essential functions of the States, maintainer of the separation of judicial power, upholder of individual rights, arbiter of justiciable controversies, champion of freedom. It is independent, impartial, practical, competent, scholarly, articulate, industrious. It has the unique capacity to transform its members so that in some mysterious way those who join its ranks do not always fulfil the expectations of those who appoint them. It has a mystique – a mystique which is born not so much of its power as of its authority. But it is a human institution and its day-to-day operations require the complementary efforts of many who are not mentioned in the *Oxford Companion*.

This is an appropriate occasion in which we could remember those others who, unsung, in a sense unnoticed, nonetheless contribute in their respective ways to the easy working of that institution. I would start with Malcolm McGann. Malcolm is a cleaner. You can see him from time to time crawling through the ducts under the floorboards, taking wires to this point or that. Or Sitiveni, the Fijian who was so proud of becoming an Australian. The attendants and Court criers. I remember, Sheila Mumberson and the late Wyn Edwards; two wonderful women who, when the Court was closed at weekends because of the absence of funds, wrote in to say that they, though retired, would love to come back voluntarily on weekends to open the Court and allow it to be seen by the visiting public. There were others of the same calibre. Today there is still the smiling face of Pat Power, one of the attendants of many years standing. The Court Reporting Service has done much to enable practitioners to appreciate the issues which are to be revised overnight and to enable the Justices to prepare their judgments away from the court building. Ruth Byrnes and Pat Callahan have done wonderful work. Then Siriporn who makes the computers work so effectively they almost make coffee for you. Tonight, I see here Jacqui Elliott who efficiently manages the magnificent library, created late in the Court's history. Joe Pelli and Margaret Neilson in administration and Ken Byron the auditor: people who have done much for the ordinary working of the Court though their identity is not always known outside the Court. Let me leave aside Chris Doogan, the Chief Executive and Principal Registrar and Carolyn Rogers, the Senior Registrar, and mention some others in the Registry: Margaret Heywood who was so dutiful in all her years there, and Lyn Donoghue who has kept the Sydney Registry running. Among the Justices' personal staff there are Russell Slater, the tipstaff to Sir Anthony Mason who now serves Justice Gummow, Trudy Watson and Helen Holmes, and my own Nessie Birchley who ensured that nothing ever went wrong. And Janet Saleh, Personal Assistant to Justice Kirby who produces an enormous volume of material – and who, indeed, deserves a medal from the Archives of Australia!

However, the Court consists, as the *Constitution* provides, of a Chief Justice and Justices — it is their work which is the subject of and the justification for, the *Oxford Companion*.

Putting aside the florid metaphors to which I earlier referred, the Court's role is at base the maintenance of the rule of law – not by exercising the power of the purse, nor by exercising the power of the sword, but only the power of judgment — as Hamilton pointed out in 'The Federalist', 200 years ago. For over a hundred years, the Court has kept the confidence of the people and, in that time, it has adjusted itself and the law to the needs of the community. It is a living, changing human institution. It maintains the rule of law by impartially declaring, expounding and applying the law applicable to the case in hand. Perhaps that work is not particularly glamorous — it is mostly a hard grind under the tyranny of reserved judgments. But on it depends the peace and order and freedom of our nation. That is a task entrusted to successive generations of judges who constitute for their time this singular entity which over arches and subsumes each of its members. It is an institution that is vital to a free and confident nation.

I would therefore ask you ladies and gentlemen, with the exception of those who are the High Court of Australia at present, to be upstanding and to drink a toast to the High Court of Australia.

6.7 Human rights, International Standards and the Protection of Minorities

Editor's note

Brennan delivered this paper at the 'High Court of Australia Centenary 1903-2003' Conference convened by Professor Peter Cane of Australian National University and the Australian Bar Association. Brennan joined Professor Hilary Charlesworth at a session held on 11 October 2003. The synopsis of his paper stated: 'Domestic law, not international law, provides practical protection of minority rights. The courts of common law countries, responsive to the culture of their respective societies, reduce international standards of human rights to legal rules applicable to concrete situations. They articulate the rules either by construing statutes which embody international standards or by developing the common law to develop those standards. The jurisprudence of this work in the High Court is still emerging. The case-by-case methodology is slow, but results in precise and effective rules which do not create unintended consequences. Yet the rules, lacking a constitutional foundation, are vulnerable to political attack.' [1]

It was the rhetoric of human rights and fundamental freedoms which was the undoing of Albert Haddock, AP Herbert's legendary litigant. You will remember that Albert appealed against his conviction on a number of charges consequent on his leaping off Hammersmith Bridge during a regatta. The Court of Criminal Appeal upheld each of his grounds of appeal until they reached the last. Albert had submitted that 'this is a free country and a man can do what he likes if he does nobody any harm.' Lord Light, LCJ dismissed the appeal, perceiving that this ground 'is like the thirteenth stroke of a crazy clock, which not only is itself discredited but casts a shade of doubt over all previous assertions'.[2] Albert had overstated his case, but he was on the right track.

A balance between freedom and legal restriction is needed in an ordered society and the courts of common law have established a methodology for achieving that balance. In the first place, they define the common law rules which impose legal restrictions and construe the statutes which create legal restrictions, leaving the individual free to engage in conduct or to enjoy their rights to the full extent that falls outside the scope of those restrictions. Thus, in *Lange v Australian Broadcasting Commission*,[3] the Court said: 'Under a legal system based on the common law, "everybody is free to do anything, subject only to the provisions of the Law", so that one proceeds "upon an assumption of freedom of speech" and turns to the law "to discover the established exceptions to it".[4] The common law torts of libel and slander are such exceptions.'

Once the restrictions are defined, the common law provides the remedies to protect the remaining freedom. In *Plenty v Dillon,*[5] the majority judgment took as its starting point the judgment of Lord Camden LCJ in *Entick v Carrington:*[6] 'By the laws of England, every invasion of private property, be it ever so minute, is a trespass. No man can set his foot upon my ground without my licence, but he is liable to an action, though the damage be nothing . . . If he admits the fact, he is bound to shew by way of justification, that some positive law has empowered or excused him.'

The fundamental freedoms recognized by the common law are jealously preserved. In *Williams v R*[7] it was noted that 'The right to personal liberty cannot be impaired or taken away without lawful authority and then only to the extent and for the time which the law prescribes.'

Exceptions to general freedom are established in order to protect the community or individuals against an exercise of freedom by those who have the power to oppress. The freedom of an attacker is restrained by the common law's torts of assault and battery in order to protect physical integrity; the common law's invalidation of contractual clauses in unreasonable restraint of trade protects (albeit to a limited extent) both the strength of the economy and the freedom of the individual trader or artisan. To the extent that the common law is the source of legal rules prescribing the boundary between freedoms and legal restrictions, its methodology works well. Although the methodology of the common law allows for the development of restrictions on freedom which protect human rights and fundamental freedoms, it starts from an assumption that the restrictions are to be narrowly defined. The assumption is that freedom, rather than legal control, is conducive to the fulfilment of the human condition. It is an assumption which is basic to a free society.

A similar approach is taken by the Court to the construction of statutes. The common law's balance between freedom and restriction is presumed to be unaffected by statute unless the legislature has manifested a clear contrary intention. In *Bropho v Western Australia*, the majority judgment explained the rationale of the presumption. It

> is to be found in the assumption that it is 'in the last degree improbable that the legislature would overthrow fundamental principles, infringe rights, or depart from the general system of law, without expressing its intention with irresistible clearness...'[8]. If such an assumption be shown to be or to have become ill-founded, the foundation upon which the particular presumption rests will necessarily be weakened

> or removed. Thus, if what was previously accepted as a fundamental principle or fundamental right ceases to be so regarded, the presumption that the legislature would not have intended to depart from that principle or to abolish or modify that right will necessarily be undermined and may well disappear.[9]

The flexibility of the common law allows the Court to adjust (subject to clear statutory provision) the balance between freedom and legal restriction so as to keep the law in harmony with the values of the community. Of course, the common law's protection of rights and freedoms is subject to statutory qualification and the Court is powerless to prevent the qualification if the statute clearly shows an intention to abrogate the protection. I pointed out in *Nationwide News Pty Ltd v Wills* that 'A court will interpret laws of the Parliament in the light of a presumption that the Parliament does not intend to abrogate human rights and fundamental freedoms[10] but the court cannot deny the validity of an exercise of a legislative power expressly granted merely on the ground that the law abrogates human rights and fundamental freedoms or trenches upon political rights which, in the court's opinion, should be preserved.'[11]

Some statutes create new rights or otherwise benefit those in need of protection. In such a case, the Court construes the statute broadly in order to give full effect to the purpose.[12] If the statute has some other purpose, the general rules of statutory interpretation apply.

There are comparatively few[13] constitutional provisions which are protective of rights and freedoms and to them I shall presently refer. Constitutional provisions may invalidate a statute whether the statute would protect or diminish rights; they may entrench rights beyond the reach of any branch of government and they may so constrain the development of the common law as to require conformity with the constitutional norm.[14] So particular attention must be given to the effect of the *Constitution* on rights, especially the rights of minorities.

Legal protection of rights and freedoms is the purpose and consequence of the rule of law as that is understood in the western democracies. The rule of law requires judges, so far as they can, to be guided by their sense of the community's values when they are called on to balance the interests in dispute. Dias comments that –

> ... it is commonplace that in this task [the judges] are guided by their sense of values according to which they balance the interests in dispute.
>
> This explanation, brief as it is, makes it possible to relate judicial

> independence to the 'rule by law'/'rule of law' dichotomy. Where 'rule by law' obtains, the judiciary is a tool of government, which, along with others, reflects and implements official policies and interests. Where 'rule of law' obtains, judges are free to decide on values of their own, and the check on power derives from their being able to hold governmental interests in balance against others. In this way the British judiciary has built up its tradition of independence over the centuries. By and large judges have contrived to preserve as much balance of power in society as they could by siding with the weaker side whenever the balance tilted against it.[15]

Dias is mistaken in his phrase 'values of their own': judges do not purport to apply their idiosyncratic sense of values, but rather to give expression to those deep and enduring values of the community which, in large measure, inform the common law. The very notion of freedom from legal restriction is such a value. Chief Justice Gleeson has pointed out that judges seek to avoid administering the law as an instrument of oppression, however popular that course might be: 'Those for whose rights we need to be zealous are the unpopular, those against whom campaigns of public vilification may be waged, those whose activities, even though lawful, are sought to be made the object of public disapproval.'[16]

That is not to say that the High Court has the role of champion of minorities or promoter of the weak; but equally it is not the voice of the majority or the agent of the strong. It stands independently to apply the law equally[17] between the government and the governed, the majority and minorities, the strong and the weak. The Chief Justice's comment, like Dias' observation, relates to the astuteness of the Court to ensure that there is no overreaching of the interests of a litigant who is one of a minority group or weaker than the adversary and that, when there is legitimate leeway for judicial decision, the balance is struck fairly, not yielding to the influence of government, the majority or the powerful.

Is this a sufficient protection of human rights and of the interests of minorities? That is the question on which the desirability of a Bill of Rights turns. This is not the occasion to enter that debate but rather to assess one side of it, to ascertain the means by which human rights and the interests of minorities have been protected under the common law methodology and, more specifically, by the High Court of Australia.

The common law is domestic law. The High Court's jurisdiction is domestic jurisdiction, while the modern movement for human rights is chiefly international. Yet it is by domestic law, applied by domestic courts and enforced by domestic agencies, which gives – or denies – effective protection to individuals. No international convention has legal effect on rights and duties under domestic law unless and until the convention is translated into domestic law by legislation.[18] It follows that the laws under which human rights and the interests of minorities are protected are the laws administered by the domestic courts. Conventions and other provisions of international law have effect only so far as they produce a response from one or other of the branches of the municipal government. It follows that, in the common law countries of the western democracies, the precise extent of legal protection for minorities often awaits the determination of individual cases, even when the protection arises from statute.

If the protection arises from the common law – for example, from the law of torts – the basic legal principle will be derived from particular judgments of the courts, though often modified by statute. As society changes, so may the legal principle be redefined in order to make it intelligible and applicable to contemporary society. If the protection arises from statute, the precise extent of legal protection may have to await judicial interpretation in order to ascertain the true scope of the statutory text. Nowhere is the need for judicial exegesis more obvious than in the case of statutes which incorporate international Conventions declaring standards of human rights and fundamental freedoms. The open-textured and unqualified definition of rights and freedoms which are characteristic of many such instruments cannot be taken at face value. An unqualified definition of a right or freedom does not necessarily imply that the right or freedom is absolute, nor does it answer the question whether it is to have, or is to yield, priority over other rights and freedoms which may be declared in equally general terms. Article 29(2) of the *Universal Declaration of Human Rights* recognizes that rights and freedoms may be subject to qualification. It declares: 'In the exercise of his rights and freedoms, everyone shall be subject only to such limitations as are determined by law solely for the purpose of securing due recognition and respect for the rights and freedoms of others and of meeting the just requirements of morality, public order and the general welfare in a democratic society.'

This declaration, like the common law, seeks a balance but the starting point is a declaration of the rights and freedoms, the residue being open to restriction. The common law, on the other hand, declares the restrictions and protects the residuary rights and freedoms. The common law method of developing the law is slow and conservative but, within the legitimate authority of the judiciary, legal rules are moulded to produce just and practical solutions.

The common law method of deciding no more than is necessary for the determination of the instant case has not been rigorously followed by many judges in recent times. The desire to elaborate judicial reasoning and to give guidance in situations not specific to the instant case, coupled with an increased complexity in the issues falling for determination, has led to an expansion in judicial dicta and a professional inclination to quote from judgments rather than to proffer analysis of the *rationes decidendi* of earlier cases. Although this change in judicial practice may assist in the elucidation of difficult and open-textured provisions in a statute, judgments do have to be understood in the context of the particular case. This means that the common law method of developing and interpreting the law is slow and conservative; but it also means that legal rules are articulated so as to produce, so far as it lies within the legitimate authority of the judiciary, just and practical solutions.

In the High Court cases involving human rights, the judgments have not always been unanimous but I venture to suggest that the judicial dialectic has sharpened the issues and, in the absence of a constitutional Bill of Rights, has enhanced the jurisprudence which protects the rights and freedoms of a free society. In each case, development of that jurisprudence has depended on the source of the governing law: the *Constitution*, statute or the common law.

The *Constitution*

The framers of the *Constitution* saw no need to insert a Bill of Rights in the *Constitution*, though they were familiar with the American precedent. They were practical politicians and they had faith 'in a system of parliamentary Government with ministerial responsibility.'[19] In *Australian Capital Television Pty Ltd v The Commonwealth,*[20] Mason CJ asserted that 'it is difficult, if not impossible to establish a foundation for the implication of general guarantees of fundamental rights and freedoms. To make such an implication would run counter to the prevailing sentiment of the framers that there was no need to incorporate a comprehensive Bill of Rights in order to protect the rights and freedoms of citizens. That sentiment was one of the unexpressed assumptions on which the *Constitution* was drafted.'[21]

But Deane J had a rather different approach. In *Street v Queensland Bar Association,* he said: 'It is often said that the Australian *Constitution* contains no Bill of Rights. Statements to that effect, while literally true, are superficial and potentially misleading. The *Constitution* contains a significant number of express or implied guarantees of rights and immunities.'[22]

The High Court has given a liberal interpretation to the express provisions and, in more recent times, has found implications in the Constitution which do guarantee, at least in the federal sphere, some rights and freedoms.

Express Protection

The first of the express provisions is section 51(xxxi). It empowers the Commonwealth to acquire property compulsorily, but the power is conditioned upon the provision of 'just terms'[23] for the property acquired. Construing the term 'property' liberally,[24] the High Court has invested the subsection with the function of protecting an extensive miscellany of private economic interests. Next, s 80, which guarantees trial by jury for indictable offences against laws of the Commonwealth precludes not only any other mode of trial[25] for such indictable offences but also any conviction by mere majority verdict.[26] But s 80 is a defective guarantee, as it is possible for the Parliament to create serious offences which are not indictable[27] or to provide increased maximum penalties for indictable offences if, after conviction by the jury, a judge finds that there were accompanying circumstances of aggravation.[28]

Section 116 is an important provision for the protection of human rights. It prohibits the establishment of a State religion.[29] It also prohibits the imposition of any religious observance or the requirement of any religious test as a qualification for public office. In *Church of the New Faith v Commissioner of Payroll Tax (Vict)*[30] Mason ACJ and I observed: 'Freedom of religion, the paradigm freedom of conscience, is of the essence of a free society. The chief function in the law of a definition of religion is to mark out an area within which a person subject to the law is free to believe and to act in accordance with his belief without legal restraint.'[31]

We expressed the opinion that 'Protection is accorded to preserve the dignity and freedom of each man so that he may adhere to any religion of his choosing or to none.' The parties in that case had agreed that the issue on which the litigation turned was 'Is Scientology a religion?' The High Court accepted this issue for determination, noting that the case would be relevant to the constitutional guarantee of freedom of religion contained in s 116. To answer the question proposed, we held: 'that, for the purposes of the law, the criteria of religion are twofold: first, belief in a supernatural Being, Thing or Principle; and second, the acceptance of canons of conduct in order to give effect to that belief, though canons of conduct which offend against the ordinary laws are outside the area of any immunity, privilege or right conferred on the grounds of religion.'[32]

Wilson and Deane JJ added three other indicia, namely, that the ideas relate to man's nature and place in the universe and his relations to things supernatural, that adherents constitute an identifiable group or groups and that the adherents see the collection of beliefs or practices as a religion.[33]

Although the Court gave a broad interpretation to 'religion', it declared that the constitutional freedom of religion does not convert adherence to religious belief or practice into a justification or excuse for contravention of the general laws which preserve and protect society.[34]

One of the strongly contested debates in the Constitutional Convention of 1898 related to the precursors of s 117 of the *Constitution*. Section 117 protects any citizen resident in one State from any disability or discrimination in another State which would not be equally applicable if the citizen were a resident of the other State. For many years, s 117 was given an extremely limited application. When Mr Henry, a Victorian legal practitioner and a resident of Victoria, sought admission to practice in South Australia, he was met with a residential requirement for those seeking admission in reliance on admission in another State. A majority of the High Court held that s 117 was not offended by that requirement as any resident of South Australia seeking admission in reliance on admission in another State would have to satisfy the same residential requirement.[35] That decision, and the general approach to s 117, was changed by the unanimous decision of the Court in *Street v Queensland Bar Association*, Mason CJ observing: 'The very object of federation was to bring into existence one nation and one people. This section is one of the comparatively few provisions in the *Constitution* which was designed to enhance national unity and a real sense of national identity by eliminating disability or discrimination on account of residence in another State.'[36]

Street, a member of the New South Wales Bar and a Sydney resident, objected to the Queensland rules for admission which contained a residential qualification. Mason CJ applied the principle – 'that s 117 renders a disability or discrimination invalid if the notional fact of residence within the legislating State would effectively remove the disability or discrimination or substantially deprive it of its onerous nature.'[37]

I expressed the view that 'The law, which today pushes open the doors of the Supreme Court of Queensland for entry by suitably qualified barristers admitted and practising in other States, opens too the doors of State universities, hospitals and other institutions for entry by subjects of the Queen resident in other States on the same terms as residents of the relevant State.'

Although discrimination on grounds of residence seems to be outlawed by s 117, opinion has been divided on the question whether Commonwealth laws should have a uniform operation throughout the Commonwealth. In *Leeth v The Commonwealth,*[38] a majority judgment denied that the *Constitution* required uniformity of operation,[39] and a minority judgment held that the *Constitution* required 'equality of the people of the Commonwealth under the law and before the courts',[40] but no clear view emerged.[41]

The notorious provisions of s 92 declare that 'trade, commerce and intercourse among the States ... shall be absolutely free'. The absolute freedom of personal movement guaranteed by the section is a freedom to pass to and fro among the States without burden, hindrance or restriction[42] but this freedom is consistent with restrictions that are an incidental consequence of a measure which is appropriate and adapted to achieving some reasonable regulation for the protection or order of the community.[43] In earlier times, s 92 was invoked to protect the individual rights of traders, but in *Cole v Whitfield*[44] the Court gave the section a more restricted operation in relation to trade and commerce, proscribing discriminatory burdens of a protectionist kind.[45]

Implied Protection

Perhaps the limitations on governmental power implied in the *Constitution* are of greater significance to the protection of rights and freedoms than the express provisions. These implications are derived not from international treaties which declare human rights or fundamental freedoms, but from the text and structure of the *Constitution*. The joint judgment of the Court in *AMS v AIF* declared that the *Constitution's* provisions 'are not to be construed as subject to an implication said to be derived from international law'.[46]

The implications relevant to the protection of rights and freedoms fall into three general categories – categories which are not exhaustive of all the implications to be found in the *Constitution*. The first, and most fundamental, is that the *Constitution* assumes the rule of law. In *Australian Communist Party v The Commonwealth*,[47] Dixon J stated that the *Constitution*: 'is an instrument framed in accordance with many traditional conceptions, to some of which it gives effect, as, for example, in separating the judicial power from other functions of government, others of which are simply assumed. Among these I think that it may fairly be said that the rule of law forms an assumption.'[48]

The rule of law itself imports the common law[49] which is the matrix in which the *Constitution* and the laws of the Commonwealth are to be found. The common law then informs the express provisions of the *Constitution* and, in particular, it affects the interpretation of Ch III – *The Judicature*. Thus, it ensures that jurisdiction is exercised in accordance with the rules of natural justice.[50]

Significant implications arise from Ch III. The separation of judicial power from the legislative and executive powers of the Commonwealth and the reposing of judicial power exclusively in courts specified in s 71 of the

Constitution[51] are features of the *Constitution* which have been seen to afford significant protection for individuals against the exercise of political power. Political power characteristically responds to majoritarian sentiment, but judicial power focuses on individual rights and liabilities.

In an early series of cases,[52] the High Court established that the judicial power of the Commonwealth can be exercised only by the courts in which federal jurisdiction can be and is vested pursuant to s 71. The concept of judicial power 'is not susceptible of precise and comprehensive definition'[53] but the definition which Griffith CJ propounded in *Huddart Parker* has been widely accepted: 'the power which every sovereign authority must of necessity have to decide controversies between its subjects, or between itself and its subjects, whether the rights relate to life, liberty or property.'[54]

In *R v Davison*, Dixon CJ and McTiernan J said that – 'the ascertainment of existing rights by the judicial determination of issues of fact or law falls exclusively within judicial power so that the Parliament cannot confide the function to any person or body but a court constituted under ss 71 and 72 of the Constitution.'[55]

The content of judicial power is established by judicial exegesis and is immune from modification or diminution by the Parliament or from influence by the Executive Government.[56] In *Chu Kheng Lim v Minister for Immigration*[57] it was said that the legislative power did not extend 'to the making of a law which requires or authorizes the courts in which the judicial power of the Commonwealth is exclusively vested to exercise judicial power in a manner which is inconsistent with the essential character of a court or with the nature of judicial power.'[58]

Although a set of exhaustive criteria for determining what is the 'essential character of a court or the nature of judicial power' has not been, and probably cannot be, settled, it has been said that 'it may well be that any attempt on the part of the legislature to cause a court to act in a manner contrary to natural justice would impose a non-judicial requirement inconsistent with the exercise of judicial power.'[59]

A court must act impartially between the parties.[60]

If Parliament purports to direct the courts as to the manner or outcome of the exercise of their jurisdiction, it would constitute 'an impermissible intrusion into the judicial power which Ch III vests exclusively in the courts which it designates.'[61] The principal limitation on legislative power – a limitation which protects the liberty of individuals and restricts the power to inflict penalties on both individuals and corporations – was established in *Waterside Workers' Federation of Australia v J W Alexander Ltd.*[62] Griffith CJ declared that 'convictions for offences and the imposition of penalties and punishments are matters appertaining exclusively to the judicial power'. In *Re Tracey; Ex parte Ryan*,[63] Deane J asserted that 'The guilt of the citizen of a criminal offence and the liability of the citizen under the law, either to a fellow citizen or to the State, can be conclusively determined only by a Ch III court acting as such, that is to say, acting judicially.'

So it was that, in *Polyukovitch v The Commonwealth*,[64] six Justices noted, without dissent, that a law which imposed penal consequences on an individual or an identifiable group without a judicial trial would amount to a usurpation of judicial power. Such a law would be tantamount to a Bill of Attainder or a Bill of Pains and Penalties and would be invalid as offending Ch III of the *Constitution*. Similarly, a law which purports to vest any part of the function of adjudging and punishing criminal guilt under a law of the Commonwealth in the executive government is a usurpation of judicial power and invalid.[65]

In *R v Kidman*, Isaacs J said that 'punishment, whether regarded as retribution or a as deterrent, is beyond the scope of the executive power.'[66] Putting to one side the instances of committal pending trial and involuntary detention in cases of mental illness and infectious disease as exceptions, three Justices in *Chu Kheng Lim v Minister for Immigration*, asserted that 'the involuntary detention of a citizen in custody by the State is penal or punitive in character and, under our system of government, exists only as an incident of the exclusively judicial function of adjudging and punishing criminal guilt.'[67]

The common law and statutory powers of arrest are no exception to this rule. Those powers can be exercised only as an incident of the judicial function unless a valid statute otherwise provides.[68] If the stated exceptions are exhaustive of the instances when executive power may be exercised to detain a citizen in custody,[69] Ch III affords constitutional protection to citizens and perhaps to non-citizens against the extra-judicial imposition of penal or punitive measures by Commonwealth authorities.[70] In the absence of valid statutory authority, the executive government cannot authorize the extra-judicial arrest or detention of a person. In *Re Bolton; Ex Parte Beane* Deane J said: 'The common law of Australia knows no lettre de cachet or executive warrant pursuant to which either citizen or alien can be deprived of his freedom by mere administrative decision or action'.[71]

The importance of maintaining the safeguards, and preserving public confidence, in the exercise of federal judicial power led the Court in *Kable v Director of Public Prosecutions (NSW)*[72] to hold invalid a State law which required the Supreme Court of the State to make a 'preventive detention order' against a named person (Kable) if, on the balance of probabilities, the Court was satisfied that he might commit a serious act of violence. A majority of the Court held that that function was incompatible with the integrity, independence and impartiality of the Supreme Court as a court in which federal jurisdiction had been invested under Ch III. An exercise of that function 'might lead an ordinary member of the public to conclude that the [Supreme] Court was not independent of the executive government of the State'.[73]

Of course, the invocation of judicial power does not prevent the Parliament from exercising its legislative power to affect rights and liabilities generally, even if the legislation affects a right which is in issue in the judicial proceedings.[74] Legislative power is not paralysed by litigation.

Section 75(v) of the *Constitution* confers on the High Court jurisdiction to issue writs of mandamus and prohibition and injunctions against officers of the Commonwealth, including the judges of federal courts.[75] The significance of that subsection was spelt out in a joint judgment of six members of the Court in *Plaintiff S157/2002 v Commonwealth of Australia* who observed that –

> The reservation to this Court by the Constitution of the jurisdiction in all matters in which the named constitutional writs or an injunction are sought against an officer of the Commonwealth is a means of assuring to all people affected that officers of the Commonwealth obey the law and neither exceed nor neglect any jurisdiction which the law confers on them. The centrality, and protective purpose, of the jurisdiction of this Court in that regard places significant barriers in the way of legislative attempts (by privative clauses or otherwise) to impair judicial review of administrative action. Such jurisdiction exists to maintain the federal compact by ensuring that propounded laws are constitutionally valid and ministerial or other official action lawful and within jurisdiction.[76]

The constitutionally vested jurisdiction of the High Court, especially the jurisdiction vested by s 75(v), is the lynchpin of freedom under the law in Australia.

The text and structure of the *Constitution* also imply a freedom of political speech and action.[77] When the incidental power (s 51(xxxix)) was relied on in *Davis v The Commonwealth*[78] to support a law forbidding the use of '1788' or '1988' in conjunction with certain other words in connection with the official celebration of the Bicentenary of European settlement in Australia, I took the view that 'freedom of speech can hardly be an incidental casualty of an activity undertaken by the executive government to advance a nation which boasts of its freedom.'

Although there is no equivalent to the 1st Amendment of the *Constitution of the United States* in the *Constitution* of the Commonwealth, the provisions[79] relating to the membership and election of the Houses of the Parliament and the constitution of the executive government mandate a legislature and executive of the Westminster kind, that is to say, responsible and representative government. This led Deane and Toohey JJ in *Nationwide News Pty Ltd v Wills* to hold that 'there is to be discerned in the doctrine of representative government ... an implication of freedom of communication of information and opinions about matters relating to the government of the Commonwealth.'[80]

I was of the same opinion.[81] The implied freedom of communication about matters relating to the government of the Commonwealth was firmly established in a series of cases – *Australian Capital Television Pty Ltd v The Commonwealth,*[82] *Theophanous v The Herald and Weekly Times*[83] and *Stephens v West Australian Newspapers Ltd*[84] – and a unanimous Court in *Lange v The Australian Broadcasting Corporation* held that '[f]reedom of communication on matters of government and politics is an indispensable incident of that system of representative government which the Constitution creates'.[85] But that freedom is not absolute. As Gaudron J pointed out in *ACTV*: 'As the implied freedom is one that depends substantially on the general law, its limits are also marked out by the general law. Thus, in general terms, the laws which have developed to regulate speech, including the laws with respect to defamation, sedition, blasphemy, obscenity and offensive language, will indicate the kind of regulation that is consistent with the freedom of political discourse.'[86]

My view was that permissible regulation could not impair unduly the freedom of informed political discussion essential to the maintenance of a system of responsible government and that the boundary of the implied freedom depended on the subject matter of the law which was impugned as attacking the freedom.[87]

How does the freedom operate? For a time, there was some dissension as to the relationship between the implied freedom and the laws of defamation. Unanimity was reached in *Lange* where it was held that the common law of libel and slander could not be developed inconsistently with the *Constitution* and that the categories of qualified privilege in Australia are extended accordingly.[88] The extended privilege is lost if the conduct of the person making the publication is unreasonable. Statutes which derogate from that privilege are invalid.

Statutory Interpretation

The High Court applied the common law presumption[89] in interpreting a variety of statutes, as the joint judgment pointed out in *Wentworth v New South Wales Bar Association.*[90] 'There are certain matters in relation to which legislative provisions will be construed as effecting no more than is strictly required by clear words or as a matter of necessary implication.[91] They include important common law rights,[92] procedural[93] and other[94] safeguards of individual rights and freedoms and the jurisdiction of superior courts.'[95]

Among the freedoms protected by the presumption, liberty of the person is especially important. Restraint on personal freedom in exercising a statutory power is not justified unless the statute necessitates a construction conferring a power to restrain. In *Re Bolton; Ex parte Beane* Deane J declared the general rule that 'subject to extradition and migration legislation, every person coming from abroad, as soon as he sets foot in Australia without breach of Australian law, is free.'[96] I noted that 'The law of this country is very jealous of any infringement of personal liberty[97] and a statute or statutory instrument which purports to impair a right to personal liberty is interpreted, if possible, so as to respect that right.'[98]

And the majority, construing a statute which authorized the arrest and detention of deserters from the armed forces of the United States, denied that the statute applied when the desertion occurred outside Australia, even though the Minister's second reading speech had asserted that the statute did so.[99]

The same limiting construction was applied to a statute relied on to justify an intrusion on the free enjoyment of property. When the owner of land in the Territory of the Cocos (Keeling) Islands challenged a purported compulsory acquisition of his land by the Commonwealth for the purpose of achieving a social policy in the Territory, the Commonwealth supported the acquisition by relying on a statutory power to acquire land for 'any purpose in relation to that Territory'. The Court construed the statute as conferring the power only for a 'purpose related to a need for or proposed use … or application of the land to be acquired.'[100] The joint judgment affirmed that 'An executive power to deprive a citizen of his property by compulsory acquisition should be construed as being confined within the scope of what is granted by the clear meaning or necessary intendment of the words by which it is conferred.'

Taking the same approach to a statute providing for the issue of search warrants authorizing intrusion on private property, the Court insisted on strict compliance with the statutory conditions, saying: 'in construing and applying such statutes, it needs to be kept in mind that they authorize the invasion of interests which the common law has always valued highly and which.... it went to great lengths to protect.'[101]

Accordingly, a statute empowering a judge to authorize the use of a listening device was not construed as empowering the judge to authorize its secretive emplacement on private property. The Court held that as: 'there is no clear expression in the legislation of an unmistakable and unambiguous intention to confer such a power... it cannot be said that there is to be implied in [the relevant section] power in a judge to authorize conduct which otherwise would amount to a trespass.'[102]

Similarly, when a process server sought to justify entry on private premises to serve a summons by relying on a statute giving the process-server an option as to the manner of service, the Court declined to construe the statute 'as conferring a right to enter private premises without consent'.[103]

Freedom from arbitrary treatment is safeguarded by judicial review of statutory discretions. When statute creates a discretionary power which may be exercised to affect the interests of an individual or a discrete group, the individual or group is presumed to be entitled to have notice of and to deal with material adverse to those interests[104] and to be heard[105] by the repository of the power. If the implied obligation of procedural fairness is not excluded by the statute conferring the power, an absence of procedural fairness will ordinarily entitle a person adversely affected by a decision taken in purported exercise of the power to have the decision set aside.[106] Even a privative clause enacted to protect decisions 'under the Act' from judicial review will be ineffective to oust the court's jurisdiction.[107]

The freedom to be silent when charged with an offence has been a tradition of administering criminal justice in the courts of the common law.[108] Consistently with that tradition, the courts have recognized the privilege of a witness to refuse to answer questions if the answer may tend to incriminate him or to subject him to a penalty. The High Court has held that those privileges may be invoked by a witness called before a statutory Commission of Inquiry[109] or a person required to answer questions by a Commission having a statutory power to require answers under the *Trade Practices Act 1974* (Cth).[110] In like manner, the common law privilege against disclosure of confidential communications between client and legal adviser is regarded as a fundamental common law right[111] which is not abrogated by statute unless the contrary appears in the clearest terms.[112]

Although the Court presumes that the common law's balance of freedom and restriction is intended to be left unaffected by the legislature unless modified by express terms or necessary intendment, that general approach is not applied if the purpose of the statute is to advance human rights and fundamental freedoms. Then the court construes the statute to give full effect to its terms. Conspicuous examples of this class of statutes are those which incorporate international instruments which declare, or international norms which reflect, human rights and fundamental freedoms. Then the governing rule of construction is that the terms in the statute corresponding with terms in the international instrument or norm are given the same meaning as the meaning which international law attributes to the corresponding term in the instrument or norm.[113] That rule is really a particular example of a rule of wider application expressed in the joint judgment in *AMS v AIF*: ' . . . it has been accepted that a statute of the Commonwealth or of a State is to be interpreted and applied, so far as its language permits, so that it is in conformity and not in conflict with established rules of international law.'[114]

By construing statutory language to accord with the meaning of corresponding language in international instruments and in the expression of international norms, Australian statutes which incorporate those instruments or norms are kept in conformity with international law and are so construed as to comply with international obligations assumed by Australia.[115] But when an international instrument is incorporated in a statute and declares human rights and fundamental freedoms in open-textured terms, difficult questions of interpretation arise and, not infrequently, those questions have significant political implications. One party may rely on the generality of a right expressed in an open-textured statute while the opponent contends for a restriction.

Thus in *Mabo v Queensland*[116] – *Mabo [No 1]* – the critical question related to the operation of s 10 of the *Racial Discrimination Act* 1975 (Cth.) which picked up the provisions of Article 5 in the *International Convention on the Elimination of All Forms of Racial Discrimination ('the CERD')*. Pursuant to that section, a particular race – the Meriam people – were entitled to enjoy the human rights to own property and to inherit to the same extent as other races in the community. When a challenge was raised to the *Queensland Coast Islands Declaratory Act 1985* (Qld) ('the Queensland Act') which purported to extinguish the title of the Meriam people to their traditional land, they invoked the *Racial Discrimination Act 1975* (Cth) to protect their enjoyment of the rights declared in Article 5 of the *CERD*. The case proceeded on the assumption that the common law recognized the title of the Meriam people to their traditional land, that is, native title – an assumption that was not verified until *Mabo [No 2]*.[117] The Court was narrowly divided in *Mabo [No 1]*. The majority held that, as native title was characteristically vested in the Miriam people, the Queensland Act which purported to extinguish their right to own and to inherit native title land placed them at a disadvantage in comparison with others who were unaffected in their enjoyment of rights over land in the Murray Islands. That operation of the Queensland Act was held to impair the human rights of the Meriam people. The minority did not perceive any relevant inequality in the enjoyment of rights. Wilson J thought that s 10 of the *Racial Discrimination Act 1975* (Cth) was not attracted as there was 'no suggestion… that there are any persons of another race who enjoy the same rights of which the [Meriam people] have been deprived by the Queensland Act.' There was divergence in identifying the human rights declared in Article 5 of the *CERD* and protected by s 10 of the *Racial Discrimination Act 1975* (Cth).

If an international instrument is incorporated in a valid law of the Commonwealth, the impact of any declaration of human rights and fundamental freedoms on the statute laws and executive powers of the States and Territories may be a source of frustration to their governments.[118] By force of s 109 of the *Constitution,* a law of the Commonwealth which embodies an international standard prevails over any inconsistent State law and may govern the exercise of executive power under State law.[119] By the combined operation of that section and s 51(xxix) – the external affairs power – international standards of human rights and fundamental freedoms may become effective constraints on the legislative and executive powers of State governments. Territory governments are similarly constrained by the directly binding effect of Commonwealth law.

Even if an international instrument or a principle of international law affecting human rights is not incorporated into Australian law, it may have some effect on the operation of domestic law in any of three ways: it may affect the interpretation given to a domestic statute; it may affect the factors material to the exercise of a statutory discretion and it may influence the judicial development of the common law. *Teoh's Case*[120] is the highwater mark of the non-statutory effects on domestic law of human rights standards expressed in international instruments which, though not incorporated into domestic law, are binding on Australia internationally. Mason CJ and Deane J held that '[i]f the language of the legislation is susceptible of a construction which is consistent with the terms of the international instrument and the obligations which it imposes on Australia, then that construction should prevail.'[121] Moreover, when by ratification the Government states that the Government and its agencies will act in accordance with a Convention, especially a Convention dealing with human rights affecting the family and children, that ratification founds a legitimate expectation that the Government and its agencies will so act. And, 'if a decision-maker proposes to make a decision inconsistent with a legitimate expectation, procedural fairness requires that the persons affected should be given notice and an adequate opportunity of presenting a case against the taking of such a course.'[122] Further, their Honours held,[123] a binding international Convention 'especially one which declares universal fundamental rights, may be used by the courts as a legitimate guide in developing the common law'.[124] Their Honours accepted that '[t]he common law does not necessarily conform with international law, but international law is a legitimate and important influence on the development of the common law, especially when international law declares the existence of universal human rights.'[125]

The Common Law Protection of International Human Rights

The protection of rights and freedoms by the common law depends upon the availability of common law rights of action.

Of course, the common law is a fragile protection of human rights in the sense that protection may be reduced or stripped away by statute. But, as we have seen, the rules for the construction of statutes go some of the way towards ensuring the integrity of the common law's protection. As there is a political inhibition tending to restrain statutory incursions into human rights, the argument against constitutionally entrenching human rights is readily understood. But does the common law provide sufficient protection of human rights assuming an absence of statutory interference? It would be impossible to canvass the entirety of the common law in order to elicit all the protective mechanisms but cases in the High Court give an indication of the scope of common law protections. I mention some of them which give a measure of protection to rights and freedoms contained in the *Universal Declaration of Human Rights*.

Article 2: Everyone is entitled to all the rights and freedoms set forth in this Declaration, without distinction of any kind, such as race, colour, sex, language, religion, political or other opinion, national or social origin, property, birth or other status.

Following *Mabo [No 1]*, the parties turned their attention to the question whether the common law recognized native title, that is to say, the rights in respect of land enjoyed by indigenous Australians by reason of their occupation of the land prior to European settlement. *Mabo [No 2]*[126] gave an affirmative answer to that question. In the present context, it is unnecessary to consider the path of judicial reasoning which led to that result. Suffice to note that the majority judgments manifested the same approach to the common law as the approach enjoined by Article 2 of the *Universal Declaration of Human*

Rights. Deane and Gaudron JJ, rejecting the propositions that in 1788 the territory of New South Wales was *terra nullius* and that the Crown took full beneficial ownership of the land unaffected by the claims of the Aboriginal inhabitants, explained the history of land settlement since 1788 saying: 'The official endorsement, by administrative practice and in judgments of the courts, of those two propositions provided the environment in which the Aboriginal people of the continent came to be treated as a different and lower form of life whose very existence could be ignored for the purpose of determining the legal right to occupy and use their traditional homelands.'[127]

Their Honours held that the common law recognized traditional native title derived from native law or custom, varying 'according to the extent of the pre-existing interest of the relevant individual, group or community.' Speaking of the proposition that Aboriginal social organization was so undeveloped that the common law could not recognize native title derived from their laws and customs, I observed with the concurrence of Mason CJ and McHugh J that 'it is imperative in today's world that the common law should neither be nor be seen to be frozen in an age of racial discrimination' and that '[t]he fiction by which the rights and interests of indigenous inhabitants in land were treated as non-existent was justified by a policy which has no place in the contemporary law of this country.'

The *Mabo* litigation has generated a vast jurisprudence as the nation strives to balance two centuries of injustice to the indigenous people with the rights which have become vested in others. The absence of immediate and simple solutions in cases involving human rights is to be expected for there will often be a contest between the rights of a majority and the interests of a minority. If open-textured standards of human rights are enacted, as in the *Racial Discrimination Act 1975* (Cth) on which *Mabo* was based, their precise content may have to be worked out in a succession of cases. That is a price worth paying when the common law needs statutory assistance to secure substantive equality before the law.

Article 3: The right to life, liberty and security of person.

The laws proscribing culpable homicide, criminal negligence, assault and battery and the torts which give compensation for personal injury are the most direct mechanisms for the protection of life. Those laws seek to balance personal integrity and the exigencies of ordinary life and human experience. Thus, the life and limb of a trespasser is entitled to protection under the general law of negligence. In *Hackshaw v Shaw*[128] where a farmer lay in wait at night for trespassing thieves and fired at their car when he should have known that a passenger might be in the car, the injured passenger was held entitled to damages. Deane J observed: 'References to the 'humane man' and 'common humanity' are not inappropriate in describing the reasonable care which should be exercised by the reasonable man of the common law when it is reasonably foreseeable that his actions or omissions are likely to injure a trespasser who has forced a relationship of proximity upon him.'

Liberty is secured by the constitutional limitation on executive power to imprison, by the writ of habeas corpus,[129] and the general provisions of the common law especially the rules of criminal law and practice and the tort of false imprisonment.

Security of the person is protected chiefly by the law of trespass, assault and battery. Those laws were invoked to protect the physical integrity of an intellectually disabled girl in *Marion's Case*[130] where a majority of the Court held that non-therapeutic surgical sterilization, albeit with the consent of the girl's parents or guardians, would be unlawful without an order of the Family Court. I dissented, holding that the common law forbad non-therapeutic sterilization, even with the consent of the parents or guardians and that the Family Court had no jurisdiction to make an order approving sterilization.[131] Cases of this kind, which raise bioethical issues affecting personal integrity and the terminal stages of life, will increase in number and difficulty with the increasing efficacy of medical science. Although the High Court has not had to grapple yet with problems of the kind faced by the House of Lords in *Anthony Bland,*[132] it is clear that the laws governing personal integrity and the terminal stages of life will grow in sophistication.

Article 10: Everyone is entitled in full equality to a fair and public hearing by an independent and impartial tribunal, in the determination of his rights and obligations and of any criminal charge against him.

Article 11: Everyone charged with a penal offence has the right to be presumed innocent until proved guilty according to law in a public trial at which he has had all the guarantees necessary for his defence.

The equality of every person before the court is at the heart of the rule of law as understood by the common law. To ensure that equality, an independent and impartial tribunal is required. In a series of cases, the High Court has laid down strict criteria of independence and impartiality. The rule is that a challenge to a decision on the ground of want of impartiality will succeed if 'in all the circumstances the parties or the public might entertain a reasonable apprehension that the judge might not bring an impartial and unprejudiced mind to the resolution of the matter before him' or her.[133] Thus, no judge may adjudicate in a case in the outcome of which he or she might have a financial interest, but the holding of a parcel of shares in a public company will not be regarded as a disqualifying interest if the effect of the litigation or its outcome cannot reasonably be expected to affect the value of those shares.[134] An 'independent and impartial tribunal' is, of course, essential for the fair trial of a person charged with a criminal offence, but fairness in that jurisdiction calls for more than an independent and impartial tribunal.

The right to a fair trial has been the subject of frequent consideration in the High Court although it is not really a 'right'. In *Jago v District Court (NSW)* Deane J observed that 'Strictly speaking, ... there is no such directly enforceable "right" [to a fair trial] since no person has the right to insist upon being prosecuted or tried by the State. What is involved is more accurately expressed in negative terms as a right not to be tried unfairly or as an immunity against conviction otherwise than after a fair trial.'[135]

In *Dietrich v R,* Mason CJ and McHugh J observed that the right to a fair trial 'is manifested in rules of law and of practice designed to regulate the course of the trial' but there had been no judicial attempt to list exhaustively the attributes of a fair trial.[136] The basic structure of a fair trial in Anglo-Australian jurisprudence follows from the approach taken to proof of guilt. In *R v Mullen,*[137] the High Court adopted the 'golden thread' of the criminal law, taken from the seminal decision of *Woolmington v DPP,*[138] that the prosecution must prove guilt beyond reasonable doubt. If, on a charge of murder, intent to kill is an element, the prosecution must prove that the accused had an actual intent and it is not sufficient to rely merely on a presumption that a person is taken to intend the natural consequences of his acts.[139] To prove that the act constituting the offence was a willed act, however, 'the prosecution may rely on the inference that an act done by an apparently conscious actor is willed or voluntary... unless there are grounds for believing that the accused was unable to control that act.'[140]

The entire complex of rules governing criminal procedure is intended to secure fairness to both the prosecution and the defence. Some of the rules relate to practice, some to the admissibility of evidence, some to the directions which a judge must or ought to give to a jury, some to the verdict and sentence. By way of example, the High Court has held that a trial should be stayed until committal proceedings are first held,[141] that similar fact evidence should not be admitted against an accused in a criminal trial unless its probative value clearly transcends its merely prejudicial effect,[142] that a warning must be given to the jury whenever needed to avoid a perceptible risk of miscarriage of justice,[143] that no adverse inference can be drawn against an accused person by reason of a failure to answer questions or provide information about the occurrence of an offence, the identity of the participants or the roles which they played[144] and that a verdict of guilty requires the agreement of all the jurors.[145]

The effect of adverse media publicity has occasioned some concern. Proceedings for contempt of court go some of the distance towards ensuring fairness of a subsequent trial. In affirming a conviction for contempt, Deane J said: 'The ability of a society to provide a fair and unprejudiced trial is an indispensable basis of any acceptable justification of the restraints and penalties of the criminal law. It is difficult, if not impossible, to envisage any situation in which countervailing public interest considerations could outweigh the detriment to the due administration of justice involved in public prejudgment by the mass media of the guilt of a person awaiting trial.'[146]

But in *R v Glennon*, the High Court balanced the accused's right to a fair trial, which was allegedly affected by extensive media coverage, against the 'community's right to expect that a person accused of a serious criminal offence will be brought to trial.'[147] In light of this competing consideration, the Court held that 'a conviction be quashed as unsafe and unsatisfactory only where the materials justify a conclusion that there was a likelihood or substantial risk of prejudice arising from pre-trial publication'.[148]

Article 20(1): Everyone has the right to a freedom of peaceful assembly and association.

Even if a peaceful assembly is declared unlawful by statute, the common law does not impose a civil liability for participation in the assembly. In *Williams v Hursey,*[149] an assembly, being a 'picket line' that was used to prevent the plaintiffs, non-union employees, from presenting themselves for employment was proscribed under the *Stevedoring Industry Act* (Cth).[150] Nonetheless, Fullagar J denied 'that taking part in an unlawful assembly was a tortious act as against the plaintiffs. Wrongful acts, giving rise to a cause of action for damages, may be committed in the course of an unlawful assembly, but the civil liability which arises is for those wrongful acts, and not for membership of the unlawful assembly as such.'

Article 22: Everyone, as a member of society, has the right to social security and is entitled to realization, through national effort and international cooperation and in accordance with the organization and resources of each State, of the economic, social and cultural rights indispensable for his dignity and the free development of his personality.

This Article goes beyond the reach of the common law. If a court were to order the satisfaction of the right, it would necessitate the making of an order requiring the exercise of governmental power in a particular way. That has been done in other countries under a Bill or Charter of Rights, but not in Australia. In the United States, when the Supreme Court held in *Brown v Board of Education of Topeka*[151] that segregation in public education deprived negro children of equal protection of the laws under the Fourteenth Amendment, the Court acknowledged that 'decrees in these cases present problems of considerable complexity'. In *Grootboom v South Africa,*[152] the State was ordered 'to devise and implement within its available resources a comprehensive and coordinated programme progressively to realize the right of access to adequate housing' and in *Minister of Health v Treatment Action Campaign*,[153] the Constitutional Court ordered the South African Government 'to devise and implement within its available resources a comprehensive and coordinated programme to realize progressively the rights of pregnant women and their newborn children to have access to health services to combat mother-to-child transmission of HIV'.

Conclusion

The common law has a long tradition of protecting rights and freedoms. No doubt rhetoric has embellished the reality. The vigour of that tradition appears in the High Court's judgments. But the common law cannot itself secure full protection of human rights and fundamental freedoms. Indeed, without a constitutional entrenching of a Bill of Rights the courts cannot secure individual rights against overreaching by the political branches of government. But should the responsibility for the protection of rights and freedoms rest solely or chiefly on the judiciary or should it rest also, perhaps chiefly, on the Parliament and the Executive? I leave the answer to others. If the judiciary is to bear greater responsibility for protecting rights and freedoms, it must be commanded to do so by constitutional amendment or statutory enactment. The language of such provisions will necessarily be open textured and new approaches to interpretation will emerge. In *Applicant A,* McHugh J said: '[I]nternational treaties often fail to exhibit the precision of domestic legislation. This is the sometimes necessary price paid for multinational political comity. The lack of precision in treaties confirms the need to adopt interpretative principles, ... which are founded on the view that treaties "cannot be expected to be applied with taut logical precision".'[154]

To determine the content of a broadly expressed right which overrides other legal rules, a court must reverse the methodology for developing the common law. The common law methodology is fact-based. From the facts of particular cases, a general rule is developed. But if a judgment starts by defining the scope of an open textured right or freedom in isolation from the facts of the case, application of that definition in particular cases may produce anomalous results.

The High Court is not unfamiliar with problems of that kind. For generations it grappled with the notion that the constitutional provision that trade among the States should be absolutely free[155] conferred individual rights on traders to carry on their activities free of governmental controls. The Court attempted repeatedly to develop a coherent and consistent body of principle to determine what controls were permissible in an ordered society but the attempts were unsuccessful. It was only when the Court rejected the individual rights theory that the problem was resolved and the section interpreted as proscribing the imposition of burdens on interstate trade and commerce which are protective of intrastate trade and commerce of the same kind.[156]

Although the introduction of broad international standards of human rights into domestic legislation raises difficulties of interpretation, it nevertheless offers opportunities for the judicial development of new principles which can eliminate instances of long standing injustice. As international human rights law expands, we can anticipate an increasing incorporation of international standards into our domestic law. We may not incorporate a Bill of Rights in our *Constitution*, but we may expect some interesting challenges as we accommodate our law and our practice to international aspirations for human rights and fundamental freedoms.

---

1. An edited version of this paper was published in Peter Cane (ed), *Centenary essays for the High Court of Australia* (LexisNexis Butterworths, 2004) 355.
2. See *Rex v Haddock: Is it a Free Country?* Reported in "Uncommon Law" (3rd Edn.) (1937) 24, 28
3. (1997) 189 CLR 520, 564.
4. See *Attorney-General v Guardian Newspapers [No 2]* [1990] 1 AC 109, 283.
5. (1991) 171 CLR 635, 639, (Mason CJ, Brennan & Toohey JJ).
6. (1765) 19 St Tr 1029, 1066.
7. (1986) 161 CLR 278, 292 (Mason & Brennan JJ).
8. See *Potter v Minahan* (1908) 7 CLR 277, 304), and see, also *Ex Parte Walsh and Johnson; In re Yates* (1925) 37 CLR 36, 93.
9. (1990) 171 CLR 1, 18 (Mason CJ, Deane, Dawson, Toohey, Gaudron & McHugh JJ).
10. See *Re Bolton; Ex parte Beane* (1987) 162 CLR 514, 523; *Potter v Minahan* (1908) 7 CLR 277, 1065 (Browne-Wilkinson LJ).
11. (1992) 177 CLR 1, 43.
12. See *Waters v Public Transport Commission* (1991) 173 CLR 349, 359, 372, 394, 406-7; IW *v City of Perth* (1998) 191 CLR 1; Kate Eastman and Chris Ronalds, *'Using Human*

Rights Laws in Litigation' in David Kinley (ed), *Human Rights in Australia Law* (The Federation Press, Sydney, 1998) 325.

13. David Kinley (ed), *Human Rights in Australia Law* (The Federation Press, Sydney, 1998) 333.
14. See *Lange v Australian Broadcasting Commission* (1997) 189 CLR 520
15. Dias RWM, "Götterdammerung – gods of the law in decline" (1981) 1(1) *Legal Studies* 3, 13.
16. Murray Gleeson, 'The Rule of Law and the Independence of the Judiciary' (1989) 1 *Judicial Officers' Bulletin* No 10, 2.
17. See *Clunies-Ross v The Commonwealth* (1984) 155 CLR 193, 204.
18. See *Victoria v The Commonwealth* (1996) 187 CLR 416, 481; *Minister for Immigration and Ethnic Affairs v Teoh* (1995) 183 CLR 273.
19. See *Attorney General (Cth.) (Ex rel. McKinlay) v The Commonwealth* (1975) 135 CLR 1, 24 (Barwick CJ).
20. (1992) 177 CLR 106, 136.
21. Dawson J expressed a similar view in *Kruger v The Commonwealth* (1997) 190 CLR 1.
22. (1999) 168 CLR 461, 521
23. See *Bank of New South Wales v The Commonwealth* (1948) 76 CLR 1, 349-350; *Nintendo Co Ltd v Centronic Systems Pty Ltd* (1994) 181 CLR 134.
24. See *Australian Tape Manufacturers Association Ltd v The Commonwealth* (1993) 176 CLR 480, 509; *Georgiadis v Australian and Overseas Telecommunications Corporation* (1994) 179 CLR 297.
25. See *Brown v The Queen* (1986) 160 CLR 171.
26. See *Cheatle v The Queen* (1993) 177 CLR 541.
27. See *Zarb v Kennedy* (1968) 121 CLR 283.
28. See *Kingswell v The Queen* (1985) 159 CLR 264.
29. See *Attorney General (Victoria); Ex rel Black v The Commonwealth* (1981) 146 CLR 559.
30. (1983) 154 CLR 120.
31. Ibid 130.
32. Ibid 136.
33. Ibid 174.
34. See *Adelaide Company of Jehovah's Witnesses Inc v The Commonwealth* (1943) 67 CLR 116; *Church of the New Faith v Commissioner of Pay-Roll Tax (Vic)* (1983) 154 CLR 120.
35. See *Henry v Boehm* (1973) 128 CLR 482.
36. (1989) 168 CLR 461, 485.
37. (1989) 168 CLR 461, 489.
38. (1992) 174 CLR 455.
39. Mason CJ, Dawson and McHugh JJ.
40. Deane and Toohey JJ at 492; Gaudron J at 502-503 held equality before the law to be 'fundamental to the judicial process'.
41. My judgment focussed on particular provisions of the impugned legislation, not on the overarching issues.
42. See *Gratwick v.Johnson* (1945), 70 CLR 1, 17; *Cole v. Whitfield* (1988), 165 CLR 360, 393.
43. See *AMS v AIF* (1999) 199 CLR 160.

44. (1988) 165 CLR 360.
45. See, in particular, 398.
46. (1999) 199 CLR 160, 180 (Gleeson CJ, McHugh and Gummow JJ).
47. (1951) 83 CLR 1, 193; cited in *Plaintiff S157/2002 v Commonwealth of Australia* (2003) 77 ALJR 454; 195 ALR 24; cf *Kartinyeri v Commonwealth* (1998) 195 CLR 337, 381 [89] per Gummow and Hayne JJ.
48. (1951) 83 CLR 1,193.
49. See *Western Australia v The Commonwealth* (1995) 183 CLR 373, 484-488.
50. See *Commissioner of Police v Tanos* (1958) 98 CLR 383, 395-396.
51. See *Reg v Kirby; Ex parte Boilermakers' Society of Australia* (1956) 94 CLR 254, affirmed *Attorney General of the Commonwealth of Australia v The Queen* (1957) 95 CLR 529; *Harris v Caladine* (1991) 172 CLR 84.
52. See *Huddart Parker & Co Pty Ltd v Moorehead* (1909) 8 CLR 330; *New South Wales v The Commonwealth* (1915) 20 CLR 54; *Waterside Workers' Federation of Australia v JW Alexander Ltd* (1918) 25 CLR 434.
53. See *Nicholas v The Queen* (1998) 193 CLR 173, 233 and cases there cited.
54. See *Huddart Parker & Co Pty Ltd v Moorehead* (1909) 8 CLR 330, 357.
55. (1954) 90 CLR 353, 369.
56. See *Re Tracey; Ex parte Ryan* (1989) 166 CLR 518, 580 (Deane J).
57. (1992) 176 CLR 1, 27. See also 37, 53, 68.
58. Cf Deane J in *Re Tracey; Ex parte Ryan* (1989) 166 CLR 518, 580; 84 ALR 1.
59. See *Leeth v The Commonwealth* (1992) 174 CLR 455, 470 (Mason CJ, Dawson and McHugh JJ).
60. See *R v Watson; Ex parte Armstrong* (1976) 136 CLR 248.
61. See *Chu Kheng Lim v Minister for Immigration* (1992) 176 CLR 1, 36-37 (Brennan, Deane and Dawson JJ)
62. (1918) 25 CLR 434, 444.
63. (1989) 166 CLR 518, 580.
64. (1991) 172 CLR 501, 535, 607, 648, 686, 706-707, 721.
65. See *Chu Kheng Lim v Minister for Immigration* (1992) 176 CLR 1, 27 (Brennan, Deane and Dawson JJ).
66. (1915) 20 CLR 425, 441.
67. (1992) 176 CLR 1, 27-28 (Brennan, Deane and Dawson JJ).
68. See *Reg v Iorlano* (1983) 151 CLR 678; *Williams v The Queen* (1986) 161 CLR 278, 283, 291-292, 305.
69. Cf Gaudron J at 55 who was not persuaded that the *Constitution* precluded the imposition of other categories of extra-judicial detention. In *Kable v Director of Public Prosecutions (NSW))* (1996) 189 CLR 51, Toohey J cited the quoted passage (at 97) and Gummow J cited Gaudron J's reservation (at 131) but neither Justice found it necessary to determine whether the specified categories of legitimate extra-judicial detention were exhaustive.
70. See *Al Masri v Minister for Immigration & Multicultural & Indigenous Affairs* [2002] FCA 1009.
71. (1987) 162 CLR 514, 528; affirmed in *Chu Kheng Lim v Minister for Immigration* 176 CLR 1, 19.

72. (1996) 189 CLR 51, 98, 106-108, 132.
73. (1996) 189 CLR 51, 117 (McHugh J).
74. See *Australian Building Construction Employees' and Builders Labourers' Federation v The Commonwealth* (1986) 161 CLR 88, 96-97.
75. See, for example, *The Queen v Ross-Jones; Ex parte Green* (1984) 156 CLR 185.
76. *Re Minister for Immigration and Multicultural Affairs; Ex parte Applicant S20/2002*; (2003) 77 ALJR 1165.
77. See *Levy v Victoria* (1997) 189 CLR 579.
78. (1988) 166 CLR 79, 116
79. Sections 1, 7, 8, 13, 24, 25, 28 and 30: see *Lange v Australian Broadcasting Corporation* (1997) 189 CLR 520, 557.
80. (1992) 177 CLR 1, 72-73.
81. Ibid 49: 'where a representative democracy is constitutionally entrenched, it carries with it those legal incidents which are essential to the effective maintenance of that form of government. The freedom of discussion which is essential to sustain it is as firmly entrenched in the Constitution as the system of government which the Constitution expressly ordains'.
82. (1992) 177 CLR 106.
83. (1994) 182 CLR 104.
84. (1994) 182 CLR 211.
85. (1997) 189 CLR 520, 559.
86. See *Australian Capital Television Pty Ltd v The Commonwealth* (1992) 177 CLR 106, 217.
87. Ibid 150.
88. See *Lange v The Australian Broadcasting Corporation* (1997) 189 CLR 520, 571-573.
89. See *Williams v R* (1986) 161 CLR 278, 292 (Mason & Brennan JJ). See fn 7.
90. (1992) 176 CLR 239, 252 (Deane, Dawson, Toohey & Gaudron JJ).
91. The judgment directed attention to *Bropho v Western Australia* (1990) 171 CLR 1,17-18 for a general statement of the rule.
92. Their Honours cited *Bropho v Western Australia* (1990) 171 CLR 1, 17,18; and also, *Corporate Affairs Commission (NSW) v Yuill* (1991) 172 CLR 319, 322, 338 and cases there cited, 346-347. As to property rights see *American Dairy Queen (Q) Pty Ltd v Blue Rio Pty Ltd* (1981) 147 CLR 677, 682-683. As to the right to carry on business, see *Commonwealth v Progress Advertising & Press Agency Co Pty Ltd* (1910) 10 CLR 457, 464.
93. As to procedural fairness, the judgment cited *Annetts v McCann* (1990) 170 CLR 596, 598 and cases there cited; *Ainsworth v Criminal Justice Commission* (1992) 175 CLR 564, 575-576.
94. As to the privilege against self-incrimination, the judgment cited *Hammond v The Commonwealth* (1982) 152 CLR 188,197-198, 200; *Sorby v The Commonwealth* (1983) 152 CLR 281, 289-290, 294-295, 309, 311; *Hamilton v Oades* (1989) 166 CLR 486, 495, 500-501. As to the right to trial by jury see *Tassell v Hayes* (1987) 163 CLR 34, 41, 50. As to the right to personal liberty see *Re Bolton; Ex parte Beane* (1987) 162 CLR 514, 523. As to legal professional privilege see *Baker v Campbell* (1983) 153 CLR 52, 96-97, 104, 116-117, 123; *Corporate Affairs Commission (NSW) v Yuill* (1991) 172 CLR 319, 322, 331, 338, 348-349.
95. The judgment cited *Clancy v Butchers' Shop Employes Union* (1904) 1 CLR 181, 196-197, 204; *Hockey v Yelland* (1984) 157 CLR 124, 130, 142; *Bropho v Western Australia* (1990)

171 CLR 1, 17; *Public Service Association (SA) v Federated Clerks' Union of Australia (SA) Branch* (1991) 173 CLR 132, 160.

96. (1987) 162 CLR 514, 532.
97. See *Cox v Hakes* (1890) 15 App Cas 506, 527.
98. See *Re Bolton; Ex parte Beane* (1987) 162 CLR 514, 523.
99. (1987) 162 CLR 514, 518.
100. See *Clunies-Ross v The Commonwealth* (1984) 155 CLR 193, 201-202.
101. See *George v Rockett* (1990) 170 CLR 104, 110-111.
102. See *Coco v R* (1993) 179 CLR 427, 439 (Mason CJ, Brennan, Gaudron and McHugh JJ).
103. See *Plenty v Dillon* (1991) 171 CLR 635, 644-5 (Mason CJ, Brennan and Toohey JJ).
104. See *Re Refugee Tribunal; Ex p Aala* (2000) 204 CLR 82, 99-101, [38-42].
105. See *Annetts v McCann* (1990) 170 CLR 596.
106. See *Plaintiff S157/2002 v Commonwealth of Australia* (2003) 77 ALJR 454; 195 ALR 24.
107. See *Plaintiff S157/2002 v Commonwealth of Australia* (2003) 77 ALJR 454; 470;195 ALR 24, [74-77].
108. See *Hammond v The Commonwealth* (1982) 152 CLR 188.
109. See *Sorby v The Commonwealth* (1983) 152 CLR 281.
110. See *Pyneboard Pty Ltd v Trade Practices Commission* (1983) 152 CLR 328.
111. See *Baker v Campbell* (1983) 153 CLR 52.
112. See *Corporate Affairs Commission (NSW) v Yuill* (1991) 172 CLR 319.
113. See *Koowarta v Bjelke-Petersen* (1982) 153 CLR 168, 265; *Applicant A v Minister for Immigration and Ethnic Affairs* (1997) 190 CLR 225.
114. (1999) 199 CLR 160, 180 (Gleeson CJ, McHugh and Gummow JJ).
115. See *Plaintiff S157/2002 v The Commonwealth* (2003) 77 ALJR 454, 462, [29].
116. (1989) 166 CLR 186.
117. (1992) 175 CLR 1.
118. See, for example, *The Commonwealth v Tasmania (The Tasmanian Dam Case)* (1983) 158 CLR 1; *Richardson v Forestry Commission* (1988) 164 CLR 261. These cases upheld the validity of Commonwealth action under legislation which gave effect to the *Convention for the Protection of the World Cultural and Natural Heritage.*
119. See *Koowarta v Bjelke-Petersen* (1982) 153 CLR 168.
120. See *Minister for Immigration and Ethnic Affairs v Teoh* (1995) 183 CLR 273
121. Ibid 287.
122. Ibid 291-292.
123. See *Minister for Immigration and Ethnic Affairs v Teoh* (1995) 183 CLR 273, 288.
124. The judgment cited *Mabo v Queensland [No 2]* (1992) 175 CLR 1, 42, (Brennan J with whom Mason CJ and McHugh J agreed); *Dietrich v The Queen* (1992) 177 CLR 292,321, (Brennan J); 360 (Toohey J); *Jago v District Court (NSW)* (1988) 12 NSWLR 558, 569, (Kirby P); *Derbyshire County Council v Times Newspapers Ltd* [1992] QB 770.
125. See *Mabo v Queensland [No 2]* (1992) 175 CLR 1, 42.
126. See *Mabo v Queensland [No 2]* (1992) 175 CLR 1.
127. Ibid 108-109.
128. (1984) 155 CLR 614.

129. As to the High Court's jurisdiction in habeas corpus, see *Judiciary Act 1903,* s 33(1)(f) and *Ex parte Eastman* (1999) 200 CLR 322

130. See *Secretary, Department of Health and Community Services v JWB and SMB* (1992) 175 CLR 218.

131. The jurisdiction of the Family Court was affirmed by the majority in *P v P* (1994) 181 CLR 583.

132. See *Airedale NHS Trust v Bland* [1993] 1 All ER 821.

133. See *Grassby v R* (1989) 168 CLR 1, 20 Dawson J citing *Livesey v New South Wales Bar Association* (1983) 151 CLR 288 and *R v Watson; Ex parte Armstrong* (1976) 136 CLR 248; *E H Cochrane Ltd v Ministry of Transport* [1987] 1 NZLR 146, 152-153

134. See *Ebner v Official Trustee in Bankruptcy* (2000) 205 CLR 337.

135. (1989) 168 CLR 23, 56-7 (Deane J).

136. See *Dietrich v R* (1992) 177 CLR 292, 299-300.

137. (1938) 59 CLR 124.

138. [1935] AC 462, 481, 482.

139. See *Smyth v The Queen* (1957) 98 CLR 163.

140. See *R v Falconer* (1990) 171 CLR 30, 41.

141. See *Barton v The Queen* (1980) 147 CLR 75.

142. See *Sutton v The Queen* (1984) 152 CLR 528, 534, 547-549, 560, 564*; Hoch v The Queen* (1988) 165 CLR 292, 300

143. See *Carr v The Queen* (1988) 165 CLR 314, 330; *Longman v The Queen* (1989) 168 CLR 79, 86.

144. See *Petty v The Queen* (1991) 173 CLR 95, 99 (Mason, Deane, Toohey and McHugh JJ).

145. See *Cheatle v The Queen* (1993) 177 CLR 541, 552; *Brownlee v The Queen* (2001) 207 CLR 278, 303-304 (Gaudron, Gummow and Hayne JJ).

146. See *Hinch v A-G (Victoria)* (1987) 64 CLR 15, 58-59 (Deane J).

147. See *R v Glennon* (1992) 173 CLR 592, 604-605 (Mason CJ and Toohey J).

148. See *R v Glennon* (1992) 173 CLR 592, 605 (Mason CJ and Toohey J)

149. (1959) 103 CLR 30, 78.

150. Section 44(1)(b): 'A person shall not, by violence to the person or property of a person, by threat, intimidation or incitement of any kind to any person, or, without reasonable cause of excuse, by boycott or threat of boycott of a person… dissuade… (b) a registered waterside worker from offering for, obtaining or accepting employment'. See (1959) 103 CLR 30, 79.

151. (1954) 347 US 483

152. See *Case No. CCT 38/00*, 21 September 2000; (2000) 10 BHRC 84.

153. See *Case No. CCT 9/02*, 5 July 2002; (2000) (5) SA 703 (CC); (10) BCLR 1075 (CC).

154. (1997) 190 CLR 225, 255-256 (footnotes omitted).

155. Section 92 of the *Constitution.*

156. See *Cole v Whitfield* (1988) 165 CLR 360.

6.8 The Parameters of Constitutional Change

Editor's note

Brennan delivered the Monash Law School's 16th Lucinda Lecture on 13 November 2008.[1] The *Lucinda* was the Queensland Government's paddle steamer which Sir Samuel Griffith had taken to Sydney during the 1891 National Australasian Convention. Between 27 and 29 March 1891, Griffith was joined on board by Edmund Barton and Charles Kingston on the Hawkesbury River. Inglis Clark was another member of the drafting committee, but he missed most of the cruise around the Hawkesbury because he had the flu. They put together a draft of the Australian *Constitution*.

Introduction

Seven years ago, we celebrated the centenary of our *Constitution*, observing how well it has served us in times of war and in times of peace; in times of prosperity and in times of poverty. Six Colonies have grown into an independent nation, free of Imperial legislative power, conducting our own affairs and responsible for our own safekeeping. Our *Constitution* has been the framework of a stable democracy, governed by the rule of law and modelled somewhat loosely on the Westminster system.

The *Constitution* could be improved in a number of respects which were identified by the Constitutional Commission's Report in 1988. They relate chiefly to the composition, tenure and powers of the Parliament. It could be improved by acknowledging the dignity of our indigenous peoples. Changes of these kinds can be effected only by referendum, but structural changes can occur and have occurred without significant change in the constitutional text. The last 100 years have seen a transformation of our form of government. A facilitator of change has been the High Court, as Alfred Deakin foretold when he introduced the Bill for the *Judiciary Act* in 1903:

> the nation lives, grows, and expands. Its circumstances change, its needs alter, and its problems present themselves with new faces. The organ of the national life, which preserving the union is yet able from time to time to transfuse into it the fresh blood of the living present, is the Judiciary ... It is as one of the organs of Government which enables the Constitution to grow and to be adapted to the changeful necessities and circumstances of generation after generation that the High Court operates.[2]

The High Court has not been the only organ of government that has responded to changing circumstances. The politico-economic exigencies of the day have worked changes in the relationship of Commonwealth and States and the relationship of Parliament and the Executive.

In retrospect, the High Court's judgment in *Amalgamated Society of Engineers v Adelaide Steamship Co Ltd*[3] – probably the most dramatic change in the constitutional landscape – can be seen as the opening of Commonwealth dominance in both legislative and fiscal power. The change was not isolated from the political sentiment of the time. As Windeyer J observed: 'in 1920 the Constitution was read in a new light, a light reflected from events that had, over twenty years, led to a growing realization that Australians were now one people and Australia one country and that national laws might meet national needs. ... As I see it the *Engineers' Case*, looked at as an event in legal and constitutional history, was a consequence of developments that had occurred outside the law courts as well as a cause of further developments there'.[4]

So, when we look at our *Constitution* today, we must be conscious of the changes that have occurred in the nature and location of political power in consequence of factors external to the law courts, notably vertical fiscal imbalance and the dominance of party leadership. Then, in the judicial branch of government, the growth of the federal court system has been criticised and a single court structure has been suggested. And finally, the issue of a Republic remains alive but dormant.

These are major structural issues and we may think that their solution should find, and perhaps need, expression in the *Constitution*. Yet I venture to suggest that constitutional amendment to change or reverse any of these movements is unlikely or, in the case of the Republic, dependent on solving a yet unsolved problem.

Vertical Fiscal Imbalance

In 1901, the collection of revenue from the duties of customs and excise passed to the Commonwealth although it was forbidden to apply more than a quarter of the net revenue towards its expenditure for a period of at least 10 years.[5] Subject to the loss of revenue from customs and excise, the States retained power to levy taxation of all kinds. They retain that power today, but in practice it can be exercised only in limited fields, including the exaction of mining royalties and stamp duty.

The reason, of course, is that the Commonwealth, by exercising its concurrent taxing power, made it politically impossible for States to impose income tax in addition to that imposed by the Commonwealth and, by exercise of its power under s 96, made financial grants to the States conditional on the States abstaining from imposing income tax. Thus, the States were legislatively excluded from the most important sources of taxation,[6] not because they were stripped of taxing power but because they were induced not to exercise it.[7]

Sections 90 and 92 of the *Constitution* ensured that the geographical Commonwealth, consisting at least of the entire mainland and the island of Tasmania, should be a free trade area [8] and that the sole authority to determine duties of customs and excise and the payment of bounties on the production or export of goods should be the Commonwealth Parliament.[9] Customs, bounties and taxation must be uniform throughout the Commonwealth.[10] In C*apital Duplicators Pty Ltd v Australian Capital Territory (No 2),*[11] the joint judgment commented that: 'ss 90 and 92, taken together with the safeguards against discrimination in s 51(ii) and (iii) and s 88, created a Commonwealth economic union, not an association of States each with its own separate economy.'[12]

The concurrent powers of the Commonwealth over currency, banking and insurance (other than State banking and insurance) have been exercised so as to cover those respective fields.[13] The consequence of these provisions is to give the Commonwealth 'control of the national economy as a unity which knows no State boundaries, by a legislature without direct legislative power over the economy as such'.[14] That was the view of s 90 taken by Sir Garfield Barwick CJ in *Western Australia v Chamberlain Industries Pty Ltd*,[15] and expanded in his dissenting judgment in *Victoria v Commonwealth*:[16] 'There is but one economy of the country, not six ... But no specific power over the economy is given to the Commonwealth. Such control as it exercises on that behalf must be effected by indirection through taxation, including customs and excise, banking, including the activities of the Reserve Bank and the budget, whether it be in surplus or in deficit.'[17]

Thus, the Commonwealth has in hand the chief regulatory levers of the national economy, both fiscal and monetary. Its influence on State borrowings has waxed and waned since the establishment of a Loan Council in 1923. The Commonwealth acquired a measure of control over State borrowing powers through the Loan Council after s 105A was inserted into the *Constitution* in 1928.[18] Today, if Commonwealth control over State borrowings were required, it would not be effected by action under the current Financial Agreement which dates from 1994,[19] but by some other policy mechanism, perhaps by attaching conditions to State grants.

In the National Economy Chapter of the Final Report of the Constitutional Commission in 1988, it was said that: 'In economic matters, Australia is not the master of its own destiny. This was made clear during the depression of the 1930s. It is just as clear today, perhaps even more so.'[20]

Recent events confirm that view. National responses – indeed, supranational responses – are needed to protect and foster the national economy and central control of fiscal and monetary policy is essential for that purpose. A de facto return of taxing powers to the States, or to the States and Territories, would today be unacceptable, not only to the Government of the Commonwealth, but to the Governments and peoples of the States and Territories. Indeed, in 2006 agreement was reached between the Commonwealth and the States on the progressive elimination of State stamp duties on various documents and transactions. I do not sense any current agitation for relinquishing the exercise of any of the Commonwealth's taxation powers in order to admit the exercise of corresponding powers by the States and Territories. Rather, accepting Commonwealth hegemony, the movement has been towards reaching agreement on the disposal of Commonwealth revenue to fund the functions of the States and Territories. The most obvious example is the allocation of GST revenue to the States and Territories.

The constitutional issue of the present time is not the exercise of taxing powers but the distribution of the revenue derived from their exercise. In principle, revenue should be so distributed as to allow each organ of government to fund the maintenance, support and regulation of the activities for which it is responsible. But there is no constitutional provision which determines which activities should fall within the responsibility of one organ of government and which within another.

The only constitutional provisions now governing Commonwealth expenditure appear to be ss 81 and 83. In accordance with established constitutional principle,[21] those sections require Parliamentary appropriation of any moneys to be withdrawn from the Consolidated Revenue of the Commonwealth.[22] An appropriation must be 'for the purposes of the Commonwealth'.[23] The meaning of that phrase has not been settled, but there is substantial support for the view that authorised purposes extend to 'such purposes as Parliament may determine'.[24]

The consequence, as the dissenting judgments in the '*AAP Case*' pointed out, is that an appropriation of funds to be expended on a subject outside Commonwealth legislative power (which includes the legislative power inherent in a national legislature)[25] erodes the amount which would otherwise be available for grants to the States under s 96 or perhaps for payments to the States under s 94.[26] The framers of the *Constitution* envisaged that there would be a surplus of Commonwealth revenue available for distribution to the States. But fluctuating economic and political factors, sometimes producing budget surpluses, sometimes deficits, destroyed any notion that the States might rely on a steady distribution of Commonwealth surpluses.

There is no constitutional provision which guarantees the payment of any Commonwealth Consolidated Revenue to the States or Territories or which specifies the subjects on which Commonwealth Consolidated Revenue may be expended. The States (and Territories) are left to carry out their functions with only their domestic revenues and such funding as the Commonwealth determines. That funding is a matter for political negotiation. The Parliament may grant financial assistance to a State pursuant to s 96, and may attach conditions to the grant. The conditions may direct the use by the States of the moneys granted,[27] thus prescribing the manner in which the State exercises its power. Attached conditions may require a State to distribute the moneys granted to particular recipients,[28] and may induce a State to take action which the Commonwealth is constitutionally prohibited itself from taking.[29] The conditions attached to a grant can become the provision which, albeit indirectly, regulates the activity which would otherwise be a State responsibility. Although the State retains and exercises its power to regulate the activity, the attached condition may make it impossible for the State to exercise its own legislative discretion.

The appropriations power seems to go further, allowing the Commonwealth to bypass the State and to regulate an activity lying outside its legislative power by funding that activity directly and attaching conditions to the funding whereby the conditions become the effective regulation. Fields of activity are brought under Commonwealth regulation not by legislation but by contract made by the Executive requiring the beneficiary to conform to specified standards and practices. Thus, for example, State universities, pursuant to individual funding agreements, have been required to conform to Commonwealth governance protocols. That has been the price of receiving Commonwealth funding, even though State laws had prescribed a different governance regime. States have had to modify those regimes in order to allow universities to receive Commonwealth funding.

Until recent times the areas of activity within Commonwealth responsibility were ascertained by reference to its allocated legislative power. The High Court was the arbiter of any dispute. Increasingly, the areas of responsibility are ascertained by reference to the source of supporting funding, a question determined by the political branches of government. The High Court has no role to play in that determination.

Although an appropriation in blank would be beyond the power of the Parliament,[30] an appropriation can, and often is, expressed in very general terms.[31] In the *Work Choices Advertising Case*, the High Court construed an *Appropriation Act* which appropriated funds as a 'departmental item', to 'be applied for the departmental expenditure'[32] of the Department of Employment and Workplace Relations. The majority held that was an appropriation for a purpose of the Commonwealth.[33] An amount listed under the heading 'Departmental Outputs' authorised the minister to direct departmental expenditure of that amount on such departmental subjects as he chose. In so holding, the majority observed: 'at least since the mid-1980s the chief means of limiting expenditures made by departments of State that has been adopted in annual appropriation Acts has been to specify the amount that may be spent rather than further define the purposes or activities for which it may be spent.' [34]

It appears that, unless the expenditure of moneys appropriated under the Combet formula is restricted by other legislation,[35] it may be expended on such departmental activities as a Minister may choose and on terms of the Minister's choosing.[36] It is difficult to postulate any constitutional limitation on the subjects to which Commonwealth funds can be channelled through departments. Thus, Commonwealth Consolidated Revenue can be expended on subjects, which have not been subjected to Parliamentary scrutiny in the budget process.

The *Combet* formula allows the Parliament to return to the executive the spending discretion it was traditionally denied.[37] The absence of constitutional restriction on the exercise of Commonwealth taxing power, on appropriations and on some departmental spending leaves the areas to fall within Commonwealth responsibility to political negotiation. The necessity for central regulation of the economy and the desirability of national standards in many fields of activity has led to a new political approach, which is termed 'co-operative federalism'. At its March 2008 meeting, the Council of Australian Governments ('COAG') agreed to 'a new model for federal financial relations, with priority being to modernise payments for specific purposes and the development of National Partnership payments'.[38]

When the Budget was brought down in May 2008, *Budget Paper No 3* declared:

> The proliferation of these payments since the 1970s has been a source of increasingly blurred roles and responsibilities, duplication and overlap, higher administration costs and cost-shifting.
>
> These payments are also subject to conditions which the Commonwealth imposed on the States to dictate the way that funding was to be used. For example, the Commonwealth used conditions known as input controls that limited the States' flexibility in how they allocated funding or pursued policy objectives.

> This overly prescriptive approach constrains the States' innovation in service delivery and leads to each level of government blaming the other for instances of poor service delivery and inadequate funding.[39]

COAG declared that it would consider a new 'intergovernmental agreement on financial relations together with drafts of each new Special Purpose Payment and proposals for National Partnership payments'.[40] A monitoring and reporting role for a COAG Reform Council is proposed. At its July meeting, COAG declared that: 'Many of the challenges facing the economy can only be addressed through more effective Commonwealth-State arrangements. By moving towards a seamless national economy through the reform of business and other regulation, COAG's reforms will make it easier for businesses and workers to operate across State and Territory (State) borders.'[41]

In October, COAG agreed to introduce national consumer protection and credit regulation laws and to deal with federal financial relations in December.

If the creation of national standards for business and industry is needed to achieve a seamless national economy, that could have been achieved by the Commonwealth alone had the Constitutional Commission's recommendation in its 1988 Report been adopted. The Commission recommended that s 51(i) of the *Constitution* be amended.[42] Presently the Commonwealth's power is to make laws with respect to 'trade and commerce with other countries and among the States'[43] and the Commission proposed that the power be more broadly stated simply as 'trade and commerce'.[44] For some reason, that power has been little-used by the Commonwealth, perhaps for fear that its use would be liable to unforeseen frustration by s 92 of the *Constitution*. That fear should have dissipated after *Cole v Whitfield*[45] when the High Court observed that: 's 51(i) is a plenary power on a topic of fundamental importance. That being so, the express conferral of legislative power with respect to interstate trade and commerce lends some support for the view that s 92 should not be construed as precluding an exercise of legislative power which would impose any burden or restriction on interstate trade and commerce or on an essential attribute of that trade and commerce. Obviously, the provision conferring legislative power (s 51(i)) and the provision restricting the exercise of legislative power (s 92) sit more easily together if the latter is construed as being concerned with precluding particular types of burdens, such as discriminatory burdens of a protectionist kind.'[46]

Whether national standards are introduced by unilateral Commonwealth legislation or pursuant to inter-governmental agreements, it seems that major initiatives for Australia in the coming years will be negotiated between the respective executive governments of the Commonwealth and the States and Territories. The complexity of modern government, the necessity for central control of fiscal and monetary policy, the interdependence of national and international policies, the growth of national enterprises and national media, the movement for national standards, the enhancement of national rather than local sentiment and identity, the mobility of the Australian population, the elimination of unnecessary duplication of bureaucracies, and general community acceptance of the present form of government are irresistibly fashioning a new distribution of governmental power. The only practical limitation on the subjects of Commonwealth expenditure and regulation is a political one. The constitutional division of legislative powers between Commonwealth and States, though relevant, has become of secondary importance. We have come a long way from the basic constitutional system envisaged by the Founding Fathers of Federation.

That does not mean, however, that federalism is dead or that the movement towards centralising governmental power will continue unabated until we arrive at a unitary system. There are significant factors, other than the *Constitution*, which indicate not only the desirability of maintaining a form of federalism but also the practical impossibility of eliminating the functions of the States and Territories and centralising those functions in Canberra. Much essential administrative expertise remains with the States and Territories, not possessed by the Commonwealth, especially in the delivery of public services.

When some of the functions of the Colonies or States were taken over, entire departments had to become part of the Commonwealth public service to provide the requisite administrative expertise. Thus, when the collection of customs and excise and the payment of bounties became the function of the Commonwealth executive by operation of s 86, the State departments dealing with those functions were immediately transferred to the Commonwealth. Subsequently, State departments dealing with posts, telegraphs, and telephones; naval and military defence; lighthouses, lightships, beacons, and buoys; and quarantine were transferred pursuant to s 69. When the Commonwealth assumed the sole power to tax income in 1942, it took over from the States the officers, premises and equipment concerned with the assessment and collection of income tax. These examples, and there are no doubt others, illustrate that the transfer of power is not effected merely by a constitutional or statutory text, nor by an intergovernmental agreement.

There are two conditions which must be met to provide efficiency in administration. Principally, there must be an efficient organisation for delivery of a governmental service; then there must be sufficient funding for the creation and maintenance of the organisation. The recent report of the Hon Ian Callinan on the outbreak of equine flu demonstrates the importance of departmental culture, interconnection of the various elements in the delivery of the service, recruitment and training and professional control of quarantine services. These are elements that develop over time and in response to local circumstances. They can be supported by adequate funding but no stroke of a drafting pen can produce them. So if the States and Territories possess administrative expertise and the Commonwealth possesses the funds, co-operative federalism is the means by which governmental services can be delivered to the Australian people.

However, the 'seamless national economy' may well require Commonwealth laws to prescribe national standards. The wide extent of the Commonwealth's power to make laws with respect to trading and financial corporations has been shown in *New South Wales v Commonwealth*[47] and the trade and commerce power is awaiting exploration. In addition there is the reference power in s 51(xxxvii) by which the States may refer to the Commonwealth power to enact laws with respect to a matter, either permanently or for a time.[48] Given co-operation, there should be no need for constitutional amendment to permit the prescription of national standards, although it may be preferable to add some heads of legislative power to s 51.[49]

Given the central role which executive governments will play in co-operative federalism, supervision of the exercise of executive power needs consideration. In *R v Kirby; Ex parte Boilermakers' Society of Australia*[50] the joint judgment remarked: 'Probably the most striking achievement of the framers of the Australian instrument of government was the successful combination of the British system of parliamentary government containing an executive responsible to the legislature with American federalism.'[51]

Now, however, the Diceyan theory of responsible government, which made the fate of the executive dependent on the confidence of Parliament, does not fully reflect the political reality. Responsible government depends more on debates in the party room than in the Parliament. Today the political fortunes of the members of the Parliament are tied to the performance of the party leaders who take major decisions. The problem is not unique to Australia; it is the consequence of, inter alia, the complexity of modern government. Lord Hailsham observed that '[we] live under an elective dictatorship, absolute in theory if hitherto thought tolerable in practice'.[52]

And, as *Work Choices Advertising Case* shows, the Parliament's constitutional authority over Commonwealth expenditure by the Executive has been diminished in practice by a device of drafting. As financial and regulatory power passes increasingly to the executive branch of the Commonwealth government, the adequacy of existing controls on its exercise may be doubted. There is a measure of supervision by the Senate which is not usually controlled by government and by Parliamentary Committees constituted by members from both sides of the House or Senate. And Commonwealth Grants Commission reports may influence expenditure and may be laid before Parliament for scrutiny.[53]

The funding of programs to be delivered by non-governmental entities raises another question of accountability. If a grant is made under s 96 or a similar grant to the Territories, the political and judicial institutions of those polities are responsible for the due administration of the funds received. But in the case of other external funding arrangements, some accountability mechanism may be required, especially if the expenditure has been authorised not by legislation but by ministerial direction. Ministerial responsibility for the actions or omissions of departmental staff in performing some function is an aspect of responsible government but if an external entity is funded to perform the function, the relevant Minister may not be responsible to the Parliament for that entity's acts or omissions. Outsourcing erodes responsible government.

Moreover, if a funded function is outsourced and is intended to provide third parties with a right to some benefit and the benefit is not provided, it is not a satisfactory remedy to impose a penalty on the recipient of the funds. The intended beneficiaries should be provided by statute with remedies similar to those available under the Commonwealth's administrative law package.[54]

Our constitutional landscape, at least in the near future, shows a continuing accession of central power, achieved in part by changing circumstances which attract one of the Commonwealth's constitutional heads of power, in part by the referral of legislative power and in part by contract or other forms of conditional funding determined largely by the federal executive.

There will be no return of taxing powers to the States, no greater Parliamentary control of the executive. Commonwealth expenditure will fund new federal programs but, hopefully, the administrative expertise of State and Territory departments will be employed in administration of many of the fields which fall within Commonwealth regulation. New review mechanisms will be required to protect intended beneficiaries of these programs. The High Court remains as the keystone of the federal arch, but the piers of the arch are coming closer together.

The Dual Court System

Moving from the political branches of government, we may consider the judicial branch. From time to time, it is suggested that the dual system of federal and state courts should be eliminated in favour of a single judiciary. The suggestion has a worthy provenance.[55] An interesting model is the German judiciary.[56] Ninety-eight per cent of the judges are members of the public service of the 16 States (or *Lander*) and they staff the trial courts and the intermediate courts of appeal.[57] The judges of the Federal Court of Justice,[58] to which appeals are brought from the lower courts on points of law, are federal judges; so are the judges of the Federal Constitutional Court.[59] The Federal Court of Justice, which has 25 senates or divisions, has the function, inter alia, of ensuring that the law is applied uniformly throughout Germany. Could such a system be applied in Australia?

In some superficial respects, the Australian system is comparable. The High Court and the Federal Court are federal and each of those courts has appellate jurisdiction. The difference lies in the vesting of original jurisdiction and its incidents.[60] The autochthonous expedient, which allows the Commonwealth to vest jurisdiction in the courts of the States, has worked well in many fields of federal jurisdiction, but not in all. A good example is the field of taxation. For many years, appeals against assessments to tax were determined by the High Court in its original jurisdiction even though the Supreme Courts were available fora.[61] In time the volume of such appeals demanded the vesting of original jurisdiction in another court and the creation of an intermediate appellate court which would ensure uniformity of application of the taxing statutes throughout the Commonwealth. The Federal Court was created accordingly. That court could also determine appeals from, or judicially review, administrative decisions which are a feature of tax administration. The Commonwealth Parliament has never been willing to vest in State courts jurisdiction to review judicially decisions taken by Commonwealth administrators in the exercise of their statutory powers,[62] that jurisdiction being vested today in the Federal Court or in the Federal Magistrates Court.[63]

Governments, whether Commonwealth or State, may be willing to vest jurisdiction in the courts of another polity in some areas, but not in others. There are sound reasons for such discrimination: some areas of jurisdiction relate particularly to local conditions – planning and mining, for example – or concern the functions of a particular government – matters of 'special federal concern'.[64] In such areas, each government needs to retain its own legislative discretion to shape the laws which the court administers. It would be neither wise nor realistic to expect that either the Commonwealth or a

State would vest original jurisdiction under all its laws in a single court of another polity.

In a federation, jurisdiction should be distributed between federal and state courts to achieve, so far as possible, two objectives: ease of access to a tribunal having jurisdiction to hear and determine a matter and uniformity of application of law throughout the relevant territory.

Jurisdictional disputes can be avoided by cross-vesting of suitable original jurisdiction with power to remit cases to the appropriate or most convenient court. State courts can be[65] and have been[66] invested with federal jurisdiction except in specified areas, but federal courts cannot be vested by State Parliaments with jurisdiction in exclusively State or non-federal matters.[67] However, federal courts can hear and determine controversies which encompass both claims arising under vested federal jurisdiction and under non-federal jurisdiction.[68]

Uniformity of application of State or Territory laws is primarily the responsibility of the Supreme Court of the State or Territory, but uniformity in the application of Commonwealth laws should be the responsibility of a single court. If it were left to the High Court alone to ensure such uniformity, the workload involved would be excessive, especially as more laws prescribing national standards are enacted, whether pursuant to referred powers or not.[69] The Federal Court now has the primary responsibility of ensuring uniformity in some areas of federal law, notably taxation, intellectual property and workplace relations. Differences in the interpretation and application of Commonwealth laws are more likely to occur if appeals in cases involving Commonwealth laws are decided by the eight appellate courts of the States and Territories than if they were decided by the Federal Court. Uniformity provides a strong argument in favour of channelling all appeals in federal jurisdiction to the Federal Court. If that were done, the Court would probably need to be restructured into an appellate and a trial division.[70]

The notion of a single Australian court system runs into several difficulties, the principal difficulty being the unwillingness of any polity to forego its ability to confer on its court the functions which it chooses – functions which, in the case of the States, may include non-judicial functions. Another difficulty is court administration – appointment of judges, staffing, court houses and facilities, services and execution of court process. Each government has made its own arrangements for court administration and the likelihood of agreeing on funding and of creating a single administration is remote. In time, if Australia becomes virtually a unitary state, the court system will follow. But not in the near future.

At present the only constitutional amendment that might be contemplated is one to allow the vesting of suitable State judicial powers in Commonwealth courts.[71] Otherwise the present system will remain, although a statutory vesting of all federal appellate jurisdictions in the Federal Court would assist in securing uniformity in the application of federal laws.

The Republic

The constitutional powers and functions presently vested in Queen Elizabeth II are, upon her death, immediately vested in her 'heir and successor in the sovereignty of the United Kingdom'.[72] If Australia were to become a Republic, the powers and functions of the Monarch would have to be vested in another repository, probably called a President.

Assuming that we would wish to retain our system of responsible government in the absence of a Monarch, how can the executive government be made responsible to the Parliament for the manner in which a President exercises his or her powers and functions? This is the central and critical question that must be resolved before, or at least contemporaneously with, deciding on the manner of the President's appointment. The present system relies chiefly on convention – long established convention, but only convention, not law. Sir Anthony Mason has explained the role of convention in the system of responsible government: 'The principle that in general the Governor defers to, or acts upon, the advice of his Ministers ... is a convention, compliance with which enables the doctrine of ministerial responsibility to come into play so that a Minister or Ministers become responsible to Parliament for the decision made by the Governor in Council, thereby contributing to the concept of responsible government.'[73]

At present the convention is supported by a Prime Minister's ability to secure the removal of a Governor-General by the Queen if the Governor-General should breach the convention. Absent the Queen, the present convention might not be sufficient to sustain responsible government if the President chose to follow his or her own judgment. Constitutional law would have to make alternative provision.

It would be easy enough to provide that the President must act only in accordance with ministerial advice but an exception has to be made for the reserve powers which are essential to safeguard stable government and, in the last analysis, to maintain the rule of law. The reserve powers, though exercised in only the most unusual and extreme circumstances, are necessary to ensure that a government does not pursue an unlawful course of conduct or refuse to enforce court orders or to ensure that the elements of our parliamentary democracy perform their intended function, especially if they should be unwilling or unable to do so. The *Constitution* would be imperilled if, for example, a Prime Minister who had lost the confidence of the House of Representatives were to refuse to resign or to advise an election. If such a situation were to arise, the President might have to act promptly without or even contrary to ministerial advice. At present, the Governor-General is solely responsible for an exercise of the reserve powers, as the dismissal of the Whitlam Government illustrates.

If the *Constitution* were to provide that the President is bound generally to act in accordance with ministerial advice, the framing of an exception to provide for the reserve powers immediately raises two questions: how to identify the reserve powers and how to prescribe the circumstances in which they might be exercised. Even if a textual amendment could answer those questions, a challenge to any exercise of the powers would be justiciable in the High Court and delay would be inevitable – probably to the detriment of the nation.

There are some reserve powers which can be exercised without ministerial advice and without the likelihood of challenge: for example, the power to dismiss a Prime Minister who refuses to resign after the government is defeated in a general election. These can be easily defined. But the exercise of other powers or in other circumstances cannot be exhaustively defined and cannot be fully foreseen. The *Constitution* must allow some flexibility while defining both the purpose of the exercise of a reserve power and the nature of the circumstances in which such a power might properly be exercised without ministerial advice. The purpose of the reserve powers is to ensure compliance with the law or the effective operation of responsible government. The only occasion for an exercise of a reserve power is when it is absolutely necessary to effect that purpose.[74] A provision drafted in these general terms would cover the constitutionally defined powers to prorogue the Parliament, to dissolve the House of Representatives, to dissolve both Houses after the Senate has twice failed to pass a proposed law and to appoint and dismiss ministers (*Constitution* ss 5, 57, 64). However, the propriety of exercising a power defined in such general terms should not be left to the judgment of the President alone. Nor should the High Court be the primary arbiter of the open-textured question whether, in the circumstances of the time, it was absolutely necessary to exercise a reserve power. But if the people (and the President) cannot have the effective protection of a High Court order, some other mechanism must be found. A Council of State can provide it.

It would be for a President to form the opinion that an exercise of any reserve power is absolutely necessary, but a Council of State, immediately available to the President, could be empowered to certify – if it sees fit – that the President's intended exercise of a reserve power is valid. The certificate and all proceedings relating to the Council of State should be immune from question in any court. Such a certificate would preclude curial challenge and the consequent delay. The jurisdiction of the High Court could be invoked only if the President had acted without first obtaining such a certificate.

But how should a Council of State be constituted? The Council should be small enough to allow speedy consultation in the event of an emergency. The issues with which the Council would have to deal would be highly political though within a legal context. I would favour a Council of three, one of whom has served as a Governor-General or President or as a Governor of a State; the second of whom has served as a Chief Justice or Justice of the High Court or as a Chief Justice of a superior federal court or the Supreme Court of a State; and the third of whom should have served in one or more of the offices just mentioned. To ensure that there is confidence reposed by the government in the Council of State I would suggest that they should be appointed by the President after consultation with the Prime Minister in the early days of any government – say, within three months after the date on which the Parliament is summoned to meet after a general election.

There is little point in debate about the way in which a President should be elected or appointed until there is agreement about the way in which Presidential powers are to be controlled. Once that is agreed, the other issues – the people's franchise, Presidential election campaigns, availability of candidates and the like – can be debated with a better understanding of the kind of Republic we should have. Unless we first determine how a President's power is to be controlled, the possibility of an Australian Republic is remote.

The events of the last 100 years have shown some shortcomings and some obsolete provisions in our *Constitution*. Perhaps the wonder is that an instrument which was a work of inspired compromise should have served us as well as it has. We now live in a different age and there are different dynamics affecting the functions of governments. Old controversies about the maintenance of State powers have been diminished by political and economic factors in the 21st century. But our basic constitutional structure can be maintained even if we choose a republican form of government. Those who occupied the cabin of the *SS Lucinda* could not have provided for the constitutional exigencies of our century but we can be grateful for their work in fashioning a Constitution which allows us to do so.

---

1. This address was first published in the *Monash University Law* Review: see Sir Gerard Brennan, 'The Parameters of Constitutional Change' 2009 35(1) *Monash University Law Review* 1.
2. Commonwealth, *Parliamentary Debates*, House of Representatives, 18 March 1902, 10967-8 (Alfred Deakin, Attorney-General).

3. (1920) 28 CLR 129 (‘*Engineers' Case*’).
4. See *Victoria v Commonwealth* (1971) 122 CLR 353, 396 (Windeyer J) (‘*Payroll Taxation Case*’).
5. See Australian *Constitution* ss 86, 87.
6. See *South Australia v Commonwealth* (1942) 65 CLR 373 (‘*First Uniform Tax Case*’).
7. See *Victoria v Commonwealth* (1957) 99 CLR 575, 610 (Dixon CJ) (‘*Second Uniform Tax Case*’).
8. See *Cole v Whitfield* (1988) 165 CLR 360.
9. See *Capital Duplicators Pty Ltd v Australian Capital Territory* (1992) 177 CLR 248; *Ha v New South Wales* (1997) 189 CLR 465; *Betfair Pty Ltd v Western Australia* (2008) 234 CLR 418.
10. Australian *Constitution* ss 51(ii)-(iii), 88.
11. (1993) 178 CLR 561, 585 (Mason CJ, Brennan, Deane and McHugh JJ).
12. See, for example, *Philip Morris Ltd v Commissioner of Business Franchises (Vic)* (1989) 167 CLR 399, 426 (Mason CJ and Deane J).
13. As to the scope of the exception of ‘State banking’, see *Bourke v State Bank of New South Wales* (1990) 170 CLR 276.
14. See *Western Australia v Chamberlain Industries Pty Ltd* (1970) 121 CLR 1, 17 (Barwick CJ).
15. (1970) 121 CLR 1. Cf the rejection of this view in *Hematite Petroleum Ply Ltd v Victoria* (1983) 151 CLR 599, 616 17 (Gibbs CJ) (‘*Pipelines Case*’).
16. (1975) 134 CLR 338 (‘*AAP Case*’).
17. Ibid 362 (Barwick CJ).
18. See Cheryl Saunders, ‘Government Borrowing in Australia’ (1989) 17 (2) *Melbourne University Law Review* 187.
19. See *Financial Agreement Act 1994* (Cth).
20. Constitutional Commission, *Final Report of the Constitutional Commission 1988* (1988) vol 2, 773.
21. See *Auckland Harbour Board v The King* [1924] AC 318, 326-7 (Viscount Haldane).
22. See *Constitution* ss 81, 83.
23. See *Constitution* s 81.
24. See, for example, *Attorney-General (Vict) v Commonwealth* (1945) 71 CLR 237, 256 (Latham CJ); 274 (McTiernan J) (‘*Pharmaceutical Benefits Case*’); *Victoria v Commonwealth* (1975) 134 CLR 338, 396 (Mason J); 417 (Murphy J) (‘*AAP Case*’); *Combet v Commonwealth* (2005) 224 CLR 494, 522 (Gleeson CJ) (‘*Work Choices Advertising Case*’).The narrower view was put by Owen Dixon KC after reviewing the American authorities in his evidence before the 1929 Royal Commission on the *Constitution*: ‘[the *Constitution*] restricts the power of Parliament to appropriate money to the subjects assigned to Federal legislative power. The function of appropriating money seems to be treated as an exercise of the power of law-making, and not as a separate power’: see Constitutional Commission, above (n 20), 780.
25. See *Davis v Commonwealth* (1988) 166 CLR 79.
26. Cf *New South Wales v Commonwealth* (1908) 7 CLR 179 (‘*Surplus Revenue Case*’); *Victoria v Commonwealth* (1975) 134 CLR 338, 357 (Barwick CJ); 374 (Gibbs J) (‘AAP Case’).
27. See *Victoria v Commonwealth* (1926) 38 CLR 399 (‘*Federal Roads Case*’); *Victoria v Commonwealth (‘Second Uniform Tax Case’)* (1957) 99 CLR 575.

28. See *Attorney-General (Vict); Ex rel Black v Commonwealth* (1981) 146 CLR 559.
29. See *Pye v Renshaw* (1951) 84 CLR 58, 76-9 (Dixon, Williams, Webb, Fullagar and Kitto JJ). Cf *Attorney-General (Vict); Ex Rel Black v Commonwealth* (1981) 146 CLR 559, 592-3 (Gibbs J).
30. See *Attorney-General (Vict) v Commonwealth* (1945) 71 CLR 237, 253 (Latham CJ) '*Pharmaceutical Benefits Case*'; *Brown v West* (1990) 169 CLR 195, 208 (Mason CJ, Brennan, Deane, Dawson and Toohey JJ).
31. See *Combet v Commonwealth* (2005) 224 CLR 494, 522 (Gleeson CJ) *('Work Choices Advertising Case').*
32. Ibid 527.
33. Ibid 568 (Gummow, Hayne, Callinan and Heydon JJ).
34. Ibid 577 (Gummow, Hayne, Callinan and Heydon JJ).
35. See, for example, *Brown v West* (1990) 169 CLR 195.
36. Although as Gleeson CJ pointed in the *Combet v Commonwealth* (2005) 224 CLR 494, 523*('Work Choices Advertising Case'*): 'While the generality of statements of outcome may increase the difficulty of contesting the relationship between an appropriation and a drawing, appropriations are made in a context that includes public scrutiny and political debate concerning budget estimates and expenditure review. The higher the level of abstraction, or the greater the scope for political interpretation, involved in a proposed outcome appropriation, the greater may be the detail required by Parliament before appropriating a sum to such a purpose.'
37. See *Auckland Harbour Board v The King* [1924] AC 318, 326.
38. Council of Australian Governments ('COAG'), *Council of Australian Governments› Meeting 3 July 2008.*
39. Australian Commonwealth, *Budget Paper No 3: Australia's Federal Relations 2008-09* (2008) 12-13 <https://archive.budget.gov.au/2008-09/bp3/bp3.pdf>
40. COAG, (n 38).
41. Ibid.
42. Constitutional Commission, *Final Report of the Constitutional Commission Summary: 1988* (1988) 64.
43. See *Constitution* s 51(i).
44. Constitutional Commission (n 42).
45. (1988) 165 CLR 360 (‹*Tasmanian Lobster Case*›).
46. Ibid 398.
47. (2006) 229 CLR 1 (Gleeson CJ, Gummow, Kirby, Hayne, Callinan, Heydon and Crennan JJ) (‹*Workchoices Case*›).
48. See *R v Public Vehicles Licensing Appeals Tribunal (Tas); Ex parte Australian National Airways Pty Ltd* (1964) 113 CLR 207.
49. For example, technology affecting human existence, nuclear energy and the ecosystem.
50. (1956) 94 CLR 254 (*'Boilermakers' Case'*).
51. Ibid 275 (Dixon CJ, McTiernan, Fullagar and Kitto JJ).
52. 1976 Richard Dimbleby Lecture : Lord Hailsham, *Elective Dictatorship* (British Broadcasting Corporation, 1976) 2.
53. See *Commonwealth Grants Commission Act 1973* (Cth) s 25.
54. See *Administrative Appeals Tribunal Act 1975* (Cth); *Ombudsman Act 1976* (Cth); *Administrative Decisions (Judicial Review) Act 1977 (Cth).*

55. Commonwealth of Australia, Royal Commission on the Constitution of the Commonwealth, *Report of the Proceedings and Minutes of Evidence* (1929) 789-90 (Sir Owen Dixon); Ian Callinan, 'Imaging a Judiciary for a New Republic', *The Australian* (Sydney), 22 August 2008, 15. See also Sir Owen Dixon, 'Sources of Legal Authority' in Sir Owen Dixon, *Jesting Pilate* (Law Book Co, 1965) 201.
56. What follows is taken from a paper by Dr Klaus Tolksdorf, President of the Federal Court of Justice (Paper presented at the Conference of Supreme Court Presidents, Abu Dhabi, 23 March 2008).
57. Local Courts (*Amtsgerichte*), Regional Courts (*Landgerichte)* and Higher Regional Courts (*Oberlandesgerichte*).
58. Bundesgerichtshof
59. Bundesverfassungsgericht.
60. And requires consideration of Australian jurisprudence about the nature of the judicial power of the Commonwealth.
61. See Robert Ellicott, 'The Autochthonous Expedient and the Federal Court' (2008) 82 (10) *Australian Law Journal* 700, 702.
62. See *Judiciary Act 1903* (Cth) s 38(e); *Administrative Decisions (Judicial Review) Act 1977* (Cth) s 9; Ellicott, 'The Autochthonous Expedient and the Federal Court' (n 61) 701: Ellicott comments: 'It has always been the Commonwealth Parliament›s view that judges appointed by it [sic] should review those decisions'.
63. See *Administrative Decisions (Judicial Review) Act 1977* (Cth) ss 5-8.
64. See Michael Black, 'The Federal Court of Australia: The First 30 Years: A Survey on the Occasion of Two Anniversaries' (2007) 31 (3) *Melbourne University Law Review* 1, 6-10.
65. See *Constitution* s 77(iii).
66. See *Judiciary Act 1903* (Cth) s 39.
67. See *Re Wakim; Ex parte McNally* (1999) 198 CLR 511.
68. See *Fencott v Muller* (1983) 152 CLR 570.
69. See, for example, *Corporations Act 2001* (Cth).
70. Cf the views of Black, Michael Black, 'The Federal Court of Australia: The First 30 Years: A Survey on the Occasion of Two Anniversaries' (n 64) 10-17.
71. See *R v Hughes* (2000) 202 CLR 535, 553 which suggests that it may be desirable also to seek an amendment allowing State administrative powers to be vested in Commonwealth agencies.
72. Covering clause 2 of the *Commonwealth of Australia Constitution Act 1900* (Imp). Succession is governed by the laws of the United Kingdom, unaffected by Australian law.
73. See *FAI Insurances Ltdv Winneke* (1982) 151 CLR 342, 364.
74. Absolute necessity was the test proposed by Professor George Winterton: George Winterton, 'Reserve Powers in an Australian Republic' (1993) 12 (2) *University of Tasmania Law Review* 249, 256; George Winterton, 'The Resurrection of the Republic' (Law and Policy Paper No 15, Centre for International and Public Law, Australian National University, 2001) 17. Both the majority and the minority of the Executive Government Advisory Committee to the Constitutional Commission endorsed a test similar to that of 'absolute necessity' their formula was 'that there is no other method available to prevent': Executive Government Advisory Committee to the Constitutional Commission, *Final Report* (1988) vol 1, 326.

Chapter 7

'I did it my way'

7.1 Swearing in as Chief Justice

Editor's note

Brennan was sworn in as Chief Justice on 21 April 1995. These were his remarks.

Mr Attorney, Mr Fowler, Mrs Crennan, Mr Sofronoff, Members of the Bar, Solicitors and Attorneys, my dear wife and family and friends, Ladies and Gentlemen:

I am grateful for the excess of generosity in the remarks you have made this morning. It comforts me to think that I must have learnt to conceal my shortcomings in the 50 years since I first entered my father's Court to arraign a prisoner at the commencement of a criminal trial. Picking up the indictment and misreading the name of the prosecutor for the name of the accused, I charged one of the dearest and most upright of men with the crime of rape. Such is the camaraderie of the Bar that counsel for the accused leapt to his feet and pleaded not guilty on behalf of his learned friend. Although your compliments sit uneasily with the truth as I know it, your words and the presence of this large gathering reveal the respect in which you, the legal profession generally and the public hold this Court and the Office which I now assume. At a personal level, your good wishes, coupled with the loving support of my family, the valued encouragement of my judicial colleagues and the loyal devotion of my staff go far to dispel the inevitable diffidence with which I enter on the duties of Chief Justice.

My first duty is to welcome those who have honoured the Court by their attendance here this morning, especially those who have come from long distances. The Court appreciates your participation in today's ceremonies. Particularly do we welcome the Right Honourable Sir Harry Gibbs and the Honourable Sir Ronald Wilson, the Chief Justices of the Federal Court of Australia and the Family Court of Australia, the Chief Justices of the Supreme Courts of the several States and Territories and the Right Honourable Sir Thomas Eichelbaum, Chief Justice of New Zealand, who sit with us today. Strictly speaking, I should welcome also Sir Anthony Mason but insufficient time has passed to separate him from the Court which he so lately led and which he leaves with our unfeigned respect and affection. We welcome his Excellency Mr Martin Burke, Dean of the Diplomatic Corps, Judges of the Federal Court and of the Supreme Courts of the States and of the Australian

Capital Territory, you Mr Attorney, the Attorneys-General of New South Wales and the Australian Capital Territory and the Solicitors-General of the several States and of the Northern Territory.

Today's ceremonies are not empty rituals. This Court's practice is to administer the Oath of Allegiance and Office in public. That is not a matter of formal procedure. It is a public witnessing of the making of two solemn promises for the performance of which the oath taker will be responsible not only to this Court and this country but also to his Creator. Statute requires that the Oath or a like affirmation be taken before a Chief Justice or Justice enters upon the duties of his or her office.

The first promise is a commitment of loyalty to Her Majesty the Queen her heirs and successors according to law. It is a commitment to the head of State under the Constitution. It is from the *Constitution* that the Oath of Allegiance, which has its origins in feudal England, takes it significance in the present day. As the *Constitution* can now be abrogated or amended only by the Australian people in whom, therefore, the ultimate sovereignty of the nation resides, the Oath of Allegiance and the undertaking to serve the head of State as Chief Justice are a promise of fidelity and service to the Australian people. The duties which the oath imposes sit lightly on a citizen of the nation which the *Constitution* summoned into being and which it sustains. Allegiance to a young, free and confident nation governed by the rule of law is not a burden but a privilege.

The second promise is to 'do right to all manner of people according to law without fear or favour, affection or ill-will'. The form can be traced back to a statute of Edward III, but its substance is of enduring relevance. In substantially that form, the oath or affirmation is taken by every judge. It is rich in meaning. It precludes partisanship for a cause, however worthy to the eyes of a protagonist that cause may be. It forbids any judge to regard himself or herself as a representative of a section of society. It forbids partiality and, most importantly, it commands independence from any influence that might improperly tilt the scales of justice. When the case is heard, the judge must decide it in the lonely room of his or her own conscience but in accordance with the law. That is the way in which right is done without fear or favour, affection or ill-will. Judges sometimes appear to be remote, belonging to what have been described as 'the chill and distant heights'. In the doing of justice that must be so. Justice is not done in public rallies. Nor can it be done by opinion polls or in the comment or correspondence columns of the journals.

The oath requires justice to be done according to law. The content of the duty thus accepted depends upon the jurisdiction to be exercised. In the trial courts of this country, the rules of law prevail. And so they must, for it would do no justice to give judgment according to an abstract notion of what is right in the knowledge that the judgment would be overruled on appeal. In appellate courts, the law may authorize a tension between abstract justice and a rule of law to be resolved by an alteration of the rule. In either case, the jurisdiction of the court is fixed by law and judgment must be rendered in accordance with the judicial method. The security which each of us has is the law. Sir Thomas More of the 'Man for All Seasons' is surely right to put to Roper :'This country's planted thick with laws from coast to coast... and if you cut them down...d'you really think you could stand upright in the winds that would blow then?'[1]

Insistence on the rule of law has a corollary which is implicit in the terms of the judicial oath. If right is to be done according to law, right will be done only if the law be just. Such tension as there is between justice and the rules of law surfaces most acutely in litigation before the High Court, partly because of history, partly because of procedure. With the abolition of the last appeals from Australian courts to the Privy Council, this Court was charged with the ultimate responsibility of declaring the law for this country. This did not mean that we were free to cast aside the priceless heritage of the common law of England, but it did mean that this Court had to examine critically those rules of the common law including the rules of statutory interpretation in the light of our own history, culture and social conditions. Long-standing rules of tort and contract, of land law, equity and administrative law have been revisited in recent years. The same factors and the ever-changing problems of government have evoked renewed examination of the spare text of our *Constitution*.

Then, with the increasing volume of appeals to this Court, it became necessary to introduce the procedural filter of a grant of special leave to appeal. The result is that a considerable proportion of the cases to be decided by this Court involve rules of law that have already proved to be questionable, or at least productive of uncertainty in the Courts below. In cases in both its original and appellate jurisdictions, the Court has had to grapple with issues on which two or more views can reasonably be held. Decisions have not always been reached by more than a narrow majority, but that is not to be wondered at. Where the review of existing rules is in question, the judicial oath to do right according to law sometimes places emphasis on abstract justice, sometimes on the existing rule. And when constitutional doctrine is to be re-examined, the frustration of powerful interests frequently follows. It is inevitable in these circumstances that the decisions of this Court would be seen by many to have a legislative flavour.

But this Court is not a Parliament of policy; it is a court of law. Judicial method is not concerned with the ephemeral opinions of the community. The law is most needed when it stands against popular attitudes sometimes engendered by those with power and when it protects the unpopular against the clamour of the multitude. But judicial method is concerned with the equal dignity of every person, his or her capacity to participate in the life of the community, to contribute to society and to share in its benefits; it is concerned with the powers entrusted to governments and the manner in which those powers are exercised. Judicial method starts with an understanding of the existing rules; it seeks to perceive the principle that underlies them and, at an even deeper level, the values that underlie the principle. At the appellate level, analogy and experience, as well as logic, have a part to play. Judgments must be principled, reasoned and objective, as Sir Anthony Mason said yesterday. And, most significantly, each step in the reasoning must be exposed for public examination and criticism.

Herein lies a difficulty. The work of this Court is rightly a subject of considerable public interest. Though the arguments heard here are often at a high level of abstraction, the emerging principles have a concrete effect on the liberties, relationships and property of individual persons, both natural and artificial. Therefore, the work of this Court should be subject to informed public scrutiny. But how is it possible for the public to be informed? It is unrealistic to expect the arid fields of law to be tilled in the popular press, much less in the brief and adversarial encounters of the television screen. Of course, there are some few highly competent legal journalists but an adequate analysis of legal principle and its significance may be precluded by limited space or may give way to a story of more gripping, if ephemeral, interest. The problem of fostering informed public appreciation of the laws by which we are governed and protected is, I venture to suggest, a problem far from satisfactory solution. It will not be resolved by superficial comment or by an expression of pleasure or disappointment in advancing policy or interest.

Nevertheless, the public interest in the judgments of this and other Courts is a clear and gratifying indication that, in this country, we are governed by the rule of law. The Courts have earned and maintained public confidence in their unfailing response to every reasonable application, to their impartiality and the fearless administration of the law. Today's focus is on the work of the High Court, but it must be remembered that the face of justice is more often the face of the magistrate and the judge at trial.

To accept the office of Chief Justice in the judicial branch of government is a signal honour. To share in the rigorous debates in this Court with colleagues who bear mutual respect for the intellectual integrity and fierce independence of one another is a continuing satisfaction. I assume this office with gratitude for their friendship and support. I thank you for your attendance here today.

---

1 Robert Bolt, *A Man for All Seasons* (Heinemann, 1960) Act 1, 39.

7.2 Retirement as Chief Justice

Editor's note

Brennan retired as Chief Justice on 21 May 1998, the day before his 70th birthday, the constitutional retirement age. These were his remarks.

Thank you all for the extremely generous remarks you have made. Your submissions are usually much more accurate but, enjoying the extravagant spirit of the occasion, I propose to accept them in their entirety, though I would act upon them at my peril.

I must say in the first place that I am delighted that we are sitting here today, Mr Attorney, in a courtroom, the roof of which does not leak. It was not ever so and, indeed, on the last occasion when I presided in this Court, counsel, and I fear sometimes the Justices, were distracted by the signs of slithers of silver coming down from the roof and landing somewhere between the Bar table and this Bench. That has now happily come to pass. As to the products that this grocery shop may produce from time to time, I hope they are to the likings of the customers.

I accept the submissions that you have made because they are offered as an expression of respect by Government, by the legal profession and by the Australian Bar for the holder of the office of Chief Justice. Respect for that office and for the Court in which the Chief Justice presides is a condition of the Court's ability to discharge effectively its constitutional duty to quell disputes by the application of the law. Occasions of this kind, though they tend to focus on the incumbent of the office, have a wider significance when they are seen as a public declaration of respect for the institution.

On behalf of the Court, I welcome the large and distinguished gathering in attendance here this morning. First, I welcome his Excellency, the Governor-General and Lady Deane. I was privileged to sit with His Excellency on this Court and on the Federal Court of Australia for many years. They were years of intense legal interest and, I venture to believe, they fostered an abiding friendship. I thank him and Lady Deane for choosing to be with us today in the character of beloved colleagues, recapturing for the moment the common period of judicial service.

I welcome the President of the Senate and the Speaker of the House of Representatives who, by their presence, affirm on behalf of the parliament as I affirm on behalf of the Court, the mutual respect which the branches of Government must have and demonstrate for the powers and functions of each. Mutual respect is the necessary acknowledgment of the constitutional distribution of powers and the manifesting of mutual respect accords with the expectation of the Australian people.

No decision of this Court refuses to follow an expression of the Parliament's legislative will, properly construed and within power. But it must be remembered that the construction of the Parliament's statutory expression of its will, the scope of its powers and the scope of the powers which Parliament confers on the executive government are firmly within the jurisdiction of the courts – including, of course, this Court. That jurisdiction is basic to the constitutional separation of powers. The rules of construction and constitutional doctrine are applied by the courts for the purpose of accurately perceiving the will of the Parliament as the Parliament has expressed it and ensuring that the *Constitution* – the charter of the political power of the people – is faithfully observed.

I welcome his Excellency, the Dean of the Diplomatic Corps. The links between this Court and the courts of other nations have grown in recent years. As the courts administer the laws embodying the ethos of each nation, the better the understanding of the actual workings of a nation's courts, the deeper the understanding of its values, its laws, its government and the relationships of its people. In recent years, some Justices have visited overseas courts and universities to examine concepts that are current in the legal systems of other countries. Thus, the tyranny of distance and the risk of intellectual isolation has been lessened.

I welcome the retired Chief Justices and Justices of this Court. I have been privileged to sit with each of those distinguished judges. By their learning, integrity and intellect I have been instructed. It is a pleasure to sit again with them at this Bench, however briefly, and to recall the friendship which accompanied the performance of our curial duties. With them, I welcome Lady Stephen, Mrs Murphy, Lady Dawson and Mrs Toohey who have graced us in the past.

I welcome the Chief Justices of the superior Courts of the Commonwealth and of the States and Territories, whose presence here is a tangible reminder of the integration of the judicial system of this nation and of the solidarity of a national judiciary who are at one in their commitment to independence and impartiality in the administration of justice according to law. I welcome especially the Chief Justice of New Zealand, Sir Thomas Eichelbaum who, as a member of the Council of Chief Justices of Australia and New Zealand, contributes not only the wisdom of his advice but the experience of the courts in that country whose judicial method most closely accords with our own.

I welcome the Bar and the Solicitors of this Court on whose knowledge, insights and industry this Court heavily depends. It is right that, as I leave this Bench, I should express my profound appreciation of the assistance I have derived from the careful preparation of cases by solicitors; from the incisive, fearless and courteous advocacy of counsel and from the illumination of problems that emerges from the joint efforts of both. It will not be taken amiss if I note with regret the absence from the Bar table of Sir Maurice Byers, a friend of many years, who is presently indisposed. His participation in the work of this Court was perhaps no less on that side of the Bar table than it would have been on this.

I welcome the many judicial and personal friends, including my Associates, past and present, for whose company on this day I am especially grateful. There are many with whom I practised at the Queensland Bar, including Sir Dormer Andrews, latterly Chief Justice of Queensland. He admitted me to his chambers and his advice 46 years ago. It is a pleasure to see these friends here today.

I will be pardoned for not expressing publicly sentiments about my family – my wife, my children and their spouses, my grandchildren and my sisters. Those sentiments belong to the deep intimacies of family life and they cannot be shared without depreciation of the gratitude I owe and the love I bear them.

Finally, I welcome the members of the public who come to this Court, as they do to every court in the Commonwealth, as of right. It is for the service of the people that the courts are created and perform their functions. The courts sit in public, think and write in private, then publishes to all the world their decisions and their reasons. No other branch of government responds so unfailingly to every application within its jurisdiction nor gives so adequate an explanation of the reasons for its decisions. The courts must be available to serve the litigants by quelling their disputes, else raw power prevails untrammelled by the rule of law.

The agenda of the courts are defined by the litigants. The courts decide the controversies that the people bring to the courts for decision. They are the people's problems. The Court has no agenda of its own. But, as the issues that arise for decision are contemporary issues arising in contemporary circumstances, the work of the Court in each generation reflects that generation's concerns.

Patterns of litigation are not hard to perceive, especially in the area of public law. In the years between the two World Wars, when the sense of Australian nationhood was gaining firm ground, there were controversies about the extent of Commonwealth legislative power; in times of war, the focus of litigation was often on the scope of Commonwealth power in respect of defence; in the period since the Second World War, which has seen a massive growth in governmental regulation and governmental benefits, the law of judicial review of administrative action has been greatly developed; then the growing community and international concerns with human rights and with the environment have evoked major judicial examination of the relevant laws. It is foreseeable that the growth of international law, the negotiation of treaties on a wide diversity of subjects and the legislative incorporation of international instruments in domestic statutes will give rise to an expanded jurisprudence affecting the relationship between international and domestic law. Thus, the cases that are brought forward for determination can be related to the social issues of the time.

They are brought forward by litigants seeking a resolution of their disputes; and so, it is with every case. The Court's role is responsive to the invocation of its jurisdiction. One of the advantages of the Court's responsiveness is that it is kept abreast of contemporary issues – not by formulating an agenda but by the demands of the litigants. Then the Court must find and apply the relevant legal rule to resolve the dispute – not a rule to fit a particular case on the day of judgment but a general rule in terms which can be applied in contemporary litigation to resolve all contemporary controversies of the same kind.

The courts do not have a free hand in formulating the rules to be applied. The courts are bound by the text of the *Constitution*, by the terms of a valid statute and by the history and precedents that constitute what I once called 'the skeleton of principle which gives the body of our law its shape and internal consistency'.

In construing the *Constitution*, this Court has had to construe the spare text in order to answer contemporary problems. It was always intended that it would be so. Ninety-six years ago, when Attorney-General Deakin spoke on the second reading of the Judiciary Bill for the constitution of this Court, he observed that:

the nation lives, grows, and expands. Its circumstances change, its needs alter, and its problems present themselves with new faces. The organ of the national life which, preserving the union, is yet able from time to time to transfuse into it the fresh blood of the living present, is the Judiciary. ... It is as one of the organs of Government which enables the *Constitution* to grow and to be adapted to the changeful necessities and circumstances of generation after generation that the High Court operates.[1]

At first, the founding Justices, whose portraits hang above us in this Courtroom today, read the text of the *Constitution* through the prism of their experience in securing the approval of six self-governing colonies to bring the Commonwealth into being. It was understandable that they should do so. Reading the text through those eyes, they espoused the doctrine of state reserved powers and implied immunities.

In time, with the First World War, the economic and commercial integration of the States and the growing sense of national identity, the doctrine of reserved powers was discarded in the *Engineers' Case*.[2] Changing conditions exposed the true meaning of the text. Sir Victor Windeyer, in the *Payroll Tax Case*, explained that the discarding of the doctrine of the implied immunity of the states occurred 'because in 1920 the *Constitution* was read in a new light, a light reflected from events that had, over twenty years, led to a growing realisation that Australians were now one people and Australia one country and that national laws might meet national needs'.[3]

In recent times, this Court has looked to the history of the constitutional text to identify the subject to which the language is directed and the nature and objectives of the federal movement. It has looked to the purpose of a provision so far as that can be elicited from the text. It has sought to examine the *Constitution* with that strict logic and high technique of which Sir Owen Dixon spoke. That is the judicial method that keeps the law in a state of good repair.

When the courts are dealing with the common law – the law created and developed at first by English judges and, in more recent times, chiefly by Australian judges – the rules of law have been changed in response to changing circumstances. It must be so, else the law would moulder into irrelevancy or, worse, produce or perpetuate injustice. Sometimes the argument is advanced that the renewal of the common law in the hands of the judges is a new departure – an attempt at social engineering that is at odds with Sir Owen Dixon's rigorous insistence on 'strict and complete legalism'. It should be remembered that the strict and complete legalism of which Sir Owen spoke pre-supposed – to use his own words – the existence of 'a definite system of accepted knowledge or thought and that judgments and other legal writings are evidence of its content'. But the law is not an ever-expanding cosmos containing rules for the solution of the problems of every generation and awaiting only a judicial telescope to capture their text. As each generation faces new problems, the rules must be crafted by the judges of the time.

This is pre-eminently the work of the High Court. If the law already provided a full panoply of appropriate and applicable rules, the occasions for this Court's interventions would be few indeed. But the Court cannot refrain from determining matters within its jurisdiction simply because a new rule has to be devised for the purpose. To perform this function the Justices must master the existing authorities and from them elicit the underlying principle. In some cases, it is necessary to perceive, if not to articulate, the community value which gives vitality to the law in question. Then, provided the value is consistent with enduring community values, the principle must be re-examined and, if need be, it must be restated in contemporary terms that can be integrated with other legal principles and a new rule, appropriate to the case in hand and expressed to apply to the instant and future similar cases, is formulated. This work, though conceptual in nature, requires more than intellectual rigour. It requires the wisdom which each Justice must bring to the task.

It has been my privilege to engage with and to be stimulated by the colleagues, past and present, who sit with me this morning. It has been a privilege impossible to convey in words for it is based in the acknowledged integrity and industry of colleagues whose work is done in the privacy of their chambers and in the isolation of each judicial conscience. The increasing burden of work places great strains on the judicial resources. The devotion of my colleagues to their duties has been a continuing encouragement in the performance of my own.

For the years of intellectual stimulation and personal friendship which I have enjoyed on this Court I give my thanks to my judicial colleagues past and present.

I thank the Chief Executive and Principal Registrar, Mr Christopher Doogan, whose efficiency and advice have steered the administration of this Court during my term as Chief Justice. I thank the Registrars and their staffs who keep the machinery of the Court in efficient working order. I thank the administrative staff and the attendants who introduce the visiting public to this building. I thank my personal staff including the Associates who have worked so constructively with me on judgments in this Court, in the Federal Court and in the Administrative Appeals Tribunal. I thank especially for her loyalty and devotion Ms Nessie Birchley, who has been with me all the years on this Court, and I thank Mr Luigi Cartolano, not only for transport but for friendship. And most of all I thank the people of Australia for the opportunity of being a member of, and presiding over, a Court which exercises its authority not to control but to serve; not to achieve a policy objective but to maintain a society where peace, order and good government are based on the rule of law. To have contributed to that endeavour has been a high honour and if, to some extent, that contribution has been beneficial, I am fortunate indeed. And if it be found that, unremarked by the generous comments from the Bar table, I have committed errors or made omissions, my only explanation can be: I did it my way.

I extend my warm congratulations to Chief Justice Gleeson as he assumes this office on the morrow. He will find it a challenge but, I doubt not, like me he will find it a privilege.

The Court will now adjourn.

---

1. Commonwealth, *Parliamentary Debates*, House of Representatives, 18 March 1902, 10966 (Alfred Deakin, Attorney-General).
2. See *Amalgamated Society of Engineers v Adelaide Steamship Co Ltd* (1920) 28 CLR 129.
3. See *Victoria v Commonwealth ('Payroll Tax Case')* (1971) 122 CLR 353, 396.

7.3 Lessons from a life in the Law

Editor's note

This was Brennan's Hal Wootten Lecture delivered at the University of New South Wales on 23 August 2012.[1] At the conclusion of the lecture Hal Wootten proposed a vote of thanks. He said:

> Sir Gerard did refer to *Mabo* in his Lecture, as an example of the High Court giving the law a little nudge in the direction the judges thought it ought to go. He was picking up a phrase I used in my 2008 Lecture, which I in turn picked up at the 1971 Australian Law Convention. In those days we couldn't have a conference without a visiting Law Lord. In opening the Convention, Lord Diplock observed that it is not often that there is an opportunity of saying as Lord Mansfield could, 'the air of England is too pure for any slave to breathe, let the black go free', but there are many more opportunities of giving a little nudge that sends the law in the direction it ought to go. The mention of Lord Mansfield was a reference to his somewhat hesitant decision in *Somerset's Case* in 1772 concerning the status of slavery under the common law.
>
> I have often quoted those words in preaching a "little nudger" philosophy, open not just to judges but to everyone. Each of us has countless opportunities every day to give the world little nudges in the right direction, and the cumulative effect of our little nudges, and those of all the other little nudgers, is a major effect on the direction the world takes. All of us, however humble, can lead worthwhile lives.
>
> I remember using the theme in responding to the extraordinary attacks that followed the *Mabo* decision. In the turbulent 18 months between the judgment and the passing of the *Native Title Act 1993* (*Cth*), I was one of those who engaged in the public defence of the decision that judges could not undertake themselves. Among dozens of occasions on which I spoke or wrote was a graduation ceremony where I told the story of Granville Sharp, a civil servant who, as one historian wrote, 'fired by the cruel usage of a negro slave in the streets of London, never rested until he had obtained the verdict [of Lord Mansfield] which forever afterwards rid the British islands of the taint of slavery.' In my anxiety to give just recognition to this little nudger, I obscured Lord Diplock's distinction between the Lord Mansfield's and the little nudgers: I did the same when I came to praise the 'little nudgers' on the High Court who had given the Mabo decision. I lumped them in with many little nudgers whose work laid the ground for the decision, people like Eddie Mabo himself, Greg McIntyre, Henry Reynolds, Ron Castan and the lawyers he led, our own Garth Nettheim (with us tonight), to invidiously name a few.
>
> But Lord Diplock's distinction is worth making. In the end we little nudgers need the Lord Mansfield's. We depend on there being people in high places who have the wisdom, the vision and the courage to seize the opportunity and bring the work of the little nudgers to fruition in a form that will

command authority and survive. As Ecclesiastes tells us, there comes a time to praise famous men and women, especially when they are so little given to self-praise as our speaker tonight.

Why had there been no appeal from Justice Blackburn's 1971 decision affirming that in the eyes of the common law Australia had been *terra nullius* prior to British annexation? Because the plaintiffs' lawyers judged, with good reason, that there would be no Mansfield moment in the Barwick High Court. Had an unsuccessful appeal been made, the possibility of overturning *terra nullius* may well have been buried, perhaps beyond resurrection. So, the issue had to wait another 20 years, until the work of many little nudgers found six receptive judges on the Mason Court.

While all six joined in the Mansfield role, one had to write what would become the leading judgment, find the words and the arguments that could command a majority – the reasons that would survive the scrutiny of future generations of judges and ultimately win the support of the community. Although one would never guess it from tonight's Lecture, that role fell to Justice Brennan.[2]

When Hal Wootten delivered his eponymous Lecture in 2008, he gave it the title 'Living in the Law'. He thought that subsequent Lecturers might be judges or others who have had an opportunity 'to give a little nudge that sends the law along the direction it ought to go'. It is an inevitable function of a Justice of the High Court that she or he can give a little nudge to the law, and I am happy to think, that life in the law can and should have a connection with the problems of the time. But I shall not trouble you with an analysis of High Court judgments to demonstrate their relationship with contemporary issues. It is manifest that cases such as the *Communist Party Case,*[3] the *Tasmanian Dam Case,*[4] the *Mabo Cases,*[5] *Lange's Case,*[6] the *Work Choices Case*[7] and the recent migration cases[8] have engaged major issues of the day and have nudged the law in a direction in which the Court thought that the law ought to go. Rather at this terminal stage of my life in the law, I should like to reflect on the way in which that legal life has taught me some lessons about the law itself, its significance for the community and about the profession which practises the law.

It is nearly 70 years since I first entered a court room presided over by my father in Rockhampton. That was in the war years when his Associate was temporarily absent and I stepped into the role and demonstrated my lack of experience – a story that I have previously told.[9] I had in one hand a pro forma sheet for charging a prisoner on trial and in the other the indictment signed and presented by the Crown Prosecutor. Mistaking the name of the Prosecutor for the name of the accused, I charged a kindly, meek and highly reputable man with the crime of rape. Counsel for the accused, in accordance with the camaraderie of the Bar, immediately announced his appearance for his learned friend and pleaded not guilty. And so, I was given the first instalment of a lesson about life in the law. It was not about the need to follow the form – that was only too obvious – it was a lesson about the relationship that is built among members of the legal profession who share a deep respect for their vocation – a respect which fosters warm personal relationships even when they are engaged as adversaries. I shall return later in this talk to discuss the significance of that relationship for the way in which the law is practised.

Every practising lawyer will have learnt a variety of lessons in the course of her or his practice. The education of the fledgling barrister might focus on how to run a case in court, how to avoid embarrassing mistakes and how to survive the first lean years of the Bar. I was taught that I should always check the facts, identify and stick to the issues and cite law that was applicable to the case. One of the doyens of the Bar told me that there is usually only one point worth pursuing, sometimes two; another said to be careful of any juror who wore a coat with a slit in the back – in those days, an indication of sartorial elegance. I discovered the wisdom of thinking carefully before speaking when I offered my leader in the High Court a quick answer to Sir Alan Taylor's barbed question only to hear him submit my answer, pause then, turning to me, say 'That's not right!' I was shown that cross-examination became more effective once the club was put away in favour of the stiletto and prospects were improved by understating the case in the opening address. The prudence of receiving a fee before starting a criminal trial was a practical lesson when a friend whom I was induced to represent was acquitted of fraud and emerged from the dock saying 'I don't know how to thank you but, as the great Darrow for the Defence observed, that is a problem that has disappeared since the Phoenicians invented money'. His historical reference had more substance than his implied promise. I am tempted to ramble on about the people I have known, the humour of events and the battles fought and won – or lost. But I think I should identify a few issues of more general importance and try to develop a few themes in the time available. I have chosen four issues: law and cultural values; the importance of the community's interest in the law and its administration; the necessity for fair procedure; and the motivation of the lawyer and the rewards of legal practice.

First, the law and cultural values

In the course of an undistinguished academic career in the post-war years, I had the good fortune to be appointed as an Associate first to my father and later to other Supreme Court judges. I learnt that the law regulates a vast area of our lives, as individuals, as parties to relationships and as members of the community. And it seemed to operate consistently with the values of the community.

When the foundations of the common law were laid in the 12th and 13th centuries, the English judges drew on the customs of the English people, albeit the content was affected by the practices of the judges and lawyers of the time assisted by scholars familiar with Roman Law.[10] In the formative years of the common law, the judges drew on the values of contemporary society, giving institutional force to the values of that society. This is the way in which the common law develops. Judge Cardozo observed: 'Law is indeed an historical growth for it is an expression of customary morality which develops silently and unconsciously from one age to another.'[11]

Sir Ninian Stephen observed in *Onus v Alcoa* that 'Courts necessarily reflect community values and beliefs'.[12] Civilisation is impossible without moral values and a community which does not share or accept a basic set of moral values is a community in chaos. A cohesive society shares a common set of fundamental community standards. In a peaceful and stable community, community moral standards give the law its normative force and the law in turn reinforces those standards. Thus, the rule of law depends upon the consensus of the community. Lord Devlin, after a lifetime of experience, observed that:

> [S]ociety means a community of ideas; without shared ideas on politics, morals, and ethics no society can exist... If men and women try to create a society in which there is no fundamental agreement about good and evil they will fail; if, having based it on common agreement, the agreement goes, the society will disintegrate. For society is not something that is kept together physically; it is held by the invisible bonds of common thought... A common morality is part of the bondage. The bondage is part of the price of society; and mankind, which needs society, must pay its price. [13]

If law and the community's cultural standards were generally at odds, either the rule of law would cease or the law would be forcibly applied in a totalitarian regime. Herein lies the distinction between the rule *of* law and rule *by* law. It may be that Nazi Germany was ruled by law, many of Hitler's heinous policies being implemented in accordance with Nazi ideology, either without judicial sanction or by the courts which were bound to apply the law without regard to justice. The rule of law, on the other hand, seeks to do justice as the community understands it and therefore to reduce to a minimum any difference between justice and legal rules. Law and community moral standards must march in unison. Professor Hart's seminal work *The Concept of Law* observed that '[n]ot only do law and morals share a vocabulary so that there are both legal and moral obligations, duties and rights; but all municipal legal systems reproduce the substance of certain fundamental moral requirements.'[14]

Community standards may not change rapidly, but they do change and, when they do, they call for corresponding changes in the law. If community standards have bypassed an old law, the old law will gradually moulder into irrelevance and cease to be enforced. Conversely, when there is a movement towards a change in community standards, a timely change in the law may hasten the change in standards. But the law cannot go so far in advance of the community's standards or alienate the approval of the general community without forfeiting the practical sanction on which every law depends, namely, a community consensus that law should be obeyed or otherwise operate according to its terms. That consensus is Lord Devlin's 'bond of common thought' that keeps society together. The common law cannot be developed inconsistently with the enduring values of contemporary society. If it were otherwise, the law would lose its authority. Nevertheless, as the majority said in the *Native Title Case,* 'The content of the common law will, in the ordinary course of events, change from time to time according to the changing perception of the courts'. [15]

When I entered practice, Australian community standards were changing. We found that, however gradually, the law changed too in order to re-establish its relationship with contemporary culture. Divorce law was a clear example. At first the laws of the several States governing divorce required proof of a matrimonial offence or breach of an order for the restitution of conjugal rights. And the three C's –collusion, connivance and condonation – were absolute bars to a decree. To give effect to these laws, the Supreme Courts of the States and Territories exercised a busy jurisdiction and briefs in undefended divorces were some of the basic fodder of the junior Bar. But community standards were changing and ultimately the Commonwealth exercised its constitutional power to legislate with respect to marriage and divorce. In 1959 Sir Garfield Barwick as Attorney-General procured the passage of the *Matrimonial Causes Bill* which introduced the concept of no-fault divorce. The concept was advanced when Senator Lionel Murphy introduced the *Family Law Act 1975* (Cth).[16] The concept of no-fault divorce was strongly opposed and was perhaps in advance of general community sentiment at the time but once it became law it confirmed a change in the community's standards. Today no reversion to fault-based divorce would be possible.

A law which is at odds with the fundamental standards of the community will not be enforced. For that reason, Australia came to reject capital punishment. It had been abolished in my home State of Queensland in 1922. In 1967, the last judicial execution in Australia – the hanging of Ronald Ryan in Victoria – met with such community abhorrence that capital punishment was ultimately removed from every statute book in this country. It took a long time but the law was ultimately brought into conformity with community standards.

Parliament is the branch of government, which is primarily capable of, and responsible for, changing the law. Of course, some legislative changes are made simply because of a political decision which does not affect the fundamental moral standards of the community. Similarly, the courts may change some common law rules simply because the existing rules are too complex or are not the most efficient in contemporary conditions. But the courts are slow to change the common law (including in that term the rules of equity) in response to a change in community standards. Yet by making a change, the law is kept in a serviceable state. If a fundamental moral standard which supported a common law rule has been supplanted by a new fundamental moral standard and the old common law rule denies the contemporary community's fundamental moral standard, application of the old rule would work an injustice. Moral standards monitor the law's operation, as they always have. A century ago, Roscoe Pound described a reaction from the common law in Tudor and Stuart England: 'The law was liberalising by an infusion of moral ideas from without; and since the hard and fast mould of common-law procedure precluded this liberalisation and this infusion through the ordinary course of the law, it was necessary to go outside of the law for a season until a readjustment could be accomplished.'[17]

Then a further reaction set in to restore the law's authority: 'If we meet the movement away from the law, therefore, by a modernising of the legal and judicial machinery which will enable it to meet more effectively the demands of the present, to attain the ends for which the legal system exists, we may be confident that now, as in Tudor and Stuart England, the law will prevail.'[18]

The courts may be constrained to change the old common law rule, but such an adventure in law reform requires a fundamental change in community standards. In *Mabo (No 2)* the High Court saw that the old rule that indigenous people were incapable of having a proprietary interest in land was incompatible with the contemporary community's standard of racial equality in the right to enjoy the exclusive occupation of land. Such cases are, however, few in number, occurring only when fundamental standards change and the law has been left behind.

Fundamental community standards are of the essence of any culture, but what happens when the community is or becomes multi-cultural? As the law will, of its nature, apply generally and uniformly, the democratic principle prescribes that the culture of the majority is determinative of the legal structure. Minority practices which offend the fundamental moral standards of the majority have to be abandoned, for there is no community if basic moral standards are in conflict.

If there is no correlation of the law and the community's culture or there is significant tension between the two, the likely result is disregard of the law or erosion of the culture or both. This was starkly illustrated by the events leading to the murder of Jack Emanuel, a District Commissioner in Rabaul in 1971. The Chief Justice of PNG described the events.[19] Land to the Tolai – the people of the Gazelle Peninsula – is the centre of their existence as a people. From the late nineteenth century there had been gradual encroachment on traditional Tolai lands by the colonial powers – Germany and Australia. The Kabaira villagers endeavoured for years to seek a solution in their favour from the Land Titles Commission, but a 1971 court decision made it clear that the courts would not support their claim. They felt that the courts were denying them protection and that they might lose all their land to a titles system which they did not understand. A leading villager argued that it was necessary to highlight their grievances by killing a 'big man', so the District Commissioner was lured alone down a pathway in the hidden presence of a number of villagers and was stabbed to death. A number of Tolai people were tried for murder. I was briefed to prosecute in the 5 month trial in Rabaul. Shortly after the start of the trial, a protest of about 6,000 Tolai was peacefully staged to demonstrate the strength of their cultural entitlement to land. Fortunately, the patient, dignified sitting of Chief Justice Sir John Minogue leading to the conviction of some accused and the acquittal of others quelled all public disturbances. Forty years later, I saw a small note in a newspaper that some land in Kabaira had been returned to the traditional owners. Law and order broke down when the law refused to recognize traditional ownership of the land, but ultimately law and practice had to be congruent with the cultural values of the people.

Later, when I was representing the Northern Land Council in the Woodward Land Rights Commission, we gathered our instructions by visiting the communities in the Top End of the Territory. It was clear that Aboriginal culture was languishing. Aborigines had lost much of their land and land is central to Aboriginal culture – indeed, to an Aborigine's identity.[20] Following Justice Woodward's report, large tracts of land were restored to Aboriginal ownership by the *Aboriginal Land Rights (Northern Territory) Act 1976* (Cth) and the cultural life of many communities, especially in Arnhem Land, was greatly strengthened. Australian law accommodated and was reconciled to essential elements of Aboriginal culture.

There have been some suggestions that, following the growth of Islam in Australia, there is room for a pluralistic legal system, a system in which at least some parts of Islamic Sharia law might operate as part of Australian law and in parallel with the common law system. Dr Rowan Williams, Archbishop of Canterbury made that suggestion for the United Kingdom. That suggestion seems to me to be misconceived. It recalls the problem of recognition of traditional Aboriginal law which the Australian Law Reform Commission reported on in 1986.[21] The Commission acknowledged that there are substantial objections to legal pluralism in the sense of two distinct legal systems operating in the one country.[22] Its recommendations for recognition of Aboriginal law did not go so far. The Commission noted that: 'The general arguments ... lead to the conclusion that any recognition of Aboriginal customary laws must occur against the background and within the framework of the general law. Indeed, the contrary has not really been argued before the Commission.'[23] In my respectful opinion, this was a wise conclusion.

No Court could apply and no Government could administer two parallel systems of law, especially if they reflect – as they inevitably would reflect – different fundamental standards. To give effect to dual legal systems would be to confirm dual cultures and, as Lord Devlin pointed out, a stable society is held together by 'the invisible bonds of common thought', that is, common thought about fundamental moral standards. The emphasis here is on 'fundamental'. In a multi-cultural society, cohesiveness depends on agreement about fundamentals, leaving ample freedom for individuals to adhere to moral standards different from those of the mainstream majority.

The beliefs, customs and practices which give an individual his or her identity as a member of a religious or national or ethnic group are respected by Australian law except in a case where the custom or practice is proscribed by the general law. Freedom of religious belief and practice is one of the essential freedoms that are a fundamental value of contemporary Australian culture. Mason CJ and I spelt out the principle in *The Scientology Case*: 'Conduct in which a person engages in giving effect to his faith in the supernatural is religious, but it is excluded from the area of legal immunity marked out by the concept of religion if it offends against the ordinary laws, that is, if it offends against laws which do not discriminate against religion generally or against particular religions or against conduct of a kind which is characteristic only of a religion.'[24]

Our law, strengthened by anti-discrimination legislation, is intended to give effect to our basic values. Australians enjoy political stability because we share the basic values of equality, tolerance and freedom of thought and action; we respect integrity, especially in public office, and we insist on the rule of law. These are the essential values of our culture that must be reflected generally in our law. This is the law that binds all Australians, and which has effect in every part of our nation.[25]

Therefore, a Muslim is free to adhere to the beliefs, customs and practices prescribed by Sharia law insofar as they are consistent with the general law in force in this country. That freedom must be respected and protected but that does not mean that Islamic Sharia should have the force of law. One version of Islamic Sharia was expounded by the President of the Federal Supreme Court of the United Arab Emirates at a Conference I attended in Abu Dhabi in 2008. The scholarly and hospitable President explained the scope of that law. He said that 'the Islamic Sharia is … comprehensive in the sense that it finds the legal rules that regulate all the aspects of daily life for individuals and societies. For instance, there are overall rules regulating civil and commercial transactions, rules regulating family relationships, rules regulating the affairs of the judiciary, litigation and criminal justice, rules related to international relations, and so on.'[26]

His Excellency further explained that the basic principles of Islamic Sharia are provided by '[b]oth the Koran and the Sunna [which] could be considered the constitution in other legislation systems, and therefore all other sources should agree with them. Thus, if juristic reasoning contradicts with them, it should be rendered invalid, and if customs contradict with them, they are also unacceptable; and this applies to all other secondary or ancillary sources.'[27]

The common law does not go so far – it leaves a gap between the mandates of the law and the conduct that we choose to engage in according to our individual moral standards. We call that gap "freedom" and it allows Australian law to protect the cultural moral values of our minorities. We value that freedom not only for the benefit of the individual but in order to maintain a free society – a society which can celebrate the rule *of* law but which rejects the notion of rule *by* law.

We are proud of our multi-cultural, multi-ethnic, multi-religious society especially because our citizens, including the Islamic community, share the basic Australian values of tolerance, egalitarianism, and individual freedom in thought and action. That consensus provides the essential cohesiveness of our society and the moral support for our integrated system of law. It secures the peace and order that we cherish.

Next, the community's interest in the administration of the law

We are so accustomed to the open administration of the law that its role in maintaining the rule of law in an ordered and peaceful society does not dawn on our consciousness. But peace and order are characteristics of our society only by reason of the community's confidence in – indeed, its ownership of – the process of administering the law. The community's interest in the administration of the law is manifest more often on the country circuits than in the metropolitan courts which depend mainly on media reports to inform the community about the work of the courts. I remember a rather notorious trial in Longreach. There had been arson of one of the three hotels in the small town of Isisford in which a young girl and her baby perished. The other two hotel keepers and the alleged 'torch' were charged with murder and the graziers and townspeople of the district packed the old courthouse and its verandahs day by day. Notorious cases stimulate public interest, but this case was rather special. The judge heard that the word had got around that the trial had become so important that it might have to be transferred to Brisbane! In his summing up, he delivered a wonderful exposition of the authority of the Circuit Court and the local jury, comparable with the authority of Her Majesty's Courts in London! This was the law in local action, involving the community and open to observation by the people. It was easy to sense the response of the gallery and, indeed, the pride of the district. The rule of law was strengthened by the public involvement, as critical spectators, in the proceedings of the trial.

In 1970, the legendary Lord Denning, accompanied by a distinguished accountant, Mr McNeil, went to Fiji to conduct what was in substance an arbitration between the 15,000 sugar growers – mainly Indian Fijians – and the sugar miller, South Pacific Sugar Mills, a subsidiary of the CSR Company, a major element in the economy of Fiji. There had been festering dissatisfaction about the terms on which growers supplied cane to the mills. A Committee sponsored by the Government Party, the Alliance, briefed me for some of the sugar growers and other growers were represented by local counsel briefed by the Opposition, the Federation Party. Fiji was fortunate in having the services of Lord Denning whose acuity of mind was equalled by his sensitivity to the history of Southern Indian immigration to Fiji. The Arbitration was held in the parish hall of Lautoka, in the sugar-growing north west of the island of Viti Levu. The public interest was enormous, manifested both by the numbers who attended each day and by the continuous media coverage. On the basis of the Denning Award, Fiji moved from colonial to independent status and the CSR Company disposed of its interest in the sugar mills. These were major developments in the history of Fiji. They would not have been possible without public familiarity with and confidence in the manner in which the contentious issues of the arbitration had been litigated before, and resolved by, Lord Denning.

And, as I mentioned earlier, during the Emanuel trial in Rabaul, there was a protest march of approximately 6,000 Tolai people. Their protest was in support of those asserting traditional interests in land but, that having been stated, the interest of the community moved to the fairness of the trial itself. There was no protest against the proceedings in the trial and the numbers in the public gallery diminished as day after long day went on. When so contentious an issue was involved, it was only community satisfaction with the fairness of the proceedings that could account for the peaceful outcome of the trial and public order in the Gazelle Peninsula.

In 1913, the High Court said[28] that the admission of the public to attend proceedings is 'one of the normal attributes of a court'.[29] Public scrutiny of curial proceedings gives the assurance of integrity in the application of the law. The administration of the law is a public function and, as Sir Frank Kitto observed:

> The process of reasoning which has decided the case must itself be exposed to the light of day, so that all concerned may understand what principles and practice of law and logic are guiding the courts, and so that full publicity may be achieved which provides, on the one hand, a powerful protection against any tendency to judicial autocracy and against any erroneous suspicion of judicial wrongdoing and, on the other hand, an effective stimulant to judicial high performance. Jeremy Bentham put the matter in a nutshell ... when he wrote ... 'Publicity is the very soul of justice. It is the keenest spur to exertion and the surest of all guards against improbity. It keeps the judge himself while trying on trial'.[30]

The community's interest in the administration of the law is partially satisfied by the media, but that is not always beneficial. The courts are not strangers to the risk of injustice flowing from prejudice sometimes created by media statements, particularly in criminal cases when statements on the part of the police or other law enforcement agencies may represent only a partisan version of the facts. The ultimate bulwark of liberty is the jury. The jury is the institution which not only assures the community of its right to participate in the administration of justice but also assures the litigants of an impartial assessment of their rights and duties. The collective wisdom of twelve jurors and the innate sense of fairness in our people is a solid bastion against injustice. After some experience in criminal cases, I recall only one instance of a jury whose verdict I suspected because of the intense feeling in a country town, but even then the verdict may well have been correct. Perhaps some of you remember the film *Twelve Angry Men* in which Henry Fonda was the questioning juror who steadily engaged the prejudices of his fellow jurors until a unanimous and just acquittal was returned. Then the jurors dispersed. It is a common experience, in civil and in criminal jury trials, for the jurors to perform their critical functions and then, anonymously and with no more than a judicial expression of appreciation, to leave the court to resume their disparate activities. Their anonymity is proof of the jurors' disinterest in the verdict they were sworn to give. They take with them, however, the consciousness that they have represented their community in administering justice and they are able to tell others about the fairness – or otherwise – of the curial process. Community participation in the trial process is one of the important bonds between the courts and the people they serve. No doubt there are some issues, particularly of a technical nature, that may be difficult for a jury to evaluate, but errors in findings of that kind can often be traced to the inaccuracy or obscurity of the technical evidence. To be sure, there can be miscarriages of justice but, when it comes to the determination of the ultimate issues in a trial, the wisdom born of the various life experiences of twelve jurors is likely to be greater than the wisdom of a single judge, however experienced and learned the judge may be. The worldly wisdom of the jury cannot be supplied by a judge. Moreover, as Latham CJ observed: 'The right to a jury is one of the fundamental rights of citizenship and not a mere matter of procedure, and so the courts have said.'[31]

I remember a trial in which my client was charged with assault. He produced ostensibly independent witnesses who gave unshaken evidence of an alibi. A judge would surely have acquitted in the light of that evidence, but the jury convicted. Juries have an uncanny ability to spot the truth, as I discovered later. One of my colleagues reported that the client, despite conviction, a hefty fine and the payment of my fee, had been pleased by my advocacy. I found the tribute difficult to understand. 'Oh', the colleague explained, 'your client thought it was all worthwhile to have had the satisfaction of hitting the rotter!' In my view, it would be a mistake to favour trial by judge alone in preference to trial by jury.

There is another great advantage which, in my view, juries confer on the administration of justice. They strengthen the independence of the Bar. In the absence of juries, advocates are obliged to respond to judicial idiosyncrasies and sometimes it is possible to detect an obsequiousness in the framing of submissions. The advocate may think that a show of independence will not be in the interests of a client and, in time, may allow servility to sap the passion for independence. In a jury trial, the advocate is primarily concerned not by the response of the presiding judge, but by the response of the jury. Mortimer's *Rumpole* not only illustrated the strength of an independent Bar but demonstrated the community's admiration of a system that accommodates, and indeed welcomes, robust independence.

The necessity of fair procedure

The primary purpose of fair procedure is the protection of the interests of the parties who are affected by the exercise of governmental power, whether administrative or judicial power. But there is another purpose – the maintenance of public confidence in the authority of the repository of the power. If a fair procedure is followed in exercising a power, even unfavourable decisions may find acceptance. An unsuccessful applicant or litigant may feel disappointed in the result, but if the decision has been reached without observing a fair procedure, disappointment will be exacerbated by a sense of fundamental injustice. Community confidence in the integrity of a system depends more upon the fairness of the procedure in the exercise of power than on the results of the power exercised.

The importance of procedural fairness in the exercise of governmental power was at the heart of the enormous reforms that introduced the new Commonwealth administrative law, leading in turn to new administrative law arrangements in the States. Traditional procedure for exercising administrative power had fallen short in achieving fairness compared with judicial procedure. That is why there was more confidence in the exercise of judicial power than in the exercise of administrative power as Sir Anthony Mason pointed out:

> Experience indicates that administrative decision-making falls short of the judicial model . ... – in five significant respects. First, it lacks the independence of the judicial process. The administrative decision-maker is, and is thought to be, more susceptible to political, ministerial and bureaucratic influence than is a judge. Secondly, some administrative decisions are made out in the open; most are not. Thirdly, apart from statute, the administrator does not have to give reasons for his decision. Fourthly, the administrator does not always observe the standards of natural justice or procedural fairness. That is not surprising; he is not trained to do so. Finally, he is inclined to subordinate the claims of justice of the individual to the more general demands of public policy and sometimes to adventitious political and bureaucratic pressures.

> The five features of administrative decision-making which I have mentioned reveal why it is that administrative decision-making has never achieved the level of acceptance of the judicial process.[32]

The *Administrative Appeals Tribunal Act 1975* (Cth) created a framework for merits review of administrative decisions which vested in the AAT the powers and duties appropriate to judicial procedure. The Tribunal was constituted by a Judge and independent members but when the Tribunal opened its doors in 1976; I was its only member. Its hearings were generally to be in public, it had to apply the law and to give reasons for the Tribunal's decision and its decisions were subject to appeal on questions of law to the Federal Court. This was a novel development under a Westminster form of government, but public and bureaucratic confidence in the Tribunal's processes was quickly shown by the rapid increase in applications on the one hand and the rapid expansion of areas subjected to review on the other. Not least among the benefits of the innovation was the following of statutory and other legal rules in place of traditional departmental guidelines and practices in the making of decisions. The winds of legal orthodoxy blew through the corridors of power.

Then the *Ombudsman Act 1976* (Cth), authorizing the investigation of administrative actions, opened the way to external supervision of the exercise of administrative power to ensure, inter alia, regularity of procedure. The *Administrative Decisions (Judicial Review) Act 1977* (Cth) conferred on the Federal Court jurisdiction to review judicially decisions purportedly made under an enactment if the decision was not made in accordance with prescribed rules or was otherwise in breach of the rules of natural justice. The package was rounded out by the enactment of the *Freedom of Information Act 1982* (Cth). The machinery was in place to ensure not only fairness but integrity in the exercise of Commonwealth bureaucratic power.

Unlike administrative procedure, judicial procedure had been well established to ensure fairness in decision-making. If judicial procedure were to fall short of ensuring fairness, public confidence in the courts' authority would be eroded. This has been demonstrated by the adverse assessment of the procedures adopted in the war crimes trials that took place in the aftermath of World War II.

As an undergraduate Judge's Associate, I had had some early experience of the shortcomings of war crimes procedure when my Judge, Mr Justice Townley, a judge of outstanding ability, was appointed to preside at the last of the Japanese War Crimes Trials which took place in 1950 on Los Negros Island, then an Australian Territory. The trials, in the form of a field general court martial, were governed by the *War Crimes Act 1945* (Cth) which provided[33], inter alia, for the reception of hearsay evidence if it appeared to be 'of assistance in proving or disproving the charge.' It was unnecessary for any eye witness to give oral testimony or to be cross-examined. The prosecution tendered affidavits that had been obtained either from witnesses to the events charged or from investigators deposing to confessional statements made by an accused. These documents were in English. If the witness or an accused spoke Japanese, his statement had been translated into English, recorded and retranslated back to him before the document was signed. There was little that the defence could do to challenge these affidavits. The procedure risked the miscarriage of justice, but the risk was frequently minimised by the accused person entering the witness box, raising a defence of superior orders. Then General Imamura Hiroshi would be summoned from his gaol on Manus Island to give evidence of the strict penalties that awaited any Japanese soldier who did not immediately carry out the instructions of a superior officer. General Imamura had been commandant of the Japanese Staff College and had served with the North Lancashire Regiment in the First World War. He bore himself with great dignity and his authority was not diminished in the least by the orange fatigues which were prison issue. However, superior orders were not a valid defence. Japanese military culture was incompatible with the international rules of war.

There was another disturbing aspect of the Los Negros trials. I was familiar with the Queensland practice that a judge who was presiding at a criminal trial would not meet with counsel for either the prosecution or the defence in the absence of counsel for the other side. But in Los Negros, all members of the 1st Australian War Crimes Section – both members of the Court and the prosecutors – were members of the same Army mess. I was the secretary who kept the accounts! The Japanese counsel, their interpreters and their support staff were accommodated in a compound nearby and there was no social communication between them and the members of the Army mess, except for the Australian liaison officer – the estimable George Dickenson who exemplified the best traditions of the Australian Bar.

These procedural shortcomings cast an increased burden on the members of the Court, and especially on the President. I think their judicial approach earned the respect of the Japanese Counsel and Dickenson, the latter commenting in an article published in the *Australian Quarterly* in 1952: 'It was a good thing for Australia that the War Crimes Court at Manus had as its president an able and experienced lawyer and Supreme Court Judge, and it was indeed fortunate that he was assisted by a bench of fair-minded officers, all with battle experience in the Second World War.'[34]

The quality of the members of the Court diminished the risk of injustice.

Nevertheless, I have not seen any indication that the decisions of that War Crimes Court have had any precedential authority.

Two years earlier the judgment in the major Tokyo War Crimes Trial was delivered. Unfairness in the procedure of that Trial has deprived the judgment of any precedential value in the view of the international community. In November 2008, the Asia Pacific Centre for Military Law at Melbourne University hosted a conference to mark the 60th Anniversary of the delivery of the judgment. The scholarly papers delivered by international authors, including Japanese academics, were subsequently published in a volume entitled 'Beyond Victors' Justice? The Tokyo War Crimes Trial Revisited'.[35] Professor Tim McCormack and Ms Sarah Finnin, writing of the continuing relevance of the Trial, observed that 'There has been sustained criticism of the rules of evidence and procedure applied by the Allies in Tokyo....[S]ome will argue that the lack of procedural fairness was so fundamental as to call into question the convictions of the accused....[I]t is unquestionably the case that contemporary international criminal procedure distances itself from the Nuremberg/Tokyo model.'[36]

The modern international criminal Tribunals are not constituted as 'Victor's Justice'. The fairness of their procedures are respected. And the result is that the cogency of international criminal law has become more firmly established even though there are notable omissions in the extent of the international tribunals' jurisdiction.

Domestically, a lifetime in the law etches the notion of fairness on the mind of every practitioner. It is a lesson that is put into practice in every field of the law. Whether the lawyer is construing statutory materials or contracts, or is weighing evidence, or assessing damages or determining punishment, fairness is a guiding concept. It ensures that the law and the practice of the law are congruent with one of the basic values of the contemporary Australian community – the fair go – and, on that account, enjoy the community's support.

The motivation of the lawyer and the rewards of legal practice

I suppose every professional is at risk of boredom as the novelty of practice wears away. Lawyers are no exception. As time passes, there is an increased knowledge of the law and an enhanced facility in performing accustomed tasks. Some lawyers change careers to find new challenges, often assisted by their legal experience. Others find new challenges in the daily practice of the law. That is not surprising. The law is an intellectual construct and there is an attraction in discovering unexplored areas of the law and in following its development. Indeed, that kind of curiosity can be satisfied even after retirement! Moreover, because of the rich diversity of humankind and the innumerable activities about which they seek legal advice, the lawyer's interest is likely to be stimulated in a wide variety of problems. Some of the most interesting days I have spent were in the Administrative Appeals Tribunal, sitting sometimes with aviators, sometimes with actuaries, sometimes with doctors. In practice, lawyers learn a great deal about human nature, society, its institutions and customs and the utilisation of material goods. They are privileged to be given access to confidences and intimacies that are hidden from others. The risk of boredom is diminished by a flow of new problems which sometimes have to be solved by research in previously unfamiliar areas of the law.

It is one thing to find some interest in the intellectual task of solving legal problems, it is another to identify why the solution of legal problems is a worthwhile lifetime pursuit. The basic motivation for practising law in any of the professional categories, I suggest, is the desire to see justice done and to see it done according to law.

Ideally, of course, the law operates justly. When justice is compared with law, however, we can see that law affects a community; justice and injustice are experienced by individuals. Law is a social regulator, justice is a moral value. In the 2nd century AD, Ulpian defined justice as 'the constant and perpetual will to allot to every man his due.' Lawyers who know how the law operates on all but who are concerned to accord justice to each are essential to a free society, especially in a diverse and pluralist democracy. It is a satisfying life to belong to a profession which is devoted to assisting in the allotment 'to every man his due'. That is why lawyers find the pursuit of individual justice a worthwhile motivation for continuing the practice of law in one or other of its categories. Whether in the representation of a client, or in the adjudication of a case, or in analysing and expounding a legal proposition or in proposing an amendment to the law, committed lawyers see themselves as administering justice. And they see one another as truly 'learned friends'. It has been my good fortune to be in the company of such lawyers from the day I entered practice.

At the Bar, it was a group of friends, opposed to one another in court, competitive but acknowledging the ability of others from whom we could learn. When the issues are significant, the contest is vigorous and the egos are unbending, the integrity of opponents who maintain the ethical standards of the Bar earns not only the respect but the friendship of colleagues. Those are friendships which last a lifetime.

On the Bench, judges are truly privileged in the friendship of colleagues of unshakeable integrity whose heavy sitting schedules are followed by the long and lonely task of judgment writing. There is no risk of boredom on the High Court Bench: the great diversity of cases are a continuing challenge and source of interest. Sometimes High Court judgments which manifested a devotion to justice according to law attracted criticism for being 'activist' but, as Lord Bingham reminded us, 'Constitutional dangers exist, no less in too little judicial activism, as in too much'.[37]

It has been a great adventure to have been in the company of those whom I have respected for their devotion to justice according to law, not least when we have not been unanimous in our definitions of the law. Among the enjoyable phenomena of life on the High Court were the lunch-time walks when four of the Justices – utterly anonymous, I am pleased to say – would walk around the Parliamentary triangle discussing shoes and ships and sealing wax and cabbages and kings. The judicial aspiration that justice should be done according to law gave no guarantee, I regret to say, of unanimity about the content of the law. Yet the aspiration of justice according to law is central to our judicial tradition as it was to the American tradition of Justice Cardozo. It was that noted jurist who told the lawyers of New York County that – 'The tradition, the ennobling tradition, though it be myth as well as verity, that surrounds as with an aura the profession of the law, is the bond between its members and one of the great concerns of man, the cause of justice upon earth.'

It is the tradition which Hal Wootten wanted to instil in the new Law School of this University. And I think that he succeeded.

---

1. The lecture was first published in *The Judicial Review*: Gerard Brennan, 'Lessons from a Life in the Law September (2013) 11 (3) *Judicial Review* 245-264.
2. See https://www.unsw.edu.au/content/dam/pdfs/law/general/events/2018-12-annual-hal-wootten-lecture/2018-12-2012-hwl-response-final-1.pdf
3. See *Australian Communist Party v Commonwealth* (1951) 83 CLR 1.
4. See *Commonwealth v Tasmania* (1983) 158 CLR 1.
5. See *Mabo v Queensland* (1988) 166 CLR 186; *Mabo v Queensland (No 2)* (1992) 175 CLR 1.
6. See *Lange v Australian Broadcasting Corporation* (1997) 189 CLR 520.
7. See *New South Wales v Commonwealth* (2006) 229 CLR 1.
8. See *Plaintiff M61/2010E v Commonwealth* [2010] HCA 41; 85 ALJR 133; *Plaintiff M70/2011 v Minister for Immigration and Citizenship; Plaintiff M106 of 2011 v Minister for Immigration and Citizenship* [2011] HCA 32 (31 August 2011); 85 ALJR 891.
9. (1995) 183 CLR ix.
10. AWB Simpson *Legal Theory and legal history: essays on the Common Law* (Hambledon, 1987) 376.
11. Benjamin N Cardozo, *The Nature of the Judicial Process* (1921 Yale University Press, 21st Printing 1963) 104-105.

12. (1981) 149 CLR 27, 42.
13. Lord Devlin, *The Enforcement of Morals* (Oxford University Press, 1965) 10.
14. H L A Hart, *The Concept of Law* (The Clarendon Press, 1961) 7.
15. (1995) 183 CLR 373, 486; see McHugh J in *Re Colina, Ex parte Torney* (1999) 200 CLR 386 at 400-401.
16. Section 48.
17. Roscoe Pound, 'Justice according to Law' *The Mid-West Quarterly,* 1:3 (April 1914), 223, 226
18. Ibid 228.
19. PNG Australia Association website http://www.pngaa.net/Library/MurderEmanuel.htm
20. Powerfully described by Professor WEH Stanner in his Boyer Lectures 'After the Dreaming' delivered in 1968 and reproduced in the book of his essays, WEH Stanner, *White Man Got No Dreaming* (Australian National University Press, 1979) 30: cited in *R v Toohey; Ex parte Meneling Station Pty Ltd* (1982) 158 CLR 327.
21. Australian Law Reform Commission, 'Recognition of Aboriginal Customary Law', (ALRC Report 31), tabled 12 June 1986.
22. Ibid par 167.
23. Ibid par 195.
24. See *Church of the New Faith v Commissioner of Payroll Tax (Vict)* (1983) 154 CLR 120, 136.
25. The unity of Australian common law was reaffirmed by the High Court in *Lipohar v R* (2000) 199 CLR 485.
26. Paper on *Scopes of Juxtaposition of Islamic Sharia as Legal System with Other Great Legal Systems of the World,* 2nd Day, Slide 20.
27. Ibid Slide 29.
28. See *Dickason v Dickason* (1913) 17 CLR 50, 51; [1913] HCA 77 (Barton ACJ for the Court).
29. Stephen J (as Sir Ninian then was) in *Russell v Russell* (1976) 134 CLR 495, 532 said that 'a tribunal which as of course conducts its hearings in closed court is not of the same character as one which habitually conducts its proceedings in open court'.
30. Sir Frank Kitto, 'Why Write Judgments?' (1992) 66 *Australian Law Journal* 787, 790.
31. See *Newell v The King* (1936) 55 CLR 707, 711, cited in *Cheatle v The Queen* (1992) 177 CLR 541, 559.
32. Sir Anthony Mason, 'Administrative Review: The Experience of the first Twelve Years' (1989) 18(3) *Federal Law Review* 122, 130.
33. Section 9(1).
34. George Dickenson, 'Japanese War Trials' (1952) 24 (2) *Australian Quarterly* 69, 71.
35. Yuki Tanaka, Tim McCormack and Gerry Simpson (eds) *Beyond Victor's Justice? The Tokyo War Crimes Trial Revisited* (Martinus Nijhoff, 2011).
36. Sarah Finnin and Tim McCormack, 'Tokyo's Continuing Relevance' in Yuki Tanaka, Tim McCormack and Gerry Simpson (eds) *Beyond Victor's Justice? The Tokyo War Crimes Trial Revisited* (Martinus Nijhoff, 2011) 356.
37. See *A v Home Secretary* [2005] 2 AC 68, 110 [41].

Index

References in italics indicate photographs

www.ingramcontent.com/pod-product-compliance
Lightning Source LLC
LaVergne TN
LVHW020413220926
848484LV00017B/2563/J
* 9 7 8 1 9 2 3 2 2 4 6 9 8 *